INTRODUCTION
TO
PUBLIC POLICY

INTRODUCTION TO PUBLIC POLICY

CHARLES WHEELAN

W. W. NORTON & COMPANY

NEW YORK • LONDON

W. W. Norton & Company has been independent since its founding in 1923, when William Warder Norton and Mary D. Herter Norton first published lectures delivered at the People's Institute, the adult education division of New York City's Cooper Union. The firm soon expanded its program beyond the Institute, publishing books by celebrated academics from America and abroad. By midcentury, the two major pillars of Norton's publishing program—trade books and college texts—were firmly established. In the 1950s, the Norton family transferred control of the company to its employees, and today—with a staff of four hundred and a comparable number of trade, college, and professional titles published each year—W. W. Norton & Company stands as the largest and oldest publishing house owned wholly by its employees.

Editor: Jack Repcheck
Editorial Assistant: Jason Spears
Managing Editor, College: Marian Johnson
Project Editor: Christine D'Antonio
Production Manager: Benjamin Reynolds
Developmental Editor: Carol Flechner
Electronic Media Editor: Eileen Connell
Design Director: Rubina Yeh
Book Designer: Fearn Cutler de Vicq
Composition: Roberta Flechner
Drawn art: John McAusland
The text of this book is composed in Bulmer
with the display set in Gotham
Manufacturing by R R Donnelley—N. Chelmsford, MA

Library of Congress Cataloging-in-Publication Data

Wheelan, Charles J.
    Introduction to public policy / Charles Wheelan. -- 1st ed.
        p. cm.
    Includes bibliographic references and index.
    ISBN 978-0-393-92665-1 (hardcover)
I. Policy sciences. I. Title.
    H97.W48 2011
    320.6--dc22
                    2010024278

W. W. Norton & Company, Inc., 500 Fifth Avenue, New York, N.Y. 10110-0017
www.wwnorton.com
W. W. Norton & Company Ltd., Castle House, 75/76 Wells Street, London W1T 3QT

3 4 5 6 7 8 9

For My Parents

Brief Contents

SECTION V | MAKING POLICY

Contents

SECTION II | WHY WE DO WHAT WE DO

SECTION II | MARKETS AND GOVERNMENT

SECTION IV | TOOLS FOR ANALYSIS

SECTION V │ MAKING POLICY

Preface

The world has its challenges at the moment. The worst of the housing-related financial crisis has passed, but there has been little progress on crafting a new regulatory regime to prevent the next crisis. The U.S. budget is woefully out of balance. At best, the accumulating debts will be passed along to future taxpayers; at worst, global creditors may balk at feeding America's borrowing habit. Then there is our unsustainably expensive health-care system. And climate change. And wars in Iraq and Afghanistan. And so on. The United States is not unique. In Japan, the economic malaise brought on by the collapse of a property bubble in the late 1980s has been going on so long that the "lost decade" will soon become the "lost decades." In Europe, public budgets are increasingly stressed by the costs of providing a generous social safety net to an aging population.

There is plenty of good news, too. India and China have enjoyed two decades of robust economic growth, which has lifted hundreds of millions of people out of poverty. But even those economic success stories have created their own challenges, such as environmental degradation, rising income inequality, rapid urbanization, inadequate infrastructure, and trade-related tensions with the rest of the world. Of course, much of the developing world should be so lucky as to have China or India's problems. I have just returned from Cambodia, where a shocking 45 percent of the population lacks access to clean drinking water and basic sanitation.

The point of this preface is not to depress the reader. In fact, most of the world in 2010 is richer, safer, and healthier than it was in 1970 or 1850. Still, there is progress to be made. There will always be progress to be made. What the challenges described above have in common—and what any society's major challenges will always have in common—is that they fall under the rubric of public policy, meaning that they cannot be addressed satisfactorily by a single individual or by one entrepreneurial firm. Instead, public policy problems require communal decisions: Who must attend school (and who must pay for it)? What substances can or cannot be dumped in a communal water source? How should a contagious disease be contained? Where should a new airport be built? What levels of jet noise and exhaust are acceptable? How should we protect ourselves against our external enemies? What is the obligation of each individual or family to that national defense?

Although these are modern policy questions, there is not a society in the history of human civilization that has not dealt with similar issues. National defense in the twenty-first century requires sophisticated border technology to protect against terrorists; national defense in the eleventh century required building walls and fortresses to protect against barbarians. It's the same basic thing—not the technology, of course, but the need to make and implement a communal decision. There is usually no right answer when making these kinds of public choices. (I suspect that in the eleventh century, some citizens found the fortresses unnecessary and/or overly expensive.) However, there are constructive ways to think about confronting social challenges. We can measure and quantify the outcomes that we care about. We can analyze when markets deliver socially optimal outcomes and when they do not. We can identify the causes of a social problem and propose a range of solutions. We can design processes for making public decisions that are transparent and democratic (though still respectful of individual rights). And once we have implemented a policy, we can evaluate whether it is effective or not. These are the basic tools laid out in *Introduction to Public Policy*.

This book was the writing equivalent of running an ultra-marathon. Without lots of people yelling encouragement and handing me water along the way, I would be face down on the pavement somewhere. W.W. Norton & Company has been a terrific partner—on this project and others. That begins at the top with Norton's president, Drake McFeely, who has the unique ability to be both charming and highly effective at enforcing deadlines. Karl Bakeman was the "founding editor" of this book. He and, later, Ann Shin did the organizational planning that put the whole project on the right trajectory. (An ultra-marathon is a lot harder to win if you begin by running in the wrong direction!) Jack Repcheck then brought the project to fruition. He is a joy to work with both because of his substantive expertise and his easygoing demeanor. Carol Flechner got the whole project ready for race day; she took a heaping manuscript and turned it into something publishable.

This book is packed with data and examples. They did not research themselves. Sujata Bhat is the most extraordinary purveyor of data I've ever encountered. If it exists, she can find it. Fast. This book would much less interesting without her help. In the final stages of production, when facts and figures needed to be checked and updated on a tight deadline, Daniel Van Deusen was extremely helpful.

If we stick with the ultra-marathon metaphor, then my agent, Tina Bennett, is coach, fitness guru, and sports psychologist all wrapped in one. Tina has remarkable commercial instincts, a keen appreciation for producing meaningful work, and a great sense of humor. Every project feels more manageable with her involved.

I have the good fortune to be a part of a great institution, the University of Chicago. At the Harris School of Public Policy Studies, I am continually surrounded by bright students, colleagues, and visitors, all of whom have contributed directly or indirectly to the contents of this book. Former dean Susan Mayer was particularly supportive in creating an academic perch from which I could work on this project and many others. I am also indebted to the Dartmouth Department of Economics and to the Nelson A. Rockefeller Center at Dartmouth College for providing me with both an academic "home away from home" during my frequent teaching stints and a fun, smart group of colleagues and friends. I would also like to thank Bruce Sacerdote, Dartmouth College; Ethan Lewis, Dartmouth College; Paula Worthington, Harris School of Public Policy, University of Chicago; and Amy Richardson, RAND Corporation.

My wife, Leah, has never met an adventure she didn't like, beginning with our trip around the world twenty years ago that left me fascinated with public policy. She is supportive of every project I take on, including those like this one that stretch on for half a decade or more. Without our children, Katrina, Sophie, and CJ, these books would be written faster but everything else in life would be less meaningful and vibrant. It is a political cliché to write about improving the world for our children. I have a more specific hope: I would like to recapture the optimism of the late 1990s, when my oldest daughter was born. The Cold War had ended. The global economy was booming. Public budgets were balanced or in surplus. There was a palpable sense that societies around the world, rich and poor, were on a steady, peaceful march in the right direction. A decade later, the world is a more uncertain and less optimistic place. Public policy comprises the tools we have for changing that. Policy analysis is at the root of diplomacy, governance, economic growth, environmental protection, education, and just about every other mechanism for transforming a society in a positive way. It can literally help to fix the world (and make it a better place for our children).

INTRODUCTION
TO
PUBLIC POLICY

WHAT IS PUBLIC POLICY?

Public Decision Making

TO SNOWMOBILE,
OR NOT TO SNOWMOBILE?

Some people like to snowmobile. Some don't. The decision to buy a snow-mobile and spend time using it is a personal one. The market will, by and large, oversee the production and sale of snowmobiles. The world operates peaceful-ly if some people pursue their private interest in snowmobiling and others choose different hobbies—up to a point.

The thrill of snowmobiling begins when an individual starts the ignition and sets out on the trail. That is also the point at which private behavior inter-sects with public policy. Snowmobiles are an exciting way to explore the out-doors. They also make noise and generate exhaust. The very places that are the best for snowmobiling—pristine forests and beautiful expanses of open space—are the same places that other outdoor enthusiasts would prefer to enjoy with-out the noise and disturbance of snowmobiles.

That issue has come to a head in America's national parks. In winter, Yellowstone National Park, with its thousands of square miles of snow-covered trails, scenic vistas, and abundance of wildlife, is one of the country's best places for snowmobiling. Or the very worst place for snowmobiling, according to others. "I think it's clear the national parks should be places where the pub-lic can go and escape traffic. And clearly these snow machines are loud, they're polluting and they cause conflict with other visitors," Bob Ekey, director of the Wilderness Society, told the *New York Times*.[1]

Whether snowmobiling should be allowed in America's national parks is a public decision (as was the decision decades earlier to set aside public land as national parks). The national parks belong to all American citizens; no matter how the issue is resolved, some of those citizens will feel that they have been made worse off. In the private sector, these differences in preferences are more easily resolved. If you walk into Starbucks and buy coffee, your neighbor will not object, even if he thinks coffee is a disgusting beverage.

---

1. Douglas Jehl, "National Parks Will Ban Recreation Snowmobiling," *New York Times,* April 27, 2000.

When private behavior does not significantly affect other people, we do not need to agree on the merits of that behavior. We can pursue our own interests and make ourselves happy—coffee, tea, or nothing. There need not be any public consensus on the merits of a grande latte. Even snowmobiling on private property is not likely to cause major disputes. If you buy 1,000 acres in northern Wisconsin and use it for snowmobiling, your activities are not likely to draw protest.

But snowmobiling in Yellowstone National Park is different. The issue cannot be resolved simply by declaring that those who approve of snowmobiling should do it, and those who don't should not, because people who do not approve of snowmobiling in Yellowstone *do not want anyone doing it.* Snowmobiling opponents perceive themselves as being made worse off by snowmobiles in Yellowstone, whether or not they are present while it is happening. Indeed, they may object to snowmobiling in Yellowstone National Park even if they never plan to go there simply because they place a high priority on the protection of the nation's natural resources.

The snowmobiling policy in America's national parks is a public policy issue. The people who "own" the national parks—the American public—have built an institution (the National Park Service) to gather information, decide on a policy, and then enforce that policy. One of the most significant features of public policy is that the decision—to allow snowmobiling or not—is binding on everyone, including those who disagree with it.

Three recent presidential administrations have disagreed over what that policy ought to be. Under Bill Clinton's administration, the National Park Service imposed a ban on the recreational use of snowmobiles in most of the nation's national parks and other recreational areas. George W. Bush's administration set aside the ban. To underscore the point, Interior Secretary Gale Norton spent a high-profile vacation snowmobiling in Yellowstone during the winter of 2005.[2] The *New York Times* reported at the time, "With a jaunty orange pennant waving from the back of her black snowmobile, Interior Secretary Gale A. Norton tootled through a snowscape of hills, steaming rivers and indifferent bison this week, giving an unusual personal endorsement to the machines that some consider a blight and others a blessing." A federal judge later placed a cap of 720 snowmobiles a day in Yellowstone. In 2009, Barack Obama's administration proposed cutting that cap by more than half, to 318 snowmobiles daily (and 78 "multipassenger snowcoaches").[3]

The snowmobile issue is emblematic of most public policy issues: there is no way to make all parties to the disagreement entirely happy. Some individuals

2. Felicity Barringer, "A 3-Day Yellowstone Tour in Support of Snowmobiles," *New York Times,* February 17, 2005, p. A16.

3. Associated Press, July 23, 2009.

would prefer that snowmobiles have unfettered access to all parts of the park at all times; others feel equally strongly that recreational use of motorized vehicles should not be allowed anywhere in the national parks at any time. And, of course, there is a continuum of opinion in between (as well as a sizable group of people who don't care about the issue at all).

Compromise is possible, such as the daily caps. But compromise does not make the disagreement go away. In fact, the parties who are most passionate about the issue—those who think snowmobiles should be banned and those who disagree with any limits at all—are both angered by some middle course of action.

Snowmobiling in a national park is just one small example of the much larger challenge inherent to public policy: finding a way for a large group of people to agree on a common course of action (or lack of action). Rarely will 10 people share identical views on an issue they have in common; consensus is nearly impossible in a town of 30,000, a country of 300 million, or a planet of 6 billion. Yet many issues of public significance—from building roads to dealing with global warming—demand some communal action.

This book presents a series of analytical tools that are essential for making good public policy decisions. These are not merely academic exercises; public policy has a profound impact on our quality of life. Sensible public policy creates an environment that promotes health, wealth, and peace. Bad public policy can literally destroy a society, as the sad example of Zimbabwe will show later in this chapter.

Chapter 1 begins with an overview of public decision making. This process is never easy, but it is essential to building a stable and prosperous society.

CHAPTER OUTLINE

1.1 DEFINING PUBLIC POLICY

When making public policy, groups act collectively—they do everything from declaring war to installing stoplights. The study of public policy enables us to do it better. This is not to say that all people can be made happy all the time, as the Yellowstone snowmobiling example makes clear. But better public policy leads to more informed decisions, a better understanding of human behavior, more effective institutions for resolving differences of opinion, and, as a result, healthier, safer, more peaceful, and more productive lives.

The key distinction between private behavior and public policy is that public policy decisions are often binding on all those who are a member of the relevant group, even those who disagree with the decision. Whatever the relevant group decides, whether the group consists of members of a church parish or the citizens of the United States, there must be a decision in the end on a single shared course of action. Because of that, good public decisions require institutions that can gather and act upon the preferences of the group—through voting and other tools of representative governance. The group will almost never agree unanimously with a decision, but it is imperative that they agree with the process through which it is reached.

Consider some examples, all of which are more contentious than snowmobiling in a national park.

- **Waging war.** The United States could not simultaneously invade and not invade Iraq. Americans disagreed sharply over policy toward Iraq and, later, Afghanistan. Yet it was obviously not possible to satisfy all parties; invading and not invading are mutually exclusive options. American citizens collectively control their armed forces; they elect a single individual as president, who also serves as commander in chief, and a Congress vested with the power to declare war. Public policy is the process by which 300 million Americans use their democratic institutions to exercise control over one army.

- **Social issues.** Abortion cannot be both legal and illegal. Some Americans believe that life begins at conception; thus, abortion is tantamount to murder and should be illegal. Others believe that the decision to terminate a pregnancy belongs exclusively to the woman carrying the fetus. There is also a continuum of opinion as to when and under what conditions abortion should be allowed. The most extreme positions are irreconcilable, yet a society must come to some resolution on whether a pregnant woman can receive an abortion legally or not. **Public policy** is the process by which a society makes and enforces decisions on what behavior is acceptable and what is not—whether it is abortion, gay marriage, or carrying a concealed weapon. At issue is not just our own private behavior, *but what we are willing to allow other people to do.*

- **Raising revenue.** Individuals cannot choose to pay taxes or not. Imagine a world in which you stepped to the cash register at Target and the cashier asked, "Would you like to pay the sales tax today?" Public policy involves collecting revenue to pay for shared goods and services. Unlike in the private sector, individuals cannot examine their tax bills and pay for the things that interest them most. Instead, we use government to make investments in public goods and services—parks, police protection, border security, public schools, and so on—and then compel citizens to pay for these shared goods and services in the form of taxation. Individuals will almost certainly disagree over what shared services are necessary and what constitutes the "fair share" for different parties; but once that decision has been made, the relevant membership—be it American taxpayers or the member nations of the United Nations—must pay up or face sanctions.

What these examples have in common is the need to act collectively in the hope of making the relevant group better off. (The difficulty of measuring and quantifying "better off" will be covered in Chapter 5.) Do all Americans agree about when and where the U.S. Army should be deployed? No. But most believe that having an army and placing it under the control of an elected commander in chief is far preferable to the alternatives: a nation with no national defense or a nation with many private militias under the command of whoever pays them.

Of course, you should recognize that most human endeavors *do not* require society to act communally. Much of a modern economy is more like ordering from Starbucks than waging war or snowmobiling in a national park. When it comes to most goods and services, there is no reason for citizens to agree on a common course of action. In fact, it can be costly, inefficient, and ideologically unacceptable for many to entrust the machinery of government with responsibilities that are better left in the private domain. One of the fundamental elements of policy analysis is recognizing when some communal action (usually coordinated by government) can make society better off, when individuals and firms are best left to act on their own, and when some existing government policy ought to be modified or eliminated because it is doing more harm than good.

Good public policy should improve the overall welfare of society. Of course, good public policy is often elusive. Indeed, the idea of what constitutes "good public policy" is frequently contentious, as will be discussed in the next chapter. Should judges be able to post the Ten Commandments in their courtrooms? Should public money be used to protect endangered species? Should the United States invade other countries in order to topple repressive governments and spread democracy?

Even when reasonable people can agree on desirable outcomes—children should not die at birth; humans should live long, healthy lives; individuals should be educated in ways that make them productive—some societies fail to achieve these basic goals. Much of the world lives in dire poverty or amid deadly violence. That failure of human potential can almost always be traced to bad public policy: a lack of good public institutions, a failure to give voice to a nation's people, a lack of public infrastructure (roads, ports, etc.), or some other policy failures that stifle human potential.

· · · · · · · · · · · · · · · | **POLICY IN THE REAL WORLD** | · · · · · · · · · · · · · · ·

Bad Policy Can Be Fatal, Literally: Zimbabwe's Self-Inflicted Wounds

In 2002, David Coltart, a member of Zimbabwe's Parliament, made the charge that Zimbabwean president Robert Mugabe was "determined to hold on to power at any cost, including the destruction of the nation and the deaths of hundreds of thousands of Zimbabweans."[4] Mr. Coltart made his accusation in the *New York Times*; if he had published such an accusation in his home country, he would most likely have been arrested and the newspaper closed.

Zimbabwe has gone from one of sub-Saharan Africa's richest nations in the mid-1990s to one of its neediest.[5] By 2003, relief agencies concluded that some two-thirds of Zimbabweans were not getting enough to eat on a daily basis. Half of the children under five were suffering from chronic malnutrition.

4. David Coltart, "Zimbabwe's Man-Made Famine," *New York Times,* August 7, 2002.
5. "The Method behind Mugabe's Madness," *The Economist,* June 26, 2004.

One in four people was infected with the HIV virus.[6] In 2008, British prime minister Gordon Brown referred to Zimbabwe's ongoing suffering as a "humanitarian emergency of colossal proportions."[7]

What has gone wrong? The short answer is bad governance.

Zimbabwe's President Mugabe has clung to power through fraud and oppression. When he was "re-elected" in 2002, the British news magazine *The Economist* noted, "The strangest fact about Zimbabwe's presidential election last weekend was not that Robert Mugabe stole it, but that he went to such extraordinary lengths to do so. How much simpler it would have been to cancel it and declare himself president for life."[8]

Mugabe's public policy misdeeds are legion: he has printed money to pay bills, imprisoned political opponents, intimidated journalists, and loaded the government with his political cronies. The most devastating policy, however, has been a particularly repressive form of "land reform," in which the government confiscated the land of hundreds of white farmers and stood aside as more than a thousand other farms were occupied by marauding gangs and soldiers.

Many of Zimbabwe's experienced farmers were replaced by individuals with little or no knowledge of agriculture. Predictably, yields plunged, and many of Zimbabwe's most productive citizens fled the country.[9] These destructive policies have taken an enormous toll: by 2004, the economy had shrunk by a third; infant mortality had doubled; school enrollment rates had plunged from 95 percent for boys and 90 percent for girls to 67 percent and 63 percent respectively; life expectancy (made worse by an unchecked AIDS epidemic) had fallen from 60 to 35.[10]

International pressure forced Mugabe into a power-sharing agreement with an opposing political party in 2008, but the eighty-five-year-old Mugabe managed to keep control of the police, the intelligence services, and the media, prompting one Western news outlet to comment: "Sadly for his many opponents, Robert Mugabe is far from being the decrepit old man some would wish."[11] The problem is not merely that Mugabe has unfairly held on to the levers of power, but also that he has used that power to implement policies that are so ruinous for his country.

. . . .

6. Michael Wines, "In Zimbabwe, Even the Farmers Are Going Hungry," *New York Times,* February 29, 2004.

7. "In Need of Strong Medicine," *The Economist,* December 11, 2008.

8. "Mugabe's Smash-and-Grab," *The Economist,* March 16, 2002.

9. "First Get the Basics Right," *The Economist,* January 17, 2004.

10. "The Method behind Mugabe's Madness."

11. "Still Adored," *The Economist,* December 17, 2000.

1.2 THE POLICY PROCESS

We study public policy in hopes that we can do it better. It is an audacious task. What activities are best handled by the market? How can we act in the face of scientific uncertainty? How can we make sense of the opinions of hundreds of millions of people? How can we evaluate trade-offs—economic growth versus environmental protection, for example? How can we even measure our success? *What is good public policy, and how does it happen?*

This book is a tool kit for understanding the public policy process and for making better public policy decisions. As a starting point, good public policy seeks to do the following:

1. **Identify a social goal.** What is the social benefit (or the elimination of a harm) that can be achieved through effective public action? This can be anything from eradicating a childhood disease to promoting income growth or reducing traffic congestion. The objective is to make life better in some specific way. This social benefit need not derive from added government responsibility or spending; it may result from a collective decision to eliminate a public program or pare back some regulatory responsibility, as in the deregulation examples discussed later in this chapter or in the Bush administration decision to lift the ban on snowmobiling in the national parks.

2. **Diagnose the problem.** What is causing the social harm or preventing the realization of some benefit? What is causing self-interested individuals to act in a way that makes society worse off? This process of inquiry is similar to how a doctor would make a diagnosis: only by understanding what is causing a bad outcome can we hope to fix the problem. In the end, policy analysis seeks to understand what behavior has to change in order to achieve the stated social goal.

3. **Identify the appropriate institution for action.** Who or what is going to take action to change behavior in a way that will bring about the desired social benefit? What is the source of his or her or its authority? No matter how someone reading this book feels about snowmobiling in Yellowstone National Park, he or she cannot show up in Wyoming and tell people to get on or off their snowmobiles. The secretary of the interior, on the other hand, does have that authority. He or she has been appointed by the president of the United States to make policy regarding the national parks and other federal property. The president, in turn, has been vested with that power of appointment by virtue of having been elected by American voters (which is a process that was created by the Constitution).

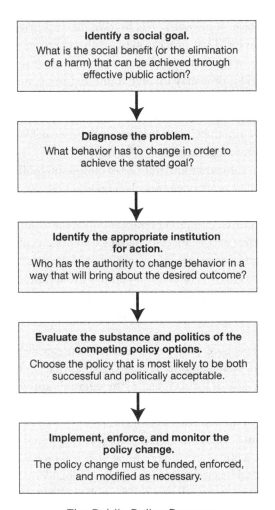

Identify a social goal.
What is the social benefit (or the elimination of a harm) that can be achieved through effective public action?

↓

Diagnose the problem.
What behavior has to change in order to achieve the stated goal?

↓

Identify the appropriate institution for action.
Who has the authority to change behavior in a way that will bring about the desired outcome?

↓

Evaluate the substance and politics of the competing policy options.
Choose the policy that is most likely to be both successful and politically acceptable.

↓

Implement, enforce, and monitor the policy change.
The policy change must be funded, enforced, and modified as necessary.

The Public Policy Process

Public action requires institutions with the authority to make or change policy. That may be anything from a neighborhood organization with the authority to grant restaurants outdoor dining permits to an international treaty that limits greenhouse gas emissions. These institutions vary in their degree of democratic control. At one end of the spectrum, many public policy issues in California are decided by direct democracy; all eligible voters are invited to vote on referenda that determine state policy, such as the 2004 referendum directing the state to spend $3 billion on stem cell research. At the other end of the spectrum, autocratic regimes control policy through sheer force or coercion, regardless of the opinions of the people whom they control.

In any case, some entity has to have the authority and capacity to change behavior. That process may involve exerting more government authority (as in the Clinton administration banning snowmobiles in the national parks), or it may involve relinquishing some authority (as in the Bush administration policy setting aside that ban). In both cases, the authority to make that decision is vested with the U.S. federal government—not the United Nations or the state of Wyoming or the private sector firms that manufacture snowmobiles.

4. **Evaluate the substance and politics of competing policy options.** What can or should be done (including the important option of doing nothing)? Policy analysis involves evaluating different courses of action—estimating costs and benefits, evaluating political implications, understanding how different parties will be affected, making trade-offs explicit, and so on. In some cases, the choices are binary (e.g., should the citizens of a jurisdiction be allowed to carry a concealed weapon or not?). More often, there are numerous, or even infinite, possible courses of action. This book introduces the most important tools for evaluating policy options, such as cost-benefit analysis.

At the same time, policy change requires political support in a democratic system. Who needs to be persuaded of what? Is it a single individual, as in the case of the secretary of the interior's authority to reverse the ban on snowmobiling in the national parks? Is it a simple majority vote, as is required for bills to pass most legislative bodies? Is it a supermajority (some fraction beyond a simple majority), as is required in the U.S. Senate to overcome a filibuster? The optimal policy choice is one that achieves the desired goal in a way that is politically acceptable.

5. **Implement, enforce, and monitor the policy change.** A good idea won't change the world until it is carried out successfully. A policy change may require funding or expertise or some other process for literally and figuratively delivering the goods. Meanwhile, we have already discussed the fact that public policy is often binding on those who disagree with it and, therefore, requires some degree of coercion in order to be effective: The sheriff evicts individuals who do not pay their rent; the United Nations imposes economic sanctions on countries that violate international norms; a state can incarcerate or even execute individuals who violate criminal statutes. A policy change without sufficient mechanisms and resources for implementing and enforcing it is not really a policy change at all.

Finally, public policy is not a pure science; outcomes are never certain or entirely predictable, especially when they are dependent on the behavior of millions or even hundreds of millions of individuals. A policy change may or may not achieve its intended effect; a policy may even have adverse consequences that were not anticipated at the time it was passed. Therefore, it is essential to monitor policies after they are implemented to determine their true costs and benefits and to recommend modifications when necessary.

Making good policy requires a set of tools to analyze the nature of a problem and implement a solution that is both effective and politically palatable. The balance of the book will introduce this set of tools. We will revisit the policy process outlined above in greater depth in Chapter 15, by which time you will be more familiar with the skills required at each step.

1.3   OVERVIEW OF THE BOOK

The book will proceed as follows:

Chapters 1 and 2 will introduce the concept of public policy and lay out the unique challenges of public decision making.

Chapters 3 and 4 will present a set of tools for understanding and anticipating individual and group behavior. It is crucial to understand why people do what they do in order to make policy that leads to better social outcomes.

Chapter 5 presents the challenge of measuring our overall well-being, or "social welfare." The first step to making better policy is attempting to define *better*.

Chapter 6 offers an in-depth look at the political process, which must be navigated to achieve any successful policy change in a democratic system.

Chapters 7 and 8 present important tools for understanding what markets can reasonably accomplish and what they cannot. In many cases, markets are an extraordinary tool for social progress. Yet government policies are often necessary to make markets work better, to modify their outcomes, or to deliver important goods and services that markets fail to provide.

Chapters 9 through 13 present a basic set of quantitative tools for making public policy decisions. As with any endeavor, good policy decisions are based on sound analysis of available data, such as the costs and benefits of different options.

Chapter 14 examines the crucial role that institutions play in making and carrying out policy.

Chapter 15 brings all of these tools together by laying out a framework for how policy makers can identify and diagnose a policy problem; evaluate possible courses of action; and implement a solution that makes society better off.

1.4 FOR-PROFIT, NONPROFIT, AND GOVERNMENT INSTITUTIONS

Public policy is not synonymous with government. Indeed, government performs some functions that could just as easily be done by private firms, such as delivering mail. And private firms sometimes perform crucial social functions, such as assisting with disaster cleanup or building advanced weapons systems. Thus, it would be helpful to draw a distinction among the three kinds of enterprises in a modern economy: for-profit firms, nonprofit firms, and government. Each of these kinds of enterprises plays an important role in public policy.

For-profit firms operate to earn a profit for their owners. Such businesses may be as small as a single person selling hot dogs from a pushcart or as large as a global business with hundreds of thousands of employees. For-profit firms perform some activity or activities in the hope that the revenues generated by doing business exceed the costs. All residual profits accrue to the owners of the firm. Public companies (traded on a stock exchange) are owned by their shareholders, the individuals or institutions who own stock in the company. Private firms, on the other hand, may be owned by an individual, a family, a partnership, or some other combination of persons.

The most salient characteristic of for-profit firms is that they exist to make money. Such firms may have other stated objectives—improving the community, investing in the workforce, making customers happy—but these objectives are predicated on the firm doing business in a way in which revenues consistently exceed costs.

For-profit firms (which are often referred to collectively as "the private sector") play an important role in public policy. Many public services are delivered by the private, for-profit sector. For example, if a local government decides to build a new highway, the actual building of the road will likely be done by a private contractor. Federal health programs like Medicaid and Medicare are funded with public money but depend on private doctors and hospitals to deliver care. When the United States sought to rebuild Iraq, enormous contracts were tendered to private American companies for everything from infrastructure projects to security.

Indeed, the notion that for-profit firms serve private interests to the exclusion of the public interest makes little sense. Most of what we need in our daily lives—food, clothes, shelter, entertainment, medical innovation, even art and literature—is produced by the private sector with the aim of making a profit. For reasons that will be discussed later in the text, most of these goods and services can be produced more cheaply, efficiently, and responsively in the private sector than they could by a government entity. There are many cases, including the airline deregulation example that will be discussed in this chapter, when overall social welfare can be improved by turning responsibility for some government service over to the private sector or by allowing for-profit firms to operate with less government restraint.

Yet it is also true that for-profit firms will not voluntarily undertake major activities that lose money in the long run:

- Real-estate developers will not build housing for people who cannot afford to buy it.
- Pharmaceutical companies will not create vaccines for rare diseases if the research costs are likely to exceed the profits that can be earned by selling the medicines, even if they are life-saving cures.

Nonprofit firms are not operated for the purpose of earning a profit. A nonprofit firm undertakes activities for which the revenues do not necessarily exceed the costs. The balance is made up through private contributions, government funding, or subsidies generated by profitable activities. Nonprofit organizations range from small neighborhood organizations with shoestring budgets to Harvard University, which has an endowment of nearly $26 billion.

There are two key distinctions between for-profit and nonprofit firms:

1. In a nonprofit organization, any excess of revenues over costs remains within the organization—there are no "owners" entitled to a profit. It is entirely possible for a nonprofit organization to generate excess revenues for some period of time, but that surplus—which would be profit in a for-profit firm—is retained by the organization rather than being distributed to shareholders, partners, or other owners.

2. In the United States, nonprofit organizations are exempt from state and federal taxes as set forth in Section 501(c)(3) of the tax code. Federal law requires nonprofits to be corporations, funds, or foundations that fall under the broad rubric of "charitable organizations." These include religious organizations, educational institutions, relief and humanitarian organizations, and so on. To preserve their tax-exempt status, nonprofit organizations are not allowed to influence legislation as a substantial portion of their activities, nor may they participate in campaign activity for or against specific political candidates.

Nonprofit organizations play a crucial role in enhancing overall social welfare by delivering goods and services that are not ordinarily provided by the private sector. Harvard University, for example, uses its extraordinary endowment to educate students who cannot afford to pay tuition and to conduct research that will generate knowledge but may not have immediate practical (and, therefore, profitable) applications. Many institutions that play an important role in public policy—schools, community hospitals, charities, environmental organizations and other advocacy groups—are structured as nonprofit organizations.

Government exercises authority over some political jurisdiction—a town, a county, a state, a country, or even a union of countries. The source of that authority varies: a governing body can be elected, appointed, passed down along family lines (royalty), or seized by force. In general, a government provides services for its unit of jurisdiction and pays for those services by raising revenues, usually through some form of taxation.

From a public policy standpoint, government has a unique power: it is the only entity that can compel individuals to do things that they might otherwise choose not to do. Most societies have vested government with coercive powers—to collect taxes, condemn property, incarcerate individuals, remove children from their families, invade other countries, and even execute criminals. It is sometimes said that government has a monopoly on the legitimate use of force.

Neither private firms nor nonprofit organizations have such powers. Consider an important distinction between the International Committee of the Red Cross (a nonprofit organization) and the U.S. government. Both institutions provided large amounts of relief to the victims of the tsunami that swept across Southeast Asia in December 2004, but there is a crucial difference in the source of that aid: the Red Cross raises its funds primarily through voluntary contributions; individuals choose to give money to the Red Cross, which in turn distributes aid around the globe. In contrast, the U.S. government raises money used for humanitarian relief through taxation, which is not voluntary. When Congress and the president decide that America will send aid to tsunami victims, American taxpayers have no choice but to pay their share, regardless of how they feel about spending money on tsunami relief. Those who refuse can be sent to prison—a power that the Red Cross obviously does not have. This distinction will be very important as we delve further into public policy.

Most of the concepts in this book assume democratic governance. In theory, an autocrat might still have much interest in public policy. He or she could design policies that enhance society's productivity, minimize conflict, improve public safety, improve health, and so on. An absolute dictator might study environmental reports, poll citizens, tour a national park, and then render a decision on whether or not snowmobiling should be allowed. In practice, the informed and enlightened autocrat has been a rare occurrence. Most developed nations have chosen democratic institutions as their mechanism for aggregating citizens' preferences. Meanwhile, nondemocratic governments have often perpetrated horrible policies on the people under their control. Winston Churchill's observation still rings true: "Democracy is the worst form of government, except for all those others that have been tried."

As was noted earlier, good public policy does not always require more government. Indeed, a key part of public policy is developing a process for determining when and how government can make our lives better and when individuals and corporations are best left alone. Too much government can be worse than too little. The World Bank, the international organization charged with fighting global poverty, released a report called *Doing Business in 2005* that documents cases around the world in which an overregulated business climate harms poor nations. Surprisingly, the report found that poor countries impose on average three times the administrative costs and twice the number of bureaucratic procedures as rich countries.[12] For example, incorporating a business takes two days in Canada compared to 153 days in Mozambique.

Public policy is in many ways analogous to medicine. Physicians must decide between offering treatment—with its attendant costs, side effects, and imperfect outcomes—and deferring to the body's remarkable ability to heal itself. Policy makers must also decide when, where, and how to intervene in a modern economy. Markets have a powerful ability to harness individual initiative and propel society forward, as will be explained in Chapter 7. Nearly every modern economy uses a market system to allocate scarce resources. The twentieth-century experiments with nonmarket-based economies, notably the Soviet Union, were abject failures. Markets, like the human body, have an extraordinary ability to fix things on their own.

But markets are not perfect. For reasons that will be explored in Chapter 8, markets fail to provide some goods and services that would improve overall social welfare. And good government can make markets work better—by ensuring everything from a sound currency to an efficient legal system. How well would the American economy work without the dollar, the court system, or the federal highways?

Yet public policies, like medical procedures, often have adverse effects, both foreseen and unforeseen. The more profound the intervention, the more significant the adverse effects are likely to be. As with medicine, public policy fixes may not work. Or they may have unintended consequences that are worse than the problem at hand.

The challenge is steering a course between policies that enhance the strength and versatility of the market and those that are too heavy-handed. The study of public policy enables us to steer that course more effectively.

12. "Breaking Poverty's Chains," *The Economist*, September 11, 2004.

··············· | **POLICY IN THE REAL WORLD** | ·················

Less Can Be More:
Deregulation in the United States

In the 1970s, there was no Southwest Airlines flying across the country—or ATA or Ted or Spirit. Air travel was operated by private firms, but every significant aspect of the business was regulated by the government: what firms could operate, where they could fly, and how much they could charge.

The Civil Aeronautics Board (CAB), a federal government agency, made all these determinations. The CAB generally prohibited new airlines from entering the market on routes already being served by existing carriers. No existing firm could compete for customers by cutting prices because the CAB dictated the fare structure. A flight from Chicago to Denver on every airline cost the same—by law.

Prior to 1978, such regulation in the American economy was not uncommon. The federal government regulated long-distance telephone rates, cable-television fees, trucking rates, and even the interest rates that banks could pay on savings accounts.

The Airline Deregulation Act of 1978, which gave airlines the freedom to set fares and made it possible for Southwest and other discount carriers to launch national service, was the beginning of a sustained effort to roll back government regulation of many consumer services.[13] Public policy experts argued successfully at the time that there was no compelling economic rationale for such regulation and that consumers would benefit from greater competition.

Long-distance phone service was partially deregulated in 1984. Cable television was deregulated in 1984 (though reregulated in 1992 and then deregulated again in 1996). Banking was deregulated in phases: Congress deregulated savings rates in 1980 and lending standards in 1982; interstate banking, which allowed banks to do business in more than one state, was allowed in 1994.[14]

How has deregulation worked? In the airline industry, fares have fallen steadily for twenty years, saving consumers billions of dollars. Service levels

---

13. Steven A. Morrison and Clifford Winston, *The Evolution of the Airline Industry* (Washington, D.C.: Brookings Institution, 1995).
14. "Deregulated: Airlines, Banking, Cable TV, Electricity, Telephones," *Consumer Reports* (July 2002), p. 30.

also fell once airlines began competing based on price rather than quality of service. Analysts had expected as much. Prior to deregulation, fares were fixed, so the only way to attract customers was with superior service—comfortable seats, good food, and frequent direct flights. After deregulation, consumers have shown a preference for cheaper flights at the expense of premium service. You may not get peanuts on your Chicago–Denver flight, but the inflation-adjusted fare is significantly lower than it was in 1978.

In several cases, poorly conceived deregulation plans have had more serious consequences. Partial deregulation of the savings and loan industry created incentives for savings and loan owners to make reckless investments with depositors' money, eventually requiring a $160-billion government bailout in the 1980s and 1990s. A botched electricity deregulation in California, made worse by market manipulation and corporate fraud, led to a year of power shortages and blackouts beginning in June 2000.

Overall, however, analysts believe that deregulation has been good for consumers, as demonstrated by the fact that few deregulated industries have later been reregulated.

. . . .

1.5 BALANCING PRIVATE LIFE AND PUBLIC POLICY

Public policy shapes most of our modern existence. It's true that most goods and services in a modern economy are provided by private firms, but public policy—the collective decisions we make and enforce as a society—create the framework in which the private sector operates.

- Most of us wake up every morning in homes that we buy or rent in the private market. Yet the size and design of those homes is usually dictated by local zoning ordinances. The construction techniques are constrained by fire and safety codes.
- We decide privately where to work and what to do for a living. Yet we have made laws that prohibit us from accepting less than a minimum wage or engaging in certain kinds of business, even when they might be highly profitable (e.g., prostitution, selling drugs, or trafficking in human organs).
- We decide privately how to raise our children. Yet the vast majority of children attend public schools. Not only are such institutions funded communally, they require a consensus on how students should be taught and what they need to learn. And, if in the process of raising children, we

do them harm or are considered at risk of doing so, we have empowered government agencies to take them away from us.

- We pursue our hobbies—playing basketball, reading a novel, watching television. We do so, however, in the belief that the defense and law-enforcement institutions we have created will protect us: the U.S. Army is searching for terrorists in Afghanistan, spy satellites are monitoring nuclear activity in North Korea, border patrol agents are monitoring who enters the United States and interdicting contraband.

One inherent challenge to public policy is balancing individual freedom against the rights and welfare of the community. By its nature, public policy often requires enforcing policies that some members of society oppose. Societies create institutions—from neighborhood zoning laws to international treaties—that constrain individual behavior in the name of some larger social good. Communities routinely demolish private homes and confiscate private property through the power of eminent domain (which enables them to take private property with compensation) in order to build roads and other public infrastructure. A handful of countries, the United States included, vest their governments with the ultimate power: the authority to put an individual to death.

Indeed, most public policies make some individuals or groups worse off. That does not make them bad public policies; the total social benefits may far exceed the total costs imposed on those who are harmed—but that is little consolation to those who are made worse off. Navigating this trade-off between private interests and the welfare of the larger community is at the heart of some of the most difficult and contentious public policy issues:

- Under what circumstances and to what extent should society attempt to protect individuals from their own behavior? Should we mandate motor-cycle helmets or ban smoking even in private establishments?
- What limits should be placed on private behavior that has little or no public impact? Twice in the past two decades the U.S. Supreme Court—the American institution often called upon to resolve such difficult questions—has been asked to rule on the constitutionality of a Texas antisodomy law that bans certain kinds of private sexual acts between consenting adults.
- What powers should law-enforcement agencies have in their efforts to fight terrorism? Should they be allowed to enter private homes or listen to private phone conversations? If so, under what circumstances? Should they be allowed to make decisions based on ethnic or racial profiling?

These kinds of trade-off arise at all levels of society—from a neighborhood policy that prohibits certain kinds of commercial signage to an international treaty that bans activities that have an adverse impact on the global environment. The process for resolving these important trade-offs is no different than the broad policy process outlined earlier in the chapter. It requires a thorough understanding of the issue (including the costs and benefits imposed on the affected parties), a process for gathering democratic input, and an institution or institutions with the capacity to evaluate competing policy options and choose (and then enforce and evaluate) a course of action.

· · · · · · · · · · · · · · · | **POLICY IN THE REAL WORLD** | · · · · · · · · · · · · · · ·

Private Behavior, Public Information: The AIDS National Mailing of 1988

When C. Everett Koop was appointed U.S. surgeon general in 1981, acquired immunodeficiency syndrome (AIDS) had yet to be identified as such. The Centers for Disease Control (CDC) reported five cases that year of homosexual men who were dying from a rare form of pneumonia usually contracted by individuals with weakened immune systems.[15]

In 1983, French and American scientists named the disease AIDS and identified the virus that caused it, the human immunodeficiency virus, or HIV. Only two years later, 12,000 cases of AIDS had been reported in the United States. What was the role for the U.S. surgeon general, an office within the U.S. Department of Health and Human Services, as "America's chief health educator"?

Koop concluded, "If ever there was a disease made for a Surgeon General, it was AIDS." But AIDS was not like typhoid or yellow fever. The earliest victims were predominantly gay men and intravenous drug users; social conservatives, including many officials within the Reagan administration, believed that victims brought the disease on themselves through aberrant and immoral behavior. What was government's responsibility, if any, for confronting the mounting HIV/AIDS epidemic?

15. "AIDS, the Surgeon General, and the Politics of Public Health," C. Everett Koop Papers (Washington, D.C.: National Library of Medicine).

In 1986, President Ronald Reagan asked his surgeon general to draft a report on AIDS. Koop himself drafted a thirty-six-page report that explained AIDS, its causes, and the ways transmission could be prevented, including the use of condoms. The explicit discussion of sex was startling for many, as was Koop's recommendation that all schoolchildren receive sex education beginning in third grade.

Two years later, Congress ordered the surgeon general to undertake a national AIDS mailing, recognizing the moral politics of the situation by ordering that the report be "distributed without necessary clearance of the content by any official, organization or office."[16] On May 5, 1988, the federal government began mailing out brochures, an eight-page summary of Koop's original report, to all 107 million American households with a postal address. It was the largest mailing in American history and the first health advisory sent directly to all American households.

The hope was that public information on AIDS would change private behavior in ways that would lessen the devastating effects of the disease.

1.6 THE ART OF THE POSSIBLE: LIFE IN A WORLD OF SCARCITY AND UNCERTAINTY

We attempt to make policy not only amid fundamental disagreements over basic values (Does life begin at conception?), but also with limited resources and imperfect information.

Scarcity. There is a finite supply of everything worth having—from oil to oceanfront mansions. In the private sector, we ration scarce resources by using prices. When the demand for some good or service exceeds the available supply—when 60,000 people would like to attend a concert in an arena with 20,000 seats—the price will rise, reducing demand until it matches the available supply. In the concert example, the ticket price will rise (either via the concert promoter or on a secondary market like eBay) until the 20,000 people who most want to see the concert are the ones who buy the tickets at the market-clearing price (the price at which supply equals demand).

In the private sector, not everyone gets everything he or she wants. We do not all live in huge houses and drive luxury automobiles. Very few of us own

16. "U.S. Will Mail AIDS Advisory to All Households," *New York Times*, May 5, 1988.

Gulfstream jets. Price is the mechanism we use to ration goods and services, even essential items like food, shelter, and health care.

Public policy also involves rationing scarce goods and services, albeit using different mechanisms. The market does not necessarily work as a mechanism for allocating shared goods and services. Imagine, for example, if the citizens of a nation were asked to make voluntary payments for a missile defense system to protect the country from a terrorist nuclear attack. Would those who valued a missile defense system most highly be willing to pay the most to fund it, as in the private sector? Probably not—because once the system was in place, it would protect everyone within the borders, even those who did not pay for it. Most citizens, even those who strongly support a missile defense system, would prefer to contribute nothing and allow others to pay for a resource from which they would benefit. This "free rider" phenomenon and other collective action problems will be covered in greater detail in Chapter 4.

Thus, the provision of shared goods and services is likely to be a political rather than a market-driven process. The relevant group must decide what goods and services should be provided and what price members should be charged for those services: a homeowners' association charges assessments for landscaping and upkeep of common areas; a municipality levies taxes to pay for schools, parks, sewers, police and fire protection; the United Nations charges member countries for administration, peacekeeping, and other global functions. The contributions required from members need not be uniform. Most governments, for example, levy higher taxes on wealthier individuals. But these contributions are rarely voluntary.

The complexity of making a collective decision on how money ought to be raised and spent explains both why the public budgeting process is so important and why it is so contentious. In a modern economy, the private sector allocates scarce resources based on the private decisions of millions of individuals as they shop, work, play, and otherwise go about life. Society does not have to vote on where Starbucks ought to put stores; the company will put them where there are the most people who want to buy coffee.

The institutions of public policy, on the other hand, do require that members of society come to agreement on how scarce resources should be raised and spent. The U.S. federal budget is over $2 trillion annually; 300 million of us must somehow come to a collective decision on exactly how money ought to be raised and where it should be spent.

Uncertainty. If public policy were a laboratory science, the world would be a much better place. It's not. Policy analysts, politicians, and others working in the realm of public policy must often make decisions in the face of imperfect information, both about the nature of the challenges they are trying to address and the effectiveness of the solutions they are considering.

For example, economists still disagree about the fundamental causes of the Great Depression more than seventy-five years after the stock market crash of 1929. (The relationship between the crash and the subsequent depression is but one source of disagreement.) Yet President Franklin Roosevelt obviously did not have seventy-five years for his advisers to come to an agreement on what ought to be done to help the country out of its economic despair. Doing nothing was not a political or economic option.

Unlike physics or chemistry, public policy does not produce consistent outcomes that can be tested with controlled experiments and, therefore, understood with certainty. It is not possible to repeat the Great Depression over and over again, each time slightly altering the policy mix of the New Deal until the full ramifications of each program were perfectly understood. By its nature, public policy decisions are likely to be complicated by certain inherent uncertainties:

- **Scientific uncertainty.** When a new threat to society is discovered, such as a disease like HIV/AIDS or an environmental phenomenon like global warming, we do not have a complete understanding of the problem. Yet the more serious the threat, the more urgent it is to act quickly, even with limited information.

- **Human unpredictability.** Unlike carbon atoms, no two human beings are exactly the same; more important, individuals cannot be expected to behave identically, even under similar circumstances. Public policy offers many tools for understanding and predicting human behavior, but there are no immutable laws. A policy problem or solution may involve hundreds, thousands, or millions of individuals, not one of whose future behavior can be known with certainty.

- **Deliberately hidden information.** In fighting terrorism, waging war, catching tax cheats, minimizing nuclear proliferation, or a wide array of other activities, there are individuals or governments that prefer to operate in secrecy. The most salient issues of the George W. Bush presidency for example—the attacks of September 11, 2001; the question of weapons of mass destruction in Iraq; the nuclear ambitions of North Korea and Iran—have involved actors who deliberately withheld information of profound importance to the United States.

- **The sheer complexity of life.** No two policy problems are exactly the same, nor are two moments in time. Economists and policy makers have studied the Great Depression for seventy years. In fact, Federal Reserve chairman Ben Bernanke has written books on the subject. Still, the financial crisis of 2008 presented new challenges. There were no credit default swaps or mortgage-backed securities in the 1930s. The Obama administration could learn from the policies of the Roosevelt administration—but only up to a point. Our accretion of knowledge allows us to live dramatically better than we did only a century ago. But no matter how much we learn from history, the present will always be different in crucial respects.

For all these reasons, policy makers must often act without any certainty of the "right" course of action, particularly if doing nothing is not an attractive option. In his autobiography, former Treasury secretary Robert Rubin describes the attempt to react to a financial crisis in Mexico in December 1994. The peso was plunging against the dollar as investors withdrew their capital from Mexico, and there was a fear around the globe that the Mexican government would not be able to pay its international debts. The question facing the U.S. Treasury secretary was what, if anything, the United States should do about it. Rubin writes:

> Mexico is a good example of a situation—often encountered by policy makers as well as by those in the private sector—in which all decisions had the potential for serious adverse consequences and the key was to find the least bad option. In this case, the dangers of not acting were severe economic distress in Mexico, a contagious decline in emerging markets, and a setback to American growth and prosperity. The risk of acting was failure—potentially endangering repayment of billions of dollars of taxpayer money—or, if we succeeded, moral hazard [the risk that bailing out Mexico would encourage lenders to make excessively risky loans in the future].[17]

The Clinton administration did not have the luxury of studying the issue in detail. As investors took their money out of Mexico, the Mexican government's reserves of foreign currency, which it would need to pay back foreign loans, were dwindling away. The country was moving quickly toward default on its debts,

---

17. Robert E. Rubin and Jacob Weisberg, *In an Uncertain World: Tough Choices from Wall Street to Washington* (New York: Random House, 2003), p. 11.

the government equivalent of bankruptcy. An American intervention would put billions of dollars of taxpayers' money at risk. On the other hand, doing nothing and allowing Mexico to default might lead to a chain reaction of international financial crises with a significant impact on the U.S. economy. Rubin continues:

> I woke up on Monday with a sense of deep concern. As I had feared, the Mexican markets began to sell off sharply, with the peso dropping almost 10 percent to more than 6 pesos per dollar, its lowest level yet. We had originally assumed that Mexico could remain solvent at least through February. But despite the assumption many people make that government has better information than the private sector, the opposite is often true. Mexico informed us that its reserves had fallen to around $2 billion on the same day the *International Herald Tribune* reported it. That could have meant a generalized financial collapse within days in Mexico.[18]

In short order, the United States made a multibillion-dollar loan to the Mexican government. The American commitment of capital, combined with a large loan from the International Monetary Fund, was sufficient to stabilize the Mexican government's finances. The outcome was favorable: Mexico repaid the loan, early and with interest. But what Rubin makes clear is that even the proponents of this policy were far from certain that it would work. They had a limited amount of time to make an informed decision with a limited amount of information. Important public policy decisions are often made under such circumstances.

1.7 CONCLUSION

Why does public policy matter? Consider a striking example from American history. The Articles of Confederation, the nation's first attempt at self-government, did not work. The institutions it put in place were not sufficient to unify and support a young country. The second attempt, the Constitution, laid the foundation for the richest, most powerful society in the history of

---

18. Rubin and Weisberg, *In an Uncertain World*, p. 22.

human civilization—the same people, the same land, the same economic system, but a different set of governing institutions and principles. In other words, better public policy.

Even that system would later break down. The Civil War resulted from a failure of America's institutions to resolve differences over the balance of power between the federal government and the states, with slavery as the irreconcilable issue that broke the country apart. The Civil War killed some 600,000 Americans. Good public policy does not require individuals to agree on every issue; it does require them to agree on a mechanism for resolving those disputes. In 1860, Americans could not agree on how to resolve the slavery issue; they turned to killing each other as a result.

Good public policy makes our lives better. It facilitates prosperity, empowers people, and builds stronger societies. Bad public policy does the opposite. It inhibits economic activity and diminishes human potential. A survey of the world at the beginning of the twenty-first century finds that many societies—comprising billions of people—have been unable to organize and govern themselves in a way that fully unlocks their potential.

The goal of public policy is to improve the way we live. The goal of this book is to provide an introduction to the most important tools for making good public policy.

FOR DISCUSSION

Maximizing Human Potential:
The First Arab Human Development Report[19]

The United Nations Development Programme (UNDP) is the organization within the United Nations that collects data on living conditions around the world. More than a decade ago, the UNDP created the human development index (HDI), a measure of average well-being for a nation's people based on a combination of indicators: gross domestic product (GDP) per capita, life expectancy, school enrollment, and the adult literacy rate.

Norway ranked first in the world in terms of human development in 2009. The United States, the world's ninth richest economy on a per capita basis, ranked thirteenth. Niger—with a life expectancy at birth of 50.8 years, an adult literacy rate of 29 percent, and GDP per capita of $627—ranked last.

What accounts for the extraordinary gap between the most and least developed nations? In 2002, the UNDP took a step toward answering this question with its first comprehensive report on a single region, the *Arab Human Development Report 2002*. A team of Arab scholars, led by Egyptian sociologist Nader Fergany, documented living conditions in the twenty-two nations that make up the League of Arab States— 280 million people, or roughly 5 percent of the world. More controversially, the report analyzed why Arab countries have consistently lagged behind the rest of the world in many measures of human development.[20] The scholars' work was "guided by the conviction that solid analysis can contribute to the many efforts underway to mobilize the region's rich human potential."

There was some good news in the report. Life expectancy in the Arab world had increased by fifteen years over the previous three decades, while infant mortality rates had dropped by two-thirds. The twenty-two Arab countries had the lowest level of dire poverty in the world (defined as the fraction of persons living on less than $1 a day).

Yet there was much evidence that the Arab nations have not made the best possible use of their human and physical endowments. The region's total factor productivity—the efficiency with which inputs are converted into outputs—actually declined between 1960 and 1990, meaning that the Arab nations' economies became less efficient at producing goods and services at the same time most of the rest of the world was growing significantly more productive.

---

19. United Nations Development Programme, *Arab Human Development Report 2002* (New York: UNDP, 2002).

20. "Self-Doomed to Failure," *The Economist,* July 6, 2002.

Meanwhile, per capita income for the Arab nations grew at a meager 0.5 percent annually between 1960 and 1990. Some income growth is obviously better than none, but at that slow rate, the income of an average Arab citizen will not double for 140 years. In other parts of the world, notably east Asia, rapid economic growth is doubling incomes every ten years. In 1960, the Arab nations were richer on a per capita basis than the "Asian Tigers." Three decades later, South Korea was twice as rich as the Arab average.

There is, of course, a broad range of performance across the countries studied in the *Arab Human Development Report 2002*. Based on the HDI, Kuwait scores in the highest category (number 46 in the world), while Djibouti (153 out of 175 countries) is near the bottom. Still, the total economic output for the twenty-two Arab countries studied was a paltry $531 billion—roughly the same economic output as Spain and slightly less than the state of Florida. The region's unemployment rate was 15 percent. The most powerful sign of distress, however, lay in the attitudes of young people: 51 percent of "older adolescents" interviewed said they would like to emigrate.

The *Arab Human Development Report 2002* concluded: "It is evident that in both quantitative and qualitative terms, Arab countries have not developed as quickly or as fully as other comparable regions. From a human development perspective, the state of human development in the Arab world is a cause for concern."

So what is going wrong?

In short, the answer is poor public policy. The report identified three broad deficits: freedom, women's empowerment, and knowledge acquisition. The authors found that policies in these areas that deviate from the norms of the developed world have made it more difficult for the Arab societies to reach their potential.

Freedom. The report's authors used a freedom index, which reflects the degree to which citizens enjoy civil and political liberties. The Arab countries have the lowest freedom score of any region in the world. The report concluded, "Compared with similar regions, the Arabs suffer from a 'freedom deficit', so that even when civil rights are enshrined in constitutions and laws, they are often ignored in practice. Popular political participation in Arab countries remains weak, as shown by the lack of genuine democracy and restrictions on liberties."

A related measure of "voice and accountability" examined the political process, civil liberties, political rights, and the independence of the media. Again, the Arab nations have the lowest value of all regions in the world. The report called for improving the institutions of governance and activating the voice of the people, including "political representation in effective legislatures based on free, honest, efficient and regular elections."

Women's empowerment. Women's economic and political participation in the twenty-two Arab nations studied is the lowest in the world. For example, women hold 11.0 percent of the seats in parliament in sub-Saharan Africa compared to 3.5 percent in the Arab countries studied. Women are precluded from voting or holding office in some countries. Roughly half of all women in the Arab world can neither read nor write. The report draws the obvious conclusion: "Society as a whole suffers when half of its productive potential is stifled."

Knowledge acquisition. As a group, the Arab nations examined spend a higher fraction of GDP on education than any other developing region; the resources are not necessarily being well spent. Some 10 million children between the ages of six and fifteen are not in school at all. The enrollment rate for higher education is 13 percent—shockingly below the 60-percent rate for the industrialized nations. And the share of women in higher education is lower still. The quality of that education has also deteriorated, according to the report. Arab schools are not teaching skills appropriate for the economy, which helps to explain slow productivity growth and relatively high levels of unemployment. Some 65 million adults are illiterate, two-thirds of whom are women.

The report identified other systemic knowledge gaps beyond weak schools and the repression of women. The Arab region has the lowest level of Internet access in the world; less than 1 percent of the population uses the Internet. Even then, much of the content on the Web is in English, which is not widely spoken in the Arab world.

The Arab world was a center of learning in the Middle Ages. Yet in the last 1,000 years, the Arab nations collectively have translated as many books as Spain translates in a single year. In the twenty-two countries of the Arab world, only 300 books a year are translated into Arabic—roughly a fifth the number that Greece translates every year.

These broad deficits are a function of public policy. To the extent that the HDI is an accurate measure of human well-being, the Arab nations are paying a high cost for poor policy.

QUESTIONS

1. Is the human development index (HDI) a good indicator of human well-being? What about gross domestic product (GDP)? What are the strengths and limitations of these indicators?
2. Is it constructive to focus on a region of the world with such a wide variance of countries?
3. Does this report matter outside the affected countries? Why, or why not?
4. How can policy makers measure and quantify something as seemingly abstract as "freedom"?
5. Why would we expect there to be a relationship between "voice and accountability" and economic strength?
6. Is the acquisition of knowledge a private endeavor or a public responsibility? Why?
7. Given the deficits identified by the report's authors, what kinds of policies would likely lead to better social and economic outcomes? What are the barriers to those kinds of policy changes?
8. Under what circumstances, if any, should the United States and other developed countries intervene to change the policies of nondemocratic countries or regions? Why?

KEY CONCEPTS

★ Public policy is the process through which we make collective decisions that are binding upon all affected parties, whether they agree with the ultimate decision or not.

★ Good public decisions require institutions that can gather and act upon the preferences of the relevant group, whether the group consists of members of a church parish or the citizens of a country. The group will almost never agree unanimously with a decision, but it is imperative that the group agree with the process by which the decision was reached.

★ For-profit firms operate to earn a profit for their owners. Nonprofit organizations do not operate with the intention of making a profit and, therefore, play a crucial role in enhancing overall social welfare by delivering goods and services that are not ordinarily provided by the private sector. Government is vested with authority, including coercive powers and even force, over some political jurisdiction.

★ Policy analysis uses a set of tools to analyze a social problem and implement a solution that is both effective and politically feasible.

★ Good public policy does not necessarily involve more government. The process of deregulation, or removing government authority over activities better coordinated by the private sector, can lower costs and improve social welfare.

★ Public policy almost always involves choosing among imperfect alternatives without perfect information on their likely outcomes.

★ Better public policy leads to more informed decisions, a better understanding of human behavior, more effective institutions for resolving differences of opinion, and outcomes that help us lead healthy, productive, safe, and peaceful lives.

CHAPTER 2

Why Is It So Hard to Make the World a Better Place?

THE PROMISE AND PITFALLS OF GENETIC TESTING

The advance in genetic research encapsulates the challenges of making good public policy in an age of rapid scientific discovery and technological change. Our growing knowledge of the human genome makes medicine easier and public policy more complex.

In 2003, researchers announced that they had successfully decoded the human genome, the genetic building blocks of human life. This mapping of our more than 30,000 genes, and the subsequent research on how specific genes affect behavior and disease, is considered to be one of the most significant medical advances in history. Already, researchers have identified genes associated with diseases ranging from breast cancer to emphysema—some 1,800 disease-related genes so far.[1]

But lurking within that extraordinary leap in science is a nettlesome public policy question: Who should have access to that genetic information? If a strand of your hair or a swab from your cheek can determine whether you are prone to Alzheimer's disease or heart disease or cervical cancer ten or twenty years before the onset of the illness, who should be privy to that information?

One intuitive solution is to allow individuals to gather the details of their genetic profile and keep such information strictly private. After all, it's *your* DNA; the case for medical privacy does not seem hard to make. But it turns out that providing individuals with genetic information about the likelihood of their becoming seriously ill has profound social implications; indeed, it could bankrupt the American health insurance industry.

---

1. http://www.nih.gov/about/researchresultsforthepublic/HumanGenomeProject.pdf.

Health insurance, like all other kinds of insurance, is based on pooling risk. A private company sells policies to thousands or millions of people, each of whom has a small risk of some very expensive event. For example, anyone who owns a home runs the risk that the house or condominium might be destroyed by fire. It's an unlikely event but one that would be financially devastating, should it strike. So most property owners buy homeowners insurance, which provides a large payout in the event of fire, hurricane, or other catastrophic event.

When a private insurance company insures millions of homes, some will burn down and most won't. The company makes money by calculating the average costs of its payouts and then charging premiums that are slightly higher. The company makes money even when some houses burn down; the firm merely needs to collect enough money from homeowners whose homes are not harmed to exceed the cost of payments to the unlucky few.

This system is built on a crucial premise: no one knows which houses will burn down and which ones will not—not the insurance company and not the homeowners. Imagine if that were not the case. Suppose homeowners knew in advance whether or not their house would burn down or even if they were at higher or lower risk than average. Owners with houses likely to go up in flames would purchase huge amounts of insurance while those with little or no risk would likely skip insurance entirely. The insurance company would be left mostly with customers whose houses are likely to burn down—a recipe for financial ruin.

On the other hand, if insurance companies know in advance which houses are likely to go up in flames, they will refuse to sell insurance to those families. The people who need insurance most—those whose homes are at high risk of fire—will not be able to buy it.

Health insurance works—or doesn't work—the same way. Some individuals will be sicker, and, therefore, more expensive to insure, than others. An insurance company need only collect enough in premiums from relatively healthy individuals to make a profit after paying the claims of those who turn out to be unhealthy.

The challenge of genetic testing is that it can tell us in advance who is most at risk of becoming sick and who is not. Who should have access to that information?

If genetic information is shared widely with insurance companies, then those individuals most prone to illness will find it difficult, if not impossible, to get any kind of coverage. In other words, the people who need health insurance the most will be the least likely to get it.

If, on the other hand, insurance companies are forbidden from gathering such information, they may face financial ruin as individuals prone to illness load up on coverage while those with a relatively healthy prognosis avoid insurance or choose the minimum available coverage.

While scientists and doctors are busy exploiting the knowledge from the Human Genome Project, policy makers must answer a question that had no relevance ten or twenty years ago: Can insurance companies ask potential customers for a strand of hair or a swab of the cheek? And, if so, what should they be allowed to do with that information?

Such questions related to genetic testing have already moved from the theoretical to the practical. At the end of the 2005 professional basketball season, the Chicago Bulls asked one of their star players, forward Eddy Curry, to submit to a DNA test to determine if he has cardiomyopathy, a potentially fatal disease of part of the heart muscle. Curry was due for contract negotiations, and critics charged that the Bulls were attempting to gauge his long-term health before signing a $40-million or $50-million contract. Chicago Bulls General Manager John Paxson told the media, "I know this is a new issue in our business right now. There's no road map here to follow. But we're just trying to do what's in the best interest of Eddy Curry."[2]

Should a team considering a multimillion-dollar contract have the right to make that request? Under what circumstances, if any, should other kinds of employers be able to ask workers for genetic information? In 2008, Congress answered this question by passing the Genetic Information Nondiscrimination Act (implemented in 2009), which prohibits employers from requesting genetic information or using such information in hiring, firing, or promotions.[3] Genetic research has changed the world, but, as with most technological or scientific leaps forward, public policy has had to keep pace—or even catch up.

This chapter explores the challenges inherent in implementing policies that make our lives better, beginning with debate over what constitutes "better." As technology and science constantly propel us forward, why does public policy appear to lag so far behind? If we can put a man on the moon, build planes that fly themselves, and decode the human genome, why do we have so much difficulty fixing the American health-care system or fighting poverty in Africa? As it turns out, there are many answers to that question.

2. Greg Couch, "About This Test of Curry's DNA . . . No Way," *Chicago Sun-Times,* June 9, 2005.

3. Steven Greenhouse, "Law Seeks to Ban Misuse of Genetic Testing," *New York Times,* November 16, 2009.

CHAPTER OUTLINE

2.1 PUBLIC POLICY SUCCESS: LIFE IS BETTER NOW

For all the challenges of modern public policy, we should not lose sight of the degree to which life in the developed world has grown steadily better by almost every important measure.

- We are living longer. Average life expectancy at birth has increased from forty-seven in 1900 to seventy-eight at present.[4]
- We're richer. Our real per capita income (meaning that it has been adjusted for inflation) is more than twice what it was in 1970.[5]
- And we work less. The number of hours the average American private-sector worker spends on the job has fallen from 39 hours per week in 1964 to 33 in 2009. We retire earlier, too. The average age at retirement for American men has fallen from an average of sixty-nine in the 1950s to

---

4. http://www.cdc.gov/nchs/data/hus/hus06.pdf#027
5. http://www.ers.usda.gov/Data/Macroeconomics/, real per capita income data set.

sixty-three at the beginning of the twenty-first century, even as we live longer, meaning that the average American spends a far lower proportion of his life on the job than he did a half century ago.[6]

- Life is better in many places outside of the developed world, too. The number of people around the globe living in dire poverty (less than $1 a day) has fallen from 40 percent in 1981 to 26 percent in 2005, according to the World Bank.

···········| **RULE OF THUMB** |·············

A Note on Numbers

Chapters 9 to 13 will deal with data and statistics in greater depth, but two important concepts should be noted here. The first is the distinction between **real figures,** which have been adjusted for inflation (the rise in average prices), and **nominal figures,** which have not. For example, if personal income grows by 5 percent but average prices have also gone up 5 percent, then the typical person is not any better off at all. His or her income has gone up, but so have the prices of the things he spends it on. His quality of life, as measured by the things he can afford to buy, is unchanged. In this case, policy analysts would say that the *nominal* growth in personal income is 5 percent, but *real* income growth is 0.

Of course, if prices are falling—deflation—then a person can buy more with the same paycheck. Real wages would be going up in that case, even as nominal wages are unchanged.

REAL = NOMINAL − ADJUSTMENT FOR CHANGES IN PRICES

Policy makers should use real rather than nominal figures in order to avoid distortion when comparing prices or incomes over time.

A second important concept when dealing with figures is **per capita,** which means "per person." If a statistic is described as *per capita,* then it has been divided by the number of people it describes. For example, the American **gross domestic product (GDP),** which is the value of all goods and services produced in the country, is roughly $14.4 trillion. By comparison, **GDP per**

---

6. U.S. Bureau of Labor Statistics.

capita—$14.4 trillion divided by the population of the United States—is roughly $47,000.

A simple example makes clear why per capita figures are often more accurate than those that do not take into account the size of the relevant population. The GDP of India in 2008 was $3.3 trillion; the GDP of Israel was only $203 billion. India has a bigger economy than Israel, but does that mean most Indians live better? No. GDP per capita is a scant $2,900 in India compared to $28,000 in Israel. Figures that do not take into account the size of the population or population growth over time can be highly misleading.

....

Life is better in the twenty-first century than it was in 1900 for many people in many places. Public policy has much to do with that, both directly via programs such as mandatory childhood immunizations and compulsory education, and indirectly through the creation of institutions that allow a modern economy to thrive. The patent system, for example, gives an inventor (or his designee) an exclusive right to produce the new product for a fixed amount of time, providing a powerful incentive for private-sector research and innovation.

Our extraordinary economic progress has been built on the solid foundation of good public institutions: clearly defined property rights, a sound legal system, a reasonable regulatory climate, efficient public infrastructure, and so on. All of these concepts will be explored in greater detail throughout the book. For now, it is important to recognize that good public policy has led to dramatic improvements in our quality of life.

.... **POLICY IN THE REAL WORLD** ....

Good Science, Great Policy: The Global Eradication of Smallpox

Smallpox, a disfiguring and often fatal disease, is one of the worst scourges ever to strike civilization. The disease, caused by a virus, is spread from human to human by direct contact. There is no known cure. The body of a smallpox victim is covered by painful pustules; the disease eventually causes death or intense scarring for those who survive. In 1967, there were 10 million to 15 million cases of smallpox worldwide, killing some 2 million people and leaving millions of others blinded and disfigured.[7]

Yet in the 1960s—and for 150 years before that—society had the technical expertise to prevent smallpox. In the late eighteenth century, Edward Jenner, an English country doctor, developed a smallpox vaccine. Jenner discovered that infecting an individual with cowpox, a milder relative of the smallpox virus, would cause the body to produce antibodies that subsequently protected humans against smallpox.[8]

As a result, routine immunizations largely eliminated the threat of smallpox in the developed world. In the 1960s, however, the disease was still raging in Brazil, Africa, the Indian subcontinent, and Indonesia. On January 1, 1967, the World Health Organization (WHO) launched the Intensified Smallpox Eradication Program—an audacious effort to wipe out the disease entirely through aggressive global vaccination.

Despite the horrific nature of smallpox, there were some features of the disease that made the public health campaign easier:

- Smallpox is easy to diagnose, largely because of the distinctive rash and pustules.
- There is no animal host. Smallpox is spread exclusively by humans (unlike malaria, which is spread by mosquitoes).
- The disease progresses quickly, which is bad for victims but makes it less likely that they will infect others before they realize that they are sick (unlike the HIV/AIDS virus).
- There is no social stigma associated with smallpox (unlike sexually transmitted diseases).

Health workers were also assisted by several new technologies: a freeze-dried vaccine eliminated the need for refrigeration and made transportation and storage easier in the tropics; a new bifurcated needle provided a cheap, easy, and effective way to give the immunization.

But the eradication of smallpox was primarily a triumph of good policy, not new medicine or technology. Since 100-percent immunization was not feasible, the WHO set a target immunization rate around 80 percent (easily measurable by the small scar that immunization leaves behind) and supplemented mass immunization with a policy of "surveillance and containment." When new outbreaks of smallpox were detected, health workers were dis-

---

7. F. Fenner, D. A. Henderson, I. Arita, Z. Ježek, and I. D. Ladnyi, *Smallpox and Its Eradication* (Geneva: World Health Organization, 1988), p. 175.

8. Jonathan B. Tucker, *Scourge: The Once and Future Threat of Smallpox* (New York: Atlantic Monthly Press, 2001), pp. 23–38.

patched immediately to isolate the victims and immunize all those who might have come in contact with them. In some cases, that involved house-to-house searches in affected and surrounding villages. Guards were even posted at infected homes to prevent further transmission.[9]

The last case of naturally occurring indigenous smallpox (*Variola minor*) was reported in Somalia in 1977. Dr. H. Mahler, WHO director-general at the time, described the success—the first time a major disease had been stricken from the planet—as a "triumph of management, not of medicine."[10]

. . . .

2.2 SO FAR TO GO

For all our progress, the world is far from a perfect place. Some 1.8 billion people live on less than $1.25 a day, which is the World Bank's definition of extreme poverty. Even in the United States, the poverty rate hit 13 percent in 2009, which is not dramatically different than it was in the 1970s. One in three black children lives in poverty.

Elsewhere in the world, societies are racked by poverty, poor health, civil war, and other horrible violence. Vast swaths of Africa actually grew poorer between 1990 and 2000. Diseases that are easily prevented or cured in the developed world continue to kill millions of people in poor nations. A staggering 20 percent of the world's population does not have access to safe drinking water, making diarrhea one of the leading preventable causes of death among the world's children. If the study of public policy enables society to produce better outcomes, then why do we still face so many challenges? Or, as the chapter title asks, why is it so hard to make the world a better place?

There is a handful of challenges inherent to public policy.

1. What is *better*? Any discussion of making the world a better place must begin with the fact that different people will define *better* differently. There is no single, quantifiable measure of public policy success. We cannot point to Japan and say that it scores 98, compared to 87 for Sweden. We can attempt to create such indices, such as the Human Development Index, discussed in the last chapter, but reasonable people will disagree profoundly over what factors ought to be included in such indices and how heavily each of

9. Jack W. Hopkins, *The Eradication of Smallpox: Organizational Learning and Innovation in International Health* (Boulder, Colo.: Westview Press, 1989), pp. 85–94.

10. Hopkins, *The Eradication of Smallpox,* p. 125.

those factors ought to be weighted. There are many possible measures of success. Aggregating them into a single public policy indicator involves the proverbial comparison between "apples and oranges"—except that with public policy it is likely to be "jobs and environmental quality" or "public safety and personal liberty" or some other trade-off that is not easily reconciled.

Which of the following policies would *you* support:

- an economic development initiative that created 100,000 new jobs in Florida but did permanent damage to the Everglades?
- a free-trade agreement that raised the overall wealth of the country but caused significant job losses in some industries?
- a criminal-justice initiative that lowered violent crime rates but increased the likelihood that some innocent individuals would be wrongfully convicted?

In other fields, success is more easily measured. In business, for example, companies can be evaluated and compared based on their profitability. Firms that consistently make a lot of money are considered more successful than companies that don't—period. There are other intermediate measures of success, such as market share or customer satisfaction, but these tend to be benchmarks along the way toward boosting the bottom line, which means earning the highest possible return for the owners of the firm. A CEO who presides over an unprofitable company will not keep his job very long if there is not some plan for making money in the long run, no matter how happy customers are.

Which company is doing better: Ford or Toyota? We can answer that question with variations on a single metric: profits. Profits can be measured and compared across firms; there is universal agreement that earning more is better than earning less. It's the proverbial bottom line.

Now let's ask a seemingly similar question from the realm of public policy: Which city is doing better—Chicago or Denver?

We certainly would not answer that question by comparing their profitability, since cities are not in the business of making money, let alone maximizing profits. (Indeed, a city could theoretically maximize profits by taking in huge amounts of tax revenue and spending very little on city services—which is not what urban residents would prefer.) We might look instead at a figure like population growth, which should tell us something about the health of the city. Healthy places tend to retain residents and attract new ones, so cities with rapid population growth are presumably doing better than those that are growing slowly or not at all.

But what if a city is growing slowly or not at all, but has had rapid growth in real per capita income? Such a city may not be getting bigger, but its residents would be growing richer, which is clearly a desirable outcome. Indeed, the people who live in a city almost certainly care more about their own income than they do about overall population growth. So, per capita income growth would appear to be a more refined measure of urban health than population growth.

But what if that increase in per capita income has been accompanied by rising levels of air pollution or by plummeting incomes for some segments of the population? (Remember, rising per capita income reflects an increase in *average* income but does not guarantee that everyone is getting richer.)

An analyst seeking to compare Chicago and Denver would likely consult many indicators: population growth, personal income growth, environmental health, the quality of municipal services relative to the tax burden, the quality of the public schools, the crime rate, the poverty rate, and so on. Different people may place different weights on the many possible outcome measures mentioned here (and on many other indicators not mentioned here). Public policy success, like beauty, is often in the eye of the beholder.

2. Disagreements over basic values. Public policy requires communal decisions that govern how we live as a society. Each of us brings a different set of core beliefs to that process. In some cases, these core beliefs clash mightily with the core beliefs of other reasonable people. There is no absolute truth (even if some of the parties involved assert as much), nor will science, technology, or any process of intellectual inquiry change minds. Instead, these are values informed by religious beliefs, cultural norms, upbringing, and other life experiences.

The ongoing debate in America over abortion is a good example. No scientific experiment can determine whether a fertilized embryo should be afforded the same rights as a fully formed human being. Scientists can measure the embryo, describe its development, even freeze it for later implantation. But they cannot answer the philosophical question at the heart of the abortion debate in America: Does human life begin when an egg is fertilized, when a child is born, or somewhere in between?

Disagreements over basic values are often most obvious in the context of social issues: abortion, guns, premarital sex, school prayer, and the like. In reality, however, values are often at the core of other policy disputes. The advent of genetic testing, discussed at the beginning of this chapter, raises issues that touch upon core values. Should prospective parents be able to test a fetus for genetic abnormalities? Should employers have access to an employee's genetic profile? Should individuals who are unlucky in life's genetic lottery have their health-care costs subsidized by those who are luckier and, therefore, healthier?

The related field of DNA testing—recognizing each individual's unique "DNA fingerprint"—raises similar questions. Should the government keep a DNA database to help solve crimes? If so, whose DNA should or should not be included in the database? These are not scientific questions: they are ethical questions that grow out of our advances in science. Public policy is complicated by the fact that society must resolve these kinds of issues despite the fact that reasonable people have strongly held, contradictory views that are not likely to be changed by new evidence or further inquiry.

3. Trade-offs among basic values. Even if we were to agree on basic values, public policy often forces us to make trade-offs that pit those basic values against one another. If asked, most Americans would say that the government ought to save money wherever possible. Indeed, the government has an obligation to taxpayers to procure goods and services as quickly and cheaply as possible.

Many of those same Americans might also say that preserving American jobs is an important priority and that the U.S. government—the army in particular—ought to procure its goods and services in the United States whenever possible.

So what happens when those values, each quite logical, conflict with one another, as happened when the U.S. Army sought to update its uniforms?

In 2001, the U.S. Army sought to modernize the appearance of its forces by providing all soldiers with black berets. The army's birthday, June 14, was set as the deadline for acquiring 1.3 million black berets. Army Chief of Staff General Eric Shinseki actually set the tight deadline for the beret switchover because he thought it would "demonstrate that the Army could accomplish this change effectively and quickly."[11]

To meet this deadline—as we expect our government to do—the army placed an order with an American firm. Since that firm did not have the capacity to make enough berets to meet the deadline, the government also placed orders with firms that make berets in China, Sri Lanka, Romania, Canada, and South Africa.[12]

Pride in the army's ability to meet a tight deadline was quickly eclipsed by the heresy of putting American troops in foreign-made uniforms. Representative Bill Pascrell of New Jersey recoiled at the "image of our guys and gals in uniform, taking off these berets to wipe their brows, and reading 'made in China.'" He declared, "Somebody should be punched for this."[13]

---

11. Gail Collins, "Hurry Up and Shield," *New York Times,* May 4, 2001.
12. "Army Recalling China-Made Black Berets," *New York Times,* May 2, 2001.
13. Collins, "Hurry Up and Shield."

Putting American soldiers in uniforms made in America trumped the government's responsibility to meet deadlines and procure goods as cheaply as possible. The army went so far as to recall and destroy hundreds of thousands of berets that had been manufactured in China.[14]

Or consider our ongoing antiterrorism efforts. Most Americans feel that protecting the nation against terrorist attacks should be one of the government's highest priorities. Many of those same individuals *also* feel that personal liberty is a core American value and that the government should be limited in its power to intrude upon the private affairs of individuals without compelling evidence that they may have committed a crime. The broad surveillance necessary to preempt terrorist attacks can cause clashes between our strong interest in national security and our equally strong interest in civil liberties. Many public policy issues force us to make trade-offs among our most strongly held beliefs and principles.

4. "Side effects" and organized interests. Nearly all policy changes generate both social benefits and social costs. Presumably, a good policy is one in which the benefits outweigh the costs. The complication is that the social costs, or "side effects," are often imposed on parties who do not enjoy the benefits, creating potential political opposition even when the policy makes society significantly better off overall.

Public policy is like medicine in that making things better sometimes makes other things slightly worse. And as with medicine, the question is not whether the solution is perfect, but whether the overall benefits exceed the overall costs. Thus, a physician may recommend surgery even when there is the risk of death or prescribe a medicine even if it has unpleasant side effects. The more serious the problem being addressed, the higher the tolerance for side effects. Treatments for cancer, for example, can cause great physical discomfort. But rarely does a patient decide to forgo chemotherapy because it will cause nausea or hair loss.

Public policy is different in one crucial respect: the individuals or groups who receive the benefits of a policy change are not necessarily the same people who bear the costs. To return to the medical analogy, imagine that, when a person is treated with chemotherapy successfully for cancer, *someone else gets nauseous and loses his hair.* The person who gets sick will not be pleased about the chemotherapy, even if the benefits of cancer treatment wildly exceed the discomfort of the side effects.

---

14. "Army Recalling China-Made Berets."

The individuals or groups harmed are not likely to be happy about their sacrifice, no matter how good the policy change is for society overall. Indeed, if the costs are concentrated, the losers may be angrier—and, therefore, more politically motivated—than the winners are happy. Imagine, for example, some kind of restriction on burning high-sulfur coal because of its adverse impact on the environment. For the sake of example, let's assume (a) that this policy would improve air quality for hundreds of millions of people and reduce global warming for everyone on the planet, and (b) a cost-benefit analysis suggests that the total environmental benefits from curtailing the use of high-sulfur coal would exceed the economic costs of making the transition, including the economic dislocation imposed on coal producers.

The costs—primarily lost coal-mining jobs—would be concentrated in a handful of coal-rich areas, such as West Virginia. Such areas would be devastated—not just the coal miners, but all the attendant businesses supported by that wealth. Those who lose lose big. Their livelihoods and communities would be at stake.

Meanwhile, the air-quality benefits of the hypothetical high-sulfur coal restriction would be highly diffuse: billions of people would enjoy a slightly better environment. The benefit to each individual person, however, might be quite small, even if the aggregate impact is enormous.

The potential losers are likely to be more politically motivated and organized than the potential winners. The political system responds not only to the number of voters who win or lose, but to the *intensity* of their preferences and the degree to which they can organize effectively. It is sometimes said that the losers scream louder than the winners sing, and that is what politicians hear. Policies with significant benefits for society overall may not necessarily survive the political process.

As a result, it is hard for a democratic political process to impose pain, even if broad social benefits far exceed the aggregate costs. The corollary is that so-called "pork barrel" projects often gain legislative approval because they lavish benefits on a concentrated group and spread the costs over a much wider population. It is the opposite of the case above: the small group that receives a special government benefit cares a lot about it; the much larger group that pays for it barely notices, even if the aggregate costs far exceed the benefits.

The role of organized interests in determining political outcomes is so important that we will return to it in Chapter 4 and elsewhere throughout the book. Public policy is complicated by the fact that the benefits and costs of a policy do not necessarily fall on the same individuals or groups. Even policies with enormous net social benefits are likely to be opposed by groups that bear a disproportionate share of the costs.

5. Balancing the present against the future. Policy change often involves imposing costs now in order to derive benefits in the future or, conversely, enjoying benefits today that must be paid for in the future. In private life, we do the same. Students pay tuition and forgo years of income to acquire a college degree. The payoff for that investment is significantly higher wages (relative to high-school graduates) for the duration of their working lives. In the long run, the benefits of a college degree generally far exceed the costs, though there is some sacrifice required in the short run.

Of course, we also sometimes make decisions that allow us to enjoy benefits in the present while deferring the costs for the future. Credit cards make it possible to purchase a television or vacation today while paying for it—with interest—in the months or even years to come.

These kinds of decisions are called intertemporal decisions because the costs and benefits occur at different times. Public policy decisions often have an intertemporal dimension. A country may limit fishing for some species, for example, to allow the stocks to replenish. Such a policy would curtail fishing incomes in the present but create more bountiful harvests in the future.

Or society may choose to incur benefits now and pay the costs later. For example, communities often pay for major infrastructure projects, such as new schools or roads, by borrowing money rather than using current tax revenues. The borrowed money must be paid back—with interest—from future tax revenues.

Humans are not particularly good at making intertemporal trade-offs even when only private behavior is involved. Individuals eat things that do not promote long-term health, exercise less than most health experts recommend, engage in behaviors like smoking and risky sexual activity that have enormous long-term costs, and so on. Some economists argue that all of these behaviors are perfectly rational—that individuals who smoke or take illegal drugs get enough pleasure out of those activities to outweigh the costs. This rich topic—the extent to which human behavior is truly rational—is crucial to policy analysis and will be covered in much greater detail in the next chapter.

For now, it is important to appreciate the degree to which intertemporal decisions complicate public policy. Many issues require that some group of people—perhaps even an entire nation—make some sacrifice in the present in order to generate benefits that accrue far in the future or even to a different generation. When analysts study an extreme case like climate change, for example, they evaluate the costs of modifying behavior today relative to the benefits that will accrue *over the next several centuries.*

Meanwhile, societies have ample opportunity to live large in the present while leaving the bill for the future. Indeed, it is entirely possible for a government to spend money on benefits for current citizens while passing much of the cost on to individuals who are not yet born. Imagine the temptation of a credit card with a bill that goes to someone else's address thirty years from now.

New York City borrowed heavily in the 1970s to ward off a fiscal crisis; repayment of that debt has been stretched out over such a long period of time that taxpayers in the year 2034 will still be paying interest and principal for government borrowing sixty years earlier. The *New York Times* noted, "Those costs would be borne by the children of taxpayers who were not even alive when Donna Summer ruled the airwaves—by people of the future who never wore mood rings or dialed rotary phones. It would be one of the longest fiscal bailouts ever."[15]

The concept of intergenerational equity—the fairness of how costs and benefits are distributed across generations—is an important concept in public policy and will be covered in more depth in Chapter 5. Successful groups, or even entire societies, must sacrifice in the present to yield benefits in the future and resist the temptation to enjoy benefits now while leaving excessive costs to the future.

6. Collective-action problems, or the "tragedy of the commons." Group behavior is often plagued by **collective-action problems**—cases in which the members of a group are unable or unwilling to organize themselves in a way that would make them better off in the long run. One of the core principles of public policy is that individuals behave in ways that make themselves better off. Individuals make millions of small decisions based on their own preferences; firms accommodate those preferences and make profits in the process. No central planning authority could ever allocate resources as efficiently. These basic assumptions are the most important principles of microeconomics and are at the core of how public policy will be approached in this book.

Yet there are many curious examples of individuals making what appear to be rational decisions based on their own self-interest that lead to bad outcomes. Consider the following: A group of coastal communities depends on fishing for its livelihood. Fish are a renewable resource (unlike petroleum or other minerals with a fixed amount in the ground that will eventually be exhausted). Basic economics tells us that the fishermen in these communities can maximize their total income and provide an infinite stream of future wealth by placing limits on current fishing. It is in the best interest of the

---

15. Michael Cooper, "New York City May Get a Free Ride to 2034," *New York Times,* May 7, 2003.

fishermen themselves to prevent "overfishing," or depleting the stock of fish to the point that future income is jeopardized.

Just as a matter of dollars and cents, we would expect fishermen to observe practices that maximize the number of fish that they can catch in the long run. That's often not what happens. Instead, fishermen act in ways that threaten the long-term viability of their own profession. Why?

The answer lies in a phenomenon known informally as **tragedy of the commons** and formally as "a collective-action problem." The incentives of the individual fishermen cause them to compromise the long-term value of the resource that they share. An example makes the case best. Assume that fishermen can make the most money in the long run by limiting their catch in such a way that the fish have time to spawn and grow larger. Further suppose that there is complete agreement that the best way to achieve this target is to have all fishermen voluntarily cut their current catch in half.

It is unlikely that this voluntary restraint will achieve its desired end. Any individual fisherman has a powerful incentive to "cheat." If he believes that other fishermen are abiding by the quota, then he can make lots of extra money by doubling or tripling his catch. Since he is just one of many fishermen (the rest of whom are supposedly observing the quota), his "cheating" will not compromise the fish stocks enough to lower his future catch, but it will significantly improve his current income.

But every individual fisherman has that same incentive, so cheating is likely to be common. Indeed, the "overfishing" will feed on itself. Once cheating becomes widespread, the future stock of fish is compromised; at that point, even the fishermen who resisted exceeding their quota in the beginning have an incentive to catch what they can before the resource is depleted.

Our understanding of communal behavior suggests that any voluntary agreement to protect a shared resource will not work in the absence of monitoring and enforcement, *even when all parties that share the resource understand that cooperation would raise their long-term incomes.* Indeed, tragedy of the commons is the observed pattern for many shared resources.

This topic and related models of group behavior are so important to understanding social outcomes that they will be covered in far greater detail in Chapter 4. Good public policy, of course, requires plans that help individuals overcome collective-action problems in order to achieve better outcomes. Collective-action problems, such as tragedy of the commons, can explain how groups of individuals acting in their own self-interest can actually make themselves worse off.

7. Nondemocratic safeguards. The policy process can be cumbersome and frustrating in part because we *deliberately* create institutions that defy or ignore the will of the majority. The connection between democratic governance and good social outcomes is well established. Nearly every developed nation in the world is a democracy. This book will make the case that many developing nations would be better served by more democratic institutions. But few, if any, nations are truly governed based only on the will of the majority. The United States certainly is not.

To understand why, consider a simple example. Imagine a classroom of twenty students. The professor announces that because democracy is a sensible process for making communal decisions, the class will operate as a pure democracy. The majority will get what the majority wants. By definition, this should be the best way to please the most people and, therefore, achieve the best outcomes for the class as a whole.

Now suppose that nineteen students vote to beat up their twentieth classmate, take his money, and use it to buy pizza. Is that a good social outcome?

Public policy requires a delicate balance between honoring the wishes of the majority and respecting the rights of the minority. Some of the most important American political institutions exist to guarantee individual rights against larger political forces:

- The framers of the Constitution insisted on the Bill of Rights as a set of absolute protections for individual citizens, regardless of the popular will. For example, the First Amendment guarantees freedom of speech, even when a vast majority of citizens might find the content of that speech hateful.

- The Constitution created both the House of Representatives and the Senate to avoid political domination by the most populous states, which would have happened with a system of pure representation. The Senate, with two representatives from each state regardless of population, is not a pure democratic institution. The **filibuster,** a rule within the Senate that allows 41 of 100 senators to thwart Senate business, is less democratic still.

- Federal judges, including Supreme Court justices, are appointed for life in order to make them immune from political vicissitudes. The net effect is that judges can make decisions that are not popular with many people. The goal is to protect certain rights and outcomes that might be trampled by a majority—the social equivalent of nineteen students voting to take money from their lone colleague.

For public policy, this inherent tension between individual rights and the will of the majority has several implications. First, it explains why many citizens, even a vast majority in some cases, are unhappy with some public outcome. Most Americans would prefer that the Nazi Party not be allowed to hold parades or recruit on the Internet. But a society that gives most people what they want all of the time might actually be a dangerous and repressive place, because it offers no protection to individuals or minority groups.

Second, many societies have found it difficult or impossible to build a democratic nation when a minority population—often a religious or ethnic minority—is unwilling to entrust its fate to the majority. For example, the efforts to build a democratic society in postwar Iraq have been handicapped by fear on the part of Sunni Muslims that the Shiite majority will abuse its power. As we have noted, it is possible to create institutional protections, such as the U.S. Bill of Rights; but this requires (a) the majority to agree to such constraints, and (b) the minority or minorities to have faith that the safeguards that have been put in place—limits on democracy—will truly afford them protection. Public policy is sometimes unresponsive to public opinion by design. Societies create nondemocratic institutions to protect individuals or minorities from the majority.

8. The challenge of changing human behavior. Humans are complex beings embedded within complex cultures. Achieving better social outcomes requires changing behavior, and changing behavior is difficult. Human beings do not act like carbon atoms or even laboratory rats. No person or institution can wave a wand and expect instantaneous and predictable changes in behavior. In many cases, we know what kinds of policies would lead to better social outcomes: parents should read to their children; students should not drop out of school; individuals should not become addicted to drugs; and so on. Yet it is often undesirable, impractical, or just plain impossible to mandate and enforce such changes in behavior.

Good policy is sometimes confounded by cultural beliefs. For example, scientists in Angola were thwarted recently in their efforts to fight an outbreak of the Marburg virus, a deadly relative of the Ebola virus, brought on by local funeral rituals. Marburg is spread through contact with the bodily fluids of an infected person or a dead victim. The disease is highly contagious; by day 8 of the infection, a single drop of a victim's blood contains 5 million viruses.[16]

To contain a Marburg outbreak, therefore, it is crucial to isolate living victims, as well as to deal carefully with dead bodies. Marburg corpses are so overrun with the deadly virus that one virologist described them as "kind of like bombs." From a public-health standpoint, the most efficient ways to stop the

---

16. Sharon LaFraniere and Denise Grady, "Stalking a Deadly Virus, Battling a Town's Fears," *New York Times,* April 17, 2005.

outbreak are straightforward: isolate victims, and quickly bury or cremate the corpses of those who die from the disease.

Such an approach encounters significant local resistance. According to the *New York Times,* "Angolans have resisted the public health messages, because they do not want loved ones taken away and put into isolation wards where family cannot visit and because they resent interference with funeral traditions of washing the body and kissing it goodbye."[17] It is believed that the lack of a proper funeral will anger the spirit of the deceased and cause it to seek vengeance.

Good policy requires strategies that are attentive to human nature and powerful social forces. One health worker remarked, "We are fighting the battle of the disease. But first we have to win the battle of the heart, and the battle of the funeral." To that end, doctors in Angola have found ways to disinfect the bodies of Marburg victims so that their families can hold safe and dignified funerals.

Chapters 14 and 15 will outline the tools that policy makers can use to change behavior in ways that are consistent with some social objective.

9. Progress breeds new challenges. Scientific and technological progress makes our lives better; yet most breakthroughs bring a host of new policy questions, as illustrated by the genetic-testing example at the beginning of this chapter. Our knowledge of the human genome will make life better; there is no doubt that it will ultimately enable us to live longer, healthier lives. But, in the process, we will have to confront some nettlesome social issues such as who is allowed access to an individual's "genetic fingerprint."

Indeed, even the eradication of smallpox—one of the most impressive policy successes of the twentieth century—has raised a contentious question: What should we do with the last remaining live smallpox viruses? The United States and Russia have the only known live stocks of smallpox (the variola virus). Should those laboratory viruses be destroyed or be preserved for some future purpose?

Some scientists have argued that the virus stocks should be destroyed to prevent accidental leakage or theft. It would also send a message to the world that stockpiling potential biological weapons is immoral. Proponents of destruction point out that the live virus is no longer needed to make more vaccine, should the disease reemerge.

Yet other experts argue that the live variola viruses may yet have some scientific or defensive purpose. The viruses might have some research value if the disease were to reemerge (spread, for example, by live viruses in victims' corpses frozen in arctic permafrost or by mutation of some other pox virus).

---

17. Denise Grady, "Deadly Virus Alters Angola's Traditions," *New York Times,* April 19, 2005.

Destroying the smallpox stocks might also leave the United States at a disadvantage if the virus were used as a weapon by a rogue state that possesses undeclared stocks of the virus.[18]

The point is that the eradication of smallpox famously ended one public policy challenge and introduced a new one. These examples are not unique. The creation of the Internet has transformed how we communicate and do business; it has also created policy challenges related to data privacy, spam, the allocation of domain names, access by minors to adult content, and even the outsourcing of jobs made possible by cheap data transmission. We must deal with these issues, even as we enjoy the profound benefits of the Internet. Whereas scientific and technological advances usually make other aspects of life easier, cheaper, and more convenient, they often make public policy harder.

10. Status-quo bias. Even flawed policies in the status quo can be more attractive than the uncertainty associated with change. We can never predict the outcomes of a policy change with certainty—for many of the reasons already discussed in this chapter. All policies are introduced into a complex world. The individuals and groups affected may or may not act in ways that had been anticipated. There are likely to be adverse consequences, both those that were expected and some that were not. Individuals and groups with ill intentions may evade the policy change or even use it to harm others.

This uncertainty inherent in policy change has two major implications. First, in most policy deliberations, the status quo—doing nothing—has a certain appeal for the simple reason that it is the condition we know best: the devil we know may be better than the devil we don't. This is not necessarily an unhealthy skepticism, since there are plenty of historical examples in which the new devil was indeed worse than the old one. (One purpose of studying public policy is to prevent that from happening.) Nonetheless, the inherent uncertainty surrounding change can create a slight bias in favor of inaction.

Second, opponents of a policy change can create "doomsday scenarios" to curry public opinion against change, even when such warnings are not supported by good data or analysis. Since the future can never be known with certainty, it can be difficult, if not impossible, to disprove such dire predictions. In 2003, New York City implemented a ban on smoking in all bars and restaurants. The benefits of such a policy were obvious: it would improve public health and create environments more comfortable for nonsmokers. The costs were less obvious: How would smokers react to the ban? Would they curtail their visits to bars and restaurants? If so, what would be the implications of that change in behavior?

18. Tucker, *Scourge.*

Critics made devastating predictions about the likely economic and political impacts of the ban: nightlife would wither; bar and restaurant business would suffer; tourists would avoid New York City; and Mayor Bloomberg would pay a hefty political price for all of this.[19]

Time proved otherwise. Two years into the ban, employment in restaurants and bars had climbed slightly, and, according to interviews conducted by the *New York Times,* "a vast majority of bar and restaurant patrons, including self-described hard core smokers, said they were surprised to find themselves pleased with cleaner air, cheaper dry-cleaning bills and a new social order created by the ban."

The important point is not that the critics of the smoking ban were proved wrong, but that their dire predictions could not be disproved at the time the ban was being considered, contributing to a phenomenon known as status-quo bias. Any policy change involves uncertainty; opponents have wide latitude to make "the devil you don't know" into a powerful, albeit not necessarily accurate, argument against change.

· · · · · · · · · · · · · ·| **POLICY IN THE REAL WORLD** |· · · · · · · · · · · · · ·

Using Research to Inform Policy: Fighting Drugs versus Fighting AIDS

Most reasonable people believe it is important to eliminate the use of illegal, addictive drugs. Drug use can destroy the lives of addicts and their families and inspire criminal behavior, both to raise money to buy drugs and as the result of the impaired judgment of those who are taking the drugs.

And most reasonable people believe it is important to fight the spread of HIV/AIDS, a potentially ravaging disease with no known cure.

But which is more important: fighting illegal drug use or slowing down the transmission of HIV/AIDS? Policy makers seemingly have to choose. Drug addicts sharing needles is one way the disease is spread; dirty needles account for one-third of all reported AIDS cases.[20] Yet providing clean needles—either allowing them to be sold over the counter or through "needle exchange" programs, where used needles can be exchanged for clean ones—obviously facilitates illegal drug use. What to do?

---

19. Jim Rutenberg and Lily Koppel, "Almost Two Years into Cigarette Ban, New York City Bars Thrive and Many Smokers Shrug," *New York Times,* February 6, 2005.

20. "Needle Points," *The Economist,* September 11, 2003.

Different countries have pursued different policies. Some European nations and Australia have created needle exchange programs and even regulated "injection sites," where medical technicians provide hard-core drug users with syringes and other sterile accoutrements.[21]

For many years, the United States resisted any programs designed to fight AIDS transmission by providing easier access to clean needles. Beginning in the 1980s, Congress banned any federal funding for local programs to provide clean needles to intravenous drug users.[22] President George W. Bush said that needle exchange programs undermine the war on drugs. Most states ban the possession of syringes without a prescription. Former California governor Gray Davis twice vetoed legislation that would have allowed pharmacies to sell syringes without a prescription.

Yet research can often inform policy. The trade-off between drug use and public health (dirty needles also spread hepatitis C) is a false dilemma. The British news magazine *The Economist* summarized the research findings: "Studies show the provision of clean needles does not increase either crime or drug use. On the other side, there is no end of evidence that dirty needles cost a lot of taxpayers' money in AIDS treatment, and shorten many lives."[23]

A 2001 article in the *Journal of Public Health*, a peer-reviewed journal, found that IV drug users were twice as likely to be infected by the HIV/AIDS virus in cities that did not allow needle sales without a prescription—13.8 percent compared to 6.7 percent.[24]

Persuaded by such evidence, groups such as the American Medical Association have come to support broader access to clean needles. In 2004, California governor Arnold Schwarzenegger signed legislation that made it legal for pharmacies to sell up to ten syringes to any adult in cities or counties where local officials also approved the policy. The legislation, which automatically expires in 2010, requires state health officials to evaluate the impact of the law. Congress lifted the ban on federal funding for clean-needle programs in December 2009. President Obama appointed former Seattle police chief Gil Kerlikowske as his "drug czar" (director of national drug-control policy). Kerlikowske supported a Seattle needle-exchange program and has called for "a new common-sense approach to drug addiction."[25]

. . . .

21. Clifford Krauss, "Canada Parts with U.S. on Drugs: Policies Lean toward Treating, Rather Than Punishing Users," *New York Times,* May 19, 2003.

22. Bob Egelko, http://www.SFGate.com, December 18, 2009.

23. "Needle Points."

24. Mark Martin and Lynda Gledhill, "Sacramento: Schwarzenegger OKs Increased Needle Sales," *San Francisco Chronicle,* September 21, 2004.

25. Beth Schwartzapfel, "Swapping Politics for Science on Drug Policy," *Nation,* December 21, 2009.

2.3 RECONCILING OUR DIFFERENCES

Good public policy requires that we understand *why* people disagree and, in particular, which disagreements are reconcilable and which are not. The following sections will explore the nature of policy disagreements in a more systematic way.

2.3.1 Values, Facts, and Theories

A **value** is a strongly held belief rooted in faith, life experience, or ideology: *life begins at conception; health care is a fundamental right; premarital sex is wrong.* Reasonable people can, do, and always will disagree over these basic philosophical questions. Most important from a public policy standpoint, further inquiry or study is not likely to change minds in a way that will reconcile the disagreement.

A **fact** is an objective reality or truth, generally informed by observation, measurement, or calculation: *the world is round; gravity forces objects to fall to the surface of the earth; the United States has a higher gross domestic product than Mexico has.* Reasonable people should agree on the facts or on a process for determining the facts. Policy analysts will often refer to an issue as an **empirical question** if a hypothesis can be accepted or rejected based on observation, experiment, or some other objective analysis.

A **theory** is a general principle supported by data or analytics: *creating competition among schools will increase school quality; the emission of greenhouse gases is gradually increasing the temperature of the earth (global warming); man evolved from more primitive creatures through a process of natural selection.* A theory can be supported, proved, or disproved by subsequent inquiry. In the meantime, credible researchers can propose different or even competing theories, and some theories are likely to be more widely accepted than others depending on the quantity and quality of supporting evidence. Reasonable people can disagree over the validity of a theory; however, subsequent data and intellectual inquiry should help reconcile this disagreement.

········· ┌─────────────────────────────┐ ·················
          │ **POLICY IN THE REAL WORLD** │
········· └─────────────────────────────┘ ·················

Peer Pressure: Peer-Reviewed Journals

Policy analysts are rarely experts in all subjects that they must tackle. More often, they have a set of general skills and tools (the kind of things taught in this book) but are not the foremost authority on many of the subjects that may require a decision. A congressional staff member, for example, may have to render judgment on subjects ranging from international trade to childhood immunizations. We have already discussed how very little knowledge in the social sciences, and even science and medicine, can be known with absolute certainty. There are likely to be theories and countertheories and even eccentric theories. How is a policy analyst supposed to tell the experts from the crackpots—sound theory from total speculation—without expertise in the subject at hand?

The peer-review process provides a tool for determining the quality of research in a field. Academic journals and other research-based institutions will often submit articles and studies for peer review, meaning that the article or proposal is distributed for critique to other experts in the field. For example, if the *Journal of the American Medical Association* is considering publication of a study on the treatment of glaucoma, it will distribute the manuscript to several glaucoma experts for their assessment of the quality of the research.

The process is "blind" at some institutions, meaning that the reviewers do not know the identity of the author or applicant; or it may be nonblind, meaning that the authors' identities are known. In either case, the intent of the process is to help editors overcome a challenge that policy analysts also often encounter: How can a generalist (or an expert in a different field) evaluate highly specialized research?

Peer review is a tool for doing that. An article that appears in a "peer-reviewed" journal has an imprimatur of credibility from experts in the field. There are not likely to be gaping methodological errors, or theories at odds with existing facts, or a blatant conflict of interest by the individuals doing the work. This is in stark contrast to papers posted on the Internet or passed out on street corners. Thus, the peer-review process is an important screen.

A conclusion published in a peer-reviewed journal may still be proved wrong in the end. It may, for example, be contradicted by further study—which would also be published in a peer-reviewed journal. In the absence of absolute consensus, the peer-review process is a tool for vetting work in highly specialized fields. As a result, journalists and policy analysts will often accept articles in peer-reviewed journals as the best extant thinking on a given subject.

. . . .

2.3.2 Sources of Disagreement

Not all disagreements are the same. Understanding why we disagree can help policy makers formulate a policy for reconciling disagreements. In some cases, that may require more evidence or study in hopes of finding a "right" answer; in others, it may require institutions for managing fundamental differences in values that will never go away.

Why can't we all just get along?

1. Differences in basic values. This chapter has noted repeatedly that different individuals are likely to have different core beliefs and that these values are not likely to be changed by subsequent inquiry or evidence. Many of society's most intractable policy disputes stem from these basic disagreements over right and wrong. Policy analysis cannot make these disagreements go away.

However, policy analysts have three important contributions in this area. First, we should recognize when a disagreement stems from a difference in values and will not be resolved by further debate. As obvious as that seems, talk-show guests, dinner-party tablemates, and politicians will often argue round and round when the real source of their disagreement is an irreconcilable difference in values. If an individual believes that stem cell research is fundamentally wrong because it requires the destruction of human embryos, then the argument that stem cell research may lead to future medical breakthroughs is both irrelevant and almost certainly futile.

Second, good policy analysis requires that our values not affect our analysis or interpretation of data. Capital punishment may or may not deter crime. This is an empirical question, the answer to which should not be affected by one's views on the morality of the death penalty. Similarly, dispensing birth control to high-school students may or may not decrease teen pregnancy; credible policy analysts examining this question should not come to different answers because of their views on the morality of premarital sex.

Last, public policy requires institutions for reconciling our differences in values. We will never agree on everything; we *can* agree on a process for dealing with those disagreements. For example, abortion is legal in the United States. The Supreme Court affirmed it as a constitutional right in the 1973 decision *Roe v. Wade*. Many Americans disagree with that decision and believe passionately that abortion should be illegal. However, most of those

Americans also believe in the legitimacy of the Supreme Court. Those who disagree with the *Roe* decision are working to have it overturned—a possibility if justices with different legal philosophies are appointed to the Supreme Court. Only a tiny minority believes that the Supreme Court should be ignored or that individuals should fight abortion outside of our extant legal institutions.

All societies have fundamental disagreements over values; functional societies have institutions to resolve those disputes. A crucial component of public policy is the process by which we build, operate, and improve such institutions. Dysfunctional societies lack such functioning institutions, and the alternative is often violence or other destructive activities.

2. Disagreements over facts or theory. Good policy requires good information. Yet public policy is not a laboratory science; we cannot test human behavior or complex macroeconomic phenomena with perfectly controlled experiments. As a result, reasonable people can interpret data differently or even debate over which data should be used to answer specific questions.

What have been the major effects of America's dramatic 1996 welfare reform? This is a complex question but one that needs to be answered if legislators are to assess the success of this radical transformation of American social policy (even as different parties may define "success" differently). What data need to be collected, and from what subset of the welfare population? How can we statistically disaggregate the effects of welfare reform from the effects of other social factors? For example, was the post-1996 drop in the welfare caseload caused by welfare reform, or by a particularly strong economy, or by some combination of the two?

Experts routinely disagree about these kinds of significant questions. All studies are not created equal. Good research facilitates good policy; poorly designed research is unhelpful or even misleading. Good policy analysts must be able to tell the difference, whether they are doing original research or interpreting the work of others. Chapters 9 to 13 cover some of the most important methodological tools for public policy research.

3. Different interests. There is an old adage in public policy that "where you stand on an issue depends on where you sit." This chapter should have made clear that even policies with enormous net social benefits will not make everyone better off. Some individuals or groups will oppose a policy change because it compromises their interests. Homeowners in the path of a proposed new runway will oppose an airport expansion. Smokers don't like higher tobacco taxes (nor do tobacco farmers). Ranchers will fight efforts to reintroduce wolves on nearby public lands.

As with ideological differences of opinion, more information or analysis will not smooth over these disagreements. The challenge for public policy is to advance policies that improve overall social welfare, even in the face of inevitable opposition. In some cases, that will involve providing compensation or some other kind of relief to groups that are adversely affected. Or it may simply involve building a political coalition strong enough to overcome pockets of resistance.

4. Disagreements over things that are at present unknowable. Is there a God? If so, what does he/she/it really think about SUVs? How will global warming affect the planet one hundred years from now, and what kind of tools will we have then to remedy those problems? Would personal retirement accounts provide greater resources in retirement for certain cohorts of Americans than Social Security? Did the United States make the world safer by removing Saddam Hussein from power?

Each of these questions is relevant to public policy. Each has a correct answer—but we don't know what it is, and we have no way of finding out. These "unknowable" questions fall into several categories:

- existential questions, such as religious doctrine, that play an important role in shaping values and beliefs about public policy.
- questions about the future. We can make inferences and informed judgments about what lies ahead, but we can never know the future with certainty until it happens (at which point it's not the future anymore).
- questions related to the counterfactual, or what might have happened under different circumstances. We don't know if the world is safer without Saddam Hussein because we will never know with certainty what would have happened had he remained in power. Any disagreement over that question, or others like it, will never move beyond mere speculation.

2.3.3 Positive and Normative Analysis

Policy analysis requires drawing conclusions and making recommendations. In that process, experts are likely to offer two different kinds of analysis: **positive analysis** and **normative analysis.** Positive analysis is a statement of fact, finding, or theory that is devoid of judgment. The analyst is merely drawing a conclusion about what did or will happen without introducing an opinion as to whether this is a good or bad thing. *Raising the minimum wage will lead some employers to hire fewer low-skilled workers.* This a conclusion based on our understanding of how labor markets work. It does not imply judgment on whether or not the minimum wage should be raised.

Normative analysis, on the other hand, introduces an explicit judgment about what *should* be done. The analyst draws a conclusion based on data, theory, and also his or her own values. For example: *Some government spending should be redirected from entitlements for older Americans to programs that alleviate poverty among children.* This statement makes a recommendation based on the value judgment that fighting child poverty is a more worthwhile way to spend government resources than providing services for the elderly.

Consider several more examples:

Positive analysis: The U.S. Fish and Wildlife Service has currently classified 607 animal species and 744 plant species as endangered.
Normative analysis: Current economic and development policies take an unacceptable toll on America's wildlife.

Positive analysis: Lower marginal tax rates are likely to increase the number of people in the labor force and the total number of hours worked.
Normative analysis: The federal government should cut income tax rates.

In short, positive analysis describes how the world *is*; normative analysis describes how the world *should be*.

2.4 CONCLUSION

If public policy were easy, then there would be no hunger, disease, or civil war. Yet the world does routinely experience such preventable hardships. Good public policy can and does improve the human condition. That process, however, requires us to understand the difficulties inherent in making communal decisions. Why can't we all just get along? Because it's hard—for all the reasons outlined in this chapter. None of these obstacles is insurmountable. The balance of the book will present tools for designing and implementing public policies that make the most of our human potential.

FOR DISCUSSION

A Bipartisan Transformation of Social Policy: Welfare Reform

In the mid-1990s, America transformed its social welfare system, changing radically the nature of government support for poor single parents (almost exclusively women) with dependent children. Welfare was changed from an entitlement program—in which benefits are offered automatically and indefinitely to all those who qualify—into a program that encourages work and has a five-year lifetime limit on federal benefits.

Welfare, known originally as Aid to Families with Dependent Children (AFDC), was designed in the 1930s to assist single-parent families. At the time, most such female-headed households were the result of the death of a spouse. Welfare benefits were structured so that a single woman could support her family without having to work until the children were grown. The implicit belief was that a widowed woman belonged at home with her children rather than in the workforce.

Over time, the AFDC caseload grew dramatically. Between 1960 and 1977, for example, the welfare caseload quadrupled from 800,000 families to over 3.5 million families. By 1994, the caseload reached 5.1 million families, or 15 percent of American families with children.[26] The growing caseload was the result of broader inclusion—including an end to practices that wrongly denied benefits to black and Hispanic families—but also a striking social phenomenon: an explosion in the number of children born outside of marriage. In 1940, for example, 4 percent of children were born out of wedlock; by 1995, that number had grown to 32 percent of children and 70 percent of African-American children.

Welfare had become a lightning rod for conservatives. They criticized abuses in the program, citing "welfare queens" who drove fancy cars and lived large on government benefits.[27] Even when the program was not abused, they argued, it discouraged work and fostered a **culture of dependency.** Welfare had become a way of life for many recipients, and that dependency was passed down across generations to children who knew nothing other than government assistance. Republican representative Clay Shaw, who helped write the 1996 reform, stated, "It was an evil thing the way it was set up. . . . Telling people you don't have to work, don't get married and the check's in the mail."[28]

26. Douglas J. Besharov, "The Past and Future of Welfare Reform," *Public Interest* 150 (Winter 2003): 4–21.
27. J. Janelle George, "The Personal Responsibility and Work Opportunities Reconciliation Act of 1996" (unpublished manuscript, 2004).
28. Kelly Smith, "Welfare Reform" (unpublished manuscript, 2004).

Liberals believed that government had an obligation to provide a safety net for the country's most disadvantaged populations. The world's richest nation should not have people, especially children, living in dire poverty. However, even those who supported a generous safety net had come to believe by the early 1990s that the system was dysfunctional. Policy analysts, including several academics who later joined the Clinton administration, made the case that America's poor would be better served by a welfare system with healthier incentives for recipients.

A political consensus for change was slowly emerging. Bill Clinton made a pledge during his 1992 presidential campaign to "end welfare as we know it." The details of that pledge left a lot of room for interpretation, but it clearly resonated with a broad swath of the political spectrum. Republican Newt Gingrich, Speaker of the House of Representatives, promulgated a 1994 election manifesto, "The Contract with America," that called for radical welfare reform.[29] Meanwhile, many states had begun to experiment with programs that encouraged or required able-bodied welfare recipients to seek work, job training, or education.

In 1996, after extensive political machinations (including two welfare reform bills passed by Congress and vetoed by President Clinton), the United States passed the Personal Responsibility and Work Opportunity Reconciliation Act (PRWORA), better known as "welfare reform." The 1996 legislation created a new program: Temporary Assistance for Needy Families (TANF). The overarching goals of the new program were to promote self-sufficiency through work and to decrease the number of children growing up in single-parent families.[30] The salient features of the legislation were

1. the end of a cash entitlement for poor single parents with dependent children;
2. work requirements so that welfare recipients must be working, looking for work, or engaged in job training in order to receive benefits;
3. sanctions, including termination of benefits, for those who violate the work requirements;
4. a sixty-month lifetime limit on federal welfare assistance;
5. more lump sum funding ("block grants") to states to encourage additional experimentation within the above parameters.

The legislation also contained provisions to decrease the number of births outside of marriage. For example, it included an abstinence education program and cash grants for states that reduced their rate of births to unwed mothers. The reform strengthened enforcement of child-support payments and set new requirements for establishing paternity as a precondition for receiving welfare.

29. George, "The Personal Responsibility."
30. Ron Haskins, testimony before the U.S. Senate Committee on Finance, February 20, 2003.

Most of all, welfare reform transformed the philosophy of the program. A sign stenciled on a job center in New York City admonished, "Be prepared to work, or be prepared to leave."[31]

Opponents of the reform, primarily on the political left, charged that welfare term limits would be a social catastrophe. Senator Edward Kennedy described a Senate version of the bill as "legislative child abuse."[32] Peter Edelman, assistant secretary of the U.S. Department of Health and Human Services and an early proponent of fixing AFDC, resigned in protest and wrote an article in the *Atlantic Monthly* entitled "The Worst Thing Bill Clinton Has Done."[33]

So what happened?

Writing in *Public Interest* in 2003, Douglas Besharov, a professor at the University of Maryland School of Public Policy, concluded: "Taking a broad view of what happened, one would have to say that both conservatives and liberals were proven right—and wrong."

Conservatives were correct to believe that different incentives would encourage many welfare recipients to find and hold jobs. By 2004, the welfare rolls had plummeted 60 percent from the peak in 1994, and most of the decline occurred after the 1996 reform. Employment among mothers who had never married rose 40 percent in the four years after 1996. All of this happened without the widespread social catastrophe that had been predicted by some welfare-reform opponents.

Yet it has not been all good news. Liberals were correct in believing that women leaving welfare would have a hard time pulling themselves out of poverty. The jobs they are likely to take pay low wages, and other government programs—transportation assistance, childcare subsidies, and the Earned Income Tax Credit (which uses the tax system to supplement the incomes of low-wage workers)—are often required to make former welfare recipients as well off as they were before. Welfare reform transformed the landscape of welfare, but not necessarily of poverty.

In the end, success may be in the eye of the beholder. If the goal of the program was to remove individuals from government dependency, then welfare reform was successful beyond what even its strongest supporters had hoped. But if the goal was to raise individuals out of poverty, then the record is less impressive.

From a public policy perspective, several important questions remain:

- **What will be the long-term impact on children whose mothers have left welfare for low-wage jobs?** In theory, these children might be better off, if having a working parent sets an important example. Or they might be worse off, if the only affordable childcare arrangements are of low quality or even dangerous.

---

31. Besharov, "The Past and Future of Welfare Reform."
32. Melissa Baker, unpublished manuscript on welfare reform, 2004.
33. March 1997.

- **What will happen to the most disadvantaged segment of the welfare population as more and more recipients hit the five-year welfare limit?** As policy analysts predicted, the early welfare leavers had the highest skills on average and were the most employable. Moving welfare recipients into work becomes more difficult as the process reaches deeper into the welfare pool.
- **What will be the workforce trajectory of those who leave welfare for low-wage jobs?** Will their earnings rise steadily, making them better off over time? Or will they spend years working full time while living at or near the poverty line?
- **How will former welfare recipients fare during economic downturns?** How will the overall caseload be affected by a weak economy, particularly the deep downturn that began in 2007?

Welfare reform remains a work in progress. There is no doubt, however, that it was one of the most radical changes in government policy in the twentieth century.

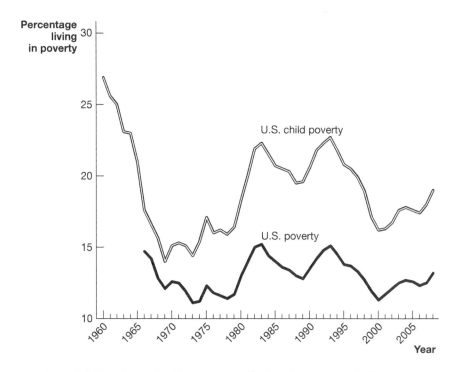

Source: U.S. Census Bureau, http://www.census.gov/hhes/www/poverty/poverty.html and http://www.census.gov/hhes/www/poverty/histpov/perindex.html. This information was retrieved on January 26, 2010.

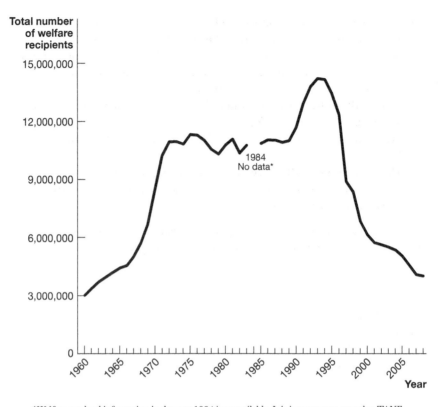

*Welfare caseload information in the year 1984 is unavailable. It is important to note that TANF—Temporary Assistance for Needy Families—which was passed under the Personal Responsibility and Work Opportunity Reconciliation Act, became effective on July 1, 1997. Additionally, welfare information is given based on calendar year, not fiscal year.

Source: The recipient information for the above figure was obtained from the U.S. Administration for Children and Families (http://www.acf.hhs.gov/programs/ofa/data-reports/caseload/caseload_recent.html#2000).

QUESTIONS

1. What should be the goal of welfare policy: to put people to work, to raise them out of poverty, or both?
2. Do you agree with the policy of placing lifetime limits on the length of time an individual can spend on welfare? Why, or why not?
3. Liberals often defend welfare and other social programs as an essential safety net for the disadvantaged; conservatives criticize such programs for fostering dependency and discouraging work. What kind of data might inform this ideological debate?
4. Should legal immigrants—foreigners who are in the United States legally but are not citizens—be entitled to welfare and other government benefits? Why, or why not?

5. Other countries with more generous social welfare policies also tend to have higher rates of unemployment. Explain a theory for the connection between welfare policies and unemployment. What kind of research might support or disprove this theory?

6. Is it wrong for a woman to have a child out of wedlock? Does it matter if she can afford to support the child financially?

7. What moral obligation, if any, do wealthy Americans have to provide a safety net for America's poor? What about for desperately poor populations elsewhere in the world?

8. One unanswered question surrounding welfare reform is its long-term impact on the children of women who have left welfare for low-wage jobs. How can this question be studied, given that we will never know how those children would have fared if their mothers had stayed on welfare? What would we like to know about these children, and how can it be measured objectively?

9. Should the government create jobs of last resort—as it did during the Great Depression—for welfare recipients who are unable to find work in the conventional labor market?

10. What kinds of programs might be a logical "next step" for welfare reform?

KEY CONCEPTS

★ Good public policy has led to dramatic improvements in our quality of life.

★ There is no single quantifiable measure of public policy success. In other fields, such as business, success is more easily measured and compared.

★ Public policy is complicated by the fact that society must come to resolution on issues where reasonable people have strongly held, contradictory views that are not likely to be changed by new evidence or further inquiry.

★ Even when we agree on basic values, public policy often forces us to make trade-offs that pit those basic values against one another.

★ Public policy is complicated by the fact that the benefits and costs of a policy do not necessarily fall on the same individuals or groups. Even policies with enormous net social benefits are likely to be opposed by groups that bear a disproportionate share of the costs.

★ Successful groups, or even entire societies, must sacrifice in the present to yield benefits in the future and resist the temptation to enjoy benefits now while leaving excessive costs to be paid in the future.

★ Group behavior is often plagued by collective-action problems—cases in which the members of a group are unable or unwilling to organize themselves in a way that would make them all better off in the long run.

★ Public policy is sometimes unresponsive to public opinion by design. Societies create nondemocratic institutions to protect individuals or minorities from the majority.

★ Humans are complex beings embedded within complex cultures. Achieving better social outcomes often requires changing behavior, and changing behavior is difficult.

★ Progress of any kind usually brings new public policy challenges.

★ Any policy change involves uncertainty; opponents have wide latitude to make "the devil you don't know" into a powerful, albeit not necessarily accurate, argument against change.

★ A *value* is a strongly held belief rooted in faith, life experience, or ideology. A *fact* is an objective reality or truth, generally informed by observation, measurement, or calculation. A *theory* is a general principle supported by data or analysis.

★ *Positive analysis* is a statement of fact, finding, or theory that is devoid of judgment. *Normative analysis* introduces an explicit judgment about what *should* be done.

WHY WE DO WHAT WE DO

SECTION II

OCEANOGRAPHY
OF THE OCEAN

CHAPTER 3

Understanding Behavior: Rational Man and Woman

WHERE HAVE ALL THE GIRLS GONE?

In the early 1990s, the *New York Times* ran a provocative headline: "Stark Data on Women: 100 Million Are Missing."[1] The main idea was straightforward: demographics suggested that there should be far more women on the planet than there actually were, particularly in Asia. If boys and girls are born at roughly equal rates (with nature slightly favoring boys at birth because they are more prone to die before reaching sexual maturity), then censuses around the globe were turning up some 100 million fewer women than nature intended. Why?

The short answer is that discrimination against girls can literally kill them. Females, particularly in the populous nations of India and China, are more likely than boys to be aborted during pregnancy, killed at birth, or neglected during childhood in ways that cause death. The longer answer—the one that gets at the source of this fatal discrimination—requires an understanding of the powerful incentives that create a preference for boys in certain societies. In China, India, and many other developing countries, girls are more expensive to a family than boys and provide fewer long-term benefits.

In rural India and China, for example, boys are more helpful with manual labor. Men also provide an important form of social insurance, since boys eventually provide for their parents in old age. When a man marries, he brings his wife to live with his family; girls, therefore, require the expense of upbringing only to leave upon marriage to join their husband's family.

In India, the disparity is compounded by the tradition of a dowry, a payment from the bride's family to the groom's family upon marriage. Dowries have been illegal for decades but are still common practice and can easily be disguised as a gift. A typical dowry can amount to several years of household earnings.

China amplified the incentive to meddle with nature by implementing a strict "one child" policy in 1979 in order to restrain rapid population growth.

---

1. Nicholas D. Kristof, "Stark Data on Women: 100 Million Are Missing," *New York Times,* November 5, 1991.

Families are allowed only a single child, with violators subject to steep fines—as much as three to ten times the average annual urban income—and other punishments, including forced abortion and destruction of property. There are loopholes. In rural areas, couples are allowed to have a second child if the first is a girl. Or if two urban parents are both only children, then they are permitted to have a second child.

China's one-child policy did play a role in curbing population growth. The **fertility rate** fell from 2.29 children per woman in 1980 to 1.69 in 2004. (A fertility rate of 2.10, the "replacement rate," is considered the point at which the population will remain roughly constant.)[2] However, the policy clearly exacerbated the harm done to females; given a strong social preference for boys and only one opportunity (in most cases) to have a child, families can and do seek to have boys, in part through selective abortion.

Advances in ultrasound technology, including portable ultrasounds, have made it cheap and easy to determine the sex of the fetus *in utero* even in poor, remote areas. As a result, female fetuses are more likely to be aborted than male fetuses. One advertising campaign for the portable ultrasound in India proclaimed, "Pay 500 rupees now and save 50,000 later."[3]

Sex tests in India are now illegal. But the ban is rarely enforced, in large part because health-care workers have an incentive to do the opposite. The ultrasound machines are widely in place (since they are an important part of normal prenatal care). Doctors make money both from bribes to do the tests and fees for the subsequent abortions. When an Indian TV network sent pregnant women to 140 health clinics in 36 Indian cities requesting a sex-determination test and possible abortion (both of which are illegal), doctors in 100 of the clinics either agreed to perform the services or referred the woman to another doctor who would.[4]

Such behavior helps to explain "100 million missing women." In India, the sex ratio fell throughout the twentieth century from 103 males for every 100 females to 108 males for every 100 females. In China, the sex ratio at birth is now roughly 118 males for every 100 females. (A ratio at birth of 105 males for every 100 females is normal.)

Chinese law forbids both sex-selection abortions and ultrasound exams for the purpose of determining the sex of the fetus.[5] The policy is not likely to

2. "A Brother for Her," *The Economist,* December 16, 2004.

3. "Missing Sisters: India," *The Economist,* April 17, 2003.

4. Julia Duin, "Lots of Stings, No Pain: Just a Wink for Doctors Who Flout Law," *Washington Times,* February 28, 2007.

5. Sherry F. Colb, "China Announces That It Will Criminalize Sex-Selection Abortions: What, If Anything, Should the U.S. Do about the Practice in This Country?" FindLaw, January 26, 2005.

have much effect since it does not affect the underlying social preference for boys. That social preference is, in turn, driven by the significant financial and social advantages of having boys, or a single boy in the case of China. Furthermore, any effort to limit sex tests or selective abortion is hindered by the fact that the only individuals in a position to stop the practices—health workers—stand to gain by doing them.

The lopsided sex ratio in countries like China and India is typical of many public policy challenges. Significant social trends are the sum of independent decisions made by hundreds of millions of individuals or families. Those individual decisions are shaped by the costs and benefits of competing alternatives. Thus, to understand why the world's population has millions fewer women than nature intended, one must first understand why a single family in Beijing might prefer to have a boy—and how that family is likely to act on such a preference.

This chapter introduces some of the most important tools for analyzing and understanding the behavior of individuals, families, and firms. Good public policy requires that we understand why individuals and organizations behave the way that they do. Policy makers must also anticipate how affected parties will react to changes in policy. The chapter will also explore the limits to "rational" behavior. Many individuals arguably make decisions that are not in their own best interest, which raises an important policy question: To what extent should government attempt to protect individuals from their own bad decisions?

CHAPTER OUTLINE

3.1 SIMPLIFYING THE WORLD

Obviously, no two individuals, families, or businesses are the same. How can analysts make sense of the behavior of thousands, millions, or even billions of people? We begin with a set of tools that helps us to simplify and understand why people do what they do.

3.1.1 The Role of Models

Policy analysts use **models**—simplified illustrations of how systems operate—to gain greater insight into how the world works. Models are designed to cut through staggeringly complex relationships in order to focus on the most important factors at work. Consider the most basic model from microeconomics: the **law of supply and demand.** It takes billions of independent, complex transactions—how consumers and producers around the world behave—and distills them into a simple but powerful model for understanding how a market economy operates.

    The model is built upon two core assumptions. First, as the market price of a good or service falls, consumers will demand more of it. If the price of salmon falls, then some consumers who would have bought a different kind of fish or a different product entirely will be induced to buy salmon instead. Other consumers who would have bought salmon anyway might buy more of it. The key insight is that when we hold all other things constant—consumer tastes, the weather, the health effects of salmon, etc.—consumers will buy more salmon when the price is lower and less when the price is higher.

The second core assumption is that when the price of a good or service rises, firms will supply more of it to the market. If we stick with the salmon example, we would expect some fishermen to respond to the higher market price by fishing longer hours; others will retrofit their boats to fish for salmon rather than some other fish; and so on. The point is that when the profit to be made by selling fresh salmon goes up, many fishermen will respond to that incentive by "producing" more.

If we plot these two basic relationships—the supply curve and the demand curve—on the same graph, they will intersect at the only point where the supply produced by firms is equal to the quantity demanded by consumers. That point of intersection determines the quantity of the good that will be produced and the price at which it will be sold.

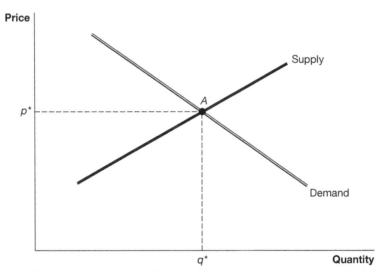

Point *A* is the market equilibrium, where the quantity produced equals the quantity demanded (supply = demand)
*p** = equilibrium price
*q** = equilibrium quantity produced and sold

Model of Supply and Demand

Of course, every assumption in the model (and all others) is oversimplified. Will each fisherman produce more salmon if the price that can be fetched at auction goes up? Probably not. We don't have the capacity to understand the individual decision of every man or woman who owns a fishing boat (e.g.,

"Jean had an argument with her husband that morning and was in no mood to take the boat out, even though the hotels were paying a premium for salmon at that time of year.") Yet we can say with near certainty that the supply of salmon overall will go up.

The same is true on the demand side. We can't say exactly how Phil is going to respond when he walks into Whole Foods in Chicago and sees that salmon is $3 more a pound than it was last month. Will he buy tuna instead? Will he grill chicken breasts? You would have to know Phil fairly well to answer that question. But you don't have to know Phil at all to understand the central insight of this model in terms of consumer demand: when the market price goes up, consumers—in the aggregate—will demand less of the good or service.

Thus, the model of supply and demand cuts through the clutter and exceptions to give us a good idea of how the market for salmon operates. Once we've formulated this basic model, we can use it to think through the implications of different changes in market conditions or public policy, such as the imposition of a sales tax, a ban on certain kinds of fishing practices, or the release of a study showing that salmon contains higher levels of mercury than previously thought. Simple models often give us intellectual traction to explore complex problems.

3.1.2 The *Ceteris Paribus* Assumption

In creating and analyzing models, policy analysts often use the term ***ceteris paribus,*** which is Latin for "all other things being equal." For example, our model of supply and demand assumes that nothing else changes in the world except for the price of the good or service being examined. Someone working with this basic model might draw the following conclusion: "A rise in the market price of fresh tuna will reduce the demand for sushi, *ceteris paribus*." If all other factors in the world remain unchanged, except for an increase in the price of fresh tuna, then we would expect the demand for sushi to fall.

The *ceteris paribus* assumption is important because researchers and policy analysts are often attempting to focus on the importance of a single factor. Policy makers who are concerned about selective abortion in India might focus on the role of dowries (the payment that a bride's family must make to the groom's family at the time of marriage). A simple model of sex preference for children would include a measure of the costs and benefits of raising a girl relative to a boy. A dowry raises the cost of having a girl (because her family pays it) and increases the benefit of raising a boy (because his family receives it). Using this basic model, an analyst would conclude that the higher the expected dowry, *ceteris paribus,* the stronger the preference for boys at birth and, therefore, the higher the rate of selective abortion.

Of course, all other things usually are *not* equal. While researchers are focusing on dowries, many other factors are likely to affect the rate of selective abortion: changing social attitudes toward abortion, the availability of educational opportunities for girls, the prevalence of ultrasound technology, and so on. One challenge of social-science research is to identify the causal link between a single variable and an outcome of interest. This causal link, in turn, enables policy makers to formulate policies that achieve a predictable and desirable outcome. Good models facilitate that process in the following ways:

- Models enable us to examine complex phenomena in ways that strip away extraneous detail and focus on the most important factors at work. What matters most?
- Models produce theories that can be tested with data. In the case of selective abortion, the model suggests that dowries (along with other factors) create a preference for boys, which in turn increases the likelihood of selective abortion. Researchers would seek to test this theory using available data, perhaps by comparing the abortion rates in parts of the country where dowries are an accepted social practice (the law notwithstanding) to abortion rates in parts of the country where dowries are less common.
- Models help us identify places where changes in policy are likely to have the most impact. By clarifying the factors that matter most, we can begin to determine which of those factors are most amenable to some kind of policy intervention. In the case of selective abortion, one's first instinct is to crack down on the practice itself. Yet basic analysis suggests that this approach may have limited success without some kind of shift in social attitudes: as long as some families have a preference for boys and health workers have an incentive to charge fees or take bribes to determine the sex of the fetus and perform abortions, then the practice will be virtually impossible to stop. Instead, a basic model suggests that the most effective policies in the long run will involve improving the economic opportunities for girls and women, thereby reducing the social preference for boys.

Good policy recognizes why people and firms behave the way they do. An effective policy solution must either be compatible with that behavior, or it must include incentives to change behavior in a way that is consistent with some positive social outcome. Bad policy often ignores the reasons that people and firms behave the way they do; the resulting "solutions" can be inefficient, ineffective, or even counterproductive. In some cases, policy changes can have unintended consequences that are worse than the original problem.

3.1.3 Individuals Seek to Maximize Their Own Utility

Why do individuals do what they do? The short answer is that they try to make themselves as well off as possible—i.e., to **maximize their utility.** **Utility** is a theoretical concept—and, therefore, not directly observable or measurable—that equates roughly to well-being. We derive utility from consuming goods, enjoying human relationships, beholding things of great beauty, and so on. Not all activities that give us utility are pleasurable. Most individuals get utility out of paying taxes, not because writing a check to the IRS makes them feel good, but because it prevents the disutility of going to jail. Similarly, we all seek to maximize utility in the long run. We may do things that are difficult, unpleasant, or expensive in the short run (e.g., graduate school or Internet dating) because we expect some payoff that will make it worthwhile in the long run.

We do not all derive the same utility from the same kinds of things. We assume that all individuals have unique preferences—likes and dislikes—that guide their behavior. In some cases, these preferences have huge social significance, as in the case of the Indian and Chinese preference for boys. In other cases, they explain more trivial differences in behavior: some people put milk in their coffee; others don't. In all cases, these preferences help to explain individual behavior.

It is crucial to note that maximizing utility is not synonymous with acting selfishly. Most individuals derive utility from helping others, donating to charities, or engaging in other altruistic activities. Basic economics does assume that individuals act rationally and, therefore, do not knowingly engage in activities that diminish their own welfare. This is an important beginning assumption because it would be virtually impossible to make sense of the world or anticipate the impact of a policy change if we were to assume that individuals routinely act in ways that make themselves worse off.

Nonetheless, there are cases in which individuals do things that do not appear to be strictly rational: dropping out of high school, gambling excessively, experimenting with addictive drugs, leading profoundly unhealthy lifestyles, and so on. Researchers in the emerging subdiscipline of behavioral economics have demonstrated that most of us make systematic errors when it comes to decisions that involve risk, the future, and other kinds of uncertainty. These findings are not merely an academic curiosity. Many public policy issues have at their heart the question of whether or not government should play a role in protecting individuals from themselves. We will discuss the limits to rationality at the end of the chapter.

POLICY IN THE REAL WORLD

Opportunity Cost: Why Those Free Concert Tickets Aren't Really Free If You Have to Wait in Line for Them

Suppose you sleep outside overnight to be the first in line to receive free tickets to see your favorite band in concert. To an accountant, those tickets are indeed free. You didn't have to pay for them. But to a policy analyst, the tickets are not free at all. You had to give up quite a bit to get them—many hours of your time.

The notion that the true cost of an activity is what we must give up in order to do it (e.g., time spent doing something else) is referred to as **opportunity cost.** In a world of scarce resources, everything we do or buy requires us to forgo doing or buying something else. With market transactions, the opportunity cost is easy to calculate: it is the next best thing that we could have done with the money. If you buy a home for $300,000, for example, then the opportunity cost represents the best investment or spending opportunity that was passed up in order to buy the house.

When it comes to nonmarket activities, such as being stuck in traffic, the opportunity cost represents the value of whatever else you may have done with that time—making money at work, spending time with friends, etc. Different individuals will have different opportunity costs, depending on the value of their time. For example, the opportunity cost of attending graduate school full time is likely to be much higher for someone who is fifty years old than for someone who is twenty-four. Why? Because a fifty year old is more likely to be leaving a high-paying job.

In fact, the opportunity cost of lost wages—stepping away from an $85,000 salary for a year or two—is a far bigger "cost" than direct expenses like tuition and books. To policy analysts, opportunity cost is a crucial concept because it is so helpful in explaining human behavior.

3.1.4 Firms Seek to Maximize Profits

Economics treats any for-profit institution—anything from a single hot-dog vendor to a multinational corporation—as a "firm." Firms organize their resources and make other decisions in order to make as much money as possible for the owners of the firm—i.e., to **maximize profits.** The basic assumption that firms seek to maximize profits offers some simple but powerful insights for public policy:

- Firms will not voluntarily do things that are unprofitable in the long run. Obviously, there are cases of corporate philanthropy; but, in general, society cannot depend on the private sector to produce goods or services that cannot be sold profitably. Real-estate developers will not build housing for families who cannot afford to buy it or to pay the rent.
- Profit is a powerful motivator. Changing the incentives for firms—namely, the opportunity to earn money (or to avoid losing money)—will change their behavior. Thus, a real-estate developer who does not ordinarily build low-income housing might embrace such a project if there were a tax credit for doing so or some other subsidy that would make the project profitable.

While firms are motivated primarily by the bottom line, nonmonetary incentives can still have a powerful effect on firm behavior, if they have an effect on profits. For example, a city may encourage more environmentally friendly buildings by offering an expedited permitting process for new construction that meets certain "green" standards. The old aphorism that "time is money" is true for most firms; the sooner a project is done, the sooner it will begin generating profits. Therefore, speeding up the permit approval process—and incentives like that—can have a powerful impact on firm behavior.

························| **POLICY IN THE REAL WORLD** |·················

Changing the Incentives: A Malaria Vaccine

Malaria is one of the world's deadliest diseases, killing some 2 million people a year in Africa, many of them children. Hundreds of millions more are made seriously ill. Because malaria does not directly affect the developed world, the scale of suffering caused by the disease is often overlooked. Wen Kilama, a Tanzanian researcher, once noted famously, "If seven Boeing 747s, filled mostly with children, were crashing into Mount Kilimanjaro each day, something might be done about it."[6] That is the magnitude of malaria's impact on Africa.

Malaria is caused by a parasite passed to humans by mosquitoes. Once the parasite is in the human bloodstream, it causes fever, chills, brain damage, and sometimes death. Some drugs have a preventive effect, but they must be taken constantly to be effective. Quinine bark, for example, was an early anti-malaria remedy, making the gin and tonic (which contains quinine) a popular cocktail in British colonial outposts.

Scientists have long believed that a malaria vaccine is feasible. With a vaccine, a single immunization would protect a person for years, most likely saving millions of lives. Yet only modest resources have been devoted to producing a malaria vaccine. Why? Because it's not likely to be profitable.

Malaria has been eradicated from the United States, Europe, and most other rich countries. Thus, the world's wealthiest citizens have no incentive to spend money searching for more effective tools against the malaria scourge. The hundreds of millions of victims of malaria each year are doubly unfortunate: first, because they fall victim to a terrible disease; second, and less intuitive, because they fall victim to a disease that only afflicts poor countries.

The vast majority of malaria victims cannot afford to spend much on medicine even for a potentially life-saving inoculation. As a result, the world's pharmaceutical companies have little incentive to invest in the research and clinical trials necessary to bring a vaccine to market because they are not likely to earn those costs back. It is far more profitable to find a cure for a minor affliction that plagues rich people in the developed world, such as heartburn or hair loss, than to find a cure for a deadly disease that kills poor people almost exclusively.

Several individuals, led by software mogul Bill Gates and former British Prime Minister Gordon Brown, have vowed to fight malaria by altering those incentives for pharmaceutical companies.[7] The plans that have been proposed are a variation on the same basic theme: replicate the profit motive by using philanthropy—billions of dollars—to reward the company or consortium of companies that is the first to produce a successful malaria vaccine.

Under one such proposal, donors would define in advance the criteria for an effective vaccine, such as the required efficacy, level of safety (particularly for young children), storability in hot climates, etc. They would then

---

6. "Africa's Other Plague: Malaria," *The Economist,* May 1, 2003.

7. Marilyn Chase, "Malaria Trial May Yield Vaccines' Finance Model: New Strategies for Funding Aim to Fight Diseases Affecting Developing World," *Asian Wall Street Journal,* April 27, 2005.

precommit to buying a certain number of doses of any vaccine meeting those criteria at a specified price. For example, a philanthropic donor might draw up an "advance purchase contract"[8] to pay $15 to $20 per dose for the first 200 million immunizations, essentially replicating the "market" in a rich country and enabling the pharmaceutical company to recoup its research and development costs. After that, the pharmaceutical company would agree to drop the vaccine price to $1 per dose or less, providing a cheap and effective tool for fighting malaria in the future.

The Bill & Melinda Gates Foundation has provided funding directly to a research arm of GlaxoSmithKline PLC to fund a study on a malaria vaccine for toddlers. Creating and testing such a vaccine is expected to cost $1 billion or more. The GlaxoSmithKline CEO told the *Asian Wall Street Journal*, "It is fair to say that we would not be where we are today [without the Gates money]. . . . We need these incentives."[9]

. . . .

3.2 THE POWER OF INCENTIVES

If the world were a perfect place, then there would be no need to modify behavior. But it's not. As a result, public policy involves encouraging some kinds of activities (work, education, savings) and discouraging others (crime, substance abuse, pollution). As the malaria-vaccine example demonstrated, incentives play a crucial role in understanding the outcomes we observe and, in some cases, improving upon them.

1. Incentives motivate and explain an extraordinary range of human behaviors. One could argue that the "missing girls" discussed at the beginning of this chapter are a response to the way certain societies have raised the "cost" of girls relative to boys. A dowry, for example, represents a literal price for marriage that must be paid for girls and not for boys. Similarly, the social custom whereby a girl leaves her family upon marriage to join her husband's family also skews the costs and benefits of the two sexes.

Gary Becker, a professor of economics at the University of Chicago, was awarded the Nobel Prize in Economics in 1992 for expanding the way we think about the role of incentives in our lives. Becker's work has consistently advanced the idea that economic analysis can explain a far broader range of

8. Chase, "Malaria Trial."

9. "Press Release: The Sveriges Riksbank (Bank of Sweden) Prize in Economic Sciences in Memory of Alfred Nobel 1992," from Nobelprize.org, last modified April 13, 2005.

human activity than previously considered.[9] He was the first to recognize that many decisions within the family, including the number of children we choose to have, are highly responsive to changes in labor-market conditions. For example, higher real wages for women can help to explain not only the increase in married women's job participation outside the home, but also the rising tendency toward divorce (better job prospects for women make it less costly to leave a bad marriage) and the declining fertility rate in the developed world (high wages for women make it more costly to leave the labor force to take care of children).

One of Becker's other major contributions involves the concept of **human capital**—the notion that individuals make decisions about investments in their own skills and education in the same way that a firm might evaluate such investments. For example, if the wages of college graduates rise relative to the wages of high-school graduates, then more individuals will choose to invest time and money in a college degree.

To Becker's way of thinking, even criminals act purposefully, responding rationally to changes in the costs and benefits of criminal activity (with the exception of true psychopaths). Becker says this line of thinking first occurred to him when he was late for an oral exam for one of his students; in deciding whether or not to park illegally on the street, he tried to calculate the likelihood of getting a ticket and the probable fine. (In the end, he parked illegally and did not get a ticket.)

We are accustomed to thinking about the role that prices play in shaping consumer decisions. Policy analysts must recognize that incentives play a crucial role in shaping a much broader range of human behavior.

2. One of the most powerful tools for changing behavior is changing incentives. If the government doubles the prison sentence for a certain kind of accounting fraud, then it would raise the expected "cost" of such activity and presumably deter the crime. (Spending more resources on enforcement might actually have a more significant effect, since it increases the probability of getting caught.) If the government cuts marginal income tax rates, allowing workers to keep more of each dollar that they earn, it provides an incentive for some workers to add extra hours or take a second job. Some individuals who are not currently working may be induced to join the workforce, since cutting the tax on labor income is essentially the same as raising the real wage—workers see a bigger number on their paychecks.

Government has the capacity to alter the prices of different activities, either directly or indirectly. The tax code has the most powerful direct effect on prices. We're used to thinking of taxes as a mechanism for raising revenue; policy analysts must recognize that any tax also has an impact on prices and, therefore, on behavior. In some cases, we recognize this explicitly: **"sin taxes"** are levied on cigarettes and alcohol; "green taxes" are levied on products or activities that pollute. Taxes have the potential to discourage whatever behavior is being taxed—including both socially harmful activities like smoking (the cigarette tax) and socially beneficial behavior like working (the income tax).

Government subsidies have the opposite effect; they make some activity more attractive than it would otherwise be. Most urban mass transit systems are subsidized, meaning that the price of a bus or train ticket does not cover the full cost of the service. Government funding covers the balance. This encourages some commuters who might otherwise drive to take transit, which has a positive impact on traffic congestion and air quality.

Government can also affect the price of many goods and services *indirectly* through regulation or other policies. An environmental regulation that bans or limits a certain input, such as lead paint, may raise the cost of producing a good, which in turn raises the cost for consumers. Major infrastructure projects like highways and airports might have the opposite effect. If the government pays for these projects with general revenues (funds collected from all taxpayers) rather than with tolls or landing fees that are paid only by the users of the highway or airport, then any product delivered by air or road is being subsidized by the general public and is, therefore, cheaper than it would otherwise be. The bottom line is that rational individuals and firms respond to incentives; good public policy will recognize the power that government exerts over those incentives.

Consider an extraordinary example from Illinois. In 2001, the state passed a law allowing parents to surrender their newborn babies at fire stations, hospitals, or other designated "safe havens" without facing any criminal sanctions. Why would a state create a law that made it easier to abandon a newborn child? Because the alternative was much worse. There had been a number of tragic cases in which infants had died after being abandoned in places where they were not found until it was too late. The safe-haven law created an incentive for women who might otherwise abandon a newborn in a deadly place to leave the baby somewhere safe instead. A 2005 assessment of the legislation found that it may have saved a dozen or more babies. Twenty-one babies were left at the designated safe havens after the legislation took effect. Over the same period, more than thirty babies were simply abandoned in the trash or on the street; eighteen of them died.[10]

3. Rational individuals and firms will seek to avoid any outcome that makes them worse off. As Chapters 1 and 2 should have made clear, any policy change is likely to create winners and losers. Of course, individuals or

---

10. "Law May Have Saved Babies' Lives," *Chicago Sun-Times,* May 18, 2005.

firms that stand to lose will look for ways to avoid whatever cost is being imposed on them. Many such strategies are perfectly legal: an individual or firm with a high tax burden will hire an accountant to find legal loopholes to shrink their tax bill; or the individual or firm may even lobby lawmakers to *create* such a loophole. Fast-food restaurants that have to pay a higher minimum wage may opt to invest in technology to mechanize some basic tasks rather than pay more for low-skill labor.

Ever since China enacted the one-child policy described at the beginning of the chapter, many families have sought to evade it, often with clever strategies. For example, rich families seek in vitro fertilization because it increases the chances of having multiple births. Or they may deliver a baby out of the country and apply for a foreign passport; such children are not counted by Chinese family planning officials.[11] There has also been evasion: in rural areas, families often hide "illegal" children from census takers.

In other cases, the response may be illegal, but understandable nonetheless. Consider the use of standardized testing as a tool for evaluating school quality. Schools and teachers are often rewarded based on the good performance of their students, or they are punished (through loss of funding or even the closing of schools) if students do poorly. This seems logical enough: teachers and school administrators should have an incentive to maximize student achievement. Analysts have always speculated, however, that teachers and school administrators might also have some less constructive incentives. To begin with, teachers may "teach to the test"—that is, they spend time instructing students on skills that will improve test scores but not necessarily leave them with a better understanding of the material being tested. In more serious cases, teachers or administrators may even cheat.

Researchers have documented exactly this kind of behavior. Brian Jacob and Steven Levitt, now professors at the Gerald R. Ford School of Public Policy (University of Michigan) and at the University of Chicago, respectively, designed an algorithm to detect cheating by teachers in Chicago public schools.[12] (It looked for unexpected test-score fluctuations combined with suspicious patterns of answers for students in the same classroom.) They estimate that "serious cases of teacher or administrator cheating on standardized tests occur in a minimum of 4–5 percent of elementary school classrooms annually." And, as theory would suggest, they conclude, "The observed frequency of cheating appears to respond strongly to relatively minor changes in

---

11. "A Brother for Her."
12. Brian A. Jacob and Steven D. Levitt, "Rotten Apples: An Investigation of the Prevalence and Predictors of Teacher Cheating," *Quarterly Journal of Economics* 118 (August 2003): 843–878.

incentives." The Chicago public schools made a policy change in 1996 that put more emphasis on standardized tests for low-achieving students. After that change, the observed incidence of cheating went up "sharply" in low-achieving classrooms but not in classrooms with average or high-achieving students.

Policy analysts must anticipate these kinds of rational responses and evaluate the likely effectiveness of a policy in light of them.

4. Policies that fail to anticipate how rational individuals and firms will respond can have serious unintended consequences. New policies may inadvertently introduce what economists refer to as **perverse incentives**—incentives that cause rational individuals and firms to behave in ways that are not consistent with the policy and may even cause serious harm. When policy makers seek to fix one problem and inadvertently create another (or make the original problem worse), it is often referred to informally as the **law of unintended consequences.** Consider a policy in the state of New York to help heart patients by keeping scorecards that evaluate the mortality rates of cardiologists performing coronary angioplasty, a treatment for heart disease.[13] Patients would presumably benefit from having information on something as important as a cardiologist's mortality rate for a specific medical procedure.

But according to a survey conducted by the School of Medicine and Dentistry at the University of Rochester, the scorecard, which ostensibly serves patients, also may work to their detriment: 83 percent of the cardiologists surveyed said that because of the public mortality statistics, some patients who might benefit from angioplasty may not receive the procedure; 79 percent of the doctors said that some of their personal medical decisions had been influenced by the knowledge that mortality data are collected and made public. The irony—and the unintended consequence—is that surgeons can make themselves look better by helping fewer people, particularly those who are the sickest!

Often, such perverse incentives can and should be identified in the course of basic policy analysis. During the Clinton administration, for example, the Federal Aviation Administration (FAA) considered a proposal requiring all young children traveling on commercial airlines to be restrained in car seats. On the surface, the policy made obvious sense: unrestrained young children can be hurt if a plane hits turbulence. The FAA also cited some cases in which young children might have survived crashes if they had been in car seats.

---

13. Marc Santora, "Cardiologists Say Rankings Sway Surgical Decisions," *New York Times,* January 11, 2005.

In the end, the FAA did not impose such a requirement, arguably because of good policy analysis. Why?

Analysts anticipated the airline car-seat policy would create a significant—and potentially deadly—incentive. The existing law allowed children under two to travel free on the lap of a parent; requiring car seats for young children would force families to incur the significant additional expense of buying one more seat on the plane. As a result, some families would choose to drive rather than fly. And driving—even with children secured in a car seat—is dramatically more dangerous than flying. In the end, the FAA concluded that requiring car seats on planes might result in more injuries and deaths to children (and adults), not fewer.[14] The mandatory car-seat policy was not implemented.

None of the behavior described in this section is irrational. (Unethical or illegal behavior can be perfectly rational, if it advances the interests of the person or persons doing it.) If individuals feel that a policy makes them worse off, then they will expend significant resources (depending on how bad off they believe it makes them) to evade it, legally or illegally. These problems never go away entirely, as public policy by its nature often involves making people do things that they would otherwise not do (or else we wouldn't need a policy intervention in the first place). If policy makers erect a wall, and individuals or firms would prefer to be on the other side, they will expend enormous effort to get over, around, or under that wall. Any sensible policy change should anticipate that response and have a mechanism for dealing with it.

RULE OF THUMB

At a minimum, an analyst should ask three basic questions about any proposed policy change: Who is affected? How are they affected? What is their likely response?

3.3 MORAL HAZARD

Moral hazard occurs when individuals or firms that are protected against some kind of loss act with less caution than they would have otherwise, thereby making a bad outcome more likely. The most obvious cases of moral hazard occur

---

14. Charles Wheelan, *Naked Economics: Undressing the Dismal Science* (New York: Norton, 2002), pp. 29–30.

when an individual is insured against some adverse outcome, such as auto theft. Under ordinary circumstances, individuals will take significant measures to avoid the huge expense of having a car stolen—parking in safe places, locking the car, using an antitheft device, etc. But once that car is insured for nearly its full replacement value, the driver has significantly less incentive to take such precautions.

This is obviously a challenge for the insurance company: How can the firm provide insurance and still encourage the driver to act responsibly? Insurance companies can charge deductibles (an amount that the insured driver will still have to pay if the car is stolen) or offer premium discounts for antitheft devices. In the end, however, the moral-hazard problem never entirely goes away: as long as insurance lowers the financial risk of some outcome (as it is designed to do), the insured individual or firm has less incentive to engage in behavior to protect against that outcome.

Moral hazard may occur in the realm of safety as well. Devices that protect us from harm might also encourage us to take greater risks. This theory of "offsetting behavior" was proposed by University of Chicago economist Sam Peltzman in the 1970s. He theorized that motorists would respond to the introduction of air bags by driving more recklessly, causing more accidents and putting pedestrians at additional risk. Subsequent empirical research suggests that making drivers feel safer may indeed lead to worse driving. For example, a study of 206 fatal Virginia crashes in 1993 found that drivers with air bags were disproportionately responsible for multicar accidents and placed their own passengers at greater risk than did other drivers.[15]

Neither the theory nor the study suggests that air bags or other safety devices are inherently bad, since they may still lower overall injury and death rates, even in the face of more reckless behavior. It *does* suggest that policy makers must be aware of the potential for moral hazard, given that many public programs provide insurance or protection that could change the behavior of the affected parties. Some observers have even argued that America's all-volunteer military creates a potential moral-hazard problem in foreign affairs. Would American voters who are not in the military make the same decisions regarding war and humanitarian interventions if they or their children faced some risk of being involved in the fighting?

Policy analysts have found ways to minimize moral hazard in the public domain. Such was the case with the National Flood Insurance Program administered by the Federal Emergency Management Agency (FEMA).

15. "Drivers with Airbags Take More Risks, Crash More, Study Suggests," *The Virginian-Pilot,* December 27, 1994.

Government flood insurance has an inherent moral-hazard problem: individuals who are insured against flooding are far more inclined to build things in places that are prone to serious flooding. (The private market does not provide flood insurance for exactly that reason.) Historically, many flood victims used government insurance money to rebuild flood-damaged properties in the same place, thus inviting future damage. Analysts argued that government flood insurance may be doing more harm than good (in terms of lost property and lost lives) by causing property owners to exercise less care in choosing where and how they build.

In the 1990s, FEMA took a step toward preserving the basic protection of flood insurance while ameliorating the moral-hazard problem. When the great Mississippi flood of 1993 washed over Valmeyer, Illinois, causing damage to 90 percent of the town's properties, FEMA paid to rebuild the town—somewhere else. Residents voted to relocate the whole town a mile and a half east (and 400 feet higher). FEMA paid for the relocation.[16] In 1994, FEMA created a formal program for "buying out" flood-damaged properties so that they can be rebuilt somewhere with a lower flood risk. In other cases, FEMA has insisted on more stringent flood-mitigation efforts before a property can be insured.

One fundamental purpose of public policy is to protect the public against harm; the concept of moral hazard suggests that policy makers must always be cognizant of the offsetting changes in behavior that may be caused by such protection or insurance.

3.4 INCOMPLETE INFORMATION

Many models of human behavior, including the basic assumptions of market economics, assume that all parties to a transaction have full information. A consumer who walks into Starbucks has a good idea of what he or she plans to buy. The same is true with most goods and services in a modern economy. If you buy a big-screen television and the picture quality is poor, then it is fairly easy to document the problem and seek some kind of redress.

In some cases, however, information relevant to a transaction is difficult or impossible to obtain. Judging the quality of open-heart surgery, for example, is more difficult than evaluating the picture quality on a big-screen television. How does one choose a heart surgeon—or even an auto mechanic?

16. "By Flood and by Fire," *The Economist*, April 24, 1997.

Quality in these cases is not easily observed, especially by those who are not experts in the field. Indeed, sometimes it is not even possible to evaluate quality *after* a good or service has been provided. If an individual has heart surgery but dies during the procedure, how can we evaluate the quality of the surgeon, assuming that there was no egregious error? Is your auto mechanic charging you for unnecessary work? How do you know?

When one party to a transaction has more information than the other, it is referred to as an **asymmetry of information.** If the information gap is significant enough, it can hinder the way markets operate or even cause them to fail entirely. Information problems are relevant to public policy for two primary reasons. First, understanding how individuals and firms act in the face of incomplete information is an important part of understanding human behavior. Second, policy makers are often called upon to ameliorate information problems; these potential remedies include everything from "lemon laws" to protect consumers from shoddy goods to mandatory food labeling.

Several kinds of behavior in the face of imperfect information are particularly relevant to public policy.

3.4.1 Principal–Agent Problems

Principal–agent problems occur when one party, the "principal," expects another party with different motivations, "the agent," to act in a way that is consistent with the principal's goals and objectives but does not have sufficient expertise or resources to monitor the agent's behavior. Principal–agent problems have two basic characteristics:

1. The principal (which can be an individual, a firm, a government agency, or any other actor) hires an agent to do some specified task; the agent has an incentive to behave in ways that are not consistent with the principal's interests. Most employer–employee relationships operate this way, for example. A firm hires a person and expects him to advance the firm's interests—everything from not stealing office equipment to working hard to please clients. But the employee might also prefer to nap in the copy room or spend much of the day surfing the Web—interests that are not aligned with the goals of the firm.

2. The principal cannot easily monitor the agent's behavior. The behavior may be difficult to monitor because the person in charge—the principal—cannot be there to observe it, as in the case of a family hiring a nanny or babysitter. Or the behavior may be difficult to monitor because the principal does not have the requisite expertise to determine whether the hired agent is doing a good job or not, as in the case of a nonphysician who might stand at the shoulder of a cardiologist and still not know if the heart surgery is being botched.

Principal–agent problems present a challenge in private life, business, and public policy because they make transactions more costly or complicated than when quality or performance can be easily observed. It is cost-prohibitive to have a manager watching every employee every hour of the day. (And who would watch the managers?) Private-sector firms often come up with clever ways to monitor their employees for behavior that is at odds with the goals of the firm. Many fast-food restaurants, for example, have a sign by the cash register offering cash or a free meal if the cashier does not provide a receipt for the transaction. Why? Because it is a relatively simple way to protect against employee theft. The easiest way for a cashier to steal money is by conducting transactions and not recording them on the cash register—selling a meal and pocketing the cash without leaving a record of the transaction. A manager at some distant headquarters would find it hard to detect this kind of theft without expensive monitoring and oversight. Instead, the firm has provided an incentive for the customer to do that monitoring. If there is no receipt, the customer calls the manager to get $5 or a free meal or whatever is offered; the employee gets fired.

Principal–agent problems were arguably responsible for many of the actions that led to the financial crisis of 2008. Employees at Wall Street firms and other financial institutions are typically paid large bonuses based on the profits that they generate for their firms. However, each potentially profitable transaction also carries some embedded risk. The problem is that the employees making huge commissions on risky transactions do not bear the full risk associated with their decisions—their firms do. When trades go well, the employee and the firm can make a lot of money. When trades go badly, the firm can lose enormous sums or even face bankruptcy (as happened with the investment bank Lehman Brothers). Heads the employee wins, tails the firm loses. The challenge is that managers at these kinds of financial firms often do not have the time or expertise to understand and monitor the risks that their employees are taking, particularly as the range and sophistication of financial products evolve (e.g., collateralized debt obligations, mortgage-backed securities, credit-default swaps, and so on). Wall Street bosses (the principals) face the same basic challenge as the managers of fast-food restaurants: to prevent employees (the agents) from doing things that are potentially detrimental to the firm and its shareholders.

Principal–agent problems complicate public policy. Policy makers cannot merely assume that their decisions will be implemented as directed. The individuals who are asked to carry out policies often have different interests from the people who designed those policies—from a different political philosophy to an incentive to minimize their own work or to make money from bribes. Consider the case of building inspectors. Policy makers have a legitimate public interest in making buildings safe. Doing that requires promulgating construction requirements and then sending out an inspector to determine if a project conforms to the requirements. If those requirements are expensive for the builder and the inspector is prone to graft, then the builder and inspector have an incentive to strike an illegal side deal. The inspector earns a bribe; the builder saves money by cutting corners. The public—those who might be hurt by an unsafe building—will find it difficult to monitor such behavior.

There is no easy solution to such problems, although any technology or process that facilitates transparency and accountability has the potential to mitigate the problem. For example, Chicago has explored the idea of installing GPS transponders in the city's snow plows to monitor how plow drivers spend their time, thereby reducing idleness, side payments for plowing private parking lots on city time, and other activities that don't benefit taxpayers.

The cases in which monitoring remains difficult or expensive create a dilemma for policy makers. Policies that allow flexibility and discretion can empower motivated, well-intentioned employees (or other "agents") to make fast, sensible decisions that are well adapted to specific circumstances. Yet the same flexibility and discretion opens the door for abuse. As a result, policy makers often choose to require layers of monitoring (e.g., formal procedures, paperwork, approval by higher levels of management) that curtail the potential for abuse but can also create a process that is slow, inflexible, and expensive—the kind of public-sector "bureaucracy" that people often complain about. One way to minimize corruption among building inspectors, for example, would be to require two or more inspections by different inspectors—a deliberately duplicative process.

Principal–agent problems complicate any process in which an individual or firm, the principal, must depend on the actions of another party, the agent, without either the expertise or the resources to verify that that agent is doing what he has been hired or required to do.

3.4.2 Adverse Selection

Adverse selection occurs when individuals use private information to sort themselves into or out of a market transaction. If this self-sorting is serious enough, it can distort the relevant market or even cause it to collapse. Some of the most serious problems with adverse selection occur in the market for health and life insurance. If individuals have more information about their health or family health history than the insurance company has (or is allowed to collect), then individuals in the poorest health or with the greatest risk of illness will be those most inclined to sign up for policies with the most generous benefits. (As the example at the beginning of Chapter 2 illustrated, genetic testing has made this potential problem even worse.) If individuals are allowed to use genetic information to gauge their relative risk of becoming seriously ill and insurance companies are denied such information, then the pool for insurance has the potential to become excessively skewed toward the unhealthy.

The problem at the core of adverse selection is an asymmetry of information. One party offers a contract that makes economic sense based on the *average* information for the pool of individuals who might take advantage of it, such as a health-insurance contract with premiums based on average health-care costs. But the individuals who sign up for that contract are *not* average. Those for whom the contract is particularly beneficial sign up; those for whom it is less attractive do not. And the firm offering the contract cannot easily tell one group from the other, leaving it with an unfavorable pool of persons or firms accepting the deal.

This is what happened to an experiment in financial aid at Yale University several decades ago. Yale offered a new aid option: rather than taking out a conventional student loan (borrowing money to pay for tuition and then paying it all back later plus accrued interest), eligible students could opt instead to repay their loans after graduation with a percentage of their income for a fixed number of years, whatever that income happened to be. Those who had higher postgraduation incomes would end up paying more for their student loans than those who had lower incomes, which was exactly the point. The plan was designed to address concerns that students graduating with large debts were forced to do well, rather than to do good.

The Yale program enabled students who took low-paying jobs, say teaching in the inner city, to repay a percentage of that low salary, rather than being saddled with a high fixed-loan payment. Students who went on to make a lot of money on Wall Street or in Silicon Valley would end up paying a percentage of those high salaries. If Yale set the required postgraduation "salary tax" correctly, the program would pay for itself. Students who went on to become brain surgeons would pay back more than average; students who fought tropical diseases in rural Togo would pay less. On average, the high and low earners would cancel each other out, and the program would recoup the same amount as a conventional financial-aid program without leaving students who take low-paying public-service jobs after graduation saddled with big debts.

Adverse selection ruined this elegant plan. There is a crucial asymmetry of information between students and the university financial-aid office. Students know more about their future career plans than loan administrators do. Students obviously don't know exactly what jobs they will have after graduation, but they do have a rough idea whether their income is likely to be higher or lower than average. Someone interested in investment banking can reasonably expect to make a high salary; someone interested in the Peace Corps would expect to earn much less. Students sort themselves into or out of this alternative financial-aid program based on private information about whether it is likely to be a good deal for them. As a result, the program attracts predominantly low earners, for whom it is a good deal. The repayment calculations—based on the assumption that both high and low earners will sign up for the program and offset one another—no longer apply. The Yale program collected significantly less in loan repayments than a conventional student loan program and was ultimately canceled.

Policy analysis often requires identifying potential adverse-selection problems in a wide array of different situations. The article below argues that compensation for public-school teachers, which pays a uniform wage that is not tied closely to productivity, invites adverse selection.

················| **POLICY IN THE REAL WORLD** |················

Pay and Productivity: Adverse Selection among Public-School Teachers*

The annual Phi Delta Kappa/Gallup poll of attitudes towards public education released this week found that a majority of Americans feel it is important to put "a qualified, competent teacher in every classroom." Bob Chase, president of the National Education Association (NEA), the main teachers' union, wasted no time in pointing out that this will require raising teachers' salaries so that more qualified candidates will enter the profession and stay there. Al Gore has won cheers from Democrats for suggesting a pay hike. Would it really help?

Work over the past five years by two economists, Dale Ballou at the University of Massachusetts and Michael Podgursky of the University of

*From "Paying Teachers More," *The Economist*, August 24, 2000. Reprinted with permission.

Missouri, suggests that the quality of America's teachers has more to do with how they are paid rather than how much. The pay of American public-school teachers is not based on any measure of performance (the NEA opposes merit pay); instead, it is determined by a rigid formula based on experience and years of schooling, factors that Mr Podgursky calls "massively unimportant" in deciding how well students do.

The uniform pay scale invites what economists call adverse selection. Since the most talented teachers are also likely to be good at other professions, they have a strong incentive to leave education for jobs in which pay is more closely linked to productivity. For dullards, the incentives are just the opposite. The data are striking: when test scores are used as a proxy for ability, the brightest individuals shun the teaching profession at every juncture. Clever students are the least likely to choose education as a major at university. Among students who do major in education, those with higher test scores are less likely to become teachers. And among individuals who enter teaching, those with the highest test scores are the most likely to leave the profession early.

Mr Ballou and Mr Podgursky have studied the effects of a nationwide 20% real increase in teacher salaries during the 1980s. They conclude that it had no appreciable effect on overall teacher quality, in large part because schools do a poor job of recruiting and selecting the best teachers. Also, even if higher salaries lure more qualified candidates into the profession, the overall effect on quality may be offset by mediocre teachers who choose to postpone retirement.

Messrs Ballou and Podgursky also take aim at teacher training. Every state requires that teachers be licensed, a process that can involve up to two years of education classes, even for those who have a university degree or a graduate degree in the field they would like to teach. Albert Einstein would have had to go back to the local community college for 12 months of training in pedagogy and first aid before he could teach high-school physics. Inevitably, this system does little to lure in graduates of top universities or professionals who would like to enter teaching at mid-career.

None of this proves that all training courses are useless—or that America's teachers are being paid enough. Many patently deserve more money. Good ones would get it under any system with merit pay. But the current system of training, licensing and pay could not have been better designed to protect bad teachers from competition.

3.5 MECHANISMS FOR OVERCOMING INFORMATION PROBLEMS

Information problems can cripple markets and lead to socially inefficient outcomes. At times, the appropriate policy remedy is to require a party to a transaction to provide certain information that might otherwise be difficult or expensive to acquire: ingredient and nutrition labels on food, safety warnings on products, lead-paint disclosure by the seller of a home, and so on. Such policies facilitate market activity by ameliorating potential asymmetries of information. (Imagine the cost and difficulty of grocery shopping for someone with a peanut allergy if there were no mandatory food labels.)

In other cases, the government may actually determine the quality of a good or service. For example, the U.S. Department of Agriculture tests assorted food products for contamination and evaluates quality—"U.S.D.A. Grade A Eggs." The Food and Drug Administration tests the safety and efficacy of prescription drugs. Or government may create policies that provide remedies for poor quality after a transaction has taken place. Some states have "lemon laws" that allow consumers to return a car if it turns out to have serious defects in a set period of time. It is crucial to recognize, however, that markets are remarkably resilient, even in the face of incomplete information; firms and individuals devise many strategies for making transactions work when there is an asymmetry of information, even without any public policy intervention.

Branding occurs when firms make large investments over time to build an identity for their products. This identity often includes important information about the quality, durability, or safety of the product that might not otherwise be observable. Most consumers, for example, cannot raise the hood of an automobile and determine how durable the engine is likely to be. Even a test drive will not help in that regard. But cars have brand names that have been built up over decades and convey important information about quality and durability. The same consumers who could not tell a V-6 engine from a V-8 would be able to make a distinction between a Hyundai and a Mercedes.

Signaling is a process by which individuals or firms undertake activities with no direct value; instead, these activities "signal" intangible information to other parties. Some educational credentials serve this purpose. An employer may be impressed that a student passed a rigorous exam, not because the exam material included anything relevant for the job, but because the strong performance on the exam is evidence that the student has attributes that *are* relevant for the job but not easily observable—perseverance, intelligence, a willingness to work hard and abide by the rules, and so on. Similarly, a law firm may invest heavily in attractive office furniture and fancy letterhead.

These things obviously do not win cases, but they do convey an aura of success to prospective clients.

One subtle point is that effective signals are difficult to "fake." Lazy or unintelligent students cannot easily do well on a rigorous exam, no matter how irrelevant the exam may be to job performance. Law firms that do not win cases cannot afford to spend lavishly on their offices. As a result, the signal enables prospective employers or clients to make inferences about quality that would otherwise require costly information gathering.

Certification is the process whereby an independent third party attests to the quality of a good or service. This firm may have some special expertise, such as the reviewers at *Car and Driver* magazine, or they may merely make the necessary investment to determine the quality of the relevant product, as in the case of movie and restaurant reviewers. Most people know if they like a movie *after* they've seen it; yet they would like to know if a movie is good *before* they plan a Saturday night. Roger Ebert makes that possible. *Consumer Reports* evaluates the quality of a broad range of consumer items by purchasing them, using them, even taking them apart, if necessary. In all of these cases, the market has provided a mechanism for providing important information without any government intervention.

Screening is a mechanism whereby one party to a transaction designs a mechanism that elicits private information from another party to the transaction. Insurance companies can use deductibles (a minimum amount that must be paid by the policyholder before the insurance kicks in) to elicit information from prospective customers. Individuals with private information suggesting that they are a good risk (e.g., good drivers or healthy individuals) will choose a policy with a high deductible and, therefore, can be offered a lower premium. Individuals who perceive themselves as worse risks will opt for a lower deductible and will likely be offered a much higher premium. Thus, the choice of insurance products causes individuals to sort themselves based on private information. A firm might use a compensation package to accomplish a similar objective. It may be difficult to determine from a résumé and interview which candidates are motivated and effective salespeople. Thus, a firm may offer a salary that is based largely on commission. Only those individuals with information to suggest that they are hardworking and good at sales will be attracted by such a compensation structure.

Missing information can inhibit market transactions. On the other hand, there are many mechanisms short of government action that can ameliorate these problems. The key to good policy analysis is recognizing when some kind of intervention will improve overall social welfare and when markets are best left to themselves to find clever mechanisms for overcoming information problems.

3.6 HOW RATIONAL ARE WE?

This chapter, this book, and most of policy analysis are predicated on the simple but powerful idea that individuals make rational decisions in order to maximize their own welfare. By and large, that is true. At the same time, researchers have produced increasingly sophisticated evidence to suggest that individuals have a tendency to make decisions that do not always appear to maximize their own utility. Indeed, a whole new field of **behavioral economics** has sprung up to examine the processes by which humans make decisions.[17] For policy makers, this subject is more than an academic curiosity. It gets to the heart of whether, or to what extent, government policies ought to protect individuals from making bad decisions. Below is a small sample of ways in which human decision making appears to deviate from what would be strictly rational.

Revenge. Researchers have found that getting revenge gives us satisfaction, even when it does not make us materially better off—and even when it makes us worse off![18] Swiss scientists set up a game of "double cross" while monitoring the brain activity of the participants with a positron-emission tomography (PET) scanner.[19] The game was set up so that two players could cooperate to share a monetary prize; or one of them could double-cross the other and keep an unfair amount. A player who was double-crossed could choose to punish his "partner" by having researchers take some of the money away. Even though this punishment does not benefit the person who was double-crossed (since they don't get the punishment money), (1) most players opted to punish a double cross, and (2) they enjoyed doing it. According to the researchers, "A brain region known to be important for enjoyment and satisfaction—the dorsal striatum—became active in those players who decided to retaliate."

But the behavior gets more interesting than that. Many players who were double-crossed opted for revenge (and again enjoyed it), even when the rules were changed so that they had to give up some of their own money in order to have the researchers punish their "partner." These players were willing to make themselves worse off in order to make someone else worse off, which does not fit the conventional definition of rational behavior.

17. "Freud, Finance, and Folly: Human Intuition Is a Bad Guide to Handling Risk," *The Economist,* January 22, 2004.

18. Lauran Neergaard, "Looking for Satisfaction? Try Revenge, Study Says," *Chicago Sun-Times,* August 27, 2004.

19. Brian Knutson, "Behavior: Sweet Revenge?" *Science* 305, no. 5688 (August 27, 2004): 1246–1247.

Assessing risk. Many individuals assign risks to certain activities that differ markedly from their real danger, as measured by the actual probability of a bad outcome. For example, following the attacks of September 11, 2001, many Americans opted to drive rather than fly. There was a perception that flying had become more dangerous because of the terrorist threat. Air traffic fell dramatically in the months after 9/11, while total miles driven on rural roads increased. Yet even after September 11, driving was still more dangerous than flying. Indeed, fatal accidents rose 8 percent, with half of the increase attributable to 9/11-induced fear of flying.[20] Gerd Gigerenzer of the Max Planck Institute for Human Development in Berlin, an expert on how humans respond to "low-probability but high consequence" events like a plane crash, calculated that 353 additional people died as the result of the increased road traffic. This defies rationality, which assumes that an individual will make utility-maximizing decisions that are consistent with actual probabilities.

Planning and saving for retirement. In theory, individuals maximize utility over the course of their lifetime. This involves saving money now in order to enjoy consumption after retirement. Economists now have more than two decades of data on how employees have managed their 401(k) retirement accounts; the data show several common savings and investment mistakes relative to what an income-maximizing strategy would be:

- **Setting too little aside.** Employers often match 401(k) contributions—which is essentially free money. Yet a striking number of workers with access to this employer match do not take advantage of this option.
- **Making investments that are too conservative or too risky.** The data on how to maximize the value of an investment portfolio are clear: young workers should take advantage of the long time horizon until retirement and invest predominantly in stocks; older investors should do the opposite, shifting their portfolio into safer investments as retirement nears. The data from 401(k) accounts find systematic mistakes: younger workers underinvest in stocks; older investors overinvest in stocks.
- **Making emotional investment decisions.** This mistake is best encapsulated by a *Wall Street Journal* headline: "This Is Your Brain. This Is Your Brain on a Surging Stock."[21] Brain imaging shows that when individuals anticipate making money, the circuits that switch on in their brains are

20. Sharon Begley, "Afraid to Fly after 9/11, Some Took a Bigger Risk—in Cars," *Wall Street Journal*, March 23, 2004.
21. Sharon Begley, "This Is Your Brain; This Is Your Brain on a Surging Stock," *Wall Street Journal*, November 15, 2002.

"the very ones that go wild when you anticipate a delectable chocolate truffle, sex or (in the case of addicts) cocaine." The Internet stock bubble proved disastrous to many Americans, even though most could have easily diversified their portfolios in ways that would have prevented the high-tech bust from compromising their retirement savings.

The question of whether individuals act rationally to maximize their own utility is at the core of many important public policy decisions. For example, if individuals make systematic mistakes in saving for retirement, then there might be a government role in providing information or even limiting the range of investment choices. This is a particularly salient point in the debate over replacing or supplementing Social Security with some kind of private retirement accounts.

3.7 CONCLUSION

Many complex policy issues can be fully understood only by learning more about the incentives of the various actors involved. When analysts get this right, they can gain intellectual traction on issues ranging from health care to global warming. But when they get it wrong—if they fail to appreciate why people do what they do and how people are likely to respond to change—the resulting policies will be ineffective or even seriously harmful.

FOR DISCUSSION

Childbearing as a Lesson in Rationality: Understanding Fertility

The decision to have a child and the number of children a woman chooses to have are highly personal matters. And yet fertility has profound public policy implications. In developing countries, rapid population growth is a source of public concern. Many developing countries have agricultural-based economies; rapid population growth puts increasing demands on farmland. Having many children also makes it less likely that the family will be able to invest in education (or other forms of human capital). Researchers have found a connection between high population growth and lower economic growth, *ceteris paribus*.

Curiously, policy makers in many developed countries are concerned about the opposite: low fertility rates. Women in rich countries tend to have far fewer children than women in poor countries. In the United States, the total fertility rate was roughly 4.0 at the beginning of the twentieth century, down from 7.0 in the early 1800s. By 2000, it had fallen below 2.0 in the United States and nearly every developed country. It had plunged to 1.2 in the Czech Republic, Italy, Spain, and several other countries.[22]

This, too, presents economic challenges. As life expectancy grows in developed countries, and women have fewer children on average, the ratio of young people to old people begins to fall. Among other social changes, a nation begins to have fewer active workers for each retiree, meaning that it becomes increasingly expensive to fund social programs for the elderly. Social Security in the United States, for example, is a **"pay as you go" program;** benefits paid to current retirees are financed by taxes on current workers.

When the law was signed by Franklin Roosevelt in 1935, the retirement age for full Social Security benefits was sixty-five, and the life expectancy at birth for men was fifty-eight. (Because child mortality rates were high, the typical male who lived to adulthood could expect to live beyond fifty-eight.) Meanwhile, population growth, as the result of immigration and a high fertility rate, was robust. As a result, there were roughly ten Americans in the workforce for every one retiree. Social Security benefits for retirees could be financed with a relatively small tax on each working person.[23]

As Americans lived longer and the fertility rate fell, the ratio of workers to retirees fell—and is projected to continue falling. By 2030, it is estimated that there will be

---

22. Population Reference Bureau staff, "Transitions in World Population," *Population Bulletin* 59, no. 1 (March 2004): 7.

23. Stephen C. Goss, Chief Actuary Social Security Administration, testimony for the Senate Finance Committee, February 2, 2005.

only two workers per retiree. To keep such programs solvent in the face of a growing number of beneficiaries per worker, it requires either collecting more money from workers or lowering benefits for retirees.

A report released recently by a group of population researchers noted the disparate population challenges in developed and developing nations:[24] less developed regions must deal with the economic, social, environmental, and political strains associated with adding several billion more people in the next fifty years. At the same time, about 40 percent of the world's population lives in countries in which couples have so few children that the countries' populations are likely to decline over the long term. These countries, which include China and most of Europe, must grapple with the social, economic, environmental, and political challenges associated with aging and eventually dwindling populations.

Are we experiencing a population explosion or a birth dearth? Policy makers might also ask: What can we do about it anyway? Fertility decisions are highly personal; most nations would not countenance a policy as coercive as China's one-child policy. And how can we understand it? The world's population seems to be moving in two directions at once, with high population growth in poor countries and much lower growth in wealthy countries.

Fertility turns out to be a perfect example of why policy makers use models. Each decision to have a child is personal and unique; yet by thinking more broadly about fertility, and examining data over time, public policy analysts can gain important insight into fertility trends. Such models, and the empirical data that support them, also provide insight into policies that are likely to affect fertility decisions in the future.

Thomas Malthus (1766–1834), a political economist, was one of the first scholars to think systematically about fertility. His 1798 *Essay on the Principle of Population* introduced a dire model of human population growth. Malthus assumed that population growth was caused by surplus crops. When there was more food, people would have more children. His pessimistic conclusion was that humans would always live on the brink of starvation, procreating away any agricultural surpluses. As incomes rose, people would marry earlier and have more kids; the subsequent population increases would dissipate the rise in income.

Malthus's model did indeed explain fertility and population trends for much of human history: population levels were relatively constant; periods of population growth were offset by deaths from wars, famine, and epidemics.[25] Yet it obviously failed to explain what is happening now in the developed world. The United States has grown richer, while fertility rates have *fallen*. We are most certainly not procreating away our growing wealth.

Nobel Prize–winner Gary Becker has offered a competing model for fertility decisions that contains a more powerful explanation for the observed population

24. Population Reference Bureau staff, "Transitions in World Population."
25. Population Reference Bureau staff, "Transitions in World Population," 6.

trends in both developed and developing nations. Becker's key insight is that families do not merely make decisions about the quantity of their children, but also about the "quality"—in terms of investments in human capital. In his Nobel lecture, Becker noted, "The very concept of *human* capital was alleged to be demeaning because it treated people as machines. To approach schooling as an investment rather than a cultural experience was considered unfeeling and extremely narrow. As a result, I hesitated a long time before deciding to call my book *Human Capital,* and hedged the risk by using a long subtitle."[26]

Becker explained where Malthus's model went wrong:

> The trouble with the Malthusian approach is not its use of economics *per se,* but an economics inappropriate for modern life. It neglects that the time spent on child care becomes more expensive as countries become more productive. The higher value of time raises the cost of children, and thereby reduces the demand for large families. It also fails to consider that the greater importance of education and training in industrialized economies encourages parents to invest more in the skills of their children, which also raises the cost of large families. The growing value of time and the increased emphasis on schooling and other human capital explain the decline in fertility as countries develop, and many features of birth rates in modern economies.

Malthus wasn't all wrong, according to Becker. Parents did spend more on children when their incomes rose—as Malthus predicted—but they spent a lot more on each child and had fewer children, as human-capital theory would predict.[27]

A fertility model that incorporates human capital suggests that children are relatively more expensive in the developed world for two reasons: (1) parents must make much larger investments in their children's upbringing, particularly schooling; and (2) the opportunity cost of having children is much higher for women in the developed world because they must take time away from productive activities—jobs that earn them a lot of money, for example—in order to raise children.

Many other factors affect childbearing, such as religion, cultural beliefs, and access to contraception. But the Becker model of fertility provides crucial insights into fertility trends. Most important, it suggests policies that might affect fertility rates in rich countries and poor.

In the developing world, providing more education and greater economic opportunity for women are likely to make large families less attractive. Indeed, the relationship between education and fertility in developing countries is striking. In Egypt, for example, the fertility rate in 2000 among women with no education

---

26. Gary Becker, Nobel lecture, December 9, 1992. The subtitle of Becker's *Human Capital* is *A Theoretical and Empirical Analysis with Special Reference to Education.*

27. Gary S. Becker, *Human Capital: A Theoretical and Empirical Analysis with Special Reference to Education,* 3rd ed. (Chicago: University of Chicago Press, 1993), p. 23.

was 4.1 children; the rate for women with secondary or higher education was 3.2 children. In Mali, the figure was 7.1 children for women with no education and 4.1 children for women with secondary or higher education. A recent report by the Population Reference Bureau concluded: "Women with more education usually . . . have their first sexual experience later, marry later, want smaller families, and are more likely to use contraception than their less-educated counterparts."[28]

Meanwhile, countries in the developed world have the opposite concern. Some governments have implemented "pro-fertility" programs that offer inducements ranging from housing subsidies (enabling couples to have children earlier) to cash payments for larger families. The human-capital model discussed here suggests that the policies that are likely to have the most long-term impact are those that lower the opportunity cost of having and raising children for educated women: childcare subsidies, parental leave, flexible working arrangements, etc.

Economists at Dartmouth College have identified an intriguing relationship between the fertility rate in a developed country and a woman's status within that country. James Feyrer, Bruce Sacerdote, and Ariel Dora Stern analyzed data on childbearing in high-income countries and concluded that changes in the status of women affect fertility decisions (rather than the other way around). They write:

> At low levels of female status, women specialize in household production and fertility is high. In an intermediate phase, women have increasing opportunities to earn a living outside the home yet still shoulder the bulk of household production. Fertility is at a minimum in this regime due to the increased opportunity cost in women's foregone wages with no decrease in time allotted to childcare. We see the lowest fertility nations (Japan, Spain, Italy) as being in this regime. At even higher levels of women's status, men begin to share in the burden of child care at home and fertility is higher than in the middle regime. This progression has been observed in the US, Sweden and other countries.[29]

Fertility is like many policy issues: it is a private decision, yet millions or billions of individual acts have important social consequences. To understand the big picture, therefore, it is often essential to understand the many little pictures that it comprises.

28. Dara Carr et al., "Is Education the Best Contraceptive?" Population Reference Bureau Policy Brief, May 2000.
29. James Feyrer, Bruce Sacerdote, and Ariel Dora Stern, "Will the Stork Return to Europe and Japan?: Understanding Fertility within Developed Nations," *Journal of Economic Perspectives* 22, no. 3 (Summer 2008): 3.

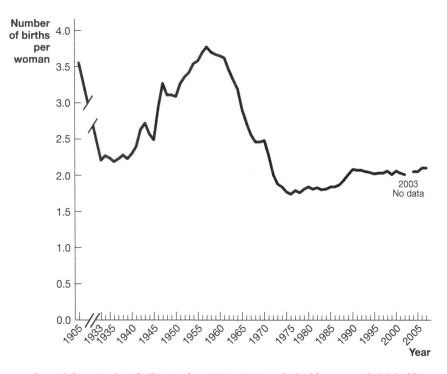

Source: Information about fertility rates from 1905 to 1998 was obtained from a report by Michael R. Haines, "Total Fertility Rate and Birth Rate, by Race and Age: 1800–1998," in *Historical Statistics of the United States: Earliest Times to the Present,* ed. Susan B. Carter, Scott Sigmund Gartner, Michael R. Haines, Alan L. Olmstead, Richard Sutch, and Gavin Wright, millennial ed., 5 vols. (New York: Cambridge University Press, 2006), I, Table Ab52–117; http://dx.doi.org/10.1017/ISBN-9780511132971.Ab40-643. Information from 1999–2007 was obtained through the World Bank's Data finder, http://datafinder .worldbank.org/fertility-rate-total.

FIVE COUNTRIES WITH THE HIGHEST FERTILITY RATES (2009)

COUNTRY	FERTILITY RATE
Niger	7.75
Uganda	6.77
Mali	6.62
Somalia	6.52
Burundi	6.33

Note: The fertility rates cited are *total fertility rates,* the average number of children that would be born per woman if all women lived to the end of their childbearing years.

Source: Central Inelligence Agency, *The World Factbook,* https://www.cia.gov/library/publications/the-world-factbook/rankorder/rawdata_2127.text. This information was retrieved on January 25, 2010.

FIVE COUNTRIES WITH THE LOWEST FERTILITY RATES (2009)

COUNTRY	FERTILITY RATE
Macau	0.91
Hong Kong	1.02
Singapore	1.09
Taiwan	1.14
South Korea	1.21

Note: The fertility rates cited are *total fertility rates,* the average number of children that would be born per woman if all women lived to the end of their childbearing years.

Source: Central Inelligence Agency, *The World Factbook,* https://www.cia.gov/library/publications/the-world-factbook/rankorder/rawdata_2127.text. This information was retrieved on January 25, 2010.

QUESTIONS

1. Does government have a role in promoting or discouraging fertility? What kinds of policies are acceptable, and what policies are not? Why?

2. Can you think of examples of how raising children becomes more expensive as a society becomes more productive?

3. One seemingly simple solution for the simultaneous "population explosion" and "birth dearth" would be to allow much more immigration in developed countries from the developing world. What might be the economic and political implications of such a policy?

4. Becker's theory, and our general understanding of incentives, suggests that fertility in developed countries might rise (or decline more slowly) if the opportunity costs for women of having children were lower. What kinds of policies might achieve that end? What might be the political or economic drawbacks to such programs or policies?

5. Are flexible working arrangements for fathers likely to lower the opportunity cost of raising children? Why, or why not?

6. One fertility expert has quipped, "Prosperity is the best contraceptive." Do you agree? Why?

7. Explain the problem of a "pay as you go" public retirement program (such as Social Security) when fertility rates are falling. Why is it difficult to transition to a system in which each generation saves for its own retirement?

8. What are likely to be the other social implications of an "aging" of the population?

9. If lower fertility in the developing world were a U.S. priority (e.g., for global environmental reasons), what kinds of policies might achieve that end?

KEY CONCEPTS

★ Good public policy requires us to understand why people act the way they do. It also requires us to anticipate how rational individuals, firms, and other affected parties are likely to react to policy changes.

★ Policy analysts use models—simplified illustrations of how systems operate—to gain greater insight into how the world works.

★ Public policy draws on two of the core assumptions of microeconomics: individuals seek to maximize their own utility, and firms seek to maximize profits.

★ Opportunity cost is the value an individual attaches to the most attractive opportunity that he or she must give up in order to do something else.

★ Taxes do not merely generate revenue; they also affect behavior by raising the cost of whatever activity is being taxed. Subsidies do the opposite.

★ Some policies that seem beneficial on the surface can have perverse incentives that cause individuals or firms to react in ways that cause significant unintended harm. This is often referred to as the law of unintended consequences.

★ Moral hazard occurs when individuals or firms that are protected against some kind of loss act with less caution than they otherwise would have, thereby making a bad outcome more likely.

★ Principal–agent problems occur when a party, the "principal," expects another party with different motivations, "the agent," to act in a way that is consistent with the principal's goals and objectives but does not have sufficient expertise or resources to monitor the agent's behavior.

★ Adverse selection occurs when individuals sort themselves into or out of a market using private information; if this self-sorting is serious enough, it can distort the relevant market or even cause it to collapse.

★ Firms and individuals devise many strategies for making transactions work when there is an asymmetry of information, even without any public policy intervention.

★ Researchers have found significant evidence that individuals do not always behave as rationally as traditional economic theory would suggest.

CHAPTER 4

Understanding Group Behavior: Collective Action

THE WORLD'S DISAPPEARING FISHERIES

In 2003, scientists published a paper in the journal *Nature* with a sobering finding: the world's stocks of large, predatory fish—including tuna, cod, marlin, and swordfish—had fallen 90 percent over the last fifty years.[1] The study noted that industrialized fishing practices are decimating some of the world's most productive fisheries. For example, in South Georgia (east of the tip of South America), a productive fishing area was "effectively fished down" in just two years.

Meanwhile, a report prepared by a science and technology committee of the British Parliament described the world's fish stocks as being "in a state of crisis." Some species are already at risk of being fished to extinction. Improving technology can temporarily mask the problem. As fishermen get better at finding and harvesting fish, the catch often increases—giving the erroneous impression that fish populations are stable or rising. In fact, the *Nature* article and many other studies demonstrate that fishermen are getting better at exploiting sharply dwindling stocks.

The curious thing about damage to international fisheries is that in the long run it will lower or destroy the incomes of people who make their living from fishing. But there is no reason that has to happen. Fish are a renewable resource—unlike oil or minerals, which exist on earth in fixed quantities. By managing the yield of a renewable resource (e.g., allowing fish to breed and produce offspring before they are caught), we can literally have our fish and eat them, too. A single large female red snapper (27.0 pounds) contains the same number of eggs—over 9 million—as 212 smaller females (2.4 pounds). Fishing

---

1. Ransom A. Myers and Boris Worm, "Rapid Worldwide Depletion of Predatory Fish Communities," *Nature* 423 (May 15, 2003): 280–283.

practices that protected the large females could put red snapper in the fish departments of supermarkets forever.

The world's fishermen are not behaving that way. In fact, they rarely have. The famous cod stocks off the coast of New England and eastern Canada were fished to the point of collapse in the 1980s and early 1990s, ending what had been a way of life since colonial times. The *Nature* article noted that the historical pattern has been one of "serial depletions," as fishermen exploit new technology, new areas, and new species. Why?

The most important answer is that international fisheries are what is known as a common-pool resource—i.e., numerous users (many fishermen from many countries) share a common resource (the world's fisheries), making it hard to manage the resource in a way that would maximize its long-term yield. The most important result is that individual fishing boats have incentives to act in ways that put the shared resource—and their own livelihoods—at risk.

To understand this paradoxical finding, consider the incentives of a fisherman who catches a 27-pound female red snapper, pregnant with over 9 million eggs. Assume that the overall red-snapper yield (and incomes for fishermen) would go up in the long run if this particularly fecund female were released rather than landed and sold. What is the boat captain likely to do? If he is acting rationally, he will keep the fish.

The reason is basic dollars and cents. If the fisherman keeps the fish, he will reap all the reward of selling an enormous red snapper at market. If he throws the fish back, it will produce thousands or millions of young red snapper—*virtually all of which will be caught by someone else.* From the narrow perspective of one boat captain, the giant red snapper is more valuable dead in his boat than alive back in the wide ocean, even if fishermen collectively would be significantly better off if he threw the large female back.

It is crucial to note that if the same fisherman somehow owned or controlled the whole fishery, he would behave differently. He would throw back the large red snapper because he would be the sole beneficiary of the larger future catch that will result from protecting those 9 million eggs.

Therein lies the challenge of a common-pool resource: the many individuals sharing the resource are often unable or unwilling to cooperate in a way that would maximize its yield. International fisheries are particularly prone to overexploitation because any plan to manage the world's catch has to be approved by all nations with access to the world's oceans; and even then, the behavior of individual fishermen is extremely difficult to monitor. Paradoxically, fishermen thinking only about their own incomes will earn less money in the long run. *Individuals acting rationally have produced a collectively irrational outcome.*

The previous chapter introduced key principles for understanding individual behavior. Public policy requires us to anticipate how individuals—whether they are acting rationally or not—are likely to respond to assorted circumstances. At the same time, we must appreciate that life is a group activity. Individual behavior is affected by how other individuals behave. Do you walk at night on a certain street? That probably depends on how many other people are walking there and who they are. Do you drive to work? That probably depends on how many other drivers are trying to use the same road at the same time.

As with individual behavior, we can model group behavior in ways that help us to understand the world better and, as a result, to make more effective policies.

CHAPTER OUTLINE

4.1 EXTERNALITIES

The market is an awesome mechanism for allocating resources in an advanced economy. Firms have an incentive to deliver what consumers want and to do it cheaper, faster, or better than their competitors. Billions of voluntary transactions, each of which makes all parties to the transaction better off, usually add up to what is best for society overall—but not always. When individuals and firms only do what is best for themselves, no one takes account of any costs or benefits that spill over to the rest of society.

A **negative externality** occurs when an individual or firm engages in some activity that imposes a cost on society that does not have to be paid by the party generating the externality. A firm tallies up the costs and benefits of some activity, such as building a new plant, and then determines whether or not to go ahead with the project. That tally of costs and benefits does *not* include any costs that may be imposed on neighboring firms and residents—noise, pollution, additional traffic congestion, and so on. Similarly, an individual takes many costs into consideration when deciding what kind of vehicle to buy and how often to drive it: car payments, insurance, gas, and so on. But that vehicle owner will not have to write a check for the broader social costs associated with driving: CO_2 emissions, wear and tear on the roads, the safety risk imposed on other drivers and pedestrians, and so on—all of which have an adverse effect on the rest of society. As a result, the private costs and benefits of some activity are different than the social costs, causing a situation in which behaviors that make perfect sense for the individuals or firms doing them do not maximize society's overall well-being.

Many of life's little annoyances are behaviors that impose externalities on others: people who talk on cellular phones in restaurants (or, worse, while driving); pet owners who don't pick up after their dogs; neighbors who mow their lawns or blow leaves at 6:30 on a Saturday morning; car alarms that go off whenever a plane passes overhead.

Many serious social problems, including nearly all environmental challenges, also stem from negative externalities. The fisherman who keeps the large female red snapper rather than throwing it back is imposing a negative externality on his fellow fishermen; his behavior will lower all of their future catch. In fact, the difference in his expected behavior when the fishery is shared compared to the hypothetical case in which he controls the whole resource is illustrative of why and how a negative externality distorts behavior in ways that harm society. When the fisherman is one of many, he bears only a tiny fraction of the cost of keeping a fish that would otherwise produce millions of offspring. But if the fisherman "owns" the whole resource, he bears the *full cost* of any diminution of the future catch—he's the one who won't catch those millions of offspring. The crucial point is that the fisherman's behavior is different when he must pay the full costs of his actions than it is when a significant portion of those costs are imposed on others who have no say in his behavior. When there is a gap between the private costs of an activity and the broader social costs, an individual is likely to do "too much" of it from the standpoint of overall social welfare.

An externality can also be positive if some private activity generates a benefit that spills over to other members of society. Imagine a blighted neighborhood that has few public or private amenities. Now suppose that a private real-estate developer is considering building a shopping center with a supermarket, a bank, and a coffee shop. As with any other private business decision, the developer will evaluate the projected costs and benefits of the project—the future rents relative to the costs of building and managing the project.

But in this case, there is an important positive externality that will not get taken into account: the new shopping center will improve the surrounding community in ways that may not be captured by the developer's financial calculations. It may raise surrounding property values, encourage other investments in the neighborhood, and even improve public safety by increasing pedestrian traffic. The developer has no way of capturing any of these additional benefits. He cannot, for example, charge surrounding homeowners for the incremental value that he has added to their properties. Nor can he collect money from people who didn't have their cars stolen because the shopping center generated pedestrian traffic that deterred crime.

It's possible that the developer will forgo the project, even if the benefits far exceed the costs for the community at large. Good public policy, therefore, may involve creating incentives or other policies that better align the private costs and benefits of the developer with the broader social costs and benefits of the project. Indeed, such programs exist at every level of government. The city may donate land to the developer, lowering his costs and making the project more attractive. Or the federal government may offer a tax credit for investments in disadvantaged neighborhoods, raising the developer's net return on the project. The objective in either case is to provide an incentive for a private party to undertake an activity that has broader social benefits and might not otherwise get done.

Externalities can distort private behavior in ways that diminish overall social welfare. A negative externality creates a situation in which rational individuals and firms do "too much" of an activity from the standpoint of society overall—whether it is fishing, driving, smoking, or any other activity with costs that spill over to parties with no say in the behavior. **Positive externalities** present the opposite challenge: private actors do "too little" of things with broader social benefits—investments in public art and architecture, conservation of endangered habitats, and so on.

············ | **POLICY IN THE REAL WORLD** | ················

To Prescribe or Not to Prescribe?: The Negative Externality of Antibiotic Misuse

Antibiotics and related antimicrobial agents have delivered stunning health gains since their invention more than a half century ago. We can now treat diseases easily and cheaply that once killed or made sick millions of people. But public health officials are worried about too much of a good thing. The misuse of antimicrobial medicines is speeding up the emergence and spread of drug-resistant germs.

Like all organisms, disease-causing bacteria and viruses evolve in ways that enhance their chances of survival, even in the face of drugs that normally kill them. According to a fact sheet from the World Health Organization, "The use of an antimicrobial for any infection, real or feared, in any dose and over any time period, forces microbes to either adapt or die in a phenomenon known as 'selective pressure'. The microbes which adapt and survive carry genes for resistance, which can be passed on."[2] To paraphrase the old aphorism—that which does not kill germs makes them stronger.

This creates the potential for a serious negative externality. Individuals who take antimicrobial drugs when these drugs are not medically necessary ("just to be on the safe side") or who fail to take their full dose of medicine because they feel better (thereby leaving the strongest microbes alive) speed up the process by which pathogens become resistant to standard "first line" drugs like penicillin. As a result, more dangerous diseases are unleashed on the rest of society.

At best, drug-resistant strains of disease must be treated with second- or third-line drugs, which are often more expensive or have more adverse side effects than standard drugs. For example, the drugs needed to treat multidrug-resistant forms of tuberculosis are over a hundred times more expensive than

---

2. World Health Organization, "Antimicrobial Resistance," Fact Sheet No. 194 (Geneva: World Health Organization, revised January 2002).

the traditional drugs used to treat nonresistant forms of the disease. At worst, diseases that were once easily treatable will develop a resistance to all available drug options—a deadly specter described by the WHO as "a post-antibiotic era."

. . . .

4.1.1 Property Rights

To understand how and why societies operate the way they do, we need a finer appreciation of how groups allocate control over resources (such as fisheries). A **property right** is the legal right to exercise control over some resource. At the most basic level, a property right involves control over literal property: real estate, automobiles, livestock, furniture, and so on. Under our legal framework, ownership of these items bestows certain rights: the right to use the property (and exclude others from using it); the right to use it as collateral when borrowing; the right to sell it, lease it, or otherwise transfer use to another party or parties. These rights are seldom absolute. It is illegal to build a skyscraper in most residential communities, regardless of whether you own the property on which it would sit. And if you build a more modest dwelling on your land, it is unlikely that you will be allowed to operate a brothel.

Property rights can also be extended to inventions, formulas, works of art and literature, and other forms of intellectual property that exist as unique ideas rather than physical things. For example, a patent bestows an exclusive right to use or produce a newly invented item, whether it is a better ice-cream maker or a life-saving heart medication. A copyright bestows control over literary, musical, and artistic works. If you violate a patent or copyright—by illegally downloading music, for example—you can be prosecuted just as if you trespassed on private land or stole clothes from a department store.

Property rights can also define the allowable behavior of firms and individuals in relation to the rights of other firms and individuals. Does my neighbor have the right to use his leaf blower at 5:30 a.m. on a Saturday, or do I have the right to sleep in peace on a weekend morning? In this case, the property right involves control of the sound waves that waft across the boundaries of physical property. Who controls that right? If there is no noise regulation, then the property right implicitly belongs to the owner of the leaf blower who can use his noisy machine whenever he wants. On the other hand, a homeowners association, or a community, or some other entity with authority over the relevant households may create a rule forbidding the use of loud machinery at certain times of day. In that case, the property right—control of the sound waves—is vested with those who prefer silence, at least until 8:00 a.m. or some other such hour.

One of the reasons that shared resources like international fisheries are difficult to manage—and, therefore, produce poor collective outcomes—is that property rights are undefined, ambiguous, or difficult to enforce. This important point will be discussed in greater detail in Chapter 8; clearly defined property rights are essential for a market economy.

4.1.2 Transactions Costs

Individuals and groups within society will make private deals with one another when it suits their interests. These voluntary agreements and transactions are the cornerstone of civil society. However, such agreements are not costless, particularly between strangers. Striking private deals requires gathering information, bargaining, drawing up legal contracts, monitoring the agreement, and undertaking other activities that consume resources. Collectively, the costs of conducting a transaction are referred to as **transactions costs.** A simple transaction, such as walking into a pharmacy and buying a candy bar, has low transactions costs. A complex transaction, such as the merger of two multinational corporations, might involve hundreds of millions of dollars of transactions costs as investment bankers, lawyers, accountants, regulators, and consultants consummate the deal. Transactions costs rise significantly as the nature of the transaction becomes more complex or as the number of parties involved grows larger.

Transactions costs are related to public policy in two significant ways. First, transactions costs can impede or prevent agreements that would otherwise make all parties better off. Think back to the fisherman who lands a 27-pound female red snapper pregnant with 9 million eggs. Lots of other fishermen will benefit if he throws it back. In a world without transactions costs, each of those fishermen could pay him a small amount to do just that. The guy who throws back the large red snapper would be compensated for giving up his catch; the other fishermen would benefit from better harvests in the future. This is a classic voluntary exchange that makes all parties better off—except that it will never happen. The costs of organizing, negotiating, and monitoring such an agreement among so many different parties would be prohibitive.

Second, good public policy can play an important role in lowering transactions costs. For example, the legal code makes it cheaper and easier to enter into commercial contracts; the court system makes it easier to enforce such contracts. Government can gather and promulgate information—such as testing a municipal water supply and publishing the results—that might otherwise be expensive for consumers to gather. One of the most fundamental tasks of government is assigning and defending property rights. It is difficult to sell a house or any other asset if there is some dispute over who actually owns the property. As basic as that sounds, governments in many poor countries either cannot or do not protect basic property rights. In the slums of Delhi or São Paulo, millions of residents have no formal title to their modest homes. They are technically squatters. As a result, they have none of the legal protections that come with formal property rights; nor can they use their homes as a financial asset, such as collateral for a small loan.

4.1.3 The Coase Theorem

University of Chicago economist Ronald Coase was awarded the 1991 Nobel Prize in Economics for exploring the role that property rights and transactions costs play in the structure and functioning of a modern economy. One of his key insights, now enshrined as the **Coase Theorem,** is that externalities will be corrected by the market without any government intervention if two criteria are met: (1) property rights are clearly defined, and (2) transactions costs are nonexistent (or very low). Moreover, Coase theorized that if two parties are engaged in activities that impinge on one another (such as a polluting leather factory next to a bottled-water plant) and the above conditions are met, the outcome in terms of which activity prevails will be the same regardless of which party begins with the relevant property right.

To better illuminate this last point, let's consider an example of the polluting factory adjacent to the bottled-water plant. For the sake of simplification, let's assume that the two activities have become mutually exclusive: the pollution from the leather factory makes it impossible to bottle water on the adjacent property. Assuming that the two parties can reach some kind of agreement cheaply (low transactions costs), the Coase Theorem dictates not only that the two parties will resolve this externality by themselves, but that the ultimate resolution—whether it is the leather factory or the bottled-water plant that continues to operate—will be invariant to which party has the relevant property right (which in this case revolves around whether or not the bottled-water company has a legal claim to stop the pollution).

Some numbers will help to clarify the theory. Let's assume that the leather factory earns profits of $10 million a year, and the bottled-water plant earns annual profits of $25 million. Suppose the law awards the property right to the leather factory, meaning that the bottled-water company has no legal claim to stop the pollution. Will the bottled-water company close its doors? No. *The leather factory will.* The central insight of the Coase Theorem is that the bottled-water company makes the most productive use of the adjacent properties and, therefore, can afford to pay the leather factory to stop polluting. Assuming low or nonexistent transactions costs, the bottled-water company could strike a deal in which it pays the leather factory $12 million a year to cease operations—more than the $10 million the leather factory makes from operating. The bottled-water company still earns $13 million in annual profits ($25 million minus the $12-million side payment to keep the leather factory shuttered), which is a far better outcome than not being able to produce water at all. The externality has been dealt with, and the resource is being put to its most productive use.

Now suppose that the original property right resided with the bottled-water plant, meaning that the leather factory was prohibited by law from emitting particulates that would despoil the adjacent spring water. The potential profits are the same as in the first case: $25 million for the bottled-water plant and $10 million for the leather factory. What happens?

The leather factory will close its doors. Even if the leather factory offered all of its $10-million profits to the bottled-water plant in exchange for the right to pollute, the bottled-water company is better off rejecting the deal. There is no sense in taking $10 million to accept pollution that will destroy $25 million in profits.

Note that the use of the ultimate resource is the same in both cases—the bottled-water plant continues to operate, and the leather factory is shuttered—regardless of which firm is originally vested with the pollution-related property right. Of course, the two scenarios have widely disparate impacts on the profitability of the two firms. In the case where the property right resides with the leather factory, the bottled-water plant must pay to make the factory close its doors. When the property right resides with the bottled-water plant, however, the leather factory also ends up closed but gets nothing as compensation.

The key insights of the Coase Theorem are threefold:

1. Private parties can deal with externalities (positive or negative) as long as the property rights are clearly defined and the transactions costs are low or nonexistent.
2. The ultimate use of the resource will be the same regardless of which party originally owns the property right. This outcome will be socially efficient because it creates the most value from the disputed resource. As the Royal Swedish Academy noted in presenting Coase with the Nobel Prize, "The right will end up with the party who can achieve the largest output."
3. If, for some reason, transactions costs were high, the parties may not be able to reach a socially efficient outcome. In such cases, the role of public policy may be to impose a solution, or to create laws and institutions that lower transactions costs, so that private parties can more easily reach an efficient solution.

4.2 STRATEGIC INTERACTION

Much of our behavior is shaped by the way others are behaving around us. **Game theory** is the study of strategic interactions between different individuals, or "agents." Many of the models developed by game theorists are powerful tools for understanding group behavior, which makes them important analytical tools for understanding public policy.

4.2.1 The Prisoner's Dilemma

The **prisoner's dilemma** is a model that depicts how two rational agents, each trying to maximize his own utility but unable to make a binding agreement with the other, behave in a way that makes both of them worse off. The model is based on a hypothetical situation in which two prisoners are accused of committing a crime together. After they are arrested, the prisoners are immediately separated and not allowed to communicate. The authorities are eager to get testimony that will lead to convictions of some sort. Thus, they are willing to offer leniency in exchange for information.

Each prisoner faces a choice: confess and share information with the authorities in exchange for a more lenient sentence, or don't confess and tell the authorities nothing, making it harder for them to get a conviction. Neither prisoner knows what the other prisoner will do (or has done). The surprising finding is that both prisoners—each of whom is concerned solely with minimizing his own prison sentence—end up with longer prison sentences than they would have been given had they behaved differently.

To understand this curious but important outcome (which can be generalized to many real-world policy situations), it helps to attach numbers to the possible prison sentences being offered by the authorities. Suppose that the two prisoners have been arrested for armed robbery. If neither prisoner confesses, then the authorities have only enough evidence to convict them both on a lesser charge, such as illegal possession of a weapon. In this scenario, each prisoner would be sentenced to 5 years in prison.

If only one prisoner confesses to participating in the robbery, then he will receive a relatively light sentence, 3 years, in exchange for his cooperation. The other prisoner who does not confess, however, will be given a harsh 30-year sentence. (For the sake of detail, assume that the confessor pleads guilty to being the getaway driver while pinning his partner with being the gunman and "brains" behind the operation.)

Finally, if both prisoners confess, then each will be charged with armed robbery and given a 20-year sentence.

A key point in this example—and a concept at the core all of game theory—is that each prisoner is making a decision based in part on what he expects the other prisoner to do. We can represent the choices and possible outcomes that the two prisoners face with the matrix below. The numbers represent the sentence that each prisoner would receive under assorted scenarios. In each box, Prisoner 1's sentence is listed first, followed by Prisoner 2's sentence. Thus, if both prisoners were to confess, each would each receive a 20-year sentence, as shown in the northwest quadrant.

		PRISONER 2	
		CONFESS	DON'T CONFESS
PRISONER 1	CONFESS	20, 20	3, 30
	DON'T CONFESS	30, 3	5, 5

Or, if Prisoner 1 were to confess but Prisoner 2 did not, the sentences would be 3 years for Prisoner 1 and 30 years for Prisoner 2, as represented in the northeast quadrant.

		PRISONER 2	
		CONFESS	DON'T CONFESS
PRISONER 1	CONFESS	20, 20	3, 30
	DON'T CONFESS	30, 3	5, 5

It should be clear that the best collective outcome for the two prisoners is for neither of them to confess; each would receive a 5-year sentence—a combined 10 years of prison time (the southeast quadrant). Similarly, the worst collective outcome would be for both prisoners to confess; each would draw a 20-year sentence—40 years of total prison time (northwest quadrant).

Of course, each prisoner is not necessarily thinking about the best collective outcome; he is thinking about the best possibility for himself. By confessing and hoping that his partner does not confess, each prisoner has the possibility of a 3-year term—albeit at a high price to his literal partner in crime, a 30-year sentence (the northeast and southwest quadrants, depending on who confesses and who doesn't).

The model has a powerful but counterintuitive prediction: both prisoners, each acting rationally, end up with long prison terms. How could that happen? This curious outcome makes sense once we analyze the options faced by each prisoner and the decisions each is likely to make, given those options.

Prisoner 1 can either confess or not confess. The sentence he would receive under each of these scenarios depends, of course, on what Prisoner 2 decides to do. Suppose that Prisoner 2 has confessed. In that case, Prisoner 1's behavior would have the following consequences:

		PRISONER 2	
		CONFESS	
PRISONER 1	CONFESS	**20,** 20	
	DON'T CONFESS	**30,** 3	

If Prisoner 1 confesses, he will draw a sentence of 20 years; if he does not confess, he will draw the harsh 30-year sentence. Neither is an attractive option, but the best choice, contingent upon Prisoner 2 having confessed, is to confess as well and take the 20-year sentence.

Of course, Prisoner 1 does not know what his partner has done, so he must also consider the possibility that Prisoner 2 has not confessed. In that case, Prisoner 1's options would have the following consequences:

		PRISONER 2	
			DON'T CONFESS
PRISONER 1	CONFESS		**3,** 30
	DON'T CONFESS		**5,** 5

If Prisoner 1 confesses, he will draw a sentence of 3 years; if he does not confess, he will be sentenced to 5 years. The better option, contingent upon Prisoner 2 having not cooperated with the authorities, is to confess and take the 3-year sentence.

It turns out that Prisoner 1's decision is very easy: *no matter what Prisoner 2 chooses to do, Prisoner 1's best option is to confess.* In game-theory parlance, Prisoner 1's **dominant strategy** is to confess because no matter what the other "player" chooses to do, confessing is the best strategy.

Meanwhile, Prisoner 2 has exactly the same options and payoffs. If Prisoner 1 confesses, then Prisoner 2 should also confess, drawing 20 years instead of 30.

		PRISONER 2	
		CONFESS	DON'T CONFESS
PRISONER 1	CONFESS	20, 20	3, 30

And if Prisoner 1 does not confess, then Prisoner 2 should still confess,

		PRISONER 2	
		CONFESS	DON'T CONFESS
PRISONER 1			
	DON'T CONFESS	30, 3	5, 5

The dominant strategy for Prisoner 2 is also to confess. With that information, we can now infer the likely outcome of the prisoner's dilemma: both prisoners will exercise their dominant strategy and confess. As a result, both will be sentenced to 20 years in prison.

		PRISONER 2	
		CONFESS	DON'T CONFESS
PRISONER 1	CONFESS	20, 20	3, 30
	DON'T CONFESS	30, 3	5, 5

This inefficient outcome (for the prisoners) reflects the fact that the two prisoners cannot cooperate while under interrogation, nor can they make any kind of binding agreement before their arrest. Even if the two conspirators promised each other at the moment of arrest to tell the authorities nothing, each has a powerful incentive to double-cross in exchange for the shorter 3-year sentence. And each, recognizing that his accomplice has an incentive to double-cross, has an incentive to protect himself against the harsh 30-year sentence by confessing.

Note that the outcome of the prisoner's dilemma would likely change if the circumstances were altered in any number of ways.

1. If the two prisoners could trust each other unequivocally, or if they could make some kind of binding contractual commitment. In this case, neither

would be tempted to sell the other out (nor would they need to protect themselves from a double cross).

2. If some form of retribution were possible to punish a prisoner who cooperated with the police—essentially raising the cost of confessing. In the real world of crime, a prisoner who cooperates with authorities in order to shorten his own sentence might find himself or his family threatened by his former criminal associates.

3. If the prisoners (or actors in a similar situation) played the game over and over again so that they were able to build some kind of trust and predictability. Game theorists call this an **iterated game,** and it allows the players to experiment with certain kinds of behavior. If one player does the equivalent of not confessing, and the other player responds by not confessing as well (earning both of them short sentences), then they can repeat this cooperative behavior in subsequent games to good effect. If one player begins to cheat, however, then the other player can immediately stop cooperating.

The model of the prisoner's dilemma explains many modern phenomena. Two (or more) companies would earn higher profits if they did not engage in "price wars." Think about American Airlines and United Airlines, for example. If the two companies keep prices high in a market where they control a large share of the flights, then both companies will earn high profits. But competitors cannot make any explicit or binding agreements about price without violating U.S. antitrust law. So United would have to hold prices high and hope that American chose to do the same.

Of course, if a competitor is holding prices high, there is an incentive to cut prices to steal customers and profits. For example, if United Airlines holds its prices high on tickets in and out of Chicago, then American has an incentive to cut fares to fill its planes with former United customers. But as soon as American cuts fares, United will have to respond to protect itself. The dominant strategy for firms is to cut fares—which is good news for airline passengers and an important feature of markets. It should also be clear why antitrust law—a prerequisite for effective markets—forbids competitors from making agreements on pricing or from even discussing prices with one another.

4.2.2 An Arms Race

An **arms race** is a variation on the prisoner's-dilemma model. The value of any weapon is relative; all that matters is whether the weapon is more or less powerful than what a military opponent has. For example, a bomber with a slightly longer range can be used to gain a major strategic advantage. The incentive for any nation, therefore, is to spend more on weapons and related items than a likely adversary.

Of course, all nations have the same incentive. The likely outcome, which has been observed historically, is that countries spend increasing amounts on armaments—the "arms race"—and make themselves worse off in the process. When all countries spend more on arms, their relative military strength does not change. The weapons are expensive, however, and citizens are left with fewer resources to spend on other goods and services. Thus, all governments would be better off if they could somehow limit arms purchases and use the saved resources on things that provide more direct value to their citizens.

Yet what is the likely outcome of such an agreement? The nations that agree to arms control are likely to cheat on that agreement for the same reason that the two prisoners are likely to rat each other out. If two or more countries have pledged to limit spending on weapons (or to desist from developing a certain kind of new weapon), then one party to the agreement has an incentive to gain a strategic advantage by spending more on weapons than the agreement allows (or by developing a new, highly sophisticated weapon).

Of course, other nations recognize this incentive and are likely to cheat themselves. The dominant strategy is to cheat, which leaves all nations spending a great deal of resources without ever gaining a long-term strategic advantage. This outcome can be improved if the parties to the agreement are able to monitor the weapons development of the other nations in the agreement, which explains President Ronald Reagan's admonition for negotiating arms agreements with the former Soviet Union: "Trust but verify."

More recently, the use of performance-enhancing drugs, such as steroids, can be modeled as an arms race. Performance in any sport is relative; a competitor is judged relative to the performance of other competitors—can he ride faster or hit more home runs than others? If few participants are using performance-enhancing drugs, then there is a powerful incentive to gain a small advantage, even at the cost of adverse health effects. Once some athletes begin to "dope," then others have a strong incentive to follow suit, lest their relative performance suffer. Yet once enough athletes are using drugs, then any relative advantage dissipates, and all users are left merely with the adverse health effects caused by the prohibited substance. As in the case of a literal arms race, the athletes themselves would be best off under a regime that bans such drugs and strictly tests for their use—a difficult policy to achieve given that that new performance-enhancing drugs are often developed faster than the capacity to test for them.

Strategic Driving: An SUV Arms Race?

Can the decision to drive a sport-utility vehicle or some other relatively large vehicle be modeled as an arms race? Yes, according to both economic theory and empirical research. According to federal safety data, SUVs are safer than small cars for the occupants inside them. According to a *Wall Street Journal* study of the 50 safest vehicles on the road, 18 were SUVs, 23 were large pickups or vans, and only 9 were passenger sedans.[3]

Yet those "safe" SUVs, trucks, and vans inflict more damage to others on the road than smaller vehicles do. For example, not only are SUVs bigger and heavier, but they have higher bumpers and stiffer bodies than other vehicles, transferring more force upon impact to smaller cars.[4]

Economist Hal Varian has described the ensuing "arms race." It is rational, he points out, for a safety-conscious family to choose a large vehicle. If there are mostly small cars in their town, the family can reduce their risk in the event of a collision by buying an SUV. The side effect of that decision, however, is that their large SUV would cause significant damage to any smaller car and its occupants in the event of an accident. That creates an incentive for other drivers to buy SUVs themselves, if only to avoid being the small car in a collision.

Like many of the phenomena described in this chapter, the SUV outcome could be "collectively irrational." Auto fatalities fell steadily in the United States for nearly 30 years, from 54,600 in 1972 to 34,900 in 1992—a 36 percent decline. But in 1992, fatalities began to rise. In 2002, there were 38,300 traffic fatalities, a 10 percent climb over the course of a decade during which SUVs became increasingly popular.

What can or should be done? In 2003, the auto industry agreed on a voluntary basis to begin implementing standards to make cars safer when hit by larger vehicles and to make SUVs and pickups less dangerous.[5] (The industry

---

3. Robert H. Frank, "Feeling Crash-Resistant in an S.U.V.," *New York Times,* May 16, 2000.

4. Hal R. Varian, "Economic Scene: Are Bigger Vehicles Safer? It Depends on Whether You're a Passenger or a Target," *New York Times,* December 18, 2003.

5. Danny Hakim, "Automakers Agree to Work Together for S.U.V. Safety," *New York Times,* February 14, 2003.

was motivated to act voluntarily in part by threats of new regulation from the Bush administration.)

Others have proposed more radical solutions. Economist Robert Frank has called for a "mass tax" that would be assessed based on the size of a vehicle. Drivers of big vehicles would be charged for the negative externality (safety and environmental) that they impose on the rest of society. Frank writes, "No one complains of intrusive government regulation when we tax trucks according to weight, because a truck's weight is a good indicator of how much damage it does to our roads. Pegging passenger vehicle taxes to weight, emission levels and fuel economy can be recommended on similar practical grounds."

. . . .

4.2.3   Zero-Sum, Positive-Sum, and Negative-Sum Games

One important distinction among strategic interactions, or "games," is whether or not the participants are competing for shares of a fixed payoff or for shares of a payoff that might get larger or smaller, depending on the participants' behavior. In other words, can the players affect the "size of the pie" or just how the slices are split? Strategic games can be classified into three categories: **zero-sum games** have a fixed payoff; **positive-sum games** have a payoff that can get larger under some circumstances; and **negative-sum games** have a payoff that gets smaller as time goes on.

Zero-sum games are those in which "the size of the pie" is fixed. If one player gets more, then other players must get less. A simple example would be splitting a sum of money, such as $20. Two players could obviously get $10 each. But if one player gets $11, then the other player can only get $9. If one player gets $12, the other gets $8. Making one party better off comes entirely at the expense of a different party.

In a world of finite resources, there are many zero-sum situations. If an organization or government has a fixed budget, then providing more resources for one program may come at the expense of another program. When the Bush administration proposed cutting federal funding for Medicaid, a health-insurance program for the poor, to help the victims of Hurricane Katrina, Iowa governor Tom Vilsack called it "morally wrong" to take money from the poor people of Iowa to help the poor people of New Orleans. Of course, Governor Vilsack, a Democrat eyeing a run for president in 2008, had his own zero-sum solution for funding Katrina-related programs: reverse federal tax cuts for the wealthiest Americans.

Positive-sum games are those in which the participants can increase the size of the pie if they behave in certain ways. Suppose the management and workers of a company are negotiating a new contract. At first glance, this appears to be a zero-sum situation: any increase in pay for workers must come at the expense of corporate profits. In fact, the negotiators may find ways to make both parties better off, such as finding ways to cut nonlabor costs, or to speed up production, or to improve product quality—all of which could increase the "pie" of revenues to be split between labor and management.

Negative-sum games are those in which the participants are competing for shares of a shrinking pie. Consider the example of labor and management negotiating during a strike. Assuming that the strike disrupts production, each day of lost profits represents money that neither side will get, no matter what deal they eventually agree to. When the National Hockey League canceled the 2004–2005 hockey season because the players and owners could not come to an agreement on a contract, a year of ticket and television revenues were lost forever. Whatever deal the owners and players ultimately cut, both would have been better off had they made the same agreement one year earlier: the parties could have agreed to the same division of a larger pie.

So why do strikes happen? You should note that although the potential total payoff grows smaller over time in a negative-sum game, one side or the other may still believe that its share of that payoff will be improved by using bargaining strategies that shrink the pie. For example, a labor union may believe that management will be hurt worse than workers by a strike. Thus, the leverage it gains from the work stoppage may earn the union a much better deal than it would have been offered otherwise, even after the lost revenues from the strike are taken into account. A larger slice of a smaller pie may turn out to be a good deal.

Of course, the rational strategy for management is to anticipate the deal that it will ultimately have to offer workers and to proffer it sooner rather than later, thereby avoiding losses from the strike. If management is going to have to offer workers a 7-percent raise, then management ought to do it *before* losing $30 million as the result of a strike. In reality, however, information is uncertain in a bargaining situation. Neither side knows with certainty the strength or resolve of the other side. Will workers really go on strike, or will they accept a 5-percent raise? Strategic information is often revealed slowly, which is one reason that bargaining can be a significant transaction cost.

In both the public and private sectors, good analysis often involves identifying the positive-sum potential in what appears to be a zero-sum or negative-sum situation. Are there ways to make the pie bigger so that nobody has to be made worse off in the process of making another party better off?

4.3 DYNAMIC BEHAVIOR

Our behavior is often shaped by the behavior of those around us. Indeed, what seems perfectly rational when other people are behaving one way may be impractical or dangerous when others are behaving a different way. Thomas Schelling, cowinner of the Nobel Prize in Economics in 2005, offers the simple example of people standing up at a sporting event. If the fans in the first few rows stand up (even though they can see fine while sitting down), then the people seated behind them have no choice but to stand up if they hope to see the game.

While this may be a trivial example, the phenomenon whereby the behavior of a small group of individuals can change the incentives of those around them and set in motion a large-scale change in behavior is crucial to understanding many public policy issues. For example, bank runs—in which customers rush to withdraw as much of their deposits as possible—were common in the early days of the United States and led to the collapse of some financial institutions that were entirely fiscally sound.

To understand how this might happen, we must first understand the nature of banking and related financial institutions. Banks accept deposits and then use that money to make loans (often many years in duration) to other customers. Thus, only a fraction of the money a customer deposits in a bank is actually sitting in the vault at any given time. This arrangement works fine as long as most of the bank's depositors do not demand most of their money at the same time.

Of course, that is exactly what happens during a bank run. For reasons that may be rooted in fact or fiction, some of the bank's customers fear for the solvency of the bank and demand their money back before it is "too late." If the sum demanded is large enough, it will be tied up in loans rather than stacked in the vault, and customers are told that their money will be made available at some future date. This process can feed on itself. As word spreads that some customers are not getting all of their deposits back immediately, other customers rush to withdraw whatever cash they can get, exacerbating the run. This dynamic process—with panicked depositors causing other depositors to panic—can render a perfectly healthy bank insolvent (not to mention a bank that may actually have some underlying financial problems).

No bank or financial institution can withstand a full-scale panic for the simple reason that the bulk of its assets cannot be converted into cash quickly or easily. The policy challenge, therefore, is to protect institutions from panics that can devastate even a healthy balance sheet. Federal Deposit Insurance was created in 1933 in response to the bank runs of the Great Depression.

The Federal Deposit Insurance Corporation (FDIC) now guarantees all commercial bank deposits up to $250,000, and, since 1989, the Savings Association Insurance Fund offers similar protection for savings and loan deposits. As a result, depositors have no need to worry about the solvency of their banks because the government will reimburse them up to $250,000 in the event that their bank or savings and loan cannot honor their deposits.

Deposit insurance has sometimes been criticized as being *too* effective because it creates a moral hazard. Customers have no incentive to monitor their banks or financial institutions for imprudent behavior.

Not all dynamic relationships are the same. In some cases, behavior can feed on itself in ways that lead to worsening outcomes, as in the case of a bank run. But in other instances, behavior can feed on itself in a positive way. We should distinguish among three different kinds of dynamic relationships.

In a **negative feedback loop,** or "vicious cycle," some incident or behavior leads to a bad outcome, which induces behavior that makes the situation even worse. A **positive feedback loop** is the opposite: some behavior or incident causes a positive outcome, which induces additional positive behavior. Finally, a situation is in **equilibrium** if there is some relatively stable outcome, even in the face of changing behavior or circumstances.

Imagine a city that is facing a slight decline in public transit use. To balance the transit budget in the face of lower fare revenues, the seemingly logical approach would be to raise transit fares and/or cut service. Yet this situation represents a potential negative feedback loop: as fares go up and service becomes less frequent, the number of riders is likely to fall further still; and as ridership falls further, the system will have to pursue additional fare increases or service cuts, discouraging even more riders; and so on. Experts in public transit recognize this potential phenomenon as the "public transit death spiral." It does not mean that all public transit systems should be immune from fare increases or service cuts. It does mean, however, that policy makers should recognize that transit use is a dynamic phenomenon.

With a positive feedback loop, or virtuous cycle, changes in behavior or policy have a positive impact, which induces other behavioral changes that have additional beneficial effects. Consider the effect of a drop in crime in a certain neighborhood (because of better policing, more vigilant neighbors, or for any other reason). Safer streets set in motion changes that can diminish crime further still. More people feel safe walking the streets at all hours, which deters criminals (and makes it even safer to walk the streets at night). With fewer crimes to solve, police have greater resources to solve the crimes that do happen and to patrol the streets proactively, both of which are deterrents to crime. And so on.

In contrast to virtuous and vicious cycles, some situations show remarkable stability in the face of change. These outcomes are said to be *in equilibrium,* meaning that even if the situation is disrupted by some kind of shock, there is a self-correcting mechanism that is likely to move the situation back toward its starting point. Most markets exhibit this tendency. For example, suppose that the equilibrium price for tomatoes in some market is $3.00 a pound. Further suppose that a late-summer drought devastates many of the local tomato farms. In the short run, this disruption of the tomato supply would cause prices to shoot up—perhaps to $4.50 or $5.00 a pound—since far fewer tomatoes come to market. Yet those rising prices will set in motion assorted behavioral responses that will begin moving the price of tomatoes back toward the original equilibrium price of $3.00 a pound: higher tomato prices will cause some consumers to buy other fruits or vegetables; growers in other markets will be attracted by the higher prices in the drought-affected area and will begin shipping more tomatoes there; the tomato growers who lost crops will be encouraged by higher prices to replant for the following year (and perhaps invest in irrigation technology to protect against drought). It's very likely that the price of tomatoes will be back near $3.00 a pound within a year, if not sooner (assuming that the drought was the only major shock involved).

Negative and positive feedback loops may be thought of as pushing a boulder downhill; once a process begins, it gains momentum for good or for ill. In contrast, a condition in equilibrium is like a marble resting at the bottom of a bowl; even if disturbed, forces will move it back toward its initial resting point.

4.4 COLLECTIVE-ACTION PROBLEMS

Public policy is the study of how we make collective decisions. If individuals act in ways that make them better off, then presumably *groups* of rational individuals will also act in ways that lead to optimal collective outcomes. In fact, for reasons related to the concepts we explored with the prisoner's dilemma, this is not always the case. **Collective-action problems** occur when each individual in a group pursues a rational strategy, yet the collective outcome is bad for all of those same individuals, creating "collective irrationality."

Many group endeavors involve shared responsibilities that produce shared benefits. Collective-action problems arise when members of the group can shirk their responsibilities and still share in the group benefits. A significant social problem can arise when there are so many "rational" shirkers that no one is left to do the work that would have made everyone in the group better off, *including the shirkers!* Those who enjoy the benefits of group action without contributing to the effort (or without desisting from some harmful activity) are known as **free riders.** The possibility of getting something for nothing creates an incentive for most members of the group to shirk their responsibilities, at which point the benefits are no longer generated and the group is made worse off.

Italian economist Vilfredo Pareto stated the situation elegantly in 1935:

> If *all* individuals refrained from doing A, every individual as a member of the community would derive a certain advantage. But now if all individuals less *one* continue refraining from doing A, the community loss is very slight, whereas the one individual doing A makes a personal gain far greater than the loss that he incurs as a member of the community.[6]

This situation is perhaps best encapsulated by the "tragedy of the commons," an example popularized by Garrett Hardin in a 1968 article in *Science*. Hardin used an English commons—a shared grassy area for grazing livestock—to illustrate the inherent challenges of collective action. Village residents—all of whom can be expected to maximize their own utility and behave rationally—derive benefits from grazing their animals on the shared commons. Each sheep, goat, or cow does some damage to the shared resource, which will repair itself naturally if not overgrazed. The commons will be a valuable resource in perpetuity if each livestock owner limits the grazing of his animals to a responsible level.

Yet each herdsman has a powerful incentive to graze additional animals beyond that level: he gets all the benefits of increasing the size of his herd but pays only a fraction of the cost of the incremental damage done to the commons. Hardin explained, "The rational herdsman concludes that the only sensible course for him to pursue is to add another animal to his herd. And another. . . . But this is the conclusion reached by each and every rational herdsman sharing a commons. Therein is the tragedy. Each man is locked into a system that compels him to increase his herd without limit—in a world that is limited. Ruin is the destination toward which all men rush, each pursuing his own best interest in a society that believes in the freedom of the commons. Freedom in a commons brings ruin to all."[7]

---

6. From the *Stanford Encyclopedia of Philosophy* (Stanford: Metaphysics Research Lab, Center for the Study of Language and Information, Stanford University, 2009).

7. Garrett Hardin, "The Tragedy of the Commons," *Science* 162 (1968): 1243–1248.

Hardin was criticized for his poor knowledge of how English commons were actually used; many were regulated, particularly as they became subject to overuse. But that does not detract from the main point; if anything, it underscores the need for groups to come up with policies (that can be monitored and enforced) to prevent collective irrationality. The fisheries example at the beginning of this chapter is a perfect example of the tragedy of the commons. The same kind of analysis can also help to explain global warming, deforestation, and other resource-depletion problems. It can even explain why some civilizations collapsed entirely, as will be explored in the For Discussion section at the end of this chapter.

Collective-action problems tend to get worse as a group gets larger for two reasons. First, the incentive to free ride grows because the impact of any one individual's efforts becomes less important to the overall effort; the free rider can still enjoy plenty of benefit without doing any work. And, second, it is far easier to monitor participation in smaller groups.

Consider an outdoor space shared by three families. If one of those families does not do its share of gardening, maintenance, and picking up after pets, then the impact will be quite significant—enough so that the delinquent family's enjoyment of the space will be diminished by its own sloth even if the other two families are doing their share of the work. Meanwhile, with only three families involved, it is not terribly difficult to identify which party is not keeping its part of the bargain.

Compare that to a park shared by 1,000 families. If 999 of those families are doing their share of the work, then the thousandth family can still shirk its responsibilities and enjoy a lovely park. And, of course, it is difficult to monitor behavior when 1,000 families have shared responsibilities.[8] The problem is that when every family thinks that it can get away with doing nothing, then nothing is exactly what gets done—no garden, even if all 1,000 families would prefer to have a garden.

You've almost certainly noticed collective-action problems in your everyday life. Group projects tend to create free-rider problems, particularly as the group gets larger. A lazy student can get the benefit (e.g., a good grade) of other hard-working group members without doing any of the work. The larger the group, the less impact one student's shirking will have on his eventual grade and the harder it is to ensure that everyone participates fairly.

---

8. Some information for this section came from the online *Wikipedia, the Free Encyclopedia,* a terrific resource, albeit one seemingly prone to free-rider problems. All *Wikipedia* content is free; the site is financed through voluntary contributions. For the record, your textbook author contributed $25.

Given that any society—from the people in a small village to those on the entire planet—must engage in cooperative activities, how is it possible to overcome collective-action problems? There are numerous potential solutions, some of which are informal and voluntary, and others that require the action of an authority with coercive powers, such as government.

Each of the following may help to alleviate a collective-action problem, depending on the nature of the situation:

- **Regulate.** Individuals can be compelled to act in a way that leads to the best collective outcome, such as setting and enforcing fishing quotas, making union dues mandatory, allowing groups to dock the grade of students who don't contribute to a project, and so on. To avoid cheating, any such regulation must be easily monitored and enforced.

- **Use government to provide the good.** Some level of government can provide a good or service—such as maintaining a park, fighting fires, or shoveling snow—and then collect taxes from all those citizens who share the benefits. Mandatory taxation leaves no room for free riding.

- **Privatize the resource.** A single owner, such as our hypothetical fisherman, has an incentive to maximize the long-run value of his resource. If we were to "enclose the commons" and allow a single owner to charge for grazing rights, he would have a powerful incentive to (1) prevent overgrazing and (2) monitor the behavior of herdsmen keeping their animals on the commons.

- **Rely on a "privileged group."** A privileged group is some subset of a larger group whose private incentives are such that they will pay the costs necessary to support a group activity even if all other potential beneficiaries choose to free ride. For example, a particularly dedicated group of neighbors may set up a "neighborhood watch," benefiting the whole neighborhood, including those who do not contribute time or money to the effort. Or a very grade-conscious student may do most of the work on a group project, much to the benefit of fellow group members, who choose to watch television instead.

- **Provide "selective incentives."** Why do people contribute to National Public Radio when they can listen for free? For some people, it's the tote bag or coffee mug that comes with a contribution. AARP (formerly the American Association of Retired Persons), which advocates on behalf of older Americans, offers a magazine and insurance discounts to those who pay to join. Free riders could enjoy some benefits of NPR and AARP without contributing anything, but there are added benefits for those who do pay their share.

- **Develop informal solutions.** Throughout the history of human civilization, groups have sought to overcome collective-action problems. Many societies have developed informal institutions to facilitate cooperation in ways that enhance overall welfare, whether it is an unwritten rule for gathering firewood in an African village or a group of neighbors who take it upon themselves to organize a communal garden.

4.5 NOBEL IDEAS: ELINOR OSTROM AND GOVERNING THE COMMONS

Must there always be a "tragedy" of the commons? Many shared resources are depleted, such as the international fisheries described at the beginning of the chapter. However, history is replete with examples of groups that develop mechanisms for successfully managing common property, sometimes for centuries. Elinor Ostrom, a professor of political science at Indiana University and at the School of Public Environmental Affairs, Indiana University, shared the 2009 Nobel Prize in Economics for her evidence "on the rules and enforcement mechanisms that govern the exploitation of common pools by associations of users."

Ostrom has spent a career studying **common-pool resources,** which are resources to which more than one individual has access but where one person's consumption reduces the potential value of the resource to others, such as with fish stocks, pastures, or water for irrigation.[9] In her seminal book *Governing the Commons: The Evolution of Institutions for Collective Action,*[10] Ostrom demonstrated that the users who depend on a shared resource often create rules, monitoring mechanisms and sanctions that preserve and protect the resource.

The Royal Swedish Academy wrote in the press release announcing the 2009 Nobel Prize:

> Elinor Ostrom has challenged the conventional wisdom that common property is poorly managed and should be either regulated by central authorities or privatized.

9. Economic Sciences Prize Committee of the Royal Swedish Academy of Sciences, "Economic Governance: Scientific Background on the Sveriges Riksbank Prize in Economic Sciences in Memory of Alfred Nobel 2009," October 12, 2009.
10. Elinor Ostrom, *Governing the Commons: The Evolution of Institutions for Collective Action* (New York: Cambridge University Press, 1990).

Based on numerous studies of user-maintained fish stocks, pastures, woods, lakes, and groundwater basins, Ostrom concludes the outcomes are, more often than not, better than predicted by standard theories. She observes that resource users frequently develop sophisticated mechanisms for decision-making and rule enforcement to handle conflicts of interest, and she characterizes the rules that promote successful outcomes.[11]

Ostrom has also documented many cases in which the local management of a shared resource has failed. From a public-policy standpoint, it is crucial to recognize when local solutions lead to wise stewardship of common-pool resources and when they do not. Based on Ostrom's empirical studies, she identifies the following principles for effective common-pool resource management:

1. Clear rules should define who has what entitlement.
2. Adequate mechanisms should be in place for resolving disputes and conflicts.
3. An individual's duty to maintain the resource should stand in reasonable proportion to his or her benefits.
4. Monitoring and sanctioning should be carried out by the users themselves or by a party acountable to the users.
5. Sanctions should be graduated, mild for a first violation and stricter as violations are repeated.
6. Governance of the resource should be democratic.
7. The right of local users to manage the resource should be clearly recognized by outside authorities.[12]

11. "Economic Governance: The Organization of Cooperation," press release from the Royal Swedish Academy of Sciences, October 12, 2009.
12. "Economic Governance."

4.6 CONCLUSION

The key insight of this chapter is that groups do not always behave in ways that maximize total welfare. One curious but powerful finding is that rational individuals seeking to advance their own interests can end up making themselves worse off. Every society in the history of human civilization has wrestled with the challenges inherent to communal decision making. One goal of public policy is to create policies and institutions that lead to better collective outcomes. As the following case study demonstrates, the cost of bad decisions—so-called collective irrationality—can literally be catastrophic.

FOR DISCUSSION

Collective Ruin: Why Do Some Societies Fail?

Good public policy can help us live better. Might it also help us to avoid the end of society as we know it? Jared Diamond, a geography professor at UCLA, has studied the collapse of societies over the course of history. His book *Collapse: How Societies Choose to Fail or Succeed* identifies common patterns in the precipitous demise of societies ranging from the Maya of the Yucatán Peninsula to the Polynesians of Easter Island in the Pacific.

Mayan civilization was the most advanced in the New World before the arrival of Columbus. The Maya were innovators in writing, astronomy, architecture and art; Mayan society peaked in terms of population and sophistication in the late eighth century."[13] And then there was a precipitous social collapse.

Diamond explains, "Between 760 and 910, kings were overthrown, large areas were abandoned, and at least 90 percent of the population disappeared, leaving cities to become overgrown by jungle."[14] Why? The primary cause was a diminishing food supply caused by environmental degradation—deforestation, soil erosion, and water-management problems. The environmental problems were compounded by drought (which may have been caused in part by human deforestation) and chronic warfare.

Diamond examines similar collapses among the Vikings on Greenland, the Anasazi (a pre-Columbian society in what is now the American Southwest), and others. The findings should interest more than historians, however. The key problem for policy analysts is how relatively advanced societies could allow themselves to spiral toward collapse. It turns out that many of the ideas in this chapter—namely, the potential among groups for "collective irrationality"—can explain the inability of some societies to reverse their decline.

Some societies begin with better physical endowments than others, such as fertile soil, a benign climate, and so on. Even in the present, geography and climate can have a profound impact on a society's ability to thrive. Economist Jeffrey Sachs has argued that much of global poverty can be explained by the harshness of the tropics, where diseases thrive (such as malaria) and agriculture does not. At the beginning of the third millennium, only 2 of the 30 countries classified by the World Bank as "rich"—Hong Kong and Singapore—lie between the Tropic of Cancer and the Tropic of Capricorn.

But historically, geography is not destiny, according to Diamond. The Maya despoiled a privileged environment, while other societies (e.g., Icelanders and

13. Jared Diamond, "The Ends of the World As We Know Them," *New York Times,* January 1, 2005.
14. Diamond, "The Ends of the World."

Australian Aborigines) have survived in some of the world's most difficult places. Diamond identifies five interrelating factors that are most important in explaining social collapse:

1. Damage inflicted on the environment, such as deforestation.
2. Climate change—natural forces making an environment colder or warmer, wetter or drier, or imposing some other significant change.
3. Hostile neighbors that can no longer be fought off or defeated (often because of some internal social weakness).
4. Changes in friendly trading partners, such as when a neighboring society can no longer provide an essential import.
5. A society's political, economic, and social responsibilities to these shifts.

Easter Island in the Pacific, which was settled by humans some time after 900 CE, provides a stark example of how a society can slowly strangle itself. Archaeological evidence suggests that Easter Island (64 square miles) was once forested, which was an important part of the ecosystem that supported human habitation. The islanders subsequently overharvested the palms and other large trees on which their society was dependent.

The deforestation did social damage on multiple levels. Wood for building and cooking gradually became scarcer. So did food from species that depended on the forest, such as birds. Crop yields suffered as deforestation led to more rapid soil erosion. The Easter Islanders even found it harder to fish and hunt marine animals because tall trees were required to build seagoing canoes. By 1722, explorers found no trees over 10 feet tall on the island. In 1774, Captain James Cook described the islanders as "small, lean, timid, and miserable."

The striking thing about the Easter Island example is that the society was unable to change its ways, particularly given that trees are a renewable resource. As Diamond asks, "What did the Easter Islander who cut down the last palm tree say while he was doing it?"[15]

How societies respond to the problems they encounter is the most significant question from a public policy standpoint. Diamond writes, "Four of those sets of factors—environmental damage, climate change, hostile neighbors, and friendly trade partners—may or may not prove significant for a particular society. The fifth set of factors—the society's response to its environmental problems—always proves significant."[16]

Some societies *do* recognize long-term problems and put in place policies to fix them. Residents on the tiny Pacific island of Tikopia (1.8 square miles) have survived for 3,000 years with one of the highest population densities in the world. The society has historically depended on fish and shellfish from the sea and the island's one lake.

15. Jared Diamond, *Collapse: How Societies Choose to Fail or Succeed* (New York: Viking, 2005), p. 114.
16. Diamond, *Collapse,* p. 11.

As we know, fisheries—like forests—are renewable resources prone to overexploitation by large groups. The Tikopian solution was simple: permission from the chief was required to catch or eat fish—the equivalent of a modern fishing quota.

And yet some societies fail to act in the face of serious but reversible challenges. Why? Diamond identifies several patterns, all of which should be familiar to readers of this book up to this point. Some cases involve conflict of interest, whereby one segment of society profits from practices that have a harmful impact on the rest of society. For example, pig farmers in medieval Greenland and Iceland contributed disproportionately to the erosion that took a serious toll on agricultural output.

In other cases, some persons or groups do serious harm because they have no long-term stake in a particular region or society—parties ranging from explorers searching for gold to modern logging companies. Diamond makes an interesting historical distinction between two kinds of Chinese warlords. A locally entrenched "stationary bandit" would exploit peasants in a way that at least left enough resources to generate more plunder in future years. A "roving bandit," on the other hand, would leave nothing standing and then move on to plunder peasants somewhere else.

Any social problem can be exacerbated when the governance structure—the process for making collective decisions—is out of touch with or unresponsive to what is happening in the broader society. Diamond explains, "A society contains a built-in blueprint for failure if the elite insulates itself from the consequences of its actions. That's why Maya kings, Norse Greenlanders and Easter Island chiefs made choices that eventually undermined their societies. They themselves did not begin to feel deprived until they had irreversibly destroyed their landscape."[17]

Finally, all societies that share collective resources—water, fisheries, forests, air—must manage them in a way that discourages short-term gains at the expense of long-term survival. Different societies—and even different groups within the same society—have historically dealt with this challenge in different ways. Shared resources can be managed "top down," in which case a centralized authority assigns property rights, monitors the health of the resource, and promulgates and enforces rules. This is how wealthy landowners in sixteenth-century Germany managed logging in the region's forests.

Shared resources can be "privatized" by subdividing them into individually owned tracts, giving each owner an incentive to maximize the long-run value of his share of the resource. In Japan during the Tokugawa era (1603–1867), for instance, a large share of village land previously held in common was divided into separate leases for individual households, thereby minimizing the potential tragedy of the commons.

Or collective resources can be managed "bottom up" by a group that recognizes its common interest and designs mechanisms to protect it. Diamond writes, "That is likely to happen only if a whole series of conditions is met: the consumers form a homogeneous group; they have learned to trust and communicate with each other; they expect to share a common future and to pass on the resource to their heirs; they

---

17. Diamond, "The Ends of the World."

are capable of and permitted to organize and police themselves; and the boundaries of the resource and of its pool of consumers are well defined."[18] These are the kinds of solution that Elinor Ostrom has identified.

In a *New York Times* op-ed drawn from the lessons of *Collapse,* Diamond writes, "When the Maya and Mangarevans were cutting down their trees, there were no historians or archaeologists, no newspapers or television, to warn them of the consequences of their actions. We, on the other hand, have a detailed chronicle of human successes and failures at our disposal. Will we choose to use it?"[19]

Our global society is the first with the opportunity to learn from the catastrophic mistakes of the past. That is, of course, one reason that we study public policy.

QUESTIONS

1. Agree or disagree: a benevolent monarch would do an excellent job of protecting society's most important resources.
2. Can you identify current social problems that have the potential to cause major long-term harm? Are they being adequately addressed? If not, why not?
3. Can you identify any organized interests whose behavior poses serious harm to society? Why hasn't the policy process stopped or limited such behavior?
4. Can you think of a policy solution that may have averted major social harm (e.g., nuclear-arms agreements)? How did such a policy come about, and why has it been effective?
5. In writing about social collapse, Diamond asks: "Could this happen in the United States? It's a thought that often occurs to me here in Los Angeles, when I drive by gated communities, guarded by private security patrols, and filled with people who drink bottled water, depend on private pensions, and send their children to private schools. By doing these things, they lose the motivation to support the police force, the municipal water supply, Social Security and public schools." Do you agree? Why, or why not?
6. Does technology lessen the likelihood that a society will experience a rapid collapse? Or might it speed the process?
7. Can you think of an important shared resource that is effectively managed "top down"? What about "bottom up"?
8. Can you think of a modern social equivalent of a "roving bandit"?

KEY CONCEPTS

★ An externality is a cost or benefit that accrues to a third party that is not taken into account by the individual or firm engaging in the activity that generates the externality. A negative externality creates a situation in which rational individuals

18. Diamond, *Collapse,* p. 429.
19. Diamond, "The Ends of the World."

and firms do "too much" of an activity that has some costs that spill over to society; a positive externality can lead to the opposite outcome.

★ A property right is the legal right to exercise control over some resource, whether it is physical property or an intangible creation, such as a work of art or an invention.

★ Transactions costs are associated with conducting a market transaction, such as gathering information, bargaining, writing a contract, and monitoring and enforcing whatever agreement is reached.

★ The Coase Theorem says that when property rights are defined and transactions costs are low or nonexistent, the parties affected by an externality will reach an agreement in which the disputed resource is put to its most valuable use, regardless of which party begins with the relevant property right.

★ The prisoner's dilemma shows how two rational agents, each trying to maximize his own utility but unable to make a binding agreement with the other, behave in a way that makes both of them worse off.

★ In an "arms race," agents spend increasing amounts on some item (weapons, steroids, etc.) that will give them a relative strategic advantage. But when all agents spend more on such "arms," their relative strength or performance does not change. The parties must pay for the costly competition, whether it is with adverse health effects (steroids), or with less consumption of other goods and services (weapons), or with some other sacrifice.

★ In a negative feedback loop some incident or behavior leads to a bad outcome, which induces behavior that makes the situation even worse. A positive feedback loop is the opposite: some behavior or incident causes a positive outcome that induces additional positive behavior. A situation is in equilibrium if there is some relatively stable outcome, even in the face of changes of behavior or circumstances.

★ Collective-action problems occur when each individual in a group pursues a rational strategy, yet the collective outcome is bad for all of those same individuals—creating "collective irrationality."

CHAPTER 5

Evaluating Social Welfare

WHAT IS POVERTY? AND WHO IS POOR?

These seem like fairly basic questions. If one goal of public policy is to minimize human suffering caused by poverty, then we ought to begin by agreeing on what constitutes poverty. The United States does indeed have **poverty thresholds** (listed below) that are used to distinguish for statistical purposes those who live in poverty from those who do not. For example, as of 2008 an American family of four is defined by the U.S. Census Bureau as living in poverty if the household income is less than $22,050. These thresholds are often referred to as the *poverty line,* although, as you can see from the table below, it would be more accurate to say that there is a series of poverty lines depending on household size.[1]

PERSONS IN FAMILY UNIT	48 CONTIGUOUS STATES AND D.C.	ALASKA	HAWAII
1	$10,830	$13,530	$12,460
2	14,570	18,210	16,760
3	18,310	22,890	21,060
4	22,050	27,570	25,360
5	25,790	32,250	29,660
6	29,530	36,930	33,960
7	33,270	41,610	38,260
8	37,010	46,290	42,560
For each additional person, add	3,740	4,680	4,300

These poverty thresholds can, in turn, allow us to calculate the fraction of the American population living at or below the poverty line—the **poverty rate.** In 2008, the American poverty rate climbed to 13.2 percent, up from 12.3 percent in 2006.

---

1. *Federal Register* 74, no. 14, January 23, 2009, p. 4200.

While these poverty statistics suggest a certain exactitude, the reality is that *poverty* is an elusive term, subject to contentious debate and even deep philosophical disagreement. To begin with, the poverty thresholds create somewhat arbitrary cutoffs. For example, a person living alone in the continental United States and earning $10,829 in 2009 would be considered poor; his neighbor earning $10,831 would not be classified as poor, even though their incomes are essentially identical.

Similarly, not all persons or families living below the poverty line are equally poor. A person earning $3,000 is obviously much worse off than someone earning $10,800, although each is technically living in poverty. The poverty rate does not capture such variations—one is either poor or not poor. The Census Bureau does use the term *extreme poverty* to denote persons or households living at half the poverty level or below, but that is a separate indicator that is not reflected in the poverty rate.

A more substantive concern has to do with the degree to which the poverty thresholds truly reflect the material deprivation that most people associate with poverty. How badly off must one be to be considered living in poverty in the United States in the twenty-first century, and do the poverty thresholds capture that notion?

The cutoffs currently used to define poverty were originally developed in the early 1960s by Mollie Orshansky, an official in the Social Security Administration, as "back of the envelope" calculations. The Department of Agriculture had done research on the cost of a nutritionally adequate diet for different size families. Meanwhile, surveys had found that families of three or more spent roughly a third of their after-tax income on food. To calculate the poverty threshold for a family of a given size, Orshansky simply took the food costs for a nutritionally adequate diet and multiplied by three.[2]

The calculations were never meant to indicate that those living above the poverty thresholds had adequate incomes, but rather that those living below the thresholds clearly were suffering some deprivation. As part of Lyndon Johnson's War on Poverty, the thresholds were adopted in 1965 as a working definition of poverty, subject to annual adjustments for inflation. Numerous proposals have been made over the years to adjust how poverty is defined and measured; so far, no substantive changes have been made to the methodology.

In 1990, Congress requested a study of the poverty thresholds by the National Academy of Sciences/National Research Council. In a summary of the final 1995 report, the panel's chairman, Robert T. Michael, noted, "The official

---

2. Gordon M. Fisher, "The Development and History of the Poverty Thresholds," *Social Security Bulletin* 55, no. 4 (Winter 1992).

U.S. poverty measure was devised more than 30 years ago. Due to its outdated concepts and data, the measure does not accurately reflect the nation's current poverty population, nor does it adequately serve policymakers or researchers."[3]

Why? Different groups have made different criticisms. Here is a sample:

- The income figures used to determine poverty do not take into account the benefits provided by many government antipoverty policies, such as food stamps and the Earned Income Tax Credit. Thus, a family whose quality of life is raised above the poverty threshold by government benefits would still be counted as poor by the Census Bureau.

- The poverty thresholds have been updated for inflation but do not take into account the fact that the standard of living for the average American family has improved significantly in the past three decades. Someone considered "middle class" in 2009 lives more comfortably than someone considered middle class in 1963—two cars instead of one, more meals in restaurants, more vacations farther from home, and so on. Should our definition of poverty, therefore, change to reflect that we are now a richer society? Does a family need more income not to be considered poor?

- Others have argued just the opposite: families living below the official poverty line live well by many objective measures and have access to goods that were considered luxuries thirty years ago. For example, a 1999 report points out that 40 percent of poor households own their own homes, nearly all poor households have color televisions, and nearly half own two or more television sets. The report notes, "While these numbers do not suggest lives of luxury, they also seem quite distant from conventional images of poverty."[4]

In the end, the National Research Council panel recommended a new measure of poverty based on a "commonly-accepted notion of economic deprivation." The thresholds would be based on the costs necessary to satisfy a family's basic needs for food, clothing, and shelter, plus a percentage to account for other personal needs. A family's income would include benefits from government programs, such as food stamps, but would subtract nondiscretionary expenses, such as child care, medical expenses, and transportation to work. The thresholds would also be adjusted for geography to take account of differences in housing costs across the country, particularly between large metropolitan areas and rural areas.

3. "Measuring Poverty—A New Approach," *Executive Summaries of Working Papers Published by the Northwestern University/University of Chicago Joint Center for Poverty Research* 1, no. 6 (1995).

4. Robert E. Rector, Kirk A. Johnson, and Sarah E. Youssef, "The Extent of Material Hardship and Poverty in the United States," *Review of Social Economy* 57, no. 3 (September 1999): 351–387.

The recommendations were never adopted. One striking finding, however, is how the definition of poverty affects the determination of who is poor and who is not. The National Research Council calculated that one in five families considered living in poverty may actually live above the poverty threshold when the tax system and social welfare programs are taken into account. At the same time, many families with large medical or child-care costs, or living in expensive areas, may not register as poor when in fact their after-tax disposable income is well below the poverty line.

So who is poor in America? It depends on what you mean by "poor."

The goal of public policy is to make our lives better. Does that mean richer? Or healthier? No policy change is good for everyone, so we must weigh total gains against total losses. But even that task is more complicated than it first appears. Total gains and losses in what? Even when gains and losses can be measured in a common denominator—such as dollars—the task of evaluating gains relative to losses is more difficult than it first appears. For example, does one dollar generate the same amount of well-being for a person on the brink of starvation as it does for a multimillionaire? Probably not. A dollar is arguably worth much more to the person struggling to stay alive. But how much more? And does that justify taking a dollar away from a rich person to help someone who is barely getting by?

This chapter examines two related challenges. First, how do we make judgments about society's well-being when it is impossible to measure welfare directly? Second, when making policy, how do we evaluate trade-offs in welfare between individuals or across large populations? For example, how do we evaluate a policy that costs the wealthiest 10 percent of taxpayers $200 each in order to increase the incomes of the poorest 10 percent of citizens by $120 each? (Assume that the lost $80 is consumed by the administrative costs of the income transfer.)

CHAPTER OUTLINE

What Is Poverty? And Who Is Poor?

5.1 MEASURING SOCIAL WELFARE

5.1.1 INDICATORS

5.1.2 INDEXES

Top Ten and Bottom Five Nations as Ranked by the Human Development Index

POLICY IN THE REAL WORLD Can We Maximize Happiness?: Bhutan's Gross National Happiness

5.1 MEASURING SOCIAL WELFARE

Public policy would be much easier if we had an objective measure that could be used to quantify the overall effect of any policy change. Assume, for example, that the concept of utility, discussed in previous chapters, could actually be measured for all individuals. Policy makers could determine that building a new airport would generate 31 million "utils" of utility for the beneficiaries and impose a cost of 15 million "utils" on other parties (such as those who would suffer from the noise and pollution).

Policy makers could immediately make two handy calculations. First, they could determine objectively that the project creates more utility than it destroys, making society better off overall. Second, they could determine exactly how much compensation the adversely affected parties would need in order to make up for "utils" destroyed by the new airport. Experts in human utility would be able to calculate that paying a family living near the new airport $753 a year would make them better off by 19 "utils"—exactly the utility they lost every year from airport noise and pollution.

Sadly, there are no such utility experts, and there is no such thing as a "util." Public policy does not provide us with any directly measurable indicator of overall human well-being. Utility is a theoretical concept rather than something that can be quantified and measured. We cannot say that playing golf gives an individual 31 "utils" of utility while playing tennis would give the same person 54 "utils." Individuals obviously make choices that reflect such preferences, but we have no scientific method for assigning meaningful numbers to the underlying utility.

Even when an individual can rank certain activities based on the amount of utility they provide (e.g., golf is better than tennis), he has no objective way to quantify *how much* better golf makes him feel than tennis, let alone how the utility of golf compares to the utility generated by a good piece of cherry pie or to the disutility caused by getting his finger caught in a car door.

Nor can we directly compare utility across individuals. If I enjoy Indian food and my neighbor likes Indian food, too, we have no objective way to compare the amount of pleasure that each of us receives from a good Indian meal. Nor, to use a counterexample, can we objectively compare unpleasant experiences across individuals in a way that would enable us to quantify and rank the disutility caused by those experiences. A student might walk out of an exam and declare that it had been an "awful" experience; a prisoner of war might also describe his captivity as "awful." Are they the same? We assume not, but we cannot quantify exactly how much worse a prisoner of war suffers than does a student who fails an exam.

Indeed, we cannot even prove that the prisoner of war feels worse than the student failing an exam. It's possible, for example, that a prisoner of war who has become habituated to his circumstances may experience less disutility from his circumstances on a given day than does a student who fails an exam and is not used to getting bad grades.

Researchers and policy makers wrestle with such challenges whenever they attempt to measure emotional well-being. For example, a survey may ask individuals to rate their happiness on a scale of 1 to 10. But a subsistence farmer in rural Africa living on $2 per day who answers that she is "happy" may have a different notion of "happy" than a brain surgeon living in Manhattan. Perhaps the African farmer is indeed as happy as the New York doctor, if we could measure such a thing directly. But it's also likely that the two individuals have vastly different ideas of what constitutes "happy."

For public policy, this creates an enormous challenge. Our goal is to maximize social welfare without the capacity to measure social welfare. Policy makers have no perfect tools for directly measuring individual utility or for comparing utility across individuals. Yet we obviously seek to make informed judgments about well-being, both for individuals and for society as a whole.

To that end, policy makers often seek quantifiable measures of the human condition that can be used as proxies for the immeasurable notion of utility or overall "well-being."

5.1.1 Indicators

Indicators are tools used to quantify and evaluate outcomes or performance. The poverty thresholds discussed in the introduction to this chapter are an indicator—albeit imperfect—of material deprivation. Policy makers seek to alleviate human suffering. We cannot measure such "suffering" directly, but we do know that it is associated with material hardship, which we *can* measure and quantify. Thus, the poverty thresholds are used to make inferences about the welfare of individuals and the nation as a whole.

For all the failings of the current poverty thresholds, they still give us important traction in dealing with America's poor. It is reasonable, for example, to focus resources on those families living below the poverty line, even if that poverty line is somewhat arbitrary. To that end, the poverty thresholds give us an objective criterion for participating in government programs or receiving benefits. In a perfect world, food stamps would be provided to the families for whom they would generate the most "utils" of incremental utility. We cannot make that judgment; a reasonable alternative is to provide benefits to those with incomes below the poverty line or below some multiple of the poverty line. (Some programs, for example, are open to individuals or families with incomes up to 150 percent of their respective poverty thresholds.)

We can also use the poverty thresholds to evaluate the general direction of poverty in the United States. The poverty thresholds allow us to calculate the poverty rate, which is the fraction of individuals in the nation with incomes below their respective poverty line. Even if reasonable people disagree over what constitutes poverty, a sharp rise or fall in the poverty rate provides important information about the direction of overall social welfare.

Test scores are another example of an indicator. We cannot directly measure "knowledge" or "quality education." These concepts are complex and contentious. In the short run, we cannot even determine the relationship between education and labor-market outcomes such as wages, since it will be many years before a third-grade student is earning a paycheck. Instead, we use test scores as an indicator of student achievement. Test scores themselves are meaningless; no one has ever earned a living by doing well on standardized tests. But a well-designed test can be an indicator of future life success—performance in college, earnings in the labor market, and so forth.

Good indicators are easily measurable and highly correlated with the underlying variable of interest, which is usually impossible to observe directly.

How well are the people of the United States living? How does that compare to Switzerland or Nigeria? Since the notion of "total well-being" is impossible for policy makers to define or measure, they are likely to use some of the following indicators instead:

Life Expectancy—(2009 Estimate)[5]

United States	75.65 (men), 80.69 (women)
Switzerland	78.03 (men), 83.83 (women)
Nigeria	46.16 (men), 47.76 (women)

Gross Domestic Product per Capita—2009 Estimate[6]
(total output of the economy divided by the population)

United States	$46,443
Switzerland	$42,948
Nigeria	$2,199

5.1.2   Indexes

In some cases, it is possible to make comparisons based on **indexes**—a combination of indicators. The human development index (HDI), developed by Pakistani economist Mahbub ul Haq in 1990, takes a series of measures of human well-being and uses a mathematical formula to combine them into a single number. The indicators incorporated into the human development index are life expectancy at birth; the adult literacy rate; enrollment in primary, secondary, and tertiary schools; and gross domestic product per capita.

The human development index, like all indexes, has the advantage of combining multiple indicators into one number, thereby getting us closer to a single measure of performance. The HDI provides more information than any one indicator and allows us to create a single ranking of countries, which we could not do if we were evaluating multiple countries using multiple indicators.

However, any index is sensitive to the way it is constructed. In creating the human development index, for example, how much weight should be given in the formula to GDP per capita as opposed to secondary-school enrollment or life expectancy? If the formula were changed slightly or a new but related indicator were added, then the HDI rankings would almost certainly change. *The rankings would not change radically, however.* Sierra Leone would not move into the top ten, nor would Norway suddenly look unattractive.

Thus, the HDI illustrates the strength and weakness of any index. On the positive side, it allows us to organize multiple indicators into a single number,

5. Central Intelligence Agency, *The World Factbook*, http://www.cia.gov/library/publications/the-world-factbook/fields/2102.html; accessed February 10, 2010.

6. International Monetary Fund, *World Economic Outlook Database, October 2009*, www.imf.org; accessed February 10, 2010.

which can in turn be ranked. On the negative side, any index is sensitive to the way in which it is designed, which involves judgments about the relative weight of the indicators that make up the index.

Most aspects of public policy depend on indicators and/or indexes to provide important information. In education policy, for example, we have no simple way of defining a "good" school or a "bad" school. Yet it is obviously important to evaluate how well a school is performing. Educators, therefore, depend on a range of indicators to provide this feedback: graduation rates, student test scores, average class size, etc.

All of this should sound familiar to sports enthusiasts, who depend on assorted statistics as indicators of performance: batting average for baseball hitters, earned-run average for baseball pitchers, passing yardage for football quarterbacks, and so on. Some sports have even created indexes. The NFL created the "passer rating" to evaluate quarterback performance. It collapses multiple statistics—passing yardage, touchdowns, interceptions, etc.—into a single number that can be used to evaluate and compare how quarterbacks perform in a game, season, or career.

. . . .

Top Ten and Bottom Five Nations As Ranked by the Human Development Index[7]

THE TOP TEN:		AND THE BOTTOM FIVE:	
1. Norway	97.1	182. Niger	34.0
2. Australia	97.0	181. Afghanistan	35.2
3. Iceland	96.9	180. Sierra Leone	36.5
4. Canada	96.6	179. Central African	
5. Ireland	96.5	Republic	36.9
6. Netherlands	96.4	178. Mali	37.1
7. Sweden	96.3		
8. France	96.1		
9. Switzerland	96.0		
Japan	96.0		
Luxembourg	96.0		
10. Finland	95.9		

. . . .

7. United Nations Development Programme, *Human Development Report, 2009,* http://hdr.undp.org /en/statistics; accessed February 10, 2010. This report is based on 2007 statistics.

················| **POLICY IN THE REAL WORLD** |················

Can We Maximize Happiness?: Bhutan's Gross National Happiness

The kingdom of Bhutan is a small country nestled in the Himalayas with a population of a mere 691,141. It is poor and undeveloped by global standards: GDP per capita is approximately $5,200; the nation paved its first road in 1961 and had no access to television or the internet until 1999.

But might Bhutan, a predominantly Buddhist nation, be the happiest place on earth? That is the explicit goal of Bhutan's government. In 1972, King Jigme Singye Wangchuck declared that the nation's most important indicator would be GNH, or Gross National Happiness.[8] The notion behind GNH is that even in a very poor country, material well-being is only one component of overall happiness. A Bhutanese government minister explained to the *New York Times,* "We have to think of human well-being in broader terms. Material well-being is only one component. That doesn't ensure that you're at peace with your environment and in harmony with each other."

The government has promulgated the four pillars of Gross National Happiness, which are rooted in Buddhist doctrine and designed to manage the inevitable forces of modernization and globalization:

1. Sustainable and equitable socioeconomic development.
2. A pristine environment.
3. Preserving and promoting Bhutan's culture.
4. Good governance.[9]

To those ends, Bhutan limits tourism and requires that at least 60 percent of its land remain forested. Hospital patients with nonacute health problems can choose Western or traditional medicine. Traditional dress is compulsory in public, which protects both the nation's heritage and the industries that produce such items.

The goals are easier in theory than practice, however. Critics say that the focus on traditional culture—"one nation, one people"—has led to discrimination against citizens of Nepalese descent, who are Hindu. More fundamentally,

---

8. Andrew C. Revkin, "A New Measure of Well-Being from a Happy Little Kingdom," *New York Times,* October 4, 2005.

9. "Bhutan's Pursuit of Happiness," *The Economist,* December 16, 2004.

the four pillars of happiness could easily contradict one another. For example, good governance generally relies on democratic representation; an elected government might easily decide that the forests ought to be developed or that requiring traditional dress in public is too coercive.

Thus, Bhutan has not discovered an elixir for well-being. However, the notion that happiness is distinct from material well-being is an idea that has gained traction. In attempting to make crude observations on happiness, researchers have found that it does not move linearly with income. People in Latin American countries report themselves as happier than their income would suggest; citizens of communist countries are less happy than citizens in noncommunist countries with similar incomes, even long after the communist governments were swept away.

Both Britain and Canada are compiling indexes of well-being. The British index will not only include income, but also indicators such as mental illness, civility, access to parks, and the crime rate. Princeton psychologist and Nobel laureate Daniel Kahneman is working with several colleagues on a new research tool for quantifying people's quality of life. The "day reconstruction method" creates an enjoyment scale by requiring participants to record their activities during the day in a journal and describe their feelings about the experiences. The researchers hope to use the tool to create a "national well-being account" that would supplement economic indicators such as the gross domestic product.[10]

French president Nicolas Sarkozy instructed the French national statistics agency in 2009 to develop an indicator of the nation's economic health that incorporates broader measures of quality of life than GDP alone. Two prominent economists and former Nobel Prize–winners, Joseph Stiglitz and Amartya Sen, chaired a panel convened by Sarkozy to examine a seeming paradox: rising GDP appears to be linked with a perception that life is getting more stressful and difficult, not less. Sarkozy wants a measure that incorporates the joys of art and leisure and the sorrows of environmental destruction and stress.[11]

The *New York Times* noted in an editorial accompanying a story on Bhutan's experiment, "To talk about gross national happiness may sound purely pie in the sky, partly because we have been taught to believe that happiness is essentially a personal emotion, not an attribute of a community or a

10. "New Research Tool Aids Study of National Well-Being," Princeton University news release, December 2, 2004.
11. Edward Hadas and Richard Beales, "Sarkozy Imagines: No GDP," *Wall Street Journal,* January 10, 2008.

country. But thinking of happiness as a quotient of cultural and environmental factors might help us understand the growing disconnect between America's prosperity and Americans' sense of well-being."[12]

So Bhutan may be on to something.

....

For now, we are left without a definitive measure of well-being. Policy makers must still make important judgments about how resources ought to be allocated—or, in some cases, redistributed—in order to make society as well off as possible. Does taking money from the rich and giving it to the poor make the populace better off overall? Revolutions have been launched over this very question.

5.2 THE PHILOSOPHY OF WELL-BEING

Philosophers have debated how society ought to allocate resources in order to maximize social welfare (including, in some cases, the welfare of non-humans) for as long as there has been social thought. Consider the following question posed by Amartya Sen, winner of the 1998 Nobel Prize in Economics, in his book *Development as Freedom* (1999). Three men have come to you looking for work. You have only one job to offer; the work cannot be divided among the three of them; and they are all equally qualified. One of your goals is to make the world a better place by hiring the man who needs the job most.

The first man is the poorest of the three. If one of your goals is to make the world a better place, then presumably the poorest man ought to get the job.

Or perhaps not. The second man is not the poorest, but he is unhappiest because he has only recently become poor and is not accustomed to the deprivation. Offering him the job will cause the greatest gain in happiness.

The third man is neither the poorest nor the unhappiest. But he has a chronic health problem, borne stoically for his whole life, which can be cured with the wages from the job. Thus, giving him the job would have the most profound impact on an individual's quality of life.[13]

12. "Net National Happiness," *New York Times*, October 6, 2005.
13. From Charles Wheelan, *Naked Economics: Undressing the Dismal Science* (New York: Norton, 2002), pp. 60–61.

To make society best off, who should get the job? Sen does not answer the question; indeed, he makes clear that there is no right answer.

A course in political theory would present the full spectrum of thinking on how a society ought to allocate its resources. For the purposes of policy makers, it is crucial to recognize the enormous range of defensible views on this subject.

At one end of the spectrum, for example, the communist governments that came to power in the twentieth century were built upon the notion that government could improve overall social welfare through redistribution of wealth and intensive management of the economy. The Marxist slogan "from each according to his abilities, to each according to his needs" encapsulates the philosophy that a society is best served by guaranteeing some level of consumption and benefits for all citizens, including those who cannot or do not make significant contributions to society's overall wealth. This is only possible, of course, by expropriating a significant amount of wealth from the most productive members of society.

The communist governments of the twentieth century, notably the Soviet Union, employed an extraordinary degree of coercion in order to redistribute resources across society. The governments did not merely tax the most productive individuals; they also dictated where citizens could live, what professions they could pursue, where and when they could travel, and so on. The most salient belief on this end of the philosophical spectrum is that society owns all wealth collectively, including the potential productive capacity of all individuals, and that the role of government is to manage and distribute these resources in a manner that maximizes overall social welfare.

Marxism as a governing ideology was largely discredited by the collapse of the Soviet Union and many of the world's other communist regimes. China remains nominally communist, but has been moving aggressively toward using markets, rather than government, to allocate society's resources. However, the idea that government can improve social welfare through significant redistribution of wealth remains a popular and defensible view around the globe.

In India, the world's most populous democracy, several states have elected communist governments; the governing coalition at the national level includes the Communist Party. Indeed, the Indian state of Kerala is often heralded as an example of what can be achieved through comprehensive social programs, even in a very poor country. In 2001, after a decade of robust growth across India, Kerala had a per capita income of just $675, which was less than India's average of $730.[14] However, the government has invested heavily in basic education and health care for all citizens. One result is that Kerala has achieved better outcomes on some social indicators than far richer states in India. Kerala's life expectancy is nearly 74 years, which is 11 years longer than the Indian average and not far from America's life expectancy of 77. Kerala's 2001 infant mortality rate, 14.00 deaths per 1,000 live births, was far better than that in every other Indian state. Statistically, the next closest state was Maharashtra, with 48.00 deaths per 1,000 live births; the figure at that time for India as a whole was 71.00 deaths.[15] The infant mortality rate in the United States is 6.26 per 1,000 live births, although it is 13.25 for African-Americans, which is just slightly lower than Kerala's rate a decade ago.[16]

The extent to which one views Kerala as a "success" depends on the indicators that one uses to define success. In particular, how does one evaluate the importance of per capita income and job creation (where Kerala ranks poorly) relative to life expectancy and infant mortality (where it ranks very well)? Or how do we compare a rich society with little or no safety net for the most disadvantaged to a much poorer society that guarantees a certain minimum standard of living for all citizens?

The collectivist economic philosophy of Marxism represents one end of the philosophical spectrum; the other end of the spectrum is the libertarian view that government has little or no right to expropriate personal wealth. As one economist recently lamented, "Three-fifths to two-thirds of the federal budget consists of taking property from one American and giving it to another. Were a private person to do the same thing, we'd call it theft. When government does it, we euphemistically call it income distribution, but that's exactly what thieves do—redistribute income."[17]

Economist and political philosopher Friedrich Hayek was one of the twentieth century's many influential thinkers who have argued that government ought to limit itself to maintaining the rule of law. Hayek's writing was influenced by the rise of communism and the Soviet Union in particular. In his 1944 book *The Road to Serfdom,* Hayek argued that extensive redistribu-

14. Jason DeParle, "Jobs Abroad Support 'Model' State in India," *New York Times,* September 7, 2007.

15. Centre for Development Studies, Thiruvananthapuram, Kerala, *Human Development Report 2005: Kerala* (Thiruvananthapuram, India: State Planning Board, Government of Kerala, 2006), p. 26: (http://data.undp.org.in/shdr/kerala/report.pdf).

16. T. J. Mathews and Marian F. MacDorman, "Infant Mortality Statistics from the 2004 Period Linked Birth/Infant Death Data Set," *National Vital Statistics Report* 55, no. 14 (May 2, 2007; rev. June 13, 2007): 6, Table A (http://www.cdc.gov/nchs/data/nvsr/nvsr55/nvsr55_14.pdf).

17. Walter Williams, "Bogus Rights," *Capitalism Magazine* (February 8, 2006).

tion of wealth requires a powerful central government, which is likely to lead to social control and perhaps totalitarianism.[18] Indeed, the communist governments of the twentieth century tightly controlled areas of life far beyond the distribution of goods and services. The Berlin Wall, constructed in East Germany to prevent citizens from escaping to democratic West Germany (where living standards were much higher, on average), was perhaps the most striking example of the repressive nature of such regimes.

Thus, the libertarian strand of political thought argues that economic freedom is inextricably linked to political freedom. All wealth, and the potential capacity to produce such wealth, belong to the individual and ought not to be confiscated by government. According to this strand of thought, there are still legitimate purposes of government. For example, individuals may decide to collectively pay for a road, or a park, or a fire department because it is more economical to share such goods and services. However, significant redistribution of wealth from one individual to another is not a legitimate function of government. No matter how wealthy or poor the individuals involved, government should not play the role of "thief."

. . . .

John Rawls and the Veil of Ignorance

What is fair? Philosophers like to debate such weighty topics, but in the world of politics, answers are often swayed more by self-interest than deep introspection. Is society better off if we raise taxes on the wealthy to provide basic health care for those who cannot otherwise afford it? That answer will be affected in part by whether one will be paying the new taxes or receiving the new health-care benefits. Hence the old public policy aphorism: where you stand depends on where you sit.

Political philosopher John Rawls proposed a thought experiment to shed light on the abstract notion of what is "fair." Rawls argued that, in theory, the optimal decisions regarding social welfare would be made under a **"veil of ignorance"** in which decision makers had no idea what role they would be assigned in the society they were designing.

Rawls described this "original position" as a situation in which "no one knows his place in society, his class position or social status, nor does anyone

18. Friedrich A. von Hayek, *The Road to Serfdom* (Chicago: University of Chicago Press, 1944).

know his fortune in the distribution of natural assets and abilities, his intelligence, strength and the like."[19] The decisions made by such actors would lead to a just society, Rawls reasoned, because individuals unaware of their own place in society would pursue the interests of society at large.

Obviously, any such decision-making process is impossible, since we all know where we stand in society (though there is uncertainty about where we might end up in the future). Still, the veil of ignorance is often a helpful thought exercise. How would you feel about the plan to raise taxes on the wealthy to expand health care if you were to be born tomorrow without any knowledge of whether you would be rich or poor, healthy or unhealthy?

. . . .

Clearly, communism and libertarianism represent the extremes of a broad continuum of thought; most people have beliefs that fall somewhere in between. It is crucial, however, to recognize how such underlying philosophical beliefs affect public policy. When policy makers argue about the "right" solution, they are often really in disagreement over philosophical issues that have no "right" answer. For example, the poverty thresholds discussed at the beginning of the chapter are merely one technical piece of the larger issue of U.S. antipoverty policy. That discussion must begin with philosophical questions such as what, if anything, the nation owes to its most disadvantaged citizens, and who ought to pay for such benefits.

5.3 TOOLS FOR MAKING INFERENCES ABOUT SOCIAL WELFARE

If many measures of social welfare are subjective, must we give up any hope of working systematically to make society better off? No. Public policy provides us with many tools for making objective judgments about the relative merits of different policies.

5.3.1 Efficiency

Efficiency is the degree to which resources are used to generate the most productive outcome. The world has finite resources. We have limited quantities of everything worth having—from clean water to vaccines to oceanfront property. Indeed, one of the most valuable commodities is our time, since there are only twenty-four hours in the day and an hour spent doing one thing requires

19. John Rawls, *A Theory of Justice* (Cambridge, Mass.: Belknap Press of Harvard University Press, 1971), p. 137.

an hour less of doing something else. All else being equal, society should prefer policies that use resources as efficiently as possible.

The concept of efficiency may be best understood by first examining several examples of an *inefficient* allocation of resources:

- One man has two left shoes and another man has two right shoes of the same size and kind. The mismatched shoes are, at best, uncomfortable for the two men; perhaps the shoes cannot be worn at all. We recognize immediately that the four shoes could be allocated differently to produce a better outcome. Giving each man a right and left shoe is a more efficient allocation of resources than the original mismatched distribution.

- Consider a lovely piece of property on a bluff with a unique view of the Pacific Ocean. Would it be more efficient to have a hotel on this property or a grain warehouse? The answer is almost certainly a hotel, since guests would appreciate and value the ocean view while farmers storing grain couldn't care less. Thus, it would be inefficient to squander the property on a building that makes no use of the property's most valuable feature.

- Imagine a four-year-old child with an extraordinary IQ and, therefore, the capacity to make extraordinary contributions to society as a scientist, teacher, artist, entrepreneur, or business person. But further suppose that this child receives a mediocre primary and secondary education, and does not have sufficient resources to attend college. If this child never achieves his extraordinary potential—or, worse, becomes a cost to society in some way—then that outcome is inefficient. A unique resource—human capital, in this case—has been squandered, not unlike passing out mismatched shoes or building a grain warehouse on a scenic overlook.

An allocation of resources is said to be **Pareto-efficient** (named for Italian economist Vilfredo Pareto) when it is not possible to make any individual better off without making another individual worse off. Conversely, an allocation of resources is Pareto-inefficient when it is possible to make one or more persons better off without making anyone worse off. In the case of the mismatched shoes, the two individuals (assuming they could find one another) would simply trade one left shoe for one right shoe, leaving both participants better off. Government need not involve itself in such a transaction, other than supporting the basic institutions that enable it to happen. The two individuals have an incentive to find each other and trade; society is made better off when they do. Indeed, the most powerful tool we have for allocating resources efficiently is our market economy. In most cases, the market economy—individuals seeking to maximize their own utility and firms attempting to maximize profits—will naturally propel resources to their most productive use.

For example, a market economy will almost certainly ensure that a hotel, rather than a grain warehouse, is built on a scenic overlook. Why? Because the hotel owner will earn higher profits by having a unique ocean view; the farmers don't care if the grain warehouse is near the ocean or not. The prospective hotel owner will, therefore, be willing to pay more than the farmers for the unique property. Even if the grain warehouse had been built on the scenic bluff decades ago, the prospective hotel owner would likely pay the warehouse operators to move to another location, leaving both parties better off. The transaction gives the hotel owner a scenic location that will generate profits; the warehouse owners get a new location that will work just as well as the old one, plus cash in their pockets from being paid to move.

One important virtue of a price system is that it allocates resources to what economists call the "highest and best use," which is really just a fancy way of saying that those who can make the best use of something are willing to pay the most for it. Again, there is not likely to be a compelling reason for government to be involved in deciding what is built atop this unique piece of property.

The example of the talented child who lives in a poor family and receives a mediocre education is different, however. There is not likely to be a market-oriented mechanism to unlock his potential. The most efficient use of society's resources would be to invest in the human capital of this promising child in order to reap large returns in the future (or avoid large costs), but there is no obvious way for a private firm to make money by exploiting this inefficiency. Suppose that investment in the early education of poor children leads to lower rates of incarceration later in life. How would a private firm that made such an investment earn its profits? By sending a bill to the government for money *not* spent on prisons?

Public policy often involves redirecting resources or changing incentives in order to achieve more efficient outcomes. One challenge is determining when markets will achieve efficient outcomes on their own and when some kind of intervention could improve on that outcome. Chapters 7 and 8 will explore this in much greater depth. For now, it is important to understand that we have one objective tool for defining a "better" public policy outcome: a more efficient use of society's resources.

5.3.2 Deadweight Loss

Public policy also provides us with tools for evaluating why and how certain behaviors or policies lead to inefficient outcomes. **Deadweight loss,** a measure of inefficiency, occurs when the loss of welfare imposed on one party exceeds the gain in welfare afforded to another party; a more efficient allocation of resources could make at least one person better off without making anyone worse off.

We have an intuitive sense for deadweight loss, even if the term is foreign. Everyday life presents many situations in which effort or resources are needlessly wasted. One way to think about it is that the losers lose more than the winners win. Consider this simple example. Assume that a thief breaks into your apartment and steals $20 from your wallet. While this may be an unpleasant incident, there is no deadweight loss, since the benefit to the thief ($20) is exactly the same as your loss ($20).

Now let's tweak the example slightly. Assume that the thief breaks into your apartment and takes your whole wallet. Several blocks away, he removes the $20 and dumps the rest of the wallet, including your credit cards, driver's license, and several sentimental photos, into a trash can, never to be recovered. That action *does* create significant deadweight loss. The loss to you includes not only the $20 in cash, but also the photos and the time that will be required to cancel and reissue your credit cards and to wait in line at the Department of Motor Vehicles to get a new driver's license. Yet the benefit to the thief is still only $20. You would likely find yourself saying, "I wish he had just taken the cash," which is a recognition of the inefficiency caused by the thief taking the whole wallet rather than just the money. You lose (including your time) more than the thief gains.

Now consider an example from the policy world: an increase in the minimum wage. Federal law requires that all employers pay workers a minimum of $7.25 per hour. Some states—and even some cities—require wages that are higher than the federal minimum. The minimum wage impacts poverty by raising the total income of low-wage workers beyond what it would have been in the absence of regulation. So would a dramatic increase in the minimum wage—to, say, $15 an hour—be an effective tool for fighting poverty?

Not necessarily. A minimum wage also creates deadweight loss. The inefficiency arises because there are some workers who are not hired for $15 an hour *but would have been hired, if the minimum wage were lower*. One of our fundamental assumptions is that firms seek to maximize profits. Thus, a firm will hire an additional worker only if the incremental revenues generated by that worker exceed the wage that has to be paid. For example, if the owner of a movie theater can earn an extra $10 an hour by hiring one more ticket taker, then he would be willing to pay the new employee up to $9.99 an hour (leaving him a penny profit!). He will not pay $15 an hour to hire a new ticket taker, since the added revenues would not justify the added expense. Therein lies the deadweight loss caused by a high minimum wage. Federal law prohibits what would otherwise have been a mutually beneficial transaction: hiring one more ticket taker for slightly less than $10 an hour. Instead, the theater owner earns lower profits and the person willing to take tickets does not get a job.

Suppose we raised the minimum wage to $15 an hour but created an exemption for movie theaters. Many workers would receive higher wages as the law intended, but the theater owner would still be able to hire one more ticket taker for $9.50 an hour. The theater owner is better off; the new employee is better off; and no one is made worse off.

The minimum wage distorts the labor market, raising the wages of many workers (at the expense of their employers) while leaving some workers without jobs. This latter category, representing those who could have been hired profitably at a lower wage, represents deadweight loss. For this reason, minimum-wage laws do sometimes exempt certain categories of workers, such as students. However, it is impossible to identify and exempt all potential sources of deadweight loss from a given increase in the minimum wage. As a result, most policy makers believe that raising the minimum wage is, at best, one piece of a broader antipoverty strategy, and some argue—reasonably— that it could actually be counterproductive.

Public policy often involves choosing the most efficient among an array of policy options. For policy makers in Oregon, providing "better" health care meant getting improved outcomes from the same level of public investment— more medical bang for the buck. As logical as that may seem, the process was far more unusual and controversial than it sounds.

································| **POLICY IN THE REAL WORLD** |················

The Efficiency of "Rationing" Health Care: The Oregon Health Plan

Health care is a large and growing expense in both the private and public sectors. Beginning in the 1980s, a broad coalition of Oregon citizens began discussing plans for achieving better medical outcomes from the state's health-care spending. In particular, leaders were considering changes to the Medicaid program, which provides a broad range of health-care benefits for eligible low-income citizens.

At the time Oregon began contemplating policy changes, the state only had sufficient funding to provide Medicaid coverage to 57 percent of Oregon residents with incomes below the poverty level. The issue of inadequate health coverage was highlighted by a single high-profile case. In 1987, a seven-year-old boy, Coby Howard, was diagnosed with a form of leukemia normally treated with a bone-marrow transplant. However, the Oregon legislature had recently disallowed Medicaid coverage for organ transplants. Coby Howard's family was not able to afford the treatment, and he died.[20]

Meanwhile, John Kitzhaber, president of the Oregon Senate from 1985 to 1993, was already aware of the shortcomings in the Medicaid program. As an emergency-room physician, Kitzhaber had seen many cases in which patients could have been treated more cheaply and effectively had they been provided earlier access to basic care. ER physicians are trained in triage, the prioritizing of cases in order to get the best possible outcomes—i.e., the medical equivalent of efficiency.

Kitzhaber believed that Oregon's Medicaid program could benefit from systemic triage. According to the *New England Journal of Medicine,* Kitzhaber wanted to address related problems: Oregon residents without health insurance were being denied life-saving treatment, while residents with health insurance through the state's Medicaid program were covered for far less serious procedures. The state's finite resources were not being targeted to have the greatest health impact.

The process of radical reform began when, in 1987, Governor Neil Goldschmidt appointed a panel of stakeholders—health-care providers and consumers, business and labor leaders, insurers and lawmakers—and charged them with answering three crucial questions, none of which had an obvious "right" answer: Who should be covered? What treatments should be covered? And how should this care be financed and delivered?[21]

The panel came to consensus on some important philosophical points, including the following:

- All citizens should have universal access to a basic level of care.
- Society is responsible for financing care for poor people.
- There must be a process to define a "basic" level of care.
- The health-care delivery system must encourage the use of services and procedures that are effective and appropriate and discourage overtreatment.

20. Thomas Bodenheimer, "The Oregon Health Plan—Lessons for the Nation," *New England Journal of Medicine* 337, no. 9 (August 28, 1997): 651–656.

21. Oregon health-services Web site: http://www.oregon.gov/DHS/ph/about_us.shtml.

From 1989 to 1993, the Oregon legislature passed a series of laws that became known collectively as the Oregon Health Plan.[22] A cornerstone of the reform was Senate Bill 27, passed in 1989, which created a prioritized list of health services—a ranking of all possible health services from most effective to least effective. The "list" was essential to making more productive use of the state's finite health budget. As the *New England Journal of Medicine* explained, "The state planned to add many uninsured people to the Medicaid program and pay for this expansion by reducing the Medicaid benefit package—more people would be covered, but for fewer services."[23]

But who would decide which health services are most essential and effective? The legislation created a Health Services Commission, made up of five primary-care physicians, a public-health nurse, a social worker, and four health-care "consumers," that was charged with the task of ranking more than 700 medical and dental services "according to comparative benefits of each service to the entire population being served." The legislature, in turn, was responsible for deciding the number of treatments on the list that would be funded but was prohibited from meddling with the prioritized ranking.[24]

In short, the Health Services Commission was charged with ranking procedures according to their overall benefit; the legislature would then draw a line at some point on the list. Those health services above the line would be paid for by the state; those below would not.

The process has continued to the present. For the period 2005–2007, the legislature allocated funding sufficient to cover treatments 1 to 530 out of the 710 health services on the prioritized list. Thus, for a low-income person covered by the plan, the state would pay for an adenoidectomy to treat chronic ear infections (530 on the list) but not for therapy for acute conjunctivitis (531) or removal of a foreign body from the ear or nose (532).

Outside of Oregon, politicians from both parties recoiled at the idea of "rationing" care. Of course, in a world with a finite amount of money to spend on health care, resources must *always* be rationed in one way or another. Oregon's previous system also rationed care, albeit by denying payment for *all* treatments to those individuals the system could not afford to cover, rather than by denying some treatments to the expanded number of people covered by the Oregon Health Plan.

After the plan took effect in 1994, the proportion of children in Oregon with no health coverage fell from 17 percent to 11 percent. By 1998, infant

22. Oregon health-services Web site.
23. Bodenheimer, "The Oregon Health Plan."
24. See http://www.oregon.gov/DHS/healthplan/priorlist/main.shtml.

mortality had dropped, and childhood immunization was up.[25] In short, the Oregon Health Plan was designed in the spirit of what political philosophers have long described as utilitarianism: providing the greatest good for the greatest number.

. . . .

Public policy aims to be efficient, thereby putting society's resources to the most productive use. But efficiency is not the only relevant criterion. Many policies that generate significant deadweight loss are politically popular because they allocate resources in a way that voters find socially desirable. While policies that promote efficiency maximize the size of the "economic pie," most citizens also care about how that pie is sliced.

5.3.3 Equity

Equity is a measure of a policy's fairness. It turns out that equity, like happiness, is a somewhat elusive concept. After all, what is fair? One simple definition of **equity** is uniformity—an equal division of resources and responsibilities. If all members of a community share the benefits from some public investment, such as a road or sewage system, then it would seem equitable for them to share that expense. Similarly, if there is some social burden to be borne, such as fighting a war, then it seems equitable for all members of society to contribute to the fighting or at least have an equal probability of doing so, as is achieved with a military draft. Yet equal is not always considered fair. We would not necessarily consider it fair to divide a resource equally if some individuals have worked much harder to produce it than others. Few students would argue that a fair distribution of grades is one in which every student gets the same grade, regardless of effort or performance in the class.

Fairness is an important social objective, despite varying interpretations of what constitutes "fair." To help think more systematically about the implications of different policies, analysts refer to three different kinds of equity: horizontal equity, vertical equity, and intergenerational equity.

Horizontal equity is a measure of the degree to which similar persons and situations are treated equally. For example, if two families both earn $50,000 a year, then they should pay roughly the same amount in taxes. Or if two manufacturing plants are doing the same thing in the same place, they should face similar rules and regulations. In an academic context, students who score the same on an exam should receive the same grade. In an employment context, those who do the same work should get the same pay. Horizontal equity requires that similar things be treated similarly.

25. "John Kitzhaber's Prescription," *The Economist*, April 25, 1998.

Vertical equity is a measure of the degree to which the rich pay more than the poor. Or, conversely, it can reflect the extent to which the poor receive greater social benefits than the wealthy. This is a more nettlesome and controversial concept of fairness than horizontal equity, since reasonable people can disagree over what constitutes the "fair share" that the wealthy should pay. While most people believe that Bill Gates should pay more in taxes than your professor, there is no obvious answer as to how much more. In fact, one could reasonably argue that Bill Gates should pay the same in taxes as your professor, if they both make use of the same basic public services. That disagreement notwithstanding, most tax and social-welfare policies around the world incorporate elements of vertical equity. In the United States, the federal income tax is graduated, meaning that individuals with higher incomes pay a higher rate on their taxable income. Similarly, many social-welfare programs are means-tested—that is, individuals or families must be at or below a certain income level to be eligible for benefits.

Intergenerational equity refers to fairness in the way that policies treat different generations. Some public policies have costs and benefits that stretch across decades or even centuries, affecting multiple generations of citizens. Taxes paid in the present may pay for benefits that accrue to future generations (such as spending on medical research or space exploration); or current benefits may be charged to future taxpayers (as when the government issues bonds to fund large deficits). Policy makers must be cognizant of this distribution of costs and benefits across generations.

Social Security, which provides benefits to working Americans upon retirement, is an example of a policy that has significant intergenerational effects. The program is paid for by a payroll tax on current workers. These revenues are not put in a dedicated account and invested to pay for future benefits. Instead, the money collected from current workers goes directly to pay the benefits of current retirees. Workers paying into the system have the promise (though no legal guarantee) that they will be paid in their retirement by taxes collected from future workers. The program has been described as a social contract between generations.

That social contract now faces a demographic challenge. Americans are having smaller families, meaning that future generations will have fewer workers paying taxes to support Social Security. Meanwhile, retired Americans are living longer, so that there are more retirees to be supported. In 1960, there were five workers for every retiree. Now, there are around three. By 2030, there will be two. Without modifications to the program soon, these demographic changes may make it difficult to finance the benefits that have been promised to the workers now paying taxes into the system. The result could violate our sense of intergenerational equity in several possible ways. Retirees may be shortchanged; they may not get their promised benefits, despite paying taxes into the system for decades. Or young workers may be treated unfairly; they may be taxed so heavily to fund benefits for the growing pool of retirees that they end up paying far more into the system than they ever get back during their own retirement.

This chapter has identified two important criteria that can be used to evaluate policy: efficiency and equity. Policy makers seek to treat citizens fairly (however they choose to define it) and to make the best possible use of society's resources. Unfortunately these goals are often in conflict.

5.4 THE EFFICIENCY–EQUITY TRADE-OFF

Public policies often involve a trade-off between equity (a fair division of resources) and efficiency (a productive allocation of resources). Imagine a society in which all citizens are promised the same income. Communist societies historically professed this goal. The philosophy of collective farms, for example, was that all residents would share equally in both the work and the rewards. Certainly, this could be interpreted as a highly equitable arrangement. Yet communism—and collective farms in particular—turned out to be a horribly inefficient way to organize a society's resources.

The drawbacks to this equal sharing of work and reward should be apparent to anyone who has ever worked on a group project. Sharing output creates an incentive for an individual to shirk his responsibilities; he can enjoy much more leisure while bearing only a small fraction of the cost of the fall in total output. Similarly, individuals have little incentive to innovate, take risks, or invest in their own human capital since the benefits from such behavior accrue primarily to the rest of the group. We should not be surprised that in places like China and the former Soviet Union (1) collective farms were notoriously unproductive and (2) the same farmers on the same land were dramatically more productive when the communal farms were divided into smaller private plots on which the owner could literally reap what he sowed.

5.4.1 The Inequity of Efficiency

Inequality is a powerful motivator. Large rewards—financial or otherwise—inspire the kinds of behavior that make society more productive: hard work, innovation, investment, risk, and so on. Conversely, sharing a resource equally weakens the connection between work and reward, thereby diminishing the incentive to achieve greater productivity. As economist Arthur Okun has noted, "We can't have our cake of market efficiency and share it equally."[26]

The cake metaphor is perhaps the easiest way to think about the efficiency–equity trade-off. Efficiency is about using resources in a way that creates the largest possible cake, regardless of how the slices are cut and allocated. Equity is about dividing the pieces in a way that society deems fair. Highly efficient policies have the potential to create a large cake that is divided unevenly, leaving some segments of society with huge pieces while others get tiny slices or nothing at all.

A market economy left entirely to its own devices will produce such an outcome. Individuals reap what they sow—no more, no less. Those who produce valuable goods and services can sell them profitably to the rest of society. Oprah Winfrey has earned hundreds of millions of dollars because people around the world enjoy watching her show on television (and then buy the products that are advertised during the commercial breaks). Oprah is rewarded handsomely for doing what she does best; viewers prefer watching her program to all other things they could be doing with their time. That is an efficient outcome that delivers a very big chunk of cake to Winfrey (and Steve Jobs, Bill Gates, Warren Buffett, and other uniquely talented individuals).

The same efficient market will leave some individuals with no income at all. The market only rewards individuals who have something valuable to sell—labor, human capital, etc. Those members of society who are unhealthy, unlucky, untalented, or otherwise unable or unwilling to do something of value will get no cake at all. The outcomes will be profoundly unequal; whether that is unfair is a philosophical question. However, any discussion of fairness must recognize that the participants in a market economy do not *begin* with the same resources and capabilities. A market economy will distribute resources as efficiently as possible from some **initial endowment,** or starting point. Obviously, the endowments of talent, health, character, and just plain luck are distributed unequally across society.

To revisit one of the simple examples at the beginning of the chapter, imagine a class of 21 students who show up to class as follows: 10 students have two right shoes; 10 students have two left shoes; and one student has no shoes at all. The students will make trades that improve the efficiency of the shoe distribution. We would expect the following outcome: 20 students have

---

26. Arthur M. Okun, *Equality and Efficiency: The Big Tradeoff* (Washington, D.C.: Brookings Institution, 1975), p. 2.

a matched pair of shoes and one student still has no shoes at all. The twenty-first student arrived with nothing of value to trade to the rest of the class and will, therefore, leave with nothing of value.

5.4.2 The Inefficiency of Equity

At the same time, some policies that promote equal slices for all can diminish the size of the cake. Any policy that seeks to promote equity by redistributing resources—taking cake from those with big slices and giving it to those who have less—creates two incentives that are likely to diminish the overall productive capacity of the economy (or shrink the cake): (1) the beneficiaries of such redistribution have less incentive to work hard on their own, and (2) the wealthier individuals who are taxed to pay for such benefits have less incentive to create such wealth in the first place.

Consider a simple program to ameliorate the effects of poverty. We know from the example at the beginning of the chapter that a significant number of Americans live below the poverty line. We can infer that many of them are in financial distress because they are unemployed. A seemingly logical social program would provide benefits to nonworking individuals that are generous enough to raise their standard of living above the poverty line. The program could be financed by levying an additional income tax on wealthy individuals.

You should recognize the incentives that such a program creates for both the recipients and the individuals who are taxed to pay for it. If poor individuals receive a generous unemployment benefit, then they have far less incentive to find a job (and a more powerful incentive to quit a job that is inconvenient or unpleasant). Meanwhile, any tax on income reduces the benefit of doing productive work or making investments that yield income. If the marginal tax rate (the tax levied on each additional dollar of income) for an individual is 50 percent, then his after-tax return on work or investment is only 50 cents for every dollar that he would have otherwise earned. A skilled worker, such as a graphic designer, who would be willing to take on an additional project for $50 an hour will be less inclined to do the work for $25 an hour—which is the after-tax wage.[27]

In the nineteenth century, economist David Ricardo warned that England's poor laws, which taxed citizens to provide modest sustenance for the poor, would "change wealth and power into misery and weakness." That

---

27. You should recognize this as deadweight loss, if the graphic designer turns down the work as a result of the 50-percent marginal tax rate. Both he and the client who was willing to pay $50 an hour for the work are made worse off. Yet the government gains nothing because no tax revenue can be collected on work that is not done.

tension has not gone away. Two centuries later, *The Economist* wrote, "Modern economists have raised similar concerns about today's redistributive welfare states: by subtracting from the rewards of work and adding to the consolations of idleness, social transfers sap economies of their vigor."[28]

Finally, it is important to note that in some cases policies that improve equity can also improve efficiency. Recall the example from earlier in the chapter of a four year old with an exceptional IQ but poor access to schooling. In many parts of the United States, access to education is inequitable; poor children are less likely to get preschool education and more likely to end up in mediocre schools.

This is not merely inequitable; it is also inefficient, because it limits the future productivity of students who receive inadequate education. James Heckman, winner of the 2000 Nobel Prize in Economics, has concluded, for example, that the benefit-cost ratio for intensive preschool for children in disadvantaged families is on the order of 8 to 1 because of its proven impact on future employment, participation in crime, and other outcomes. He wrote in the *Wall Street Journal*:

> It is a rare public policy initiative that promotes fairness and social justice and, at the same time, promotes productivity in the economy and in society at large. Investing in disadvantaged young children is such a policy. The traditional argument for providing enriched environments for disadvantaged young children is based on considerations of fairness and social justice. But another argument can be made that complements and strengthens the first one. It is based on economic efficiency, and it is more compelling than the equity argument, in part because the gains from such investment can be quantified—and they are large.[29]

Policy makers often face trade-offs between equity and efficiency; policies that promote fairness are not necessarily efficient, and vice versa. However, one important purpose of policy analysis is to minimize this trade-off. For example, America's 1996 welfare reform implemented a work requirement for welfare recipients—anyone receiving government antipoverty assistance must be in school, looking for a job, or working. This aspect of the legislation was

28. "Taxing the Poor to Pay the Poor," *The Economist*, April 1, 2004.
29. James J. Heckman, "Catch 'Em Young," *Wall Street Journal*, January 10, 2006.

designed to address the long-standing belief that welfare benefits discouraged work. Similarly, the Oregon Health Plan was designed to use the state's finite health resources more efficiently—and, arguably, more fairly, too.

5.5 ABSOLUTE VERSUS RELATIVE WELL-BEING

Although policy makers do not have a perfect tool for measuring utility, researchers are constantly seeking to understand more about the factors that determine our sense of well-being. Economists have been working with psychologists recently to explore questions that have significant implications for public policy: To what extent is an individual's utility determined by the consumption of those around him? Do we evaluate our own well-being solely on the goods and services that we consume? Or is our personal utility affected by what others are consuming around us? In other words, does our relative income matter?

Economists long assumed that "envy" does not enter our utility functions. Our sense of well-being should be determined by the goods and services that we can enjoy rather than by the things that other people have or don't have. Yet we know from everyday life that humans are acutely aware of status and relative consumption. Researchers now believe that H. L. Mencken may have been right when he noted that a wealthy man is someone who earns $100 a year more than his wife's sister's husband.

For example, take the following quiz:

Which world would you rather live in?
 A. A world in which you earn $110,000 and everyone else earns $200,000.
 B. A world in which you earn $100,000 and everyone else earns $85,000.

In world A, your absolute income (and the consumption it buys) is higher than in world B. In world B, your relative income—what you have relative to those around you—is higher than in world A. You would be richer in world A; you would be less wealthy in world B but richer than everyone around you.

So which would you choose?

When Cornell economist Robert Frank polled Americans, asking that question, a majority chose B, suggesting that individuals care as much or more about what they have relative to the rest of society as they do about their absolute level of consumption.[30] The notion that well-being may be

30. Robert H. Frank, "Why Living in a Rich Society Makes Us Feel Poor," *New York Times Magazine*, October 15, 2000.

determined in part by what we have relative to those around us has significant implications for public policy. For example, the task of defining poverty introduced at the beginning of the chapter is made even more complicated by philosophical disagreements over the importance of income inequality. Should we consider someone poor if his basic needs are being met but he still has much less than everyone around him?

Absolute poverty reflects the degree to which a person's basic needs are being met—food, housing, health care, and so on. **Relative poverty** measures an individual's consumption relative to other members of society. Both measures of poverty have advantages and limitations. An absolute measure of poverty defines some basic level of consumption and measures the number of individuals or families who fail to achieve it. Policy makers identify a basket of basic necessities, such as food, transportation, and health care, and then set the poverty "line" at the amount of income required to purchase those items. That minimum level of consumption does not change over time, even as society gets richer (though the actual income thresholds are updated to reflect changes in prices).

As a social indicator, the advantage of an absolute measure of poverty is that it provides a clear indication of the degree to which society is meeting certain fixed basic needs for its poorest citizens. Because the definition of *basic needs* does not change over time, it is possible to compare data from 1960 to 1990 to 2010 and evaluate progress. Using some absolute measure of poverty, if the poverty rate in 1960 was 15 percent and it falls to 11 percent in 2010, then we can conclude that the fraction of the population living below some basic level of consumption has fallen by 4 percentage points. An absolute measure of poverty (or of anything else) allows for an "apples to apples" comparison over time.

The drawback of an absolute measure of poverty is that it does not reflect changing lifestyles and expectations as a society grows richer. The "basic necessities" of 2010 may be significantly different than they were in 1960. Thus, having sufficient income to purchase some minimum level of consumption as defined in 1960 may provide a lifestyle that most people in 2010 still consider to be impoverished. Suppose a society decided in 1900 that the poverty threshold for a family of four would be a level of income sufficient to pay for a two-room apartment, trolley fare for basic errands, and food, including meat at least once a week. That was a comfortable existence relative to the rest of society at the beginning of the twentieth century, even in the wealthiest countries.

At the beginning of the twenty-first century, the same existence would be considered a lot less comfortable. Families of four who share a two-room apartment, eat meat once a week, and rely exclusively on public transportation are living a life more disadvantaged relative to the rest of society than they would have been 100 years ago. They cannot afford a car, a computer, access to the internet and many other goods and services that might now be considered essential items. Do you think this family is poor or not?

Any measure of relative poverty is anchored to the rest of society. As a community or nation grows richer, the perception of what constitutes deprivation likely changes, too. In the United States, an automobile was a novelty in 1920, a luxury in 1950, and a basic need in most parts of the country in 2000. Thus, relative poverty is a "moving target," which suggests both its primary strength and weakness as an indicator. On the positive side, relative poverty is an important measure of how an individual or family is living in the context of society overall. This is particularly important in light of recent evidence indicating that our sense of well-being is often shaped by what we have relative to those around us, rather than simply by the absolute level of our consumption. As the last section demonstrated, many people report that they would be happier having less income or fewer goods, as long as they have more than everyone else!

Obviously, policy makers need not depend on a single indicator. Yet several important philosophical questions arise when dealing with the distinction between absolute and relative poverty and with the broader issue of income inequality. First, does society have any obligation to deal with relative poverty once it has met the basic needs of the most disadvantaged individuals and families? Should public policy strive constantly to keep the bottom from falling too far behind the middle, or is that an unreasonable moving target that asks too much of social policy?

Second, if relative income is an important determinant of well-being, then is there a case for restraining incomes at the top? Could higher tax rates for the wealthy (or capping executive pay) be justified not merely as tools for raising revenue, but also as a means of improving overall social welfare by lessening inequality across society? In other words, should policy makers aim to bring the bottom up or also to bring the top down?

These are obviously explosive political issues, but they lay at the heart of social policy. One cannot make decisions regarding welfare policy, tax policy, or a whole host of other policy issues without rendering judgment on these kinds of contentious philosophical questions, either explicitly or implicitly.

5.6 CONCLUSION

The goal of public policy is to improve overall social welfare. In some respects, this is an impossible task, since we have no objective way of measuring human well-being. And even if we did, many of the most important questions related to how society ought to allocate resources are better left to philosophers than policy analysts. Nonetheless, policy analysis can inform and improve the way in which we allocate society's resources. We can create indicators that are reasonable proxies for outcomes that we care about. We can evaluate policies based on objective criteria, such as efficiency. We can also evaluate policies based on equity, which is an important but less objective criterion.

FOR DISCUSSION

Animals, Infanticide, and Ethics: Peter Singer's Modern Utilitarianism

Peter Singer is a professor of bioethics at Princeton University. Trained as a philosopher, Singer ascribes to a view known as utilitarianism, which argues that society should seek to achieve the "greatest good" by maximizing happiness and minimizing suffering.

This does not sound terribly controversial. So why did Princeton have to buy Singer a machine to scan his mail for bombs? Why did billionaire Steve Forbes, a Princeton alumnus and trustee, vow when he was running for president in 2000 that he would cut off all financial contributions to the university until Singer left?[31]

Peter Singer's work includes several twists on traditional utilitarian thinking. He believes that society should take into account the happiness of all species who can feel pain and pleasure, not merely humans. This line of reasoning has important—and controversial—implications for public policy toward both animals and humans. Singer's 1975 book *Animal Liberation: A New Ethics for Our Treatment of Animals* helped to create and provide intellectual underpinnings for the animal-rights movement. Singer does not argue that animals are identical to humans, only that they are entitled to some rights. He explains, "There are obviously important differences between humans and other animals, and these differences must give rise to *some* differences in the rights that each have."[32]

Thus, to maximize social welfare (including the welfare of animals), society must demonstrate that the incremental pleasure generated by eating animals (above and beyond a vegetarian diet) is greater than the pain and other disutility caused to the animals raised and killed for food. (Singer is a vegan.)

Should we allow experiments on animals? Singer says yes, if the likely benefits, such as new medical treatments that will minimize future suffering, exceed the harm done to the experimental subjects. But here is the twist that helps to explain why Singer's mail is scanned for bombs and his beliefs have been compared to the Third Reich: he argues that if we are going to experiment on animals, then we also ought to experiment on humans with similar or lesser sentience and mental capacity.

Indeed, he argues that infants or mentally incapacitated humans might be more easily justifiable as experimental subjects because they are less sentient than monkeys.

---

31. Debra Galant, "Peter Singer Settles In, and Princeton Looks Deeper; Furor over the Philosopher Fades though Some Discomfort Lingers," *New York Times,* March 5, 2000.

32. See Peter Singer, *Animal Liberation: A New Ethics for Our Treatment of Animals* (New York: New York Review, 1975), p. 2.

Inflicting pain on animals with superior mental capacity over humans with less mental capacity is "speciesist."

Singer's approach to utilitarianism has controversial implications for a wide array of social issues. He believes that the right to life is grounded in the capacity to plan and anticipate one's future. As society attempts to achieve "the greatest good," creatures without that sentient capacity—human or otherwise—should be treated differently than those that have it. Such beliefs can be used to justify abortion, euthanasia, and infanticide. For example, Singer's beliefs argue for painlessly ending the lives of severely disabled infants whose lives would cause suffering for themselves and their parents. He has also argued that the parents of a severely disabled child (a hemophiliac, for example) might be justified in ending the life of the child, particularly if they were able to have another child without the disability. Singer explained to the *New Yorker*:

> When the death of a disabled infant will lead to the birth of another infant with better prospects of a happy life, the total amount of happiness will be greater if the disabled infant is killed. The loss of happy life for the first infant is outweighed by the gain of a happier life for the second. Therefore, if killing the hemophiliac infant has no effect on others, it would, according to the total view, be right to kill him.[33]

Singer also argues that all humans have a moral obligation to improve the lives of all others who are living less well on the planet, just as if these less fortunate people were their children. "It makes no moral difference whether the person I can help is a neighbor's child ten yards from me or a Bengali whose name I shall never know, ten thousand miles away," he says. The theoretical implication of this belief is that the wealthy of the world should give away nearly all of their wealth, until their standard of living is reduced to the point where any further donations would make them worse off than the poorest person whom they might help. (As a practical matter, Singer recommends that people give 10 percent of their income to charity; he contributes 20 percent of his income.)

Singer's beliefs are outside of mainstream thinking; however, they are perfect evidence that the challenge of maximizing social welfare begins with the debate over defining social welfare itself.

33. Michael Specter, "The Dangerous Philosopher," *New Yorker*, September 6, 1999.

QUESTIONS

1. Assuming that you disagree with any or all of Peter Singer's "modern utilitarianism," what is your philosophy for defining and achieving "the greatest good"?

2. Singer would argue that killing and eating sentient animals is morally indefensible. Do you agree? Is your lifestyle consistent with that belief?

3. Are you guilty of "speciesism"?

4. Do you believe that the enormous disparities in wealth—within the United States and around the globe—are morally justifiable? Why, or why not? Is your lifestyle consistent with this belief?

5. Singer sees no ethical distinction between withdrawing life support for a severely disabled infant and ending such an infant's life with a lethal injection. Do you? Why, or why not?

6. The *New York Times* has written: "Nor does Peter Singer always live up to his own ethical standards. For instance, he does not give every cent of his disposable income to alleviate suffering overseas, even though that is what [his article] 'Famine, Affluence and Morality' calls for." Does this diminish the validity of Singer's beliefs?

7. Singer has sold more books than any other modern philosopher. A century from now, do you think that society will look back on Singer as a visionary or as an eccentric and irrelevant academic? Why?

KEY CONCEPTS

★ Public policy has no objective tool for measuring utility or for comparing utility across individuals. This creates an enormous challenge: Without the capacity to measure social welfare, how do we maximize it?

★ Indicators and indexes are tools used to quantify and evaluate outcomes or performance.

★ For as long as there has been social thought, philosophers have debated how society ought to allocate resources in order to maximize social welfare (including, in some cases, the welfare of nonhumans).

★ The collectivist economic philosophy of Marxism represents one end of the philosophical spectrum ("From each according to his ability, to each according to his needs"). The other end of the spectrum is the libertarian view that government has little or no right to expropriate personal wealth.

★ Efficiency is the degree to which resources are used to generate the most productive outcome.

★ An allocation of resources is said to be Pareto-efficient when it is not possible to make any individual better off without making another individual worse off.

★ Deadweight loss, a measure of inefficiency, occurs when the loss of welfare imposed on one party exceeds the gain in welfare afforded to another party; a more efficient allocation of resources could make at least one person better off without making anyone worse off.

★ Equity is a measure of fairness: between comparable situations (horizontal); between rich and poor (vertical); and between generations (intergenerational).

★ Public policies often involve a trade-off between equity (a fair division of resources) and efficiency (a productive allocation of resources).

★ Absolute well-being reflects the degree to which a person's basic needs are being met—food, housing, health care, and so on. Relative well-being measures an individual's consumption relative to other members of society.

MARKETS AND GOVERNMENT

CHAPTER 6

The Political Process

THE BRIDGES TO NOWHERE

One of the primary responsibilities of the U.S. Congress is to raise tax revenues and spend those funds in ways that benefit American citizens. Presumably, projects that provide the broadest benefits will have the most congressional support. So how is it that the first spending bill signed by President Barack Obama contained nearly 9,000 "earmarks"? **Earmarks** are the mechanism by which members of Congress insert pork into bills; an earmark directs federal money to a specific project in a member's district and is, therefore, insulated from any formal review as to whether the project makes sense or not. Most of those 9,000 projects would probably be rejected as unwise federal spending by most Americans—the people whose taxes are paying for them. Did this happen because a new Democratic administration had run amok? Or was it a unique response to a deep recession? No, and no. Earmarks are a natural product of the democratic political process. In 2005, when the economy was strong and the Republicans controlled the White House, the federal transportation bill included funding for the infamous "bridge to nowhere," a project that would have connected a mere 8,000 people in coastal Alaska to an island airport that was already accessible via a 7-minute ferry ride?[1] Congress, which presumably represents the interests of all fifty states, provided $223 million in federal funding for a bridge (planned to be longer than the Golden Gate) that would have benefited a small number of voters in a relatively unpopulated state. And that bridge was only one egregious component of what *U.S. News & World Report* described as Alaska's "$1 billion in pork-barrel goodies."[2] The same transportation bill included funding for another Alaskan bridge of equally dubious economic value that would have run for nearly 2 miles, connecting Anchorage to a nearby port.[3]

---

1. Rebecca Clarren, "A Bridge to Nowhere," Salon.com, August 9, 2005.
2. Bret Schulte, "Congress Watch: Pork to Nowhere Wins Again," USNews.com, October 21, 2005.
3. Timothy Egan, "Built with Steel, Perhaps, but Greased with Pork," *New York Times*, April 10, 2004.

The Alaskan bridges were funded by Congress even as seemingly more worthwhile projects were neglected. On August 1, 2007, a bridge in Minneapolis across the Mississippi River collapsed during the evening rush hour, killing 13 people and injuring 145 as cars plunged into the river. In 2005—at the same time the transportation bill was being loaded up with "pork"—roughly one in four of America's existing bridges had been deemed in need of repair. Senator John McCain wondered aloud after the Minneapolis tragedy whether it could have been averted if transportation funds had been more wisely spent. He mused, "Maybe if we had done it right, maybe some of that money would have gone to inspect those bridges and other bridges around the country. Maybe the 200,000 people who cross that bridge every day would have been safer than spending $233 million of your tax dollars on a bridge in Alaska to an island with 50 people on it."[4]

Alaskan bridges were not the only dubious projects in the now infamous 2005 legislation. The final $286-billion highway bill included 6,000 other earmarks.[5] Earmarks are not inherently wasteful, but there is no vetting process to ensure that they are the best use of taxpayers' money. As the *New York Times* has explained, "Many pork projects may have local value. But few would be ranked as priorities by state highway and transit professionals, who are the qualified experts on what's truly needed." Earmarks short-circuit many of the important processes that have been put in place to ensure that public funds are allocated to projects that offer the greatest net social benefits. In short, earmarks are a poor way of allocating public resources.

The "bridges to nowhere" were eventually canceled by Congress when a spotlight was shined on their sheer absurdity, but the earmark process is alive and well. Several years after the infamous transportation bill of 2005, Congress and the Obama administration were criticized for the Christmas tree of pet spending projects included in the fiscal stimulus bill passed at the beginning of 2009. Why do the pet projects of individual legislators get funded, even as seemingly more worthwhile projects are neglected? The electoral math does not seem to make sense. How can 1 legislator in a chamber of 435 representatives get his or her way when there are 434 other representatives—all with votes—who presumably have no interest in spending their constituents' money to support a local project in someone else's district?

A deeper understanding of the American political process offers insight into how projects like the "bridges to nowhere" get funded and why earmarks

---

4. Associated Press, "Alaska Seeks Alternative to Bridge Plan," *New York Times,* September 23, 2007.

5. Carl Hulse, "Two 'Bridges to Nowhere' Tumble Down in Congress," *New York Times,* November 17, 2005.

persist. The first lesson is that Alaska's federal legislators were far more powerful than most. In theory, all elected representatives have an equal voice in Congress—that is the whole point of a representative democracy. In practice, the nature of Congress vests more power in the hands of some lawmakers than others. Alaska is a sparsely populated state with only a single representative in the House of Representatives. (California, in contrast, has 53.) But Alaska's lone representative, Don Young, was chair of the House Committee on Transportation and Infrastructure when the 2005 transportation bill was drafted and passed. As chair of the committee, Young had far more influence over infrastructure spending than all other members of the House. On the Senate side, Alaska senator Ted Stevens was the senior Republican member of the Senate Committee on Finance, giving him disproportionate control in the Senate over spending priorities, including transportation.

Second, the "bridges to nowhere" were originally politically viable in part because the benefits were concentrated on a small community while the costs were spread across the rest of the country. Most Americans were made losers by the projects; but when we consider intensity of preference—the degree to which Alaskans would have benefited from the projects relative to what everyone else paid—the political calculus looks different. A small group of Alaska residents would have benefited significantly both from having the bridges and from the jobs generated during their construction. When the $400-million cost for the two bridges is spread around the rest of the country, *the burden is little more than $1 per person, which is barely enough to notice!* The political process is often highly responsive to situations in which the per capita gains are large and concentrated, while the per capita losses are small and diffuse. *There are more losers than winners, but that's not the point. The winners are much happier about their gains than the losers are upset about their losses.* It's sometimes said that the winners sing louder than the losers cry, and that's what elected representatives hear.

Finally, earmarks like the "bridges to nowhere" do not happen in a vacuum; legislators make agreements among themselves to deliver lots of pet projects in lots of districts around the country. Individual members of Congress are rewarded by voters for bringing home federal largesse to their district: money, jobs, infrastructure, and so on. (It's only "pork" when someone else gets it.) Congress—or any legislative body—has no incentive to reward just one member; however, the elected representatives do have an incentive to cut deals among themselves that spread rewards around broadly. Members support each other's projects, so that they can all go home and cut the ribbon on a new bridge, museum, library, or highway. This kind of deal making, or "logrolling," explains why it is more likely for a bill to pass with 6,000 earmarks than with just 1 or 2.

This chapter explores the political process, which is the process by which a democratic society makes governance decisions. A democratic system must somehow aggregate the preferences of thousands, millions, or even billions of people into a single course of action. There is no perfect process for doing that. Different mechanisms for casting and counting votes—all reasonable—can produce different outcomes from the same set of citizen preferences. Politics is the process by which policy happens—good policy and bad. Policy analysts need a sophisticated understanding of the political process for a number of reasons: (1) an understanding of the political process can explain some policy outcomes, such as the "bridges to nowhere," that might not otherwise make any sense; (2) an appreciation of the political process can help us design effective democratic institutions or to refine the institutions that we already have; (3) policy analysts who understand the political process can operate strategically and, therefore, effectively within the system.

CHAPTER OUTLINE

6.1 AGGREGATING PREFERENCES

Public policy requires collective decisions, meaning that communities or
nations must decide upon a single course of action from many possible choices, often in the face of deep disagreement about what the correct choice ought
to be. A municipality must decide whether or not to raise property taxes in
order to build a new indoor swimming complex. A nation must decide
whether or not to make a military strike against another country. The international community must decide whether or not to reduce global greenhouse
gas emissions. How does a community or a nation or a group of nations make
such decisions? Any democratic process requires **aggregating preferences,**
or somehow organizing the beliefs and opinions of many actors into a communal decision. A condominium association may perform this function for
the property owners in a high-rise building; the House of Representatives and
the Senate do it for the citizens of the United States (although the president
and the courts also play a role in this process). There is no single process for
aggregating preferences that is guaranteed to produce the best policy outcome. In fact, you should recognize that the Senate and the House of
Representatives are different kinds of representative bodies: one apportions
representatives equally by state regardless of population (two senators per
state); the other apportions representatives by state based on population. As a
result, the two chambers often produce different outcomes, even though both
bodies represent the same American citizens! All political processes have
strengths and weaknesses. **Comparative politics** is the study of how different
political systems operate around the world. Even within a single country or
state, there are likely to be numerous political mechanisms for giving voice to
the relevant stakeholders.

6.1.1 Direct and Representative Democracy

A system of **direct democracy** enables all actors with a voice in the decision-making process to vote directly on whatever matter is being considered. Many New England towns still have annual town meetings in which all residents are invited to attend and vote on major items of town business. The state of California makes many decisions by referendum, in which major policy questions are put directly to all voters on a statewide ballot. In the 2008 election, for example, California voters were not only asked to vote for president, but to vote yes or no on twelve different referendum questions, or ballot initiatives. The advantage of direct democracy is that it provides a voice to every affected party on a particular issue, leaving no doubt about whether the outcome reflects the preferences of voters. For this reason, contentious political issues are often left to referendum, even when some other legislative body has the authority to make such a decision. Many European nations put the issue of whether or not their country should join the European Union to referendum. The drawback to direct democracy is that it can be unwieldy, expensive, and time-consuming to gather the opinions of all citizens on every item of communal business. Referenda can work well on issues with a yes or no answer, but they are not practical for making more complex decisions, such as the design of a subway system or the allocation of funds across state agencies. Some governance decisions also require background information or technical expertise. Individual voters facing choices on a wide range of issues may not have the time, interest, or capacity to make an informed decision on all the communal decisions that a modern society requires.

As a result, most democratic societies adopt some form of **representative democracy,** in which voters choose representatives who make decisions on their behalf. In the United States, voters choose the members of the House of Representatives, the members of the Senate, and the president, all of whom are empowered to make governance decisions subject to the Constitution and other rules and institutional constraints that have evolved over the past two centuries. The less obvious point is that the rules for assigning representation—and for electing those representatives—can have a profound impact on democratic outcomes. Consider something as seemingly simple as voting for president of the United States. What became obvious during the election of 2000 is that the electoral college, a voting process whereby the winner of the popular vote in a state is awarded all of that state's electoral votes, is merely one of many possible ways of choosing a president. A different voting mechanism might produce a different winner, even if the same votes were cast and counted.

If the president of the United States were determined by popular vote, with the winner being the candidate with the most total votes nationwide, then Al Gore would likely have been elected in 2000.[6] The electoral college and the debate over whether it ought to be reformed is the subject of the For Discussion section at the end of this chapter.

6.1.2 Methods of Assigning Representation

One of the most important insights of political science is that not all methods of electing representatives will produce the same governance outcomes. The rules for allocating representation in a decision-making body have a profound effect on the relative power of the different groups represented. The framers of the U.S. Constitution recognized this fact. One of the crucial debates at the constitutional convention was over the number of legislative representatives from each state. If each state had been granted the same number of legislators, then the small states would have had a disproportionately large voice. If the legislative seats were allocated in proportion to a state's population, however, then the small states would have had virtually no influence at all. The constitutional compromise was to create both the House of Representatives (in which state representation is proportional to population) and the Senate (in which each state has two representatives, regardless of population).

In an **at-large legislature** or council, all of the representatives are elected by all of the eligible voters in the relevant geographic area. So if a city has a ten-person city council, then every voter in the city can vote for ten members of the council. In other words, all members of the council represent all citizens in the city. U.S. senators are elected this way; there are two senators in each state, and every voter in a state can vote for both senators.

A legislature can also be made up of **single-member legislative districts,** in which the relevant geography (e.g., a city, state, or country) is divided into individual districts with one representative from each district. For example, the

---

6. Al Gore had more popular votes nationwide than George Bush in 2000. However, we cannot say with certainty that Al Gore would have won the 2000 election if the winner were determined by popular vote because the candidates would have campaigned differently, which might have resulted in a different pattern of votes cast. Under the electoral college, the winner of a state gets all of that state's electoral votes (with several small exceptions). As a result, candidates have no incentive to campaign in states that they are likely to lose. For example, a Republican candidate would not spend time or money in the heavily Democratic state of New York since he or she would still lose the state. However, if the election were determined by nationwide popular vote, all candidates would have an incentive to campaign everywhere. This different kind of campaign would likely have led to a different tally in the nationwide popular vote.

ten-person city council could be made up of ten representatives from different districts within the city; each citizen would vote only for the representative from his or her district. The U.S. House of Representatives is constituted this way. Large states have more seats in the House than small states, but voters in any given state can vote only for the representative from their congressional district.

These seemingly arcane rules have an extraordinary impact on outcomes. Consider the following hypothetical political entity, with three relevant electoral groups—A, B, and C—that make up 45 percent, 25 percent, and 30 percent of the population, respectively. They could be groups that share a political identity or perhaps a racial or ethnic identity. In any case, groups A, B, and C would like to be represented by a member of their own group in the three-person elected body. For the sake of the example, assume that members of each group tend to live near one another. Look at how the nature of the electoral system and the electoral rules can change the nature of representation in this community:

CASE 1 Three representatives elected at large with a plurality.

A **plurality** means that the person with the most votes wins, regardless of whether that candidate achieves a majority or not. Assume that the rules work like the U.S. Senate, and that every citizen can vote for each of the three members of the elected body, and that voters cast their votes strictly according to their group or party identity. Because group A is the largest segment of the population (45%), candidates supported by group A will win all three seats. *Representative outcome: A: 3; B: 0; C: 0.*

CASE 2 Three representatives elected at large, but requiring a majority.

Again, we'll assume that voters cast their votes along group or party lines, but this time the A candidates get only 45 percent of the vote and cannot win the election outright. The most likely process is to hold a runoff election between the top two vote getters for each spot on the council: the A and C candidates, with the B candidate eliminated. From here, the outcome is indeterminate: it will depend entirely on the second choice of the B group. They could support the A candidates, the C candidates, or split their votes between the two. *Representative outcome: uncertain. The council could be made up of three As and no Cs; or three Cs and no As; or any combination in between.*

CASE 3 Three representatives elected by district, with districts drawn roughly to coincide with population densities for groups A, B, and C.

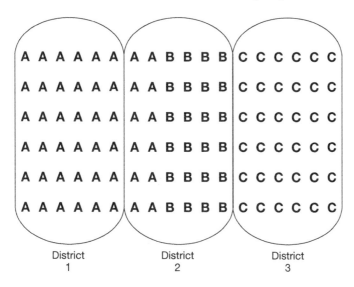

District 1   District 2   District 3

Electoral Map Showing Encircled Districts

We assume in this case that voters with similar preferences live in proximity to one another (which is not an unreasonable assumption in many cases) and that the boundaries for the electoral districts honor those residential patterns. Each group will win its own district, and the three-person council will be split among them. *Representative outcome: A: 1; B: 1; C: 1.*

CASE 4 Three representatives elected by district, the districts having been "gerrymandered" (see the figure on the next page).

It is important to remember that elections are political. But so is the process for designing electoral systems. Electoral boundaries are not drawn at random or by dispassionate computers (though the latter has been suggested). They are drawn by politicians. For example, the boundaries of each state's congressional districts are redrawn by that state's legislature and governor every ten years based on census data. **Gerrymandering** is the process of drawing electoral boundaries in ways that give a political advantage to a particular group. Consider the same hypothetical community, with different districts. Group A dominates each district and, therefore, will win all the seats. *Representative outcome: A: 3; B: 0; C: 0.*

District 1

A A A A A A A A B B B B C C C C C C
A A A A A A A A B B B B C C C C C C

District 2

A A A A A A A A B B B B C C C C C C
A A A A A A A A B B B B C C C C C C

District 3

A A A A A A A A B B B B C C C C C C
A A A A A A A A B B B B C C C C C C

Electoral Map Showing Gerrymandered Districts

CASE 5 Proportional representation.

In some electoral systems, voters cast their ballot for a party, rather than for an individual representative. Seats within the legislature are then allocated to the parties based on their electoral performance—a party that gets 31 percent of the votes will get 31 percent of the legislative seats. The individuals who then hold those seats are determined by the party. Traditionally, a party will compile a numbered list of prospective legislators prior to the election; a party that wins ten seats will send the top ten candidates from its list into the legislature. (Number 11 will have to wait until the next election!) Proportional representation is generally used for large legislative bodies, not for a council with three members. So assume instead that our hypothetical political entity has a council with a hundred members. An election with proportional representation would produce an outcome consistent with the population makeup of groups A, B, and C. *Representative outcome: A: 45; B: 25; C: 30.*

Proportional representation seems straightforward, but electoral rules matter here, too. Most countries with legislatures elected by proportional representation have a minimum threshold that a party must achieve in order to get any seats at all. For example, the Israeli Knesset has a 2-percent threshold for a party to win representation; the Turkish parliament has the highest threshold in the world, requiring a party to get 10 percent of the votes cast before it can earn even a single seat. If the threshold for gaining seats in a legislature is too low, then parliament is at risk of becoming an unwieldy collection of small, narrow parties. Italy and Israel are notorious for unstable legislative coalitions that contain numerous small fringe parties. (In 2009, the Israeli Knesset included representatives from twelve different parties.[7]) If the threshold is too high, then some important groups may be denied representation at all. In Turkey, the Kurdish minority complains that the uniquely high 10 percent threshold denies them their due representation in the Grand National Assembly.

POLICY IN THE REAL WORLD

Who *Isn't* Running for Governor?: The California Recall Election

There are democratic processes for electing public officials—and for getting rid of them. In 2003, California became the first state in eighty-two years to hold a vote on whether or not the governor, Gray Davis, should be turned out of office, or "recalled." The major problem with the California recall election was not that it was unusual, but rather that the process was poorly designed to reflect the preferences of the state's voters.

California's recall election asked voters two questions. First, do you support the recall of Governor Gray Davis? If a majority of voters said yes, then Davis would be removed as governor.

The same ballot posed a second question for all voters, regardless of how they voted on the first question. If Davis is removed as governor, who should replace him? The ballot had 135 candidates with the winner chosen by plurality, meaning that the candidate with the most votes would win, with or without a majority. From the standpoint of representative democracy, this strange, two-step process created numerous problems.

First, in this poorly conceived recall election, a majority vote was required in order to recall Governor Davis, but only a plurality was required to choose the next governor. This meant that Governor Davis could easily be replaced by a candidate *preferred by far fewer voters*. Suppose that 52 percent of voters had chosen to recall Davis and 48 percent had voted to keep him. The governor would lose his job. But then suppose that the new governor won from

---

7. Bernard Lewis, "Israel's Election System Is No Good," *Wall Street Journal,* April 1, 2009.

among the crowded field of candidates with only 30 percent of the vote. He or she would be the new governor, *even though far more of the state's voters (48 percent) had opted to keep Davis than had voted for the new governor (30 percent).* (The eventual winner, Arnold Schwarzenegger, won by a large enough margin that this did not prove to be the case.)

Second, supporters of the sitting governor Davis, a Democrat, were put in a strange position. They urged Californians to vote no on the recall, but they also wanted to put forward an acceptable candidate in case the recall passed. (Governor Davis was forbidden by the state constitution from being one of the candidates on the ballot after his own recall.) Lieutenant Governor Cruz Bustamante, a former Davis ally, became a reluctant candidate. He ran a complicated campaign: "No on recall; yes on Bustamante."[8]

Third, the hurdle for getting on the recall ballot was low enough so that the field of candidates became ridiculously large—135 in the end. To appear on the ballot, potential candidates needed to do one of two things: (1) gather 10,000 signatures from registered voters or (2) gather a mere 65 signatures and pay a $3,500 filing fee. The candidates included a stripper; a former child actor who argued repeatedly that he was unqualified for the job; and the publisher of *Hustler* magazine (a self-described "smut peddler who cares"). The myriad candidates created a circuslike atmosphere; they also made it likely that the votes cast would be split widely. The *New York Times* calculated that if the votes were split evenly, the governor of America's most populous state (about 37 million residents) could be chosen with as few as 60,000 votes.[9]

In the end, Davis was recalled, and movie actor Arnold Schwarzenegger was elected to replace him. Schwarzenegger won enough votes to make the outcome legitimate, but that was a function of unique circumstances, not a well-designed recall process.

. . . .

6.1.3 Deliberately Nondemocratic Institutions

Democratic systems seek to make the institutions of governance accountable to the citizens of the state. Yet some institutions in democratic systems are deliberately shielded from the control of voters in the belief that those institutions will perform better if they do not function at the whim of short-term

8. Jim Rutenberg, "TV's Intense Glare Makes the Odd California Campaign Seem Even Odder," *New York Times,* October 2, 2003.

9. Rick Lyman, "California Voters Wonder: Is Anyone Not Running?" *New York Times,* August 16, 2003.

political pressures. Members of the U.S. Senate serve six-year terms and are insulated from reelection politics for longer stretches than their peers in the House of Representatives, who must face reelection every two years. (Not surprisingly, the House is considered the more populist of the two institutions.) The president of the United States cannot serve more than two terms and is, therefore, beyond the reach of voters in his or her second term. Some institutions are even more nondemocratic than that. The justices of the Supreme Court never have to face voters. Once a justice is appointed by a president, he or she serves a lifetime term and cannot be recalled by voters or by the president, no matter how unpopular his or her decisions. (Justices can be impeached, but that must be for misconduct, not for unpopular legal rulings.) Many presidents have been disappointed not only by some of the decisions issued by their appointees, but by their overall performance on the bench—a performance that can go on for decades.

This insulation from politics is by design. Supreme Court justices are meant to make decisions based on the Constitution, not on popular opinion. Many of the Court's decisions concern race, abortion, civil liberties, and other contentious issues; what the Constitution says about the law may not always be what the public wants to hear. In fact, many constitutional protections, such as freedom of expression, were designed explicitly to protect unpopular minority views from a "tyranny of the majority." Citizens can affect the decisions of the Supreme Court, albeit indirectly and over a long period of time, by voting for presidents whose philosophy regarding appointments to the Court is similar to their own. The paradox of institutions like the Supreme Court is that citizens in a democratic society can make themselves better off by creating institutions that are at least partially insulated from their own control.

Democratic political systems often distribute power across different institutions to provide a system of "checks and balances," or **separation of powers.** The logic is that concentrated authority, even in a democratically elected official or body, is a recipe for tyranny (or merely very bad judgment). Both the early Greek and Roman democracies contained elements of checks and balances; the term *separation of powers* is attributed to the Enlightenment thinker Montesquieu. Political power in the American federal system is spread over three coequal branches: the executive, the legislature, and the judiciary. Congress has the exclusive power to pass laws; however, the president must sign bills into law. (If the president refuses to sign legislation, Congress has the authority to override his veto.) Meanwhile, the Supreme Court can invalidate legislative and executive actions that violate the Constitution; however, the judicial branch has no independent enforcement power. When the governor of Arkansas refused to integrate a public high school in Little Rock in

1957 despite the Supreme Court's decision in *Brown v. Board of Education* that America's public schools could not exclude children based on race, it was President Dwight Eisenhower—not the Supreme Court justices or their staff—who enforced the integration decision using federal troops.

Most state and local governments have similar checks and balances, as do democratic governments around the world. The value of these institutions lies not in how they function under ideal circumstances, but rather how resilient they are in the face of stress, change, and political abuse.

6.2 ARROW'S THEOREM

Isn't there a "best" way for making democratic decisions? Not necessarily. Kenneth Arrow was awarded the 1972 Nobel Prize in Economics in part for his work on what has become known as Arrow's impossibility theorem. In his Ph.D. thesis, Arrow demonstrated that when any group is making a decision among three or more alternatives, no voting system will satisfy a set of reasonable criteria that most individuals would expect from a fair, democratic process.[10] Arrow's work examined the social welfare function, which is a process of converting the preferences of many individuals into the preferences for the group as a whole. All voting systems are a form of social welfare function. Arrow's striking finding is that when three or more options are being considered, no social welfare function is capable of generating a group decision from individual preferences without violating one of the following basic conditions:

- **Unrestricted domain.** The process should be able to take all possible sets of rational individual preferences and generate some preferred ordering for the group. If all individuals rank their preferences (e.g., 1 = Bush; 2 = Gore; 3 = Nader), then the social welfare function should be able to rank the preferences for the group as a whole.
- **Completeness.** Any voting system or social welfare function must deliver a clear answer (e.g., Bush is preferred to Gore; or Gore is preferred to Bush; or voters are indifferent between the two).
- **Transitivity.** The group's preferences must be transitive, meaning that if Bush is preferred to Gore, and Gore is preferred to Nader, then Bush must also be preferred to Nader.

10. Kenneth Arrow, "A Difficulty in the Concept of Social Welfare," *Journal of Political Economy* 58, no. 4 (August 1950): 328–346.

- **Pareto optimality.** If every individual in a group prefers A to B, then the group must also prefer A to B.
- **Nondictatorship.** The social welfare function cannot merely reflect the preferences of one individual while ignoring the preferences of the remaining voters.
- **Independence of irrelevant alternatives.** The social ordering of two choices—say, Bush and Gore—should not be affected by a third alternative, such as Nader. If voters prefer Gore to Bush when the two candidates are running alone, then voters should also prefer Gore to Bush when Nader is in the race.

These seem like weak requirements, yet Arrow's (highly mathematical) proof supports the important but surprising conclusion that no voting system or decision rule can satisfy all of these basic conditions. Consider a simple example. Three graduate students plan to see a movie. They must decide among the three choices at the local theater: *Scream 8* (a horror film); *Massive Impact* (an action thriller); or *The Mollusk* (a French documentary on bivalve marine life). See the table below for the students' preferences.

STUDENT 1	STUDENT 2	STUDENT 3
Scream 8	*The Mollusk*	*Massive Impact*
Massive Impact	*Scream 8*	*The Mollusk*
The Mollusk	*Massive Impact*	*Scream 8*

A simple vote does not solve the problem, since each student prefers a different movie. Instead, student 2 proposes a two-stage vote, which will eliminate the group's least favorite movie and then make it a choice between the remaining two. She asks who in the group prefers *Scream 8* to *Massive Impact*. Two of the three students (students 1 and 2) prefer *Scream 8* to *Massive Impact*.

With *Massive Impact* now eliminated, student 2 asks whether the group would like to see *Scream 8* or *The Mollusk*. Again, two of the three students (students 2 and 3) prefer *The Mollusk* to *Scream 8*. The group has ostensibly picked its preferred movie for the evening, *The Mollusk*. Student 2 proposes that they buy tickets (for her first choice from the beginning).

Student 1, who has studied Arrow's impossibility theorem, is not ready to buy tickets just yet. She demands that they vote again, slightly differently. First, she asks if the group prefers *Massive Impact* or *The Mollusk*. Two of the three students (students 1 and 3) prefer *Massive Impact,* so *The Mollusk* is eliminated. She then asks her fellow students to vote between the remaining movies, *Scream 8* and *Massive Impact*. *Scream 8* is the winner (which happens to be student 1's first choice).

Different voting processes yield different outcomes without any change in the underlying student preferences. Individuals or groups who recognize this fact can manipulate a selection process in order to get their desired outcome. Notice that student 3 could have also designed a voting process that would have made her first choice, *Massive Impact*, the "preferred" film for the evening. The movie-selection situation violates Arrow's condition of unrestricted domain: there is no process for taking the preferences of the students and creating a single ordering of preferences for the group.

The example with three students and three movies may appear trivial; in fact, it could easily represent three broad groups of voters choosing among three political candidates or three factions within Congress considering three different health-care proposals. The key idea is that democratic decision making does not automatically solve the challenge of aggregating preferences. Instead, the design of our democratic institutions often plays an important role in the outcomes they produce. The concept of institutional design will be covered in greater depth in Chapter 14.

6.3 THE LEGISLATIVE PROCESS

Most democratic governments around the world vest power in both an executive branch and a legislative branch. The legislative branch consists of elected representatives endowed with the authority to make laws. The executive branch is usually represented by a single individual with powers independent of the legislative branch. In the United States, for example, the president is head of the executive branch. He has the authority to veto legislation, appoint judges, negotiate treaties, and so on.

6.3.1 Parliamentary versus Presidential Systems

The world's democratic governments tend to fall into two systems: a presidential system, as in the United States, or a parliamentary system, as in the United Kingdom, India, Israel, and many European countries. In a presidential system, voters elect the legislature and the chief executive separately. As a result, the majority party in the legislature may or may not be the same political party that the president belongs to. A parliamentary system is led by a prime minister, who is elected by a majority of the members of parliament. If a single political party controls a majority of the seats in parliament, then the prime minister will be the leader of that party. If the prime minister's party loses power in parliament, then his or her tenure as prime minister will end.

Or his own party may turn him out of office in a **vote of no confidence** and replace him or her with a new leader of the party, who would become prime minister. In 1990, after eleven years as prime minister of Britain, Margaret Thatcher was challenged in a party election as leader of the Conservative Party. Although she did not lose this party election, she subsequently resigned as leader of the Conservative Party and, therefore, as prime minister. She was replaced by John Major, who took over as leader of the Conservative Party and prime minister. Parliamentary systems will often have a president as well, although it is usually a ceremonial post with relatively little formal power.

Both presidential and parliamentary systems have strengths and weaknesses. A presidential system has a powerful independent executive who provides a voice separate from that of the legislature. He or she is directly elected by the people, presumably with a mandate to carry out certain policies. However, the presidential system is prone to "gridlock" when the presidency and the legislature are controlled by different political parties (this is arguably one of the checks and balances built into the system). A parliamentary system will not face this situation; by design, the prime minister must be supported by a majority of the members in parliament. When a single party controls that majority of seats, as Margaret Thatcher and her Conservative Party did in Britain from 1979 to 1990, they have both the mandate from voters and the formal power necessary to make sweeping changes. If no single party controls a majority of parliamentary seats, two or more parties must join together to support a prime minister and form a **coalition government.** The resulting government can be constrained and unstable, often because of the ideological compromises necessary to hold a disparate coalition together. For example, when Manmohan Singh, leader of the Congress Party in India, became prime minister in 2004, his efforts to reform the government through privatization, deregulation, and other market-based reforms were often stifled by the fact that the Communist Party of India was one of his coalition partners. If one political party withdraws support from a coalition, then the government "falls" and the prime minister must build a new majority. (If that fails, new parliamentary elections are usually held.) Italy, with five major political parties and many more fringe and regional parties, is famous for its short, unstable coalition governments. The Italians have had more than sixty governments since World War II.

6.3.2 Rules, Committees, and "Gatekeepers"

All institutions need rules; governments are no exception. These rules are not mere bureaucratic niceties. They have a profound impact on the distribution of political power and, therefore, on policy outcomes. Even when we hold voters' preferences constant, different rules within democratic institutions can produce radically different outcomes. Rules are so important in Congress that the House of Representatives has a Committee on Rules. (The Constitution directs each legislative chamber to determine its own rules.) The Rules Committee has broad discretion over when and how a bill is debated within the House, including the number and kind of amendments that can be offered. In some cases, legislation can be killed by loading it down with amendments that make the bill unwieldy or unpalatable; in other cases, allowing an amendment can salvage legislation that might otherwise lack sufficient support. Most other legislative bodies vest similar powers in a committee or a legislative leader. Because the rules affect legislative outcomes, the ability to make the rules can be a source of great political power.

The Rules Committee is one of twenty-five standing committees in the House of Representatives; the Senate has twenty standing committees, such as the Senate Finance Committee and the Senate Armed Services Committee. Most of the business of Congress—as well as in other legislative bodies in the states and around the world—is done by committees organized around policy areas. When a bill is introduced in the House or Senate, it is referred to the committee with oversight over that substantive area. (In some cases, a bill that touches upon multiple policy areas can be referred to more than one committee.) The political parties are generally represented on committees in proportion to their numbers in the legislature overall; if Democrats control 60 percent of the seats in the House, then they will control roughly 60 percent of the committee seats. Each committee is chaired by a member of the majority party. The bulk of legislative work is done in committees, which can be described as "little legislatures."[11]

Committees hold hearings to gather information relevant to pending or prospective legislation. The witnesses before a congressional committee may be experts in a certain field, such as a health-care economist or a health-care researcher, or they may be other individuals from whom Congress is demanding information. When Wall Street executives or CEOs of tobacco companies squirm uncomfortably in a hearing before Congress, they have usually been summoned by a specific committee. When former professional baseball player Mark McGwire testified before Congress about the use of performance-enhancing drugs, he appeared before the House Committee on Oversight and Government Reform. Many committees also have subcommittees that specialize in certain substantive areas within the broader purview of the committee.

Committees do much of the work related to writing and revising legislation, a process referred to as **committee markup,** or **marking up** a bill. When a committee has finished its work, a majority of members can vote the bill out

11. U.S. Senate, description of Senate committees.

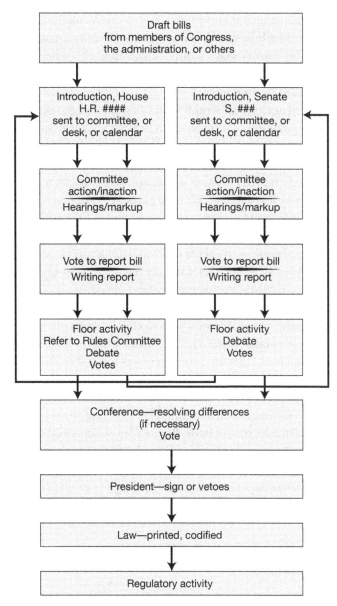

How a Bill Becomes Law

of committee for consideration by the full House.[12] The proposed legislation is **reported** to the House along with a committee report that includes background information on the measure: its purpose and cost; the position of the executive branch on the proposal; a record of committee votes on the

---

12. Judy Schneider, "House Committee Organization and Process: A Brief Overview," Congressional Research Service Report for Congress, updated February 25, 2005.

measure and all amendments considered; and so on. A committee is under no obligation to consider bills that have been referred to it; as a matter of fact, the vast majority of bills never make it out of committee either because they are voted down or they were never considered at all. This explains the expression that a bill "died in committee."

Committee chairs have important formal powers over the conduct of business before the committee. The chair often decides what legislation is considered, how it will be considered, and even what kind of vote will be held. A **roll-call vote** requires every member to go on record for or against a measure; a **voice vote** merely records whether a measure has passed or not, leaving any individual legislator less accountable for a particular outcome. The latter can be politically expedient at times, as any wily committee chair will recognize.

Committee chairs are an example of legislative **gatekeepers,** individuals whose institutional powers give them disproportionate influence over legislative outcomes. A legislative chamber usually has a speaker or majority leader with important administrative responsibilities—similar to a committee chair, only for the whole chamber. For example, the U.S. House of Representatives is run by the Speaker of the House, who is elected by its members (and, therefore, represents the majority party). The Speaker chooses the committee to which bills are referred, calls for a vote on issues before the House, appoints House members to the conference committees that reconcile different versions of bills passed by both the House and the Senate, and so on. These gatekeepers can also leverage their formal powers into informal influence over other members in the legislative body. Because legislators need the support of their committee chairs and other legislative leaders in order to accomplish their own legislative priorities, they must often follow orders from this leadership or risk legislative impotence. A single gatekeeper can often make or break a bill, regardless of how fellow legislators feel about it.

················· | **POLICY IN THE REAL WORLD** | ·················

Bill Clinton Is Schooled on the Senate: The "Byrd Rule"

One of President Bill Clinton's top priorities at the beginning of his presidency in 1993 was to pass major health-care reform. He knew it would not be easy. Clinton's fellow Democrats controlled a majority of seats in both the House and the Senate. However, a majority in the Senate is not good enough. Senate Majority Leader George Mitchell had warned President Clinton that it would be hard to get more than 51 votes in the Senate, let alone the 60 needed to defeat a filibuster.[13]

Clinton and his aides developed a plan to avoid a filibuster: he would append health-care-reform legislation to his first budget. Congress has developed special rules to facilitate deficit reduction. Every year, the House and Senate pass a budget reconciliation bill that combines into a single bill all the work done in individual committees related to raising revenue and cutting spending. Most important for President Clinton, a budget reconciliation bill cannot be filibustered, according to Senate rules. If the Clinton health-care plan were attached to the budget reconciliation bill, then it could be passed with a simple majority in both houses.

Senator Robert Byrd of West Virginia would have none of it. Senator Byrd, chairman of the Appropriations Committee, was a fellow Democrat. He favored health-care reform but respected the Senate rules even more. Byrd had been in the Senate for more than thirty years. He was the author of a four-volume collection on the U.S. Senate and a self-appointed "guardian of Senate procedure." He was also the creator of the **Byrd rule,** which stipulated that only legislation germane to the budget should be included in the budget reconciliation bill. The reconciliation process was designed to act expeditiously on budget matters; the Byrd rule was there to prevent the process from being hijacked for other legislative purposes (which was what Clinton was trying to do).

Senate rules allow only twenty hours of debate on a reconciliation bill—far too little deliberation for a topic as complex as health care, Byrd argued. He told the president, "I cannot go along with putting this into the reconciliation bill. I believe the Senate was created to deliberate. This is such a complex bill, little understood. People have a right to be informed. Woodrow Wilson said the informing function of this body is superior even to its legislative function."

President Clinton pursued health-care reform through a separate legislative process. He was never able to get a major reform bill passed.

. . . .

6.4 UNDERSTANDING POLITICAL OUTCOMES

Our analysis of the political process contains two basic assumptions about the actors involved: (1) politicians behave in ways that are likely to get them reelected by their constituents; and (2) citizens vote in ways that advance their

13. Haynes Johnson and David S. Broder, *The System: The American Way of Politics at the Breaking Point* (Boston: Back Bay Books, 1997), pp. 125–127.

own interests. Note the parallel to the core assumptions underlying a market economy—that firms maximize profits and individuals maximize their own welfare. As with economics, these core assumptions regarding political behavior are oversimplified; nonetheless, they present an important starting point.

6.4.1 The Median Voter Rule

The **median voter theory** suggests that under certain circumstances politicians can maximize the number of votes they get by adopting positions favored by the median voter. For example, if a community contains a broad difference of opinion about spending on public education, then an election will produce an education budget consistent with the preferences of the median voter—the center of the political distribution. Consider the following example. Both politician A and politician B can expand their number of political supporters by adapting their position more toward the median.

This simple model is broadly consistent with what we often observe in electoral outcomes: politicians seek to carve out the "political center"; voters with extreme views have no choice but to support a candidate whose views may be far from his own but better than the alternative. However, the median voter theory depends on a handful of strong assumptions, including the following:

- There are only two candidates. Adding candidates C, D, and E to the above graphic would vastly complicate the likely school-funding outcome.

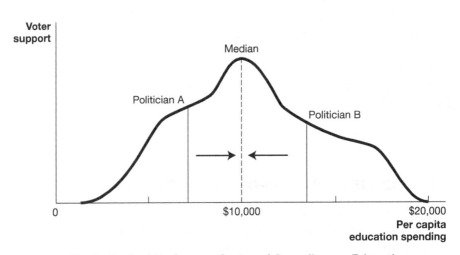

Single-Peaked Preference for Local Spending on Education

- Voters have single-peaked preferences. We assume in the school-spending example that every citizen has a preferred school budget—say, $6,000 per student—and that any amount more or less than that is less preferred. And the further away from the optimal budget, the less preferred it is ($4,000 is preferred to $3,000, and $7,000 is preferred to $8,000). But suppose that voters do not have continuous preferences of this sort. Instead, assume that many voters' first preference would be to spend $10,000 per student so that their children can go to excellent public schools. Further assume that the second choice of many of those voters would be to spend just $500 per student on education, in which case they will keep their taxes low and send their children to private schools. This kind of scenario has two possible equilibriums: a very high school budget or a very low one. Something in the middle might make everyone unhappy!

- Voters care about just one issue. Suppose that in the same municipal election the candidates must address a spike in crime and environmental concerns related to a large hog farm. With multiple voters holding preferences on multiple issues, there is no median voter (at least not in two dimensions).

- All voters are equally informed and engaged, an assumption that can be challenged with anecdotal evidence from most elections and with more rigorous empirical data.

6.4.2 The Power of Organized Interests

The median voter theorem is often at odds with what we frequently observe in the political process when organized interests successfully advance their relatively narrow interests—which don't benefit the median voter at all. If you think back to the example at the beginning of the chapter, it's clear that the median American voter had no interest in paying to build bridges in Alaska. In fact, the political system is often less responsive to the number of voters who feel one way or another than it is to their **intensity of preference,** which is *how much* the winners and losers care about their respective costs or benefits. Intensity of preference is what determines whether "the winners sing louder than the losers cry," and that, in turn, is what politicians hear.

We can explore the behavior of organized interests in the political process in a more formal way, beginning with the following basic assumptions:

1. Organized interests use the political process to compete for benefits (subsidies, tax breaks, tariff protection, etc.) and to avoid costs (taxes, regulation, etc.).

2. Any voter's intensity of preference on a given issue rises with the size of the benefit he may receive or with the cost that may be imposed upon him.

3. The cost of organizing a group to participate in the political process, especially overcoming the free-rider problems introduced in Chapter 4, rises with the size of the group. All else being equal, better-organized groups will fare better in the political process.

The key insight from these basic observations is that small organized interests have an advantage in terms of winning benefits from the political system—for two reasons. First, for any given level of per capita benefit, such as a tax break or government subsidy, the corresponding costs are spread out over a much larger segment of the population. As a result, the per capita pain of the losers is small compared to the per capita gain of the winners. Second, small groups are easier to organize than large groups, which reduces the chances of free riders creating a collective-action problem.

A numerical example will help clarify the point. Suppose a country has a population of 100 million adults, all of whom vote and pay taxes. Further suppose that 1 million of those adults grow corn and are using the political process to seek a public fertilizer subsidy of $1,000 for every farmer. The $1,000 subsidy is a significant benefit for farmers; because they make up only 1 percent of the population, however, the cost of the $1 billion program (1,000,000 × $1,000) is only $10 for every taxpayer. (Note that the net benefit to farmers would be $990 since each would presumably pay $10 as a taxpayer and receive $1,000 as a farmer.) The number of voters adversely affected by this program is 99 times larger than the number of voters who benefit, but each winner wins more than each loser loses. As a result, we should not be surprised when the farmers organize themselves for political success. This example is not real, but it is strikingly similar to the real example of America's ethanol subsidy, a program that uses government funds to pay part of the cost of converting corn into gasoline. The program raises the market demand for corn and, therefore, the incomes of farmers; the cost of the subsidy is spread across all taxpayers, roughly 99 percent of whom are not farmers.

To provide an important contrast, now imagine the same country of 100 million adult taxpayers, 80 million of whom are car owners. Suppose that the car owners are attempting to use the political process to win a $1,000 annual fuel subsidy—the same size payment as the farmers received in the previous example. Will they succeed? Probably not. Their situation is different in several important respects:

1. The total cost of the subsidy will be $80 billion—or *80 times more than the total cost of the fertilizer subsidy for farmers.* As a result, the cost to each of the 100 million taxpayers is $800.

2. Since all car owners are also taxpayers, their net benefit from the $1,000 subsidy is only $200. (All will receive the $1,000 fuel subsidy but also pay $800 in new taxes.) The $200 is still a significant benefit, but it's only a fraction of the net benefit that the farmers received ($990) for a seemingly similar $1,000 subsidy. The car owners will still sing but not as loudly as the farmers did.

3. The cost of the fuel subsidy for every non–car owner is $800, *compared to a mere $10 for the nonfarmers in the case of the fertilizer subsidy.* The losers will cry—very, very loudly. In fact, if the noise that the losers make while crying is proportional to their financial pain, they will be 80 times louder than the losers in the farming example!

The car owners have more votes than the farmers, but they are less likely to gain favors from the political process. This nuanced understanding of organized interests can help to explain many real-world political outcomes that would otherwise be puzzling.

6.4.3 Coalitions and "Logrolling"

In the movie *Mr. Smith Goes to Washington,* the actor James Stewart gives an impassioned speech to his fellow lawmakers, eventually persuading them to support his cause. That's not how Congress usually works. Individual members of Congress rarely affect outcomes by virtue of their rhetorical skills alone. Instead, successful legislators build coalitions so that their bills eventually have support from both key legislative gatekeepers and a majority of their fellow legislators. The key to building a coalition usually involves sweetening a bill in ways that attract additional support (or stripping out provisions that draw particularly strong opposition). Legislators or members of the executive branch exchange favors in order to create a mutually beneficial bill—e.g., "If you support a tax cut for manufacturers in my district, then I will support the subsidy for farmers in your district." Or legislators may trade promises across different pieces of legislation—"I will support the defense appropriations bill if you will support my tobacco legislation when it comes up." This kind of behavior, in which politicians trade and withhold favors in order to advance their own political goals, is called **logrolling.**

One example of this kind of successful deal making involves Senator Arlen Specter's role in the stimulus bill passed early in the Obama administration. President Obama and his Democratic colleagues were eager to see that the stimulus bill be perceived as bipartisan. To that end, they needed to attract at least some Republican votes. Senator Specter, who was then a Republican from Pennsylvania, delivered one of those votes and was amply rewarded in terms of his own legislative priorities. Specter had survived open-heart surgery and two bouts of cancer, so one of his key priorities in the Senate was securing funding for medical research. The *New York Times* reported, "Even lobbyists are stunned by the coup Mr. Specter pulled off this week. In return for providing one of only three Republican votes in the Senate for the Obama Administration's $789 billion economic stimulus package, he was able to secure a 34 percent increase in the [National Institutes of Health's] budget—to $39 billion from $29 billion." That's $10 billion for one vote![14]

Many of the legislative specifics that emerge from political logrolling—the so-called pork—may not always be strictly in society's best interest. On the other hand, the process of governing any large group requires compromise. An outcome that seems absurd in isolation, such as the bridges to nowhere, often makes more sense in the larger political context (the challenge of designing and passing an $286 billion transportation bill). As one longtime political observer has noted, "You need a little fat to cook the meat."[15]

6.5 RENT SEEKING

Rent seeking is the process by which political interests use the powers of government, such as regulation and taxation, to secure some kind of economic advantage. The term is derived from the concept of **economic rent,** which is an economic profit that is not bid away by the usual competitive forces. Under normal circumstances, if an entrepreneur sets up a hot-dog stand on a busy street corner and earns huge profits, we would expect other hot-dog vendors to follow suit. The new vendors would compete by offering lower prices or higher-quality products. This competitive market would quickly bid away the easy profits enjoyed by the original hot-dog vendor. But suppose that the original vendor could prevent such competition and, therefore, keep his profits high. He obviously does not have the power to prevent competition—at least not legally—but the government does. In fact, it is not uncommon for a local government to require street vendors to have a license to operate; nor would it be unusual for the government to limit the number of licenses issued. In other words, the government has the power to do what the hot-dog vendor cannot: limit competition in a way that raises his profits. This is the essence of rent seeking. Individuals, firms, and organized interests cannot simply advocate for large cash payments from the government to themselves, since such brazen public giveaways would never pass political muster. However,

14. Gardiner Harris, "Specter, a Fulcrum of the Stimulus Bill, Pulls Off a Coup for Health Money," *New York Times,* February 14, 2009.

15. Paul Green, Roosevelt University, conversation with author, date uncertain.

they *can* use the political process to secure advantages for themselves that are equally valuable but less transparent and, therefore, more likely to escape public scrutiny.

In a seminal 1971 article, George Stigler, winner of the 1982 Nobel Prize in Economics, proposed a theory in which political actors use regulation as a tool for advancing their own economic interests.[16] Stigler used the example of occupational licensure, the requirement by state governments that members of a particular profession obtain a license to practice their trade—doctors, dentists, and electricians, for example, but also teachers, tattoo artists, barbers, manicurists, and practitioners of hundreds of other occupations. Occupational licensure can, in theory, protect the public from incompetent service providers. Incompetent electricians create a potential negative externality; shoddy electrical work poses a fire risk to neighboring buildings. At the same time, licensure creates a barrier to entry in the licensed profession. Licensure limits the supply of service providers by raising the cost of entering the profession (particularly the time costs associated with taking courses or other kinds of mandatory training). One of the core principles of economics is that restricting supply, all else being equal, will raise the market price of a good or service. Thus, members of a profession can raise their incomes by using professional regulation to restrict entry into their field. This benefit can be particularly significant if existing members of the profession can get themselves "grandfathered" in the licensure legislation, meaning that new entrants to the profession must fulfill certain requirements but existing practitioners do not.

The key point is that if government has the capacity to dispense financial favors via tax and regulatory policy, then firms and individuals will engage in "rent-seeking behavior" in order to acquire such benefits. Rent-seeking behavior is often a nonproductive use of society's resources because it consumes time, energy, and talent without generating gains in productivity or output (e.g., firms spend money on Washington lobbyists rather than on new capital equipment or research and development).

6.6 STRATEGIC POINTS OF ENTRY

The hallmark of a federalist system with diffuse sources of authority is that there are usually multiple ways of accomplishing a policy objective. Effective policy actors will operate strategically across the system, seeking out favorable

---

16. George J. Stigler, "The Theory of Economic Regulation," *Bell Journal of Economics and Management Science* 2, no. 1 (Spring 1971): 3–21.

points of entry in order to maximize the chances of getting an outcome that they desire. The most obvious path to policy change in the United States involves legislative action followed by approval of the executive branch, at the federal, state, or municipal level. However, there are many other sources of potential authority within the system, as listed below.

Referendum. Many states and other institutions have provisions that allow major decisions to be made directly by the citizens affected. California allows its citizens to amend the constitution, overrule laws passed by the legislature, and create new state statutes via statewide vote. In 2008, California had twelve referendum questions, or ballot initiatives, including Proposition 1A funding high-speed rail (passed); Proposition 2 creating minimum standards for the treatment of farm animals (passed); and Proposition 8 creating a constitutional amendment eliminating the right of same-sex couples to marry (passed). Other states and localities have similar mechanisms, though the hurdle for getting a referendum on the ballot (in terms of cost, signatures, or other prerequisites) is often higher than it is in California.

Executive order (national security directive). An executive order is arguably the opposite of a referendum—it is a directive from the executive without input from the legislative branch or the voters. Most executives, from a mayor to the president, have some form of executive authority. The president of the United States has the authority to issue an executive order, which is a directive to officers within the executive branch clarifying or directing certain executive-branch operations. In theory, executive orders cannot create new laws or appropriate powers from the legislative branch; in practice, their impact can be more far-reaching. For example, President Franklin Roosevelt issued Executive Order 9066, creating military authority to remove civilians in a military zone; this authority was used to send all Japanese-Americans on the West Coast of the United States to internment camps until the end of World War II. Presidential directives, or national security directives, are a form of executive order related to national security. They are often issued in secret because they involve classified information or circumstances. These directives are issued with the advice and consent of the National Security Council.

Agency rules. Agencies within the executive branch are responsible for carrying out the laws passed by the legislative branch. However, legislation often leaves significant discretion to the agency charged with carrying it out. As a result, decisions made within an executive agency can have a profound effect on policy. For example, the Clean Air Act, originally passed by Congress in 1963 and updated periodically since then, regulates hazardous air pollutants. The statute makes no mention of greenhouse gases, but it does empower the head of the Environmental Protection Agency to "revise such list [of pollutants] by rule, adding pollutants which present, or may present through inhalation or other routes of exposure, a threat of adverse human health effects." Near the end of the George W. Bush administration in 2007, the EPA sent an e-mail to the White House concluding that greenhouse gases are pollutants that could be regulated under the Clean Air Act.[17] The White House refused to open the e-mail containing the report, sending it to what the *New York Times* described as "e-mail limbo, without official status." At the beginning of the Obama administration, the EPA declared greenhouse gases to be dangerous pollutants.[18]

The courts. The courts are charged with interpreting laws (and, in the United States, with upholding the U.S. and state constitutions). When policy actors cannot get the legislative response that they desire, they will often turn to the courts. The level and nature of public education spending in many states has been determined by state supreme court decisions. School funding would appear to be a legislative matter; however, many state constitutions have guarantees related to the "efficiency" and "equity" of their public education systems. Proponents of higher or more equitable spending have sued in many states on the grounds that these constitutional rights are being violated. Some lawsuits have been successful, resulting in major changes to the school-funding formula; others have not. The outcome usually depends on the specific language of the state constitution and the ideological makeup of the state supreme court. There have been no successful school-funding lawsuits in federal court because the U.S. Constitution offers no guarantees related to education.

. . . . POLICY IN THE REAL WORLD . . . .

Executive Order 9981:
Harry Truman Integrates the U.S. Armed Forces

Following World War II, federal civil-rights laws were routinely blocked by Southern Democrats who controlled key Senate committees. But in 1948,

17. Felicity Barringer, "White House Refused to Open Pollutants E-Mail," *New York Times,* June 25, 2008.
18. Kate Galbraith and Felicity Barringer, "The Fight Plan for Clean Air," *New York Times,* March 23, 2009.

with one signature of the pen, President Harry Truman integrated the U.S. military.[19] On July 26, Truman issued Executive Order 9981:

> NOW, THEREFORE, by virtue of the authority vested in me as President of the United States, and as Commander in Chief of the armed services, it is hereby ordered as follows:
>
> 1. It is hereby declared to be the policy of the President that there shall be equality of treatment and opportunity for all persons in the armed services without regard to race, color, religion or national origin. This policy shall be put into effect as rapidly as possible, having due regard to the time required to effectuate any necessary changes without impairing efficiency or morale.

From that point forward, there could be no legal discrimination based on race in the U.S. armed forces. Truman's power to integrate the military via executive order emanated from his constitutional role as commander in chief.

Some forty-five years later, Bill Clinton, newly elected as president and commander in chief, sought to eliminate discrimination in the armed forces based on sexual orientation. Could he do as Truman had done and merely lift the ban with the stroke of a pen? No, he could not. Clinton was the commander in chief, but Congress has authority over the legal code governing military behavior, the Uniform Code of Military Justice (UCMJ), which explicitly bans homosexuality. Any executive order from the president allowing gay soldiers to serve in the military would require a corresponding change in the UCMJ, which Congress was unwilling to do.[20]

Instead, Congress passed legislation creating the current "Don't ask, don't tell" policy. The ban on gays in the military remained; but recruits would not be asked about their sexual orientation, and the military would not proactively investigate homosexual behavior. Any soldiers who were discovered to be gay would still be subject to expulsion from the armed forces. In an ironic twist, during the wars in Iraq and Afghanistan, some soldiers began to reveal their homosexuality in order to avoid combat deployment. In response, the military began delaying legal proceedings until after combat deployment,

---

19. Harry S Truman, Executive Order 9981, July 26, 1948.
20. Based on research done by Laura Williams.

a curious reaction given that the ostensible reason for excluding gay soldiers in the first place was to avoid compromising the combat ability of the armed forces.

....

6.7 CONCLUSION

The fundamental challenge in any democratic society is to gather the opinions of the stakeholders and coordinate them into some action consistent with those preferences. This is an inherently imperfect process, since there is no single accepted mechanism for aggregating the preferences of thousands, millions, or even billions of voters across a complex range of issues. (And when the majority is in clear agreement about some course of action, we may find that it violates basic rights that we have agreed upon for the minority.) As a result, democratic societies have developed a complex array of institutional mechanisms for acting upon the diverse preferences of its citizens. Successful policy actors recognize that the nature of these rules and institutions can have a profound impact on policy outcomes, even without any changes in the underlying preferences of citizens.

FOR DISCUSSION

The Candidate with the Most Votes Loses: The Election of 2000

In November 2000, Americans went to the polls to elect a president. The two major candidates were Vice President Al Gore, a Democrat, and Texas governor George W. Bush, a Republican. They were not alone on the ballot, however. Because each state has its own legal requirements for earning a place on a presidential ballot, voters across the country had a variety of choices beyond the mainstream candidates. For example, the presidential ballot in Illinois had six candidates, including representatives from the Green, Reform, Libertarian, and Natural Law parties.[21]

The most significant challenger outside of the two main parties was Ralph Nader, head of the Green Party. Nader was on the ballot (either as a Green Party candidate or as an Independent) in forty-four states (including the District of Columbia).[22] Polls prior to the election showed that Nader would get less than 5 percent of the popular vote for the country as a whole but that his presence on the ballot could affect the outcome between Bush and Gore in eight states.[23] Pat Buchanan was also on the ballot in forty-nine states, either as the representative of the Reform Party or as an Independent.[24]

Americans voted on November 7. The immediate election results were confusing and controversial. It would be more than a month before the U.S. Supreme Court clearly determined that George W. Bush would be the forty-third president of the United States. Most of the postelection political and legal wrangling focused on counting votes in Florida, where the intent of a significant number of voters who cast ballots using a punch-card voting system was ambiguous. (The country would soon be familiar with terms like *hanging chads* and *pregnant chads*.) But the larger lesson—significant long after George W. Bush had taken the oath of office—is that America's voting system is not sacrosanct. Many groups have argued since the election (and some before) that America's electoral college is not the best way to translate the "will of the people" into a president of the United States.

One salient feature of the system is that a president does not need to win a majority of the votes cast in order to be elected. Bill Clinton was elected in 1992 with only

---

21. CNN, "President Results Summary for All States," http://www.cnn.com/ELECTION/2000/results/index.president.html.
22. CNN, "President Results Summary for All States."
23. "The Home Stretch," *The Economist*, October 31, 2000.
24. CNN, "President Results Summary for All States."

43 percent of the total votes. An alternative system of voting, common in other countries and in many other kinds of elections in the United States, would require a runoff election, if no candidate wins a majority of votes cast. The top two finishers would face each other in a second round of voting to determine the winner.

In fact, the American presidential voting system is such that the winning candidate need not even get the most votes. Rutherford B. Hayes was elected in 1876, even though his challenger, Samuel Tilden, won not only more votes, but a majority of the votes cast. America selects its president using the electoral college. Each voter goes to the polls and votes for an elector representing a presidential and vice-presidential candidate. Different states have different numbers of electors, depending on population. The number of electoral votes in every state is determined by the total number of senators (two for every state) plus the number of representatives (at least one). Wyoming has a mere 3 electoral votes while California has 55.

All of a state's electoral votes are cast for the presidential candidate who wins a plurality of votes in that state (except for Maine and Nebraska, which allow for some splitting of electoral votes). There is a total of 538 electoral votes (100 senators plus 435 representatives, plus 3 for the District of Columbia). A candidate must receive a majority of electoral votes cast (270) to be elected president.

Late in the evening of November 7, it became apparent that the election was going to be very close.[25] In an historic first, Vice President Al Gore conceded defeat at 2:15 a.m. on November 8 in a phone call to Governor George W. Bush, only to retract his concession 45 minutes later.[26] Bill Clinton noted on the morning after the election, "The American people have spoken. It is not yet clear what they said."[27] With the candidates essentially tied in the electoral college, an uncertain outcome in Florida quickly became the focal point of the whole election. The candidate who won Florida's 25 electoral votes would capture the 270 votes necessary to become the forty-third president of the United States.

The tally in Florida was clouded by confusion over the mechanics of the ballot. Florida has a punch-card voting system in which voters indicate their choice by using a stylus to punch out the box next to the candidate of their choice; ballots are ordinarily counted by machines that read the missing squares. A significant number of voters did not completely dislodge the squares on the ballot, creating the now famous "hanging chads" and other incompletely marked ballots. After an initial count of the votes, Bush was declared the winner. There was a strong belief among Gore supporters that a manual recount would more accurately capture the intent of Florida voters. A manual recount could swing the state—and, therefore, the whole election—in Gore's favor.

25. CNN, "How We Got Here: A Timeline of the Florida Recount," http://transcripts.cnn.com/2000/ALLPOLITICS/stories/12/13/got.here/index.html, December 13, 2000.
26. CNN, "How We Got Here: A Timeline of the Florida Recount."
27. "Is America Heading for a Constitutional Crisis," *The Economist*, November 10, 2000.

The subsequent battle over improperly marked ballots masked four general criticisms of America' presidential election process:

1. The candidate chosen by the most Americans does not necessarily become president. In the final tally, Gore received 50,999,897 votes (48.38 percent) nationwide to Bush's 50,456,002 (47.87 percent).[28] In the electoral college, however, Bush won 271 to 266.[29] Ironically, the same thing could have easily happened to Bush in 2004. Although he defeated John Kerry by some 3 million votes, a switch of just 60,000 votes in Ohio would have made Kerry the winner in the electoral college.[30]

2. Not every vote counts equally. Because the electoral votes are allocated based on Senate seats (2 per state, irrespective of population) plus the number of representatives, small states have a disproportionate voice in the electoral outcome. Wyoming has 1 electoral vote for every 164,594 citizens;[31] California has 1 electoral vote for every 627,253 citizens.[32] Voters in Wyoming and other small states have a disproportionate impact on the outcome.

3. Because of the "all or nothing" nature of the electoral college, the presidential election focuses on certain key "swing states" and ignores states that are firmly in the column of one candidate or the other. If New York is clearly going to go to the Democratic candidate, then it makes little sense for a Republican candidate to spend time or money there. Similarly, a Democratic candidate will not devote significant resources to reaching voters in states that usually go Republican, such as Georgia or Texas. As a result, a close national election is likely to be waged in only a handful of "battleground states."

4. Because a candidate can win a state with a mere plurality (getting more votes than any other candidate) rather than a majority (getting more than half the total votes cast), third-party candidates can skew the outcome in a way that is inconsistent with voters' preferences. The final tally in Florida was Bush (2,912,790), Gore (2,912,253), Nader (97,488), and Buchanan (17,484).[33] Bush was awarded all of the state's electoral votes. He did not, however, win the majority of the votes cast. If a runoff election had been required—a second round of voting with all candidates but Bush and Gore eliminated—then the "second choice" votes of those who originally supported independent candidates could easily have changed the outcome.

---

28. "2000 Presidential Electoral and Popular Vote," http://www.fec.gov/pubrec/fe2000/elecpop.htm.
29. "2000 Presidential Electoral and Popular Vote."
30. Hendrik Hertzberg, "Count 'Em," *New Yorker,* March 6, 2006.
31. My calculation is based on census data from 2000 (http://quickfacts.census.gov/qfd/states/56000.html): 3 electoral votes per 493,782 citizens.
32. My calculation is based on census data from 2000 (http://quickfacts.census.gov/qfd/states/06000.html): 54 electoral votes per 33,871,648 citizens.
33. "2000 Presidential General Election Results," http://www.fec.gov/pubrec/fe2000/2000presge.htm#FL.

If one assumes for the sake of example that Nader voters would have preferred Gore to Bush once their candidate was eliminated and that Buchanan voters would have preferred Bush, then Gore would have won the Florida runoff by 79,467 votes: 3,009,741 to 2,930,274.[34] In short, the presence of three or more persons on the ballot makes it possible for one candidate to be elected despite the fact that another candidate is preferred by more voters. Would a different system have made Al Gore president? Not necessarily. Obviously, he won the popular vote. *But if the winner had been determined by popular vote, then the candidates would have run different campaigns.* They would have visited different places, emphasized different issues, and otherwise changed their behavior in ways that would likely have changed the way that votes were cast.

The point is not to dwell on who could have or should have won America's 2000 presidential election, but rather to recognize the profound impact that voting systems have on voting outcomes. Critics of the electoral college would like to see it replaced by a different process for electing a president and vice president. Polls have consistently shown that some 70 percent of the American population would favor scrapping the electoral college in favor of a straight popular vote.[35]

But the electoral college is enshrined in the Constitution, and changing it would involve a distinct voting process of its own. Amending the Constitution requires approval by two-thirds of both houses of Congress plus ratification by three-quarters of the state legislatures—something that's not likely to happen, given the advantage that the electoral college confers on some states. Thus, the democratic process for choosing a president is significantly affected by the democratic process for amending the Constitution, both of which may or may not be the best way to aggregate the diverse preferences of several hundred million Americans.

QUESTIONS

1. Would you support a change in the U.S. electoral system so that the winner of the popular vote would be elected president? Why, or why not?

2. How would presidential campaigns be different if the winner were selected by the popular vote? In what ways would this strengthen or weaken the democratic process?

3. Would you require the winning presidential candidate to receive the majority of votes cast, even if it required a runoff election? Why, or why not?

4. Suppose that the electoral system were changed so that a state's electoral votes were awarded only to a candidate who receives a majority of votes cast in the state. This could be accomplished with an instant runoff, an electoral process in which voters rank their preferred candidates rather than voting for a single candidate. On Election Day, the candidate with the least votes is eliminated first; the

---

34. Calculated from the Federal Election Commission numbers quotes in note 33, above.
35. Hertzberg, "Count 'Em."

votes cast for that candidate are transferred to the voter's second-choice candidate. This process is repeated until a candidate receives a majority of votes cast. Is this system feasible for a presidential election? How might it affect voting patterns and support for nonmainstream political parties?

5. In some countries, such as Australia, Brazil, Turkey, and many others, voting is compulsory for all adults. Those who do not vote are subject to a fine. Would you support a policy like this? Why, or why not?

6. The electoral college is a reflection of the U.S. Senate, in which small states also have disproportionate influence (since all states have two Senate seats, regardless of population). How does the composition of the Senate affect public policy? Is this good for the country? Why, or why not?

7. How might history be different if the United States had had a different system in place for electing the president in 2000?

KEY CONCEPTS

★ Democratic governance requires a process for aggregating the preferences of many actors into a communal decision.

★ Comparative politics is the study of how different political systems operate around the world.

★ A system of direct democracy enables all actors with a voice in the decision-making process to vote directly on whatever matter is being considered.

★ In a representative democracy, voters choose representatives who make decisions on their behalf.

★ The rules for allocating representation in a decision-making body have a profound effect on the relative power of the different groups represented.

★ Gerrymandering is the process of drawing electoral boundaries in ways that give a political advantage to a particular group.

★ Some institutions in democratic systems are deliberately shielded from the control of voters in the belief that those institutions will perform better if they do not function at the whim of short-term political pressures.

★ Democratic political systems often distribute power across different institutions to provide a system of "checks and balances," or separation of powers.

★ In a presidential system, voters elect the legislature and the chief executive separately. A parliamentary system is led by a prime minister, who is elected by a majority of the members of parliament.

★ The rules within a representative body, such as the House or Senate, have a profound impact on the distribution of political power within the institution and, therefore, on policy outcomes. Even when we hold voters' preferences constant, different rules within democratic institutions can produce radically different outcomes.

★ Most of the business of Congress, as well as in other legislative bodies in the states and around the world, is done by committees organized around policy areas.

★ Legislative gatekeepers are individuals whose institutional powers give them disproportionate influence over legislative outcomes.

★ The median voter theory suggests that under certain circumstances politicians can maximize the number of votes they get by adopting positions favored by the median voter.

★ The political system is often less responsive to the number of voters who feel one way or another than it is to their intensity of preference, which is *how much* the winners and losers care about their respective costs or benefits. Intensity of preference is what determines whether "the winners sing louder than the losers cry," and that, in turn, is what politicians hear.

★ "Logrolling" is a process in which politicians trade and withhold favors in order to advance their own political goals.

★ Rent seeking is the process by which political interests use the powers of government, such as regulation and taxation, to secure some kind of economic advantage. Rent-seeking behavior is often a nonproductive use of society's resources because it consumes time, energy, and talent without generating gains in productivity or output.

★ The hallmark of a federalist system with diffuse sources of authority is that there are usually multiple ways of accomplishing a policy objective. Effective policy actors will operate strategically across the system, seeking out favorable points of entry in order to maximize the chances of getting an outcome that they desire.

CHAPTER 7

The Market System

HELP WANTED: THE LABOR POOL

You have probably had a job at some point. Did you earn $10 million a year? No. Yet some Americans do earn pay packages of that magnitude or even larger. In 2006, Derrek Lee, first baseman for the Chicago Cubs, signed a five-year contract extension promising him $65 million. The year before, Exxon CEO Lee Raymond earned $51 million. He subsequently retired and was awarded another $400 million in retirement benefits.

At the same time and in the same country, millions of workers earn the minimum wage ($7.25 an hour in 2009) and would likely earn less if such a law did not exist. To put that contrast in perspective, Exxon CEO Raymond's pre-retirement compensation worked out to roughly $20,000 an hour, assuming two weeks of vacation and a fifty-hour workweek.

The gap between those at the top and bottom of the labor pool is growing. According to *The Economist*, the ratio between the compensation for the average American CEO and the average American factory worker climbed from 42 in 1980 to 475 in 2000.[1] Rising inequality is showing up in other places as well. Over the last three decades, America has grown steadily richer. When adjusted for inflation, per capita income grew from $14,000 in 1968 to $39,000 in 2007.[2] But low-skilled workers are actually doing worse. Over roughly the same time frame, the median real wage for high-school dropouts fell 27 percent. Despite thirty years of sustained economic growth, the lowest-skilled Americans are likely earning significantly less in terms of real purchasing power than their fathers or mothers did a generation ago.

What is going on?

The most important insight is that the market for human talent is not significantly different from any other market. Just as prices reflect the relative supply and demand for a good or service, wages reflect the relative supply and demand for different kinds of human labor. Why do some professional baseball players earn tens of millions of dollars a year? Because they can hit or field in a

1. "Wanted: More Brains, Less Brawn," *The Economist*, September 21, 2000.
2. U.S. Census Bureau. Income given in 2007 dollars.

way that few others can. As a result, they win games, enabling their teams to earn huge ticket and broadcast revenues. Many of us would gladly play professional baseball for a fraction of what the top players earn, but we simply don't have the requisite skills. The supply of extraordinary players is tiny (and can't be expanded), and the demand for their skills is huge among teams willing to pay a great deal of money to win.

Individuals with unique skills or advanced education have always earned more than those with less talent or education. Has this trend become more pronounced in recent decades? The answer is yes. For reasons that have to do with both the supply of and the demand for different kinds of talent, highly skilled workers are doing better than ever while low-skilled workers are losing ground.

On the demand side, many of the new jobs being created in the American economy require technical skills, whether it is designing a Web page or selling a sophisticated insurance product. Even traditional manufacturing tasks, such as building a car or making steel, now require a far greater amount of technical expertise. Meanwhile, that same technology is replacing the jobs previously done by low-skilled workers: voice mail has replaced secretaries; ATMs have replaced bank tellers; automation has replaced workers on the assembly line. In short, information technology has made highly skilled workers even more productive (e.g., graphic designers, engineers, business executives) while making many less-skilled workers redundant.

As *The Economist* concluded, "Most of the jobs being lost as the result of IT are concentrated among the low-skilled, whereas many of the new jobs require good education and skills. As the demand for brains has risen relative to the demand for brawn, so wage differentials have widened in favor of the better educated. Since 1979, average weekly earnings of college graduates in America have risen by more than 30% relative to those of high-school graduates."

When it comes to understanding the market for human capital, the supply side matters as well. The supply of low-skilled workers has increased due to growing trade with China, India, and other developing countries. The plummeting cost of communications technology, for example, has made it possible to do jobs in India—outsourcing—that would have been unimaginable thirty years ago. There is also evidence that immigration, both legal and illegal, expands the pool of low-skilled workers and pushes down wages for low-skilled workers who are already in the United States.

Basic economics can also help to explain the stunning rise in compensation at the top end of the labor market. In 1981, Sherwin Rosen of the University of Chicago wrote a paper entitled "The Economics of Superstars"[3]

3. Sherwin Rosen, "The Economics of Superstars," *American Economic Review* 71, no. 5 (December 1981): 845–858.

in which he used basic analysis of markets to explain the increasingly common phenomenon in which star CEOs, athletes, and entertainers earn not merely large amounts of money, but multiples of what others who are nearly as talented in their fields are paid.

Rosen's insight was that certain markets have a **"winner take all"** nature; one need only be slightly better or more popular than the competition in order to win most or all of a very large market. Consider television news, where there is unlikely to be a huge quality difference between one broadcaster and the next. But if one broadcaster is just slightly more popular than others, then most viewers will tune in to watch him or her. That can account for millions of viewers and hundreds of millions of dollars in incremental advertising revenue for the network. A tiny difference in quality or popularity leads to a huge difference in profits, which helps to explain why CBS offered Katie Couric nearly $40 million over three years to become anchor of the *Evening News.*

The same is true in professional sports. A great baseball hitter may have a batting average of .310. A marginal hitter has an average of .285, a difference of only twenty-five hits per thousand at bats. But one need only be a little better than the competition to win a lot more games, translating into better attendance and huge broadcast revenues.

Contrast that with a profession like teaching, where being slightly better than others—or even significantly better—does not lead to huge incremental profits. An outstanding elementary-school teacher will always have twenty or

GRAND AVENUE   *BY STEVE BREEN*

thirty students and can never sell his services to tens of millions of consumers, like John Grisham or Oprah Winfrey or Katie Couric or Peyton Manning does.

Markets are one of the most important organizing principles in our everyday life. Good public policy requires that we understand how markets work, when and why they fail, and how society can be made better off by expanding or curtailing the use of markets as a mechanism for allocating resources.

CHAPTER OUTLINE

7.1 ALLOCATING SCARCE RESOURCES

One key challenge for any society is allocating scarce resources. Who gets an apartment overlooking Central Park? Who gets tickets to the Super Bowl? What firms can drill for oil on federal lands? What airlines can use the best gates at Chicago's O'Hare International Airport during peak travel hours? Each of these things has value; none of them is shared equally. Most Americans will never attend the Super Bowl or live in an apartment overlooking Central Park. So who does? And why do they receive those valuable privileges?

The answer to these questions may seem obvious: Super Bowl seats and Central Park apartments go to those who buy them. And those who buy them are generally those who are willing and able to pay the most. Most resources in our society are allocated using a market system in which sellers and buyers are free to agree on the terms of their transactions. Price is the mechanism that keeps this process in equilibrium. If the demand for some good (such as Super Bowl tickets) exceeds the supply, then sellers will raise their prices until only the most eager buyers remain. At that price, the demand for tickets will be roughly equal to the number of seats available.

As obvious as all that seems, markets are not the only way to allocate resources. In communist nations like the former Soviet Union, markets were shunned or even outlawed. Prices had little relation to supply and demand; goods and services were allocated by the government or rationed using non-market mechanisms, such as waiting in line. China, the world's most populous country, is a hybrid of markets and communist central planning. The United States and most developed nations use markets to allocate some goods but not others. During World War II, for example, America distributed scarce goods like meat and butter using ration booklets rather than allowing markets to allocate them to whoever was willing to pay the most. In this case—and there are many modern examples as well—policy makers believed that equity (ensuring some basic rations for all citizens, regardless of income) was more important than efficiency (allocating goods to those with the greatest willingness to pay for them).

Many contentious public policy issues involve questions over when markets should be used to allocate resources and when they should not. Should health care be available only for those who can pay for it? Should motorists using congested roads at peak travel hours pay higher tolls than other drivers? Should businesses have to pay a minimum wage, even if some employees would be willing to work for less? Other policy challenges involve markets that are thriving—with eager buyers and sellers—when most members of society prefer that they be shut down, such as the market for cocaine or child pornography.

7.2 FEATURES OF MARKETS

Markets are an extraordinary tool for making our lives better. They organize and allocate a staggering amount of information and economic activity without the need for any direct government intervention. Economists sometimes ask the rhetorical question: Who feeds Paris? The point is to draw attention to the extraordinary amount of activity that takes place everyday just to make modern life possible—whether it is restaurants having just the right number of fresh oysters or students buying the latest music over the Internet. By and large, government has nothing to do with producing or distributing these highly specialized goods and services. (In the next chapter, we will discuss what effective governments must do as a precondition for this kind of market activity.) All markets share a number of key features that help to explain their strengths and potential weaknesses as a mechanism for organizing human activity.

1. All markets bring together utility-maximizing consumers with profit-maximizing firms. Markets—from a flea market to the New York Stock Exchange—are mechanisms for voluntary exchange. Some markets have a physical location: a store, a town square, or even an abandoned building used for a clandestine drug deal. Other markets are virtual, such as eBay or craigslist. The purpose is always the same: to bring buyers and sellers together to consummate a mutually beneficial transaction.

Market transactions need not involve money. **Barter,** in which one good is exchanged for another good, is also a market transaction. Money is merely a mechanism for making transactions easier. Market transactions are by definition voluntary. (Robbery is not a market transaction, nor is any other coerced activity, such as forced labor.) The key is that both the buyer and the seller (or both sides of a barter transaction) feel that they are made better off by the deal. If that were not the case, then, presumably, the transaction would not take place. A major assumption in public policy is that individuals do not knowingly enter into transactions that they expect to make them worse off. A consumer who walks into Starbucks believes that he will be better off with a cup of Sumatra coffee than he would be with the $2.00 that he must hand over in order to get it. Indeed, we can even infer that for this particular customer, the cup of coffee is the *best* possible use of $2.00, or else he would spend the money somewhere else.

This line of reasoning recalls the important concept of opportunity cost, first introduced in Chapter 3. The true cost of the Starbucks coffee, or anything else, is whatever goods or services an individual has to give up to consume it. Obviously, as the price of a cup of coffee (or anything else) goes up, it becomes less attractive to consumers, all else being equal. If coffee were $2.50 or $3.00, the customer would have to forgo more consumption of other goods and services in order to enjoy a cup. Would anyone pay $5 for a cup of coffee? Yes, some consumers probably would. Each of us derives our utility in different ways; as a result, we place a different value on all kinds of goods and services. (Some people will pay a lot of money to eat snails; others would pay even more *not* to have to eat them.) Overall, however, we can draw an unequivocal conclusion: fewer customers will demand coffee at $5 a cup than they would at $3.00 or $1.98 a cup. The opposite is true as well: a good or service becomes more attractive, all else being equal, as its price falls. Thus, we can derive one crucial relationship necessary to understand basic markets: demand for any good or service will increase as the price falls, *ceteris paribus*. In microeconomics, the demand curve, therefore, slopes downward.

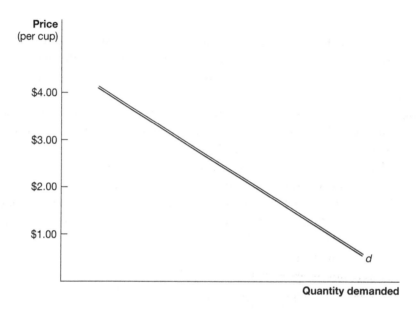

Aggregate Demand Curve (Coffee)

At the same time, the local Starbucks earns a profit on the transaction. Starbucks buys coffee beans, processes and distributes those beans, hires baristas, and rents space for operating stores. Presumably, Starbucks can do all of those things, sell coffee for $2.00 a cup, and still earn a profit for its shareholders. In fact, as long as there are significant profits to be earned selling premium coffee, other firms will have an incentive to enter the market (and Starbucks will have an incentive to open new stores). Obviously, the higher the price for which a cup of coffee can be sold, the greater the potential profits and the more incentive for new firms to enter the market and for existing firms to expand. This is the underpinning of the second important market relationship: the supply of any good or service will rise as the price increases, *ceteris paribus*.

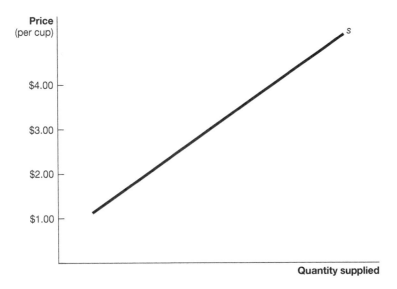

Aggregate Supply Curve (Coffee)

2. Price is the mechanism that brings supply of a good or service into equilibrium with demand. In a market economy, prices send crucial signals to consumers and producers that, in turn, induce behavioral changes. As you have no doubt observed, consumers react very quickly to changes in price. For anyone who has grown up in a capitalist economy, it is second nature to recognize that the best way to move unsold merchandise is to lower the price. In the language of economics, the "giant semiannual blowout sale" is simply a move along the demand curve; more consumers will find the merchandise worth purchasing at the new lower price.

On the supply side, a farmer contemplating spring planting may look at the market prices for corn and soybeans before deciding what crops to put in the ground. If prices are higher for one crop relative to another, he will shift some land to the more lucrative commodity. A hotel company looking to build or acquire a new hotel will examine room rates in different cities to determine the most profitable place to add capacity. The same company may close a hotel in a city where the market room rate is not high enough to enable the hotel to operate profitably, thereby reducing the aggregate supply of rooms in that city. The rational response of consumers and producers to changes in market prices—the intersection of supply and demand—is what ensures that firms are producing what consumers want to buy. Consider the example

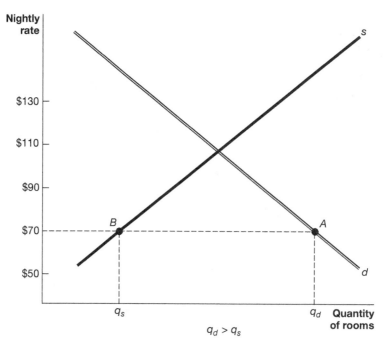

Hotel Rooms: A Shortage of Rooms for $70 a Night

above of a simple market for hotel rooms (though it could just as easily be soybeans, gasoline, or cocaine).

Consider the figure above, where hotel rooms have an average rate of $70 a night. At this price, the demand for rooms (point *A*) far exceeds the supply (point *B*). When hotels recognize that they are fully booked with a waiting list, they raise their prices. This has two effects. First, it induces more supply of hotel rooms. Other hotel chains will look to enter the market; existing hotels will add room capacity. At the same time, consumers will demand fewer rooms as the nightly rate rises.

As the figure below demonstrates, firms move upward along the supply curve, adding room capacity and raising prices as long as they continue to have more customers than they can accommodate. Meanwhile, consumers will move upward along the demand curve in the other direction; they will demand fewer rooms as long as the nightly rate is rising. The point of intersection is *C*—say, $107 a night—where the supply of rooms is equal to the demand. Firms have no incentive to raise prices or add capacity, since either would leave some rooms empty. At this point—the **market equilibrium**—customers are willing to book all of the available rooms at the market price—no more, no less.

This simple model can explain why an American supermarket is likely to have in stock all the goods that you would like to buy, while the former

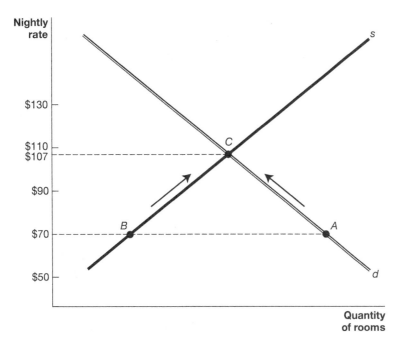

Hotel Rooms: Price Moves Supply and Demand toward Equilibrium

Soviet Union was notorious for shortages of some items and an oversupply of others. There was no price mechanism to fix the misallocation. If the demand for some product—for instance, fresh bread—exceeded the supply, the price was not allowed to rise. This had two impacts. First, consumer demand was not diminished in any way. Customers waited in line for the available bread until the supply ran out, leaving those in the back of the line with nothing at all. Second, since prices were not allowed to rise (and firms were paid a fixed stipend rather than earning profits), there was no incentive for any firm to bake more bread. That would simply require extra work for the same basic compensation from the government. (If bakeries did produce extra bread, they had an incentive to sell it on the black market out the back door.)

Conversely, workers and firms were paid to produce unwanted goods that piled up on store shelves. There were no falling prices or diminished profits to signal to producers that they were using resources inefficiently. The government did seek to control this process through elaborate **central planning.** Bureaucrats would collect data on production and consumption, and issue government edicts to reallocate resources. But this process was slow and inexact relative to the speed and precision with which prices convey such information in a market economy.

3. Markets are a powerful force for innovation and progress. In a market economy, firms thrive by finding ways to do things faster, cheaper, and better. They have a powerful incentive to make their customers happy—and to seek out new customers and make them happy, too. Why? Because that's how they earn profits and avoid going out of business. The firm that designs the proverbial "better mousetrap" will sell more mousetraps and earn higher profits. Consider the beginning of this *Wall Street Journal* story from the spring of 2004:

> As Tiger Woods cruised toward victory at the Masters in Augusta, Ga., in April 2002, executives at Nike, Inc. looked on in horror. By the 18th hole, Mr. Woods was 12 under par, but the heat and humidity were laying waste to the collar of his signature Nike polo shirt. Watching Mr. Woods receive the winner's green jacket, his collar a crumpled mess, was the "best and worst moment of my life," says David Hagler, the director of apparel for Nike Golf. There was Tiger's burgundy collar, decomposing on national television. It didn't help that the same image showed up on the cover of that week's *Sports Illustrated*.[4]

The very next morning, Nike directed its apparel maker, a subsidiary of the Hong Kong shirtmaker Esquel Group, to reengineer its shirt collars to withstand heat and humidity. According to the *Wall Street Journal* report, "Esquel designers and chemists in China began work on a new fabric using special technologies to create resilient fibers. Within weeks, the Chinese company flew six prototypes to Florida, where the May weather was humid enough for Nike to stress-test them."

By October—only six months after Tiger's victory at the Masters—shirts with new collars were rolling off the assembly line. Nike had created a better golf shirt. There was no government involvement or need for members of society to define a better golf shirt or agree to spend resources developing one. Instead, Nike executives appreciated the fact that most golfers would prefer a shirt that does not wilt in the heat and that producing one would help to earn the firm higher profits. Of course, Nike would later have other headaches related to product endorsements by Tiger Woods that the engineers could not fix.

---

4. Gabriel Kahn, "Tiger's New Threads: Champ's Wilted Polo Collar Appalled Nike, but Proved a Boon to Chinese Shirt Maker," *Wall Street Journal,* March 26, 2004.

Profit-seeking firms have a powerful incentive to discover and deliver what consumers will buy—from life-saving pharmaceutical products to quirky kitchen gadgets. In some cases, entrepreneurs have to envision a future market long before consumers have any idea that they might desire a certain product or service, as was the case with something like the iPod or even the personal computer. For policy makers, the important point is that private firms can anticipate and respond to consumer demand faster and more efficiently than any entity without a similar profit incentive. Firms also seek to maximize profits by minimizing cost. Thus, firms can succeed by finding new ways to do old things more cheaply. When oil prices were climbing steadily in 2006, the *Wall Street Journal* reported that one brickmaker began putting larger holes in its bricks because the lighter bricks require less energy to produce.[5] When energy prices are high, energy-intensive firms do not need to be shamed or cajoled into using less energy; they will do it to improve the bottom line—the same reason that Nike designed a better golf shirt.

4. Regulating markets, or otherwise limiting the degree to which prices are allowed to bring supply and demand into equilibrium, will also dull the mechanism by which markets "heal" themselves. The price system is the mechanism that enables markets to restore themselves to equilibrium, or "heal" themselves, in cases where there is some shock to the system. These kinds of shocks happen all the time. On the supply side, a frost may damage much of the Florida orange crop, or a tropical storm may knock out several large oil refineries. On the demand side, a diet craze may make some kind of food suddenly popular, or a large plant closing may leave a town with far less demand for everything from housing to restaurant meals.

These kinds of unexpected disruptions can throw markets into temporary disequilibrium. However, the immediate change in prices are what provide the incentives for consumers and firms to change their behavior in ways that begin to fix the problem. Therefore, the most logical and effective policy response to a market disruption is often to do nothing. In fact, meddling in markets, which may be politically attractive in times of disruption, can be counterproductive. For the sake of example, assume that a political event in the Middle East has caused a disruption to the oil supply, driving up not only the price of oil and gasoline, but also the price of all energy-intensive products. Policy makers in the United States would feel enormous pressure to ease consumers' pain. They ought to do *something* about high energy costs.

What might they do? Consider two possible policy responses to address high gasoline prices:

---

5. Timothy Aeppel and Melanie Trottman, *Wall Street Journal*, April 22, 2006.

- The federal and/or state governments could provide a subsidy to help offset the higher gas prices, such as a tax credit for fuel purchases. So if the price of gas has climbed from $3.00 to $3.50, the government could provide a $.50 tax rebate for every gallon purchased.
- The federal or state government could use its regulatory power to impose a cap on the price of gasoline at the pump.

Each of these policies would dampen the pain for consumers in the short run. However, both policies would also short-circuit the signals that higher prices would normally send to consumers, thereby diminishing the kinds of behavioral changes that would help to bring oil and gas prices down without any kind of policy intervention. Let's look at each option in greater detail:

Providing a subsidy to consumers to help offset the cost of gas purchases lowers the effective price that consumers pay at the pump. If the market price for gasoline is $3.50 a gallon, and consumers get a $0.50 "tax rebate," then their real cost is $3.00 a gallon. As a result, consumers behave as if gas costs $3.00 a gallon, rather than its real price at the pump of $3.50. The subsidy causes motorists to drive more than they would otherwise, increasing the demand for gasoline. That higher demand pushes prices up, offsetting at least some of the impact of the subsidy. In this case and others like it, the subsidy is not only expensive, but it is also somewhat self-defeating: the government spends money (or forgoes revenue) in order to ameliorate the effect of higher gas prices; but the subsidy itself induces behavior that exacerbates the problem.

Now let's consider the other proposed political fix: regulating the retail price of gasoline. This is not a hypothetical case. During the Arab oil embargo of the 1970s, one policy response in the United States was to cap the price at which gasoline could be sold. The result was exactly what basic economics would predict: shortages and long lines at gas stations. Suppose that the market price of gasoline is $3.50 (point *A* in the graph). But to offer relief to consumers, the government caps the price at $3.00 a gallon. As you can see from the graph on the next page, demand for gasoline at $3.00 a gallon (point *C*) exceeds the supply of gasoline at $3.00 a gallon (point *B*). Consumers want to purchase more gasoline than is available for sale. Under normal circumstances, firms would raise prices until the market returns to equilibrium. Any driver could pull into a service station and buy gasoline, albeit at the market price of $3.50.

The price caps prohibit such a market response. Instead, gas stations are forced to sell gas at a price at which demand exceeds supply. Thus, service stations will sell their supply of gasoline until it runs out, at which point there will still be some motorists who would like to buy gas but cannot—a situation

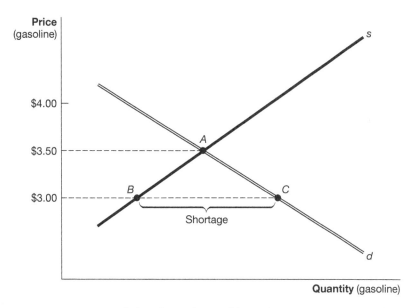

Price Caps Cause Shortages

like the bread lines in the former Soviet Union. This is what happened as the result of the price caps in the 1970s. Because some gas stations ran out of gasoline, motorists lined up early to make sure they would be able to fill their tanks. Those at the end of the line were out of luck.

5. Market outcomes are amoral. A market outcome may or may not conform to what society considers fair or socially desirable. Should teachers be paid a fraction of what professional basketball players earn? Should companies be allowed to lay off workers in the United States and hire cheaper replacements in developing countries? Should adults be allowed to exchange sex for money? Should desperately poor individuals be allowed to enhance their incomes by selling a kidney? In each of these cases, the market provides a clear answer. When firms maximize profits and individuals maximize their own utility, professional athletes earn a thousand times what teachers are usually paid; companies do lay off workers and replace them with cheaper labor or machines if that will maximize profits; there is a thriving market for sex; and there is even a black market for human organs. Are these socially desirable outcomes? The answer to that question is more ambiguous; different individuals, depending on their particular values and ideology, are likely to come to different conclusions on each of these issues.

Chapter 5 explored the tradeoff between equity and efficiency. Markets do a terrific job of maximizing efficiency; firms and individuals make decisions that are likely to maximize the "size of the pie." However, markets do not guarantee an equitable outcome. A farmer will logically sell his produce to the person willing to pay most for it, not to the person who is hungriest. Indeed, those who are starving—and, therefore, the most in need of food—are likely to be the least able to afford it. Markets distribute resources efficiently, *given some initial endowment of resources*. That **initial endowment of resources**—the distribution of land, wealth, human capital, and other assets—may or may not be considered fair in any individual's eyes. The market will merely produce the most efficient outcome, given whatever hand has been dealt. Thus, if a few families control the vast majority of a nation's arable land, market forces will likely maximize the productivity of that land. However, that bountiful harvest will belong to a small group of rich families, perhaps even as some large fraction of the population is desperately poor. Some kind of land reform, such as breaking up the large landholdings into smaller parcels owned by a broader segment of the population, would almost certainly be inefficient. It would likely lower the total harvest, since smaller parcels lose some economy of scale in farming methods, yet might still be considered desirable social policy because it yields a more equitable distribution of a smaller harvest.

To return to the example at the beginning of the chapter, market forces can explain why high-school dropouts have seen their real wages plummet over the past several decades. Over that period, those with the least human capital have been most easily replaced by technology or low-skilled labor in developing countries. The fact that the market can explain this phenomenon does not make it a desirable or inevitable outcome. Policy makers may choose to invest more of society's resources in upgrading the education and skills of workers most adversely affected by global economic trends. If that were the case, then a different distribution of human capital would result in a different labor-market outcome. Whether this is a better outcome, and whether it is justified relative to the public investment required, must be decided by policy makers and voters.

The market might reasonably be compared to the laws of physics, which explain how objects behave under different circumstances. An object will fall toward earth when dropped. That does not provide us with any moral guidance on whether or not a certain object ought to be dropped from a window. It does make clear the consequences. In light of that information, citizens must attach their own judgment to determine whether a specific market outcome is desirable or not.

6. The same features of markets that make our lives steadily better also make it difficult to stop socially pernicious behavior for which there are markets, whether it is selling guns, drugs, sex, or even human organs. Two specific features of markets make these kinds of behaviors particularly difficult to stop. First, market transactions are voluntary exchanges between parties who perceive themselves as being made better off by doing a deal, regardless of the fact that it is illegal or that it may impose significant costs on the rest of society. Just as a pharmaceutical company has a powerful incentive to discover and sell a life-saving drug and a cancer patient has a powerful incentive to buy that drug, the parties to an illegal transaction are also eager to find one another and consummate a deal. Illegal immigrants are eager to find work; firms have an incentive to hire them for wages that are lower than wages for legal workers. A drug user is eager to buy cocaine; his dealer is eager to earn profits selling it. Indeed, the parties benefiting from the transaction will cooperate to make detection by law enforcement as difficult as possible.

Second, illegal markets have the same "healing" properties as any other market. But what is healing in the market for oil or soybeans is more troublesome in the market for cocaine or child pornography. If law enforcement successfully disrupts the supply of an illicit substance like heroin, prices will rise. The good news is that this will indeed diminish demand; evidence shows that even consumers of addictive drugs are sensitive to price. The bad news is that rising prices create higher potential profits, which will induce new sources of supply. Some farmers will switch from legal crops to illegal crops; smugglers may be willing to take greater risk; new dealers will take over for those who have gone to prison; and so on. This new supply will push prices back down, which will restore demand for the illicit substance and move the market back toward its original equilibrium.

Policy makers must be cognizant of the inherent limitations of a law-enforcement strategy that focuses strictly on the "supply side" of a socially undesirable activity. In fighting illegal drugs, for example, most experts believe that it is essential to implement policies that diminish demand while also attempting to curtail supply. Thus, policy makers might also choose to spend resources on education, drug treatment, or other programs that curb overall demand for drugs. A teenager who never starts using cocaine or a prisoner who has successfully kicked the habit will not be affected by the street price of the drug—even if it were free.

··············· | **POLICY IN THE REAL WORLD** | ···············

Using Incentives to Change Behavior: London's "Congestion Charge"[6]

Traffic congestion is a bane of modern life. Nearly every metropolitan area in the world finds itself plagued with gridlock at peak travel hours. In Bangkok, Thailand, the average speed at rush hour is now 2 miles an hour. Although America's cities have not yet reached that level of congestion, time spent stuck in traffic is likely to get worse as more drivers make ever longer commutes. Over the next twenty years, for example, the average daily commute time in Los Angeles is expected to double.

One policy option is to build and expand roads. This is an expensive strategy, and experts warn that it may not work. New highways bring new drivers, since the expanded road capacity makes it easier to commute by car or to commute ever longer distances. Instead, most authorities argue that the only long-term solution is to apply the logic of the market: raise the cost of driving, particularly during the hours of peak demand.

Ken Livingstone, the mayor of London from 2000 to 2008, had the political temerity to implement such a policy to deal with London's traffic problems. Beginning in 2003, London began charging a £5 ($8) congestion fee for all drivers entering an 8-square mile section of central London between 7:00 a.m. and 6:30 p.m. In 2005, the congestion charge was raised to £8 ($13); and in 2007, the size of the zone for which the fee must be paid was expanded.

Drivers are responsible for paying the charge by phone, via the Internet, or in selected retail shops. Video cameras were installed in some 700 places to scan license plates and match the data against records of motorists who have paid the charge. Motorists caught driving in central London without paying the fee are fined £80 ($130).

The plan was designed to take advantage of the most basic feature of markets: raising the cost of driving will discourage some drivers and improve the flow of traffic. Mayor Livingstone promised a 15-percent reduction in traffic. Experts also predicted an increase in the use of public transit, both because it is a cheap alternative to driving and because buses would be able to move more quickly through central London. (Faster trips lower the opportunity cost of taking public transit.)

6. "Avoiding Gridlock," *The Economist*, February 17, 2003.

How has it worked? Within a month, the results were striking. Traffic fell 20 percent (settling after several years at 15 percent). Average speed in the congestion zone doubled; bus delays were cut in half; and the number of bus passengers climbed 14 percent. The only unpleasant surprise was that the program had such a significant deterrent effect on car traffic that revenues from the fee were lower than expected.[7]

London was not the first city to experiment with a congestion charge, but it was the largest and most high profile. Such programs are likely to become more common as policy makers seek to deal with the dual challenges of rising traffic congestion and limited budgets (and space) to build new road infrastructure. At the same time, technology has delivered simpler methods for collecting tolls, making the London system seem quite primitive. Global positioning satellites, for example, can collect fees from autos equipped with sensors. Such systems also have the advantages of (1) allowing the fee to vary at different times of day and (2) collecting the toll anonymously, thereby assuaging privacy concerns.

. . . .

7.3 ELASTICITY

If the price of coffee goes up, then consumers will buy less of it. But how much less? Similarly, if the price of Florida real estate is going up, then we would expect developers to build more units. But how many more? **Elasticity** is a measure of the degree to which supply or demand change in response to a change in price. Specifically, the **price elasticity of demand** (see formula 7.1) is the percentage change in demand associated with a 1-percent increase in price. The **price elasticity of supply** (or just **elasticity of supply**—see formula 7.2) is the percentage change in supply associated with a 1-percent increase in price.

$$\text{Price elasticity of demand} = e_{QP} = \frac{\text{Percentage change in quantity demanded}}{\text{Percentage change in price}} \quad (7.1)$$

$$\text{Price elasticity of supply} = e_{QS} = \frac{\text{Percentage change in quantity supplied}}{\text{Percentage change in price}} \quad (7.2)$$

7. "Ken's Coup," *The Economist*, March 20, 2003.

You should recognize intuitively that the demand for some products is more elastic than the demand for others, meaning that it will be more responsive to a change in price. For example, we would expect the demand for orange juice to be more elastic than the demand for cigarettes. There are more close substitutes for orange juice (e.g., apple juice) than there are for cigarettes. Also, cigarettes are an addictive product, and orange juice is not. When the price of orange juice goes up, we would expect orange-juice drinkers to curtail their consumption more dramatically than smokers would in response to a comparable increase in the price of cigarettes.

Similarly, the supply of some products will be more elastic than the supply of other products. The supply of beachfront property in Florida will have a far lower price elasticity of supply than property inland because there is a fixed amount of coastline on which to build and most of it has been developed already. So when the price of Florida real estate rises, we would expect many more new units inland—where there is a lot of land left for development—relative to the number of new beachfront units. When the supply or demand for a product is relatively invariant to price, it is described as **inelastic.**

You should also recognize that consumers and firms have far more opportunity to adapt their behavior to changes in prices in the long run than they do in the short run. Consider the effects on consumers of an increase in the price of gasoline. In the short run, most consumers can't easily change their behavior in a way that would dramatically decrease their gasoline consumption: they already own a car that may not be fuel-efficient; they live in places that require a commute to work; and so on. Over the long run, however, consumers have much more flexibility to make lifestyle changes in response to higher gasoline prices: the next car they buy will be more fuel-efficient; they can join a carpool or take a job that requires a shorter commute; etc. According to research by the Congressional Budget Office, a 10-percent rise in gasoline prices reduces consumption by just 0.6 percent in the short term, but it can cut demand by about 4 percent if sustained over fifteen years or so.[8] Elasticity is an important concept in policy analysis because policy makers must often anticipate how consumers and firms will respond to a change in prices. To what extent does a cigarette tax discourage smoking? Would more generous tuition assistance encourage more students to attend college? You

---

8. Ana Campoy, "Americans Start to Curb Their Thirst for Gasoline," *Wall Street Journal,* March 3, 2008, p. A1. Using the formula above, you should recognize the following:

the short-term price elasticity of demand for gasoline is $-.006/.1 = -.06$;
the longer-term price elasticity of demand for gasoline is $-.04/.1 = -.4$.

will recall that one surprise associated with the London congestion charge was the degree to which it reduced the number of cars entering the congestion zone; as a result, the number of cars paying the fee was lower than projected.

7.4 CREATIVE DESTRUCTION

Markets reward the firm that produces the proverbial "better mousetrap"; the often-unstated corollary to that truism is that markets punish the firm that produced the old mousetrap. **Creative destruction** is a term introduced by Austrian economist Joseph Schumpeter (1883–1950) to describe the constant process by which innovation makes older skills, technology, or processes less valuable or even useless. Wal-Mart has become a retail giant not by selling unique products, but by creating a hyperefficient process for ordering, storing, shipping, and selling merchandise. Wal-Mart makes consumers better off by selling merchandise cheaper than conventional retailers, which has the same practical effect as raising the incomes of Wal-Mart shoppers. Of course, Wal-Mart is also controversial, in part because of its impact on smaller local businesses. When consumers go to Wal-Mart for lower prices, they are opting *not* to shop at the grocery store, shoe store, hardware store, or other retail establishment that used to get the business. That is good for Wal-Mart, good for consumers, and not good for businesses that cannot compete with Wal-Mart's low prices.

Such is the nature of creative destruction. The word processor and laser printer are terrific innovations for anyone who writes; they were devastating for the manufacturers of typewriters. Blockbuster profited mightily from the creation of the video recorder, which brought with it a demand for VHS tape rentals. When the DVD was introduced as a better medium for watching films at home, the producers of VHS tapes were not the only victims. So were businesses like Blockbuster. The DVD is flat and can be mailed cheaply, thus making it possible for new firms like Netflix to deliver the same basic service in a completely different way. Of course, it is now possible to stream video over the Internet. Will we still be renting DVDs by mail in ten years?

Creative destruction makes most lives better—and some lives worse. From a public policy standpoint, that introduces several related challenges. Potential losers will often attempt to use the political process to thwart competition, even when the prospective gains to society would far exceed the losses. As has been explored earlier in the book, the benefits from competition are usually large but diffuse. In the case of trade, for example, millions of American consumers may be able to buy shoes more cheaply when they are manufactured in China and exported to the United States. The losses from such competition are often relatively small but highly concentrated. Thus, several thousand workers at a U.S. shoe company may lose their jobs. Those displaced employees are likely to care more about losing their jobs than millions of consumers are likely to care about saving $7 on a pair of running shoes.

As was discussed in the last chapter, the losers often cry louder than the winners sing, even when there are more winners than losers. The political process is disproportionately responsive to small, organized groups who seek to protect themselves from creative destruction. Unemployed shoe workers will call their member of Congress to express their views on trade; runners who got cheaper shoes generally do not.

Second, public policy may often be called upon to provide a safety net to cushion the blows cast by competition and creative destruction. A society may choose to compensate the losers from creative destruction as a matter of compassion. Or it may be a matter of political expediency. Passing legislation that has net positive benefits for society may require political concessions to groups likely to be harmed. For example, the North American Free Trade Agreement included a compensation fund for workers who could tie their job losses directly to new competition from Canada or Mexico. (Of course, any attempt to cushion the blow of creative destruction faces an unavoidable trade-off: the more generous the safety net, the less incentive there is for a person or firm or region to adapt to change, which is a necessary response as a market economy evolves and even reinvents itself.)

················| **POLICY IN THE REAL WORLD** |················

Fighting Technology to Save Jobs: The Luddites

Creative destruction often comes in the form of innovative technology that replaces human labor. Think about ATM machines, voice mail, automated ticket kiosks, self-serve gas pumps, and so on. Is it possible to save jobs by fighting the advance of technology? The Luddites, a social movement that began in 1811 in England, certainly tried.[9] At this time, the industrial revolu-

9. *Wikipedia, the Free Encyclopedia.*

tion was gaining momentum, and the production of cloth was being taken over by machines in new, large wool and cotton mills. The Luddites (named for leader Ned Ludd, who may or may not have actually existed) were workers who sought to protect jobs by destroying textile machines, even entire mills. The British army was called out to put down the revolt, and "machine breaking" was classified as a capital crime. Seventeen members of the movement were executed in 1813; others were banished as prisoners to Australia. In a modern context, the term *Luddite* is used to describe someone who is opposed to technological change.

7.5 PRODUCTIVITY

Productivity is a measure of output relative to inputs. Just as productive individuals get more done with their available time and talent, the most productive societies are those that have the greatest output of goods and services relative to the inputs required to produce them. Productivity turns out to be the single most important determinant of our standard of living.

A society must either produce everything that it consumes or produce items that can be traded for goods and services that are consumed. Thus, a society that can generate more goods and services from its available inputs will have a higher level of consumption and a better material standard of living than a society that produces less output from comparable inputs. One good way to understand productivity is by thinking about it in an agricultural context. A farmer uses assorted inputs—labor, seed, fertilizer, equipment—in order to grow crops. A bigger harvest is obviously better, because it enables the farmer to consume more, either by eating what he grows or trading it away for other goods and services. What can a farmer do to grow more crops?

One way for the farmer to increase the size of the harvest is to add more inputs: more land, more labor (hours of work), more fertilizer, and so on. In terms of actually making the farmer's life better, however, this approach is limited in two respects. First, adding more inputs also adds more costs, since the farmer has to pay for extra fertilizer, land, labor, etc. The farmer's consumption will increase only if the revenue generated by the larger harvest exceeds the costs of the additional inputs. Second, additional inputs will eventually produce what economists refer to as **diminishing marginal returns.** Each unit of additional input (holding the level of all other inputs constant) will produce a diminishing improvement in the total harvest. For example, adding fertilizer to an acre of land will improve the crop yield. But doubling the amount of fertilizer will not necessarily double the crop yield. And quadrupling the amount of fertilizer could actually *lower* the total harvest and cost the farmer a lot more money.

We would expect a similar relationship between other inputs and the crop yield. If the farmer doubles the amount of labor (by working twice as many hours himself or hiring another worker), then presumably his crop yield would go up. He could spend more time weeding, tilling the soil, and doing other things that are beneficial to the harvest. But, again, adding labor involves an expense (either the cost of hiring labor or the opportunity cost of the farmer's time) and will not necessarily produce a corresponding increase in the size of the harvest—there is only so much weeding that needs to be done.

In your own life, you may recognize the concept of diminishing marginal returns from studying for an exam. The first few hours are likely to be highly productive—you are most alert and learning the most important concepts. As you study longer, however, the time spent on the task is likely to have a less positive impact on your exam performance, since you've already mastered the most important concepts and your attention is beginning to wander because of boredom or fatigue. Finally, studying beyond a certain point could actually harm your performance as you deprive yourself of sleep or begin to confuse things that you previously understood.

In the context of studying for an exam, productivity is about becoming better at studying, not merely doing more of it. A more productive student is one who can accomplish more in two hours than a less productive student. Thus, if you were to become more productive at studying, you would be able to get better grades by studying the same number of hours; or you could get the same grades but study less, thereby leaving more time for other activities. Of course, if you became productive enough, you might even be able to study less *and* get better grades! In any case, rising productivity makes your life as a student better.

And so it is with the farmer. The key to raising his income lies in making more productive use of farming inputs, which means farming better and smarter. Rather than simply adding extra fertilizer, he will seek to find a fertilizer that is more effective for the same price (or one that is just as effective but cheaper). At the same time, the farmer can improve his yield by expanding his own knowledge of farming methods—by making each hour of labor more productive. Economists refer to this kind of knowledge as **human capital.** As with inputs like fertilizer or equipment, a farmer will invest in acquiring additional human capital if the expected return exceeds the cost of acquiring the education or experience. Modern farmers are likely to have college degrees in fields related to agronomy or even highly specialized graduate degrees.

The concept of productivity helps to explain many of the labor-market outcomes introduced at the beginning of this chapter. Why do some workers earn so much more than others? Because they are significantly more productive. The Chicago Cubs are willing to pay Derrek Lee millions of dollars a season because he is a uniquely talented player, thereby helping the team to win, sell tickets, and earn broadcast revenues. Each hour of his time generates huge potential revenue for the Cubs. Productivity also helps to explain the growing wage gap between high-school and college graduates. In a modern economy, college graduates are more likely to possess the skills and experience that add value to a firm. They are significantly more productive at the tasks that matter in a modern economy.

The incremental output produced by one additional unit of labor (holding all other inputs constant) is the **marginal product of labor.** In a competitive labor market, workers will be paid a wage closely related to their marginal product of labor. Suppose a graphic designer can generate roughly $100,000 of annual revenues for an advertising firm. We would expect her salary to be somewhere in the range of $100,000. Why? Suppose that her salary is only $50,000. In a competitive labor market, other firms (and likely the graphic designer herself) will recognize that this worker can be hired for far less than the incremental revenues she would create for the firm hiring her. Thus, other firms could afford to pay her much more—$70,000 or $80,000 or even $90,000—and still make higher total profits. In theory, firms would bid up her annual salary until it reaches somewhere close to the value she would add to the firm, which is $100,000 a year. You should also see that this graphic designer is unlikely to be paid $150,000 or $200,000. If a firm is paying $200,000 a year to a graphic designer who produces only $100,000 a year in incremental revenues for the firm, then the rational decision is to fire her (or not hire her in the first place). In these examples, we have defined a "unit of labor" as a year of work by a single employee.

In the real world, it is obviously difficult to determine a worker's exact marginal product of labor. Unfortunately for the Chicago Cubs, Derrek Lee broke his wrist shortly after signing his $65-million contract extension. As he recovered on the bench, his value to the team was zero. In other cases, workers contribute collectively to a firm's bottom line, and it may be difficult to isolate the exact contribution of any single worker. Nonetheless, a competitive market for labor ensures that there will be a strong correlation between productivity and wages. Firms will not knowingly pay workers more than their marginal product of labor; at the same time, workers will not knowingly accept less. Thus, a competitive labor market will push wages toward the point where pay and productivity are closely related, if not necessarily identical.

The concept of marginal product of labor should also help you understand the limitations of a policy like the minimum wage. Any student of public policy is aware that many Americans live in dire poverty. The introduction to this chapter illustrated the plight of low-skilled workers, who, on average, have seen their real income shrink over the past three decades. Many low-skilled workers have full-time jobs and still do not earn enough to support a family. It is certainly a reasonable goal of public policy to seek to improve the lives of poorly paid workers. Given our understanding of markets and the marginal product of labor, how would we expect a raise in the minimum wage to affect such workers?

In short, an increase in the minimum wage makes low-skilled workers more expensive without making them more productive. If a low-skilled worker generates $6 an hour in incremental revenues for a fast-food restaurant, then his wage would be in that vicinity. If the law requires that the fast-food restaurant pay such workers $8 an hour, then it no longer makes sense to have them on the job. Many economists would argue that making public investments to raise the productivity of low-skilled workers is a better strategy in the long run, even though it is expensive to fund such programs and challenging to find strategies that truly make the most disadvantaged workers more productive.

Productivity is arguably one of the most important ideas in terms of understanding why some individuals—and even entire societies—live so much better than others. Paul Krugman, winner of the Nobel Prize in Economics and a *New York Times* columnist, famously commented, "Productivity isn't everything. But in the long run, it is almost everything."[10] The reason is relatively simple. Productive societies, like productive individuals, are able to produce more from the same basic inputs. A country that has productivity growth of 3 percent a year can produce and consume 3 percent more goods and services every year from the same basic resources—land, human capital, etc.[11] A society that grows 1 percent more productive every year will see its standard of living improve by 1 percent every year. The difference between 3 percent and 1 percent annual productivity growth may not sound like much, but that difference is magnified

---

10. Paul Krugman, *The Age of Diminished Expectations: U.S. Economic Policy in the 1990s* (Cambridge, Mass.: MIT Press, 1990), p. 11.

11. Alternatively, 3 percent annual productivity growth would enable a society to produce the same output each year using 3 percent fewer inputs than the year before. This would provide a constant level of consumption, while using fewer natural resources and leaving members of society with more free time (since they would be working 3 percent less each year). Or a productivity gain could lead to some combination of the two: greater output and more leisure time.

enormously over time. A society that grows 3 percent more productive every year will see its standard of living double in roughly twenty-four years. A society with 1 percent annual productivity growth will not see its standard of living double for over seventy years—almost three times as long.

So how does a nation become more productive? Some parts of that answer are obvious. Education makes workers more productive. Research and innovation enable societies to steadily improve how they do nearly every task (and discover some new tasks in the process!). Sometimes productivity is a matter of geographic luck. Economist Jeffrey Sachs has made a compelling case that nations located in the tropics (between the Tropics of Cancer and Capricorn) are disproportionately poor in large part because of unique climate-related challenges. For example, malaria and other diseases that have been eradicated in more temperate climates continue to take a huge toll on the productivity of workers in Africa, India, and other subtropical regions.

But one of the most important determinants of productivity is public policy. The decisions that a society makes about how it will organize and govern itself have a profound impact on how productively its assets are put to use. Some unique historical accidents, such as the post–World War II division of Germany into two countries with radically different economic and political systems, have enabled us to appreciate just how radically different public policies can change the trajectory of otherwise similar nations.

Mancur Olson, Jr., a distinguished scholar in both economics and political science, wrote an essay near the end of his career addressing the question of why some nations are rich and others are poor. He ultimately came to the conclusion that good policy is what unlocks the potential of a nation:

> Those countries with the best policies and institutions achieve most of their potential, while other countries achieve only a tiny fraction of their potential income. The individuals and firms in these societies may display rationality, and often great ingenuity and perseverance, in eking out a living in extraordinarily difficult conditions, but this individual achievement does not generate anything resembling a socially efficient outcome. There are hundreds of billions or even trillions of dollars that could be—but are not—earned each year from the natural and human resources of countries.[12]

---

12. Mancur Olson, Jr., "Big Bills Left on the Sidewalk: Why Some Nations Are Rich, and Others Poor," *Journal of Economic Perspectives* 10, no. 2 (Spring 1996): 3–34.

7.6 SPECIALIZATION AND GAINS FROM TRADE

Markets, and the government policies that support them, are a crucial tool for facilitating productivity because they enable a workforce to become highly specialized and, therefore, more productive at specific tasks. In a modern economy, we need not wake up in the morning and milk our own cows and then patch our own clothing before heading out to the fields to harvest our own food. Instead, each of us is likely to perform a highly specialized task (such as writing a public policy textbook) and then trade that good or service via the market to others who perform different specialized tasks.

Adam Smith recognized the importance of specialization in his influential work *An Inquiry into the Nature and Causes of the Wealth of Nations* (1776), using the example of a pin factory. He reckons that one man would be lucky to make a single pin in a day. But many men, each expert at some specialized part of the process, can make far more than a pin per person per day:

> But in the way in which this business is now carried on, not only the whole work is a particular trade, but it is divided into a number of branches, of which the greater part are likewise peculiar trades. One man draws out the wire, another straights it, a third cuts it, a fourth points it, a fifth grinds it at the top for receiving the head; to make the head requires two or three distinct operations; to put it on is a peculiar business, to whiten the pins is another; it is even a trade by itself to put them into the paper.[13]

That was just making pins in the eighteenth century! A Boeing 767 has 3.1 million parts, made by more than 800 suppliers.[14] Of course, each one of those manufacturing processes is further specialized. Two concepts are particularly important to understanding how specialization and trade facilitate productivity and wealth creation: **absolute advantage** and **comparative advantage**.

7.6.1 Absolute Advantage

Persons, firms, or nations have an absolute advantage in production if they are better at doing something than other persons, firms, or nations. The gains from trade when different parties have different absolute advantages are rela-

---

13. Adam Smith, *An Inquiry into the Nature and Causes of the Wealth of Nations* (1776), bk. 1, ch. 1.
14. Boeing corporate Web site.

tively obvious: each party produces what it does best, and then they trade. Consider Saudi Arabia and Iowa. Saudi Arabia has an absolute advantage in producing oil; Iowa has an absolute advantage in growing corn. Thus, both Saudi Arabia and Iowa are best off if they specialize in the product that they are best endowed to produce and then trade for what they need but don't produce. A similar example would hold true for individuals: Steve Jobs is best off designing electronics and then using the revenue from his expertise in that specialized field to pay someone else to fix his car or make his clothes.

By specializing on what they do best, individuals, firms, and nations can maximize the total output of all goods and services. A simple numerical example can help to make the point. Assume that there is no international trade. Iowa must grow corn and produce its own oil, despite the dearth of petroleum deposits in the American Midwest. Meanwhile, Saudi Arabia must produce oil and grow corn, despite the arid climate and the sandy soil. The total output and consumption might look something like this:

	IOWA	SAUDI ARABIA	TOTAL PRODUCTION
Corn	1,000,000 bushels	50,000 bushels	1,050,000 bushels
Oil	50,000 barrels	1,000,000 barrels	1,050,000 barrels

Now suppose that both Saudi Arabia and Iowa specialize in producing the product for which each has an absolute advantage, devoting all of its resources to that endeavor. The total production of both goods is dramatically higher, meaning that the world has been made richer by this more productive use of resources.

	IOWA	SAUDI ARABIA	TOTAL PRODUCTION
Corn	2,000,000 bushels	0	2,000,000 bushels
Oil	0	2,000,000 barrels	2,000,000 barrels

Finally, the two countries can trade. Assume for the sake of simplicity that they agree to trade one bushel of corn for one barrel of oil. The consumption of the two places would be the following:

	IOWA CONSUMPTION	SAUDI ARABIA CONSUMPTION
Corn	1,000,000 bushels	1,000,000 bushels
Oil	1,000,000 barrels	1,000,000 barrels

You should see the two important effects of specialization and trade: (1) total production of both goods is higher; (2) total consumption in both places is higher. Both parties are better off.

It is obvious why there are benefits to trade when different regions are good at different things. But what about when one person, firm, or country is better at everything? Is there any reason for the United States to trade with Bangladesh if American workers are more productive at producing all goods and services? The surprising answer is yes.

7.6.2 Comparative Advantage

A person, firm, or country has a comparative advantage in the production of a good or service if it has the lowest opportunity cost of producing that good. You will recall from Chapter 3 that the opportunity cost of some activity is the forgone value of the next-best use of the same resources. Thus, the opportunity cost of spending an hour studying for an exam is the value of whatever you would have done instead, such as playing Frisbee, sleeping, or studying for a different exam. In an industrial context, the opportunity cost of producing some good is the value of whatever could have been produced with the next-best use of the same resources.

Even when individuals, firms, or countries have vastly different levels of productivity, trade can improve overall output by allowing highly productive persons, firms, or countries to specialize on what they do best. Consider a highly skilled individual such as Tiger Woods. Woods is extraordinarily good at two things: (1) playing golf and (2) selling golf-related merchandise. Given his coordination and concentration, he is likely to be good at lots of other things, too, such as cutting his lawn and cleaning his clubs. In fact, Woods is probably better than anyone else at cleaning his clubs, since he knows exactly how he would like it done.

So should Woods clean his own clubs? Definitely not. He may be slightly better than anyone else at cleaning his clubs, but he is much, much better than anyone else at playing golf and selling merchandise. By paying someone else to clean his clubs, he frees up resources (his time) to play more golf and sell more merchandise—the places where he can add the most value. Relative to the rest of the population, Woods has a comparative advantage in playing golf and selling golf merchandise to the golfing public. And the opportunity cost of anything that prevents him from doing those two things is huge. Consider some basic numbers. Suppose that Woods can hire someone to do a mediocre job of cleaning his clubs for $500 a month. Further suppose that this club cleaner saves Woods enough time to do one additional commercial endorsement per month, for which he is paid $500,000. For Woods, the opportunity cost of cleaning his own clubs is, therefore, $500,000. That makes the decision fairly easy: hiring someone to do the job (albeit not as well as he could do it himself) costs $500; cleaning the clubs himself "costs" $500,000.

The same basic principle explains the benefits of trade between highly productive countries and less productive countries. Assume that both China and the United States have the capacity to manufacture two goods: jet engines and televisions. Further assume that the United States has an absolute advantage in the production of both jet engines and televisions, as the chart below shows.

	PRODUCTION CAPACITY PER HOUR	
	JET ENGINES	TELEVISIONS
China	1	50
United States	5	100

If the United States devotes all of its resources to producing jet engines, it can produce 5 per hour, whereas China can produce only 1. Or the United States could devote all of its resources to making 100 televisions per hour while China could make only 50 televisions per hour. At first glance, it would appear that there are no opportunities for trade since the United States is more productive in making both goods. However, we can recast the same information in terms of opportunity cost: Every time either country produces a television, it must produce fewer jet engines—and vice versa. What must the United States and China give up in terms of jet engines in order to produce a television? And what must they give up in terms of televisions in order to produce a jet engine?

China can produce 1 jet engine or 50 televisions in an hour. Thus, the opportunity cost of producing a jet engine is 50 televisions. Conversely, the opportunity cost of producing a television set is 1/50 of a jet engine, or .02 jet engines. For the United States, the opportunity cost of producing 1 jet engine is 20 televisions; the opportunity cost of producing 1 television is 5/100 or .05 jet engines. These figures are listed in the table below.

	JET ENGINES (OPPORTUNITY COST PER ENGINE)	TELEVISIONS (OPPORTUNITY COST PER SET)
China	50 televisions	.02 jet engines
United States	20 televisions	.05 jet engines

You should see that the United States has a lower opportunity cost of producing aircraft than China does (20 televisions, compared to 50). And China has a lower opportunity cost of producing televisions than the United States does (.02 jet engines, compared to .05). As a result, there is an opportunity for trade that could make both countries better off. Suppose China, offers the United States 40 televisions in exchange for 1 jet engine. For China, this is clearly a good deal, since it would require giving up 50 televisions if it were to devote resources to producing the plane itself.

What about for the United States? Producing 40 televisions in the United States would require forgoing production of 2 jet engines ($40 \times .05$), rather than the 1 jet engine that China is asking for in the trade! Both sides are made better off by producing the good in which they have a comparative advantage and then trading. In this case, the United States trades with China for the same reason that Tiger Woods does not clean his own clubs: trading with a less developed country frees up resources so that they can be put to their most productive use. In our hypothetical example, the United States is better at making televisions but much, much better at making jet engines. (If you go back to the original table, you'll see that the United States is twice as productive as China in making televisions—100 per hour compared to 50—but five times as productive in making jet engines). This explains why highly productive countries benefit from trading with less productive countries and vice versa. Each country can specialize on products where it has a comparative advantage; both countries are made richer by the ensuing trades. Markets that cross international borders are no different than markets within a country: they facilitate the specialization and trade that boost our productivity and, therefore, our standard of living.

7.7 CONCLUSION

Markets are a powerful tool for organizing economic activity. The incentives of voluntary exchange are aligned in such a way that all parties acting in their own self-interest will maximize the productive value of existing resources. In most cases, markets are a force for progress and wealth creation, delivering an ever-improving array of goods and services that make our lives better. However, a market outcome may or may not conform to what society considers fair or socially desirable. Markets will not deliver essential goods to those who cannot afford to pay for them. Meanwhile, some thriving markets, such as the market for addictive drugs, impose significant costs on the rest of society. Even innovation has costs. Policy makers are often called upon to deal with the effects of creative destruction as individuals—and even entire communities—find their lives disrupted by economic change.

FOR DISCUSSION

Why Are We So Rich?: Understanding Productivity Growth (and Its Mysteries)

As this chapter has explored, productivity growth is what creates a rising standard of living. Why are you likely to live better than your grandparents did? Because you are more productive, as are most of the people around you. You are more likely to enter the workforce with a college diploma or an advanced degree. You have a greater access to technology—everything from a personal computer to the Internet. You can travel (or ship goods) across town or around the world faster and cheaper. You are likely to live longer and avoid diseases that might have debilitated workers a century ago.

Output per worker has climbed steadily in the United States for as long as we have been collecting data. Gross domestic product (GDP) is the value of all goods and services produced in a country; GDP per capita is that measure of total output divided by the size of the population. Wages and per capita personal income have climbed steadily as well, since a nation's income reflects its capacity to produce goods and services.

Similarly, a snapshot of the productive capacity of different nations around the globe can explain a lot about why some countries are rich and others are poor. Why is Japan a much richer nation than Zimbabwe? Because the typical Japanese worker is much, much more productive.

As clear as that concept may seem, it raises some fundamental questions: What causes productivity growth? If rising productivity is what makes us richer, why can't policy makers speed up the process? And why can't poor nations learn from richer nations in order to become more productive and, therefore, wealthier? Why can't Zimbabwe simply do what Japan does?

Productivity has not turned out to be an outcome that policy makers can turn on or off like a faucet. Indeed, the exact connection between specific policies and productivity growth turns out to be strikingly elusive. Economists can agree on many of the factors associated with productivity growth: education, investment, dependable public infrastructure, sensible taxation, good governance, and so on. But that is a long way from specific policy prescriptions—just as one cannot make a cake simply by adding random amounts flour, sugar, baking powder, and eggs to the bowl, even if those are the ingredients of a very good cake. Indeed, doubling the amount of flour without proportionally changing the other ingredients is likely to make the concoction worse, not better.

One of the most important ingredients of productivity growth—innovation—is by definition unpredictable. Why did the Internet transform society in the 1990s

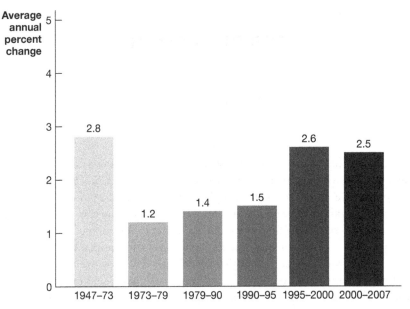

Productivity Change in the Nonfarm Business Sector, 1947–2007

Source: U.S. Bureau of Labor Statistics.

and not twenty years from now? Why did the industrial revolution happen when it did?

History presents a number of provocative questions regarding productivity growth. By understanding the path of progress in the past, researchers hope to gain clues to how the human condition can be improved in the future.

1. Why now? Human society has not grown steadily wealthier over time. Rather, humans lived at the same basic level of development for several millennia before enjoying a stunning rise in standard of living beginning in the nineteenth century. Economic historian Angus Maddison has compiled data on economic output over the course of modern history. While humans did indeed produce more, the population also increased, so that per capita wealth was largely unchanged for the vast expanse of human existence. It is not clear what factors conspired to change the trajectory of development so dramatically on the eve of the industrial revolution. Global GDP per capita did not grow at all between the year 0 and 1000; it grew only .05 percent a year from 1000 to 1820.

What happened? From the end of World War II through the 1960s, the American economy experienced productivity growth of nearly 3 percent a year. Beginning in the 1970s, however, average productivity growth slowed to 1 percent a year—a precipitous decline that lasted for nearly two decades.[15] Economists have

15. "Readjusting the Lens," *The Economist,* November 20, 1999.

offered a number of possible explanations: diminishing returns from World War II technological innovations, the rapid increase in oil prices caused by Arab oil embargos in the 1970s, excessive government regulation, declining school quality, and others. There is no definitive answer on what factor or combination of factors caused the productivity slowdown of the 1970s.

2. A "new economy"? The 1980s ushered in the era of the personal computer and the many attendant improvements in information technology. But there was a curious impact—or lack of impact—on productivity. America's productivity growth remained stubbornly low into the 1990s, prompting Robert Solow, a Nobel laureate in economics, to remark in an oft-repeated comment, "You can see the computer age everywhere but in the productivity statistics." How could the personal computer not make Americans more productive?

It just took a while, apparently. In the second half of the 1990s, productivity growth—labor productivity in particular—began to pick up sharply. Economists now believe that the productivity benefits of new technology operate with a lag; workers and firms need time to adapt their ways of doing business to take full advantage of new technological opportunities.

What will happen to American productivity growth going forward? Some experts have predicted that the wave of recent innovations could lift productivity growth to 3 or 4 percent a year. In 2003, *The Economist* predicted a more modest long-term annual average growth rate of 2.5 percent, noting at the time, "But even that rate would be a huge gain over the 1.4% average growth of the two decades to 1995. And such an increase would have a colossal impact on wealth creation, doubling real incomes every 28 years instead of every 50."[16] Private-sector productivity grew 1.8 percent in 2007 and 1.9 percent in 2008.

If policy makers could learn with some degree of certainty how to "turn up" productivity growth—in the United States or anywhere else in the world, particularly in the world's poorest countries—the positive impact on human lives would be enormous.

QUESTIONS

1. How can rising real per capita income in the United States be reconciled with the introduction at the beginning of the chapter, which showed that real wages have been falling for some workers for more than two decades?
2. Consider some jobs in a modern economy—from selling airline tickets to writing poetry. How have the firms and individuals who do these tasks become more productive over the past twenty years?
3. Would it be possible for a country to have negative productivity growth? What would that mean and how might it happen?
4. Explain why a nation's per capita income—and, therefore, its standard of living—cannot deviate for any significant period of time from its GDP per capita.

16. "Paradox Lost," *The Economist,* September 13, 2003.

5. Which is a better measure of a nation's economic strength: gross domestic product or GDP per capita? Why? Can you think of exceptions to that answer?

6. Can you think of some examples of how breakthroughs in information technology have improved the productivity of different kinds of businesses?

7. What kinds of factors would you expect to have the most significant *negative* impacts on productivity in poor countries? Why can't the situation be fixed?

KEY CONCEPTS

★ Markets are mechanisms for bringing buyers and sellers together to consummate a mutually beneficial transaction.

★ In a market economy, prices send crucial signals to consumers and producers that, in turn, induce behavioral changes. The rational response of consumers and producers to changes in market prices—the intersection of supply and demand—is what ensures that firms are producing what consumers want to buy.

★ In a market economy, firms thrive by finding ways to do things faster, cheaper, and better; as a result, they are a powerful force for innovation and progress.

★ Regulating markets, or otherwise limiting the degree to which prices are allowed to bring supply and demand into equilibrium, will also dull the mechanism by which markets "heal" themselves.

★ A market outcome may or may not conform to what society considers fair or socially desirable. Markets deliver the most efficient allocation of resources, given some initial endowment. Neither the initial endowment nor the subsequent outcome is necessarily equitable. Meanwhile, some thriving markets, such as the market for addictive drugs, impose significant costs on the rest of society.

★ Elasticity is a measure of the degree to which supply or demand changes in response to a change in price. The price elasticity of demand is the percentage change in demand associated with a 1-percent increase in price. The price elasticity of supply is the percentage change in supply associated with a 1-percent increase in price.

★ Productivity is a measure of output relative to inputs. The richest societies (and the richest individuals within any society) are those that have the greatest output of goods and services relative to the inputs required to produce them. Productivity is the single most important determinant of our standard of living.

★ Markets facilitate specialization and trade, which enhances society's overall productivity and wealth by enabling each of us to focus on the tasks that we do particularly well.

★ Persons, firms, or nations have an absolute advantage in production if they are better at doing something than other persons, firms, or nations. Persons, firms, or countries have a comparative advantage in the production of a good or service if they have the lowest opportunity cost of producing that good.

★ Even when an individual or country is more productive than another individual or country at all tasks, trade between the two parties can improve overall output by allowing each party to specialize on what it does best.

CHAPTER 8

The Role of Government

THE TRUE COSTS OF "ALL YOU CAN EAT":
GOOD GOVERNMENT AND THE MARKET ECONOMY

In 2003, Red Lobster learned an expensive lesson. The seafood restaurant created an "all you can eat" crab promotion. For a fixed price, customers were allowed to refill their plates with crab until they could eat no more.[1] For the Red Lobster customers, each additional helping of crab was free; a rational customer would continue to order more helpings until the incremental utility generated by another plate of crab reached zero.

Of course, serving each new helping of crab was *not* free for Red Lobster. In fact, the market price of crab was going up at the time. Red Lobster incurred a significant cost for buying, cooking, and serving each additional helping of crab—so much so that the promotion became a financial disaster. The restaurant chain had seriously miscalculated how much crab customers would eat when each new helping was free. Darden Restaurants (owner of Red Lobster) fired its president over the promotion gone bad. "It wasn't the second helping on all-you-can-eat but the third," the company chairman told reporters. The new president added, "And maybe the fourth."

To economists, Red Lobster had made the mistake of pricing its crab below marginal cost, which is the cost of producing one additional unit of a good or service. When something is priced too cheaply relative to its cost of production, people will use "too much" of it. In the case of Red Lobster, customers ordered additional crab as if it were free because it was for them. But additional servings of crab were *not* free for Red Lobster.

Assume that each additional helping of crab cost the restaurant $2. If the restaurant charged $2 for each additional helping of crab, then customers would demand extra helpings up until the point where one more serving generated $2 in incremental utility—the amount it cost on the menu. Instead, customers were

1. Richard Gibson, "Red Lobster Endless Crab Offer Gobbled Up Chain's Profits," *Wall Street Journal Online,* September 24, 2003.

demanding far more than that. Red Lobster created a winning recipe for losing money!

(Red Lobster may also have made an analytical error in not recognizing the adverse selection associated with any all-you-can-eat offering. Those customers with the largest appetites are most likely to select the unlimited option, so if Red Lobster based its financial projections for the promotion on how much crab the *average* customer eats, they would have underestimated the demand for second, third, and fourth helpings.)

So what does Red Lobster's bad experience have to do with public policy? Quite a bit, it turns out. Many public policy problems arise when the private marginal cost of some activity (that which must be paid by the individual or firm doing it) is significantly different from the social marginal cost (those costs borne by all the rest of society). At present, spam—unwanted e-mail solicitations blasted to multiple addresses—is a lot like the Red Lobster problem. In this case, the marginal cost of sending such e-mail is essentially zero. Solicitors can blast millions of messages for free.

For the recipients, there is no monetary cost for this spam. But it clutters the e-mailbox, carries viruses, and generally creates a nuisance. If a vendor sends out 10 million e-mails advertising an herbal sex enhancer and one person buys the product, then the blast e-mail was a profitable venture—for the sender. Of course, that person does not have to bear the cost imposed on the 9,999,999 other e-mail users who never wanted the solicitation in the first place. More than half of all e-mail is now spam, and the share is rising.[2] From society's standpoint, there is too much spam because the senders do not have to bear its full cost.

Many observers, including Bill Gates, have proposed some kind of e-mail "stamps," such as a penny or quarter penny per e-mail. Spammers would not be prohibited from buying such e-stamps, but the economics of sending out blast e-mails would change significantly. As *The Economist* has noted, "For most hawkers of penis enlargements, one can assume, the numbers would not add up, so they would not buy postage."

Many environmental problems share the same features of this problem. Economists point out that the private costs of driving do not reflect the full social costs of driving. Yes, driving has significant private costs, such as buying gas, insurance, and the car itself. But there are also costs associated with driving that are borne by society as a whole, such as the environmental costs of vehicle emissions. Most vehicles give off carbon dioxide (CO_2), which scientists now believe contributes to global warming. In making a decision whether or

2. "Make 'Em Pay," *The Economist*, February 14, 2004.

not to commute by car to work, a driver does not need to weigh this social cost in his calculations, since he will never be presented with a bill for his contribution to global warming. Thus, the private marginal cost of driving is lower than the social marginal cost; in the eyes of economists, many of us drive "too much."

This chapter explores the role that government can play in promoting social welfare. A fundamental responsibility of government is to intervene in markets when the private cost of some activity is different than the social cost. If the private cost is below the social cost, then individuals will do "too much" of it—such as driving or blasting spam—from the standpoint of overall social welfare.

Of course, government does not merely refine market outcomes; sensible government policy makes it possible for markets to operate in the first place. All modern societies use government to create and defend property rights, to build and operate infrastructure, to defend against external threats, to circulate the currency used to conduct transactions, and to carry out many other functions that facilitate market transactions. Finally, government is often called upon to redistribute resources. The most efficient outcome is not always considered the best outcome in the eyes of many citizens. Governments are vested with the authority to transfer resources from some groups in society to other groups for reasons of fairness, even at the expense of efficiency.

Good government is a prerequisite for a thriving market economy. At the same time, the coercive powers of government can be put to use in ways that serve narrow organized interests, including the government employees themselves. One of the most important tasks for policy analysts is determining when, where, and how government ought to involve itself (or not involve itself) in a modern economy.

CHAPTER OUTLINE

The True Costs of "All You Can Eat": Good Government and the Market Economy

8.1   MARKET FAILURE

8.1.1   CREATING AND ENFORCING PROPERTY RIGHTS

8.1.2   LOWERING TRANSACTIONS COSTS

8.1.3   PROMOTING COMPETITION
POLICY IN THE REAL WORLD Why Does Your Student
ID Get You a Discount?: Price Discrimination

8.1   MARKET FAILURE

Markets are an extraordinary tool for allocating resources as efficiently as possible. They are not infallible. A **market failure** is a situation in which market transactions do not lead to a socially efficient allocation of resources. In some cases, market participants are not able to make potentially mutually beneficial trades, such as when property rights are vague or transactions costs are excessively high. In other cases, private transactions impose large negative externalities on third parties, so that what is good for the market participants is not necessarily good for everyone else. Government can play a potentially constructive role in preventing market failures or dealing with their effects.

8.1.1   Creating and Enforcing Property Rights

Government creates and enforces a **property right,** which is the ownership or control of a parcel of property, an asset, or even an idea or artistic creation. The concept of ownership is a precondition of functioning markets. At the most basic level, individuals will not engage in voluntary exchange if it is not clear who owns the goods that are being exchanged. (One basic step in any modern real-estate transaction is a title search, which verifies via government records that the seller in fact owns the property that is being sold.) Similarly, no rational firm will make a business investment without an explicit assurance that it can keep the profits generated by the investment. A farmer will not plant, water, and fertilize a field of corn if there is some legal doubt about whether he alone can reap and sell the subsequent harvest.

It is sometimes easiest to understand the importance of property rights by envisioning what would likely happen in their absence. If all the citizens of a village can freely take corn from a farmer's field at harvest time, then the farmer will not invest the time and resources required to produce such a harvest. *As a result, the field will be less productive than it is when the farmer can exclude others from taking his harvest.* Elsewhere in the economy, a company would not spend hundreds of millions of dollars searching for oil if once a well was drilled other firms could come along and fill barrels of their own. We take for granted that individuals can "own" cars, homes, factories, and other forms of property. Property rights bestow ownership of an asset and everything that it is used to create, which makes it possible for the property owner to maximize the value of the asset.

In many cases, "property" is intangible, as in the case of inventions, ideas, works of art, and other forms of **intellectual property.** Your textbook author created this book in large part (though not exclusively) so that it could be sold profitably. But books are not likely to be profitable if other individuals or firms can reproduce them without permission. Instead, the U.S. government grants a copyright to the artists and writers who produce songs and written material. If this book or large sections of it are photocopied, then the person doing the copying must pay a royalty to the author or face criminal sanctions. If that were not the case, there would be little incentive to produce such terrific textbooks in the first place.

Government is also responsible for defending property rights. If your car is stolen or a vagrant is sleeping on your front lawn, you will likely call the police. If an individual or firm "steals" intellectual property by violating a copyright or patent, the victimized party can sue in court. This issue was brought to a head in the early days of online music. Napster, the firm that sells music via the Internet, began by giving music away free. Individuals could download songs and albums at no cost and without the permission of the artist. A consortium of songwriters successfully sued Napster for copyright infringement, arguing that the firm was essentially stealing artists' work. There was even evidence that free music downloads were leading to less song creation. The courts ruled against Napster, leading to the current arrangement in which music can be sold online only with permission of the artist.

Defining and defending property rights is considered to be one of the most fundamental and important responsibilities of government because it provides the foundation on which a market economy operates.

8.1.2 Lowering Transactions Costs

Government can facilitate markets by providing information, institutions, infrastructure, and other kinds of support that make private market transactions less costly. A stable currency is a good example of a government activity that lowers the transactions costs associated with doing business. Imagine going through a normal day without the American dollar or some other official currency. Would it be possible? Yes, although it would make most kinds of commerce much more difficult. You might barter for goods, or you could use some medium of exchange like gold or bags of rice. But nearly every transaction, from buying a cup of coffee to paying university tuition, would be more time-consuming and complex. Instead, the federal government maintains a currency that serves as a convenient medium of exchange in the United States and around the world. One irony of the Cold War was that the American dollar was the preferred currency on black markets in communist countries because citizens had little faith in the purchasing power of their own currencies.

Consider some other examples of government activities that facilitate private commerce:

- **Information.** Each of us assumes that when we pull up to a gas station and pay for 10 gallons of gas, we will actually get 10 gallons of gas in our tank. However, that is not a particularly easy thing to monitor; the process of buying gas would be far more inconvenient if each of us had to spend time verifying that the gas station delivered exactly what it promised. Instead, we empower a government agency to certify the accuracy of the pumps. We pay one person to test the pumps (or the quality of our drinking water or the cleanliness of a restaurant kitchen) so that the rest of us don't have to. In other cases, government can require firms to provide certain kinds of information, such as mandatory food labeling. The goal of such policies is to reduce the costs of gathering information, which are a significant component of transactions costs.
- **Regulation.** Laws that protect consumers can spare them the time and expense of taking extraordinary measures to protect themselves. Consider basic financial transactions such as buying a mutual fund, opening a retirement account, or even putting money in a checking account. Each of these acts involves handing over large amounts of money to complete strangers; in the absence of legal protection, each would be a very risky act. Individual investors would have to spend a great deal of time researching all of the institutions with which he does business. Instead, we have created institutions (albeit imperfect) such as the Securities and Exchange Commission that guard against deception, fraud, and other

misdeeds. We can mail off a check to Vanguard or Fidelity, or deposit a check in a savings account, and be relatively certain that the money will not be stolen (and that the government will act on our behalf if it is). Although government regulation is often blamed for higher costs—and, indeed, that can be the case, as will be covered later in this chapter—regulation can also *reduce* the cost of doing business by reducing risk and uncertainty.

8.1.3 Promoting Competition

A key benefit of markets is that they inspire competition among firms, which promotes innovation, lower prices, and better service. All of this is good for consumers. Firms, on the other hand, would prefer to avoid such competition. They can earn higher profits if they are the only firm doing a certain kind of business (a **monopoly**) or if they can somehow agree with other firms in the same business to avoid competing on price (**collusion**). Government enforces antitrust regulations to ensure that markets are competitive and to prevent firms from colluding.

Consider a simple example. If an entrepreneur is selling lemonade on a street corner for $1.00 a cup and it only costs $0.10 a cup to make (the marginal cost), then we would expect other vendors to enter the market. A second entrepreneur could sell lemonade for $0.50 a cup on the opposite corner and still make handsome profits. And a third vendor might soon enter the market and drive the price down to $0.25; he might also add different flavors and sell food, too. Every time a new vendor enters the market and lowers the price, all of the other vendors must follow suit or risk losing all of their sales. No one is going to pay $1.00 for lemonade if it is on sale across the street for $0.25. In a highly competitive market, we would expect the price of the good to be driven down near its marginal cost. In this case, a vendor could enter the market and sell lemonade for $0.11 a glass—just above its marginal cost—and still earn a profit. All of this is terrific for thirsty lemonade drinkers. It is not necessarily good for the profits of the lemonade vendors. Each new entrant to the market drives down the market price of lemonade, lowering the profit margin on every cup sold.

For that reason, a monopolist, a firm that controls the entire market, will behave differently. How will he choose to price his product in order to maximize profits? The less he charges, the more cups he will sell—but he will also earn a lower profit on each cup sold. Because he controls the entire market, the monopolist can choose the price and quantity that he will sell, as the graph on the next page illustrates.

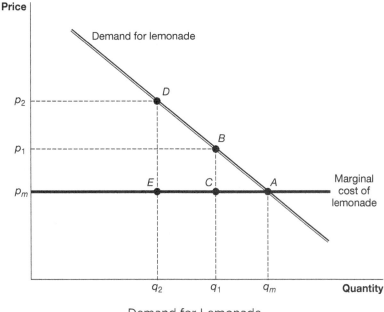

Demand for Lemonade

In a competitive market, we would expect the price to be driven down to the marginal cost of lemonade p_m, which results in an output of q_m (point A). Any vendor who tries to sell lemonade at a price appreciably above marginal cost will lose all of his sales to a rival firm willing to sell for less. A monopolist is different, however, in that it has **market power,** or **pricing power.** Since a monopolist controls the whole market, the firm's production decisions determine the market price and output of a good. If a monopolist sells a product at a price above marginal cost, there are no competing firms to steal away business.

As you should see from the diagram, the monopolist lemonade salesman does not earn the highest profits by pricing his product at the price for which it would be sold in a competitive market. Instead, the monopolist can earn higher profits by selling fewer cups of lemonade at a higher price. If he prices the product at p_1, he will sell q_1 cups and earn profits represented by the rectangle p_1BCp_m. At p_2, he will sell q_2 cups and earn profits represented by the rectangle p_2DEp_m.

To understand why the monopolist would choose a different level of production than the competitive equilibrium, we must understand a crucial feature of monopoly pricing: if a monopolist lowers his price, he will sell additional units, *but he will receive a lower price, not only for the incremental sales, but for all the units that he would have sold anyway.* Thus, by lowering price, a monopolist earns more revenue from the incremental sales but *less revenue* from the buyers who would have been willing to pay more. Since the vendor must decide on his price when he makes his sign at the beginning of the day, he cannot charge $1.00 to some buyers and $0.50 to others. He would like to do this (see the box on price discrimination, p. 259). For now, we will assume that he must offer the same price to everyone, regardless of their underlying willingness to pay.

As a result, a monopolist will choose a lower level of production and a higher market price than a competitive market would produce. The monopolist's decision to produce less than the quantity that would be produced in a competitive market does not merely transfer money from consumers (paying higher prices) to the monopolist (earning higher profits); it also generates deadweight loss, which is the source of the market failure related to noncompetitive markets. Because the monopolist is selling the product above marginal cost, there are potential welfare-enhancing transactions that do not take place, as the graph below illustrates.

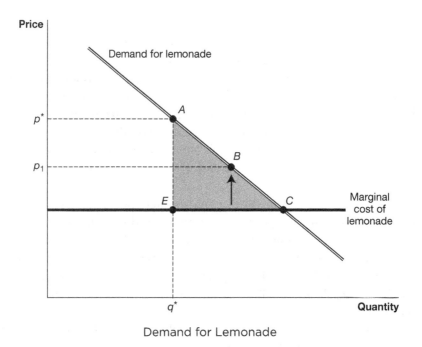

Demand for Lemonade

Assume that the monopolist maximizes profits by selling q^* cups of lemonade at price p^* (point A). As the demand curve shows, some consumers would be willing to pay p_1 for a cup of lemonade; p_1 is greater than the marginal cost of producing a cup of lemonade, so it would be a profitable sale (point *B*). Because of a monopolist's decision to maximize profits by holding price above marginal cost, transactions that would have benefited both buyer and seller do not take place. The total deadweight loss is represented by triangle *ACE*.

You should recognize that a group of firms has an incentive to behave like a monopolist, reducing their collective output, and then share the higher profits. Suppose four lemonade vendors are operating on the four corners of an intersection. In a competitive market, each will aggressively cut prices in order to steal business away from the others, driving down the price of lemonade toward the marginal cost of $0.25 a glass. But further suppose that a monopolist would maximize profits by selling fewer glasses of lemonade for $1.00 each. The four lemonade vendors could increase their collective profits if they agreed not to compete, but instead to set a common price of $1.00. This collusion among firms generates the same deadweight loss as if a monopolist were running a single stand. Firms that agree to collude and act like a monopolist are called a **cartel.**

The incentive for merchants to collude rather than compete has long been recognized. Adam Smith wrote in the *Wealth of Nations,* "People of the same trade seldom meet together, even for merriment or diversion, but the conversation ends in a conspiracy against the public, or in some contrivance to raise prices." One role of government is to make and enforce antitrust laws that (1) forbid monopolies or, in cases where that may not be practical, regulate their output or prices in ways that maximize overall social welfare; (2) forbid firms from colluding in markets that would otherwise be competitive.

················· | **POLICY IN THE REAL WORLD** | ·················

Why Does Your Student ID Get You a Discount?: Price Discrimination

In the monopoly examples above, the lemonade vendor faces a quandary: in order to sell more cups, he must reduce the price on all cups sold, including those to people who would have paid more. This suggests a better way for maximizing profits. What if the vendor could charge different prices to different customers, depending on their willingness to pay? That is exactly what many firms seek to do. The practice is called **price discrimination.** It maximizes profits for the firm, since the firm can sell lemonade to some customers for $1.00 and to others for only $0.11. It also eliminates the deadweight loss, since all profitable transactions will take place. The vendor will sell additional glasses of lemonade up to the point at which price equals marginal cost, *provided that he doesn't have to lower the price for other customers willing to pay much more.*

But how is that possible? The lemonade vendor—and most other retail establishments—has to post a price. How can that price be different for different customers? The answer is that firms find very creative ways to use differential pricing. For example, grocery stores have long used coupons to offer discounts to some customers. Those with a lower willingness to pay will take the time to cut out the coupons; other customers will pay the retail price without the discount.

Movie theaters charge different prices based on the time of day. The film is not different, but the matinee is usually cheapest, offering a chance for those with the lowest willingness to pay to see the movie at a less popular time. Department stores use sales to charge different customers different prices. Some customers pay full price when merchandise is first offered for sale, such as the new spring clothes. After some time has passed, the store will mark down the remaining merchandise, and other customers will buy merchandise "on sale."

Of course, the Internet makes it very easy for retailers to price-discriminate, since there is no longer a single posted price. Different customers may be offered different prices online based on the frequency of their past purchases, the way in which they reached the site, or other information that provides insight into their willingness to pay.

Even our hypothetical lemonade vendor could use price discrimination to boost his profits. Suppose, for example, that he recognized that tourists have the highest willingness to pay ($1.50), that local customers are willing to pay $1.00, but that students can seldom afford more than $0.25. Obviously he could not post a price charging tourists $1.50, since no one would identify himself as such. Instead, he would post a price of $1.50 but offer a "frequent lemonade card" to his regular customers, entitling them to a discounted price of $1.00. And all students with a valid student ID would pay only $0.25!

. . . .

8.1.4 Ameliorating Externalities

Markets will fail to achieve a socially efficient outcome when the activity involved harms a party or parties who are not represented in the transaction. As you will recall from the examples in the introduction, "spammers" do not consider the inconvenience they impose on e-mail users when they choose to blast an e-mail advertising vitamin supplements to millions of users who would prefer not to receive it. Nor do many drivers take into account the quantity of carbon dioxide (CO_2) that their cars emit when they buy a vehicle or make a commuting decision—and yet those emissions impose a cost on the rest of the planet, literally. These are examples of negative externalities, which arise when individuals or firms engage in an activity that imposes a cost on a party or parties not involved in the transaction, as was explained in greater detail in Chapter 4. In the case of positive externalities, market participants do not necessarily take into account the positive benefits that their private behavior generates for a third party or parties.

When some market behavior is associated with a significant positive or negative externality, the market outcome will not be consistent with what is best for society overall. In the case of a negative externality, a private transaction imposes a cost on the rest of society that the participants in the transaction do not take into account. Most environmental problems are the result of negative externalities. Consider the case of a private firm that burns coal in the process of making steel, which it then sells to private customers. Burning coal emits pollutants into the air such as sulfur dioxide (SO_2) and CO_2, which impose a cost on members of society *regardless of whether or not they buy steel.* Indeed, neither the steel producer nor its customers takes this cost into account in making production and consumption decisions.

As with most other market transactions, the level of output and the market price of steel will be determined by supply and demand. We assume that steel companies in a competitive market will produce steel up until the point where the marginal cost of producing a ton of steel is equal to the market price. Thus, if the market price of steel is $30 a ton and a company can produce it for $25 a ton, the company will produce as much as it can. Other firms will also be increasing their production. As overall steel production goes up, however, at some point the price of scarce inputs—coal, labor, etc.—will likely rise as well. This will push up the marginal cost of making a ton of steel. Firms will continue to increase supply until it is no longer profitable—which is the point at which a ton of steel can be produced for exactly the price at which it can be sold. Thus, if steel is selling for $30 a ton, no rational firm will expand production beyond the point where a ton can be produced for $30. But if the market price of steel rises to $45, producers will expand their output until the marginal cost of production reaches $45 a ton. The key insight here is that the supply curve for any given firm is determined by the marginal cost of production for the relevant good or service.

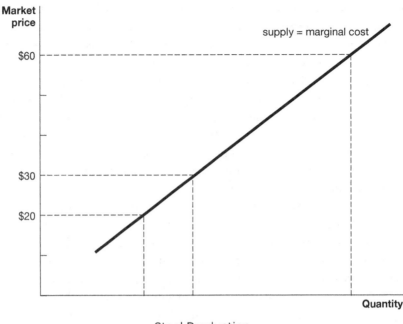

Steel Production

Meanwhile, the consumers of steel are making similar calculations. Consumers will purchase steel up until the point where the marginal benefit (the incremental utility derived from consuming one more unit of steel) is equal to the market price. If a consumer derives $50 of utility from a ton of steel that can be purchased for $30, then he will demand as much as possible. If for some reason the price of steel rises to $55 a ton, the same consumer will buy none. No rational consumer will pay $55 for a product from which he derives only $50 of incremental utility.

In the case of the Red Lobster example, the problem with the unlimited crab special was that the price for refills was zero; customers kept going back until they got absolutely no incremental utility from one more helping. If those extra helpings cost $5 instead, some customers would have stopped going back earlier—at the point at which the marginal benefit of one more serving of crab was worth $5. And if the extra helpings cost $15, even fewer customers would have gone back for the refill—only the real crab lovers, those for whom the marginal benefit of another helping is at least $15.

Again, the important point is that an individual's demand curve is determined by the underlying marginal benefit that he or she receives from the

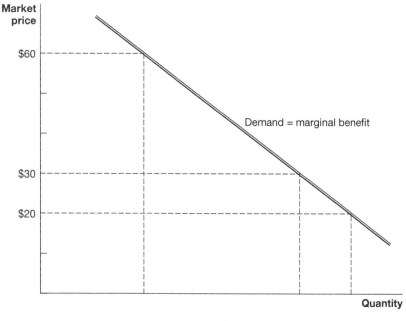

Steel Consumption

relevant good or service. If the market price of steel is $50 a ton, then any individual consumer will buy steel up until the point where the incremental benefit from one more ton is $50. Think about it. If a consumer derives $52 in utility from a ton of steel that can be purchased for $50, then he will keep buying more. We can assume that each ton of steel generates slightly less benefit than the last, perhaps because the buyer is slowly exhausting the most productive uses for it. (In the case of the crab legs, we assume that each additional refill generates less utility because the customer is slowly becoming satiated.) Whether it is crab, steel, or any other good or service, we can assume that for the last unit sold—the so-called marginal sale—the benefit generated for the purchaser is equal to the market price.

Thus, the market price and output for a good like steel is determined by the intersection of supply and demand (point *A* in graph on p. 264). We can now also infer that this market equilibrium is the point at which the marginal cost of producing one more unit of steel is exactly equal to the marginal benefit provided to the consumer. This outcome helps to explain why markets are so efficient in allocating society's resources: firms will produce a good or service up until the point where the costs incurred in production are equal to the benefits provided for consumers—no more and no less.

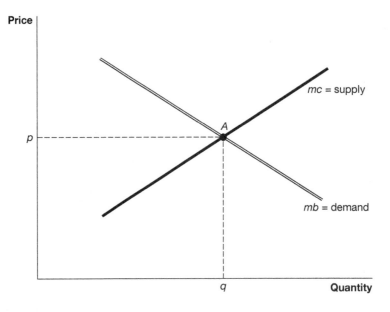

Steel Production: Private Marginal Cost and Benefit

Unfortunately from the standpoint of society overall, there is a problem— or market failure—associated with the steel example. The environmental costs of burning coal to produce steel do not appear in the calculations of either the firms producing steel or the consumers buying it. Both parties behave as if their decisions have no impact on the rest of society, which is not the case. From a social-efficiency standpoint, we need to make an important distinction:

- The **private marginal cost** of manufacturing steel is the cost borne by the steel companies (coal, iron ore, labor, etc.) to produce one additional unit of steel.
- The **social marginal cost** is the cost borne by *all of society* to produce one additional unit of steel. This includes the private costs paid by the steel company *plus* the additional costs that the negative externality imposes on third parties, such as the health and environmental costs associated with CO_2 and SO_2 emissions.

From the standpoint of overall social welfare, the optimal level of steel production is the point at which *social* marginal cost is equal to *social* marginal benefit. In other words, the benefit to society from producing one more unit of steel is equal to the cost to society of producing that steel. (We will assume that

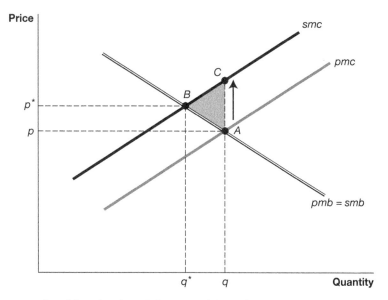

Steel Production: Private and Social Marginal Profit

the social marginal benefit of consuming steel is equal to the private marginal benefit, since there is no significant externality associated with the consumption of steel.)

You should note that the optimal level of steel production from society's standpoint is point *B*, which represents a lower level of output and a higher market price compared to the market outcome when only private incentives are taken into account (point *A*). As a result, the triangle *ABC* represents the social inefficiency, or deadweight loss, associated with the negative externality. At each point in that triangle, the social cost of producing steel exceeds the social benefit, and yet that steel still gets produced as long as there is no correction for the negative externality. In other words, the market will produce *too much* steel from an overall social-welfare standpoint because neither producers nor consumers take into account the costs imposed on the rest of society as the result of their private behavior.

A negative externality can also be caused by the *consumption* of a good or service—smoking, for example. There are no significant social costs associated with the production of cigarettes. However, smoking cigarettes imposes assorted costs on parties beyond the smoker: the annoyance and adverse health effects of secondhand smoke, the extra health-care costs for smokers that must be paid by other taxpayers, and so on. Each cigarette has a private

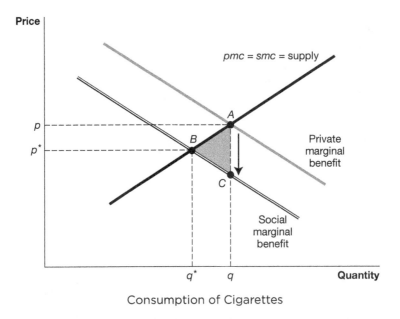

Consumption of Cigarettes

marginal benefit for the smoker but also some marginal damage imposed on nonsmokers. Thus, the social marginal benefit of smoking is lower than the private marginal benefit. Once again, the result is that smokers consume too many cigarettes from an overall social-welfare perspective.

You will note that the market outcome, point *A*, is a higher level of output and higher market price than point *B*, which is the socially optimal level of production. Triangle *ABC* represents social inefficiency, or deadweight loss, because the social marginal cost of smoking each of those cigarettes is greater than the social marginal benefit that they generate. From an overall social-welfare standpoint, smokers are consuming too many cigarettes because their consumption decision does not take into account the costs that their puffing imposes on the rest of society.

Private activities can also generate significant positive externalities. The economic logic is essentially the same: a private actor does not take into account the *positive* impact that his or her behavior has on the rest of society; as a result, the individual or firm will engage in too little of this behavior from the standpoint of overall social welfare. Consider the preservation of an historic home. In such a case, a homeowner will weigh the private costs and benefits of investing in the property and act accordingly. But an attractive historic home also benefits neighboring property owners: it is attractive to passersby, adds character to the neighborhood, and may even raise property values for the whole neighborhood. Thus, the social marginal benefit of exterior investments in the property is higher than the private marginal benefit; as a result, the property owner is likely to invest too little in the repair and upkeep of his historic home from the standpoint of the surrounding neighborhood.

One important role of government is to attempt to align private behavior with what is best for society overall. In the above examples, society would be better off if steel companies produced less steel, smokers consumed fewer cigarettes, and some property owners invested more in the exterior upkeep of their homes. How can that be accomplished? The Coase Theorem (Chapter 4) predicts that the parties affected by an externality will reach a private agreement to produce an efficient outcome if (1) the relevant property rights are clearly defined, and (2) the transactions costs are low. When these conditions are violated and a private agreement is not possible, public policy offers a number of tools for dealing with significant positive and negative externalities.

Regulation. A government entity can prohibit or limit behavior that has an adverse effect on third parties. Environmental regulations prohibit firms from dumping chemicals into the air or water. Smoking regulations spare airline passengers and office workers from breathing secondhand smoke. Blood alcohol limits protect innocent persons from dangerous drivers. In these cases, government acts on behalf of citizens who could potentially be harmed when a market activity generates a significant externality. Though it is less common, regulation could also be used to encourage or require activities that generate a positive externality. Some communities or housing associations enforce zoning regulations that enhance the overall aesthetic appeal of the neighborhood or community by setting standards for landscaping or even requiring certain colors of exterior paint. In other cases, government can designate buildings or even entire neighborhoods as historic landmarks, which prohibits private property owners in the designated area from destroying the buildings or making changes that are not consistent with the buildings' historic character.

Government has coercive power that can be used to compel outcomes that are different from what the market would otherwise deliver.

Pigovian tax (or subsidy). One elegant solution for dealing with a negative externality is to assess a tax on the offending activity that is equal to the difference between its private marginal cost and its social marginal cost. This remedy is named for English economist Arthur Pigou (1877–1959), who first formulated the concept of economic externalities. In theory, a **Pigovian tax** can induce market participants to behave in ways consistent with overall social welfare. Let's revisit the example of steel production. Suppose that the production of each ton of steel causes $2 in environmental damage. (The challenge of converting environmental damage and other intangible social costs

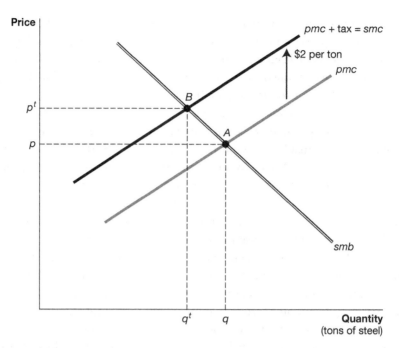

Steel Production with Pigovian Tax

into dollars and cents will be covered in Chapter 12.) A $2 tax levied on every ton of steel produced would raise the private marginal cost of steel production so that it is roughly equal to the social marginal cost. As a result, the market outcome, inclusive of the tax, produces a level of output at which social marginal benefit is equal to social marginal cost.

In the case where an externality results from consumption, a similar tax could be levied on consumers. Taxes on cigarettes and alcohol—and other so-called sin taxes—are often designed to discourage the consumption of goods that have broader social costs.

Subsidies obviously have the opposite effect; they encourage private activities with positive social spillovers by making the activities cheaper. Federal, state, and local governments provide significant funding for public transit in large part because moving commuters from private cars to trains or buses reduces traffic congestion and improves air quality, benefits that accrue to the public at large. The fare for riding public buses and trains is significantly lower than it would be if the system had to operate without a subsidy. (You should recognize why many localities offer free transit rides on New Year's Eve, when the social benefits of keeping drunk drivers off the road are potentially huge.) Similarly, governments often provide tax breaks or other incentives for property owners who restore historic buildings or leave open space undeveloped. In all of these cases, the goal of the subsidy is to encourage private activities that have broader social benefits.

Cap and trade (or allowance trading). Some recent policies for dealing with environmental externalities have combined the regulatory powers of government with the efficiency of the market. Under a **cap-and-trade system,** the government or some other regulatory body sets a cap for the total emissions of a certain pollutant, such as SO_2 or CO_2. The regulatory body then distributes emissions permits, or allowances, up to that cumulative level. If the program allows 1 million tons of some pollutant, then the agency in charge will distribute 1 million permits, each of which allows the permit holder to emit 1 ton of the pollutant. No individual or firm without a permit is allowed to emit the pollutant; the total allowable amount of a particular pollutant is fixed. That is the regulatory component of the program. The permits can be auctioned off by the government, or they can be distributed based on historical emissions or some other formula.

Once the permits are issued, they can be bought and sold, which leads to the same kinds of efficiencies as any other market. The firms that put the greatest value on the right to pollute will have the greatest willingness to pay for the permits. If firm A generates $10 million in profits in the process of emitting a ton of pollutant and firm B generates only $10,000, then firm A will buy up all the permits. From society's standpoint, that is an efficient outcome, since it generates the most economic output per ton of pollutant. The government can reduce total emissions over time by withdrawing allowance permits from the market or by reducing the quantity of emissions allowed for each permit.

A cap-and-trade system is already in place for several airborne pollutants. The U.S. Environmental Protection Agency (EPA) uses an allowance trading system to manage and reduce emissions of SO_2, a major cause of acid rain. In 1980, U.S. electric utilities generated 17.5 million tons of SO_2. In 1995, the EPA implemented a cap-and-trade program in which total allowable emissions will shrink annually to 8.95 million tons by 2010. Each allowance permits a utility to emit 1 ton of SO_2 annually; each year, the EPA will reduce the number of allowances in circulation until the target is hit.[3] The permits are traded on the New York Mercantile Exchange (NYMEX).

According to the EPA, the U.S. Acid Rain Program "has achieved greater emission reductions in such a short time than any other single program to control air pollution." And it has done so even less expensively than the cap-and-trade proponents expected. The reason lies in the efficiency of the system. The pollution externality is internalized, meaning that emitting SO_2

3. http://www.epa.gov/airmarkets/trading/index.html.

becomes a cost of doing business; firms must buy the right to pollute. Thus, profit-maximizing firms have an incentive not only to reduce emissions, but to do so as cheaply as possible. Firms that cannot or will not reduce their emissions must buy extra permits; as a result, they have a higher cost structure and will be punished in the marketplace. And they are likely buying those permits from firms that have been more successful in reducing emissions, exacerbating the cost advantage of low-emissions firms.

Allowance trading combines the precision of government regulation with the efficiency of the market. Government stipulates what must be accomplished; the market determines how that target can be achieved most efficiently. Any proposal to address global warming will almost certainly involve allowance trading, not only among firms, but between countries as well. The European Climate Exchange already facilitates trading of CO_2 permits in order to help member nations meet their commitments under the Kyoto Protocol. (As of January 2010, a 1-ton CO_2 allowance was selling for about €13, or $18.) The Chicago Climate Exchange hosts trading among American firms that have entered into a voluntary compact to reduce CO_2 emissions.

One thing you should recognize is that the party with the greatest willingness to pay for an emissions permit might be an individual or environmental group who would prefer not to have the pollutant emitted at all. Such a party can buy an emission allowance and then choose not to exercise it, effectively reducing the total output of emissions by whatever quantity the permit allowed. The next time you are searching for a birthday present for an environmentally minded friend, consider buying him the right to emit a ton of SO_2! If he owns the permit and doesn't use it, then the world will have 1 ton less pollution.[4]

8.1.5 Providing Public Goods

Some goods and services enhance overall social welfare but will not necessarily be provided by the market. That seems at odds with what we have learned about markets, which thrive by providing exactly what consumers want. If a good or service would generate social benefits in excess of social costs, why would profit-maximizing firms not produce it? The answer lies in the two specific attributes of a certain class of goods and services known as **public goods:**

---

4. The general public cannot buy and sell emissions permits at the New York Mercantile Exchange (NYMEX), where the SO_2 permits are traded. One must be a member of the exchange to have trading privileges. However, other firms act as emissions permits brokers. One can buy permits at www.cleanairconservancy.org/purchase.php.

1. **Nonrivalry.** A nonrival good or service can be offered to additional consumers at extremely low or even zero marginal cost. In other words, the good or service does not get "used up." A classic example is a lighthouse. There is a significant cost to building and maintaining a lighthouse. But once it is operational, there is zero cost associated with allowing more ships to use the lighthouse for navigational purposes. Or, to think of it another way, it is not significantly more expensive to protect a thousand ships from running aground than it is to protect just one.

2. **Nonexclusivity.** If a good or service is nonexclusive, then it is difficult or impossible to exclude individuals who have not paid for it from using it anyway. Again, a lighthouse illustrates the point. If a ship captain has not contributed to the cost of constructing and maintaining a lighthouse, there is no practical way of excluding him from using the lighthouse to navigate along shore. Counterterrorism is a more modern example. If some airline passengers pay for the security to prevent a hijacking, then every other passenger on the plane is made safer, too. It's not possible to protect some passengers on the plane from a hijacking and not others.

Goods and services that are nonexclusive create a powerful incentive for free riders, those who enjoy the benefits of some activity without contributing to its cost. If someone else has built a lighthouse that I can use free, why should I pay for it? Private firms cannot easily make profits by producing and selling nonexclusive goods, even when the total benefits they would provide far exceed the cost of production. Suppose that the 100 residents of a small fishing village would each derive $10,000 a year in higher income from a fish hatchery that restocked the waters with fish hatchlings to keep the commercial fishing industry viable—$1 million in higher annual earnings for the village in total. Further suppose that the hatchery only costs $100,000 a year to operate, or $1,000 per resident. This should be a business "no-brainer." A private firm could earn massive profits by operating the hatchery and charging each resident $5,000 a year—only half what the business is worth to each resident ($10,000) but much more than the hatchery costs to operate on a per capita basis ($1,000).

But who would actually pay the $5,000? The fish hatchlings released into the ocean are there for anyone to catch—both those who are customers of the hatchery and those who are not. Once the firm has a single customer, then no one else in town has any incentive to pay for the hatchery's service. But a single customer is not enough to make the business profitable. This business, which creates value far in excess of its costs, would likely go bust. Meanwhile, any voluntary effort by the residents of the fishing village to operate a hatchery would be plagued by similar free-rider problems. Many residents would be motivated by altruism to contribute to the hatchery; many others would opt instead to skip the contribution and catch the fish that others have paid for. The project would likely struggle to cover its costs.

Government can improve overall social welfare in these kinds of situations by providing public goods and then mandating contributions in the form of taxation. In the case of the fish hatchery, a local government would carry out this function. Alternatively, costs of the fish hatchery could be folded into the price of a commercial fishing license, which would be mandatory for all residents using the resource. In either case, the coercive power of government (or even an entity like a homeowners association) can enable groups to overcome free-rider problems and provide goods and services that improve overall social welfare.

The qualities of rivalry and exclusivity (or nonrivalry and nonexclusivity) can go a long way toward explaining how different kinds of goods and services are produced in a modern economy. Consider the following 2×2 matrix:

	RIVAL	NONRIVAL
EXCLUSIVE	1. PRIVATE GOODS Tennis shoes Automobiles iPods	2. CLUB GOODS Swimming pools Workout equipment Golf courses
NONEXCLUSIVE	3. COMMON-POOL RESOURCES Clean air International fisheries Wildlife	4. PUBLIC GOODS National defense Counterterrorism Lighthouse

The goods in quadrant 1 are rival and exclusive, meaning that they do get used up (the marginal cost is positive) and it is possible to prevent those who haven't paid for them from using them. If Adidas makes a pair of shoes, the marginal cost is not zero. And if you were to buy those shoes, it would be fairly easy for you to prevent anyone else from using them. The private sector can profitably produce and sell these kinds of goods and services.

The goods in quadrant 2 are exclusive but nonrival, meaning that it is possible to keep someone from using them, but they do not get "used up." At least up to some point, the marginal cost of allowing others to use the good is low or zero. If you were to build and maintain a golf course for yourself, the marginal cost of allowing other golfers to play would be very low (until the course became crowded). At the same time, if someone did not pay to play on your course, they would be easy to spot and remove. This category of goods is referred to as **club goods** because it may be practical to share them among the members of some group. The costs of building and maintaining the resource, such as a golf course, swimming pool, or fitness center, can be spread over the group; yet it is still possible to exclude those who have not paid their fair share. These goods are sometimes provided by membership organizations (e.g., country clubs), but they may also be provided by government (a municipal pool) or by the private sector (a private health club).

The goods in quadrant 3 are rival but nonexclusive, meaning that they do get "used up" (the marginal cost of producing them is greater than zero) but it is difficult or impossible to exclude those who haven't paid from using the resource. International fisheries are an example. When a fisherman catches a haul of tuna, there is, indeed, a marginal cost to harvesting that resource. There will be fewer tuna left for everyone else, and far fewer if the fishing method is particularly intense. Yet because property rights in international waters are ambiguous and difficult to enforce, it can be nearly impossible to exclude fishermen from exploiting the resource. In fact, even if property rights were allocated and enforced throughout the oceans, migratory species would still present a problem. Tuna or salmon might spend different parts of their lives in different areas, making it difficult to prevent one "property owner" from overexploiting the resource as it passes through his particular river or ocean. As you can probably infer, these **common-pool resources** present some of the greatest public policy challenges; neither the public nor private sector is well equipped to ensure that they are used in a socially efficient manner.

Finally, the goods and services in quadrant 4 are public goods. Government can enhance overall social welfare by providing these kinds of goods and services, which would otherwise be underprovided by the market due to their nonrival and nonexclusive nature.

··············· | **POLICY IN THE REAL WORLD** | ················

Autopsies as a Public Good: Why Plummeting Autopsy Rates May Endanger the Living

An autopsy is an examination of a body after death by a pathologist to determine the cause of death and other medical information. Obviously, an autopsy comes too late to help the person who has died. Autopsies are very important for the health of the rest of us, however. *The Economist* once noted that "an autopsy is perhaps the only way for the dead to speak to the living."[5] There are many potential benefits to listening.

Some medical relationships that are now obvious, such as the connection between smoking and lung cancer, were confirmed through autopsy. Other diseases were discovered by studying the dead, such as AIDS and Alzheimer's disease.[6] Autopsies help to teach medical students. Autopsies can also identify malpractice and even an occasional murder that might have otherwise passed as an accident.

Despite that, autopsy rates in the United Stattes have been falling steadily for decades, much to the consternation of public-health officials. In the 1940s, roughly half of all Americans who died were autopsied; that rate has now fallen to below 1 in 10.[7] *The Journal of the American Medical Association* devoted an entire issue in 1988 to the theme "Declaring War on the Nonautopsy."[8]

Why do we do too little of something that has the potential to make society better off? Because autopsies have a lot in common with lighthouses.

In short, autopsies have the key attributes of a public good. The benefits are nonrival; once a medical discovery is made or refined through autopsy, the marginal cost of sharing that knowledge with the rest of society is essentially zero. And the benefits are nonexclusive; it would be impossible to exclude particular individuals from the benefits of medical discoveries that were made as the result of autopsies.

While there are potentially large social benefits associated with autopsies, the parties associated with any individual autopsy decision have little to gain from an autopsy and may even have an incentive to discourage it.

- An autopsy is not something pleasant for the family of the deceased to contemplate.
- As hospitals and health-insurance companies look to trim costs, they are less likely to pay the cost of a postmortem exam.
- Doctors may believe that advanced tests and other medical technology provide enough information to make an autopsy unnecessary. (Unfortunately, they are wrong: studies have found that, as the result of autopsy, more than 25 percent of medical diagnoses are found to be wrong or questionable.[9]) Less well-intentioned doctors may be worried

---

5. "Autopsies: Dial One Yourself," *The Economist,* January 2, 1999.

6. Anahad O'Connor, "Deaths Go Unexamined and the Living Pay the Price," *New York Times,* March 2, 2004.

7. O'Connor, "Deaths Go Unexamined."

8. "Autopsies: Dial One Yourself."

9. O'Connor, "Deaths Go Unexamined."

about malpractice lawsuits. As *The Economist* points out, "The attending physician is the logical person to suggest a post-mortem exam; yet all too often a doctor's primary concern is covering his own *gluteus maximus*. An autopsy may prove a doctor wrong, or even negligent."[10]

Autopsy rates remain extremely low by historical standards. Hence, the recent headline in the Health and Fitness section of the *New York Times:* "Deaths Go Unexamined and the Living Pay the Price."[11]

....

8.2 PROVIDING A SOCIAL SAFETY NET

The chapter up to this point has focused on government's role in dealing with market failures. Well-designed government policy can lead to more efficient market outcomes. In other cases, although unfettered markets will deliver a perfectly efficient outcome, society will use government to reallocate resources to achieve some other social objective. Government policies may redistribute resources for equity purposes, even at the expense of efficiency. Policy makers may also implement policies that protect individuals from themselves; these paternalistic policies are predicated on the belief that a market outcome is not socially optimal, because some of the participants are not sufficiently informed or rational to act in their own best interest.

8.2.1 Redistribution

You should recall from Chapter 5 that society often faces a trade-off between equity and efficiency. Markets do an excellent job of allocating resources as efficiently as possible, meaning that they lead to outcomes in which resources are put to their most productive use. Yet you should also recall from Chapter 5 that any efficient outcome follows from some initial endowment of resources, which may be highly unequal. There is nothing inherently inefficient about a situation in which some individuals have 10,000 acres of fertile land and others have no land at all (and no other source of income). Such an arrangement may maximize the total harvest, since there are economies of scale associated with farming; it is more cost effective to have a single landowner farm one large plot than to have many farmers toiling on smaller plots. Yet this arrangement is inequitable and arguably unfair. A society may reasonably decide that overall welfare could be enhanced by taxing the income of the large landowners in

10. "Autopsies: Dial One Yourself."
11. O'Connor, "Deaths Go Unexamined."

order to feed the landless peasants or even by confiscating (with or without compensation) and redistributing some of their land. Government is often vested with these kinds of power.

Any policy designed to address the inequitable distribution of land described above would almost certainly be inefficient. If the government implemented land reform—breaking up large farms and distributing smaller parcels to landless peasants—the large landholders would expend resources to fight the redistribution. The beneficiaries of land reform would likely be less efficient farmers. Other property owners (of farmland and everything else) would consider their property rights less secure and would have less incentive to make investments in those assets. (A private firm is far less likely to spend hundreds of millions of dollars drilling for oil or prospecting for minerals if there is a significant chance that the government might expropriate the returns from those investments.) Similarly, a tax imposed on large landowners to provide some minimum income for landless peasants would have an efficiency cost. Depending on the size and design of the tax, the landowners might have an incentive to grow less or even leave some land uncultivated. Meanwhile, the beneficiaries of the income redistribution would have less incentive to invest in their own human capital and find nonagricultural work. The programs described here—and many other programs that use government to transfer wealth within society—are likely to reduce total economic output, or "shrink the pie."

But might they improve overall social welfare by leading to a fairer distribution of wealth—a smaller pie more evenly divided? The most important thing to remember is that there is no objective or uniform measure of utility, so what is best for society is in the eye of the beholder. Nonetheless, most societies believe, at least to some extent, that the total gain in social welfare from providing benefits to the indigent outweighs the total loss in social welfare from taxing wealthier individuals to pay for those benefits. Individuals are likely to disagree strenuously over the appropriate amount of redistribution; no data, discovery, or analysis can provide a "right" answer. As a result, programs that redistribute income—or have that effect—are among the most controversial of government activities because there are such strong ideological differences of opinion over the appropriate relationship between the individual and the larger community. What do the most privileged members of society owe to the least privileged, if anything? What should society be willing to give up in terms of overall economic output in order to provide a more equitable distribution of that wealth, if anything? There is no correct answer to those questions; both are likely to provoke fierce debate. Yet every society has to answer such questions, either implicitly or explicitly, in the process of designing its social safety net.

8.2.2 Paternalism

Government is sometimes called upon to protect people from themselves. According to classical economic theory, this should be unnecessary; individuals are rational actors who behave in ways that maximize their own utility. But life is sometimes more complex, and there is now abundant evidence that individuals engage in behaviors that are arguably irrational—from dropping out of high school to saving inadequately for retirement. **Paternalistic policies** seek to improve overall social welfare by preventing individuals from engaging in behavior that is likely to cause them harm in the long run.

Paternalistic policies are also a matter of sharp ideological disagreement. Does the fact that smoking is likely to cause premature death make it irrational? Not necessarily. Smokers may simply derive enough utility from the pleasures of smoking that it outweighs the adverse health effects. Economists Gary Becker (winner of the 1992 Nobel Prize in Economics) and Kevin Murphy have proposed a theory of rational addiction, which argues that consumers of addictive substances behave in ways that are consistent with maximizing utility over time.[12] On the other hand, researchers have compiled evidence that smokers underestimate the health risks of cigarettes and overestimate the likelihood that they will quit, suggesting that the behavior is not entirely rational. If that is the case, should government intervene in ways that effectively force individuals to maximize their own utility, such as making it harder for them to start smoking in the first place?

Consider the case of "payday lending." Suppose you are just a few dollars short, and payday is still a week away. Where might you get cash? For Americans without savings, one option is a payday loan. For a hefty fee, a payday lender—one facet of the larger "subprime" credit market—will lend money in exchange for a personal check that is held but not deposited. When the loan comes due, typically in a week or two (on payday, for example), the customer can have the lender deposit the check, get the check back in exchange for cash, or pay another fee to extend the loan. Payday loans are convenient and shockingly expensive. When the fees are converted into an annualized interest rate, the cost of borrowing can be 500 percent or more, prompting the Consumer Federation of America to label the business "legal loan-sharking."[13]

Some twenty states ban payday lending because it violates usury laws (which cap the rate of interest that can be legally charged). Are these states making consumers better off by protecting them from usurious loans that

---

12. Gary S. Becker and Kevin M. Murphy, "A Theory of Rational Addiction," *Journal of Political Economy* 96, no. 4 (August 1988): 675–700.

13. "Consumer Finance: Pay Dirt," *The Economist*, June 5, 1999.

would diminish their utility? Or are these states overstepping their bounds by preventing responsible adults from making up their own minds about payday loans and perhaps leaving some citizens much worse off as a result? As *The Economist* has noted, "For someone who is truly hard-up, the only thing worse than borrowing $200 at 600 percent APR may be not borrowing $200 at all." There is a clear economic rationale for limiting behavior that harms an innocent party; there is no similar consensus on the role of the state in protecting individuals from themselves. Nonetheless, paternalism (explicit or implicit) is a frequent rationale for government action in areas ranging from gambling to seat-belt use to retirement saving.

8.3 THE LIMITATIONS OF GOVERNMENT

Government can, in theory, make markets work more efficiently in order to improve overall social welfare. That does not guarantee, however, that a government solution will have its intended effect. Policy solutions are products of a political process; what emerges from that political process may bear little similarity to the theory that inspired government action in the first place. Thus, it is important that the chapter end on a cautionary note. While market outcomes often leave much to be desired, the cure may still be worse than the disease.

Just as markets have limitations in their capacity to deliver optimal outcomes, government policies also have limitations. Even when a market failure is clear, the policy adopted to ameliorate the problem may not work, or it may introduce new problems. Something that seems clear in theory, such as the negative environmental externality associated with driving, may not have a simple and elegant solution. Auto emissions contribute to climate change. But what is the appropriate Pigovian tax? What gasoline tax—the exact number of cents per gallon—would equate the social costs of driving (many of which are still uncertain) with the private costs? Even if experts could determine the optimal tax with certainty, there is no guarantee that Congress would implement that particular solution.

Meanwhile, "government" is not some monolithic entity. It is an institution made up of individuals who respond to incentives just like everyone else. The incentives for officials within government—both those who are elected and those who are otherwise hired—may not be consistent with a desired policy outcome, for several reasons. Individuals within government may act in their own interests—something as simple as protecting wasteful spending in order to preserve their own jobs, or something more insidious, such as making regulatory decisions that improve their chances of getting a job in the regulated industry after leaving government. Chapter 6 explained how organized interests can use the political process to secure benefits for themselves (e.g., subsidies, exclusive contracts, costly regulation imposed on competitors, etc.) that have no redeeming social purpose and are likely to diminish overall social welfare. The more expansive the powers of government, the more opportunities there are for bureaucrats, politicians, interest groups, and other actors to co-opt that power for personal gain.

Finally, when a government entity takes on a task, it often has neither the incentives nor the competitive pressures that inexorably lower costs and improve service in the private sector. This has two implications. First, a government agency or program is less likely to be as efficient or responsive as the private sector. An employee behind the counter at FedEx has more incentive to be friendly and helpful than an employee behind the counter at the Department of Motor Vehicles—which is a function of their respective institutional incentives. If the quality of service is poor at FedEx, then the company will lose customers (and profits) to competitors. The Department of Motor Vehicles has no competitors. Anyone who needs a driver's license must go there by law. He will not go less frequently if the service is bad, nor will he go more frequently if the service is good!

Second, there is no self-correcting mechanism for bad government. If a restaurant serves bad food or charges exorbitant prices, then customers will stop going there. The restaurant will either improve or close. If government imposes overly costly regulation or ineffective policies, there is no immediate market feedback. True, voters can punish elected officials, but that is a blunt instrument relative to the speed and intensity with which consumers can punish inefficiency in the private sector. A governor is unlikely to be voted out of office because of bad service at the Department of Motor Vehicles. And even if that were the case, it might take years!

Obviously, the goal of policy analysis is to find the most effective, least costly solution for any social problem and to design programs that do not fall prey to the problems described above. (For example, the Department of Motor Vehicles could solicit input on the quality of customer service and pay bonuses to its employees based on that feedback.) Still, it is crucial to recognize that what government *does* is not always synonymous with what government *should do*. Governments are vested with extraordinary powers, all of which can be used to enhance social welfare in ways outlined in this chapter or for less benign purposes.

The World Bank's *Doing Business* Report: The Staggering Costs of Bad Government

Would it be faster to register a new company with the government in Australia or Haiti? One would hope Haiti, a nation with a GDP per capita of only $612 in 2007, before the nation was further ravaged by a massive earthquake in 2010. The government presumably has better things to do than make entrepreneurs wade through red tape.[14]

Wrong. According to a World Bank study *Doing Business in 2005,* it takes an average of 203 days to register a new company in Haiti, compared to 2 days in Australia. What about the cost of starting a new business? One might expect countries most in need of development to make it cheapest to begin new ventures. Wrong again. In Sierra Leone, a potential entrepreneur must pay more than a year's worth of income for the average person to register a new business with the government. In Denmark, it's free.

The World Bank study of the costs of doing business around the globe provided striking evidence for what development experts had long believed: governments in poor countries often erect pointless and expensive regulatory hurdles that impinge significantly on economic growth. The study estimated that if the worst bureaucratic offenders would modify their regulatory requirements to resemble the best, it would boost their annual growth rate by 2.2 percentage points.

Petty regulation and corruption often go hand in hand. *The Economist* noted in its review of the World Bank study, "The more irksome the rule, the greater the incentive to bribe officials not to enforce it." For their part, poorly paid bureaucrats are keen to erect or maintain such roadblocks because the bribes make up a significant portion of their compensation.

One of the most illuminating examples of this process comes from Peruvian economist Hernando de Soto. In a seminal book published in 2000, the *Mystery of Capital,*[15] he and fellow team members documented their efforts to open a one-person clothing stall on the outskirts of Lima as a legally registered business. He and his researchers vowed that they would not pay

---

14. "The Global Business Environment: Measure First, Then Cut," *The Economist,* September 11, 2004.
15. Hernando de Soto, *The Mystery of Capital: Why Capitalism Triumphs in the West and Fails Everywhere Else* (New York: Basic Books, 2000).

bribes so that their efforts would reflect the full cost of complying with the law. (In the end, they were asked for bribes on ten occasions and paid them twice to prevent the project from stalling completely.) The team worked six hours a day for forty-two weeks in order to get eleven different permits from seven different government bodies. Their efforts, not including the time, cost $1,231, or thirty-one times the monthly minimum wage in Peru—all to open a one-person shop.[16]

The sad irony, of course, is that while such governments are imposing costly and needless regulations on prospective businesses, they are failing at many of the most basic and essential functions of government, such as defining property rights and enforcing the rule of law.

8.4 CONCLUSION

Government plays a crucial role in making a modern economy work. At the most basic level, good public policies create the institutions that make markets possible, such as property rights and the rule of law. Government can also improve overall social welfare by intervening in cases of market failure and by providing public goods. But not all government is good government. Government can and should perform certain roles and avoid others. The essence of good public policy, of course, is telling the difference.

16. This paragraph is from my *Naked Economics: Undressing the Dismal Science* (New York: Norton, 2002), p. 211. The original research is from "No Title," *The Economist,* March 31, 2001.

FOR DISCUSSION

The Drug Problem: Pharmaceutical Pricing

There is good news for victims of Gaucher's disease, an enzyme deficiency that causes fatty material to collect in the spleen, liver, kidneys, lungs, brain, and bone marrow. The Genzyme Corporation produces a drug called Cerezyme that can treat the disorder. There is bad news, too. The annual dosage of Cerezyme for an adult can cost as much as $500,000—roughly 90 percent of which is profit. Each unit of the drug costs $0.37 to produce; Genzyme sells it for ten times that price.[17]

Pharmaceutical products improve the lives of millions of people every year. In many of those cases, the drugs are literally the difference between life and death. But at what price should those pills or injections be sold? If the price is too high, then some sick individuals will not be able to afford the drugs that could save or improve their lives. If the price is too low, then pharmaceutical companies will have little or no incentive to develop such drugs in the first place. Unfortunately the "market" for these potentially life-saving drugs doesn't resolve this tension.

Prescription drugs are different than televisions or designer clothes. The distinction is not merely that people can live without a television or a fancy handbag, but also that prescription drugs have the key attributes of a public good. First, they are largely nonrival, meaning that the marginal cost of providing the life-saving drugs to additional people is usually quite low. That is because the bulk of the expense is in the discovery, not the production. The Tufts Center for the Study of Drug Development has pegged the average cost of bringing a new prescription drug to market at roughly $1 billion, including the cost of false starts and the clinical trials necessary to prove that a drug is safe and effective.[18] But once a drug is discovered and proved safe and effective, the cost of manufacturing the medicine is likely to be much lower. The pills are actually quite cheap.

And drugs are nonexclusive. The *knowledge* is what is valuable about prescription drugs; once a discovery has been made, imitators can easily copy the formula. As health economist Henry Grabowski has explained, "Imitators could free ride on the

17. Geeta Anand, "Why Genzyme Can Charge So Much for Cerezyme," *Wall Street Journal,* November 16, 2005.

18. Joseph A. DiMasi, Ronald W. Hansen, and Henry G. Grabowski, "The Price of Innovation: New Estimates of Drug Development Costs," *Journal of Health Economics* 22, no. 2 (2003): 151–185; updated by e-mail correspondence with Peg Hewitt, research librarian at the Tufts Center for the Study of Drug Development, January 26, 2010.

innovator's FDA approval and duplicate the compound for a small fraction of the originator's costs."[19]

As a result, we would expect private firms to underinvest in innovative prescription drugs. Private firms would be wary of spending hundreds of millions of dollars on the requisite research and development as long as imitators can steal the profits once a compound has been proven effective and safe. Is that what happens? No—because government plays a crucial role in shaping the private market for pharmaceutical products. In the United States and other developed countries, governments grant patents to individuals and firms that make discoveries, giving them the exclusive right to produce and sell the new product for a certain period of time. Here, pharmaceutical patents are granted for twenty years from the date of application. Since the application is usually made while the drug is in development, the commercial lifetime is likely to be shorter (an average of twelve years).[20] Once a patent has expired, other companies are free to copy, produce, and sell chemically equivalent versions of the drug, which are known as generic drugs.

As economic theory would predict, patents do appear to have a significant impact on private investments in research and development. A survey of pharmaceutical executives found that research and development expenditures would be 64 percent lower in the absence of patent protection. This is consistent with real-world experience. In countries that have changed their laws to provide more expansive patent coverage (Japan in 1976 and Canada in 1987), private research and development expenditures increased sharply as a result. There is no country in the world with an innovative pharmaceutical industry that does not also have significant patent protection for new drugs.[21]

But patent protection solves one problem (underinvestment in pharmaceutical research and development) and creates a new one: patent protection enables companies to charge prices far above marginal cost for important new drugs. When the *Wall Street Journal* examined why Genzyme could sell its drug for Gaucher's disease for ten times its cost of production, the answer turned out to be simple: "Because it can. There is no competition, patients are desperate and most insurers pay."[22]

The resulting outcomes are both imperfect from a social-welfare standpoint and highly politically contentious. Consider some of the major public policy challenges:

- **Monopoly pricing.** A patent creates a legal monopoly for the firm that owns or acquires it. As we learned earlier in the chapter, monopolists charge prices

19. Henry Grabowski, "Patents, Innovation and Access to New Pharmaceuticals," *Journal of International Economic Law* 5, no. 4 (2002): 849–860.

20. Grabowski, "Patents, Innovation"; updated by e-mail correspondence with Dr. Grabowski, Duke University, January 26, 2010.

21. Grabowski, "Patents, Innovation."

22. Anand, "Why Genzyme Can Charge So Much."

significantly above marginal cost, creating deadweight loss. In the case of new drugs, that wedge between the marginal cost of producing a drug and the price at which a company chooses to sell it can have enormous social welfare consequences: some patients may not be able to afford drugs when they are sold at market prices, even though they could afford to buy the drug if it were sold at marginal cost. It is a potential human tragedy when a patient cannot afford a treatment that costs $10,000 a month; it's all the worse when the cost of actually producing that medicine is only $75.

- **Price discrimination.** To economists, the most efficient solution to the monopoly pricing problem is to allow pharmaceutical companies to sell drugs to different consumers at different prices. Wealthy consumers would pay higher prices, and less wealthy consumers would pay prices closer to marginal cost, enabling the drug company to maximize profits without generating any deadweight loss. This price disparity can be particularly pronounced across countries. Consumers in poor African countries, for example, can only afford to pay a fraction of what American consumers can afford to pay for drugs to manage HIV/AIDS. But while it makes economic sense for pharmaceutical companies to charge based on "willingness to pay," consumers and politicians often recoil at the practice. In the 2000 presidential campaign, Al Gore sharply criticized a drug company for selling a prescription arthritis drug for $38 a month for dogs *and the same drug* for $108 a month for humans. Meanwhile, some pharmaceutical companies have balked at charging lower prices for drugs in developing countries—leaving many poor people without medicine at all—for fear that the cheap drugs would be reimported to the United States and sold on the black market.

- **Rare diseases.** Pharmaceutical companies are profit-maximizing firms. They make money (and generate enormous social benefits) by creating products that large numbers of people are willing to pay for. However, this equation does not work well when it comes to rare diseases. It is just as costly to develop treatments or cures for rare diseases as it is for common afflictions, but the potential market is much smaller. Drug companies can make more money by focusing on common but relatively minor maladies than they can by developing cures for serious but rare illnesses. To use an extreme example, a rational firm would invest far more in research to find a cure for male-pattern baldness than for Huntington's disease, a fatal genetic disorder that affects fewer than 10 people per 100,000.[23]

Congress recognized this incentive problem and passed the Orphan Drug Act in 1983, which provides assorted financial incentives (such as grants for research and tax credits for R & D) to pharmaceutical companies working on

---

23. *Wikipedia, the Free Encyclopedia.*

diseases that afflict fewer than 200,000 persons. The effect has been significant: the number of drugs introduced for such diseases increased twelve-fold in the ensuing years, and the number of deaths from rare diseases fell both in absolute numbers and relative to deaths from other causes.[24]

- **Common diseases in poor countries.** Malaria kills roughly 1 million people a year; virtually none of those deaths occurs in the developed world. Many other serious diseases affect predominantly poor people in the tropics. The sad fact is that it is difficult to earn profits developing drugs to help populations with little cumulative purchasing power. As a result, only 13 of the roughly 12,000 new drugs introduced between 1975 and 1997 were intended specifically to deal with tropical diseases.[25] Some philanthropic ventures have attempted to fill this market void. The major pharmaceutical companies have developed and donated drugs for diseases such as river blindness and leprosy. The Bill & Melinda Gates Foundation has made "fighting the forgotten diseases" of the developing world a major thrust of its grant-making efforts. These efforts should not obscure the basic economics of pharmaceutical research: profit-maximizing firms will not devote significant resources to developing drugs to fight diseases that afflict primarily poor populations.

- **Patent length and scope.** Patents promote innovation and are indispensable in the pharmaceutical industry. But for how long should a firm have an exclusive right to sell a new drug? Pharmaceutical patents involve a public policy trade-off: they encourage beneficial innovation but then make such innovation less accessible. The length of the patent is what intermediates these social benefits and social costs. A longer patent period raises the economic return to innovation; of course, it does so by allowing pharmaceutical companies to hold prices above marginal cost for a longer period. A shorter patent period obviously does the opposite. Policy makers must navigate this balance while simultaneously entertaining more radical notions, such as using government funds to "buy out" patents for important drugs. In this scenario, the government would buy a patent from the innovating company for a sum equal to the drug's expected revenues while under patent. The government would then immediately put the drug in the public domain, enabling generic producers to sell it cheaply years before the patent would have expired.

The market for prescription drugs is, in fact, a hybrid of public and private activity. Government makes innovation possible in the first place by creating and enforcing a property right for intellectual property. But that is only the beginning of the complex and imperfect process for using public policy to steer private behavior in a way that improves health and saves lives to the greatest extent possible.

24. Grabowski, "Patents, Innovation."
25. Grabowski, "Patents, Innovation."

QUESTIONS

1. Given that government-bestowed patents give firms monopoly pricing power, do governments also have the right, or even the obligation, to regulate drug prices while under patent? Why, or why not?

2. Should Americans be allowed to purchase prescription drugs in countries with lower prices, such as Canada? Why, or why not? Why are prices lower in those countries?

3. How would you explain to a congressional candidate why it may be ethical for a drug company to charge one customer five times as much as another customer for the same drug—indeed, why it is arguably *unethical* to forbid the practice?

4. Leaders in developing countries have argued that they should be able to "copy-cat" patented life-saving drugs that their citizens could not otherwise afford. Do you agree?

5. Should the U.S. government allocate funds—taxpayers' money—to provide incentives for pharmaceutical companies to develop drugs and immunizations that may save millions of lives in the developing world, such as a malaria vaccine? Why, or why not?

6. Agree or disagree: the only thing worse than becoming seriously ill is becoming seriously ill with a disease that rich people don't usually get.

7. Explain the difference between basic and applied research. Given that many lucrative drugs are developed using knowledge generated by government-financed research, should drug companies have to reimburse the government for this "input"? How could that be achieved in practice?

8. Under what circumstances, if any, should government use taxpayers' money to buy out a patent? Could you envision circumstances in which a drug or treatment were so valuable that the government should simply revoke the patent?

KEY CONCEPTS

★ A market failure is a situation in which market transactions do not lead to a socially efficient allocation of resources.

★ Government creates and enforces a property right, which is the ownership or control of a parcel of property, an asset, or even an idea or artistic creation.

★ Defining and defending property rights is considered to be one of the most fundamental and important responsibilities of government because it provides the foundation on which a market economy operates.

★ Government can facilitate markets by providing information, institutions, infrastructure, and other kinds of support that make private market transactions less costly.

★ Firms can earn higher profits if they are the only firm doing a certain kind of business (a monopoly), or if they can somehow agree with other firms in the same business to avoid competing on price (collusion). Government enforces antitrust regulations to ensure that markets are competitive and to prevent firms from colluding.

★ Price discrimination maximizes profits for a firm with market power by selling the same product or service to different consumers at different prices, depending on their willingness to pay. It also eliminates the deadweight loss, as all profitable transactions will take place.

★ A negative externality arises when individuals or firms engage in an activity that imposes a cost on a party or parties not involved in the transaction. In the case of a positive externality, market participants do not take into account the positive benefits that their private behavior generates for a third party or parties.

★ Public goods have two salient characteristics that make it hard for the market to provide them, even when the potential social benefits far exceed the social costs: they are nonrival, meaning that the good or service can be offered to additional consumers at extremely low, or even zero, marginal cost; and they are nonexclusive, meaning that it is difficult or impossible to exclude individuals who have not paid for the good or service from using it anyway.

★ Government policies may redistribute resources for equity purposes, even at the expense of efficiency. Policy makers may also implement policies that protect individuals from themselves. These paternalistic policies are predicated on the belief that a market outcome is not socially optimal because some of the participants are not sufficiently informed or rational to act in their own best interest.

★ Government can, in theory, make markets work more efficiently in order to improve overall social welfare. That does not guarantee, however, that a government solution will have its intended effect. Governments are vested with extraordinary powers, all of which can be used to enhance social welfare in ways outlined in this chapter—or for less benign purposes.

TOOLS FOR ANALYSIS

CHAPTER 9

Gathering and Measuring Information

QUESTIONS AND ANSWERS

As a student of public policy, you are likely to be interested in the answers to the following seemingly basic questions:

Is Global Income Inequality Growing or Narrowing?

The graphic on the next page suggests that rich countries are the primary beneficiaries of recent economic trends. Each circle represents a country. The x-axis represents the nation's real per capita GDP in 1980; the y-axis plots the nation's growth in GDP per capita over the ensuing twenty years. When a line is fitted to map the relationship between GDP per capita for a sample of countries in 1980 and subsequent economic growth in those countries over the next two decades, it slopes upward, demonstrating that the richest countries in 1980 tended also to grow faster over the next two decades. Opponents of globalization might seize on such data as evidence that globalization merely exacerbates global inequality—rich nations are growing richer faster than poor nations.

That conclusion may be technically accurate and yet misleading in an important way. A different look at the same data show that income inequality *among the world's people* has actually fallen over the past several decades. The key distinction lies in the unit of observation: countries versus people. In comparing how countries have fared over the past two decades, we obscure the important fact that some countries are much larger than others. Comparing the economic performance of nations gives equal weight to China and New Zealand, even though China has over 1 billion people and New Zealand has around 4 million. Thus, the second graphic contains the same circles as the first, but the circles have been drawn in proportion to the nation's population. As you can see, India and China, each with populations over 1 billion, grew rapidly over the past twenty-five years. Those two countries alone are so large that their rapid growth has narrowed income inequality among the world's people.

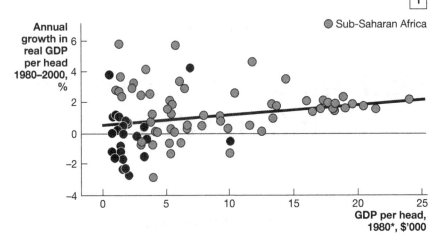

An Alternative View: Growth in GDP per Head

Growth GDP per Head, Proportional to Population

*1996 prices.

Source: From "Global Economic Inequality: More or Less Equal?" *The Economist,* March 11, 2004; for the graphic material, see Penn World Tables and Stanley Fischer. © The Economist Newspaper Limited, London (2004). Reprinted with permission.

How Large Is America's National Debt?

Huge! The United States is an enormous debtor. As of February 10, 2010, at 11:15 a.m., America's total public debt (which does not include debt held by government entities, such as the Social Security Trust Fund) was a staggering $12,404,916,929,124.77.[1] In 230 years of history, the U.S. government has never

1. See http://defeatthedebt.com.

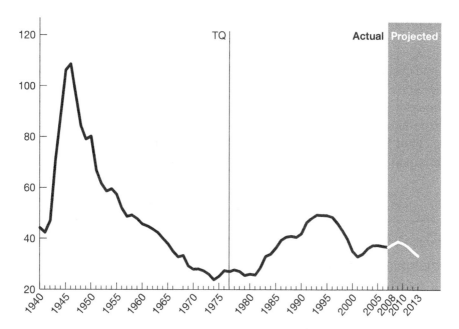

Public Debt as a Percentage of GDP over Time

Source: Office of Management and Budget, "Table 7.1—Federal Debt at the End of Year: 1940–2013," *Budget of the United States Government, Fiscal Year 2009: Historical Tables* (Washington, D.C.: U.S. Government Printing Office, 2008), pp. 127–128; see http:www.whitehouse.gov/omb/budget/fy2009/pdf/hist.pdf.

owed so much money to its creditors (those who buy Treasury bonds). Nor has any other nation in the history of civilization ever had such a large public debt.

In a different context, however, the public debt is *not* so huge, although perhaps it is a growing source of concern. While the absolute size of the debt looks large, the most important factor is the size of the debt relative to the U.S. economy. After all, our total economic output is the best measure of our capacity to pay back the debt, just as an individual's income would be considered in evaluating the size of a personal debt. (A $100,000 credit-card bill is a huge debt for someone earning $28,000 a year and a mere accounting footnote for Bill Gates.) As a proportion of GDP, the U.S. national debt appears more manageable both by historical standards or compared to many other nations around the world. As the chart above shows, the federal debt held by the public was around 40 percent of GDP in 2009, which is consistent with where it has been for seventy years and far below the World War II peak, when the public debt was over 100 percent of GDP. When the debt held by other government entities is included, the total debt rises to 69 percent of GDP, which is still lower than that of many other countries, such as Canada (72 percent of GDP), Israel (84 percent of GDP), and Japan (192 percent of GDP).[2]

2. Central Intelligence Agency, *CIA World Factbook,* 2009 estimates; see www.cia.gov/library/publications /the-world-factbook/, accessed February 22, 2010.

As you have just seen, seemingly straightforward information can be conveyed in different ways. The benefit of descriptive statistics is that they simplify data in ways that make them easier to understand and present. Of course, the choice of what information is selected and how it is simplified can radically shape the story that the numbers tell. This chapter will explore the most important tools for gathering, organizing, and expressing information—all of which are important given the role that good data play in making good policy.

CHAPTER OUTLINE

9.1 DESCRIPTIVE STATISTICS

Consider the following numbers: 47, 23, 31, 12, 19, 40, 7, 14, 23, 39, 22, 22, 27. What do they tell you? Not much. Now suppose that they are the points scored by a high-school basketball player. That tells you a lot more, although it is still not obvious whether this particular player is highly talented. The irony of the numbers presented above is that they give us all the relevant raw data—the number of points this player scored in every game—without conveying much in the way of information. To make sense of these numbers, we need two things: some summary of the player's performance and some context for evaluating it. Descriptive statistics give us a set of tools for doing that.

9.1.1 The Mean

The **mean,** or average, of a set of numbers is the sum of the numbers divided by the number of observations **(n).** For the basketball player just described, his mean points per game is 25.1. We can use that figure to compare the player's performance against other high-school players. If the league scoring average, for example, is 11.7, then we know that this player is far above average. On the other hand, if the school's all-time record for a player's single-season scoring average is 32.1, then we know that this player is good but certainly not the best to have ever played at this school. In this example, the individual basketball player is the **unit of observation,** meaning that the data we are collecting describe that player's performance. If we were interested in how the team has done, then we might collect data on the team's scoring average or its season record. This would make the team the unit of observation.

    Data points are individual observations that collectively make up the data that we are trying to describe. In the basketball example, each game's performance represents a data point, or **observation:** 47 points, 23 points, 31 points, and so on. Because there were 13 games, we have 13 data points ($n = 13$). The number of observations in a data set will take on greater significance in the next chapter, when we begin to draw inferences from the data. In general, the more data points we have, the more dependable the conclusions are that we can infer from that information. For example, we would have greater confidence in a basketball player who averaged 30 points a game over 200 games ($n = 200$) than we would in a player who scored 30 points in a single appearance ($n = 1$).

RULE OF THUMB

A Note on *Data*

The word *data* is plural—it represents multiple items of information. The singular form of the word is *datum,* which describes just one observation. Thus, a researcher might say, "The data are quite compelling," *not* "The data is quite compelling." This may sound awkward at first, but those who are comfortable working with data should also be comfortable with the appropriate subject-verb agreement!

In the case of the basketball points, we can derive the mean for the season by adding up the point totals for each game and dividing by the number of games ($n = 13$). The player scored a total of 326 points over the course of the 13-game season; he averaged 25.077 points per game (326/13). The mean is a common descriptive statistic. You are likely familiar with the use of averages to describe sports statistics or exam scores. The most attractive feature of the mean is that it collapses multiple data points into a single descriptive statistic. Thus, we can recount a player's performance over an entire season without describing the point total for each game. This feature is even more attractive, obviously, when dealing with huge data sets that may have thousands or even millions of observations. One could not reasonably describe household income in the United States by listing the incomes of 60 million or 70 million households. Instead, analysts often refer to GDP per capita, which is the gross domestic product for a nation (the value of all goods and services produced) divided by the population. GDP per capita in the United States was $46,400 in 2009, compared to $38,400 for Canada and $1,600 for Bangladesh.[3] This figure is a useful indicator of a nation's relative wealth.

In gaining simplicity, however, we do give something up: the mean does not tell us anything about the pattern of the underlying distribution. In fact, using the mean may actually disguise some important trends or patterns. Let's go back to our basketball example for a moment. Assume that a second player had a scoring average of 21.1 points per game, which was 4 points lower than the first player. Does that mean that he is really the less talented player? His

---

3. *CIA World Factbook.*

pattern of scoring over the course of the season is the following: 3, 10, 7, 9, 0, 19, 18, 31, 27, 27, 45, 40, 38. This player had a terrific second half of the season, which is obscured by his relatively poor performance in the first five games. Describing this player's average points per game for the whole season misses an important trend: he has improved dramatically. Indeed, he averaged 34.7 points per game in the final six games of the season.

Similarly, the use of GDP per capita may also obscure some important information. Because the mean is calculated by adding up the total wealth of a nation and dividing by the population, it does not tell us anything about the distribution of wealth in the country. For the sake of example, assume that in country A every resident produces $50,000 worth of goods and services per year. The country would have a GDP per capita of $50,000.

Country B is quite different. In that nation, 20 percent of the population produces $200,000 of goods and services per capita annually; the other 80 percent of the population produces only $12,500 per capita annually. This country will also have a GDP per capita of $50,000 per year. Obviously, the distribution of wealth in the two countries is strikingly different. Although country B has a GDP per capita of $50,000, *most people in the country produce much less than that*. In this case, the mean does not give an accurate portrait of the nation; as a descriptive statistic, it is skewed by the small proportion of the population who are highly productive. This is one potential drawback of using the mean to describe certain distributions. An alternative statistic, the median, is not prone to such distortions.

9.1.2 The Median

The **median** is the midpoint in a distribution of numbers when they are organized in increasing or decreasing order. If the number of observations is odd, then the median of the distribution is the middle observation. (For example, if there were 13 data points ranked in ascending or descending order, the median would be the seventh observation.) If the number of observations is even, then the median is the average of the middle two observations. In a distribution with 12 data points arrayed in ascending or descending order, the median would be the average of the sixth and seventh observations.

By definition, half the observations in a distribution lie above the median and half lie below. Analysts typically refer to statistics such as the U.S. median hourly wage, which is the midpoint of the distribution of hourly wages in the United States. If that figure is $13.52, then half of all working Americans would be earning more than $13.52 per hour and half would be earning less.

Statisticians use the related concepts of deciles, quartiles, and percentiles to describe where an observation falls within a distribution. A **decile** represents 10 percent of the distribution. Thus, if wage earners in the United States were ranked from bottom to top, the bottom decile would comprise the 10 percent of the population earning the lowest wages. The top decile would comprise the 10 percent of Americans with the highest wages. A **quartile** divides a distribution into quarters. A student who scores in the third quartile on a standardized test has performed better than half of the test takers but not as well as the top quarter. Finally, the distribution can be divided into **percentiles,** or hundredths. A one-year-old child who is in the 87th percentile for height would be taller than 86 percent of other children that age and shorter than all children in the 88th percentile and above.

As you can see in the diagram below, the median divides the top two quartiles from the bottom two quartiles; the bottom two quartiles comprise the bottom five deciles; and so on.

Both the median and the mean are important tools for describing the "middle" of a distribution. They are not identical, however. It is important to understand how choosing one or the other can present a different—or even misleading—description of the underlying data.

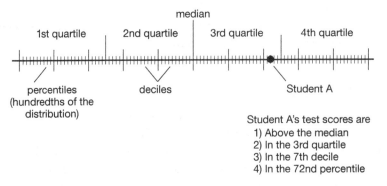

Distribution of Observations for Student Test Scores

9.1.3   Mean or Median?

The mean is affected by **outliers,** a relatively small number of observations that lie particularly far from the rest of the distribution; the median is not. While both the median and the mean describe the "center" of a distribution, the median does not give any weight to *how far* some observations may lie from that midpoint. Rather, the median is merely positional; half of the observations lie below and half lie above. Suppose the basketball player described above had scored 100 points in his best game instead of 47. Assuming his scoring for the rest of the season remained the same, his median points per game for the season would not change at all. The midpoint of the distribution of his scoring for the 13-game season is still the same: 7, 12, 14, 19, 22, 22, 23, 23, 27, 31, 39, 40, 100. The fact that 100 has replaced 47 as the highest observation does not change the midpoint.

The mean is different in this respect. Because the mean is calculated by adding up all of the scores for the season and dividing by the number of games, changing any one of those numbers will change the mean. Extreme observations, such as the 100-point game, can have a significant effect on the mean. In this case, if the player had scored 100 points in his best game of the season rather than 47, his mean points per game for the season would have gone up from 25.1 to 29.1. The effect is true going in the other direction as well. If the player had been sick with the flu for one game and scored 0 points instead of 22, then his scoring average for the season would fall while his median points per game would not.

Thus, the mean and median tell slightly different stories about this basketball season. Which is the more accurate summary of the distribution? That depends on whether or not a small number of extreme observations, or outliers, affect the mean in a way that can give a misleading impression of the data. Consider an extreme example. A small town has 100 houses, each of which is worth roughly $200,000. Thus, both the mean and median home price is $200,000. But suppose that Bill Gates decides that this town would be an excellent place to build a new summer home. He buys a parcel of land and builds a $40-million mansion. Bill Gates's new summer home affects the mean and median home values differently. Which statistic provides a better description of what has happened to the local real-estate market? Both, depending on how the information is being used.

The median home value in this town is unchanged when Bill Gates builds his mansion. If we were to rank home prices from lowest to highest, the midpoint of the distribution would still be $200,000. Because Bill Gates's $40-million home is an extreme outlier, however, it will have a significant effect on the mean. To calculate the mean, or average, we add up the value of all homes in the town and divide by 101. When Bill Gates moves in (and the value of all other homes in the town stays the same), the mean home value shoots up from $200,000 to roughly $594,000!

Now suppose that a policy analyst is preparing a report on affordable housing in this town. In particular, she is concerned about whether local workers can afford to buy homes near where they work. It would be both misleading and irresponsible to declare that the town has developed an affordable housing problem because the average home price has climbed to $594,000, which is far more than a typical worker can afford to pay. The mean is skewed by Bill Gates's new mansion; *all of the town's original 100 homes are just as affordable as they were last year*. The median home price is unchanged, which would be the most relevant and enlightening statistic for the affordable housing report.

But in some cases, the opposite may be true. Now suppose that state education officials are trying to determine which towns need extra state money to fund their local public schools. Because communities raise revenue using taxes based on the market value of local property, the state is interested in any significant changes in property values. If a town's property values go up sharply, then the community will collect more in property tax revenues and will need less assistance from the state. If property values fall sharply, the opposite would be true.

So should state officials look at mean or median property values to make this judgment? They should use the mean for reasons that our hypothetical town should make clear. As we've discussed, the median home value does not change when Bill Gates builds his summer home. If the town levies a 2 percent property tax annually, then the median property tax bill won't change either. The "median homeowner" will pay $4,000 a year in property taxes—before and after Bill Gates moves in. If state officials use the median home value to gauge a community's financial resources, then this town should receive the same assistance from the state after Bill Gates builds his mansion as it did before.

That would be a very misleading conclusion. When Bill Gates builds his vacation home, *he will pay $800,000 a year in new property taxes* (2 percent of $40 million). Although the tax bill of the typical homeowner will not change, the community will enjoy a huge increase in total property tax revenues. And since total revenue is all that matters in terms of funding local public schools, the community now has much greater financial capacity and should probably get less support from the state. In this case, the outlier—Bill Gates's huge house—is important. Neglecting it by using the median to describe local property values would disguise a significant change in the community's capacity to fund its local public schools.

Of course, an analyst need not choose between presenting the mean or the median. In many cases it is acceptable to use both. However, if a situation requires one descriptive statistic or the other, then good policy analysis requires recognizing how outliers will affect the mean relative to the median and making a judgment as to which statistic more accurately answers the question at hand.

9.1.4 Measures of Dispersion

Variance and **standard deviation** are **measures of dispersion,** or how far a set of observations spread out from their midpoint. Consider the three distributions below, each of which has a mean and median of 0. What makes them different? Obviously, a distribution with many observations that lie far from the mean (1) or with a few observations that lie very far from the mean (2) is more dispersed than a distribution that has most of its observations tightly arranged around the mean (3). How can that be quantified?

Variance and standard deviation are the most common statistical mechanisms for measuring and describing the dispersion of a distribution. The variance is calculated by determining how far the observations within a distribution lie from the mean.

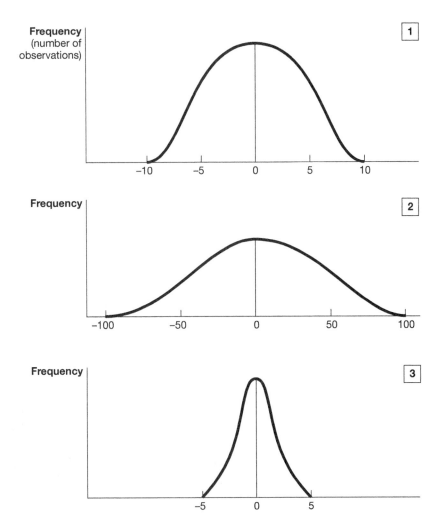

Specifically,

for any set of N observations $x_1, x_2, x_3 \ldots x_N$ with mean μ,
variance $= [(x_1 - \mu)^2 + (x_2 - \mu)^2 + (x_3 - \mu)^2 + \ldots (x_N - \mu)^2]/N$

The variance has a unique feature that puts particular weight on observations that lie far from the mean, or outliers, as the following table illustrates.

	HEIGHT (μ = 70 INCHES)	DISTANCE FROM THE MEAN = ABSOLUTE VALUE OF $(X_N - \mu)$*	$(X_N - \mu)^2$
Group 1			
Nick	74	4	16
Elana	66	4	16
Dinah	68	2	4
Rebecca	69	1	1
Ben	73	3	9
Charu	70	0	0
		14 = total	46 = total
			46/6 = variance
Group 2			
Sahar	65	5	25
Maggie	68	2	4
Faisal	69	1	1
Ted	70	0	0
Jeff	71	1	1
Narciso	75	5	25
		14 = total	56 = total
			56/6 = Variance

*Absolute value is the distance between two figures, regardless of direction, so that it is always positive. In this case, it represents the number of inches between the height of the individual and the mean.

Both groups of students have a mean height of 70 inches. The heights of students in both groups also differ from the mean by the same number of total inches: 14. By that measure of dispersion, the two distributions are also identical. However, the variance for group 2 is higher because of the weight given in the variance formula to values that lie particularly far from the mean—Sahar and Narciso, in this case.

Variance is rarely used as a descriptive statistic on its own. Instead, the variance is most useful as a step toward calculating the standard deviation of a distribution, which is one of the most important tools for making statistical inferences such as sampling and polling. The standard deviation for a set of observations is the square root of the variance:

for any set of N observations $x_1, x_2, x_3 \ldots x_N$ with mean μ,
standard deviation = σ =
$$\sqrt{[(x_1 - \mu)^2 + (x_2 - \mu)^2 + (x_3 - \mu)^2 + \ldots (x_N - \mu)^2]/N}$$

The standard deviation is particularly valuable in the case of a normal distribution, which is a set of observations that are symmetrical, or "bell-shaped," around their mean. Both of the distributions below are normal distributions:

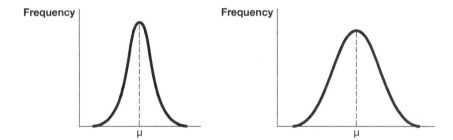

Normal distributions have an important feature: roughly 68.0 percent of the observations in the distribution lie between one standard deviation above the mean ($\mu + \sigma$) and one standard deviation below the mean ($\mu - \sigma$); roughly 95.0 percent of the observations lie between two standard deviations above the mean ($\mu + 2\sigma$) and two standard deviations below the mean ($\mu - 2\sigma$); and 99.7 percent of the observations lie within three standard deviations above or below the mean.

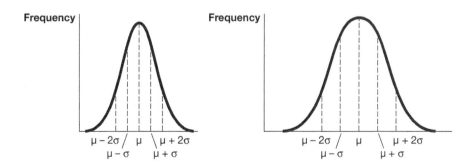

Because of this special property, the standard deviation can help us interpret data by evaluating where observations lie relative to the rest of the distribution. Suppose you go in for a blood test, and the doctor informs you that you have an elevated level of a particular liver enzyme. The figure considered normal (most likely the mean) for this particular enzyme is 1.8. Your result is 2.5. What exactly does that mean? Very little until we know what the distribution looks like for this particular lab result. Suppose the standard deviation for this result among healthy people is 1.1. In this case, your result is within one standard deviation of the mean, which could easily be explained by natural variation across individuals.

But suppose that the standard deviation for this particular liver enzyme is 0.2. In that case, your result lies more than three standard deviations above the mean. It is still possible that you are healthy and simply have a naturally high count for this enzyme. However, we know from studying the distribution that only about 3 in 1,000 healthy people would normally have such a high count (because 99.7 of the observations lie within three standard deviations from the mean). The more likely explanation is that your count for this particular enzyme has been elevated by some underlying illness or biological change. If a physician were to see a lab result that is more than three standard deviations above or below normal, he or she would almost certainly conclude that something is abnormal and do further tests.

9.1.5 Correlation

Correlation is a measure of the degree to which two variables are associated with one another; variation in one is associated with variation in the other, positively or negatively. We are familiar with this term from everyday usage. Height and weight are correlated, for example: people who are taller than average also tend to be heavier than average. But that is not always the case. There is no mathematical equation connecting height and weight. Some very tall people are also very skinny, and some short people are quite heavy. If you were given some unknown person's height, there would be no way for you to calculate his or her weight with any precision. Yet we know that there is a positive relationship between height and weight for the population as a whole.

A positive correlation tells us that two variables move in the same direction, such as height and weight. A negative correlation tells us that if one variable moves in one direction, the other variable is likely to move in the other direction, such as GDP growth and the unemployment rate. The correlation coefficient is the statistical tool used to capture this relationship. The correlation coefficient for two variables can range from –1 to 1. If two sets of observations have a correlation of 0, then they are entirely independent of one another, such as your exam score and the winning percentage of your favorite baseball team. Such observations or events are said to be **independent:** the outcome of one is unrelated to the outcome of the other. If two sets of observations have a correlation coefficient of 1, then they are perfectly correlated, meaning that they have a precise and predictable relationship. If two sets of figures have a correlation of –1, then they are perfectly inversely correlated—a precise and predictable relationship, albeit in opposite directions. The formula used to calculate the correlation between two sets of numbers is more advanced than this text but would be covered in a basic statistics course.

One of the most important concepts related to all statistical work is the distinction between correlation and **causation.** Two variables that are correlated will vary in a way that suggests a pattern or association between the two. Causation, on the other hand, implies a much stronger relationship: variation in one variable *causes* variation in the other. This distinction is crucial to doing good public policy research and interpreting the research of others. For example, researchers seek to understand as much as they possibly can about why some students drop out of high school and others do not. Dropping out of high school leaves a person poorly equipped to function in a modern economy. Thus, we would like to know which students are most prone to drop out and how we might change that behavior.

In that vein, suppose a researcher were to discover that students with iPods are significantly less likely to drop out than students without iPods. Furthermore, the researcher discovers in subsequent research that other kinds of electronic equipment are also correlated with high-school success, notably large televisions in the home. The students with the biggest, most, and best televisions in their homes are the least likely to drop out of high school. They also have higher SAT scores and are more likely to go to college than students with fewer and less expensive televisions in their homes.

Have we discovered the solution for America's high-school challenges: iPods and large televisions? Certainly not. The association between expensive electronic equipment and high-school performance is not causal, meaning that the electronic equipment is not what is making some students do better than others. Instead, it merely reflects the fact that students with wealthy and highly educated parents are also more likely to have iPods and nice televisions in their homes. The real variable of interest here—the factor that does determine why some students drop out and others do not—is the socioeconomic status of the family. Thus, a policy that attempted to improve high-school graduation rates by passing out iPods and televisions would have no impact at all, because it confuses correlation (the association between electronic equipment and high-school performance) with causation (the true factors that make some students perform better than others).

········| **POLICY IN THE REAL WORLD** |·······

The SAT: The Statistics behind the World's Most Famous Exam

The SAT Reasoning Test (formerly known as the Scholastic Aptitude Test) was introduced in 1926 as a tool for colleges and universities to gauge the capabilities of prospective students. Many of the traditional ways for evaluating high-school student performance, such as grades or class rank, do not allow for meaningful comparison of students across different schools. Obviously, a student in an undemanding high school may have a higher GPA or better class rank than a more capable student in a more demanding high school. The College Board, a nonprofit membership organization of some 5,000 colleges, universities, and other membership organizations, created the SAT as a mechanism for objectively evaluating high-school students around the world. Ever since, it has been a right of passage for high-school students applying to college and a lightning rod for critics of standardized tests. For both reasons, the SAT and related exams require extraordinary statistical expertise to ensure that they are fair, consistent, and relevant.

The numbers. In 2009, roughly 1.5 million students took the SAT Reasoning Test, made up of the Critical Reading, Mathematics, and Writing sections. Each exam is scored on a scale from 200 to 800. The exam is designed to have a mean near 500. In 2009, for example, the mean for the Critical Reading, Mathematics, and Writing sections were, respectively, 501, 515, and 493.

The point of the SAT is to create a dispersion of outcomes that provides meaningful information on students' relative capabilities. The standard deviation for the Critical Reading section was 112; the distribution of scores is roughly normal, so we can infer that about 68 percent of test takers will score within one standard deviation above or below the mean—or between 389 (501 – 112) and 613 (501 + 112). The 75th percentile for the Critical Reading exam is 580; the 25th percentile is 420.

The relevance. The most fundamental question surrounding the SAT is its accuracy in assessing student capabilities. Is the SAT a good predictor of how students will do in college, or does it simply reward students who are good at taking standardized tests? The most important criterion for answering that question is the degree to which the SAT is correlated with subsequent academic performance. According to research conducted by the College Board, the correlation between composite SAT scores (a combination of math and verbal scores) and first-year college grades is 0.53. That compares to a correlation of 0.54 between students' high-school GPAs and their first-year college GPAs.[4] According to the College Board, the best predictor of all is a combination of high-school GPA and SAT scores, which has a correlation of 0.62 with first-year college grades. Broadly speaking, the SAT does seem to have a strong relationship with academic performance, although, as with any correlation, the relationship may not hold up for specific individuals.

Bias? Is the SAT fair? This is a crucial question asked of all standardized tests. SAT scores demonstrate significant disparities based on race, income, and gender. For example, the mean Mathematics score for 2009 college-bound seniors was 534 for males and 499 for females. (For Critical Reading, the gap is much smaller: 503 for males compared to 498 for females; for the new Writing section, the mean score for females was higher than for males, 499 compared to 486.) Does the large gender disparity in math reflect underlying differences in ability, does the test provide some kind of gender advantage unrelated to true ability, or is there some other explanation for the gap? These kinds of gender-based questions have proved to be contentious. The controversial remarks by Larry Summers, former president of Harvard University, on the topic of gender and science are included at the end of this chapter for discussion.

There are significant racial and income gaps as well. For example, the mean Mathematics score for students with family incomes between $20,000 and $40,000 is 475, compared to 579 for students with family incomes over $200,000. Does that nearly 100-point gap reflect differences in ability that are likely to be correlated with wealth, such as parents' education? Or might the relationship between income and SAT scores be causal, meaning that wealthy families can "buy" better results by investing in prep courses and other tools that raise scores in ways that do not necessarily reflect true ability. The College Board, which produces the SAT, points out that coached student are only

4. The College Board, "2009 College-Bound Seniors: Total Group Profile Report, 2009," http: //professionals.collegeboard.com/profdownload/cbs-2009-national-TOTAL-GROUP.pdf.

5. The College Board, "New SAT for the Press," www.collegeboard.com/about/news_info/sat /faqs.html.

slightly more likely to have large score gains than uncoached students.[5] Roughly a third of coached students have no change in scores or do worse.

As for racial differences, the test designers have a simple and effective method for determining if specific questions are biased. They can examine whether some subgroup performs particularly poorly on a specific question relative to their performance on the rest of the exam. If the College Board were testing a new question for racial bias, for example, they would examine how black and white test takers with similar scores on the rest of the exam score on the new question. If the new question is free of bias, then black and white test takers of similar abilities should do equally well. If there is a significant gap, however, then it suggests a possible bias. Of course, there is no comparable method for determining with certainty that the whole exam is free of bias.

Some colleges and universities have recently opted to make the SAT optional, presumably because they do not find it an essential tool in the applications process. However, such a decision should be interpreted with a skeptical statistical eye. Students who opt not to submit SAT scores are likely to be those with the lowest scores. As a result, schools that make SATs optional can raise the average score of their entering class (without actually changing the composition of that class!), which makes the school look more highly selective when compared to other schools in guidebooks and the like.

....

9.1.6 Absolute versus Relative Figures

Absolute figures are presented in some units of measure, such as dollars or degrees; **relative figures** are presented as a proportion of some other quantity. How much does the United States spend on public education compared to other countries? That question could be answered reasonably in two ways. If we were to answer in absolute terms, we would compare the amount of money (converted into a common currency) per pupil that nations around the world spend on schooling. Obviously, these figures provide us with meaningful information on the amount of resources that each country spends on education inputs. The United States spends nearly $10,000 per primary school student, which is the second highest in the OECD. (The OECD, the Organisation for Economic Co-operation and Development, comprises thirty developed countries that are broadly comparable to the United States.) Only Luxembourg spends more; the OECD average is $6,400.[6]

6. Organisation for Economic Co-operation and Development, "Education at a Glance 2009: OECD Indicators," http://www.oecd.org/document/62/0,3343,en_2649_39263238_43586328_1_1_1_37455,00.html.

However, most nations are less wealthy than the United States, and we would expect them to spend less on public education simply because they have less resources overall. Thus, we might also calculate a relative measure of education expenditures: Which countries spend the most on public schooling *relative to their overall economic capacity*? To make that determination, we would likely calculate education spending for each nation as a fraction of its annual GDP. Because GDP is the value of all goods and services produced in a country, it is the most common measure of economic capacity. When expressed as a proportion of economic capacity, the education spending figures look dramatically different. Education spending in the United States is just below 6.0 percent of GDP, which ranks thirty-seventh in the world, behind countries such as Israel (7.5 percent), Malaysia (8.1 percent), and Cuba (18.7 percent).

Which figure is more accurate? Once again, that depends on the nature of the question being asked. If we would like to know which nations have the most capacity to buy books, build classrooms, and pay teachers, then the absolute measure is probably most appropriate. As a rich country, the United States can afford to spend a great amount on those kinds of schooling inputs.

However, if we are trying to measure which nations are making the greatest financial commitment to public education, then the relative figure may be more appropriate, since it tells us how much each country spends relative to its economic capacity. Yemen is a much poorer country than the United States, but it devotes a greater fraction of its productive capacity (9.5 percent) to education.

You will recall that the introduction to this chapter asked a question about the U.S. national debt. This is a case where the relative figure is the preferred statistic; indeed, using absolute figures can be misleading. The national debt represents the accumulated borrowing of the country, which must eventually be paid back. The most important consideration when evaluating the size of the debt—in the United States or anywhere else—is the capacity of the country to pay it back. Thus, the size of the debt must be evaluated relative to the size of the economy. A $100-billion debt would be huge in a country with a GDP of only $50 billion; the country would owe its creditors an amount equal to twice the value of all the goods and services that the entire nation produces in a year. The same $100-billion debt would be relatively small in an economy like that of the United States, the annual GDP of which is $14 trillion.

The U.S. national debt is large in absolute terms—it amounts to $12,404,916,929,124.77. As the introduction pointed out, however, it is smaller as a fraction of GDP than the public debt of many other nations, such as Japan. It is also smaller relative to the size of the economy than it was at other points in history, such as World War II.

9.1.7 Percentage Change

Percentage change represents the extent to which some number or quantity has changed relative to its initial value. We are routinely bombarded by statistics that use percentages. A department store has slashed prices by 25 percent; the Dow Jones Industrial Average closed down 2 percent; median home prices are expected to climb 6 percent; and so on. Yet there are subtle elements of using percent change as a descriptive statistic that are important to understand.

The first important point is that percentage change is a relative statistic, meaning that it only has meaning in comparison to something else. If you look at the examples above, each one has an implied comparison: the department store will slash prices 25 percent *relative to what those items normally cost;* the Dow Jones Industrial Average closed down 2 percent *compared to where it closed yesterday;* median home prices are expected to be 6 percent *higher than they were last year.* As a result, we do not actually have much information without that larger context; if we know only that median home prices are expected to be 6 percent higher next year, we still would not know how much a typical house would cost.

Percentage change is simple to calculate:

percentage change = (new figure – old figure)/old figure

If a department store lowers the price of a pair of shoes from $120 to $99, how much is the reduction in percentage terms? We simply plug in the numbers:

percentage change = (99 – 120)/99
percentage change = –21/99
percentage change = –.2121 or –21%

The department store has lowered prices by 21 percent.

As simple as those calculations appear, percentage change can be misunderstood or manipulated because of its role in comparing one quantity *relative to* another. Answer the following question quickly in your mind. Suppose a stock is selling for $100.00. If the price falls 25 percent the first day and then climbs 25 percent the following day, how much will it be worth? If you answered $100.00, then you have missed one of the important nuances of percentage change. The correct answer is $93.75.

Here is how the figure is calculated. On the first day, the $100.00 stock falls in value by 25 percent, or $25.00. Thus, the stock is now selling for

$75.00. On the second day, the stock climbs by 25 percent, but that is 25 percent of its *new price*, or .25($75.00) = $18.75. Thus, the stock gains $18.75 to close at $93.75.

Finally, consider one more case in which percentage change can provide bizarre or misleading impressions of the underlying data: situations in which the point of comparison is very small, making the relative change appear large.

Consider the XYZ Corporation, which has been struggling to earn profits in recent years. Last year the company barely broke even, earning a paltry $10,000 in profits. Meanwhile, its chief competitor, the robust BCD Corporation, earned a robust $50 million last year. Suppose that both companies have just closed their books for this year: XYZ had another terrible year, earning only $18,000 while BCD Corporation registered a record profit of $60 million.

How might the CEO of the XYZ Corporation use descriptive statistics to present positive, arguably misleading, data to his shareholders? He might choose to describe the company's performance relative to its chief competitor in percentage terms, rather than using the absolute numbers.

- Profit growth at XYZ this year was an impressive 80 percent: ($18,000 – $10,000)/$10,000.
- Profit growth at BCD was a less impressive 20 percent: ($60 million – $50 million)/$50 million.

The CEO of the XYZ Corporation might even claim that its profits grew *four times as fast* as profits at BCD. Of course, assuming the companies are the same size, any rational investor would prefer to own shares in the BCD Corporation, which is earning far larger profits and had larger profit growth in dollar terms. The profit growth at XYZ looks impressive only because it earned so little last year—which is the reference point when calculating the percentage change in profits.

Percentage change can be a valuable descriptive tool because it provides context for a change in quantity. When used properly, it can also help us make comparisons. If a corporate CEO gets an 18 percent raise while the average raise for other CEOs in the same industry is only 6 percent, then we have a simple expression of the disparity in compensation growth. As with all descriptive statistics, however, there can be a tension between simplicity and accuracy.

9.2 EXPECTED VALUE

Expected value is the mean outcome from a series of events for which we know the probability of all possible outcomes and the "payoff" for each of those outcomes. Many events in life have uncertain outcomes. Expected value is a tool that enables us to make informed decisions in the face of that uncertainty by evaluating the likelihood of different outcomes.

$$EV = p_1[E_1] + p_2[E_2] + p_3[E_3] + \ldots p_n[E_n]$$
for all possible outcomes 1 to n, where p is the probability of the outcome and E is the value of that outcome.

Consider a simple example: the expected value of the roll of a single die. As you know, a die has six sides with dots representing the numbers 1, 2, 3, 4, 5, 6. Assuming the die is fair, the probability of getting any number is 1/6. So what is the expected value of a single roll of the die?

$$EV = 1/6[1] + 1/6[2] + 1/6[3] + 1/6[4] + 1/6\,[5] + 1/6[6]$$
$$EV = 1/6 + 2/6 + 3/6 + 4/6 + 5/6 + 6/6$$
$$EV = 21/6$$
$$EV = 3\tfrac{1}{2}$$

Thus, the mean outcome for a single roll of the die is 3½. Of course, you should immediately realize that 3½ is not a possible outcome! A die has only whole numbers. However, if you were to repeatedly roll the die, the expected mean of your rolls would be 3½.

Expected value is an important tool for making decisions related to future events for which we know the probability of different outcomes. For example, most insurance, such as homeowner's insurance, is based on this concept. It is highly unlikely that any individual house is likely to burn down in the next year. Yet if that event were to happen, the fire would be financially devastating for the homeowner. Thus, most property owners purchase homeowner's insurance, which provides compensation in the event of a serious fire or other catastrophe. How much should it cost?

The answer can be calculated using expected value (or **expected loss,** as the concept is called in the insurance business). Most insurance companies are for-profit firms; they collect regular premiums from their customers, and they make payouts to customers who suffer losses. In order to make money on a regular basis, the premiums collected from customers must, on average, be larger than the payouts made to customers who suffer losses. Thus, an insurance company will begin by calculating the expected loss from any given policy. Suppose, for example, that the firm is insuring a home that would cost

$250,000 to rebuild in the event that it was destroyed by fire. Further assume that the probability that a home in this neighborhood would be destroyed by fire in any given year is 1/1,000.

Thus, the annual expected loss from this policy is 1/1,000[$250,000] = $250. As in the case of the single die, you should recognize that the insurance company will never actually make a payout of $250. Instead, the company will either pay a policy holder $250,000 (if the house burns down) or nothing (if the house does not burn down). Still, the expected loss figure is extremely important from a business standpoint, since it provides two important and related pieces of information. First, the company can calculate the expected loss for each policy *on average*. For example, if the expected loss is $250 per policy, and the company sells 100,000 policies, then the expected payout for any given year would be $25 million. We will learn in the next chapter that as the number of observations gets large, such calculations become increasingly accurate.

Second, the company can calculate the fair price for any given insurance policy. If the expected loss from fire equals $250 per year, then an insurance policy that is **actuarially fair,** meaning that the premium is set at the expected loss, would cost $250. In reality, insurance companies also seek to earn a profit, so the policy would likely cost more than $250 a year. Will consumers buy an insurance policy that costs more than their expected loss from some contingency, such as fire? The answer is yes, for reasons that will be explained below.

Risk aversion explains how insurance companies can make profits by selling policies that cost more than the expected loss from the event that is being insured against. A risk-averse person will choose to pay a regular, fixed amount in order to avoid the possibility, however small, of some catastrophic event. If the expected loss from fire is $400 a year for a $400,000 house, a risk-averse person will choose to pay $450 a year to avoid the possibility of losing $400,000 in property. The insurance company, on the other hand, can pool its risk across many houses. Some will burn down, but most won't; on average, the insurance company will collect more in premiums that it will pay out in claims.

9.3 SOURCES OF DATA

Good public policy requires good information. One crucial difference between research in the hard sciences, such as biology and chemistry, and the social sciences, such as economics and public policy, is the capacity to do controlled experiments. Are children who suffer abuse or neglect more likely to commit crimes as adults? This is an important public policy question, but it is obviously not a subject that can be studied using a controlled experiment. Instead, researchers must gather large amounts of data, including information on whether children were neglected or abused, and then attempt to establish important relationships based on the data available. The tools for determining such relationships from large data sets will be explored in greater depth in the next chapter.

9.3.1 Data Sets

In the absence of laboratory experiments, social-science researchers depend on several different sources of data.

- **Cross-sectional data** are made up of observations for a set of individuals, countries, or some other unit of observation at a particular time. Suppose we were studying the relationship between childhood abuse and adult crime. A cross-sectional data set might give us detailed information on 10,000 individuals at one point. For each individual, we might know his age, race, and level of educational attainment. Given the research question at hand, we would also need to know (1) if he was abused or neglected as a child and (2) if he committed a crime as an adult. Given this cross section of information on a large group, we can begin to look for relationships that might inform public policy, such as whether individuals who report being abused/neglected as children are more likely to have committed criminal acts as adults.

- **Longitudinal data** (also called **time-series data**) consist of observations for some unit of analysis at multiple times. For example, if we were interested in crime, we might collect annual data on the incidence of violent crime in Chicago over some period, say 1990–2010. For each year in that range, we would have data on crimes of interest in Chicago, allowing us to observe trends over time.

- **Panel data** are a combination of cross-sectional and longitudinal data. A panel data set comprises observations on a set of individuals, countries, or other units of observation at multiple points in time. A panel data set may include income data for 1,000 individuals in 1980, 1990, 2000, and 2010. Panel data are a rich source of information because they allow researchers to observe how different variables affect different individuals (or some other unit of observation) over time.

- **Natural experiments** occur when circumstances create a situation that approximates a controlled experiment. Humans cannot be manipulated like petri dishes or laboratory rats; yet sometimes chance events create two groups that are identical but for some policy intervention. Suppose that researchers were trying to determine the impact of sending low-income children to private schools rather than to public schools. The researchers could not merely compare the life outcomes for poor children who attended private schools to those who attended public schools; the difference in outcomes for these two groups might have nothing to do with the education they received and everything to do with the family attributes that caused them to select a private school in the first place. (This is a potential selection bias, which will be covered in the next section.) The real question is whether the private school *causes* better outcomes. But this seemingly simple question is confounded by the fact that the students who attend private schools are different just for having chosen a private school.

    This is the kind of situation where a natural experiment might provide unique insight. Suppose that a city creates a new program that provides scholarships for children from low-income families to attend private high schools. Further suppose that the program is oversubscribed; not all of the families who have signed up can be accommodated, so the participating students are chosen by lottery. This situation can be exploited to study the life effects of attending a private school in a way that approximates a laboratory experiment. The students who win the scholarship lottery and attend a private high school can be compared to the students who applied for the program—therefore demonstrating the same motivation—but were not accepted. The random selection into the program eliminates the selection bias that would otherwise plague any comparison of students in public and private schools. The difference in outcomes for these two groups might reasonably be attributed to the schools involved rather than the kinds of students who opt into those schools.

9.3.2   Representative Samples

Data analysis often requires gathering an accurate sample of some underlying population; an unrepresentative sample can yield inaccurate or even wildly misleading results. Suppose you are attempting to gauge how audiences feel about a film that was released in theaters over the weekend. It would obviously be cost- and time-prohibitive to interview every person who saw the film.

Instead, a researcher might attempt to interview some smaller segment, or sample, of the filmgoers. If done correctly, this kind of **statistical sampling** can produce strikingly accurate findings. If done incorrectly, the conclusions may bear little relationship to what most people who saw the movie actually thought of it. In particular, a **biased sample** is not representative of the larger population and will produce inaccurate results.

Suppose, for example, that the person doing market research interviews only individuals who saw a matinee showing of the film on the Friday it was released. How might that sample be biased? *People who see movies in the middle of the day on a Friday are not like most other filmgoers in several important respects.* They are more likely to be elderly and less likely to be employed. Or they may be so wildly enthusiastic about the film that they have taken a day off of work to see it during the first available screening. Thus, a sample of opinions drawn only from matinee filmgoers would not provide accurate feedback on how the movie has been received overall. To provide meaningful data, a sample must be representative of the whole population of interest.

Selection bias occurs when the process used to collect data generates a nonrepresentative sample. Suppose, for example, that researchers were conducting a telephone survey of Americans to determine what proportion of the population had experienced a spell of homelessness. No matter how large the sample, the final results would be significantly biased by the mechanism used to collect the data: *individuals who are homeless or most at risk of being homeless are far less likely than the general population to have a telephone.* Thus, the data generated by the telephone survey will almost certainly underestimate the frequency of homelessness among the U.S. population. (On the other hand, a face-to-face survey conducted on a street corner two blocks from a homeless shelter would have a selection bias in the opposite direction.)

Self-selection bias is a related problem caused when individuals can sort themselves in or out of a group being studied in a way that will affect the composition of the group being studied. Suppose a market-research firm is gathering data on consumer attitudes about new cars. The firm contacts a **representative sample** of consumers and offers them $100 to participate in a focus group. No matter how representative the sample of consumers invited to participate in the focus group, the group that ultimately chooses to participate will *not* be representative of all consumers. We can assume that those who are willing to participate have a lower cost of time, a greater interest in earning $100, a particularly strong interest in cars, or other attributes that set them apart from those who decline to participate.

Self-selection is a particularly nettlesome issue when trying to evaluate the effect of voluntary programs. Suppose prison officials are trying to evaluate the effectiveness of a voluntary prerelease substance-abuse program on recidivism rates. Does substance-abuse treatment in prison help keep inmates from returning to crime once they are released? A finding that inmates who participated in the program have lower recidivism rates than those who did not participate would not prove that substance-abuse treatment works. *The inmates who volunteered for the program may be qualitatively different than the general prison population.* Thus, it may be the selection process rather than the treatment that is responsible for the positive outcome.

Survivorship bias (or **survivor bias**) occurs when observations are lost or discarded before the analysis is conducted, thereby skewing the remaining sample. Consider a researcher who is studying the members of a high-school class who return for their sixtieth high-school reunion at age seventy-eight. A survey finds that only half of the class members has exercised regularly over the course of their lives while the other half has been sedentary. Since both groups are alive and generally healthy, one might conclude that exercise has little effect on longevity or health in old age. That would almost certainly be wrong for the simple reason that the members of the class who did not return to the reunion are most likely sick or dead, and many of them may not have exercised regularly. Thus, the relationship between exercise and good health may be obscured because the sickest members of the class are not counted.

Positive-findings bias (or **positive-publication bias**) occurs because studies with some positive findings, such as the effectiveness of a certain medical treatment, are more likely to be published than studies with no significant findings. After all, who wants to read that something doesn't shrink a tumor? But the basic laws of probability suggest that if studies with no significant findings are less likely to be published, the result may be misleading to experts in the field. Consider a simple numerical example. Suppose that ten teams of researchers are independently examining whether or not a new drug is effective in shrinking a certain kind of tumor. Further assume that nine research teams find that it is not effective while one team finds positive results. This positive finding could easily be the result of chance; a reading of all ten studies would cast serious doubt on the effectiveness of the treatment.

But medical experts may not get to see all ten studies. The researchers with negative findings may not submit their research for publication; and, if submitted, medical journals may not be inclined to publish it. On the other hand, the positive findings are more likely to be published or receive other public attention. The overall result is misleading because medical experts are exposed to the positive findings of one study but not to the far larger number of other studies with more discouraging results. Medical journals are now attempting to remedy this problem by requiring that all studies to be considered for publication be registered *before* they begin, so that the journal will have a greater awareness of all the research being done on a topic and the proportion of positive findings.

Good data are essential to good policy. Gathering such data requires both expertise and extraordinary resources. One important role of government and the nonprofit sector is gathering information that is essential for the public policy research that helps to improve our lives.

··············· POLICY IN THE REAL WORLD ···············

Twenty-one Years and $2.7 Billion Worth of Data: The National Children's Study

Why has autism become significantly more prevalent among children in the United States? Why are American youth getting fatter? Does exposure to air pollution during childhood cause asthma? These are all important research questions with no complete answers at present. The National Children's Study is a longitudinal study funded by the U.S. government to examine these important issues and many others.[7]

The National Children's Study will examine the effects of assorted environmental influences on the health and development of children in hopes of improving overall health and well-being. The study will gather data on more than 100,000 children from across the United States, beginning before birth and continuing until the subjects reach age twenty-one. Researchers will use the accumulated data to examine the health and development impacts of genetics, culture and family, physical surroundings, environmental contaminants, geography, and other factors.

For children enrolled in the study, the process begins before birth with data on their prenatal care and home environment. Researchers will gather samples of the air, water, dirt, and dust from the family's home. (Researchers would like to test the theory that childhood exposure to some allergens, such as dirt or pet hair, might actually reduce the subsequent likelihood of asthma by desensitizing the immune system.) The study participants will also donate samples of hair, blood, umbilical-cord blood, and baby teeth.[8]

---

7. See www.nationalchildrensstudy.gov.

8. Jim Ritter, "21 Years Will Be Spent Finding What Makes Kids Unhealthy," *Chicago Sun-Times*, February 14, 2005.

As the children grow up, they will meet with researchers on fifteen occasions for physical exams and developmental assessments; researchers will gather ongoing information on the children's family life and living environment.[9] The study has been designed to draw a representative sample of children from around the United States. The 105 sites around the country where families will be recruited and enrolled—79 in metropolitan areas and 26 in rural areas—were selected by statistical experts to provide a sample of American children that is representative of the youth population overall in terms of race, ethnicity, geography, income, and living environment. As the study's designers have noted, "Together the children from these 105 locations will represent the face of all of America's children." The data will be used to inform policies ranging from disease prevention to school reform to crime reduction.

Of course, such a study is remarkably expensive to design and carry out. Some 2,400 researchers have been involved in the study design and execution. Overall, the project—the largest long-term study of children in history—is expected to cost $2.7 billion.

9.4 THE TIME VALUE OF MONEY

Which would you rather have: $100 today or $100 in ten years? Most people would prefer to have the money now—for several reasons. To begin with, $100 has more purchasing power today than it is likely to have in a decade. Because of inflation (the rise in prices over time), the $100 would buy fewer goods and services a decade from now. Of course, you might also worry about actually receiving the $100 in ten years (or being alive then to spend it), so there is an element of uncertainty that makes the future payment less valuable. Finally, even if you would prefer to have the money in the future, you would still be better off accepting $100 today, investing it to earn some return, and then spending the $100 *plus accumulated interest* in ten years. At a rate of 5 percent interest, a $100 investment would be worth $162.89 in ten years.

The important point in terms of public policy is that $1 today is not the same as $1 next year (or even $1 tomorrow, in extreme cases). Yet policy analysis often requires us to compare dollar values at different times. Suppose we are considering spending $100 million to build a new government research laboratory that is expected to generate $200 million in social benefits—but not for twenty years. How can we evaluate the costs and benefits of the project if

9. Ritter, "21 Years Will Be Spent."

the dollars spent today are not comparable to the dollars that will be generated twenty years from now? The answer lies in a series of growth-related formulas that can be used to calculate the value of a quantity that is growing or shrinking at some steady rate over time, such as a population growing at 2 percent a year or a bank account earning 5-percent interest annually. The same basic principles can be used to determine the present value of a monetary sum that will be received in the future.

9.4.1   Future Value

The **future value** (*FV*) of a quantity is the value that it will grow to at a specified time in the future at a specified rate of interest or growth. Suppose a city has a current population of 1 million and a rate of population growth of 3 percent a year. What will the population be in five years? The process for answering that question is the same as the process for calculating compound interest. Each year's growth becomes the base on which the next year's growth is calculated. So the city will grow by 3 percent in the first year = 1,000,000(1.03) = 1,030,000. In the second year, the population again grows by 3 percent = 1,030,000(1.03) = 1,060,900.

Here is the key insight: the population at the end of the second year can also be expressed as the following: 1,000,000(1.03)(1.03) = (the original population)(growth in the first year)(growth in the second year) = 1,060,900. This process can be carried on for as long as the city grows annually at 3 percent. In answer to the original question, at the end of five years, the population will be 1,000,000(1.03)(1.03)(103)(1.03)(1.03) = 1,000,000(1.03)^5 = 1,159,274.

This is the source of the general formula:

$$FV = PV(1 + r)^n$$

where

> *PV* = the present value of the sum;
> *r* = the annual rate of interest or growth; and
> *n* = the number of periods.

How much will $1,000 will be worth in ten years if you deposit it in a bank account that pays 6 percent interest a year? In this case,

$$PV = \$1,000$$
$$r = .06$$
$$n = 10$$
$$FV = \$1,000(1 + .06)^{10}$$

$$FV = \$1,000\,(1.06)^{10}$$
$$FV = \$1,000\,(1.79)$$
$$FV = \$1,790$$

9.4.2 Present Value

Policy analysis often requires us to do this kind of analysis in the opposite direction—converting some future quantity into its value in the present. For example, if some project will yield $100 million in benefits a decade from now, how much is that $100 million worth today? The concept of **present discounted value,** or simply **present value (PV),** enables us to do that calculation. This tool is crucial to benefit-cost analysis and any other situation in which we must compare the value of monetary sums at different times.

The concept of present value turns some of the concepts from the previous section on their head. Suppose an investor has access to a safe investment opportunity that pays 7-percent interest a year. Such an investor (assuming that she has no immediate cash needs) ought to be indifferent to the choice of receiving $1,000 today or $1,070 a year from now. This relationship underscores the concept of present value. Assuming an interest rate of 7 percent, the present value of $1,070 to be received in one year is $1,000 *because that is the sum that a person could receive today and invest at 7 percent for one year in order to end up with $1,070 a year from now.*

The formula for present value can be derived from the formula for future value introduced in the previous section:

$$FV = PV\,(1 + r)^n$$

A simple algebraic manipulation gives us the following:

$$PV = FV\,/\,(1 + r)^n$$

where

    PV = present value
    FV = the nominal value of the sum at some point in the future
    r = the annual interest rate
    n = the number of years in the future

So what is the present value of a bond that will pay $10,000 at the end of ten years, assuming an interest rate of 7 percent? We can do the calculation:

$$PV = \$10,000\,/\,(1.07)^{10}$$
$$PV = \$10,000\,/\,(1.97)$$
$$PV = \$5,100$$

The present value of $10,000 to be paid ten years from now is only $5,100, meaning that at a prevailing interest rate of 7 percent, a rational investor should be indifferent between receiving $5,100 today or $10,000 ten years from now. When calculating present value, the interest rate used to make the calculation is often referred to as the **discount rate,** since it represents the rate at which some future sum is discounted to the present. Similarly, the term *present discounted value* is often used synonymously with *present value*.

We will conclude our discussion of the time value of money with a decision that each of us thinks about making: Should we take our lottery winnings in one lump sum or as a series of annual payments? Suppose you have won $5 million in the Pick 5 game and the Lottery Commission has offered a choice between five annual payments of $1 million or an immediate lump-sum payment of $4.5 million. The five payments of $1 million each seems like the better option, since it adds up to more money. But much of that cash will be paid in the future, when the dollars will be worth less. The $4.5 million, on the other hand, would be paid immediately. The concept of present value can help us evaluate this decision by calculating the present value of each of the future $1-million payments.

Assume that the first $1 million will be paid immediately and the four subsequent payments will be made each year thereafter. Assume once again that you have an opportunity to make safe investments at an interest rate of 7 percent. Thus, the present value of the annual lottery payments using a 7-percent discount rate is the following:

$$PV = \$1,000,000 + \$1,000,000/(1.07) + \$1,000,000/(1.07)^2 +$$
$$\$1,000,000/(1.07)^3 + \$1,000,000/(1.07)^4$$
$$PV = \$1,000,000 + \$1,000,000/(1.07) + \$1,000,000/1.14 +$$
$$\$1,000,000/1.23 + \$1,000,000/1.31$$
$$PV = \$1,000,000 + \$934,579.44 + \$877,192.98 + \$813,008.13 +$$
$$\$763,358.78$$
$$PV = \$4,388,139.33$$

The immediate lump sum payment of $4.5 million is the better option, as it is worth more than the present value of the five annual payments of $1 million each. Most lotteries stretch their large payments out over many years, so that the present value of the "jackpots" is often significantly lower than advertised.

9.5 CONCLUSION

Gathering good data is a crucial step in policy analysis, as is recognizing data that are biased or otherwise misleading. Analysts must also present complex information in ways that make it easier to understand and act upon. This chapter presents some of the most common tools for summarizing the kind of data that are likely to be relevant to public policy. Any summary statistic involves some simplification; that is the point of it. However, policy analysts must ensure that data and the descriptive statistics that summarize them are presented in a way that most accurately reflects the underlying reality.

FOR DISCUSSION

Women in Science?: The Controversial Comments of Former Harvard President Larry Summers

In 2005, Harvard president Lawrence Summers addressed the National Bureau of Economic Research on the topic of women in science. His remarks precipitated a firestorm of controversy that contributed in part to his subsequent resignation. The data clearly show that women are underrepresented as tenured professors in science and engineering at America's top universities. The data do not make clear why this is the case. President Summers's discussion of this topic and his hypotheses for the dearth of female scientists and engineers proved extraordinarily controversial. The full speech cannot be reprinted here. Instead, the speech has been summarized.

President Summers began by explaining that he would take "an entirely positive, rather than normative approach, and just try to think about and offer some hypotheses as to why we observe what we observe." He also pointed out that the gender patterns seen in the academic sciences are similar to those at large law firms, in major corporations, at the top of prominent teaching hospitals, and so on. Summers then laid out three broad hypotheses that might explain the dearth of female academic scientists and engineers.

- **The high-powered job hypothesis.** Women may steer away from careers that place extraordinary demands on their time and make it hard to balance other life activities. Summers explained, "Another way to put the point is to say, what fraction of young women in their mid-twenties make a decision that they don't want to have a job that they think about eighty hours a week. What fraction of young men make a decision that they're unwilling to have a job that they think about eighty hours a week, and to observe what the difference is." Gender-based personal preferences might explain some or all of the gap.

- **Different aptitude at the high end.** Because superstars in many professions, but particularly science and engineering, tend to come from the extreme tail of the talent distribution, some of the male-female gap in tenured academics in those fields may be explained by gender differences among the extreme "outliers." In other words, there may be more men than women when one looks at only the extremely talented. This was the most controversial aspect of Summers's speech since it suggested that innate differences may explain the gender gap. Therefore, it is worth quoting a lengthy excerpt from his explanation:

> It does appear that on many, many different human attributes— height, weight, propensity for criminality, overall IQ, mathematical

ability, scientific ability—there is relatively clear evidence that whatever the difference in means—which can be debated—there is a difference in the standard deviation, and variability of a male and a female population. And that is true with respect to attributes that are and are not plausibly, culturally determined. . . . If one is talking about physicists at a top twenty-five research university, one is not talking about people who are two standard deviations above the mean. And perhaps it's not even talking about somebody who is three standard deviations above the mean. But it's talking about people who are three and a half, four standard deviations above the mean in the one in 5,000, one in 10,000 class. Even small differences in the standard deviation will translate into very large differences in the available pool substantially out.

Summers referenced test data for twelfth graders across different subjects; at the high end of the distribution, males tend to be overrepresented. He pointed out explicitly that his methodology for the calculations was crude and could be improved upon. Nonetheless, his rough calculation of the male-female ratio at the extreme end of the test score distribution for twelfth graders was five to one. He explained the potential implications:

If my reading of the data is right—it's something people can argue about—that there are some systematic differences in variability in different populations, then whatever the set of attributes are that are precisely defined to correlate with being an aeronautical engineer at MIT or being a chemist at Berkeley, those are probably different in their standard deviations as well. So my sense is that the unfortunate truth—I would far prefer to believe something else, because it would be easier to address what is surely a serious social problem if something else were true—is that the combination of the high-powered job hypothesis and the differing variances probably explains a fair amount of this problem.

- **Socialization and discrimination.** Girls may be taught from a young age, in subtle and nonsubtle ways, that some activities and professions are more appropriate for women than men. The cumulative effect of this socialization may be that both men and women are more likely to pursue certain career paths than others (e.g., women are more likely to choose nursing). Meanwhile, discrimination might explain part of the gender gap in terms of who is chosen for highly selective positions, such as academic jobs. Summers queried: "To what extent are there pervasive patterns of passive discrimination and stereotyping in which people like to choose people like themselves, and the people in the previous group are disproportionately white male, and so they choose people who are like themselves, who are disproportionately white male. No one who's been in a university department or who has been involved in personnel processes can deny that this kind of taste does go on, and it is something that happens, and it is something that absolutely, vigorously needs to be combated."

Summers concluded by listing a series of research questions that would help inform the issue. He reiterated that the purpose of the speech was to raise awareness of the gender gap and that his thinking "may be all wrong." He concluded by pointing out that his purpose will have been served if the talk provoked thought, discussion, and research on the significant issue of gender differences in the sciences, which are "too important to sentimentalize rather than to think about in as rigorous and careful ways as we can."

President Summers's speech did provoke attention, though not necessarily deep thinking on the issues he raised. Much of the ensuing controversy surrounded his audacity at raising the points he did, rather than the merits of his hypotheses.

QUESTIONS

1. President Summers was accused of denigrating the skill and intelligence of women. Having seen excerpts of his comments in context, do you think that that is a fair criticism?
2. Summers says that he is attempting "to adopt an entirely positive, rather than normative approach." What does that mean in this context?
3. Summers argues that in examining data on scientific and mathematical aptitude, the difference in standard deviation between the sexes is more important than the difference in mean. Explain.
4. Can you think of subtle social biases that might help to explain the science and engineering gender gap?
5. If you were a university president concerned about this issue, how would you proceed?
6. What kind of data might help to inform this issue?
7. Agree or disagree: This is exactly the kind of issue that the president of Harvard should be speaking about.

KEY CONCEPTS

★ The mean, or average, of a set of numbers is the sum of the numbers divided by the number of observations (n).

★ The median is the midpoint in a distribution of numbers when they are organized in increasing or decreasing order.

★ While both the median and the mean describe the "center" of a distribution, the mean is affected by outliers, a relatively small number of observations that lie particularly far from the rest of the distribution, while the median is not. If a situation requires one descriptive statistic or the other, then good policy analysis requires recognizing how outliers will affect the mean relative to the median and making a judgment as to which statistic more accurately answers the question at hand.

★ Variance and standard deviation are measures of dispersion, or how far a set of observations spread out from their midpoint.

★ Correlation is a measure of the degree to which two variables are associated with one another; variation in one is associated with variation in the other, positively or negatively.

★ Normal distributions, which are symmetrical around the mean, have an important feature: roughly 68 percent of the observations in the distribution lie between one standard deviation above the mean ($\mu + \sigma$) and one standard deviation below the mean ($\mu - \sigma$); roughly 95 percent of the observations lie within two standard deviations above or below the mean ($\mu \pm 2\sigma$).

★ The distinction between correlation and causation is crucial to doing good public policy research and interpreting the research of others. Two variables that are correlated will vary in a way that suggests a pattern or association between the two. Causation, on the other hand, implies a much stronger relationship: variation in one variable *causes* variation in the other.

★ Absolute figures are presented in some units of measure, such as dollars or degrees; relative figures are presented as a proportion of some other quantity.

★ Expected value is the mean outcome from a series of events for which we know the probability of all possible outcomes and the "payoff" for each of those outcomes. $EV = p_1[E_1] + p_2[E_2] + p_3[E_3] + \ldots p_n[E_n]$ for all possible outcomes 1 to n, where p is the probability of the outcome and E is the value of that outcome.

★ Cross-sectional data are made up of observations for a set of individuals, countries, or some other unit of observation at a particular time. Longitudinal data consist of observations for some unit of analysis at multiple times. Panel data are a combination of cross-sectional and longitudinal data, such as data collected annually on a large group of countries.

★ Natural experiments occur when circumstances create a situation that approximates a controlled experiment; chance events create two groups that are identical but for some policy intervention.

★ Data analysis often requires gathering an accurate sample of some underlying population; an unrepresentative sample can yield inaccurate or even wildly misleading results.

★ The future value (*FV*) of a quantity is the value that it will grow to at a specified time in the future at a specified rate of interest or growth.

★ Present value (*PV*) is the value in today's dollars of a quantity that will be paid at some point in the future; the future sum is discounted to the present using a specified interest rate, or discount rate.

CHAPTER 10

Basic Data Analysis

A GRAVE MISCARRIAGE
OF JUSTICE

An improper use of statistics does not often lead to grave miscarriages of justice—but sometimes it can. This was the case in Britain in the 1990s, when 258 cases of murder were built upon expert testimony that made improper inferences from basic probability.[1] The cases involved parents accused of killing their infant children. There was no physical evidence to suggest foul play in these cases; rather, the infants had died with no obvious medical explanation in families where other infants had died under similarly mysterious circumstances. One pediatrician, Sir Roy Meadow, testified for the prosecution that multiple "cot deaths," or what Americans call sudden infant death syndrome (SIDS), could not be explained by coincidence. These deaths occur in infants under one year of age and have no medical explanation, even after autopsy. Dr. Meadow convinced jury after jury that it was a near statistical impossibility for two babies in the same family to die under such unexplainable circumstances. The more likely explanation, he explained, was murder.[2]

Meadow's testimony was predicated on basic probability: the probability of two independent events both happening is the product of their independent probabilities. Thus, if the chance of a coin toss coming up heads is 0.5, then the probability of flipping heads twice in a row is $(0.5)^2$, or 0.25. Meadow testified that the probability of a baby dying a cot death in a middle class, nonsmoking family is 1 in 8,500; thus, the probability of having two infants die of the syndrome is $1/(8,500)^2$, or 1 in 73 million. Juries were persuaded by the alternative hypothesis—that the parents who suffered multiple such infant deaths had a homicidal streak.

1. "The Probability of Injustice," *The Economist*, January 22, 2004.
2. "The Baby and the Bathwater," *The Economist*, January 22, 2004.

Unfortunately, Meadow's statistical inference was wrong. His 1-in-73-million calculation is accurate only if two events are truly independent, meaning that the outcome of one has no correlation with the outcome of the other. For example, the probability of flipping heads twice in a row would *not* be 0.25 if the coin were somehow fixed; in that case, flipping heads once may indicate that heads is far more likely than tails to come up in the future. Scientists now believe that sudden infant deaths are more like the fixed coin than an honest one. *The Economist* explained in 2004, when British courts began overturning criminal prosecutions for infant deaths: "The probability calculation works fine, so long as it is certain that cot deaths are entirely random and not linked by some unknown factor. But with something as mysterious as cot deaths, it is quite possible that there is a link—something genetic, for instance, which would make a family that had suffered one cot death more, not less, likely to suffer another."

Researchers now believe that there may be a genetic link to sudden infant death syndrome; the fetus might also acquire a physical defect while in the womb, particularly if the mother is a smoker or drug user.[3] Both such factors, of course, would be correlated across pregnancies, meaning that the parents of one child who died a cot death would have a higher likelihood than average of suffering another such tragedy.

Bad statistical analysis was compounded by another factor. Beginning in the 1990s, the number of sudden infant deaths began to drop sharply. Public health officials had learned that putting infants to sleep on their backs and not smoking around them dramatically cut the risk of sudden infant death (even though it is still not fully understood why these changes in behavior are so effective). As infant deaths became less common, the ones that happened were increasingly treated with suspicion. For example, the Canadian government instructed its investigators to "think dirty." In the language of statistics, the "null hypothesis," or the starting assumption to be disproved, was that the parent or parents involved were guilty rather than just tragically unlucky. This default assumption among investigators was compounded in the courts (where the presumption of innocence remained) by Meadow's flawed statistical inferences. *The Economist* concluded, "Justice seems to have miscarried on a grand scale."

This chapter introduces the most important tools for using data to draw conclusions. In the social sciences generally and in public policy in particular, statistics can rarely *prove* much of anything. Because researchers are often

---

3. "Researchers Gain New Insights into SIDS," MedlinePlus, March 7, 2008.

unable to conduct controlled experiments on human subjects, we must instead gather data and look for relationships and trends that offer insight into questions of interest. Does smoking cause cancer? We are likely to observe that smokers have a higher incidence of cancer than nonsmokers, but this observation alone does not prove a causal relationship between cigarettes and cancer. The observed difference may simply be a function of chance; suppose the smokers in the study were an unlucky bunch and just happened to have a particularly high incidence of cancer unrelated to their smoking. Basic statistical analysis enables us to determine the likelihood that the observed difference in the incidence of cancer between smokers and nonsmokers is a function of chance alone. Such calculations, combined with other kinds of data (such as biological studies examining the impact of tobacco on cell growth), enable policy makers to make informed decisions.

When used properly, basic statistics enables researchers and policy makers to draw important inferences from relatively small samples of data. When the analysis is poor, however, the conclusions can be wildly wrong—sometimes tragically so, as the example above demonstrates. This chapter outlines the basic tools for gathering a representative sample of data from a population of interest, such as a poll of registered voters, and making inferences based on such data. It will also explore the process for making decisions based on the probability of different outcomes. Policy makers rarely have perfect information. Probability and statistics can help them make better decisions with the data they have.

CHAPTER OUTLINE

10.1 SAMPLE POPULATIONS

The United States has an adult population of over 200 million, of whom roughly 70 percent are registered to vote in a presidential election. Only when all of the ballots have been cast do we know for certain how Americans have cast their votes (and even then there is some dispute). Yet leading up to such elections, presidential polls often provide remarkably accurate insight into voters' attitudes by interviewing a seemingly tiny proportion of the population. How is that possible? And when might the conclusions be misleading or wrong?

In a different context, public health experts can often estimate the prevalence of a disease, such as HIV/AIDS, in a region, or even in an entire country, by testing only a small proportion of the population. How do researchers make such sweeping conclusions based on what appears to be a relatively small amount of data?

The answer in both cases is statistical sampling. **Sampling** is the process of selecting a set of individual observations from some larger population, often with the intent of using the sample to make inferences about the full population. Suppose a masochistic boss sets an urn of 10,000 black and white marbles on the floor of your office and assigns you the task of determining how many marbles are black and how many are white. One obvious option is to sort all 10,000 marbles by color, giving you a precise answer (assuming that you do not make any counting errors). There is a far less time-consuming approach that would give you an excellent approximation of the proportion of colors; you could draw a sample of 100 marbles and make an inference about the fraction of black and white marbles in the larger population.

For example, if you were to draw 31 white marbles and 69 black marbles, then you might estimate the total population at 3,100 white marbles and 6,900 black marbles. This estimation is unlikely to be exactly correct. However, it will provide a reasonable approximation of the color split with far less effort than counting all 10,000 marbles. We can also use statistical techniques explained later in this chapter to build a confidence interval around our estimation, meaning that we can specify the statistical likelihood that some attribute of a population falls within a certain range. In the case of the 10,000 marbles in the urn, if we take a sample of 100 marbles and find that 31 are white, then we can say with 95-percent confidence that the true number of white marbles in the urn lies between 2,200 and 4,000. This is how modern political polls are conducted. Pollsters contact a sample of likely voters and use their answers to make an inference for the full electorate. (Just imagine Republican and Democratic voters instead of the black and white marbles.)

Obviously, the larger the sample, the more confidence we will have in our estimation. If we draw 1,000 marbles and 310 are white (and 690 are black), then we can infer with 95-percent confidence that the true number of white marbles in the urn is between 2,800 and 3,400. The technique for building such confidence intervals will be covered later in the chapter. For now, the most important point is that we don't have to count all 10,000 marbles in the urn in order to get a reasonable approximation of the proportion of black and white marbles.

10.1.1　Simple Random Sampling

A **simple random sample** is drawn from a population in such a way that any individual observation in the population has an equal probability of being included in the sample. In the marble example, drawing 100 marbles from the urn would generate a random sample (assuming the marbles had been thoroughly mixed and that we did not replace the marbles that had already been drawn). If we were conducting a political poll and had the phone numbers of all registered voters, then dialing phone numbers at random (with no repeats allowed) would give us a random sample of registered voters.

In practice, a purely random sample is difficult to achieve. For example, even if we had the phone numbers of all likely voters, not all of them will answer the phone and provide information to the pollster. The factors that affect whether or not a voter answers the phone may well be correlated with their political opinions. We could certainly imagine that wealthy voters, for example, would be more likely to invest in caller ID, which will screen out nuisance phone calls. Thus, the sample of individuals who *answered* the phone survey would be skewed toward the less wealthy, which might diminish the accuracy of the poll. It is crucial for researchers and policy makers to recognize potential sources of **sampling bias,** since they can lead to profoundly misleading conclusions. While no sample is likely to be perfect, some methods have more serious flaws than others:

- The daytime call-in radio show in which ten callers in a row express their rage at the incumbent governor. Perhaps every resident of the state is angry at the governor—or perhaps not. The callers are different than the population in key respects: they are listening to a specific station, they are listening to the radio in the middle of the day, and they are angry enough to phone the show.
- The first 1,000 names in the phone book. Those phone numbers might represent a random sample of all residents in a given jurisdiction—but probably not. Last names are not randomly distributed at birth; a family name often reflects ethnic heritage. Thus, the names at the beginning of the alphabet may be skewed toward a certain ethnic group, such as Hispanics or Armenians, who are not representative of the population as a whole.

As a policy analyst, you should begin to develop a sense of how data collection can be skewed by a biased sample. Some samples are deliberately nonrandom because an alternative selection method is deemed more cost effective at compiling a representative sample of the population of interest; the efficiencies outweigh any potential biases. For example, one of the most famous longitudinal studies ever conducted is the Framingham Heart Study. Researchers chose a single New England town to gather in-depth medical information on residents (and their children and grandchildren) over the course of decades. The residents of Framingham are wealthier and more likely to be white than the U.S. population as a whole. However, these drawbacks are presumably outweighed by the ease of gathering longitudinal data in a single location.

Moreover, racial and geographic diversity matter less when gathering data for medical studies than they do when gathering data for studies on subjects like poverty or political attitudes.

10.1.2 Stratified Sampling

A **stratified sample** randomly chooses observations from within a set of defined subpopulations, or strata, to ensure that observations from each stratum are represented in the sample in proportion to their share of the overall population. Suppose that a university would like to survey its students on their overall satisfaction with their educational experience. The university has four classes (first year, second year, third year, and fourth year), each with 2,000 students, as well as a small graduate program with 100 students. The researchers gathering the data want to make sure that the survey is representative of the whole student body. If they have a budget sufficient to survey 10 percent of students, then a stratified sample would randomly survey 200 first-year students, 200 second-year students, 200 third-year students, 200 fourth-year students, and 20 graduate students.

A simple random sample would, on average, achieve exactly the same distribution of students to be surveyed. If the researchers picked 820 university students at random to survey, the expected number of first-year students included would be 200, the expected number of second-year students would be 200, and so on. However, **sampling error,** the natural variation that comes from choosing a sample instead of the whole population, makes it possible that one class could be seriously over- or underrepresented. In particular, researchers would likely be concerned about graduate students because of their small share of the student body. A survey of 820 students could easily include just a few graduate students whose views are not representative of their peers or even no graduate students at all. In cases where the relevant nonoverlapping strata can be easily identified, a stratified sample ensures each group is proportionately represented in the overall sample.

10.1.3 Cluster Sampling

A **cluster sample** is created by dividing the population of interest into many similar or identical clusters, such as rural counties or high-income zip codes, and then drawing observations from one or several randomly chosen clusters. Suppose a researcher is interested in studying drug use in rural communities throughout the United States. Rural counties are relatively inaccessible and spread across the country, making both a simple random sample and a stratified sample impractical or cost-prohibitive. Instead, the researcher could define all the possible clusters of interest, such as all American counties with fewer than 5,000 residents, and then randomly pick one or several of those counties from which to gather data. If the clusters are properly defined, the results should be applicable to the larger population of interest.

10.1.4 Oversampling

In some cases, a data-gathering strategy may deliberately **oversample** some subgroup of the population, which means that members of the subgroup are included in the sample in excess of their share of larger population. This is usually done to ensure that the sample has sufficient data to draw meaningful conclusions on the subgroup of interest. To compensate for this oversampling, the relevant observations are likely to be **weighted** in any subsequent statistical analysis to avoid biasing the results. To more fully understand this process, imagine that researchers are attempting to learn more about the distribution of poverty among racial and ethnic groups, including Native Americans. They plan to conduct a survey of some proportion of American households. While a simple random sample might include some Native American households, it might not—or at least not enough to make meaningful inferences about that particular subpopulation. Thus, researchers may decide to oversample counties with large Native American populations. For example, they might collect three times as many observations in counties with significant Native American populations as they collect in other counties. This would provide sufficient observations on Native American households to provide information on mean household income, educational attainment, and so on.

Of course, it also means that the sample is no longer representative of the country. When the data are used to draw conclusions about the American population as a whole, the observations from the oversampled counties must be weighted so that they count less. To use a simple numerical example, if three times as many observations are collected from certain counties relative to their actual share of the population, then each of those observations would count as one-third. You should see how collecting income data for ten Native American households and then weighting each observation by one-tenth will give a more accurate snapshot of Native American household income than simply collecting data for a single household.

Good studies depend on sound strategies for gathering data. No amount of statistical wizardry can make up for a data-collection process that is inherently flawed—or, as researchers like to say, "Garbage in, garbage out."

················| **POLICY IN THE REAL WORLD** |·················

When More Data Are Not Better Data: The Subscription Bias[4]

In the fall of 1936, the *Literary Digest* conducted a poll of some 10 million Americans on how they were likely to vote in the upcoming presidential election between Kansas governor Alf Landon and incumbent president Franklin Roosevelt. The result: Landon would beat Roosevelt soundly with 57 percent of the popular vote. In fact, Roosevelt won in a landslide, capturing 60 percent of the popular vote and winning every state except Maine and Vermont.

How could a poll of 10-million Americans be so wrong, given that contemporary polls almost always get more accurate results with much, much smaller samples? Very easily. The *Literary Digest* mailed ballots to its subscribers plus a list of automobile and telephone owners, whose addresses could be culled from public records. In 1936, subscribers to the *Literary Digest* were more affluent than most Americans, as were households with autos and/or phones. Wealthy households are more likely to vote Republican. Thus, the sample was huge but not representative of the country as a whole, which went for Roosevelt.

···

10.1.5 Data Danger

One of the most important tools in policy analysis is anticipating the incentives of the stakeholders affected by any policy decision. This is true even when it comes to data analysis. When subjects or institutions are evaluated using data over which they have some control, they will seek to manipulate the data in ways that lead to more favorable evaluations. Suppose, for example, that we are trying to improve health-care policy by collecting and disseminating data on surgical outcomes. It seems perfectly reasonable to evaluate surgeons and hospitals based on their survival rates for different procedures. Patients would presumably benefit from information on the survival rates for open-heart surgery that they could compare when choosing a surgeon or hospital. Such data are easy to collect and seemingly objective.

---

4. Cynthia Crossen, "Fiasco in 1936 Survey Brought 'Science' to Election Polling," *Wall Street Journal*, October 2, 2006.

And perhaps completely misleading. It is crucial to recognize that surgeons can improve their survival rates without improving the outcome of a single patient. How? By refusing to operate on the patients who are the least likely to survive surgery. The irony is that surgeons can make themselves look better by helping fewer people, particularly those who are the sickest! This is not mere theory. The state of New York keeps scorecards that evaluate the mortality rates of cardiologists performing coronary angioplasty, a treatment for heart disease. According to a survey conducted by the School of Medicine and Dentistry at the University of Rochester, the scorecard, which ostensibly serves patients, also may work to their detriment: 83 percent of the cardiologists surveyed said that because of the public mortality statistics some patients who might benefit from angioplasty may not receive the procedure; 79 percent of the doctors said that some of their personal medical decisions had been influenced by the knowledge that mortality data are collected and made public.[5]

Educational testing is another realm where the use of data as a tool for accountability can lead to similar behavior. Society obviously has a stake in measuring educational outcomes and holding teachers and principals accountable for student performance. While standardized tests are not perfect measures of student achievement, they can provide meaningful feedback on students, schools, or entire systems. So what is the potential problem with using test scores as an evaluation tool?

Teachers and school administrators can improve test scores by improving the effectiveness of their teaching—or by manipulating the pool of test takers. For schools with control over admissions, such as private schools and some selective public schools, this is most easily accomplished by excluding students who are likely to test poorly. This is the same basic behavior as the heart surgeons: the data look better because the hardest cases are excluded. Once again, society is likely made worse off, not better, by giving schools an added incentive to refuse admission to the most disadvantaged students.

But schools need not have selective admissions in order to manipulate their test-taking population; they need only do things to exclude the scores of students most likely to do poorly—anything from encouraging them to stay home on test day to making it easier for them to drop out of school. Once again, this is not mere theory. When Florida introduced an accountability system in 1996 based on the Florida Comprehensive Assessment Test, the

---

5. Marc Santora, "Cardiologists Say Rankings Sway Choices on Surgery," *New York Times,* January 11, 2005.

test scores of students classified as disabled were not included in a school's evaluation.[6] Of course, teachers and principals at the school level have control over which students are classified as disabled. Researchers found that low-income and low-performing students were more likely to be classified as disabled after the accountability system was introduced and that this kind of reclassification was most likely to happen in schools at greatest risk of being sanctioned as the result of the program.

What these examples have in common is that the individuals or institutions being evaluated have some control over the data that are being used to evaluate them. As a result, they have an incentive to manipulate the data in ways that are not consistent with the goals for which the data-driven assessment has been designed. And, of course, the higher the stakes in the evaluation, the more incentive there is to engage in such behavior.

10.2 DRAWING STATISTICAL INFERENCES

Public policy often requires drawing inferences from sample data. Suppose, for example, that we are interested in obesity. How much does an average American adult male weigh? (Public health officials might then compare this figure to those of other countries or perhaps to the average for American adult males a decade ago.) Obviously, we cannot weigh all American adult men. Thus, we must use sample data and draw our conclusion based on those data. For the purposes of this example, let's assume that we are able to collect unbiased sample data with weights of 1,000 American adult males. If the mean weight for the current sample of men is 182 pounds, what broader significance can we attribute to that finding, if any? What is the likelihood that a different sample of 1,000 men would have yielded dramatically different results? Basic statistics offers tools for answering these kinds of questions.

10.2.1 The Sample Mean and the Central Limit Theorem

First, we must introduce the concept of the **sample mean,** represented as $\bar{x}$, which is the mean, or average, for any sample set of observations. If we invite a randomly selected sample of 1,000 American adult males to our research center and weigh each of them, then the mean of their weights would be our sam-

---

6. David N. Figlio and Lawrence S. Getzler, "Accountability, Ability and Disability: Gaming the System," Working Paper 9307, National Bureau of Economic Research, October 2002.

ple mean—say, 182 pounds. If we were then to select a different random sample of 1,000 American adult males and weigh each of them, we would likely get a different sample mean—say, 179 pounds. These sample means turn out to have a very elegant and powerful property. According to the **central limit theorem,** the sample means for any population will be distributed roughly as a normal distribution around the true mean for the population (regardless of the shape of the underlying population distribution). The larger the number of samples, the more closely the distribution of sample means will approximate a normal distribution.

Although it is nearly impossible to do, let us suppose that we know the true mean weight for all American adult men, or the population mean μ, and that it is 180 pounds. The central limit theorem tells us that (1) the sample means will be distributed symmetrically around the population mean μ and (2) the mean of the sample means will converge to μ. Each time we weigh a random sample of 1,000 men, we will likely get a slightly different sample mean, as depicted below.

Some of the sample means deviate significantly from the real population mean; however, most cluster around the true population mean of 180 pounds. Indeed, that is the statistical property that makes the central limit theorem so useful, as we shall explore in the balance of the chapter.

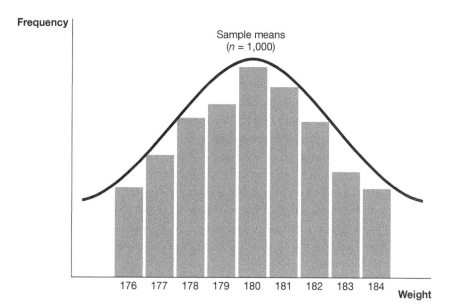

Expected Distribution of Sample Means
According to the Central Limit Theorem

10.2.2 The Standard Error

We need one more tool in order to be able to draw inferences about a population using sample data: the standard error. If we were to weigh a sample of 1,000 American adult men and calculate a sample mean of 182.5 pounds, what, if anything, would that tell us about the weights of all American adult men? It turns out that we can make a meaningful inference using this sample mean; we can calculate the likelihood that the sample mean lies within a certain distance of the true population mean. For example, depending on the specifics of our sample, we might be able to infer that there is a 95-percent probability that the true population mean (the average weight of all American men) lies between 3.0 pounds below the sample mean and 3.0 pounds above it (182.5 pounds +/– 3.0 pounds). This kind of inference could be very helpful for researchers or public health officials with an interest in obesity among Americans or other health-related issues, and it would spare them the expense of weighing tens of millions of people.

The **standard error,** which measures the dispersion of the sample means, is what makes such a calculation possible. Specifically, for some population with mean μ and standard deviation σ, the standard error of the sample means is $\sigma/\sqrt{n}$, where n is the size of each sample.

You should see from the equation that the standard error gets smaller as the sample size gets larger. This should make intuitive sense. Large samples are less prone to be affected by a handful of observations that lie far from the mean. If the true population mean for American adult males is 180 pounds, it is unlikely that a random sample of 1,000 men will have a mean weight of 211 pounds. If the sample consists of only 5 men, however, it is much more likely that we may get a sample mean of 211 pounds.

Similarly, you should see that the standard error is smaller when the standard deviation of the underlying population is smaller. A population with less dispersion will produce sample means with less dispersion. Suppose, for example, that researchers are now interested in the weights of male marathon runners. This distribution of weights is more compact than the distribution of weights for the male population overall; as a result, the sample means are less likely to lie far from the true population mean. It would be virtually impossible to draw a sample of marathon runners (even a small sample) with a mean weight of 211 pounds.

. . . .

The Summation Sign

The figure Σ is a handy character in statistics. It represents the summation of the quantity that comes after it. For example, if there is a set of observations x_1, x_2, x_3, and x_4, then $\Sigma (x_i)$ tells us that we should sum the four observations: $x_1 + x_2 + x_3 + x_4$. Thus, $\Sigma (x_i) = x_1 + x_2 + x_3 + x_4$. We can make the formula even more adaptable by writing $\sum_{i=1}^{n} (x_i)$, which sums the quantity $x_1 + x_2 + x_3 + \dots$ x_n, or, in other words, all of the terms beginning with x_1 (because $i = 1$) up to x_n (because $i = n$). Our formula for the mean of a set of observations could be represented as the following: mean $= \sum_{i=1}^{n} (x_i)/n$ for any set of n observations.

. . . .

In many cases, researchers do not know the standard deviation of the population from which a sample is being drawn. (If we knew the standard deviation for the full population of interest, then we would probably also know the population mean and wouldn't need to do all this sampling.) Thus, in most cases, we must improvise by using a standard deviation that is calculated from a population sample instead. The formula for calculating a standard deviation for a sample is similar (but not identical to) the formula for calculating the standard deviation for the full population. Specifically, the standard deviation for a sample $= s = \sqrt{\sum_{i=1}^{n} (x_i - \bar{x})^2/(n-1)}$, where n is the number of observations in the sample. Note that the sum is divided by $n - 1$, rather than n, which (for technical reasons beyond the scope of this book) compensates for the fact that we are calculating the standard deviation from a sample rather than from the full population.

If we substitute the sample standard deviation to calculate the standard error for the sample means, then the standard error $= s/\sqrt{n}$, where n is the sample size.

The properties of the standard error are what make sampling such a powerful tool. Because the sample means are distributed roughly as a normal distribution, we can draw on what we know about normal distributions to infer the following:

- Roughly 68.0 percent of the sample means will lie within one standard error of the population mean.
- Roughly 95.0 percent of the sample means will lie within two standard errors of the population mean.

- Roughly 99.7 percent of the sample means will lie within three standard errors of the population mean.

To return to our weight example, if we were to take a random sample of 1,000 American adult men, we would expect that sample mean to be within one standard error of the true population mean for all American men roughly 68 percent of the time. Or to put it slightly differently, if we were to take 100 different random samples, each of 1,000 men, we would expect the means for roughly 68 of those samples to be within one standard error of the population mean. And we would expect 95 of the sample means to be within two standard errors of the true population mean. On average, only five of the sample means would lie more than two standard errors from the population mean. These probabilities are what enable us to use sampling to make reliable inferences about the underlying population.

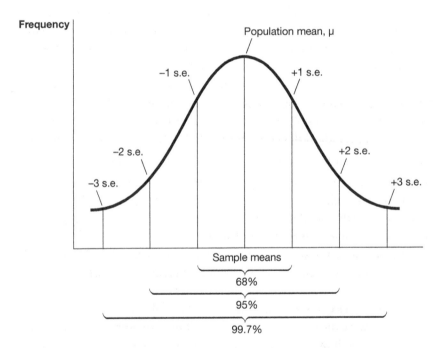

Frequency Distribution of Sample Means

10.2.3 Confidence Intervals

The standard error enables us to build a **confidence interval** that expresses the likelihood that the population mean lies within a certain distance of the observed sample mean. Suppose that our variable of interest is the average weight of an American adult male. Further suppose that we compose a random sample of 1,000 American men and find that their mean weight is 178 pounds and that the standard deviation for this sample is 42 pounds. Based on these data, what can we infer about the average weight of an American adult male?

First, we can calculate a standard error for our sample of 1,000 men: standard error = $s/\sqrt{n}$ = 42/31.6 = 1.33. We know from the central limit theorem that roughly 95 percent of sample means will lie within 1.96 standard errors of the population mean in either direction, or within the range 178 +/– 1.96(1.33) = 178 +/– 2.61 pounds. This gives us a range of 175.4 pounds to 180.6 pounds, which enables us to make the following statement: at the 95-percent confidence level, the average American adult male weighs between 175.4 and 180.6 pounds.

Of course, this is an inference based on probability. Roughly 5 times out of 100, the true population mean will *not* lie in the interval suggested by the sample mean. For some research purposes, that degree of statistical uncertainty may not be good enough. If we needed to construct our interval at the 99-percent confidence level—meaning that we would expect the true population mean to lie outside the confidence interval only 1 time in 100—then we would use a variation on the same basic approach. We know from the central limit theorem that roughly 99 percent of the sample means will lie within 2.58 standard errors of the population mean.[7] Thus, we can say with 99-percent confidence that the population mean is in the range of 178 pounds +/– 2.58(1.33) = 178 +/– 3.43. That is, we can say with 99-percent confidence that the average weight for American adult males lies between 174.6 pounds and 181.4 pounds. This is broader than our 95-percent confidence interval; the trade-off is that we can predict with greater certainty that the population mean lies within the specified range.

---

7. The exact figures for the number of standard errors that must be added or subtracted to the sample mean in order to create a confidence interval is known as a **z-value.** Most statistics texts will have tables listing the z values that correspond to different confidence intervals. The most commonly used z values are the following:

CONFIDENCE LEVEL	Z-VALUE
90	1.64
95	1.96
99	2.58

10.3 POLLING

Polling is a common form of statistical inference. A **poll** uses a sample of the population to calculate a confidence interval for the proportion of the population who share some attribute or opinion, such as support for a particular political candidate. Suppose we are conducting a presidential poll of likely voters in the weeks leading up to the general election. (You should recognize that a poll must target *likely voters* rather than citizens or even registered voters in order to produce an accurate sample.) Suppose that a news organization is interested in the likely outcome of a statewide election in Ohio. The sponsors of the poll would contact a representative sample of likely voters, as time and budget allow. Suppose the pollsters contact an unbiased sample of 400 likely voters and get the following response: 201 respondents support the Republican candidate, 115 support the Democratic candidate, and 84 are undecided. What, if anything, can this tell us about the likely electoral outcome when all Ohio voters go to the polls?

It turns out that by speaking to just 400 representative voters, we can use the basic tools of sampling to make a powerful inference about Ohio voters overall. We begin by calculating a standard error, though the standard error for a poll is calculated differently than for a sample mean.

> **The standard error for a sample proportion is $\sqrt{\hat{p}(1 - \hat{p})/n}$, where $\hat{p}$ is the proportion of the population who fall into some category of interest (such as the proportion of respondents who support one candidate or the other) and n is the sample size.**

In the above poll of Ohio voters, the sample proportion who supports the Republican candidate would be 201/400, or .5025. Thus, $1 - \hat{p}$ is .4975. The sample size is 400. The standard error for the poll based on stated support for the Republican candidate is the following:

$$\text{standard error} = \sqrt{.5025(.4975)/400}$$
$$\text{standard error} = \sqrt{.000625}$$
$$\text{standard error} = .025$$

We can repeat the same exercise for the Democratic candidate:

$$\text{standard error} = \sqrt{.2875(.7125)/400}$$
$$\text{standard error} = \sqrt{.000512}$$
$$\text{standard error} = .023$$

We can use the standard error the same way we used it in our previous sampling examples—to calculate the likelihood that the sample proportion (the percentage of voters preferring one of the candidates) lies within a certain range of the true proportion of Ohio voters who feel that way. Most polls use a 95-percent confidence level to create a confidence interval, which is often referred to in a polling context as the **margin of error.** Once again drawing on the central limit theorem, we can infer that 95 percent of the sample proportions will lie within 1.96 standard errors of the population proportion (the actual proportion of all Ohio voters who support the Republican candidate). In other words, if we were to conduct 100 different polls of representative samples of Ohio voters, we would expect roughly 5 of those polls to give us figures for support of the Republican and Democratic candidates that lie more than two standard errors away from the true proportion of Ohio voters who feel that way. Plugging in the numbers:

- Of the 400 likely voters polled, 201 (.5025) supported the Republican candidate. Thus, at the 95-percent confidence level, we can infer that the true proportion of Ohio voters who support the Republican candidate is .5025 +/- (1.96)(.025), or .5025 +/- .049. Doing the math and rounding off, we can say with 95-percent confidence that the proportion of all likely Ohio voters who support the Republican candidate lies between 45 percent and 55 percent. (The news outlet would likely report the results slightly differently: the Republican candidate has the support of 50 percent of likely voters, with a margin of error of 5 percent.)
- Of the 400 likely voters polled, 115 (.2875) supported the Democratic candidate. We can infer at the 95-percent confidence level that the true proportion of Ohio voters who support the Democratic candidate is .2875 +/- (1.96)(.023), or .2875 +/- .045. At the 95-percent confidence level, we can say that the proportion of all likely Ohio voters who currently support the Democratic candidate lies between 24 percent and 33 percent.
- Based on all of this, we can conclude with 95-percent confidence that the Republican candidate currently has more support among all likely voters in Ohio than the Democratic candidate does—not merely because the Republican candidate is leading in the poll 50 percent to 29 percent, but because the lowest value in the Republican candidate's 95-percent confidence interval (45 percent) is higher than the highest value in the Democratic candidate's 95-percent confidence interval (33 percent).

It's still possible that the poll is wrong, perhaps because the sample just happened to contact an improbable number of Republican households—not unlike flipping a coin and getting four heads in a row. It happens. Nonetheless, the probable explanation for the poll's findings is that more likely voters across the state of Ohio support the Republican candidate than support the

Democratic candidate. This is a powerful conclusion. From our sample of only 400 likely Ohio voters, we can infer with 95-percent confidence that the Republican candidate is indeed leading the race.

··············· | **RULE OF THUMB** | ···············

The Central Limit Theorem

Most statistical inference derives from the powerful central limit theorem, which holds that distribution of sample means will be roughly normal around the population mean. However, this result may not hold if the sample size is too small. For the central limit theorem to hold, the rule of thumb is that the sample mean must be generated from a sample of 30 or more. For sample proportions, $n(\hat{p})$ needs to be at least 5, as does $n(1 - \hat{p})$.

···

In modern polling, the challenge is not necessarily doing the statistics, but rather ensuring an accurate sample. In an era in which most busy families have caller ID and may not necessarily choose to spend time responding to a survey or poll, the challenge for firms collecting such data is ensuring an unbiased sample.

··············· | **POLICY IN THE REAL WORLD** | ···············

The Science of Polling: Getting Accurate Answers in the Age of Caller ID[8]

The Pew Research Center for the People & the Press is a widely respected polling organization that conducts polls on topics ranging from national political races to Americans' attitudes toward gun control and climate change. The accuracy of the results depends on a rigorous methodology for gathering an unbiased sample of opinion.[9] For a national survey, the process consists of the following:

8. Summarized from the Pew Research Center Web site "About Our Survey Methodology in Detail."
9. http://people-press.org/methodology/about.

1. The survey respondents are drawn from a random-digit sample of telephone numbers in the United States, including both landlines and cell phones. The random-digit process generates both listed and unlisted numbers, avoiding a possible "listing" bias. An American telephone number consists of 10 digits: the area code (3), the telephone exchange (3), and the bank number (4). Only the last two digits of the bank number are randomly generated. The first 8 digits of the sampled telephone numbers are selected to be proportionately stratified by county and by telephone exchange within the county. That is, the number of telephone numbers randomly sampled from within a given county is proportional to that county's share of telephone numbers in the United States.

2. The stratified sample is divided into subsamples, or replicates, each of which is also representative of the population of interest. Each replicate is surveyed before moving on to the next replicate. Thus, if the goal is to reach 100 residents in each of 20 urban counties, the first replicate may contain 25 potential respondents in each of those counties. The next replicate would contain another 25 potential respondents in each county. The primary advantage of working with replicates is that the data gathered at any point in the survey will be roughly representative of the overall population. Thus, it may be possible to draw some meaningful inferences while the survey is in progress—or if the budget runs out! (The standard errors obviously grow smaller as the sample gets larger.) For example, if political pollsters are attempting to reach as many households in the sample as possible in a twenty-four-hour period, then it is essential that they work with representative subsamples. If the poll is interrupted, then the results are still valid, albeit with a larger standard error than if the full sample had been contacted. On the other hand, if pollsters had instead contacted potential respondents state by state, and the poll was interrupted before they had time to contact any voters west of the Rocky Mountains, then the poll would not be representative of American voters, and the results would be meaningless.

3. At least seven attempts are made to complete an interview at every telephone number selected for the sample. The calls are staggered throughout the day and week to maximize the chances of making contact with a potential respondent. Interviewers are trained to ask for "the youngest male, 18 years of age or older, who is now at home." If there is no eligible male respondent, then interviewers ask for the youngest female over age eighteen. According to Pew, this process produces a sample of respondents that closely resembles the American adult population in terms of age and gender.

4. Despite the methodology described above, the possibility of nonresponse with telephone surveys produces a potential bias. To compensate, the sample data are weighted in the analysis to ensure that all subgroups of interest are represented in proportion to their makeup of the U.S. population. So, if households with income over $100,000 were undersampled, then those respondents might receive extra weighting in the analysis.

According to the National Council on Public Polls,[10] a scientific poll of 1,000 Americans will have a small enough standard error that it will accurately reflect the opinions of America's almost 218 million adults. The council notes, "That means interviews attempted with all 210 million adults—if such were possible—would give approximately the same results as a well-conducted survey based on 1,000 interviews."[11]

10.4 DECISION TREES

RULE OF THUMB

Probabilities

The probability of two independent events happening is the product of their individual probabilities. (Two events are independent if their correlation is zero; the outcome of one event has no association with the outcome of the other.) Thus, the probability of flipping heads three times in a row (with a fair coin) is $(1/2)(1/2)(1/2) = 1/8$, or 0.125. The probability of one independent event happening or another independent event happening is the sum of the individual probabilities. Thus, the probability of rolling a 1 or a 2 or a 3 with a die is $1/6 + 1/6 + 1/6 = 3/6$, or 0.5.

10. http://www.ncpp.org.
11. Sheldon R. Gawiser and G. Evans Witt, "20 Questions a Journalist Should Ask about Poll Results," 3rd ed., National Council on Public Polls, http://www.ncpp.org/?q=node/4.

Good data and sound statistical analysis are at the heart of good policy analysis. Yet policy makers rarely have the luxury of perfect information. Indeed, the more serious the policy challenge, the less likely it is that public decision makers will have complete information before taking action. A **decision tree** is a tool for evaluating possible courses of action when the future is uncertain but it is possible to estimate the probabilities and "payoffs" of different outcomes.

Imagine that you face the following business situation. Your company makes and sells T-shirts and hats to commemorate sporting events such as the Super Bowl and the World Series. You are considering producing 20,000 T-shirts for an upcoming outdoor concert. Your supplier in China will charge you $2 for each shirt; however, he has informed you that there is a 10-percent chance that the shirts will get stuck in customs and will not arrive in time for the concert, in which case the entire investment will be lost. Meanwhile, the sale of T-shirts is also uncertain. Historically, T-shirt sales have been dependent on concert attendance, which is determined primarily by the weather. When the weather is excellent, you project that the concert will be packed, and you will be able to sell all of the T-shirts at an average price of $20 per garment. If the weather is fair (overcast but not raining), attendance will be lower, and you will have to reduce your prices to an average of $12 per garment to unload all of your shirts. Finally, there is the possibility of rain. Historically, you have sold only 1,000 T-shirts at an average price of $10 per garment when it rains during an outdoor concert. The weather forecast for concert day is predicting a 30-percent chance of sunshine, a 60-percent chance of overcast skies with no rain, and a 10-percent chance of thunderstorms.

Should you try to sell the T-shirts? You must decide now, because you must place the order with your supplier.

This seems like a complex question, given the many contingencies and uncertainties. In fact, the answer is fairly straightforward once the information is manageably organized. A decision tree organizes such contingencies in a way that enables us to calculate when the T-shirt sales are likely to be profitable, on average. It will not tell us whether the T-shirt sales *will* be profitable—that will be determined by the outcome of future events. Instead, the decision tree will tell us whether the expected value of this venture is positive, zero, or negative. (You should recall from Chapter 9 that expected value of any event is the sum of all possible payoffs, each of which has been multiplied by its probability.) If we are risk neutral and the assorted probabilities and payoffs are accurate, then we ought to undertake any business opportunity that has a positive expected value; such a venture will, on average, be profitable. Or, to put it slightly differently, if you were to do a venture with a positive expected value over and over

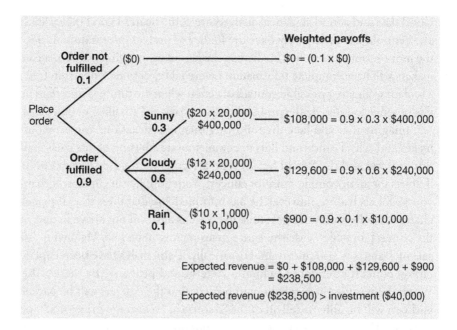

Weighted payoffs

Decision Tree: Concert T-Shirt Sales (investment = $40,000)

again (such as selling T-shirts at multiple concerts), you would make money with near certainty in the long run.

The decision tree maps all possible contingencies, their respective probabilities, and their payoffs. As a result, we get a graphic description of all possible outcomes and their relative likelihood. In this case, the decision tree helps us to calculate an expected value for the concert T-shirt sales.

In the first branch, we face the possibility that the Chinese supplier will not be able to fulfill the order. Thus, there is a 10-percent chance that there will be no return on the investment at all. On the other hand, there is a 90-percent chance that the supplier will deliver the shirts in time. But assuming the shirts arrive on time, we now face another branch with assorted possible outcomes. (You should recognize that if the shirts don't arrive on time, then the weather on concert day becomes irrelevant.) If the entrepreneur has shirts to sell at the concert, there is a 30-percent chance (sunny day) that he will earn $400,000 (20,000 shirts at $20 per shirt); there is a 60-percent chance (cloudy day) that he will earn $240,000 (20,000 shirts at $12); and there is a 10-percent chance that he will earn only $10,000 (1,000 shirts at $10). The column on the far right sums all the possible payoffs, each weighted by its probability. He obviously makes nothing if the shirts don't get out of customs. The "sunny day" expected payoff is $400,000 (the expected profits from selling T-shirts) multiplied by 0.3 (the probability of sun) multiplied by 0.9 (the probability that he has shirts to sell) for a total of $108,000. You can do the calculations for the other branches on the tree. The total expected revenues for the concert-T-shirt venture are $238,500, which vastly exceeds the required investment of $40,000.

This is a very good business idea. However, the entrepreneur could still lose all of his money if the shirts get stuck in customs, or he could make a mere $10,000 if he gets the shirts but it rains on concert day. It is crucial to recognize that a good decision—as measured by the expected outcome—could still have a bad outcome. And a bad decision—meaning that the expected outcome is negative—could still turn out well (like winning at the slots in Las Vegas). Robert Rubin, a former secretary of the treasury and Wall Street bond trader, used this strategy successfully both when making trades at Goldman Sachs and when making major decisions in the Clinton administration. Jacob Weisberg explained Rubin's "probabilistic decision making" in a story for the *New York Times Magazine:*

> What was paradoxical about Rubin's risk-taking was how reasoned it was. "Arbitrage is an actuarial business, just like so much of life," Rubin says. "Each judgment was probabilistic. What you needed to do was make sure you didn't get so big in one position, even if the odds were very good, that if it went bad it wiped out everything else. You had to maintain your balance."
>
> Put another way, Rubin played arbitrage the way a mathematician plays poker, keeping track of cards and weighing odds so as to reduce the factor of luck. In considering whether to take arbitrage positions, Rubin would muster all available information, constantly recalculate the percentages and make a decision only when necessary. Although a player with this kind of discipline will sometimes lose—and sometimes lose big—over time he has a significant advantage over those who behave less rationally.

Rubin used the same basic strategy as Treasury secretary when contemplating currency interventions or other major economic moves, such as the 1995 Mexican bailout led by the Treasury Department. Weisberg explained:

What is telling about Rubin, and what makes him ulti- mately such an unusual character in Washington, is how he thinks about something like the Mexican support program in retrospect. He points not to the happy result—that Mexico paid us back ahead of schedule, with a tidy profit for the Treasury—but to the sound decision. "If the Mexican support program had gone bad, I would still have said that it was the right thing to do," he says. "But it was judged successful because it worked. I don't think that's actually the way it should have been judged. It should have been judged based on whether it was the right judgment for our national interest in terms of every- thing that could be known at the time." Rubin says that focusing on the result rather than the decision is what's wrong with Washington, because it deters people from "acting optimally."[12]

10.5 HYPOTHESIS TESTING

Hypothesis testing consists of proposing a hypothesis and then accepting or rejecting it with some level of statistical confidence. Suppose a gambler were to propose a game with the following rules: He will roll a single die. If the number 1 comes up, you win $1,000. If the number 6 comes up, he wins $1,000. If 2, 3, 4, or 5 come up, he will roll again. The game will consist of 10 rolls of a die that he has brought with him.

This is a fair game, meaning that you both have the same expected payoff. Now suppose that after you agree to play the game, he proceeds to roll a 6 ten times in a row, winning $10,000 from you. Can you prove, based on the out- come alone, that the die is "loaded" (manipulated in some way to make a cer- tain number more likely to come up)? The answer is no. It is possible to roll a 6 ten times in a row with a fair die; indeed, if you were to roll a die for weeks on end, every once in a while you might roll ten consecutive 6s. However, both common sense and basic probability suggest that the gambler has rigged the die.

Nonetheless, it is theoretically impossible to prove that the die is loaded, based on the outcome alone (which is why the British government should

12. Jacob Weisberg, "Keeping the Boom from Busting," *New York Times Magazine,* July 19, 1998.

never have sent parents to jail simply because their innocence was highly unlikely). Hypothesis testing takes a different approach: rather than seeking to *prove* some premise—that the die has been tampered with, for instance—hypothesis testing derives its power and significance by using statistical inference to *accept or reject* some proposition with some level of statistical confidence. We reject those propositions that are highly statistically unlikely.

The theory or proposition that is being tested is known as the **null hypothesis,** or H_0. We simultaneously propose an **alternative hypothesis,** or H_a, which must be accepted if the null hypothesis is rejected. In this case, the null hypothesis would be that the die is fair. The alternative hypothesis is that the die has been manipulated in such a way as to deliver a nonrandom outcome. Thus:

H_0: the die is fair.
H_a: the die is "loaded."

Researchers generally determine the level of statistical confidence required to reject a null hypothesis *before* conducting the analysis. Thus, we may decide *ex ante* that we will reject the null hypothesis if we observe an outcome that would happen less than 1 time in 100 if the null hypothesis were true. This is called the 99-percent confidence level, since the probability that chance alone can explain the outcome is 0.01 or lower. A less rigorous benchmark would be the 95-percent confidence level. In this case, we would reject the null hypothesis if we observe an outcome that would happen less than 5 times in 100 if the null hypothesis were true.

Our null hypothesis in this case is that the die is fair. In other words, our presumption is that the gambler is not cheating. Yet we might also decide to reject that presumption if we observed a highly unlikely outcome that worked to the gambler's advantage. If we were to choose a 99-percent level of confidence, for example, a judge might ask to inspect the die if the gambler rolled a winning combination of numbers that would turn up by chance less than 1 time in 100. Once again, this low probability outcome does not prove that the gambler is cheating; it does seem a reasonable justification for inspecting the die. Indeed, casinos will take a particular interest in blackjack players who win improbably large amounts of money; such casino patrons may be lucky, or they may be counting cards.

What are the odds of rolling a 6 ten times in a row—the feat that enabled the gambler to win $10,000 from you in our hypothetical example? The probability of rolling ten consecutive 6s is $(1/6)^{10}$, or just over 1 in 60 million! That's far more improbable than the threshold we set up for rejecting the null hypothesis *ex ante,* which was 1 in 100. It is highly unlikely that this event occurred by chance alone. Inspect the die!

Most statistical inference is based on hypothesis testing. When researchers examine large data sets, such as health data for thousands or tens of thousands of people, they are looking for patterns that cannot be explained by chance alone. Suppose, for example, that researchers were attempting to probe the connection between smokeless tobacco and heart disease. Presumably they would have some theoretical reason to believe that there might be a connection. In the case of smokeless tobacco, perhaps biologists had observed that nicotine was associated with higher rates of heart disease in laboratory animals. Since researchers cannot conduct similar laboratory experiments on humans, they would look for statistical confirmation in a large data set with information on both smokeless tobacco use and heart disease. Is there a connection between the two that cannot be explained by chance alone? The data cannot *prove* that smokeless tobacco contributes to heart disease, even if every smokeless-tobacco user in the data set died of a heart attack. It's always possible that such an outcome is simply a product of chance—just as it is theoretically possible that an honest gambler could win a lot of money by rolling ten consecutive 6s. But that is not the most likely explanation for the pattern.

Thus, researchers use hypothesis testing to draw meaningful statistical conclusions from data. In this example, we would set up the following hypotheses:

H_0: smokeless-tobacco use is not associated with higher rates of heart disease.

H_a: smokeless-tobacco use is associated with higher rates of heart disease.

Researchers will reject the null hypothesis (and, therefore, accept the alternative hypothesis) if the data suggest a connection between smokeless-tobacco use and heart disease that is not likely to be explained by chance alone. The 95-percent confidence level is a generally accepted threshold for empirical research. Thus, researchers will reject the null hypothesis if the data reveal a pattern between smokeless tobacco and heart disease that has less than a 0.05 probability of occurring by chance alone. (*Note:* such research would attempt to isolate the connection between smokeless tobacco and heart disease by controlling for any differences between smokeless-tobacco users and nonusers that might be relevant to their health outcomes, such as education, income, access to health care, etc. The statistical technique used most often to isolate the effects of individual variables is multiple regression analysis, which will be covered in the next chapter.)

When researchers do find a statistical association between two variables of interest that cannot easily be explained by chance alone, the relationship is said to be **statistically significant.** For example, the study authors might conclude, "The data show a statistically significant relationship between smokeless-tobacco use and heart disease." Such a finding would not automatically prove causality, since there is still a chance that the finding is a statistical aberration, or that smokeless-tobacco users do have higher rates of heart disease but that the smokeless tobacco is not causing the illness. Authors of individual studies often deliberately use words like "association" and "relationship" that stop short of declaring causality. The broader goal in fields like public policy and public health, of course, is to compile enough consistent evidence from different sources to convince policy makers that there is a causal relationship between the variables of interest (or to reject that causal relationship). For example, it is now nearly universally accepted that smoking causes heart disease and cancer, whereas early research merely documented a connection between the two.

10.6 TYPE I AND TYPE II ERRORS

Hypothesis testing is prone to two possible kinds of errors. A **type I error** occurs when the null hypothesis is rejected even though it is true and the alternative hypothesis is falsely accepted (a false positive); a **type II error** occurs when the null hypothesis is accepted even though it is false and the alternative hypothesis should have been accepted (a false negative). These mistakes are best understood in the context of an example. Consider the case of an individual who is on trial for some crime. The U.S. judicial system offers the accused a presumption of innocence—innocent until proven guilty. Thus, the null hypothesis is that the accused is not guilty. The alternative hypothesis, of course, is that the accused is guilty.

H_0: the defendant is innocent.
H_a: the defendant is guilty.

The jury can make two possible mistakes. First, the members of the jury can find the accused guilty when he is innocent. This would involve wrongly rejecting the null hypothesis—a type I error, or false positive.

Or the jury could find the accused not guilty when he has in fact committed the crime. In this case, the members of the jury would fail to reject the null hypothesis even though it is wrong—a type II error, or false negative.

The crucial point for policy analysts is that there is an inherent trade-off between type I and type II errors. The more rigorous the standard for rejecting a null hypothesis, the more likely it is that we accept a null hypothesis that is not true. Think about it in the judicial context: The higher the standard of evidence required to convict a criminal, the more likely it is that a guilty individual will be set free (a type II error, or false negative). Conversely, the more easily an accused person can be convicted (rejecting the null hypothesis of not guilty), the more likely it is that an innocent person will be erroneously found guilty (a type I error, or false positive).

Given this tradeoff, policy makers must often decide whether a type I or a type II error would be more damaging. Consider two contemporary challenges: filtering spam and apprehending potential terrorists. Obviously, one challenge is gravely more serious than the other, but both situations involve screening in the face of imperfect information. In the case of spam, we would like to screen out unwanted e-mails without having any important communications caught in the filter. In the case of potential terrorists, we would like to catch those who are planning terrorist activities without arresting or detaining innocent persons. Let us consider the nature and costs of a type I and type II error in each case.

A spam filter searches for e-mail characteristics that suggest that a message is unwanted—certain words, certain senders, suppressed distribution lists, etc. In the context of our current discussion, the null hypothesis is that an e-mail message should be delivered; the filter then looks for attributes that are sufficient to reject that hypothesis, thereby diverting the message to a junk folder. Thus, we have the following possible errors:

- Type I error (false positive): the filter determines that a message is spam (rejecting the null hypothesis) when it is an e-mail that the recipient would prefer to receive.
- Type II error (false negative): the filter does not screen out an e-mail (accepts the null hypothesis) even though it is spam.

For most people, a type I error in this situation is far more potentially harmful than a type II error. If the filter screens out an e-mail message that should have been delivered, the recipient may miss important information. And since we don't always know what e-mail is coming, we may not know to look for the message that has been improperly screened out. In the case of a type II error (false negative), the filter allows some spam to get through. This is an inconvenience to the user but has no other costs. Thus, a type I error is potentially far more costly than a type II error; an optimal spam filter should be designed to err on the side of letting too much spam in. If your spam filter does not allow any spam through, who knows what else you have been missing?

Now, let's consider a different example: the capture and incarceration of potential terrorists. Once again, we are making decisions based on imperfect information. Because there is a presumption of innocence in our judicial system, we begin with the null hypothesis that a particular individual is not a terrorist. It is the government's responsibility to prove otherwise, or reject the null hypothesis. The crucial policy and legal question is how much evidence should be required to reject that null hypothesis and accept the alternative hypothesis—that an individual is a potential terrorist and should be treated as such. You have probably already recognized that either a type I or type II error is extremely costly in this case. Consider each of them in turn:

- Type I error (false positive): in this case, we would wrongly reject the null hypothesis of not guilty and treat an innocent person as a terrorist. This person could be wrongly incarcerated for years, or even life. In less serious cases, we may reject immigration visas for foreign students or visitors who have no ill intentions, which also imposes a social harm.
- Type II error (false negative): in this case, we would fail to reject the null hypothesis of not guilty even though the individual has malevolent intentions. We would allow the person to enter the country, or pass through security and get on an airplane, or leave government custody without being prosecuted—each activity of which could have catastrophic results.

In the spam example, we could easily err on the side of making a type II error, since the cost of allowing some spam to slip through is a mere inconvenience. In the terrorism example, we do not have that luxury. Both a type I and a type II error have enormous costs—either by treating some innocent persons as potential terrorists or by allowing some terrorists to slip through. Without perfect information, we will never get it just right, which explains why the post–September 11 debates over security have been so contentious.

We can combine our knowledge of hypothesis testing and decision trees to shed some light on a particular kind of type I error: false positives when screening large populations. When some mechanism prone to false positives is used to screen a large population for a disease or other condition that is rare, it is likely that a high proportion of the positive results will be false positives. For example, if the entire American population were screened for some rare disease, most of those who tested positive would not have the disease, even if the test used to screen for the disease were highly accurate. How could that be the case? A variation on the decision tree will illuminate this important phenomenon.

Assume that 200 million people are to be screened for a disease that has an incidence of only 1 in 10,000, or 0.0001. Further assume that the test used to screen for this disease has a false positive rate of 1 in 1,000. Thus, for every 1,000 persons who test positive, one of them does not have the disease. For simplicity's sake, assume that the test never produces a false negative—all of those who are ill will test positive. This is a very accurate test—the results are correct 99.9 percent of the time. Yet hundreds of thousands of people will wrongly be told that they have the disease! To understand how this happens, we can use a variation on the decision tree:

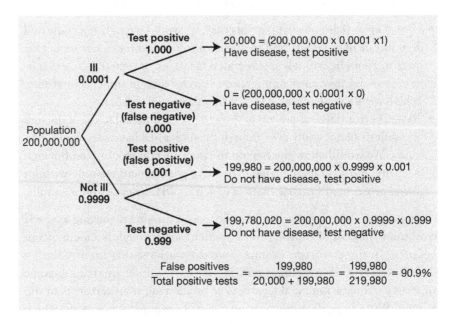

False-Positive Diagram: Testing for a Rare Disease

Two hundred million people are tested. One in 10,000 has the disease (20,000 people) and is correctly diagnosed. The balance of the population (199,980,000) does not have the disease. Among this large group, 1 in 1,000 will test positive even though they do not really have the disease. That means there will be an expected 199,980 false positives. That means nearly 200,000 people will be told that they have a disease (presumably serious or else there would be no reason to screen for it) when in fact they do not. Furthermore, of all the people who test positive, 91 percent (199,980/219,980) do not really have the disease!

As a result of this phenomenon, public-health experts sometimes recommend *against* widespread screening for rare diseases. In some cases, resources may be used more efficiently if specific groups at high risk are screened, rather than the entire population. With HIV/AIDS, for example, finite public-health budgets may best be put to use by screening groups with the highest risk of contracting the disease, such as gay men or intravenous drug users. In other cases, experts warn that widespread screening may do more harm than good, particularly if false positives lead to unnecessary treatment that is costly or potentially harmful.

10.7 CONCLUSION

Good data are essential for good public policy decisions. Bad data, however, can be useless or even dangerously misleading. The most fundamental responsibility of any policy researcher is to ensure that the data on which decisions are based are truly representative of the population of interest. With good data, statistical sampling provides a powerful tool for using a relatively small sample to draw meaningful conclusions about a much larger population. It is important to recognize, however, that statistical sampling does not prove anything about the larger population. Rather, it enables us to draw conclusions based on the likelihood that what we observe in a sample is consistent with what we would expect to observe for the whole population.

FOR DISCUSSION

Is Screening for Lung Cancer a Good Thing?: When Knowing More Can Be Bad for Your Health[13]

Lung cancer kills more than 100,000 Americans every year. Like most kinds of cancer, the disease can be treated more successfully when diagnosed early. A CT scan is a fast and painless way to test for lung cancer; it is also a far more powerful tool for detecting lung abnormalities than X-rays, which had been the traditional diagnostic tool. CT screening is bolstered by impressive statistics: patients whose disease is caught by CT screening have a five-year survival rate of 80 percent, compared to 15 percent for lung-cancer victims whose disease is detected later by other means.

Given the ease of the test and the impressive outcomes, shouldn't all of us be screened for lung cancer and sooner rather than later? Not necessarily, according to medical professionals. Their skepticism toward routine CT screening has two explanations: (1) when it comes to lung cancer, a false positive might actually kill you or at least cause great expense and discomfort; and (2) early detection can make cancer survivorship statistics highly misleading.

Some forms of lung cancer do not progress rapidly and kill the victim. Such "indolent" cancers would likely never be diagnosed in the absence of CT screening because the person would not become noticeably ill. In one study, researchers found ten times as many lung cancers using CT scans as they found among similar patients using X-rays. Steven Woloshin, Lisa Schwartz, and H. Gilbert Welch, all physician researchers, highlighted the resulting medical dilemma in the *New York Times,* "Because we can't distinguish a progressive cancer from a nonprogressive cancer on the CT scan, we tend to treat everybody who tests positive. Obviously the patients with indolent cancers cannot benefit from treatment; they can only experience its side effects." Treatment can cause discomfort or even death, particularly in older patients.

The same physicians explained why the statistics supporting CT screening can be misleading or even illusory. "Even if CT screening raised the five-year survival rate to 80 percent [from 15 percent], it is entirely possible that no one gets an extra day of life." The physicians explain this seeming paradox with two clever thought experiments:

Consider a group of people with lung cancer who will all die at age seventy. If they first receive the diagnosis when they are sixty-seven, their five-year survival rate would be 0 percent; not one of them lives for five years after the diagnosis. But if these

---

13. Steven Woloshin, Lisa Schwartz, and H. Gilbert Welch, "Warned, but Worse Off," *New York Times,* August 22, 2005.

same people had received their diagnosis earlier—at, say, age sixty-three—the five-year survival rate would be 100 percent. Yet death would still come at age seventy for all of them. Earlier diagnosis always increases the five-year survival statistic, but it doesn't necessarily mean that death is postponed.

Here is their second thought experiment. Imagine a city in which 1,000 people are found to have progressive lung cancer following evaluation because they have reported certain symptoms, such as a cough and weight loss. This is a targeted approach in which only those individuals who are most at risk of serious disease are tested for the cancer. Assume that five years after diagnosis, 150 of the patients are alive and 850 have died: a five-year survival rate of 150/1,000, or 15 percent.

Now assume that everyone in the city is screened using a CT scan, regardless of their risk profile or symptoms. The physicians posit that perhaps 5,000 people would be given a cancer diagnosis, although 4,000 would actually have indolent forms. These 4,000 would not die from lung cancer in five years simply because they don't have a virulent form of the disease, not because their illness was caught early. The five-year survival rate would increase dramatically (to 83 percent) because these healthy people would be added to the pool of survivors, making the survivorship rate 4,150/5,000 rather than 150/1,000.

But what has really changed? Some people have been unnecessarily told they have cancer (and may have experienced the harms of therapy), and the same number of people (850) have still died from the disease.

Obviously, screening for disease is a good idea in many situations, particularly when a certain population can be identified as most at risk. Thus, the case for CT screening of smokers is strongest, because smokers have a far greater risk of contracting lung cancer than the general population. But widespread screening of the general population may do more harm than good, particularly if a false positive results in unnecessary treatment that is expensive or potentially harmful. Drs. Woloshin, Schwartz, and Welch conclude, "Someday we will know if CT lung cancer screens help more than they hurt (the results of a major National Cancer Institute trial will be available in about five years). But until then, everyone should know that screening is a two-edged sword."

QUESTIONS

1. Given what you've read, would you choose to have a CT screening for lung cancer? Why, or why not?
2. Would you consider it fair for insurance companies to refuse to pay for CT screening? Under what circumstances?
3. Would you ever support mandatory testing/screening for some disease, such as HIV/AIDS? Why, or why not?
4. Would you ever support mandatory testing/screening for a disease such as HIV/AIDS among specific populations, such as prison inmates or drug offenders? Why, or why not?

5. Agree or disagree: To help rein in health-care costs, policy makers will have to impose constraints on how new medical screening technology is used.

6. Agree or disagree: Public-health officials should recommend against screening/testing some populations for certain diseases (e.g., CT scans for nonsmokers with no family history of lung cancer) even if it means that some individuals will die for lack of early detection.

KEY CONCEPTS

★ Sampling is the process of selecting a set of individual observations from some larger population, often with the intent of using the sample to make inferences about the full population.

★ A simple random sample is drawn from a population in such a way that any individual observation in the population has an equal probability of being included in the sample.

★ A stratified sample randomly chooses observations from within a set of defined subpopulations, such as racial groups within the United States, to ensure that observations from each stratum are represented in the sample in proportion to their share of the overall population.

★ A cluster sample is created by dividing the population of interest into many similar or identical clusters, such as rural counties or high-income zip codes, and then drawing observations from one cluster.

★ A data-gathering strategy may deliberately oversample some subgroup of the population—that is, members of a subgroup are included in the sample in excess of their share of larger population—in order to ensure that the sample has sufficient data to draw meaningful conclusions on the subgroup of interest. To compensate for this oversampling, the relevant observations are likely to be weighted in any subsequent statistical analysis to avoid biasing the results.

★ The sample mean, represented as $\bar{x}$, is the mean, or average, for any sample of observations.

★ According to the central limit theorem, the sample means for any population will be distributed roughly as a normal distribution around the true mean for the population (regardless of the shape of the underlying population distribution). The larger the number of samples, the more closely the distribution of sample means will approximate a normal distribution.

★ For some population with mean μ and standard deviation σ, the standard error of the sample means is $\sigma/\sqrt{n}$, where n is the sample size.

★ In cases where we do not know the standard deviation for the population of interest, we must improvise by using the standard deviation for a population sample instead: $s = \sqrt{\sum(x_i - \bar{x})^2/(n-1)}$, where n is the number of observations in the sample.

★ Because the sample means are distributed roughly as a normal distribution, we infer the following: roughly 68.0 percent of the sample means will lie within one standard error of the population mean; roughly 95.0 percent of the sample means will lie within two standard errors of the population mean; roughly 99.7 percent of the sample means will lie within three standard errors of the population mean.

★ The standard error enables us to build a confidence interval that expresses the likelihood that the population mean lies within a certain distance of the observed sample mean.

★ The standard error for a sample proportion is $\sqrt{\hat{p}(1-\hat{p})/n}$, where $\hat{p}$ is the proportion of the population who fall into some category of interest (such as the proportion of respondents who support one political candidate or the other), and n is the sample size.

★ Most polls use a 95-percent confidence level to create a confidence interval; we can infer that 95 percent of the sample proportions will lie within 1.96 standard errors of the population proportion.

★ A decision tree is a tool for evaluating possible courses of action when future events are uncertain but it is possible to estimate the probabilities and "payoffs" of different outcomes.

★ Hypothesis testing consists of proposing a hypothesis and then accepting or rejecting it with some level of statistical confidence.

★ A type I error occurs when the null hypothesis is rejected even though it is true and the alternative hypothesis is falsely accepted (a false positive); a type II error occurs when the null hypothesis is accepted even though it is false and the alternative hypothesis should have been accepted (a false negative).

★ When some mechanism prone to false positives is used to screen a large population for a disease or other condition that is rare, it is likely that a high proportion of the positive results will be false positives.

CHAPTER 11

Introduction to Regression Analysis

THE FRAMINGHAM HEART STUDY

Smoking increases the risk of heart disease and stroke. Exercise, on the other hand, may prevent heart disease. As basic is this knowledge now seems, none of it was known in 1950. In fact, the process of drawing such medical conclusions is far more difficult than it would appear. Suppose that researchers have data showing that smokers have a higher incidence of heart disease than nonsmokers. Is that sufficient to draw a causal link between smoking and heart disease? No. Smokers might be more likely to eat poorly than nonsmokers. Or they may have less education on average. Or they may work in more stressful professions. From a research standpoint, it would not be clear whether it is the smoking causing heart disease or the other factors that set smokers apart from nonsmokers. Suppose smoking *does not* cause heart disease but stressful jobs do. Further assume that people who are stressed at work are more likely to smoke. In that case, the relationship between smoking and heart disease would be misleading; physicians who counseled their smoking patients to quit would be missing the real health risk—stress on the job.

Researchers in the social sciences rarely have the luxury of designing controlled experiments to examine variables of interest. It would be neither legal nor ethical, for example, to designate an experimental group of middle-school students as illegal drug users and then compare their high-school dropout rates to non–drug users. Instead, researchers must make use of whatever data are available—such as a longitudinal study that might ask middle-school students about drug use and later collect information on their high-school performance—and then use statistical tools to isolate the effects of the variable or variables of interest.

The Framingham Heart Study is a longitudinal study that has been collecting detailed health and lifestyle information on thousands of people in the town of Framingham, Massachusetts, for more than fifty years. Researchers have used the rich Framingham data to understand the risk factors associated with cardiovascular disease. In 1948, researchers recruited over 5,000 Framingham men and women between the ages of thirty and sixty-two with no overt signs of cardiovascular disease to participate in the study. Each participant was given a detailed physical examination and a lifestyle interview and agreed to return every two years for follow-up exams, tests, and interviews. At the time the study was initiated, death rates from cardiovascular disease had been climbing steadily for fifty years, but doctors knew little about the causes. That would change over the ensuing decades as the Framingham Study gradually unveiled so many of the risk factors that we now take for granted: high cholesterol, diabetes, smoking, obesity.

In 1971, a "second generation" study enrolled 5,124 new participants drawn from the original participants' adult children and their spouses. A third generation, consisting of 3,500 grandchildren of the original participants, is now underway. The multigenerational aspect of the study enables researchers to examine the genetic factors associated with cardiovascular disease.

So far, the Framingham data have led to a stunning 1,200 articles in leading medical journals, each of which expands the frontier of knowledge in ways that improve human health all over the world. Health research is similar to detective work. A longitudinal data set like the Framingham Heart Study provides the clues. (The study's sponsors are keen on quoting Sherlock Holmes). But the data alone rarely present clear answers. After all, the question posed at the beginning of this chapter—Does smoking causes heart disease, or do people at risk of heart disease for some other reason just happen to smoke?—is not easily answered by poring over interviews from thousands or even tens of thousands of Framingham residents. Regression analysis is the statistical tool that gives power to these kinds of data by isolating the association between a single variable and an outcome of interest, such as smoking and heart disease. Regression analysis enables researchers to take into account, or **control for,** other factors that may distinguish smokers from nonsmokers (such as education or stress), so that the relationship between smoking and heart disease can be quantified apart from other risk factors. When researchers report their findings, for example, they may conclude that smoking is associated with a higher incidence of heart disease, *ceteris paribus,* meaning that for people who are similar in all other respects (education, race, stress on the job, etc.), smokers are more likely to get cancer than nonsmokers.

Done properly, regression analysis enables researchers to do with statistics and data what they cannot do in many situations with a laboratory experiment:

isolate the effect of a single variable. This chapter will introduce the strengths and limitations of regression analysis as a research tool, explain the process for interpreting results, and warn against the most common regression-related mistakes and misapplications. The chapter is not a substitute for a more rigorous and mathematical study of the underpinnings of regression analysis; it is designed to introduce policy students to the most common tools used in policy research and to illustrate the important role that advanced statistical methods like regression analysis play in expanding our frontier of knowledge.

CHAPTER OUTLINE

11.1 LINEAR REGRESSION

Regression analysis seeks to explain some outcome, the dependent variable, as a function of one or more independent variables. Does eating oat bran reduce the risk of getting colon cancer? Does watching television impair the cognitive abilities of young children? What is the relationship between educational attainment and lifetime wages? It would be impractical or unethical to examine these important research questions using controlled experiments on human subjects. The best alternative is to gather data on the variables of interest and use regression analysis to gain insight into the association between them.

11.1.1 Dependent and Independent Variables

The **dependent variable** is the outcome that researchers are trying to explain. In the above examples, that would be colon cancer, the cognitive ability of young children, and lifetime wages. An **independent variable,** or **explanatory variable,** is a factor that researchers believe has some causal relationship with the outcome of interest. Regression analysis alone cannot prove causality, as will be explained in greater depth later in this chapter. However, it can prove a statistical correlation that can be used to help confirm causality when combined with other kinds of theoretical or empirical evidence.

A **control variable** is an independent variable that is likely to have an effect on the outcome of interest but is not the primary focus of inquiry; researchers must include it in the regression analysis to improve the validity of the results. Suppose that researchers were trying to determine whether playing golf has a positive impact on health. Their specific outcome of interest is heart disease. Are people who play golf regularly more or less likely than nongolfers to suffer from heart disease? A simple comparison of the cardiac health of golfers compared to nongolfers would almost certainly find that golfers are less healthy. Does that mean that golf is dangerous? Should doctors be warning their patients to stay off the course? Of course not. You may have already figured out the flaw in this analysis: golfers tend to be much older on average than nongolfers since golf is a popular retirement sport. So a simple comparison of golfers to nongolfers is really just comparing the cardiac health of older people to younger people; we wouldn't be surprised to find that heart disease is positively associated with age. In this case, researchers would have to include age as a control variable. The subsequent analysis would quantify the relationship between heart disease and playing golf, *con-*

trolling for age, meaning that the statistical analysis has made inferences based on the cardiac health of golfers and nongolfers *of the same age.*

What other control variables are likely to be significant in this case? This is always an important question to ask, since missing control variables can lead to profoundly misleading conclusions. Researchers looking at the relationship between golf and heart disease should also control for income, education, and other measures of **socioeconomic status.** Golf can be an expensive sport; as a result, golfers are likely, on average, to be more affluent than nongolfers, meaning that they have greater access to health insurance, high-quality medical care, and other health inputs that affect cardiac health in ways that have nothing to do with stepping on the golf course.

We must also be concerned about the direction of causality in this case. Researchers are presumably examining the relationship between golf and heart disease because they hypothesize that the exercise and social aspects of the game might have a positive impact on health. However, even with the appropriate controls in place, a positive statistical association between playing golf and good cardiac health does not prove that playing golf is good for your heart. In fact, it's plausible that having a healthy heart causes people to play golf! Even when we control for age, it's possible that people who are healthier at any given age are more able and willing to play golf than their less healthy peers. Causality may even run in both directions: good health makes it possible for people to play golf, but playing golf provides exercise and social engagement, which improve health. Regression analysis is a powerful tool; however, the conclusions established using regression analysis are only as valid as the data and analysis that support them.

. . . .

Endogenous and Exogenous Variables

Researchers often make a distinction between **endogenous** and **exogenous variables.** *Endogenous* literally means "caused by factors inside the organism or system";[1] in a statistical context, it refers to a variable affected by the outcome that it is being used to explain. Thus, we would not try to explain GDP growth as a dependent variable using the unemployment rate as an independent variable because it is not truly independent. Instead, the causality runs both directions—GDP growth would affect the unemployment rate, making

1. http://www.merriam-webster.com.

the unemployment rate an endogenous variable. An *exogenous variable,* on the other hand, is caused by factors outside the system. We might examine the effect of hurricanes on GDP growth. Since GDP growth cannot reasonably affect the severity of the hurricane season, the causality can only run in one direction: hurricanes affect economic growth (by destroying property, interfering with business, etc.). Thus, a measure of hurricane activity would be exogenous to GDP growth—it comes from outside the dependent variable of interest.

11.1.2 Establishing a Linear Relationship

The goal of regression analysis is to quantify the association between variables of interest. To understand the mechanics of this process, it is easiest to begin with the most basic form: an analysis of the linear relationship between two variables, or **bivariate regression analysis.** Consider a very basic relationship, such as height and weight. We would expect there to be a causal relationship between the two attributes, since tall people, on average, will weigh more than short people. Thus, weight would be the dependent variable, or outcome of interest, and height would be the independent variable that we expect to have a causal association with weight.

If we were to plot the heights and weights of a group of people, such as a classroom of graduate students with height in inches on the x-axis and weight on the y-axis, it might look something like the following:

As you can see, there is a clear positive association between height and weight. Yet looking at the graph, it is not obvious how that relationship could or should be quantified. Linear regression is a method for **fitting a line** that best expresses the relationship between the independent variable and the dependent variable. If we revisit the scatter plot of heights and weights, it is easy to draw a line that summarizes the positive association between height and weight. But which line is the best fit? And how would we define "best fit"?

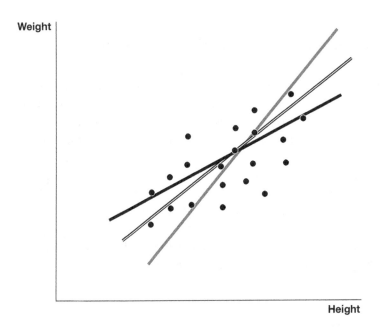

Note that each line (and, therefore, the relationship between the independent and dependent variable) can be described mathematically by its intercept (the point at which it intersects the y-axis) and its slope (the change in y produced by each one unit change in x).

$$y = a + bx$$

Every observation—each of which represents the height and weight for an individual student—can be described mathematically in the same way as long as we include one additional term to represent the distance between the point and line, which is not explained by the regression equation. Thus, any individual

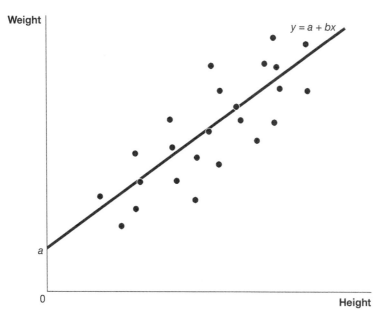

observation i for the population as a whole (all graduate students) can be expressed mathematically as the following: $y_i = a + bx_i + e_i$, where a is the intercept, b is the slope of the line, and e_i is the remaining vertical distance between the point and the line, or **error term.** For our sample of graduate students, the distance between each observation and the regression line, $\hat{e}$, is referred to as the **residual** because it represents the portion of the dependent variable that remains unexplained by the regression equation. In our simple model of height and weight, the residual would reflect other explanatory factors such as age, diet, genetics, exercise, and so on.[2]

The slope of a line fitted to the observations for height and weight expresses a relationship between the two variables since the slope, by definition, is the change in y generated by every one unit change in x. But we have not yet answered the most important question in this example: What line offers the best fit for the data? How can we even define *best fit?*

---

2. *A note on notation:* A regression line drawn for an entire population (e.g., all graduate students) would be $y = a + bx + e$. A regression line fitted for a sample of that population is written $\hat{y} = \hat{a} + \hat{b}x + \hat{e}$. This reflects the fact that if we were to draw a different sample of graduate students, our estimated regression line would also be slightly different.

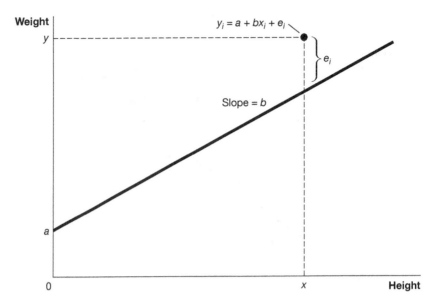

11.1.3 Ordinary Least Squares

The most common way of determining the best fit for a regression line is known as **ordinary least squares,** or OLS. A line fitted using OLS creates a regression line in which observations are as close as possible to the line—or, put differently, the error terms are as small as possible. Specifically, OLS minimizes the distance between the regression line and the sum of the squares of the error term. Imagine a very simple data set with the heights and weights of five students; the OLS regression line would minimize the sum of the five error terms: $(e_1)^2 + (e_2)^2 + (e_3)^2 + (e_4)^2 + (e_5)^2$.

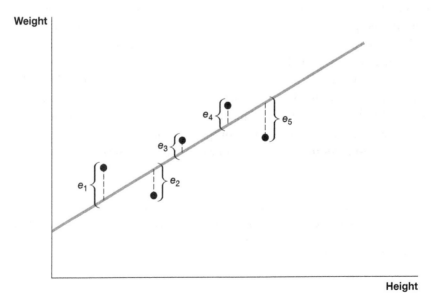

In a more advanced statistics or econometrics class, you will explore the mathematics underlying OLS. Any basic statistical package can calculate an OLS regression line once the relevant data have been entered (such as the height and weight of each student). The result expresses a linear relationship between the dependent and independent variables. Indeed, we can calculate a basic relationship for height and weight based on the seven observations below.

STUDENT	HEIGHT (INCHES)	WEIGHT (POUNDS)
Lea	66	135
Jacob	70	181
Jermaine	69	165
Madura	73	210
Cate	70	140
Felicity	60	110
Charlie	75	195

Weight is the dependent variable (y) and height is the independent variable (x). The relationship between height and weight for this small group of students can be described as

$$Y = -44.8 + 3.06x + e$$

The slope of the line is 3.06. This is also known as the **coefficient.** In the context of our example, this means that every 1-inch increase in height is associated with roughly a 3-pound increase in weight. The y-intercept is –44.8, a meaningless number in this case since there is no student who is 0 inches tall. No student actually has a height and weight that lies exactly on the regression line. Still, the regression line is a powerful tool for quantifying the relationship between the variables of interest for two primary reasons. First, the regression coefficient is the best description we have of the general relationship between two variables of interest. The height-and-weight example may be trivial from a public policy standpoint, but for researchers using large data sets to examine important policy-related questions, such as the connection between drug use and educational attainment, establishing and quantifying a relationship between an independent and dependent variable is extremely important. Second, the regression line enables us to predict the weight of a student not included in the data. Suppose a student missed class on the day these measurements were taken (but is like the rest of the other students in terms of other basic characteristics, such as age). If we know that this student is 5 feet 9 inches (69 inches) tall, what is our best estimate of his weight? Since our regression line has established a general relationship between the heights and weights for students in this class, we can plug the height information for the missing student into the regression equation and make an estimate of his weight:

$$Y = -44.8 + 3.06x_i + e_i$$

One of the standard assumptions of regression analysis is that the mean of the error term is 0, meaning that the expected value of the error term for any particular observation is 0. (If the predicted error were *not* 0, then presumably our regression line could be improved.) Therefore, our best estimate for the missing student's weight is the following:

$$Y = -44.8 + (3.06)(69) = 166.34, \text{ or roughly 166 pounds.}$$

Will the student really weigh 166 pounds? Probably not, but it is the best estimate that we can make, given the available data. Our regression equation may not be a good predictor of the relationship between height and weight for other populations since it was calculated using data for a group of graduate students. The relationship between height and weight would almost certainly be different for a group of elementary-school students or for players in the National Football League. Regression results should not be used to make inferences about populations that are **outside the range of the data,** meaning that they are likely to be different in key respects from the population for which the data were collected.

11.2 MULTIPLE REGRESSION ANALYSIS

Multiple regression analysis quantifies the linear relationship between a dependent variable and more than one independent variable. For example, cardiovascular disease has many contributing factors: smoking, diet, genetics, and so on. Even our simple model for estimating the weight of graduate students could be improved by adding other independent variables, such as age, sex, diet, and exercise. When an outcome is affected by many factors, multiple regression analysis enables us to isolate the association between the dependent variable and each independent variable. The general form of such an equation is the following:

$$Y = a + b_1x_1 + b_2x_2 + b_3x_3 \ldots + b_ix_i + e,$$

where Y is the dependent variable; a is an intercept; $x_1, x_2, x_3, \ldots x_i$ are independent variables; and e is an error term. The coefficients on the independent variables—$b_1, b_2, b_3, \ldots b_i$—quantify the relationship between that independent variable and the dependent variable, *ceteris paribus*. Unlike simple linear regression, this relationship cannot be easily graphed, since it would involve multiple dimensions.

The power of multiple regression analysis is best explained in the context of the Framingham Heart Study, introduced at the beginning of this chapter. The study sponsors have gathered a large amount of personal data on the participating subjects. Different medical researchers will make different uses of the data, but one possible line of inquiry may be the connection between cocaine use and heart disease. In this case, the dependent variable—the outcome of interest—is heart disease. Researchers are attempting to probe a potential causal relationship between cocaine use and some measure of cardiovascular disease.

The independent variable of interest in this case is self-reported cocaine use. This could be measured as a **binary variable** (also called a **dummy variable**), which is 1 if the subject is a cocaine user and 0 if he is not. Or perhaps researchers would have data on frequency of use, such as the number of times per month the drug is used or the number of years the individual has been using the drug. The obvious comparison would be with smoking, where researchers might attempt to measure the impact of being a smoker versus being a nonsmoker, or they might measure smoking behavior in a more refined way in order to study the impact of smoking intensity. The exact nature of the independent variable will always depend on the data available and the specific interests of the researchers conducting the study. For purposes of the example, assume that the independent variable is binary: the study participant is either a cocaine user or not a cocaine user (using a dummy variable).

Now suppose that we examine the data collected for the Framingham Heart Study and discover that cocaine users have a higher incidence of heart disease than those who don't use cocaine. What does this tell us about the relationship between cocaine use and cardiovascular disease? Not much, actually. As we have discussed throughout this chapter, it is possible that cocaine users are different from nonusers in other ways that explain their differences in health outcomes. *In fact, the cocaine use may have nothing to do with the incidence of heart disease.* Suppose that cocaine users also have little concern for their health and, therefore, eat poorly and don't exercise. Or cocaine users may be far more likely than nonusers to smoke. Since diet, exercise, and smoking are all contributing factors to heart disease, the cocaine variable may simply be picking up these effects.

With good data and sound analysis, multiple regression analysis has the potential to ameliorate this problem and isolate the impact of cocaine use, *ceteris paribus*. The goal of regression analysis is to measure the effect of each independent variable, holding all other variables constant. In a laboratory experiment, a researcher would accomplish this by making the independent variable of interest the only difference between the experimental subjects and the control group. Thus, a researcher would have an experimental group who used cocaine; he would have a control group who did not use cocaine but were identical *in all other respects*—age, sex, educational background, smoking behavior, and so on. The researcher would then observe the occurrence of heart disease in the two groups and could reasonably attribute any significant difference to cocaine use. Of course, everything about this experiment is impractical, beginning with the prospect of experimenting with cocaine on human subjects. With adequate data, multiple regression analysis is the next best thing. A basic statistical package can calculate a regression equation using ordinary least squares; the coefficients on each independent variable are the values that provide the best fit for the regression equation using OLS. (Once again, we will reserve the mathematics underlying the process for a more advanced class.) The coefficient on the dummy variable for cocaine use will isolate the association between using cocaine and heart disease, controlling for other personal attributes and behavior. Specifically, researchers would be interested in the **sign** of the coefficient (Does cocaine use make heart disease more or less likely?); the **size** of the coefficient (How big is that effect?); and the **significance** of the finding (What is the likelihood that the observed relationship between cocaine use and heart disease is merely a product of chance, not biology?) This process for interpreting regression coefficients will be examined in more detail later in the chapter.

To return to our simple height-and-weight example, assume that we have a much larger data set (such as all students in the graduate program) and that we are able to collect information not just on their height and weight, but also on their sex, age, eating habits, and exercise behavior. While sex and age are very specific variables, the concepts of "eating habits" and "exercise behavior" are vague. For purposes of running the regression, the researcher would have to specify how such behaviors can be measured and quantified. One approach would be to use a dummy variable in both cases. The first dummy variable might be VEGETARIAN; students in the data set are classified as either vegetarian, in which case they are classified as a 1, or nonvegetarian, in which case they are classified as a 0. Similarly, we can capture exercise behavior with a dummy variable. Students who engage in some kind of aerobic activity at least three times a week for 30 minutes are classified as EXERCISERS; those who work out less or not at all are nonexercisers.

To see how this would work in practice, we can revisit our table on heights and weights.

STUDENT	HEIGHT (INCHES)	WEIGHT (POUNDS)	SEX (1 = FEMALE)	AGE	VEGETARIAN (1 = VEGETARIAN)	EXERCISER (1 = EXERCISER)
Lea	66	135	1	28	1	1
Jacob	70	181	0	23	0	1
Jermaine	69	165	0	33	1	1
Madura	73	210	0	29	0	0
Cate	70	140	1	35	0	0
Felicity	60	110	1	26	0	1
Charlie	75	195	0	22	0	1

We can estimate the following regression equation:

$$\text{WEIGHT} = a + b_1\text{HEIGHT} + b_2\text{SEX} + b_3\text{AGE} + b_4\text{VEGETARIAN} + b_5\text{EXERCISER} + e,$$

where WEIGHT is the dependent variable, a is a constant, e is an error term, and HEIGHT, SEX, AGE, VEGETARIAN, and EXERCISE are all independent variables. Any meaningful data analysis would require information on far more students. (Each student is considered an **observation** in this analysis.) Assume that we gather data for the rest of the students in the graduate program and that a statistical program generates the following OLS regression results:

$$\text{WEIGHT} = -39.2 + (2.96)\text{HEIGHT} + (-2.44)\text{SEX} + (1.19)\text{AGE} + (-2.19)\text{VEGETARIAN} + (-5.36)\text{EXERCISER}$$

Each coefficient quantifies the association between that independent variable and the dependent variable, *holding the other independent variables in the regression constant.* Thus, we can conclude for our graduate student sample that every inch of height is associated with 2.96 additional pounds. Similarly, each additional year of age is associated with 1.19 extra pounds. The dummy variables are interpreted slightly differently. Since female students are categorized as having SEX = 1, they weigh 2.44 pounds less than male students, *all else being equal.* Similarly, since vegetarians are classified as VEGETARIAN = 1, vegetarian students weigh 2.19 pounds less than nonvegetarians. Finally, exercisers weigh 5.36 pounds less than nonexercisers, controlling for other variables in the regression.

Once again, we can use these results to infer the weight of a graduate student in the same program who is not included in the data set. Suppose we know that Michael is 5 feet 8 inches (68 inches) tall, male, twenty-eight years old, nonvegetarian, and an exerciser. We can plug those values into the regression equation and generate an estimate for Michael's weight:

$$\text{WEIGHT} = -39.2 + (2.96)(68) + (-2.44)(0) + (1.19)(28) +$$
$$(-2.19)(0) + (-5.36)(1)$$
$$\text{WEIGHT} = -39.2 + 201 + 0 + 33.32 + 0 - 5.36$$
$$\text{WEIGHT} = 189.74$$

This may or may not be a close approximation of Michael's weight. However, it is likely to be a better estimate of his weight than we would be able to make in the absence of the regression results.

11.3 INTERPRETING REGRESSION RESULTS

One important purpose of regression analysis is to use sample data to make meaningful inferences about some larger population. In the case of the Framingham Heart Study, the data analysis is designed to learn lessons from the Framingham participants that can be applied to the rest of the country or even the world. But how can researchers assume that an association established between smoking and heart disease for several thousand volunteers in Massachusetts is likely to hold true for millions of people elsewhere? The answer is that regression analysis draws on many of the statistical tools introduced in Chapter 10 to give larger meaning to the results generated by sample data. It is crucial to recognize that regression analysis never *proves* anything; instead, researchers quantify an association between two variables and use statistical analysis to determine the likelihood of observing such an association if it does not hold true for the larger population. It's possible, for example, that many smokers in Framingham became sick with heart disease because they were unlucky and not because smoking had anything to do with it. If that were the case, then mounting a national or international antismoking campaign would be a waste of public resources. However, regression analysis gives us the tools to show that it is highly unlikely that the relationship between smoking and heart disease was observed for so many participants in Framingham if there is in fact no association between smoking and heart disease among the population as a whole.

11.3.1 Sign, Size, and Significance

The interpretation of a regression coefficient focuses on three key attributes: size, sign, and significance.

Sign. We should first note whether the independent variable has a positive or negative association with the dependent variable. A positive sign on a coefficient means that the independent variable and the dependent variable are positively correlated; an increase in one is associated with an increase in the other. A negative sign means that they are negatively correlated; an increase in the independent variable is associated with a *decrease* in the dependent variable. In the Framingham Heart Study, we would expect the coefficient on smoking to be positive: an increase in smoking is associated with an increase in heart disease. We would expect the coefficient on exercise to be negative: more exercise is associated with a decrease in heart disease.

Size. How big is the observed relationship between the independent variable and the dependent variable? A regression coefficient quantifies the change in the dependent variable associated with a one unit change in the independent variable, *ceteris paribus*. In a previous example, we regressed weight on height, sex, and several other explanatory variables. The coefficient on height was 2.96, meaning that every one unit change in height is associated with 2.96 units of change in weight. Of course, we know what those "units" are in this case: height is measured in inches, and weight is measured in pounds. Thus, our regression coefficient tells us that 1 additional inch of height is associated with 2.96 additional pounds in weight for our sample of graduate students. For dummy variables, the coefficient is a measure of the effect of "turning on" the dummy variable. Consider the effect of gender on weight in our earlier example. We coded the data so that females were a 1 and males were a 0. The coefficient on sex was –2.44. We can interpret this to mean that being female (dummy = 1) is associated with weighing 2.44 pounds less than being male (dummy = 0).

The size of the coefficient gives us a sense of how big of an effect a dependent variable has in explaining our outcome of interest. From a public policy standpoint, this can be helpful in determining how resources ought to be allocated. Multiple regression analysis can identify the association between several explanatory variables and an outcome of interest. If the goal of policy makers is to change that outcome, they will want to focus on the factors that have the largest impact. In the Framingham Heart Study, researchers would be interested not only in the fact that smoking has a positive association with heart disease, but that the coefficient on smoking is large compared to other explanatory variables. Public-health officials can, therefore, infer that reducing smoking would have a large impact in reducing heart disease.

Significance. For a regression result to be meaningful from a public policy standpoint, we must have confidence that it was not an aberration based on a particular data sample. Regression analysis draws on the laws of probability introduced in the last chapter to calculate the likelihood that the association between an independent and dependent variable observed in some sample of the population is the product of chance. We begin by recognizing that the regression equation estimated using our sample data, such as the data from the Framingham Heart Study, is an estimate of the true regression equation (which we could calculate only by having data on all adults everywhere). Our regression equation using the sample data is the following: $\hat{Y} = \hat{a} + \hat{b}_1 x + \hat{e}$, to distinguish it from the theoretical regression equation for the population as a whole (which we cannot observe): $Y = a + b_1 x + e$.

To establish the statistical significance of the findings from our regression on the sample data, we will draw on the concept of hypothesis testing introduced in the previous chapter. Specifically, we will accept or reject the null hypothesis that the true coefficient b_1 for the population as a whole is 0, meaning that there is no true association between the independent and dependent variables. In the graduate-student weight regression, our null hypothesis would be that the coefficient on HEIGHT for all graduate students in the program is 0, meaning that height has no association with weight among graduate students. The null hypothesis can be expressed as the following:

$$H_o: b_1 = 0$$

If we reject the null hypothesis, then we implicitly accept the alternative hypothesis:

$$H_a: b_1 \neq 0$$

In our weight example, the alternative hypothesis is that height does have a meaningful association with weight among the population of graduate students.

We will accept or reject the null hypothesis by calculating the probability of observing $\hat{b}_1$ for the sample population if the true coefficient b_1 is in fact 0. To put it in the context of the Framingham study, suppose that a study using the Framingham data finds that smoking a pack of cigarettes or more a day is associated with a decrease in life expectancy by 7.3 years, so the coefficient on SMOKING, $\hat{b}_1$, is –7.3. Our null hypothesis is that for the population of all Americans (or all adults in the world), there is no relationship between smoking a pack of cigarettes a day and life expectancy. We can reject that null hypothesis and accept the alternative hypothesis—that smoking has an impact on life expectancy—by calculating the probability of getting our observed sample result if the true population coefficient is 0. If that probability falls below some predetermined level—usually 1 percent, 5 percent, or 10 percent—then we will accept the alternative hypothesis that there is indeed a statistically significant relationship between smoking and life expectancy. The probabilities described above are known as the **significance level.** A researcher will describe the coefficient on a variable as being significant at the .01 level if there is a 1-percent chance or less that the true coefficient is 0. Similarly, a coefficient is significant at the .05 level if there is a 5-percent chance or less that the true population coefficient is 0; a .10 significance level indicates that there is a 10-percent chance or less that the true coefficient is 0 and that the observed association is simply a product of chance.

The mechanics of calculating statistical significance are beyond this introductory chapter. However, the following terms are important to understand in the general idea of statistical significance.

Standard error. The standard error of a regression coefficient is a measure of the likely dispersion we would observe in the coefficient if we were to conduct the regression analysis on repeated samples drawn from the same population. For example, we can revisit the Framingham example in which the coefficient on the dummy variable for SMOKING, $\hat{b}_1$, is –7.3, meaning that smoking a pack or more of cigarettes a day is associated with a decrease in life expectancy of 7.3 years. If we were to conduct the same analysis on a different sample of adults from Framingham or on a sample from some other American city that is similar in size, how much variation would we expect in our different estimations of $\hat{b}_1$? Two elements of the formula for the standard error are most important. (1) The larger the residual in the regression equation, which is the unexplained variation in the dependent variable, the larger the standard error will be, *ceteris paribus*. This should be intuitive: the more unexplained variation in the regression, the more "noise" there is to create variation in $\hat{b}_1$ from sample to sample. (2) The standard error will fall as the number of observations, or **sample size,** gets larger, *ceteris paribus*. Again, this should be intuitive. In our graduate-student weight example, we would certainly expect our estimates of $\hat{b}_1$ to vary less with samples of 100 students than we would with samples of 5 students.

Any basic statistical package will generate the standard errors for the coefficients in a regression equation. A standard error in isolation cannot be interpreted in any meaningful way. Instead, we typically compare the size of a coefficient to the size of its standard error. The larger the standard error relative to the coefficient, the more difficult it is to reject the null hypothesis that the true coefficient is 0. For example, assume that in our graduate-student weight model we add a dummy variable for whether or not the student lives on campus; assume that the coefficient $\hat{b}_1$ on CAMPUS is 1.4 with a standard error of 3.3. We can interpret this to mean that living on campus is associated with weighing an extra 1.4 pounds. The standard error tells us that if we were to conduct this analysis on repeated samples of graduate students, a high proportion of our observations for $\hat{b}_1$ would fall within the range of 1.4 pounds ± 3.3 pounds. Think about what that means. For some of our samples, we would likely find that $\hat{b}_1$ is 0 or even negative, meaning that living on campus has no effect on weight or may even be associated with weighing less!

Compare that to another hypothetical case in which we add a dummy variable for the weight regression indicating whether the student is a marathon runner or not. Assume that the coefficient on MARATHON is –11.4 with a standard error of 3.4. The standard error tells us that if we were to conduct the same analysis on different samples of graduate students, a high proportion of observations for $\hat{b}_1$ would fall in the range of –11.4 ± 3.4. In other words, we would expect to consistently find that being a marathon runner is associated with weighing less.

A **t-statistic** is what quantifies the relationship between the coefficient and the standard error, and enables us to determine whether or not a coefficient is statistically significant at some level of confidence. If our null hypothesis is that $b_i = 0$, then $t = \hat{b}_i/se(\hat{b}_i)$.[3] The larger the t-statistic, the less likely it is that the observed relationship is a product of chance and the more likely we are to reject the null hypothesis. Of course, that does not yet give us a specific level of confidence with which we can reject the null hypothesis. For that, we conduct one final calculation.

RULE OF THUMB

The t-Statistic

A t-statistic of 2 or higher is generally considered to be statistically significant.

The **p-value** represents the probability of observing a particular value for $\hat{b}_1$, if the null hypothesis is in fact true. (For our purposes, we'll continue to assume that the null hypothesis is $b_1 = 0$.) You may recall the example from the last chapter in which a gambler comes into town with his own die and pro-

---

3. If the null hypothesis is that b_1 is equal to some number other than 0, then $t = (\hat{b}_1 - b_{null})/se(\hat{b})$.

ceeds to win a lot of money by rolling the number 6 ten times in a row. We cannot prove that the gambler has cheated by using a "loaded" die. However, we *can* demonstrate that it's highly unlikely that the gambler would have such a string of good luck if the die is fair. (The probability of rolling ten consecutive 6s is $(1/6)^{10}$, or just over 1 in 60 million!) Social-science research employs the same basic logic. Regression analysis using data from the Framingham Heart Study cannot *prove* that smoking causes heart disease among the general population. However, researchers can conclude that the observed relationship between smoking and heart disease among the Framingham participants would be highly unlikely if there is in fact no association between smoking and heart disease for all adults.

A basic statistics package will calculate a *p*-value based on the *t*-statistic and the number of **degrees of freedom** in the regression equation. The degrees of freedom are a function of the amount of data on which the results are based. Specifically, the degrees of freedom are the number of observations in the sample (n) minus the number of variables in the equation (k). One degree of freedom is also subtracted for the intercept.

Degrees of freedom = $n - k - 1$.

A *p*-value of 0.021 indicates that there is only a 2.1 percent chance that we would observe b if the null hypothesis were true. In other words, if we reject the null hypothesis that $b_1 = 0$, roughly 2 times out of 100 we will make a type I error, which means that we have rejected a null hypothesis that is indeed true.

Researchers pay attention to both the size of a coefficient and its statistical significance. It's important to recognize that a variable that is statistically significant may not be "significant" in the broader public policy sense, meaning that its size is not substantial. For example, a researcher examining the impact of a job-training program on earnings might find that some aspect of the program has a positive and statistically significant effect on the future earnings of participants but that the size of the impact—say, \$3 a month—is not meaningful given the purpose of the program. (Such an increase will not appreciably change a person's quality of life, which is the goal.) Similarly, a coefficient may be large but not statistically significant. This is particularly likely to happen with a small sample of data. A researcher examining the effect of a new drug on a rare disease may have only a small number of patients for which he has outcome data. The effects of the drug may be large and positive, but the small sample will make it hard or impossible to reject the null hypothesis (that the drug has no effect) with any degree of confidence. Such results are not meaningless, but they would have to be replicated with a larger sample before we could conclude with confidence that the effect is real.

11.3.2 Goodness of Fit

A regression equation can be evaluated not only based on the sign, size, and significance of the individual coefficients, but also on the extent to which the regression as a whole explains our outcome of interest, or the **goodness of fit.** The R^2 for a regression equation is a measure of how much variation in the dependent variable is explained by the regression equation relative to the total variation in the dependent variable. In the context of our earlier regression example for graduate-student weights, the R^2 would reflect how much of the variation in weight among graduate students is explained by our model.

In the weight example, $Y_i - \bar{Y}$ represents the distance of each observation from the mean weight for the sample of graduate students. If the mean weight for the students is 160 pounds and Sophie weighs 127 pounds, then $Y_i - \bar{Y}$ for this observation is –33 pounds. The **total sum of squares** for the model, TSS, is the sum of $(Y_i - \bar{Y})^2$ for all of the students in the sample, or $\sum_{i=1}^{n}(Y_i - \bar{Y})^2$. This represents the total variation in the dependent variable.

In the same example, $\hat{Y}_i - \bar{Y}_i$ represents the difference between the predicted value for an individual student and the mean for all graduate students in the sample—or the explained variation. The model predicts that Sophie will weigh 136 pounds; the mean for the sample is 160 pounds. As a result, $\hat{Y} - \bar{Y}$ is 136 – 160 = –24. This represents the amount by which our regression equation improves on the mean in terms of explaining the weight of an individual graduate student in the sample. The **explained sum of squares,** ESS, is the sum of $(\hat{Y} - \bar{Y})^2$ for all observations in the sample.

Finally, each observation in the sample has residual term $Y_i - \hat{Y}_i$, which is the portion of the student's weight that is not explained by the regression equation. Sophie's predicted weight is 136 pounds; her actual weight is 127 pounds, so the unexplained variation is –9 pounds. The **residual sum of squares,** RSS, is the sum of $(Y_i - \hat{Y}_i)^2$ for all the students in the sample, or $\sum_{i=1}^{n}(Y_i - \hat{Y}_i)^2$.

To recap, the total variation of Sophie's weight from the mean is 33 pounds. Of that, the model explains 24 pounds; 9 pounds are not explained. The better the "fit" of the model, the less unexplained variation there will be. The R^2 evaluates the fit of the model for the whole sample. Specifically, the

$$R^2 = \text{ESS/TSS} = \frac{\sum_{i=1}^{n}(\hat{Y}_i - \bar{Y}_i)^2}{\sum_{i=1}^{n}(Y_i - \bar{Y}_i)^2}$$

The R^2 can range in value from 0 (the model explains nothing at all) to 1 (the model perfectly explains every observation). A high R^2 suggests that a regression equation does a good job of explaining variation in the dependent variable. On the other hand, a regression equation with a low R^2 can still have substantial public policy value if it provides insight into an important outcome of interest. For example, a study using data from the Framingham Heart Study may find a statistically significant link between exercise and a lower incidence of heart disease but only have an R^2 of .27. Much of the variation in the incidence of heart disease remains unexplained, but we would at least have made progress toward understanding an important public health challenge.

The *F-test* is a test of statistical significance for the regression equation overall. Specifically, it examines the likelihood that *all* of the coefficients in the regression equation are collectively worthless. We can use an *F*-test to reject or accept the following hypotheses:

$$H_0\text{: } b_1 = b_2 = b_3 = \ldots b_i = 0$$

$$H_a\text{: at least one coefficient} \neq 0$$

A basic statistical package can calculate an *F*-statistic for a regression equation. This figure is interpreted in the same way as a *t*-statistic. If the *F*-statistic for the regression is high enough, we can reject the null hypothesis with some degree of confidence, such as at the .01 level. If the *F*-statistic is low, then we cannot reject the null hypothesis that the coefficients collectively have no explanatory power. The *F*-test is not redundant with the *t*-test on individual coefficients, because it is sometimes possible that the *F*-test will show that a regression equation as a whole is statistically significant even when none of the individual coefficients is statistically significant. This can be interpreted to mean that we cannot reject the null hypothesis for any individual coefficient that $b_i = 0$. However, it is extremely unlikely that *all* of the coefficients equal 0.

11.4 LINEAR TRANSFORMATIONS

One of the key assumptions of regression analysis is that there is a linear relationship between the independent variables and the dependent variable. Obviously, not all relationships that researchers may care about will be linear. Take a look at the following graph, which plots the average salary in an industry over time. As you can see, the salary is increasing at an increasing rate. Thus, linear regression would not produce an equation of the form $y = a + bx + e$, since the slope is different at different points on the line. The salary increases more sharply in the later years than it does in the early years. For example, a person could expect a larger raise between the twenty-third and twenty-fourth year on the job than between the third and fourth year.

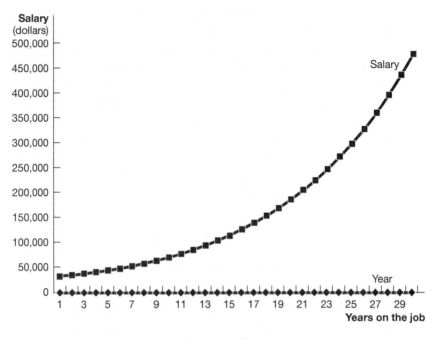

Salary over Time

In fact, there *is* a potential linear relationship between salary and years on the job in this case: a worker receives a 10-percent raise every year. Researchers would clearly consider this to be a clear, consistent, and meaningful relationship. But when measured in dollars, it does not appear to be linear, since each year's raise is 10 percent of an increasingly large base—a 10-percent raise based on a $50,000 salary in year 5 is much less in dollar terms than a 10-percent raise on a $350,000 salary after many years on the job. There is an easy mathematical fix for these common kinds of situations. Researchers will sometimes use logarithms to transform data so that they can be analyzed using linear regression. Specifically, logarithms have an elegant property: the logarithm transforms an exponential relationship (such as the salary that is increasing at an increasing rate) into a potentially linear arithmetic relationship for which regression analysis is appropriate.[4] The table below should illuminate the relationship.

4. The general rule of logarithms is the following: If $x = b^y$, then $\log_b x = y$. Some specific examples will make the relationship clearer: $10^2 = 100$; therefore, $\log_{10} 100 = 2$
$$10^3 = 1,000; \text{ therefore, } \log_{10} 1,000 = 3$$
$$10^4 = 10,000; \text{ therefore, } \log_{10} 10,000 = 4$$
$$10^5 = 100,000; \text{ therefore, } \log_{10} 100,000 = 5$$
That progression should enable you to infer that the $\log_{10}$ of 50,000 will be somewhere between 4 and 5. In fact, $\log_{10} 50,000 = 4.7$.

YEAR	SALARY	INCREASE	LOG(SALARY)	INCREASE
1	$30,000		4.477121	
2	$33,000	$3,000	4.518514	0.041393
3	$36,300	$3,300	4.559907	0.041393
4	$39,930	$3,630	4.601299	0.041393
5	$43,923	$3,993	4.642692	0.041393
6	$48,315	$4,392	4.684085	0.041393
7	$53,147	$4,832	4.725477	0.041393
8	$58,462	$5,315	4.766870	0.041393
9	$64,308	$5,846	4.808263	0.041393
10	$70,738	$6,431	4.849655	0.041393

The graph of the relationship between time on the job and log(Salary) looks different—and more conducive to regression analysis.

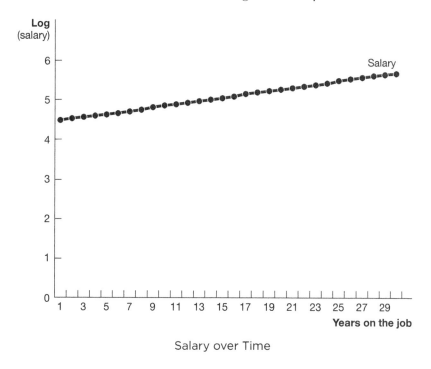

Salary over Time

We can specify the following regression equation: log(Salary) = $a + b$ (YEARS) + e. In this case, the coefficient on b turns out to be .1, meaning that every one-unit change in x (years on the job) is associated with a .1 unit change in log(Salary). How does one interpret that? (Would you be happy or sad if your boss told you that the log of your salary next year would be .1 higher than the log of your salary this year?) It turns out that logs have a particularly attractive property: if the dependent variable (income, in this case) is measured in logs, then a one-unit change in x creates a b-percent change in Y. In this case, every additional year on the job is associated with a 10-percent increase in salary—which is what we saw in the original salary chart.

When both the dependent variable and the independent variable are measured in logs, the interpretation is also easy: the coefficient on the independent variable is the percent change in the dependent variable associated with a 1-percent change in the independent variable. To see a potential application, examine the following graph, which plots the relationship between oil prices and consumption. The correlation is negative, as we would expect. Higher prices are associated with less consumption. But the relationship is clearly not linear, meaning that researchers would seemingly have a difficult time using regression analysis to quantify this relationship.

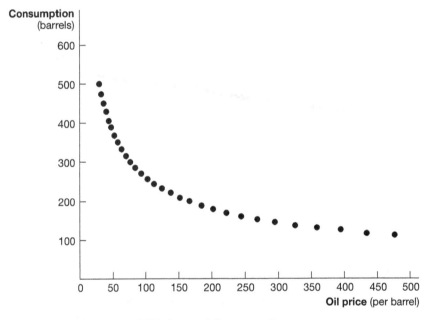

Oil Price and Consumption

Once again, however, there is a meaningful linear aspect to this relationship. The price elasticity of demand for oil represented by this graph is –.5, meaning that every 1-percent increase in the price of a barrel of oil is associated with a 0.5-percent decrease in consumption. This becomes apparent when the same relationship is graphed after taking the log of both the dependent and independent variables. A simple linear regression would find log(barrels consumed) = a + –.5 log(barrel price) (there would be no error terms since we've plotted a precisely linear relationship).

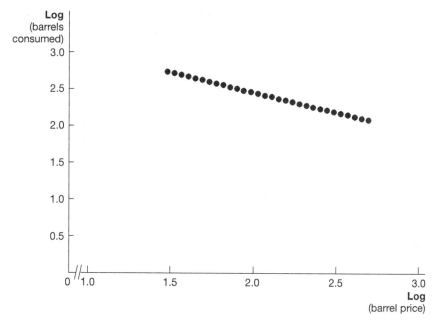

Oil Price and Consumption (Logs)

·············· POLICY IN THE REAL WORLD ···············

Two-Year Degrees:
Do Community Colleges Increase Wages?

Thomas Kane of Harvard University and Cecilia Rouse of Princeton University asked a very important question: Does a community college education have any value? From a policy standpoint, this is a significant question, since roughly half of all students who enter college today will begin at a two-year institution.

From a research standpoint, assessing the value of a community-college education is surprisingly difficult. Previous studies had shown that community colleges have little or no effect on lifetime wages, compared to time spent at a four-year institution. However, such studies were prone to two potentially serious methodological errors. First, community-college students have lower high-school grades and test scores, on average, than students who begin at a four-year institution. Might it be that the value added by community colleges in terms of wages later in life is disguised by the fact that the students who attend two-year programs had less earning potential to begin with?

Second, the data on educational attainment are limited. Data sources like the census typically gather information on an individual on his or her years of postsecondary education, but they do not differentiate by the type of institution. Someone who drops out of a four-year institution after two years is treated the same as someone who completes a degree at a two-year community college—both will show up as having two years of postsecondary education.

Kane and Rouse solved both methodological problems with a regression analysis using data from the National Longitudinal Study of the High School Class of 1972 (NLS-72), which contains extensive data on a sample of 22,652 high-school seniors across the United States in 1972. The data set has information on family background, high-school performance, postsecondary education (including transcripts), and labor-market experiences (including hourly wages and annual income) up to fourteen years after high-school graduation.

Kane and Rouse formulate several different regression equations with some measure of income fourteen years after high-school graduation as the dependent variable. One equation uses log hourly wages as the dependent variable; the other uses log annual earnings. Both regressions include attendance at a community college as an independent variable, with control variables for student background and ability. The results are broadly consistent: the returns to studying at a community college are large and significant. Each year of community college is associated with a 4-percent increase in annual earnings for men and a 7-percent increase for women, controlling for the assorted background characteristics described above. The authors find that a year of study at a community college is just as valuable in terms of future income as a year of study at a four-year college.

This is a significant finding, given the number of Americans who attend community colleges and the role that the public sector plays in funding such programs, both directly and indirectly through student aid. Professors Kane and Rouse conclude, "As an increasing proportion of high school graduates seek to improve their skills in the face of rising wage inequality, the community college is an increasingly vital institution in the U.S. labor market."

. . . .

11.5 COMMON REGRESSION ERRORS

Although this chapter is intended only as an introduction to regression analysis, there are several common regression errors that any policy analyst should recognize.

1. **Correlation does not equal causation.** Regression analysis identifies an association between two variables; it cannot prove causality. A researcher should have strong theoretical reasons to believe that the relationship between the independent and dependent variables is causal before doing the regression analysis. Thus, the researchers using the Framingham data would likely have physiological evidence suggesting that smoking causes heart disease (and no reason to believe that having heart disease would cause someone to start smoking). A regression finding that the coefficient on smoking is significant would confirm the researcher's *a priori* hypothesis that smoking causes heart disease.

2. **Endogeneity (or reverse causality).** In some cases, the statistical analysis may have the causality backward; the outcome of interest may be what causes the explanatory variable, rather than the other way around. For example, suppose that a researcher did an analysis attempting to prove that higher spending on K–12 education at the state level leads to more robust economic growth. This theory seems reasonable; we have strong theoretical and empirical reasons to believe that investments in education would yield higher incomes. But suppose that we were to perform a regression analysis with state per capita income as the dependent variable and state spending on K–12 education as the independent variable of interest (plus assorted control variables). If the coefficient on K–12 education spending is large and significant, can we conclude that spending more money on education at the state level causes incomes to rise? Not necessarily. The causality in this case may well run in the other direction: wealthier states may simply spend more on education. Thus, the significant statistical correlation does not prove that education spending raises incomes; a sensible person would infer that the causality could run in the other direction or even that causality could run in both directions.

··············· | **POLICY IN THE REAL WORLD** | ···············

A Clever Research Strategy: Do More Police Mean Less Crime?

Does putting more police officers on the street reduce criminal activity? This is obviously an important public policy question, since crime is a major social problem. Yet quantifying any meaningful causal relationship between policing and crime turns out to be surprisingly difficult. In fact, a simple association often shows that more police are associated with *more* crime—not because police breed crime, but because when crime is bad, jurisdictions put more police on the street. The "crime is causing the police" rather than the other way around.

Researchers needed some way to solve this identification problem—to isolate not only the association between police presence and crime, but to do so in a way that gets at the important policy question: What happens to crime when a jurisdiction puts more police officers on the street, *ceteris paribus*? Jonathan Klick of Florida State University and Alexander Tabarrok of George Mason University came up with a clever strategy for answering this question.[5] They found a situation in which the increases in police presence were exogenous, or caused from the outside, and had nothing to do with the current or expected crime rate: terrorism alerts.

In 2002, the Office of Homeland Security introduced the Homeland Security Advisory System (HSAS) that rates the terrorism risk on a given day on a five-color–coded scale: green (low); blue (guarded); yellow (elevated); orange (high); and red (severe). On high-alert days, cities—Washington, D.C., in particular—put more officers on the street. On high alert, Washington, D.C., also activates a Joint Operations Center with other law-enforcement agencies and turns on a closed-circuit television monitoring system around the National Mall that is otherwise not in use. The net effect on high-alert days is more police officers on the street and heightened law-enforcement surveillance for reasons that have nothing to do with the daily crime rate.

Professors Klick and Tabarrok examined whether there is less crime in Washington, D.C., on high-alert days. Their dependent variable is the daily

---

5. Jonathan Klick and Alexander Tabarrok, "Using Terror Alert Levels to Estimate the Effect of Police on Crime," *Journal of Law & Economics* 48, no. 1 (April 2005): 267–279.

crime rate, which is drawn from data gathered by the Washington, D.C., police department. The most basic analysis regresses the daily Washington, D.C., crime rate on a dummy representing the terrorism threat level (0 for elevated, 1 for high). The regression also includes dummy variables for day of the week to pick up any potential confounding factor. (Friday turns out to be a big crime day.) The authors report, "The coefficient on the alert level is statistically significant at the 5 percent level and indicates that on high-alert days, total crimes decreased by an average of seven crimes per day, or approximately 6.6 percent."

But are the police making things better. Klick and Tabarrok also test and reject two alternative explanations. Perhaps the terrorism warning keeps tourists at home, giving criminals fewer potential victims (in which case the police deserve no credit at all). In one regression, the authors include a variable for ridership on the Washington, D.C., Metro as a proxy for the number of tourists in the city, since visitors rather than locals are more likely to be riding the Metro in the middle of the day. This control variable does not change the original results in any significant way. The authors also point out that burglaries, which are committed against local property owners rather than tourists, fall on high-alert days along with other kinds of crimes.

Second, the authors test whether the high-alert days might simply have coincided with spells of bad weather or some other random cycles in crime, in which case the heightened police presence had nothing to do with the fall in crime. This does not appear to be the case either. Washington, D.C., has seven police districts. District 1 gets the most police attention on high-alert days because it includes the White House, the Capitol, and the National Mall; it is also the only area where closed-circuit monitoring is activated. The authors find that on high-alert days, crime falls much more sharply in district 1 than in any other district. (Almost half of the total drop in crime on high-alert days is in district 1 alone.) A confounding factor like weather or random variations in crime would presumably affect all districts in Washington, D.C., similarly.

The authors make a rough calculation based on the D.C. experience that every 1.0-percent increase in police presence is associated with a 0.3-percent drop in crime. This figure is inexact because, for national security reasons, the Washington, D.C., police will not say exactly how many additional police officers are on patrol on high-alert days. However, the general conclusion is more robust. The authors conclude, "Using daily crime data during the period the terror alert system has been in place, we show that the level of crime decreases significantly, both statistically and economically, during high-alert periods."

. . . .

3. **Omitted variable bias.** In some cases, an independent variable in a regression may simply be acting as a proxy for some important factor or characteristic that has been omitted from the regression equation. To use an absurd example, suppose that cancer researchers find that workers who report leaving their offices for short breaks from work during the day are at significantly higher risk of contracting heart disease and cancer. How could leaving the office for several five-minute breaks during the work day compromise a person's health? Should the surgeon general warn against taking short breaks from work? Of course not. The obvious explanation is that when workers report leaving the office for many short breaks, they are most likely smoking. If some measure of smoking is not included in the regression, then the short-break variable will really be picking up the effects of the smoking that happens on those breaks. A researcher might say that the "break" variable is acting as a proxy for smoking. As a result, if a variable were introduced into the regression that was a measure of smoking activity, we would expect the significance of the "break" variable to disappear entirely. If a researcher does not recognize the impact of an important omitted variable, he or she may erroneously attribute causality to whatever variable is picking up its effects.

4. **Multicollinearity.** The purpose of multiple regression is to isolate the relationship between an independent variable and some dependent variable of interest, holding all other factors constant. This objective can be compromised if two independent variables are included in the regression that are so highly correlated with one another that it is difficult or impossible to ascertain accurately their independent effects. For example, suppose that we are interested in the relationship between student test scores and family background. Do students with highly educated parents do better on standardized tests, *ceteris paribus*? The dependent variable would be the standardized test score; the independent variables would likely include some measure of the student's parents' education level, such as mother's educational attainment. However, the regression would probably *not* include a variable measuring father's educational attainment as well. Why? Because married couples tend to have very similar educational backgrounds; there may not be sufficient variation in the data to separate the effect of mother's education from father's education. As a result, the regression result could obscure the relationship. For example, if either father's education or mother's education is included alone in the regression, the coefficient would likely be large and significant. If both variables are included, however, it's possible that neither would be significant.

5. **Data mining.** Loading up a regression with lots of explanatory variables for which there is little or no theoretical association with the dependent variable is known as **data mining.** Simple probability suggests that some of these junk "explanatory" variables will appear to be correlated with the dependent variable, even though the relationship is spurious. If a variable is significant at the 5-percent level ($p < .05$), we must still recognize that there is a 5 in 100 chance that the observed relationship is a product of coincidence. Careful research combines a theoretical reason to believe that two variables might be related with an empirical test of the hypothesis. Suppose a researcher loads up a regression with scores of independent variables regardless of whether or not we have any *a priori* reason to believe that they would help to explain our dependent variable of interest. If the data were available, a researcher trying to explain student test scores could load up the regression with variables like shoe size, number of times a week the student eats popcorn, color of the family car, a dummy for whether or not the student's school has a volleyball team, and so on. We would not expect any of these variables to have any meaningful effect on student test scores. However, it is plausible that we might observe some patterns by coincidence. We could have a data set in which the students with the highest test scores ate a lot of popcorn—just because. In fact, the rules of probability suggest that if we put 100 silly variables in a regression equation, the coefficients on 5 of them would, on average, appear to have a statistically significant association with the dependent variable. To avoid drawing inferences that are the product of coincidence rather than meaningful association, researchers need some justification for including explanatory variables in a regression. And when empirical findings do seem curious—such as a statistically significant relationship between eating popcorn and higher test scores—other researchers would seek to replicate the results using different data.

11.6 CONCLUSION

Regression analysis is one of the most powerful statistical tools in social-science research. It allows us to identify meaningful relationships between variables and outcomes in situations where it is not possible to do controlled laboratory experiments. Regression analysis enables us to isolate the effect of a single variable on some outcome of interest, while controlling for other possible confounding factors. With good data and sound analysis, we can make meaningful inferences about the factors that affect outcomes we care about: crime, income, public health, and so on. The ultimate goal, of course, is to use this analysis to improve public policy and produce better outcomes. Regression results are only as good as the analysis and data that are used to generate them. Most important, regression cannot prove causality—that A causes B. Instead, it can quantify an association between A and B that is unlikely to have been caused by chance alone. Done properly, regression analysis can provide crucial insight into important policy challenges. If the analysis is flawed, however, the conclusions can be dangerously wrong.

FOR DISCUSSION

Is It Discrimination?: Explaining the Wage Gap between Men and Women, Blacks and Whites[6]

Men earn more than women in America, on average. The median annual earnings of women are only 76 percent of that for men. And whites earn more blacks. The ratio of black earnings to white earnings is 78 percent for men and 87 percent for women. We know that both women and African-Americans have historically suffered from discrimination in the labor market, and there is plenty of anecdotal evidence to suggest that discrimination may still be a factor. However, the presence of a wage gap is not proof of discrimination. Wages are determined by many factors, including age, education, and work experience. Women may earn less than men because they face discrimination in the workforce. Or they may earn less than men because they are more likely to be employed in professions with lower average pay. Or they may earn less than men because they are doing similar jobs but have fewer years of experience.

A wage gap alone does not prove discrimination. However, policy makers would obviously like to know as much as possible about what is causing the observed gap in wages between men and women, and blacks and whites. If a large wage gap persists even after we control for factors such as education, work experience, and job types, then discrimination would be a likely culprit. On the other hand, if politicians or advocacy groups focus on discrimination when the real culprit is a productivity-related outcome like education or experience, then they will miss the most important policy remedies, such as improving the educational outcomes and job experience of the affected groups. Which factors best explain the wage gaps that we observe in the labor market?

June E. O'Neill and Dave M. O'Neill, professors at the Centre for the Study of Business and Government at Baruch College, CUNY, have written a paper for the National Bureau of Economic Research (NBER) that uses many of the tools explained in this chapter to probe the relationship between the wage gap and discrimination. Their objective is to use regression analysis to analyze workers' wages and determine what factors best explain the observed patterns by race and gender. The research is a good example of how sophisticated data analysis can inform important policy issues.

---

6. June E. O'Neill and Dave M. O'Neill, "What Do Wage Differentials Tell Us about Labor Market Discrimination?" National Bureau of Economic Research, Working Paper 11240 (April 2005), http://www.nber.org/papers/w11240.

The theory. Direct discrimination is difficult or impossible to measure. The O'Neill and O'Neill paper takes a different approach: to what extent can differences in productivity across workers explain the differences in their wages? The residual, or unexplained component of the wage differential, may be the result of discrimination. (Or it could be the result of some other omitted variable.) Wages should roughly reflect an individual's marginal product of labor; the more valuable an individual is to the firm, the more he or she is likely to be paid. Productivity is often hard to measure directly. (For example, how productive is an individual school teacher or accountant?) However, productivity is highly correlated with factors that are more easily measured, such as education, years of experience, and so on. In the case of the gender gap, the authors point out that wages may also reflect differences in "lifetime career paths." If women are more likely to leave the labor market to take on family responsibilities, then they will accumulate less workforce experience and may earn lower wages as a result. The broad goal of the paper is to quantify the relationship between wages and productivity-related variables, recognizing that any significant gaps in wages that are not explained by productivity may be caused by discrimination.

The data. The data for the analysis come from the National Longitudinal Survey of Youth (NLSY79). Like the Framingham Heart Study discussed at the beginning of this chapter, the NLSY is a study that collects longitudinal data (repeated interviews over time with the same subjects) on a large, representative sample of Americans. The NLSY includes information on educational attainment, work experience, and other personal attributes that are likely to be associated with earnings. The authors examined the NLSY cohort that had reached ages 35–43 in 2000. One unique feature of the NLSY data is that nearly all participants were given the Armed Forces Qualification Test (AFQT). The AFQT measures cognitive ability, which is an important component of productivity. The authors also used data from the 2000 census, which contains earnings information for large samples of minority groups.

The method. The authors of the study first examine the wage gaps by sex, race, and ethnicity using data from the 2000 census. They use OLS to regress the log hourly wage on different explanatory variables, including dummy variables for different races and national origins. The coefficient on each dummy variable expresses the differential between some group (e.g., black non-Hispanics) and the comparison group (white men). In subsequent analysis, the authors add additional control variables, such as years of education, to see how these explanatory variables affect the wage gap.

The study subsequently uses the NLSY data for a more in-depth examination of the observed wage gaps. The sample used for analysis includes 5,600 workers. (Black and Hispanic workers have been oversampled to provide a sufficient number of observations for in-depth analysis of these groups.) Once again, the authors use OLS regression to explain the observed log wage differential.

The findings. What, if anything, can the observed wage gaps between different groups tell us about that discrimination in the labor market? Using many of the tools explained in this chapter, the authors conclude, "Not very much." Nearly all of the observed wage gaps between men and women and between workers of different races and ethnicities disappear once other productivity-related attributes such as educational attainment and work experience are included in the regression analysis. Space does not allow a complete discussion of all the results, so we shall focus here on the results explaining the observed wage gaps for men of different races and ethnicities.

The authors present a series of regression equations using data from the 2000 census. The dependent variable is the log hourly wage for men ages 25–54. They begin with a simple equation in which the log hourly wage is regressed on a series of dummy variables, each of which represents a specific race, ethnicity, or national origin. The coefficient on a dummy variable represents the effect of being part of that group relative to the comparison group, which, in this analysis, is white men. Since the dependent variable has been transformed into a logarithm, we can interpret the coefficients as a percentage—being a member of a certain group represented by the dummy variable is associated with a certain percentage difference in hourly earnings.

Model 1 in the chart below presents the observed difference in hourly wages across different racial and ethnic groups. The coefficient on Black non-Hispanic tells us that men in this group earn 27.3 percent less than the white men in the sample. The t-statistic suggests that this is a statistically significant finding. On the other hand, the coefficient for Asian Indian suggests that such men earn 22.7 percent more than the white men in the census sample. Again, the coefficient is highly significant.

In models 2, 3, and 4, the authors add other control variables to examine the degree to which they can help explain the observed wage gaps. In model 4, for example, the authors include information on age, geography, schooling, and other controls. Once again, the dummy variables on race and ethnicity are the point of interest; these dummies represent the disparity in wages that remains after controlling for some productivity-related attributes. In model 4, the coefficient on Black non-Hispanic shrinks to –.181, meaning that the hourly wage gap between white and black men shrinks from 27 percent in model 1 to 18 percent in model 4, once we control for some work-related differences other than race. Meanwhile, the gap between white men and Asian Indian men nearly disappears. The coefficient on the Asian Indian dummy in model 4 falls to .037, meaning that Asian Indian men earn 3.7 percent more than white men, once we control for other attributes—a dramatic drop from the 22.7-percent difference observed in model 1.

Log Hourly Wage Differentials between Men of Detailed Race/Ethnicity and White Non-Hispanic Men, Ages 25–54, in 1999, Controlling for Different Sets of Explanatory Variables (2000 Census)

	MODEL 1		MODEL 2		MODEL 3		MODEL 4	
	COEF.	*T*-STAT	COEF.	*T*-STAT	COEF.	*T*-STAT	COEF.	*T*-STAT
Race/Ethnicity Indicators								
American Indian	−0.253	−24.78	−0.212	−21.75	−0.131	−14.59	−0.125	−13.96
Black non-Hispanic	−0.273	−80.64	−0.273	−82.97	−0.182	−59.31	−0.181	−59.29
Chinese	0.037	3.57	−0.104	−10.46	−0.198	−21.44	−0.101	−10.48
Japanese	0.241	13.44	0.131	7.62	0.011	0.71	0.068	4.30
Asian Indian	0.227	20.27	0.166	15.49	−0.039	−3.93	0.037	3.52
Korean	0.143	6.29	0.089	4.10	−0.038	−1.91	−0.003	−0.17
Vietnamese	−0.034	−1.71	−0.045	−2.36	0.005	0.31	0.064	3.63
Filipino	0.099	5.56	0.053	3.13	−0.013	−0.80	−0.016	−1.00
Other Asian	−0.166	−12.85	−0.226	−18.32	−0.190	−16.64	−0.125	−10.71
Mexican	−0.448	−122.36	−0.439	−118.82	−0.200	−53.56	−0.102	−22.50
Puerto Rican	−0.220	−22.24	−0.262	−27.57	−0.135	−15.37	−0.087	−9.62
Cuban	−0.181	−12.48	−0.148	−10.69	−0.110	−8.60	−0.016	−1.21
Dominican	−0.418	−21.47	−0.504	−27.08	−0.310	−18.03	−0.190	−10.86
Other Central American	−0.489	−44.74	−0.510	−48.76	−0.256	−26.14	−0.132	−12.85
South American	−0.241	−18.17	−0.301	−23.74	−0.243	−20.76	−0.132	−10.92
Other Hispanic	−0.318	−41.70	−0.304	−41.45	−0.145	−21.32	−0.081	−11.44
Control Variables								
Age			X		X		X	
Region, MSA, Central City			X		X		X	
Schooling					X		X	
Works part-time (20–34 hours a week)					X		X	
Class of worker					X		X	
Yrs. since migration to U.S.							X	
English-speaking ability							X	

Note: The log wage differentials are the partial regression coefficients of the dummy variables (0, 1) for each of the racial/ethnic groups listed above, from a series of multiple regressions shown as Models 1–4. The other variables controlled for are also listed above for each model. The sample, excluding active military and unincorporated self-employed persons, is restricted to wage and salary workers who worked twenty hours or more a week and twenty-six weeks or more a year. Hourly wages are obtained by dividing annual earnings by the product of weeks and hours worked during the year.

Source: Census 2000, Public Use Microdata Sample (PUMS), 1 percent.

From a policy standpoint, it is important to note that the census data show a significant gap in the log hourly earnings of white and black men—18 percent—that is not explained by productivity-related attributes. What do the NLSY data show?

Once again, the authors use a series of regression equations to clarify the factors that explain the observed gap in hourly wages based on race and ethnicity. We shall focus here on the black–white differential and the Hispanic–white differential. The NLSY data have a richer set of control variables than the census data, including scores from the Armed Forces Qualifying Test (AFQT, an aptitude test normally given to recruits). Thus, it is possible to include in the regression equation a measure of cognitive ability for each of the men in the sample. Once again, the authors regress the log hourly wage on a series of explanatory variables, including dummies for race and ethnicity. The table below shows separate regressions examining the black–white differential and the Hispanic–white differential. Both gaps shrink steadily as additional control variables are added in regressions 1–4.

For example, the black–white differential is –.339 when all black workers are compared to all white workers, meaning that blacks in the sample earn 33.9 percent less than whites. In regression 4, that coefficient actually turns positive (.009) once variables such as geography, schooling, AFQT score, and work experience are added to the regression, meaning that black workers earn 1 percent more than white workers after controlling for these other factors. Among college-educated men, blacks earn 2.9 percent less than whites.

The Hispanic–white differential shows a similar pattern. For all men in the sample, the coefficient falls from –.198 (representing nearly a 20-percent gap) to –.031 (a 3-percent gap) once the other control variables are added. It is also worth noting that in both the black and Hispanic cases, the coefficients on race and ethnicity are no longer statistically significant after the other control variables have been added.

The authors conclude, "We find that differences in years of schooling, and, more importantly, AFQT scores, explain most of the black–white wage gap among men and all of the Hispanic–white wage gap. When years of work experience are included in the regression, the black–white gap is virtually closed." Although the results are not presented here, the gender gap also diminishes as additional control variables are considered, though for different reasons. Differences in schooling and AFQT scores explain little of the observed gap in wages between men and women. Instead, factors such as work experience and part-time status—variables that the authors summarize as "choices made by women and men concerning the amount of time and energy devoted to a career"—better explain the gender gap.

Overall, the authors conclude, "We find that differences in productivity-related factors account for most of the observed (unadjusted) wage differentials. This is an important finding because the belief that employment discrimination is the major source of wage differentials can divert attention away from serious problems generating differentials, such as inadequate schooling." This paper is certainly not the last word on discrimination in the workplace; any single study should always be viewed merely as one item of evidence. Nonetheless, it is an excellent example of how statistical analysis can inform important policy issues.

Black-White and Hispanic-White Log Hourly Wage Gap among NLSY Men, Ages 35-43 in 2000, Controlling for Different Sets of Explanatory Variables

	BLACK-WHITE DIFFERENTIAL			HISPANIC-WHITE DIFFERENTIAL		
	TOTAL	HS GRAD OR LESS	COLLEGE GRAD OR MORE	TOTAL	HS GRAD OR LESS	COLLEGE GRAD OR MORE
Unadjusted log wage differential	-0.339*	-0.244*	-0.262*	-0.198*	-0.086*	-0.059
Log wage differential controlling for:						
1. Age, MSA, central city, region	-0.277*	-0.192*	-0.227*	-0.205*	-0.094*	-0.040
2. Variables in 1 plus schooling	-0.186*	-0.190*	-0.193*	-0.089*	-0.068*	-0.040
3. Variables in 2 plus AFQT	-0.062*	-0.075*	-0.050	-0.021	0.003	0.019
4. Variables in 3 plus Weeks worked in civilian job since age 18 ÷ 52, Weeks worked in military since 1978 ÷ 52	0.009	-0.019	-0.029	-0.031	0.001	0.014

Note: The log wage differentials are partial regression coefficients of dummy (0, 1) variables for black (Hispanic) from a series of OLS regressions containing the explanatory variables noted. For each racial/ethnic comparison, regressions were conducted for the following: total (all education levels): H.S. graduate or less; college graduate or higher. The reference group is white non-Hispanic. The analysis is restricted to wage and salary workers. The statistical significance of the black and Hispanic coefficients is indicated as follows (two-tailed test):

*significant at the 5-percent level or less

Source: National Longitudinal Survey of Youth (NLSY79).

QUESTIONS

1. Explain the following conclusion: "We find that differences in productivity-related factors account for most of the observed (unadjusted) wage differentials."
2. Do these findings persuade you that women and minorities do not face significant discrimination in the workplace? Why, or why not?
3. If discrimination were to disappear entirely, would you expect the wage gap between different demographic groups to disappear as well? Why, or why not?
4. Can you think of a way to measure discrimination directly?
5. The authors ask rhetorically: "Is it appropriate to include work experience in an analysis of the wage gap that aims to determine the role of employer discrimination?" What does this mean, and why would the authors raise such a methodological question?

6. In the NLSY sample used in the paper, 13 percent of black men had been interviewed in prison at least once in the survey (compared to 6 percent of Hispanics and 3 percent of whites). Why is this significant in the context of the subject being examined?

7. How might supporters of affirmative action use these results to bolster their case? What about opponents of affirmative action?

KEY CONCEPTS

★ Regression analysis seeks to explain some outcome, the dependent variable, as a function of one or more independent variables.

★ The dependent variable is the outcome that researchers are trying to explain. An independent variable, or explanatory variable, is a factor that researchers believe has some causal relationship with the outcome of interest.

★ A control variable is an independent variable that is likely to have an effect on the outcome of interest but is not the primary focus of inquiry; researchers must include it in the regression analysis to improve the validity of the results.

★ Bivariate regression analysis quantifies a linear relationship between a dependent variable and one independent variable. Multiple, or multivariate, regression analysis quantifies the linear relationship between a dependent variable and more than one independent variable.

★ The most common way of determining the best fit for a regression line is known as ordinary least squares, or OLS. A line fitted using OLS minimizes the sum of the squares of the error term.

★ Multiple regression analysis takes the form $Y = a + b_1x_1 + b_2x_2 + b_3x_3 \ldots + b_ix_i + e$, where Y is the dependent variable; a is an intercept; $x_1, x_2, x_3, \ldots x_i$ are independent variables; and e is an error term. The coefficients on the independent variables—$b_1, b_2, b_3, \ldots b_i$—quantify the relationship between that independent variable and the dependent variable, *ceteris paribus.*

★ One important purpose of regression analysis is to use sample data to make meaningful inferences about some larger population.

★ The interpretation of a regression coefficient focuses on three key attributes: sign (What is the direction of the association?), size (How big is that effect?), and significance (What is the likelihood that the association observed between an independent and dependent variable for some sample of the population is the product of chance?).

★ The standard error of a regression coefficient is a measure of the likely dispersion we would observe in the coefficient if we were to conduct the regression analysis on repeated samples drawn from the same population. The larger the standard error, the less confidence we are likely to have in our estimate of the coefficient.

★ A *t*-statistic measures how far an observed regression coefficient deviates from the null hypothesis relative to its standard error. If our null hypothesis is that

$b_i = 0$, then $t = \hat{b}_i / se(\hat{b}_i)$. Otherwise, $t = (\hat{b}_i - b_{null}) / se(\hat{b}_i)$. The larger the t-statistic, the less likely it is that the observed relationship is a product of chance and the more likely we are to reject the null hypothesis.

★ The p-value represents the probability of observing a particular value for $\hat{b}_1$, if the null hypothesis is in fact true. If we reject the null hypothesis, then the p-value is the likelihood of making a type I error (rejecting a null hypothesis that is true).

★ Statistical significance is often described in terms of a significance level, typically .01, .05, or .10. These figures represent upper boundaries for the likelihood that $b_1 = 0$, given the observed sample coefficient $\hat{b}_1$.

★ The R^2 measures the goodness of fit of a regression model. It measures the amount of variation in the dependent variable that is explained by the regression model as a proportion of the total variation in the dependent variable. $R^2 = \text{ESS/TSS}$.

★ The F-test is a test of statistical significance for the regression equation overall. Specifically, it examines the likelihood that *all* of the coefficients in the regression equation are collectively worthless.

★ Researchers will sometimes use logarithms to transform data so that they can be analyzed using linear regression. Logs have a particularly attractive property: if the dependent variable is measured in logs, then a one-unit change in x creates a b-percent change in Y.

★ Regression results are only as good as the analysis and data that are used to generate them. Most important, regression cannot prove causality—that A causes B. Instead, it can quantify an association between A and B that is unlikely to have been caused by chance alone. Done properly, regression analysis can provide crucial insight into important policy challenges. If the analysis is flawed, however, the conclusions can be dangerously wrong.

CHAPTER 12

Cost-Benefit Analysis

DDT USE AND PUBLIC POLICY

DDT, a powerful organic toxin that is highly effective in killing insects, is one of the more infamous chemicals used in the developed world. In the 1960s, when farmers were routinely spraying their fields with DDT, the chemical was found to be damaging the ecosystem. In particular, DDT was absorbed by animals ingesting insects and passed up the food chain.

DDT played a role in the launch of the modern environmental movement. Rachel Carson highlighted the damage done by DDT in her influential 1962 book *Silent Spring*. Because of its impact on birds, DDT was also blamed for endangering America's bald eagle population. Given the symbolic importance of the bald eagle, DDT became a notorious environmental villain. The U.S. Environmental Protection Agency banned the use of DDT in 1972, except in an emergency. The United States also pressured countries that received U.S. aid to stop using the chemical.[1]

So it may seem surprising that at the beginning of the twenty-first century, environmental groups like the Sierra Club, the Endangered Wildlife Trust, and the Environmental Defense Fund—the last of which launched the anti-DDT campaign in the 1960s—are now calling for more DDT use in some parts of the world, not less.[2] In 2006, the World Health Organization also embraced the use of DDT for some purposes in some parts of the world. Why are these organizations advocating the use of an environmental pollutant that is still banned in the United States and most of the developed world?

Because DDT is, as *The Economist* has described it, a "useful poison."[3] More specifically, DDT is the most cost-effective way of fighting malaria, a disease that kills more than a million people every year in poor countries, many of

---

1. Tina Rosenberg, "The Revival of a Notorious Solution to a Notorious Scourge," *New York Times*, October 5, 2006.
2. "WHO Gives Indoor Use of DDT a Clean Bill of Health for Controlling Malaria," news release by the World Health Organization, September 15, 2006.
3. "DDT: A Useful Poison," *The Economist*, December 14, 2000.

them children. Malaria is spread by the *Anopheles* mosquito; the disease was eradicated long ago in the United States and Europe but still plagues hundreds of millions of people in poor countries around the world. Many developing countries made great strides in fighting malaria in the 1950s and 1960s, often with the use of DDT. By 1970, DDT had saved some 500 million lives. But when countries stopped using the powerful poison—often at the insistence of aid agencies in the United States and other developed nations—malaria rates shot back up.[4]

As a result, malaria still ravages poor nations in the tropics, where mosquito control is more difficult. Tanzanian researcher Wen Kilama once famously pointed out that if seven Boeing 747s, mostly filled with children, crashed into Mt. Kilimanjaro *every day,* then the world would take notice. That is the scale on which malaria kills its victims.[5] The disease also has a profound economic impact since it weakens local workers and makes them less productive (which, in turn, discourages foreign investment). Economist Jeffrey Sachs has estimated that the countries in sub-Saharan Africa would be a third richer today if they had eradicated malaria in 1965.[6]

The most effective tool for fighting malaria in Africa and other poor tropical countries is indoor residual spraying (IRS). Surfaces inside homes and animal shelters are sprayed periodically with a long-acting insecticide to drive away mosquitoes or kill those that land there. U.S. senator Tom Coburn, a proponent of aggressive malaria control efforts, has compared IRS to "providing a huge mosquito net over an entire household for around-the-clock protection."[7]

The most effective insecticide for IRS is DDT. The best alternatives to DDT, a class of insecticides known as pyrethroids, are both less effective and more expensive.[8] Just as important, the World Health Organization has declared that when used properly for indoor spraying, DDT poses no harm to humans or wildlife.[9] The quantities required for effective IRS are tiny. One academic has estimated that the volume of DDT used to protect for a year the entire population of Guyana at high risk from malaria is roughly equivalent to what one farmer might spray to protect a single field of cotton.[10]

As the World Health Organization has pointed out, banning DDT was the right decision—for the United States, where the costs/risks of DDT outweigh

---

4. "DDT: A Useful Poison."
5. "Fighting Malaria," *The Economist,* May 1, 2003.
6. "DDT: A Useful Poison."
7. "WHO Gives Indoor Use of DDT a Clean Bill of Health."
8. "DDT: A Useful Poison."
9. "WHO Gives Indoor Use of DDT a Clean Bill of Health."
10. "DDT: A Useful Poison."

the potential benefits. The sad irony is that in trying to be virtuous, the developed nations caused serious harm by imposing the same decision on poorer countries more at risk from malaria. In these parts of the world, the potential benefits of DDT are much higher relative to the risks. The WHO has explained, "People in rich countries felt it would be perceived as hypocritical to push a product in poor countries that they banned at home. Even malariologists who knew DDT could be used safely dared not recommend it."

William Ruckelshaus, who made the decision in 1972 as head of the U.S. EPA to ban DDT, has said more recently, "If I were a decision maker in Sri Lanka, where the benefits from use outweigh the risks, I would decide differently. It's not up to us to balance risks and benefits for other people."[11]

Good public policy requires balancing costs and benefits. Sometimes using a notorious poison is much better than not using a notorious poison. The United Nations recently decided as much. When 120 nations met in 2000 in Johannesburg to ban "persistent organic pollutants," the delegates agreed to exempt DDT in situations where it is being used to fight malaria.[12]

Making policy is a complex process. Even leaving politics aside, there are nearly an infinite number of policy areas in which changes can be made. And each policy area has a multitude of options. Where do we begin? How do we evaluate competing proposals and priorities? **Cost-benefit analysis (CBA)** is the process by which the benefits of a project are tallied up and compared to its costs; any project for which the total benefits exceed the total costs will make us better off, provided that we are comfortable with the distribution of those costs and benefits (i.e., which parties or segments of the population incur the benefits and which parties bear the costs). This is a standard tool in the private sector; any profit-maximizing firm will use cost-benefit analysis to evaluate investment options and deploy capital in the most productive manner possible. Individuals also implicitly use cost-benefit analysis when making important decisions, such as deciding whether the cost of graduate school (both tuition and forgone earnings) is worth the higher salary or increased career satisfaction that will likely come after graduation.

When it comes to public decision making, however, cost-benefit analysis has two unique challenges. First, policy makers must tally the costs and benefits that accrue across some large group, or even all of society, rather than to just a single individual or firm. And it must be done without using any objective tool for measuring utility gains and losses directly. Instead, all gains and losses are converted into monetary values—an admittedly imperfect process—

11. Rosenberg, "The Revival of a Notorious Solution."
12. "DDT: A Useful Poison."

so that we can more easily compare "apples to apples." Second, policy makers must place a value on intangible costs and benefits, such as the social benefit of a pristine mountain lake or even the cost of a human life. Many of us initially recoil at the task of attaching dollar values to things that we might consider "priceless," yet without such calculations we are left with no objective criteria for making policy decisions in a world that forces trade-offs. Cost-benefit analysis helps us to make decisions that generate the best possible social outcomes in a world of finite resources.

CHAPTER OUTLINE

12.1 BASIC TOOLS OF COST-BENEFIT ANALYSIS

Making good public policy requires evaluating the costs and benefits of the available options. Obviously, the most desirable policies are those that provide the greatest benefits relative to their costs. Suppose a community is considering two proposals for alleviating traffic congestion. Which of the following would you choose?

Plan A: highway expansion. This plan calls for building a new lane in each direction of travel on the major highway that passes through the community. This is estimated to cost $400 million, which will be raised by selling bonds to be paid off over the next thirty years. The new lanes will save roughly ten minutes for all of the commuters who use the highway. However, this increase in the average speed of travel will cause an estimated thirty-one additional traffic fatalities annually; the additional vehicle traffic will also increase the emission of CO_2 and other air pollutants by 7 percent per year.

Plan B: commuter rail system. This plan calls for building a light rail system parallel to the congested highway and will cost $500 million, but the funds can be borrowed interest-free for thirty years from the federal government. The light rail system will have less impact on auto commute times, which are projected to fall by an average of only three minutes. Commuters who switch to the light rail system will actually spend an average of eighteen extra minutes commuting, but the cost of their daily commute will be 34 percent lower than if they were traveling by car. Meanwhile, since the light rail system will reduce the number of autos on the road, it is projected to reduce the number of annual traffic fatalities by six; it will also reduce several key air pollutants by 5 percent per year.

Which is the better plan? Based on the information presented here, there is no obvious answer. How can we compare the benefits of faster commutes to the costs of more projected traffic fatalities? Or how can we evaluate the net benefit of a commute that would take longer by light rail but cost less? Even the direct costs of the two plans are not easily compared. Which is more expensive in the long run: $400 million, which must be repaid over thirty years with interest, or $500 million, to be repaid over the same time frame without interest? And whose costs and benefits are we taking into account—just residents of the community? What about federal taxpayers, who will bear the cost of the interest-free loan in plan B? Or people all over the world, who will benefit from plan B's reduction of air pollution?

12.1.1 Establishing Common Units, or "Monetizing"

Comparing two (or more) projects requires all of the costs and benefits to be converted into a single unit of measure, which is usually dollars. Only then can we avoid the seemingly intractable challenge of comparing dissimilar things—the classic "apples and oranges." The fundamental challenge of cost-benefit analysis is to assign dollar values to the kinds of costs and benefits outlined above. When all of the costs and benefits for competing projects are tallied up using a single measure, then the merits can be compared directly—apples to apples.

Is it really possible to put a dollar value on things like faster commutes, diminished air quality, or even the loss of human life? The reality is that we have no choice as long as the goal of policy analysis is to use society's resources most productively. We must constantly make trade-offs, and cost-benefit analysis is a crucial tool for informing such decisions. Even when one simply refuses to put a price tag on some outcome—the extinction of a species or the loss of companionship from a spouse—cost-benefit analysis still makes the decision-making process explicit and transparent: this is what society is getting from a policy or proposal; this is what we must give up. The Office of Management and Budget, which is the office within the White House that advises the executive branch on budget and regulatory issues, advises its senior managers: "A comprehensive enumeration of the different types of benefits and costs, monetized or not, can be helpful in identifying the full range of program effects."[13]

Shouldn't we just spend enough public money to avoid adverse outcomes like traffic fatalities, so that we don't have to put a price on lost human lives? At first glance, this seems a reasonable and humane strategy. Suppose the cost of saving the 31 projected traffic fatalities in the previous example would be an additional $200 million, perhaps for extra safety features or additional police patrols. The facile answer is that we ought to commit those additional public resources, since it would be immoral to "put a price tag on human life." Yet any such decision is made in the face of finite resources. In another department of the same municipal government, a program analyst may be advocating for better prenatal care. An additional $200 million could save 236 lives and improve the health of thousands of other children and families. Or $200 million might be spent expanding early childhood education or fighting violent crime—both of which would also improve the lives of many people. Or the $200 million could be returned to taxpayers, who could invest in their own health or otherwise spend the money in ways that would make their lives better.

The goal of public policy is to make the best use of society's finite resources, which requires some mechanism for evaluating decisions toward that end. Cost-benefit analysis is a powerful but imperfect tool for allocating resources efficiently. The alternative is to make decisions without any objective metric at all.

---

13. Office of Management and Budget, Circular No. A-94 Revised (October 29, 1992).

12.1.2 Present Discounted Value (Net Present Value)

Even before we begin the task of assigning dollar values to outcomes such as lost lives or improved water quality, we face a more basic challenge as we attempt to compare "apples to apples." A dollar today is not the same as a dollar tomorrow or next year or fifty years from now. On an intuitive level, you already understand this. If an employer were to offer you a choice between a $1,200 bonus today and a $1,200 bonus at the end of one year, you would almost certainly take the bonus now. The **time value of money** was explored in greater depth in Chapter 9. To recap, there are several reasons that payment today is preferable to payment in the future. The most important one is that you could invest your $1,200 and earn a return on it over the next year. If you took the cash and bought a bond that pays a 6-percent annual rate of interest, you would have $1,272 at the end of the year, which is more attractive than the $1,200 your employer was offering after one year. You may also have concerns about inflation, which erodes the purchasing power of money over time. It's likely that $1,200 will buy fewer goods in a year (and certainly in ten years) than it can buy today. Finally, you may simply have some preference for consumption today rather than in the future. Life is uncertain; something might happen to you or your employer (who has pledged to pay you the money) over the next year. Even if there is no uncertainty about payment, you may simply prefer the immediate gratification of consumption today, rather than waiting for consumption in the future. In fact, you may prefer receiving $1,000 today—because you can buy a new stereo *this afternoon*—to a bonus of $1,100 next year.

For all these reasons, cost-benefit analysis does not treat a dollar that is to be spent or received in the future the same as a dollar to be spent or received in the present. Suppose a highway project will cost $100 million in the present and generate $120 million in benefits at the end of twenty years. We know that the $120 million in future benefits are worth less than if we received them today. But how much less? The most common tool for dealing with this problem is to discount all future cash flows to their equivalent value in the present, so that we can accurately compare costs and benefits that accrue at different points in time. You should recall from Chapter 9 that the formula for calculating the **present discounted value** (often also referred to as **net present value,** NPV, or simply **present value**) of some future sum is the following:

$$\text{Present discounted value (or net present value)} = N/(1 + r)^t$$

where

$N=$ the nominal value of the future cost or benefit
(also called future value, or FV)

r = the discount rate

t = the number of periods in the future at which the cost or
payment will be incurred

In our example, the highway project will cost $100 million in the present and generate $120 million in benefits at the end of twenty years. We can use the formula for present discounted value to evaluate whether the investment makes sense. If the Highway Department uses a discount rate of 4 percent for purposes of project evaluation, then the present value of the project's benefits would be the following:

$$\text{Present discounted value} = \$120,000,000/(1 + .04)^{20}$$
$$= \$120,000,000/2.191$$
$$= \$54,769,512$$

This project does not make financial sense. The amount that must be spent to do the project exceeds the value of the future benefits when they are discounted to the present. That capital can be put to better use, either on another project or by not collecting it from taxpayers in the first place.

Why does the Highway Department use a 4-percent discount rate? This turns out to be a surprisingly difficult question. Unlike private firms, public entities often do not have obvious financial benchmarks that can be used as a discount rate. Indeed, the choice of a social discount rate is so crucial to cost-benefit analysis—and often so controversial—that this discussion has been reserved for a later section.

12.1.3 Evaluating Uncertainty

Many public projects are likely to involve elements of uncertainty when it comes to costs and benefits. If our objective is to tally up the total costs and benefits for a proposed project or policy, how can we account for something that might or might not happen? The answer is that we weight any cost or benefit by our best estimate of the probability that it will occur. Suppose, for example, that a construction project involves building a bridge across a river. The contractor assumes that the cost of building the pylons will be $2 million. However, the contractor has informed the decision makers that once drilling for the pylons has begun, there is a 10-percent chance that the foundation will be softer than expected and the drilling will have to go deeper, which would require an additional $3 million in excavation work (or $5 million total). Unfortunately, this determination cannot be made until the work has commenced. For purposes of cost-benefit analysis, should the pylon drilling be treated as a $2-million expense or as a $5-million expense?

The answer is neither. For purposes of cost-benefit analysis, the cost should be treated as a weighted average of the two possible outcomes. Since there is a 90-percent chance that the drilling will cost $2 million and a 10-percent chance that the drilling will cost $5 million, the weighted average would be the following:

$$\text{Expected cost of proposed pylon drilling} = (.9)(\$2 \text{ million}) + (.1)(\$5 \text{ million})$$
$$= \$1.8 \text{ million} + \$500,000$$
$$= \$2,300,000$$

As in the case of any expected value, this figure must be treated with some caution. After all, we know that the real cost will *not* actually be $2.3 million; it will be either $2 million or $5 million. A later section will explore conditions under which a risk-averse decision maker may forgo a policy option with the highest expected net benefits because it includes the possibility of some unacceptably bad outcome.

12.1.4 Opportunity Cost versus Cash-Flow Accounting

The opportunity cost of any activity reflects the value of whatever has to be given up in order to pursue that activity. For an economist or policy analyst, the "free" concert tickets that you receive after standing in line for three hours are not free at all; their cost is represented by the value of the next best thing that you might have done with those three hours of your time. If you have a campus job that pays $25 an hour and you took three hours off work to wait in line, then the opportunity cost of your "free tickets" is $75. (An accountant, however, would not see the world this way. Since you did not have to write a check for the tickets, there is no debit in your account and the tickets are treated—from a cash-flow standpoint—as free.) Cost-benefit analysis always values an input or output using its opportunity cost, since that is the best reflection of what an individual or society must give up (or no longer has to give up) as the result of some course of action.

Consider an activity like graduate school. How much does graduate school "cost"? The conventional answer would present an accounting of the assorted out-of-pocket costs of attending a graduate program: tuition, books, housing, and so on. The opportunity cost, on the other hand, is a measure of the value of what you would be doing if you didn't go to graduate school. For most people, that means working. Thus, the primary opportunity cost of a two-year graduate program would be two-years of forgone earnings. In fact, for most people, that is a much more significant cost than tuition!

In considering the concept of opportunity cost, we would do well to heed the old aphorism that "time is money." Programs and policies that involve time—saved or wasted—must take account of the productive value of that time. How we determine the value of that time will be discussed in a later section. For now, it is important to recognize that any cost-benefit analysis must include not only out-of-pocket costs (direct expenses that an accountant might tally up), but also any opportunity costs.

12.1.5 Economic and Noneconomic Values (Use and Nonuse Values)

Most policies generate both economic and noneconomic costs and benefits. An **economic cost or benefit** is a direct pecuniary gain or loss. For example, a college scholarship program may raise the future wages of the participants. Or an intensive substance-abuse treatment program for prison inmates would reduce the costs associated with future recidivism. On the other hand, a **noneconomic cost or benefit** is an intangible gain or loss. The same college scholarship program would likely provide recipients with a greater range of career choices, enhanced personal satisfaction, and so on; the substance-abuse program might reduce domestic violence and enable more children to grow up with a parent in the home rather than in prison.

The same basic concepts arise in an environmental context, where costs and benefits are often broken down into use and nonuse values. The **use value** of a resource derives from the ways in which it can be used directly, either for recreation or for commercial purposes. The use value of a lake would include things like the benefits provided to swimmers and boaters, and the income generated for commercial fishermen. **Nonuse value** is intangible; citizens may reasonably attach value to a resource for a variety of reasons that don't stem from direct use. They may want to preserve it for use by future generations; they may want to protect the opportunity to use it in the future; they may believe that the resource has the potential for future commercial value (such as pharmaceutical products derived from rare plants in the Amazon); or they may simply want to protect it because they derive utility from knowing that it exists, even if they will never directly experience it. When the Exxon *Valdez* ran aground off the coast of Prince William Sound in Alaska and spilled 11 million gallons of oil, people around the world were disturbed by the environmental damage, even though the vast majority of them have never been to Prince William Sound nor are they likely ever to visit.

Cost-benefit analysis always seeks to value both economic and noneconomic costs and benefits (and use and nonuse values). However, the distinction between the two kinds of values is important for two reasons. First, noneconomic costs tend to be much harder to quantify objectively. Consider the substance-abuse treatment example: it is much easier to attach a monetary value to reduced prison costs than it is to the benefits associated with not having a father in prison. Second, many institutional processes will break out economic and noneconomic values separately. For example, legal judgments are often broken down into economic and noneconomic damages. The For Discussion section at the end of this chapter describes the process used to calculate compensation payments from the U.S. government to those injured by the terrorist attacks on September 11 and to the families of those who were killed. Kenneth Feinberg, the expert designated by the attorney general to determine the size of each award, was directed by Congress to make separate determinations for economic loss (medical costs, lost income, etc.) and noneconomic losses (the pain and suffering caused by the attacks for the victims and their families).

············· | **POLICY IN THE REAL WORLD** | ················

The Copenhagen Consensus: Smart People Using Cost-Benefit Analysis (in Copenhagen)[14]

The world has no shortage of challenges. Developing nations in particular are afflicted with miseries ranging from civil war to malnutrition. If cost-benefit analysis is a powerful tool for efficiently allocating resources, then presumably it could be used to help wealthy nations make decisions about how their development aid can best help the world's poor.

This was the logic of the Copenhagen Consensus, a project organized by Bjørn Lomborg, head of the Environmental Assessment Institute in Denmark. Eight of the world's preeminent economists, including four Nobel Prize–winners, were invited to Copenhagen in 2004 to answer a deceptively simple question: If the rich countries of the world were to commit new resources to helping the world's poor, how should that money be spent in order to have the greatest impact? The exercise was repeated with a similarly esteemed group of experts in 2008.

14. "Putting the World to Rights—Copenhagen Consensus," *The Economist*, June 3, 2004; "Bolton v Gore: How to Save the World," *The Economist*, June 22, 2006.

As *The Economist* explained, "The organizing idea was that resources are scarce and difficult choices among good ideas therefore have to be made. How should a limited amount of new money for development initiatives, say an extra $50 billion, be spent? Would it be possible to reach agreement on what should be done first?" (*The Economist* magazine was invited to observe the proceedings and report on the findings.) The panel began by considering ten broad challenge areas that rose to the top based on United Nations assessments and other background information: civil conflicts, climate change, communicable diseases, education, financial stability, governance, hunger and malnutrition, migration, trade reform, and water and sanitation.

Outside experts were then invited to prepare "challenge papers," laying out extant information on 38 different specific proposals for action within those broad challenge areas. The experts were charged with ranking these proposals based on the proposals' social benefits relative to their social costs. Even the most rigorous application of cost-benefit analysis required judgment. The experts had to decide, for example, what discount rate ought to be applied to the prospective harms caused by global warming and what the appropriate value of a statistical life ought to be in poor countries. Often, the analysis was done using multiple values to determine how sensitive the conclusions were to these different assumptions. In the end, the panel of experts decided that they had sufficient information to rank only 17 of the 38 proposals.

With so many global problems, what interventions rose to the top? The panel identified four proposals "very good" in terms of benefits relative to costs. The first was a combination of measures for controlling HIV/AIDS, such as distributing condoms and treating sex workers for sexually transmitted diseases (which facilitate the transmission of the HIV virus). One of the commissioned papers concluded that these measures had the stunningly low cost of $4 for every disability-adjusted life year[15] saved and a ratio of social benefits to social costs of 500 to 1.

The second was a program for combating malnutrition by using targeted food supplements. The third was action by the developed nations to reduce trade barriers and eliminate agricultural subsidies, thereby allowing greater access to their markets for exports from poor countries. The fourth was a series of measures for fighting malaria, such as the distribution of bed nets treated with insecticide.

By definition a ranking of projects means that some seemingly worthwhile endeavors must come at the end of the list. Given $50 billion in additional

---

15. The World Health Organization defines disability-adjusted life years (DALYs) as the sum of years of potential life lost due to premature mortality and the years of productive life lost due to disability.

aid, the panel of experts would *not* expend the resources on programs to address climate change. The panel was in agreement that the phenomenon of global warming is both real and potentially harmful, but the large costs required in the present could not be justified by the uncertain benefits in the distant future.

Of course, the $50 billion in additional aid from the developed world is hypothetical. So was there really any point to all of this? Yes, for two reasons. First, the exercise in cost-benefit analysis is a good example of prioritizing government decisions. As *The Economist* noted of the process, "Cost-benefit analysis must be the organizing method for any such analysis—even if one thinks of this approach as inconclusive on its own, or as little more than a way of ordering one's thoughts more logically."

And second, the Copenhagen Consensus inspired diplomats at the United Nations to pursue a similar endeavor. In 2006, two years after the panel of eminent economists first met in Copenhagen, ambassadors from the United States and seven other countries convened to rank 40 proposals for tackling 10 global challenges. Their conclusions (which were "strikingly similar" to the Copenhagen Consensus) are not binding—other diplomats must yet be persuaded that the process has merit. Ranking life and death matters can be distasteful, particularly if it requires saying "no" to programs that would save lives. The more politic approach is to describe all serious issues as "priorities." But, as the American ambassador to the UN has pointed out, "When you have 9,000 priorities, you have none."

. . . .

12.2 MAKING A DECISION USING COST-BENEFIT ANALYSIS

Any project or policy for which the total expected social benefits exceed the total expected social costs should be adopted, since it will expand society's net resources.

> **NPV = net present value of the project or program**
>   **= NPV of total social benefits – NPV of total social costs**
> **If NPV > 0, then society is made better off.**

When choosing among several options, policy makers should choose the one that has the largest NPV. Because of uncertainty and imperfect information, the actual outcome may differ—for better or for worse—from the expected outcome. If no policy under consideration has a positive NPV, then policy makers may seek other options.

The objectivity of cost-benefit analysis does not obviate the need for judgment and discretion. To begin with, policy makers must decide what parties should be considered in the analysis, or who has **standing.** Whose costs and benefits should be counted? If a municipality is considering a new zoning ordinance that will allow the construction of a shopping mall, local officials will likely consider only the costs and benefits that accrue to citizens of that town. Citizens of neighboring towns will almost certainly bear some of the costs (increased traffic congestion) and benefits (more shopping opportunities) from the project, but they do not have standing in the analysis. In the transportation example at the beginning of the chapter (highway expansion versus commuter rail system), presumably only the citizens of the community making the decision would have a standing in the cost-benefit analysis. On the other hand, if state officials were to do the cost-benefit analysis, they would include the costs and benefits imposed on surrounding towns as well. Policy makers must be explicit about what parties or what geographic or political entities have standing in the cost-benefit analysis. For example, the Office of Management and Budget, which is accountable to American taxpayers and voters, explicitly advises its personnel: "Analyses should focus on benefits and costs accruing to the citizens of the United States in determining net present value. Where programs or projects have effects outside the United States, these effects should be reported separately."[16]

It is possible under some circumstances that the policy with the highest NPV is not the most desirable option. Risk-averse policy makers may prefer an alternative that has a lower NPV but a greater degree of certainty. For example, transportation officials may choose a project with a fixed positive net return of $1 billion over a competing project with an *expected* positive net return of $1.3 billion but a range of possible outcomes stretching from negative $500 million to positive $2.5 billion. It may even be rational to adopt a policy with negative expected return if it minimizes or eliminates the possibility of a catastrophic outcome. Public policy often involves contemplating extremely unlikely events that would have horrible consequences: a nuclear attack; a virulent flu epidemic; a cataclysmic change in climate. When these outcomes are weighted by their extremely low probabilities, the analysis may show that the costs of policies that would ameliorate the risk may not be justified by the expected benefits. However, policy makers may decide that some outcomes, however unlikely, are so serious that they justify action, even if the costs will *on average* outweigh the benefits. For example, the United States might choose to invest in laser technology to destroy an asteroid hurtling

---

16. Office of Management and Budget, Circular No. A-94.

toward Earth. The probability of such an event is low (but not zero), and the cost of developing the technology would be extremely high. Nonetheless, the project would be defensible, even if the expected net benefits are negative, if it protects against an unacceptably bad outcome like destruction of the planet.

Finally, policy makers may reject a policy or program with a large NPV because of its **distributional effects**—or how the costs and benefits are spread across society. Cost-benefit analysis compares total social benefits to total social costs without any regard for which members of society accrue those costs and benefits. Suppose a policy such as eliminating subsidies for home heating oil would generate positive net social benefits. From an efficiency standpoint, this is a desirable policy because it makes better use of society's finite resources. However, the costs of the policy would fall most heavily on low-income citizens since they spend the largest proportion of their income on home heating oil; the benefits would be diffused more broadly across society. Policy makers may reject the policy on equity grounds if they deem the distribution of costs and benefits—rather than the net total—unacceptable. Cost-benefit analysis is blind with regard to which groups (with standing) bear the benefits and costs; public policy most certainly is not.

12.3   VALUING INPUTS AND OUTPUTS

How much is something worth? Economics—and cost-benefit analysis in particular—usually adopts a deceivingly simple answer to that question: something is worth what people are willing to pay for it. More specifically, the **willingness to pay (WTP)** principle argues that the most accurate measure of the value of any good or service for a particular individual is what he or she is willing to give up in order to get it. This is most intuitive in a market context: a consumer who is willing to pay $78 for a pair of tennis shoes must forgo $78 of other consumption, meaning that the purchase price represents the true opportunity cost of the good. However, willingness to pay can also be extended to intangible items as well. Better air quality or an extra two years of life are worth, in theory, what the recipient would be willing to pay for them. As strange as that seems, individuals do often pay for these kinds of individual benefits, albeit indirectly. When a consumer pays a premium to buy a house with a view of the Rocky Mountains rather than a nearly identical house across the street with no such view, then the purchaser is essentially "buying" the view; we can infer the value of that view from the price premium that it commands.

Similarly, costs that are imposed can be valued according to an individual's theoretical willingness to pay to avoid whatever harm is being done. (If some activity makes you $10 worse off, then you should be willing to pay up to $10 to make it stop.) Thus, if a municipal project will destroy a small forest that has no commercial value but is used for hiking and recreation, the cost associated with that lost resource would be equal to the amount that the affected citizens would be willing to pay to protect the land from development.[17] Of course, the art of cost-benefit analysis often lies in converting this theoretical willingness to pay into actual dollars and sense.

12.3.1 Tradable Goods

When a project uses resources that can be bought and sold in a competitive market, the market price is the best measure of the social cost of those inputs. For example, suppose that a government construction project will pay workers a wage of $20 an hour, which is the prevailing wage for similar work elsewhere in the economy. In this case, the accounting cost of the labor and the opportunity cost are the same: employing these workers on the government project denies them their next best alternative, which would also pay $20. (For purposes of introduction to cost-benefit analysis, we will ignore cases in which the government hires so much labor, or any other input, that it changes

---

17. A more advanced treatment of cost-benefit analysis will likely point out the distinction between willingness to pay (WTP) to avoid some harm and the **willingness to accept (WTA)** voluntary compensation in order to endure the harm. In the forest example above, the citizens' WTP would be the amount that they would be willing to spend to protect the forest from development. If the forest were for sale and a developer was going to buy it, what would be the maximum that the citizens would bid to keep the land out of the developer's control? This would be a reasonable approximation of the cost imposed on the citizens if the forest were developed.

The WTA criterion would be slightly different in this example. The WTA assumes that the citizens have control over the forest and would have to be paid to give it up to the developer. How much would the developer have to pay them to get control of the forest?

The disparity between these two methodologies can be significant for two reasons. First, there may be a wealth effect, meaning that the wealth of the affected parties would limit their willingness to pay relative to their willingness to accept compensation. If the citizens living near the forest in this example had low incomes, their willingness to pay to protect the land from development would be low—not because they don't care about the forest, but because they simply don't have much money to pay to protect it. On the other hand, if the low-income citizens owned the forest, they might demand a much higher price to sell it to a developer since their willingness to accept compensation would not be constrained by their low incomes.

Second, for reasons that have more to do with psychology than economics, there is a tendency for individuals to demand more compensation to give up something than they would be willing to pay to acquire it. This is called the **endowment effect.** In one famous experiment, a professor randomly gave coffee mugs to half of his class and then created a market on which the mugs could be bought and sold. The price at which the students who received the mugs were willing to sell (around $7) was much higher than the price that students who did not receive a mug were willing to pay (around $3). Since the mugs were distributed randomly, it makes little sense from a rational economic standpoint that the students who received them would value them more (based on their WTA) than the students who did not (based on their WTP). The endowment effect has been confirmed in other experiments using different objects and circumstances.

the market price for those inputs; a more advanced class would explore these kinds of contingencies.) Similarly, the market price can often provide an appropriate value for benefits generated by a project. If a government housing project creates one hundred new rental apartments for low-income residents, then the market price of similar private housing units should accurately reflect the value of the new apartments.

In many cases an item will not have a price tag, but the market can still help us assign it a dollar value. Consider the value of an hour of your time. Unfortunately, you cannot go to eBay and buy a twenty-fifth hour in the day, nor during a slack period can you sell three hours of your day to someone who would prefer to have twenty-seven hours tomorrow. Yet realistically, most people buy and sell their time every day—by working for a wage. If you accept a job that pays $18 an hour, then you are giving up whatever else you might have done with that hour. On the margin, we can assume that you are willing to trade an hour of your time for $18. Thus, if you are stuck in a traffic jam for half an hour every day, we might reasonably infer that the daily economic cost to you of that traffic congestion is $9. (Of course, you should recognize that if you use your cell phone to do work during that delay, then the opportunity cost of being stuck in the traffic jam will fall or even disappear!) This mechanism for assigning a dollar value to time is obviously not perfect; few people have the opportunity to choose exactly how many hours they can work at a given wage. Nonetheless, it will often give us a reasonable approximation of the value of time saved or lost.

In other cases, we may not be able to assign a value to an intangible outcome—diminished air quality, noise from low-flying commercial aircraft, or a despoiled fishing hole—but we may be able to put a market price on the cost of dealing with those problems: treating more children for asthma; installing air-conditioning and soundproofing in homes affected by a new airport; or driving to a new fishing hole that is farther away than the old one. Behavioral responses that minimize or eliminate the harm associated with some adverse outcome are referred to as **averting behavior.** In many cases, the dollar cost of the requisite averting behavior is a reasonable approximation of the cost associated with some otherwise intangible social harm. For example, when Los Angeles approved an $11-billion plan to expand its international airport, the plan included $500 million for projects to ameliorate the impact on surrounding communities, such as installing soundproofing, air-conditioning, and air-filter systems in nearby schools.[18]

18. John M. Broder, "Los Angeles Groups Agree to Airport Growth, for a Price," *New York Times*, December 17, 2004.

Market prices are not necessarily an accurate gauge of social costs and benefits when a market is somehow distorted—by monopoly, by taxes, by regulation, by an externality, or by any other factor that causes prices and production to deviate from their socially efficient level. As an example, consider how unemployment (which occurs when the labor market is out of equilibrium) might affect how we value labor used in a public project. Suppose a local government is evaluating the costs and benefits of building a local park. The project will hire workers who are currently unemployed and pay them a wage of $20 an hour. For purposes of cost-benefit analysis, is $20 an hour the true social cost of this labor? The answer is no. The opportunity cost of time for the formerly unemployed workers represents what they have to give up—which, in this case, is leisure, not paid work elsewhere in the economy. Since the unemployed have an abundance of leisure, the opportunity cost of going to work would almost certainly be much lower than $20 an hour.

In other cases, the opportunity cost of a project may be *more* than the accounting cost. Suppose, for example, that a nation has mandatory military service. Young men and women are conscripted into the armed services and paid an annual wage of $25,000 a year. Is this the full economic cost of the program? Definitely not. One of the major social costs of such mandatory service (military or otherwise) is that it precludes young people from doing other things. Thus, the opportunity cost of the program is equal to the wages that the military conscripts would have earned if they had been free to enter the labor market. These wages would likely have been much higher than what the government pays its soldiers.

12.3.2 Shadow Pricing

In theory, cost-benefit analysis is straightforward: tally up the expected benefits, and compare them to the expected costs. But what is the cost of a mountain stream that becomes despoiled by pollution? What is the benefit of three extra years of life? These would appear to be philosophical questions. Yet if we are going to prioritize the use of society's resources, we must make informed judgments about the costs and benefits of inputs and outputs that are not easily measured in dollars and cents. **Shadow pricing** is the process of assigning an opportunity cost to resources with no obvious market price. While it is not easy to put a price on the "priceless," the alternative is to have no intellectual traction when making important policy decisions. The following are the most common economic tools for attaching monetary values, or **shadow prices,** to inputs and outputs that do not normally have price tags.

Contingent valuation. In the absence of market feedback, one approach for placing a value on some cost or benefit is to ask individuals in a survey or questionnaire how much they would be willing to pay for some intangible benefit, or, alternatively, how much they would be willing to pay to avoid some harm. The term **contingent valuation** is derived from the fact that the respondent's answer is contingent upon the hypothetical situation presented in the survey. Environmental economist Paul Portney has described the three elements that typically characterize a contingent-valuation approach:[19]

1. The survey contains a scenario or description of a program (often highly detailed) that the respondent is being asked to evaluate, such as a federal program to protect a certain endangered species. The survey will describe the effects of the program and perhaps the most likely outcome if the program is not implemented.
2. The survey must elicit the respondent's willingness to pay for the program described. It may ask the maximum amount that the respondent would be willing to pay for the program. Or it may solicit the input in a more roundabout way, such as asking if the respondent would support the program if it meant that his or her taxes would go up by $18 a year.
3. The survey should collect relevant demographic information, such as income, race, age, political ideology, and so forth. The goal is to understand the relationship between these personal characteristics and the willingness to pay for the described program so that the results can be applied more generally.

Consider an activity like protecting an endangered species. The contingent-valuation approach is straightforward: we would construct a survey that asks a representative sample of citizens how much they would be willing to pay for a specific program to protect a particular endangered species. Different people will have different answers. In theory, the cumulative willingness to pay across the affected members of society will represent the value that policy makers should attach to this benefit.

The primary advantage of a contingent-valuation approach is that it provides data in cases where we are dealing with strictly hypothetical courses of action; we have no behavior to observe, nor do we have any market transactions to use as a benchmark. The contingent-valuation approach has several serious drawbacks, however. First, there is an incentive for individuals to misrepresent their willingness to pay. Suppose that we are attempting to determine how much compensation should be paid to homeowners who will be affected by the odor from a recycling plant. In theory, the harm imposed by

19. Paul R. Portney, "The Contingent Valuation Debate: Why Economists Should Care," *Journal of Economic Perspectives* 8, no. 4 (Fall 1994): 3–17.

the odor is equivalent to the amount of money that homeowners would be willing to pay to get rid of it. In practice, however, these homeowners do not actually have to pay that sum. By overstating the cost of the harm, they can attempt to inflate the value of the compensation that will be paid to them.

In general, the key problem with contingent valuation is that survey respondents do not have to act on their stated preferences; they don't have to "put their money where their mouth is." Thus, even when respondents do not deliberately misrepresent their preferences, there is ample evidence that the survey results may be a poor measure of the true willingness to pay. For example, something as simple as the order of the questions in a survey can affect how respondents answer.[20] In a simple experiment, a group was asked for its willingness to pay to protect seals and its willingness to pay to protect whales. However, the group was split in half. One subgroup was asked how much it would pay to protect seals and then how much it would pay to protect whales. The order of the questions was reversed for the other half of the respondents.

It turns out that respondents are willing to spend more to protect seals when it is the first question asked. Other such inconsistencies have cast doubt on the validity of contingent valuation. For example, the willingness-to-pay to protect a resource falls when it is placed alongside questions about paying to protect other resources. In one study, the willingness to pay to protect the visibility at the Grand Canyon was five times higher when the question was asked alone as it was when the question was placed third on a survey with other such questions.[21]

Revealed preferences. Often, the behavior of individuals can give us excellent information on how much value they place on certain nonmonetary outcomes or attributes—we can watch what people do, rather than what they say. A **revealed preference** assigns a value to a cost or benefit based on this observed behavior. What is the value of a "priceless" beautiful mountain view? In fact, we can examine real-estate data to get a pretty good estimate of the value that homeowners place on a view of the mountains. (There is some irony in the fact that the "priceless" mountain view is often described in a real-estate advertisement that places a price on that view.) As was mentioned earlier in the chapter, any community with mountain views is likely to have some houses that have unobstructed views of the mountains and others that do not. Thus, if two houses in a community are nearly identical—same size,

20. Peter A. Diamond and Jerry A. Hausman, "Contingent Valuation: Is Some Number Better Than No Number?" *Journal of Economic Perspectives* 8, no. 4 (Fall 1994): 45–64.

21. George S. Tolley et al., "Establishing and Valuing the Effects of Improved Visibility in the Eastern United States," U.S. Environmental Protection Agency, Washington, D.C., 1983.

same schools, same general location, and so on—but one house has a mountain view and the other does not, then we can infer that the price differential between them reflects the value of the mountain view.

If a three-bedroom house in Boulder, Colorado, with a full view of the Rockies sells for $650,000, and a nearly identical house around the corner with no view sells for $500,000, then it is reasonable to assign a monetary value of $150,000 to that view of the Rockies. We need not ask individuals in Boulder how much they value mountain views; we can observe their home-buying patterns instead. Of course, using revealed preferences to place a value on costs and benefits also has limitations. One challenge is that different individuals have different preferences; as a result, the observed behavior may not necessarily reflect the willingness to pay of the population at large. In the mountain-view example, the individuals with the greatest appreciation for a mountain view will have the greatest willingness to pay for it. The people around the corner may care less about scenic views—which is why they live around the corner. Thus, it may be inaccurate to impute the value of some cost or benefit based on the willingness to pay of a subgroup who may not be representative of the population as a whole. In the mountain-view example, the revealed preference would best serve as an upper bound for the value of that view; it represents the willingness to pay for the view among those who are likely to have a strong preference for it.

Hedonic market analysis. Can two houses in Boulder, Colorado, really be identical but for the mountain view? Perhaps not. Perhaps the "mountain view" homes are also nicer, newer, slightly bigger, or closer to schools. **Hedonic market analysis** uses a tool from the previous chapter—regression analysis—to isolate the value of a specific intangible cost or benefit, such as the scenic mountain view. The process requires a data set with information for each observation on the outcome of interest (e.g., housing prices) as well as on the independent variables that might affect that outcome, such as square footage, local school quality, and, finally, the intangible variable of interest, such as whether the house has a mountain view. A hedonic market analysis would then regress the dependent variable on the independent variables in order to isolate the unique effect of each potential explanatory factor. You should recall from Chapter 11 that when the analysis is done correctly, the coefficient on each independent variable can be interpreted as its effect, holding all other factors constant, on the dependent variable.

Suppose, for example, that policy makers are attempting to determine the cost that would be imposed on homeowners by the noise and pollution from a proposed new airport. We know that houses near other airports sell at a discount to similar houses in communities that are not affected by airport noise.

But it is difficult to make a direct comparison, since the homes near existing airports may also be older or slightly smaller. Or they may have some positive attributes, such as better access to transit, that would mask the adverse impact of the airport noise on real-estate prices. A hedonic market analysis would regress home prices on a series of explanatory variables: square footage, school quality, access to transit, age of the home, lot size, *and* some variable that reflects the airport noise in a quantifiable way, such as the number of flights per day that can be heard from inside the house. The coefficient on the independent variable of interest (airport noise) gives us the impact of that specific explanatory variable on the dependent variable (home price), *ceteris paribus*. The regression results may show, for example, that each daily flight that is audible from inside the house is associated with a $5,500 reduction in the value of the home, holding constant all other variables that typically affect housing prices. Thus, if we have good data on a large number of real-estate transactions, we can isolate the specific relationship between airport noise and home values, and use that figure in our cost-benefit calculation for the proposed airport expansion.

None of these tools is perfect. For that reason, analysts will often use several different methods in the hope of finding a consistent range of values for a nonmonetary cost or benefit. As with many other aspects of public policy, experience and discretion will ultimately influence the conclusion.

12.4   VALUE OF A STATISTICAL LIFE

Many policy proposals are likely to save lives or to cause additional deaths. For example, an investment in childhood immunizations would save lives; a plan to raise the speed limit or allow truckers to drive longer hours without rest would likely lead to more highway fatalities. Obviously, analysts do not know the specific persons who will be killed or saved, but they can use data to project the most likely impact in terms of overall lives saved or lost. When human lives are a cost or benefit, policy makers must assign a monetary value to each life—the **value of a statistical life (VSL)**—in order to conduct a cost-benefit analysis of the policy under consideration.

Each of the approaches explained above can be used to derive the value of a statistical life, or a range of values:

- **Contingent valuation.** We can ask people to place a value on human life by constructing a survey instrument that forces respondents to make trade-offs that implicitly place a value on human life. For example, respondents may be asked if they would support a $100-million highway safety construction project that is expected to prevent twenty-five traffic fatalities over the life of the project. Analysts can then use such data to calculate a willingness to pay to save lives.

- **Revealed preferences.** We can observe how much individuals are willing to pay to protect their own lives and then make inferences based on that behavior. People routinely pay for safety features that lower the probability of death; or they may opt not to purchase available safety features because they prefer to use that money for additional consumption instead. The revealed-preferences methodology uses data from these real trade-offs to calculate a willingness to pay to protect a statistical life. Before airbags became a standard safety feature on American automobiles, for example, individual car buyers could pay extra to have them installed. By observing how much car buyers are willing to pay to reduce their probability of dying by some small amount, researchers can then calculate the trade-off that real consumers make between safety and risk. For example, a consumer who pays $250 for an auto safety feature that lowers the risk of death by 0.0001 is implicitly putting a lower bound on his or her VSL of $2.5 million.[22] Of course, such calculations require the individuals making such decisions to have an accurate understanding of both the risks involved and the degree to which certain safety investments will mitigate that risk.

- **Hedonic market analysis.** Presumably workers who risk death on the job must be paid a premium for taking that risk, *ceteris paribus.* This wage differential is not easily observed, since workers with risky jobs may also have less education or lower skills. However, we can use regression analysis to isolate the risk premium, or **compensating differential,** that must be paid to induce workers take jobs that involve a greater risk of death. (The compensating differential can be negative as well; workers may demand lower wages for jobs that are comfortable, prestigious, or otherwise attractive in nonpecuniary ways.) A hedonic market analysis would quantify the trade-off that workers make between cash and a higher risk of death by using regression analysis to examine data for a large number of workers in many different professions—some safe and others with significant risks. The wage would be regressed on a variety of variables that typically explain pay differentials—education, years of experience, industry, geography, and so on—as well as on some measure of the

22. $0.0001 \, (\text{VSL}) \geq \$250$

$$\text{VSL} \geq \frac{\$250}{0.0001}$$

$$\text{VSL} \geq \$2,500,000$$

risk of dying on the job. The coefficient on the risk variable would provide insight into the willingness of workers to accept higher compensation in exchange for endangering their own lives. From there, analysts can attempt to calculate more general figures for society's willingness to trade off consumption and risk of death, recognizing, of course, that workers who choose risky professions may be less risk-averse than the population in general (or even risk-loving in some cases).

······· | **POLICY IN THE REAL WORLD** | ···············

Putting a Number on Life: Your Life Is Worth $1 Million Less Than It Used to Be!

In July 2008, the Associated Press reported a strange finding: the Environmental Protection Agency (EPA) had lowered its figure for the value of a statistical life from $7.8 million in current dollars to $6.9 million.[23]

Officials at the EPA explained that the change was based on economic studies that offer a more refined understanding of Americans' willingness to pay to avoid death. The director of the EPA's Office of Policy, Economics, and Innovation explained, "It's our best estimate of what consumers are willing to pay to reduce similar risks to their own lives."

Environmentalists, however, were immediately skeptical. One group accused the George W. Bush administration of "cooking the books" in order to make environmental regulations less attractive. Changing the value of a statistical life lowers the net benefits of life-saving environmental regulations. The Associated Press story explained, "Consider, for example, a hypothetical regulation that costs $18 billion to enforce but will prevent 2,500 deaths. At $7.8 million per person (the old figure), the lifesaving benefits outweigh the costs. But at $6.9 million per person, the rule costs more than the lives it saves, so it may not be adopted."

The U.S. federal government does not have a uniform figure for the value of a statistical life (VSL). The Department of Transportation uses $3 million as the VSL when contemplating regulatory changes related to airline safety.[24] Even departments within a single agency can choose different values. The water division within the EPA not only opted against the VSL reduction, but

23. Seth Borenstein, "EPA Reduces Value of Life by $1 Million," *Valley News*, July 11, 2008.
24. W. Kip Viscusi, "A Price on Your Head," *Forbes.com*, January 7, 2008.

has used a figure as high as $8.7 million. Most government agencies use VSL figures in the $5-million to $7-million range, according to W. Kip Viscusi, an economist who has done extensive work on the subject.

According to Mr. Viscusi, such numbers do "not imply that people would accept certain death if paid $7 million or that they could come up with $7 million to buy out of certain death. Rather, it captures the rate at which people are willing to spend money to reduce risk." Studies using behavior in the U.S. labor market (where workers can accept higher wages in exchange for a greater risk of death and vice versa) has found values for a statistical life in the range of $4 million to $9 million.[25]

There is obviously no single number for the value of a statistical life. However, it is unusual for the figure to go down over time, rather than up. As people become wealthier—and, therefore, willing to pay more to reduce the risk of death—the value of a statistical life should go up, not down.

. . . .

12.5 CHOOSING A SOCIAL DISCOUNT RATE

One of the most contentious issues in cost-benefit analysis is deciding how social costs and benefits in the present ought to be compared against social costs and benefits in the future. How much should society be willing to invest today to avert damages that may occur years from now or even generations in the future? At what rate should the cost of those future damages be discounted to the present—if at all?

In the world of finance, choosing a discount rate is relatively straightforward; investors can use their typical return on capital as a benchmark for discounting future costs and benefits. If a corporation earns an average of 9 percent on its invested capital, then it would likely choose 9 percent as its internal discount rate. Given a choice between $1.00 today and $1.07 next year, the firm should choose $1.00 today, since it can be invested at 9 percent to yield a total of $1.09 next year. Similarly, individuals can make their own judgments about the value of consumption today relative to consumption in the future. Saving money in the present reduces current consumption but makes it possible to enjoy higher consumption in the future, such as in retirement.

In the realm of public policy, comparing costs and benefits that occur at different points in time is more difficult in part because they may accrue not

---

25. W. Kip Viscusi and Joseph Aldy, "The Value of a Statistical Life: A Critical Review of Market Estimates throughout the World," John M. Olin Center for Law, Economics, and Business, Discussion Paper No. 392, November 2002.

only to different people, but to different generations. When policy makers tabulate social costs and benefits, should $1.00 of consumption 50 years from now have less value than $1.00 of consumption in the present? For example, should a candy bar that I enjoy today be given greater weight than a candy bar that *someone else* will enjoy in 50 years? Why? The two candy bars will taste the same and presumably provide the same amount of utility. This philosophical question applies to much more than candy bars and has a profound impact on cost-benefit analysis.

The rate used to discount social costs and benefits to the present is called the **social discount rate.** The discount rate that is selected can have a profound impact on cost-benefit analysis, particularly when costs or benefits occur in the distant future. The following table shows the value of $100 at different points in the future using different discount rates. You should see that even with a seemingly small discount rate of 5 percent, the discounted value of $100 in 100 years (a reasonable time frame when dealing with issues like climate change) is less than $1.00. With a rate of 3 percent or greater, any cost or benefit that occurs 400 years in the future has essentially no present value at all.

Value of $100 at Different Points in the Future Using Different Discount Rates

	1 YEAR	5 YEARS	25 YEARS	100 YEARS	400 YEARS
0%	$100	$100	$100	$100	$100
1%	$99	$95	$78	$37	$2
3%	$97	$86	$48	$5	$0.0007
5%	$95	$78	$30	$0.76	$0
7%	$93	$71	$18	$0.12	$0

There are strong philosophical arguments for any number of different social discount rates. Some academics and policy makers have argued that the appropriate social discount rate is zero. This line of thinking values $1 of consumption today exactly the same as $1 of consumption at any point in the future. If some policy being considered in the present will impose $200 billion in damages on a future generation, then that harm should not be discounted. Rather, it ought to be valued in our cost-benefit calculations at $200 billion. From a policy standpoint, this means that policy makers should be willing to spend up to $200 billion in the present to raise the consumption of a future generation—even hundreds of years from now—by anything more than $200 billion. Consider the case of the value of a statistical life. If policy makers have determined that the value of a statistical life is $10 million, it may feel ethically awkward to discount the value of lives lost in the future. For example, a cost-benefit analysis that adopted a discount rate of 5 percent would value a statistical death in 20 years at only $3.8 million. Yet few would argue that saving a life in the future has less inherent value than saving a life in the present.

As economist and *New York Times* columnist Hal Varian has written, "Some very intelligent people have argued that giving future generations less weight than the current generation is 'ethically indefensible.'"[26] The British government took this approach toward climate change in the *Stern Review on the Economics of Climate Change,* a report released in 2006 on the future costs of climate change. The *Stern Review* adopted a social discount rate near zero. The actual rate was 0.1 percent; the report concluded that the only acceptable reason to discount the consumption of future generations is because they may never exist. The *Review* adopted 0.1 percent as the likelihood in any given year that a cataclysmic event, such as a nuclear conflagration or a comet hitting the earth, would destroy all life. Other than that, all future costs and benefits are valued the same as present costs and benefits.

Yet there are equally compelling reasons to adopt a nonzero discount rate. To begin with, a social discount rate of zero can produce nearly meaningless results and leave policy makers without any intellectual traction on important issues. For example, consider a public investment that would cost $1 million and produce only $1 of social benefits annually in perpetuity. With a social discount rate of zero, the social benefits of the project will eventually exceed the social costs. After 1,000,001 years, the project will have generated total benefits of $1,000,001, which exceeds the initial investment cost. By any conventional measure, this would be a rotten investment. But with a discount rate of zero, cost-benefit analysis suggests that we ought to do it.

If future benefits are not discounted at all, then any project with even a tiny stream of benefits can be justified, if the time horizon is long enough. As a result, cost-benefit analysis would dictate that policy makers forgo nearly all current consumption in the present in order to raise the consumption for individuals who will live 10, 50, or even 1,000 years from now.

A second challenge to a social discount rate of zero is that individuals who will live 10, 50, or 1,000 years from now are likely to be richer—potentially much richer—than individuals who are alive today. Because most of us assume that there is a declining marginal utility of income—that $1 of extra consumption will provide less incremental utility to someone with an income of

26. Hal R. Varian, "Recalculating the Costs of Global Climate Change," *New York Times,* December 14, 2006.

$250,000 than to someone with an income of $25,000—then we should discount the value of future consumption because society will likely be richer. By that logic, a candy bar in 100 years *will* provide less utility than a candy bar today because wealthier citizens will have a lot more candy bars.

This is one critique of the near-zero discount rate used in the *Stern Review*. The report calculates that global per capita income is (in 2006) $7,000 per year but will grow in real terms to $94,000 by 2200. Efforts to curtail global warming will reduce current consumption in order to raise consumption in future centuries, prompting one critic to query, "Is it really ethical to transfer wealth from someone making $7,000 a year to someone making $94,000 a year?"[27]

Third, there is a social opportunity cost to expending resources in the present. A dollar today can be invested in ways that will make future generations richer. Thus, every $1 of wealth dedicated to some policy, such as curtailing CO_2 emissions, will preclude some private or public investments that would have otherwise raised the consumption of future generations. Using that logic, we can revisit the policy that would cost $1 million and produce only $1 of benefit annually. If this money were instead left in the hands of the private sector, the bulk of it would be spent on current consumption, with some of it used to make productive investments that raise the consumption of future generations. If only $100,000 were invested, for example, with a real annual return of 3 percent, then it would raise the future income of members of society by $3,000 a year—a much more attractive outcome than the $1 annual benefit produced by the government program. (As with public policy in general, the distribution of this income—who shares in the higher wealth—matters as well.)

The social discount rate should represent some social opportunity cost of capital; by this calculation, the value of costs and benefits should not be invariant to when they occur. A cost that does not occur for 100 years should be discounted relative to a current expense because it leaves society 100 years to invest that capital before the expense comes due. Similarly, a benefit in the present is worth more than a benefit in the future because the capital can be put to work immediately. Economist Gary Becker, winner of the 1992 Nobel Prize, has described a discount rate of 3 percent as "typical" for policy analysis because it approximates the long-run real return on investments in physical capital.[28]

27. Varian, "Recalculating the Costs of Global Climate Change."
28. Becker-Posner blog: http://www.becker-posner-blog.com/archives/2007/02/discounting_gre.html.

Finally, the social discount rate reflects uncertainty surrounding future costs and benefits, particularly the possibility that new technology may deliver cheaper ways to ameliorate social costs. This is relevant in the context of climate change, storage of nuclear waste, or any other policy issue with a long time horizon. It is plausible that science will deliver new and cheaper ways of mitigating harms that will occur decades or centuries in the future.

In a 2001 article in the *American Economic Review,* Harvard economist Martin Weitzman noted, "The most critical single problem with discounting future benefits and costs is that no consensus now exists, or for that matter has ever existed, about what actual rate of interest to use."[29] For that article, Weitzman surveyed 2,160 economists in 48 countries and asked them to reply with their "professionally considered gut feeling" to the following question:

> Taking all relevant considerations into account, what real interest rate do you think should be used to discount over time the (expected) benefits and (expected) costs of projects being proposed to mitigate the possible effects of global climate change?

The answers are summarized in the histogram below:

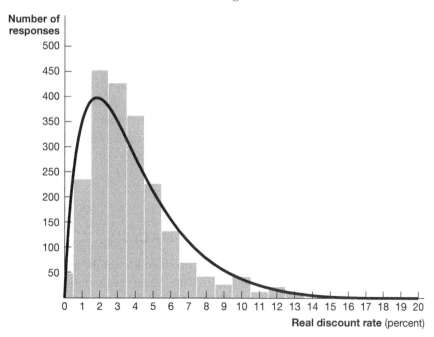

29. Martin L. Weitzman, "Gamma Discounting," *American Economic Review* 91, no. 1 (March 2001).

Every cost-benefit analysis must have a discount rate since a central part of the analysis involves calculating the present value of future costs and benefits. Although there is no single correct social discount rate, there should be some intellectual rationale for the rate or rates that are chosen. This choice of a discount rate can have a profound effect on the outcome of the analysis, particularly for issues like global warming that have costs or benefits that occur in the distant future.

12.6   SENSITIVITY ANALYSIS

Analysts will often conduct cost-benefit analysis using several different discount rates to determine how robust the conclusions are across a range of discount rates. A program for which the social benefits exceed the social costs for all reasonable discount rates is obviously preferable to a program that has positive net benefits using one reasonable discount rate but not another. This process of evaluating how the analysis is affected by changes in some of the key assumptions is called **sensitivity analysis.** For example, assume that a municipality is considering equipping some of its buildings with solar panels to produce electricity. A key benefit of such a policy would be lower future energy bills; the value of that benefit, however, will depend on the future price of energy, which is uncertain. Thus, the cost-benefit analysis may incorporate a sensitivity analysis using varying estimates for future energy costs. If the policy makes sense when oil is selling at $100 a barrel but would lose money if the price of oil drops below $85 for a sustained period of time, then policy makers may not be persuaded to take the risk. On the other hand, if the benefits exceed the costs for all reasonable estimates of future oil prices, then the case for the solar panels would be far more compelling.

12.7   COST-EFFECTIVENESS ANALYSIS

Cost-benefit analysis will not necessarily produce a scientific answer for the most socially beneficial course of action. Policy makers may decide to pursue some objective regardless of how its costs and benefits compare to competing projects. Or perhaps there is no reasonable consensus on how the relevant costs and benefits can be evaluated. In such cases, it is still possible to implement policy in a way that makes the most efficient use of society's resources. **Cost-effectiveness analysis** ranks policies based on their costs for achieving some defined objective. For example, if policy makers decided to reduce CO_2 emissions by 10 percent in order to ameliorate climate change, there would be innumerable ways of achieving this goal, some much more expensive than others. Analysts can evaluate and rank the various policy options based on cost, thereby enabling policy makers to choose the most efficient way to achieve the stated objective. Cost-effectiveness analysis does not evaluate the worthiness of a project based on its benefits relative to costs; instead, it takes some outcome or goal as given and evaluates the efficiency of the various options for achieving it.

In fields such as public health and public safety, the cost effectiveness of various policies can be strikingly different. For example, consider the variance in cost effectiveness of the safety regulations in the table below:

Cost per Life Saved

U.S. REGULATION (YEAR ISSUED)	COST PER LIFE SAVED (2002 DOLLARS)
Child-proof lighters (1993)	$100
Logging safety rules (1998)	$100
Steering-column standards (1967)	$200
Hazardous waste disposal (1998)	$1,100,000
Drinking-water quality (1992)	$19,000,000
Formaldehyde exposure (1987)	$78,000,000
Landfill restrictions (1991)	$100,000,000

Source: John Morrall, Office of Mangement and Budget, as cited in "The Price of Prudence," *The Economist,* January 22, 2004.

12.8 CONCLUSION

Cost-benefit analysis provides an objective tool for analyzing how society should best deploy scarce resources. As the Office of Management and Budget advises its staff: "Where all benefits and costs can be quantified and expressed in monetary units, benefit-cost analysis provides decision makers with a clear indication of the most efficient alternative, that is, the alternative that generates the largest net benefits to society (ignoring distributional effects). This is useful information for decision makers and the public to receive, even when economic efficiency is not the only or the overriding public policy objective."[30]

Cost-benefit analysis for most policies or projects involves the following steps:

1. Identify the policy or policies to be evaluated and the parties or political jurisdiction that has standing in the analysis.
2. Enumerate all associated costs and benefits.
3. Attach a dollar value to each cost and benefit.
4. Choose a social discount rate.
5. Calculate the net present value of each policy under consideration.
6. Perform sensitivity analyses for important assumptions, including the social discount rate.
7. Choose the most attractive policy based on the cost-benefit analysis and any other relevant considerations, such as risk aversion.

30. Office of Management and Budget, Circular A-4, September 17, 2003.

FOR DISCUSSION

The Grief Factor: Calculating the Compensation for the Families of the 9/11 Victims[31]

On Saturday, September 22, 2001—only eleven days after the tragic terrorist attacks of September 11—President George W. Bush signed into law the Victim Compensation Fund. The law would eventually provide over $7 billion in government funds to individuals injured on 9/11 and to the families of those who were killed on that morning.[32] In the haste to draft and pass legislation, two fundamental questions were not discussed in any significant way.

First, why should the American government provide compensation for the 9/11 attacks when no such funding had been allocated after previous incidents? The government did not provide any compensation after the 1995 bombing of the Alfred P. Murrah Federal Building in Oklahoma City, nor after the al-Qaeda attacks on the U.S. embassies in Kenya and Tanzania in 1998, nor even after the first attack on the World Trade Center in 1993, which killed six people and injured more than a thousand. Kathleen Treanor lost her four-year-old daughter in the Oklahoma City bombing. She asked poignantly in 2002, "Why is it right for a New York stockbroker's widow to be given millions of dollars and not a poor farmer's family in Oklahoma? It's been nearly eight years since the Oklahoma City bombing. It took them days to pass this legislation. Why is my daughter worth less than these people?"[33]

Second, how much compensation should be paid to the families of the deceased? Should it be uniform, treating all victims the same regardless of their age and likely future income? Or should it recognize, as legal verdicts often do, that the value of a human life for purposes of compensation is related to the economic loss to the family of the deceased? When economic loss is considered, the lives of high earners are worth more than the lives of low earners, and the families of some 9/11 victims would get much, much more than the families of others.

Indeed, Congress did not even specify the total amount of compensation to be paid. The legislation stipulated instead that the attorney general would appoint a special master with sweeping authority to determine the compensation levels. Attorney General John Ashcroft appointed Kenneth Feinberg, a former chief of staff for Senator

---

31. Lisa Belkin, "Just Money," *New York Times Sunday Magazine,* December 8, 2002.
32. Kenneth R. Feinberg, *Final Report of the Special Master for the September 11th Victim Compensation Fund of 2001, Volume 1* (Washington, D.C.: United States Department of Justice). The full *Final Report of the Special Master for the September 11th Victim Compensation Fund of 2001* can be found at (http://www.usdoj.gov/final_report.pdf.)
33. Belkin, "Just Money," p. 95.

Edward Kennedy. Feinberg's most relevant experience was negotiating a $250-million settlement between Dow Chemical and a group of Vietnam veterans who blamed health problems on Agent Orange, a defoliant produced by Dow and used during the Vietnam War.

According to the September 11th Victim Compensation Fund legislation, Feinberg's decisions as special master could not be appealed.

Feinberg has offered a short answer to the philosophical question of why the government ought to compensate victims of terrorism, and why some victims are eligible and not others: "Because Congress decided."[34] The slightly more complete story is that Congress decided to pay compensation to the victims of September 11 as part of legislation drafted to subsidize America's airlines for the economic disruption caused by the terrorist attacks. The Victim Compensation Fund was part of the larger Air Transportation Safety and System Stabilization Act, which offered cash, loans, and liability protection to the airlines.

Some legislators argued that if the federal government was going to cap the liability awards that 9/11 victims and their families could claim from the airlines, then it ought to offer something to those victims instead. The legislative compromise, which included relief for the airlines and open-ended compensation for 9/11 victims, passed the House of Representatives 356 to 54 and the Senate 96 to 1.

But who should get how much? The legislation stipulated that eligible victims would be compensated for their economic losses, which is defined as "the loss of earnings or other benefits related to employment, medical expense loss, replacement-services loss, loss due to death, burial costs and loss of business or employment opportunities." The process required Special Master Feinberg and his staff to convert tragic, irreplaceable loss into dollars and cents. And it required him to determine if some tragic, irreplaceable losses deserved more compensation than others.

Feinberg determined that each award would be based on two components:

1. The economic loss caused by the attack. For the families of the deceased, this would consist of forgone lifetime earnings, or the economic value of nonmarket services provided by the victim. What economic cost has been imposed on the family of the deceased? For those injured by the 9/11 attacks, the economic loss included lost income, any expected future loss of income, and any costs associated with the injury (such as home nursing care).

2. The noneconomic loss caused by the attack, or so-called pain and suffering. For those injured, this was compensation for pain, disfigurement, emotional trauma, or other noneconomic harms associated with the injury. Based on the severity and duration of the injury, these awards ranged from $500 to $6 million. Feinberg decided that the noneconomic loss for deceased victims would be set at a uniform $250,000, plus an additional $100,000 for a spouse and each dependent. Thus, the pain and suffering associated with all 9/11 deaths was deemed to be equal. Feinberg explained, "I refuse to go down the road of 'He was on the 103rd floor

34. Belkin, "Just Money," p. 96.

and died a slow death; she was on the 84th floor and was killed instantly.' I'm not getting into that."[35]

The concept of basing compensation on economic loss is much simpler in theory than practice. The families of the deceased were given awards based on the market value of what they lost because of September 11. But how exactly was that calculated? Here is a sample of the kinds of decisions made by the special master:

- For full-time workers, projected lifetime earnings were calculated using wage data and an estimation of the rate of real increase over time. The base compensation was calculated using an average for the years 1998 to 2001 to capture any fluctuations, particularly for workers in the financial-services industry.

- For those victims without wage data who would likely have entered the labor force, such as students and minors, the compensation fund used average wage data for the country.

- Projected future income was based on the number of years left in the workforce using average figures for retirement age. Although data show that men typically spend more years in the labor force than women, the figures for men were used in all cases to avoid a gender bias.

- All victims of the 9/11 attacks and their families were eligible for compensation from the U.S. government, including foreigners and illegal aliens.

- For homemakers and retired persons, the economic loss was calculated using "replacement services loss analysis," which placed a market value on the household services provided by the victim. The *Final Report* explained, "Such services include cleaning, cooking, child care, home maintenance and repairs, and financial services, among many others."

- All awards were reduced for any "offsets," which were benefits paid to the family of the deceased as the result of the death, such as life insurance and pension benefits. The award was also reduced by projected federal, state, and local taxes as well as by "self consumption," which is the portion of future income that would have been consumed by the deceased and, therefore, is not a loss for the family.

- All future costs and benefits were discounted to the present using after-tax yields on mid- to long-term U.S. Treasury securities. (Thus, if the yield on a Treasury bond with the appropriate maturity is 6 percent and half of that is taxable, then the after-tax yield would be 3 percent, which would be used as the discount rate.)

- When computing projected lifetime earnings, the base compensation of the highest-earning workers was capped at the 98th percentile of the American wage distribution, or $231,000 per year. Thus, a financial-services executive earning $10 million a year was treated as if he had been earning only a fraction of that. This means that the families of the highest earners still received the highest awards, but they received less than if the special master had not decided to cap the incomes used to calculate lifetime compensation.

---

35. Belkin, "Just Money," p. 97.

And that was just a starting point. All potential beneficiaries were entitled to a hearing in which they could present information or other special considerations that might have a bearing on their compensation. The compensation fund held a remarkable 3,962 hearings, most of which Feinberg attended personally.

By the time Special Master Feinberg made his *Final Report* in 2004, the September 11th Victim Compensation Fund had made payments to 97 percent of the families of the victims killed in the terrorist attacks; the average award was over $2 million. The fund also paid an average of nearly $400,000 to 2,680 individuals who were injured in the 9/11 attacks or in the subsequent rescue efforts. In total, American taxpayers provided $7.049 billion in compensation.[36]

Breakdown of Death Claims by Income Levels

INCOME LEVEL	NO. OF CLAIMS	PERCENT OF CLAIMS	PERCENT OF TOTAL AWARDED
$24,999 or less	180	6.25	3.22
$25,000 to $99,999	1,591	55.24	40.34
$100,000 to $199,999	633	21.98	24.30
$200,000 to $499,999	310	10.76	17.55
$500,000 to $999,999	89	3.09	7.05
$1,000,000 to $1,999,999	52	1.81	4.92
$2,000,000 and over	25	0.87	2.62
Total	2,880	100.00	100.00

The whole process left many parties unhappy. The concept of "economic loss" means that some deaths have far less value than others. As the table above demonstrates, the families of the highest-paid victims received a disproportionate share of the compensation funds. And yet some of those families also have complaints. The compensation fund was designed as a substitute for the tort system and litigation. In a court verdict, the deceased victim's income is not usually truncated at the 98th percentile of the American wage distribution, as it was by the special master. From an economic-loss standpoint, the families that got the most arguably should have received even more.

Feinberg has spoken about the tension between calculating economic loss and treating all victims equally. He told the *New York Times,* "If I were writing the program today—and I don't fault Congress; they were acting under the gun—I would have clarified the public-policy foundation. Is it tort or is it social welfare? And I'd think long and hard about this: Is a flat sum better than variations? I think perhaps it might be."[37]

36. Feinberg, *Final Report.*
37. Belkin, "Just Money," p. 97.

One hopes that it is not a lesson that has to be applied in the future. The *Final Report of the Special Master* offers a concluding thought: "Hopefully, the September 11th attacks will remain a unique historical event, never to be repeated. And there will be no need to cite the September 11th Victim Compensation Fund of 2001 as precedent for establishing a similar program."[38]

QUESTIONS

1. Should the U.S. government provide compensation to the victims of terrorism? Why, or why not?
2. Do you agree that the families of some 9/11 victims are entitled to more compensation than the families of others? Why, or why not?
3. Should victims of major natural disasters receive similar compensation? Why or why not?
4. The special master was required by the legislation to reduce all awards by the amount that the claimant would receive from "collateral sources," such as life insurance. Is that fair?
5. If a similar terrorist incident were to befall the United States or another country, would you recommend that victims be compensated in this manner? Why, or why not?
6. Do you believe that it was fair to truncate the economic loss for high earners at the 98th percentile for income ($231,000)? Why not the 95th percentile or the 99th?
7. How can you explain the fact that the families of the deceased were offered a uniform award of $250,000 to compensate for the noneconomic harm (e.g., pain and suffering) done to their loved ones, while some victims who *survived* the attacks were awarded more than $250,000 in noneconomic compensation, even as much as $6 million?
8. Do you believe that the U.S. government should pay compensation for the September 11th attacks to illegal aliens and their families? Why, or why not?

KEY CONCEPTS

★ Cost-benefit analysis (CBA) is the process by which the benefits of a project are tallied up and compared to its costs; any project for which the total benefits exceed the total costs will make us better off.

★ Comparing two (or more) projects requires all of the costs and benefits to be converted into a single unit of measure, or monetized.

★ All future costs and benefits must be discounted to their value in the present, so that we can accurately compare costs and benefits that accrue at different points

38. Feinberg, *Final Report,* p. 84.

in time. Present discounted value (or net present value) = $N/(1 + r)^t$, where $N =$ the nominal value of the future cost or benefit, r = the discount rate, t = the number of periods in the future at which the cost or benefit will be incurred.

★ When a project involves uncertainty, the range of possible costs and benefits are weighted by their respective probabilities, generating expected costs and benefits that can be used in the cost-benefit calculation.

★ Cost-benefit analysis always values an input or output using its opportunity cost, since that is the best reflection of what an individual or society must give up (or no longer has to give up) as the result of some course of action.

★ Cost-benefit analysis always seeks to value both economic and noneconomic costs and benefits. An economic cost or benefit is a direct pecuniary gain or loss. A noneconomic cost or benefit is an intangible gain or loss. (In an environmental context, these concepts are often referred to as use and nonuse values).

★ Any project or policy for which the NPV of total social benefits exceeds total social costs should be adopted, since it will expand society's net resources. When choosing among several options, policy makers should choose the one that has the largest NPV.

★ According to the willingness to pay (WTP) principle, the most accurate measure of the value of any good or service for a particular individual is what he or she is willing to give up in order to get it. Similarly, costs that are imposed on some party can be valued according to his willingness to pay to avoid whatever harm is being done.

★ When a project uses or generates resources that can be bought and sold in a competitive market, the market price is often the best measure of the social cost or benefit of those inputs or outputs.

★ Market prices are not necessarily an accurate gauge of social costs and benefits when a market is somehow distorted—by monopoly, by taxes, by regulation, by an externality, or by any other factor that causes prices and production to deviate from their socially efficient level.

★ Shadow pricing is the process of assigning an opportunity cost to resources with no obvious market price.

★ Contingent valuation seeks to assign value to an intangible cost or benefit by giving individuals a survey or questionnaire with a hypothetical situation that elicits how much they would be willing to pay to obtain some benefit or to avoid some harm.

★ A revealed preference assigns a value to a cost or benefit based on observed behavior.

★ Hedonic market analysis uses regression analysis to isolate the value of a cost or benefit.

★ When human lives are likely to be lost or saved as the result of a policy, policy makers must assign a monetary value to each life—the value of a statistical life (VSL)—in order to conduct a cost-benefit analysis of the policy under consideration.

★ The rate used to discount social costs and benefits to the present is called the social discount rate. The discount rate that is selected can have a profound impact on cost-benefit analysis, particularly when costs or benefits occur in the distant future.

★ The process of evaluating how the analysis is affected by changes in some of the key assumptions, such as the discount rate, is called sensitivity analysis.

★ Cost-effectiveness analysis ranks policies based on their costs for achieving some defined objective.

CHAPTER 13

Program Evaluation

ELITE COLLEGES—WORTH THE PRICE?

Does attending a highly selective college actually matter? That may seem like a silly question. Obviously, the graduates of places like Harvard, Princeton, and other elite universities do very well by many objective measures. For example, a recent survey by *Forbes.com* found that graduates of Dartmouth had the highest earnings of graduates from any undergraduate institution (a median salary of $134,000 for alumni with ten to twenty years of work experience). But to social-science researchers, such figures don't prove much of anything. The students at such highly selective institutions are also highly talented when they arrive to matriculate. What we don't know is how much those Dartmouth alumni would be earning now if they had attended a different college or even no college at all.

Suppose, for example, that we are trying to measure the impact on earnings from attending Harvard, one of the world's preeminent universities. We might reasonably hypothesize that a Harvard education would raise one's lifetime income. However, we also know that Harvard only accepts extremely intelligent, motivated students who are likely to do well in life no matter where they go to college. We cannot simply compare the earnings of Harvard graduates with the earnings of graduates from a local community college and conclude that attending Harvard is responsible for the difference. The students who walk in the doors of those two institutions are appreciably different.

Thus, measuring the "value added" from a Harvard education—or the treatment effect, as a researcher might call it—turns out to be a surprisingly difficult evaluation problem. We have data on the salaries of Harvard graduates, but we have no data on the counterfactual: the salaries that those same students would have earned had they not attended Harvard. We cannot conduct a scientific experiment to establish the value added at Harvard or any other highly selective university. While it would be theoretically possible to randomly assign students to competitive and less competitive institutions and then to compare their life outcomes, it's unlikely that either the students or the universities would agree to participate.

So it would appear that we cannot answer the question of interest: Are these institutions merely selecting the most talented students, or are they adding value—taking talented individuals and making them more productive? After all, Bill Gates dropped out of Harvard. Would more courses and a degree have improved his life outcomes? We can gain insight into these kinds of questions using the tools of program evaluation. Economists Stacy Dale and Alan Krueger developed a clever mechanism for measuring the impact of attending a highly selective college.[1] Their research strategy exploited the fact that many students apply to multiple colleges, including both highly selective and less selective institutions. Some of those students are accepted to a highly selective college and choose to attend; other students are accepted at a highly selective college but choose to attend a less selective college instead.

Dale and Krueger used several longitudinal data sets to compare the earnings of students in the two groups. This comparison is valuable because it helps to separate the impact of who gets accepted to highly selective colleges (the selection effect) from the value added once they get there (the treatment effect). Obviously, the Dale and Krueger study is not a perfectly controlled laboratory experiment; it does, however, provide information on the life trajectory of students who were talented enough to get into a highly competitive college but opted to go someplace else. And it informs the question raised at the beginning of this chapter: Do elite colleges launch students on the path to success, or do they merely admit students who would have been on that path anyway?

Dale and Krueger's findings should assuage the anxieties of overwrought high-school students and their parents. They write, "Students who attended more selective colleges earned about the same as students of seemingly comparable ability who attended less selective schools." The one exception was students from low-income families, who earned more if they attended a selective college. Earnings are an imperfect measure of the value of attending an elite college; there are many other reasons to attend Harvard besides a higher paycheck down the road. Nonetheless, the Dale and Krueger study helps to sort out the treatment effect (spending four years at an elite institution) from the selection effect (the most talented students are admitted to those institutions). In a summary of the research for the *New York Times,* Krueger offered the punch line for the research: "Recognize that your own motivation, ambition and talents will determine your success more than the college name on your diploma."[2]

1. Stacy Berg Dale and Alan B. Krueger, "Estimating the Payoff to Attending a More Selective College: An Application of Selection on Observables and Unobservables," *Quarterly Journal of Economics* 107, no. 4 (November 2002): 1491–1527.

2. Alan B. Krueger, "Children Smart Enough to Get into Elite Schools May Not Need to Bother," *New York Times,* April 27, 2000.

Public policy often involves implementing policy changes in an effort to make society, or some segment of society, better off. This process inevitably raises a fundamental question: Did it work? If society devotes resources to immunizing children against disease or encouraging literacy or helping to prevent ex-offenders from returning to prison, then we ought to ask if those resources had their intended effect. Public officials have an obligation to account for the effectiveness of the programs to which they commit resources. However, this evaluation process is often far more difficult than it appears. The goal of **program evaluation** is to use analysis and quantitative tools to determine the impact of a program, policy, or other intervention.

CHAPTER OUTLINE

13.4 CONCLUSION

FOR DISCUSSION The Economics of Political Incorrectness: Does Abortion Lower Crime?

13.1 THE TREATMENT EFFECT

The fundamental challenge of program evaluation is determining what outcomes have been caused by a particular program or intervention. As the introductory example with selective colleges should have made clear, the fact that the participants in a program (or the attendees of a particular college) have some positive outcome relative to nonparticipants is not sufficient to prove that the program is responsible for that positive result.[3] Policy analysts refer to the causal impact of a policy, program, or intervention as the **treatment effect.** There is an obvious analogy to medicine. If one set of patients is given a particular treatment and a similar set of patients are not given that treatment then we can infer that the difference in outcomes between the two groups was likely caused by the treatment.

Public policy rarely offers us such elegant comparisons. The basic problem is that we are often unable to compare the outcome for an individual who participates in a program with the outcome for *an identical person* who did not participate in the program. We cannot (yet) clone an individual; nor can a single person both participate in a program and not participate. We do not often have the luxury of controlled experiments using human subjects (although these experiments can be done). Instead, we are often left to observe one group who received some treatment (such as attending Harvard) relative to another group who did not receive the treatment but might also be different in other ways (such as not having good enough grades to get into Harvard). The challenge is separating the treatment effect (the Harvard education) from other underlying differences in the subjects.

In some cases, we have no comparison group because we are unable to observe the **counterfactual,** which is what would have happened to the same set of actors under an alternate set of circumstances. For example, politicians and policy makers have vigorously debated the wisdom of the U.S. invasion of Iraq in 2003. That debate takes place, however, without crucial (and ultimately

---

3. Much of the material in this section is drawn from presentations given by Robert LaLonde, professor of public policy at the Harris School of Public Policy Studies, the University of Chicago. I am indebted to him for his assistance.

unknowable) information—the counterfactual. What would have happened if the United States had *not* invaded Iraq? Since the United States opted for a different path, we will never know with certainty what would have happened if Saddam Hussein had remained in power.

The goal of program evaluation is to isolate the treatment effect—to determine what happened as the result of some policy intervention relative to what would have happened to the same actors in the absence of the intervention—which is harder than it appears.

13.2 Confounding Factors

13.2.1 Selection Effect (Selection Bias)

A **selection effect,** or **selection bias,** occurs when the participants in some treatment are significantly different in some important respect from the nonparticipants to whom they are being compared. This difference in the composition of the participants and nonparticipants, rather than the treatment, may account for some or all of the difference in outcomes. To return to the medical-treatment analogy, assume that one group of patients is given a particular medical intervention and that another group of seemingly similar patients *at a different hospital* are not given the treatment. The treatment may account for the difference in outcomes; but so may some difference between the two hospitals, such as the quality of the doctors, the demographics of the patients, or some other factor not easily observed.

Consider an important line of research that is often confounded by this selection effect: comparing the effectiveness of public and private schools. Researchers would like to know whether students learn more effectively in private schools than they do in public schools. At first glance, this appears to be a simple exercise. We have objective measures of student outcomes, such as standardized test scores, which should enable us to compare the outcomes of students in the two kinds of schools. It seems a simple question: Do third-grade students in private schools perform better on tests than third-grade students in public schools?

Yet those test data won't actually tell us much about the quality of the underlying public and private schools. Why? Because private-school students are likely to be different than public-school students in key respects. For example, they may have wealthier or more educated parents. And it may be this difference in the student bodies, rather than what happens at the schools they attend, that accounts for the difference in test scores. Even if we were to use regression analysis to attempt to control for differences in the student bodies—including data on parents' education, family income, etc.—it is still extremely difficult to make the selection effect go away. *Students in private schools are different because their families have chosen to enroll them in a private school (and to pay for it).* Even two families who look identical "on paper"—same income, same education level, same residential location, etc.—are likely to be different in significant but unobservable ways if one family opts to send the children to a private school and the other family does not.

This selection effect could bias the comparison of test scores in either direction. If families who place the highest value on education choose private schools, then this commitment to education in the home may be what accounts for the superior achievement of private-school students, not what they are doing in that private school. Or it could go the other direction. Suppose that families who feel that their children need extra academic attention are more likely to choose a private-school environment. In this case, private schools may attract students with below-average abilities; private-school test scores could lag behind their public-school peers because they attract more struggling students, not because they are doing a poor job of teaching.

Consider another subtle example in the field of education policy research. Do students learn better in smaller classes? Once again, we have objective measures of student achievement, such as test scores, so we should be able to make a comparison between student performance in big classes and small classes. But suppose that the data show that students in small classes actually do significantly *worse* than their peers in large classes. It is plausible that smaller classes don't improve student achievement, but how could they make it worse?

A selection bias could easily generate such an outcome. In general, students are not randomly assigned to big or small classes. Principals and teachers usually make such decisions. It's possible that difficult or disruptive students are placed in smaller classes, where they can be managed more easily. It's also possible that principals give their least experienced and/or least capable teachers the smallest classes so that they will not be overwhelmed. In both of these cases, it is the selection effect—the way in which teachers and students are assigned to the classroom—rather than the number of students in the class that accounts for the outcome.

Any nonrandom assignment to treatment is prone to a selection effect, particularly when participation in the intervention or program is voluntary, such as postprison employment or substance-abuse programs. The ex-inmates who volunteer for such opportunities are likely to be different in significant ways than ex-inmates who don't volunteer for such opportunities. In the absence of counterfactual data—how volunteers would have done had they not participated in the programs and how nonvolunteers would have done had they participated—we cannot separate out the effects of the program from the selection effects biases.

13.2.2 Distinguishing Causation from Correlation (or Just Coincidence)

Suppose that the government implements a tax cut, and the following year the rate of economic growth increases significantly. Did the tax cut *cause* the higher rate of growth? There are economic reasons to believe that lower taxes might spur economic growth. For example, a lower tax burden might encourage investment, which leads to job creation and growth. In this case, the tax cut would *cause* better subsequent economic performance. But there are also reasons to be skeptical about such a conclusion. Since economic growth tends to be cyclical, it is plausible that politicians would implement a tax cut just as the economy was beginning to recover on its own. In this case, the economic recovery followed the tax cut, but the relationship is not causal. The rate of economic growth would have accelerated even without the tax cut. This distinction is crucial to researchers, who are tasked with understanding what policy interventions have led to what outcomes, rather than merely coinciding with them.

Two variables are **correlated** if a movement in one is associated with a movement in the other. Two variables have a **causal relationship** if a change in one brings about a change in the other. Good public policy depends on identifying and measuring causal relationships—when a certain intervention causes a certain outcome—but also recognizing when two outcomes do not have a causal relationship. For example, people who are in hospitals die at a much higher rate than people who are not in hospitals. Obviously, the hospitals are not causing the extra deaths (although in the case of infections, that is possible); instead, the higher death rate is a function of the fact that hospitals have more seriously ill people in the first place.

- **Causality.** A is responsible for changes in B. For example, inoculating children against polio prevents outbreaks of the disease.
- **Correlation.** A and B are associated with one another, but A does not necessarily cause B. For example, the economy recovers after a tax cut is implemented; the tax cut may or may not have contributed to the recovery.
- **Reverse causality.** B causes A, rather than the other way around. Death rates from heart disease are highest in the areas with the most cardiologists. Obviously, the heart specialists are not causing the extra deaths; instead, they are moving to places where there is the most demand for their services.

- **Omitted variable.** C is responsible for both A and B. For example, the more automobiles a family owns (A), the higher that family's children are likely to score on the SAT (B). The omitted variable (C) is the family's education level. Highly educated families are likely to be wealthier and, therefore, own more cars; they are also likely to have children who do well on the SAT. For any given family, buying another automobile will not raise the test scores of its children.
- **Coincidence.** A and B have moved together over some period simply by chance and are not likely to be correlated in the future. A and B have no real association, causal or otherwise. For example, in the Policy in the Real World section below, we will discuss the suspected relationship between small amounts of mercury contained in the measles, mumps, and rubella (MMR) vaccine and the rising incidence of autism. In places where the mercury compound was removed from the vaccine, autism rates have continued to climb.

Proving causality is difficult in a complex world. Just as Congress implements some policy, many other factors also affect the economy: "baby boomers" are retiring; China is experiencing unprecedented growth; the dollar is falling in value relative to other currencies; the price of oil is rising; the Yankees won the 2009 World Series; men's ties are becoming narrower; and so on. With all of that going on, how can we isolate the effect of any single policy? No laboratory scientist would design an experiment in which the subjects are given five different treatments at once; it would be impossible to sort out which treatment, or which combination of treatments, caused the observed effects. And yet that is routinely what is required of program evaluation in the real world. Researchers must adopt strategies for identifying the causal effects of a policy change amid all the world's other complexity.

·············· | **POLICY IN THE REAL WORLD** | ··············

Cause or Coincidence?: Childhood Vaccinations and Autism

One of the striking medical developments in the United States over the past twenty years has been the sharp rise in the incidence of autism spectrum disorders. These disorders, which are often lumped together under the term *autism*, reflect a spectrum of disorders characterized by impaired communication and social skills and repetitive behaviors or interests.[4] Some adults with high-functioning autism can function effectively in society, albeit often with communication difficulties and an impaired ability to read social cues. Individuals with the most serious disorders on the autism spectrum have severe cognitive and social disabilities, making it difficult or impossible to participate meaningfully in mainstream society.

The diagnosis of autism has grown much more prevalent: from roughly 1 case per 10,000 births in the 1980s to 1 case in 150 births in 2007.[5] Parents of autistic children and public-health officials are asking the same question: What is responsible for such a dramatic increase? (The first challenge is determining whether the illness is becoming more common or is just more commonly reported. The former appears to be the case.) Thomas Insel, director of the National Institute of Mental Health, has said, "Is it cellphones? Ultrasound? Diet sodas? Every parent has a theory. At this point, we just don't know."[6]

In the 1990s, one prominent theory emerged: childhood vaccines. The alleged culprit was thimerosal, which is a mercury-based preservative used in vaccines. The amount of ethyl mercury in each vaccine is roughly the same as the amount of methyl mercury (a more toxic compound) found in a tuna sandwich. Nonetheless, in 1999, the Food and Drug Administration calculated that the amount of mercury included in the vaccines recommended for American infants exceeded a government guideline. Are the vaccines that are supposed to make children healthier actually poisoning them with a toxic metal?

In 1998, researchers published a study in the *Lancet,* a British medical journal, demonstrating a different link between the measles, mumps, and rubella (MMR) vaccine and autism. The paper provided inferential evidence that the live measles component of the vaccine causes harm to the gastrointestinal tract, which in turn releases toxins that damage the central nervous system and cause autism spectrum disorders. In February 2010, the *Lancet* took the unusual step of formally retracting the 1998 paper because of ethics violations by the paper's lead author.

Nonetheless, the connection between vaccines and autism makes intuitive sense and has remained anchored in the public psyche. The illness often

---

4. National Institute of Mental Health: http://www.nimh.nih.gov/health/publications/autism/complete-index.shtml.

5. Benedict Carey, "Study Finds Increased Prevalence of Autism," *New York Times,* December 19, 2009.

6. Gardiner Harris and Anahad O'Connor, "On Autism's Cause, It's Parents vs. Research," *New York Times,* June 25, 2005.

appears abruptly at the age when young children have been recently immunized. In 10 to 25 percent of cases, the illness appears "almost overnight," often between a child's first and second birthdays. Dan Burton, a member of Congress from Indiana, is typical of many parents and grandparents who point to vaccines as the cause of the autism epidemic. He told the *New York Times,* "My grandson received nine shots in one day, seven of which contained thimerosal, which is 50 percent mercury as you know, and he became autistic a short time later."

The scientific community has come to an entirely different consensus. The thimerosal theory has been rejected based on numerous large studies. The compound was removed from vaccines in the 1990s in Denmark, Sweden, and Canada; there was no reduction in the incidence of autism over the ensuing years. Similarly, a study of more than 100,000 children born in Britain between 1988 and 1997 found that children who had received the *most* thimerosal in vaccines had the lowest incidence of autism spectrum disorders.

The gastrointestinal theory has also been "soundly refuted." The earlier findings of the *Lancet* have never been replicated. The *Lancet* retracted the study in part because the lead author of the MMR study had received previously undisclosed research funding from lawyers seeking to sue vaccine makers. Ten of the coauthors on the article had already disavowed the study before the *Lancet* took its formal action. More recently, a team of researchers from Columbia University, Massachusetts General Hospital, and the Centers for Disease Control did a study of children with gastrointestinal illnesses, some of whom had autism and others who did not. The *New York Times* reported, "Only 5 of the 25 autistic children had been vaccinated before they developed gastrointestinal problems—and subsequently autism. Genetic tests found remnants of the measles virus in only two children, one of whom was autistic, the other not."

The cause of rising rates of autism spectrum disorders remains elusive. In the meantime, the confusion between correlation and causation has its costs. A *New York Times* editorial recently noted, "The big losers in this debate are the children who are not being vaccinated because of parental fears and are at risk of contracting serious—sometimes fatal—diseases."[7]

----

7. "Debunking an Autism Theory," *New York Times,* September 9, 2008.

13.2.3 Dropout Effect (Survivorship Bias)

Program outcomes can be seriously skewed if a nonrandom group of participants quit or are removed from a program during the period of analysis. This effect is also sometimes referred to as the **dropout effect** or **survivorship bias.** For example, suppose that 41 percent of eighth graders in a school district are reading at grade level, according to a new state test. In response, the district implements a new reading curriculum and reports four years later that 83 percent of twelfth-rade students are reading at grade level—more than twice the percentage as when the same class of students was in eighth grade. Clearly, this is a sign of major educational improvement. Or is it?

Based on the data presented above, the honest answer is that we don't know if the program improved student reading. In many states, students are allowed to drop out of high school beginning at age sixteen. So while it may be the same class of students who are tested in eighth and twelfth grades, the composition of that class has likely changed in a significant way. Many of the most troubled students—and, therefore, those who are most likely to be the worst readers—have dropped out of school by twelfth grade. As these poor readers drop out, the proportion of students who are reading at grade level will go up, even if not a single student becomes a better reader!

The bias can go the other way as well. Suppose analysts are attempting to evaluate the degree to which a two-month job-training program improves the marketable skills of welfare recipients. The participants are tested at the beginning and the end of the program on several job-related skills, such as computer proficiency, basic writing, etc. Given the potential survivorship bias, it is possible that the class adds value even if the average skills of the participants are lower at the end of the course than the beginning. Why? Because participants will drop out if they find a job before the program is over; the most skilled participants—and those who are the fastest learners—are the most likely to find work quickly. The dropout effect is likely to change the composition of the group in a way that masks the treatment effect of the program.

13.2.4 Evaluator or Participant Bias

In some situations, the person or persons doing the evaluation of a program may improperly affect the evaluation itself. Obviously, there is the possibility of fraud or misrepresentation when individuals have some stake in the program they are evaluating, such as continued funding or some other kind of financial gain. In other cases, the evaluator bias may be more subtle. For example, suppose that a teacher is asked to evaluate the reading skills of students who have received special reading intervention relative to those who have not. There is some inherent subjectivity in evaluating reading skills; the teacher may inadvertently give some benefit of the doubt to the students who have received the extra instruction. This explains why some professors choose to grade exams "blind," meaning that the student's name is not on the exam or is on the back of the exam instead of the front. This can prevent a professor's impression of a student's previous work from influencing the evaluation of the exam at hand.

A related problem may occur when personnel involved in a program behave differently with the treatment group than they do with the control group. A doctor may pay more attention to a patient receiving an experimental treatment; a job-placement professional may work harder to employ someone who has completed an experimental job-training program. The extra attention, rather than the treatment itself, may cause a different outcome. For this reason, most pharmaceutical trials are performed **double-blind,** meaning that neither the doctor nor the patients are aware of who is getting the experimental drug and who is getting a placebo. The patients are not informed because they, too, may behave differently if they know that they are part of an experimental group, such as reporting less pain if they think they are getting medicine. Some experiments go so far as to conduct fake surgeries: patients are treated as if they are being operated on, when in fact only half are getting the surgery that is being evaluated. A 2008 study of knee surgery published in the *New England Journal of Medicine* compared outcomes for a surgical procedure to relieve arthritis pain to outcomes for a control group who received a "sham operation." (The real surgery was found to be no more effective than the fake one.)[8] Obviously, public policy does not often present the equivalent of a "sham operation"; participants in a job-training program are likely to know whether they are actually receiving job training or not (it presumably cannot be done under anesthesia). Nonetheless, policy analysts should be aware that both the evaluators of a program and the participants in it might behave differently because of the evaluation itself.

13.3 EVALUATION STRATEGIES

Despite the challenges identified above, it is important to determine if a policy or program is having its intended effect. To the extent possible, policy makers should design an evaluation strategy at the time a program is created in order to ensure that the data, funding, and professional expertise necessary to conduct

8. Gina Kolata, "A Study Revives a Debate on Arthritis Knee Surgery," *New York Times,* September 11, 2008.

the program evaluation are in place. Given that humans cannot usually be studied in a laboratory like rats or bacteria cultures, the following are the most common strategies for evaluating policies and programs.

13.3.1 Randomized Experiment

Researchers sometimes do have the luxury of designing experiments to test the effectiveness of a policy program. The **randomized experiment** is the gold standard of program evaluation: a large, eligible population is identified for some kind of policy intervention, and a random mechanism is used to separate those who will receive the treatment from those who will not. Although the individuals in the treatment and control groups can never be identical, we can assume that if the groups are large enough, the important individual differences will average out over the two groups. For example, suppose that a school is testing a new reading curriculum. Five hundred students will be randomly assigned to participate in classes using the new curriculum, and five hundred students will continue to use the old curriculum. Clearly, some students are more gifted at reading than others, and the distribution of talented students across the two groups will affect the evaluation of the new curriculum. However, basic probability allows us to assume that if the experimental and control groups are large enough and if the mechanism for creating the two groups is truly random, then the talent pool in the two groups will be roughly equal. We can also assume that any external factors that might affect student achievement, such as a new video-game craze, will affect both the treatment and control groups the same. Finally, the random assignment to the two groups will eliminate any potential selection effects.

······················· POLICY IN THE REAL WORLD ·················

The Revolving Prison Door: Do Postprison Employment Programs Reduce Recidivism?

By any objective measure, America has a huge prison population. In 2008, there were roughly 1.6 million inmates in America's state and federal prisons.[9] America's incarceration rate is 504 per 100,000 population, which is higher than every country in the world[10] (and more than five times the rate of

9. William J. Sabol, Heather C. West, and Matthew Cooper, "Prisoners in 2008," *Bureau of Justice Statistics Bulletin* NCJ 228417 (December 2009): 1; http://bjs.ojp.usdoj.gov/content/pub/pdf/p08.pdf.

10. Sabol, West, and Cooper, "Prisoners in 2008," 6.

France or Germany). Roughly one-third of African-American males will spend time in state or federal prison during their lifetime,[11] if present trends continue.

Contrary to popular opinion, most prisoners serve relatively short sentences. For example, the average state prison sentence is less than five years (excluding those serving life sentences or on death row). However, the proportion of prisoners who are released and subsequently rearrested for another crime—the recidivism rate—is shockingly high. According to federal data, roughly two-thirds (67.5 percent) of prisoners released from the criminal justice system will be rearrested within three years, and more than half will return to prison during that time either for a new offense or for a parole violation.[12]

Recidivism has an enormous social cost. Clearly, it is bad for the individuals who are unable to turn their lives around upon leaving prison. It is also expensive for taxpayers. The annual cost of incarcerating an individual in a federal prison was $25,327 in 2003.[13]

The obvious goal for public policy is to make it easier for ex-offenders to re-enter society and stay out of prison, which is no easy task. As *The Economist* has noted, "The typical inmate is released from prison with all the problems he went in with—plus a prison record that makes finding a job or a place to live even harder."[14] Can programs that help ex-offenders find jobs upon their release from prison help keep them from lapsing back into crime?

That turns out to be a surprisingly difficult research question. There is plenty of evidence to indicate that ex-offenders who participate successfully in such programs are less likely to go back to prison. However, such data alone do not prove that the employment programs *cause* the reduction in recidivism. These programs suffer from two potential selection biases. First, many such programs are voluntary; as a result, the individuals who volunteer for the programs may be different from the individuals who opt not to participate. In particular, inmates who commit to postprison programs may be more intent upon staying out of prison. That attribute alone, rather than the program they sign up for, may account for the better postprison outcomes relative to nonparticipants.

Second, the individuals who successfully complete such programs may have skills, support networks, or the like that set them apart from those who

11. Thomas P. Bonczar, "Prevalence of Imprisonment in the U.S. Population, 1974–2001," Bureau of Justice Statistics Special Report, NCJ 197976 (August 2003).

12. Patrick A. Langan and David J. Levin, "Recidivism of Prisoners Released in 1994," Bureau of Justice Statistics, NCJ 193427 (June 2, 2002).

13. http://www.usdoj.gov/jmd/budgetsummary/btd/1975_2002/2002/html/page117-119.htm.

14. "A Stigma That Never Fades," *The Economist,* August 8, 2002.

drop out of the programs or don't sign up. In this case, the characteristics that enable the ex-offender to succeed in the program are similar to the ones that enable him to stay out of prison. *But success in the program does not cause those characteristics—it reflects them.* Indeed, these individuals would likely have stayed out of prison even without participating in the program.

For all that, there are also strong reasons to believe that postprison employment programs might cause better outcomes. Most inmates leave prison with limited skills and a tenuous connection to the workforce. It is reasonable to believe that helping individuals find and hold jobs when they leave prison would reduce recidivism.

So, should society spend money on such programs or not?

Two nonprofit groups in Chicago set out to answer that question.[15] The Safer Foundation and the Joyce Foundation are sponsoring a controlled study that will examine the employment and recidivism rates of 2,000 newly released male inmates in Chicago, Detroit, Milwaukee, and St. Paul. All of the ex-offenders will have roughly similar educational and work backgrounds. However, half of the men will get limited counseling and aid: résumé preparation, job-search assistance, etc. The other half will get the same basic aid but will be placed in a temporary job, giving them a transition into the workforce.

The outcomes for both groups will be tracked for three years. The Manpower Development Research Corporation, a firm that specializes in program evaluation, has been hired to analyze the results. Either way, the findings will be significant. If the temporary jobs improve the outcomes for newly released inmates, then the program can be used as a model for reducing recidivism across the country. If the postprison programs don't have a significant positive effect, then policy makers can look to other possible solutions for America's expensive and socially destructive "revolving prison door."

....

13.3.2 Natural Experiments

Researchers do not always have the luxury of creating experimental and control groups, but sometimes circumstances create them. **Natural experiments** occur when some unintentional intervention creates the opportunity to compare a group that participated in a program with another group that was similar in all important respects but was randomly excluded from receiving the

15. Erik Eckholm, "Experiment Will Test the Effectiveness of Post-Prison Employment Programs," *New York Times*, October 1, 2006.

relevant treatment. Suppose, for example, that researchers are seeking to understand the effect of a school-choice program for low-income students. (Such a program would offer low-income students vouchers to attend private schools.) For reasons that have already been discussed in this chapter, it would not be meaningful to compare the academic outcomes for students who received the vouchers to those who did not; the families who took the initiative to apply for the vouchers might be significantly different in ways that account for the different academic outcomes of their children. But suppose that there were only a limited number of vouchers available and that they were allocated by lottery. For the sake of example, assume that 1,000 families applied for 500 available vouchers. Such a scenario would present natural treatment and control groups. Only 500 students received the vouchers, but all 1,000 families tried to get into the program, which negates any potential selection effect. The families who did not get the vouchers were just like the families who did in one crucial respect: they proactively tried to get their child into the voucher program. The fact that they did not receive a voucher was simply a matter of chance. Because of the oversubscribed lottery, researchers can more easily compare the achievement of students who received the vouchers with those who applied but did not get accepted.

13.3.3 Nonequivalent Control Group (Nonrandomized)

In the ideal experimental case, subjects are assigned randomly to the treatment and control groups. In the case of a **nonequivalent control,** the subjects in the control group are thought to be largely similar to the subjects in the treatment group, but the assignment is not random. Suppose, for example, that all of the students in an elementary school are introduced to a new reading program. The fact that student reading scores are higher at the end of the program than they were at the beginning does not tell us much at all, since students may have become better readers at that school for all kinds of reasons. To get a sense of the counterfactual—how students would have fared in the absence of the reading program—we might compare the reading scores of the participating students at the end of the program to the reading scores of students at a similar elementary school who did not participate in the program. To the extent that the two groups of students are roughly similar, we might infer that any significant improvement in the treatment group relative to the nonequivalent control is due to the special program.

Since all students in the treatment school are participating in the program, there is no risk of a selection effect at the student level; this is not a case where only the best students are the ones offered an opportunity to participate in the program. However, there is the possibility of a selection effect at the school level. Suppose that the best educators are the most likely to be offered a chance to participate in the program or, conversely, that the most staid schools are more likely to reject such innovations. Because of the nonrandom nature of the comparison, it is more difficult to reject the possibility that factors other than the reading program are responsible for the observed difference in reading scores between the treatment and control students.

13.3.4 Time-Series Analysis

Time-series analysis uses longitudinal data to compare some outcome of interest before and after a particular intervention or treatment. Suppose a county implemented a new program in 2008 to reduce domestic violence. A simple time-series analysis might evaluate domestic violence rates before and after the program went into effect. A significant change in the rate of domestic violence that coincides with the introduction of the program might suggest that the new measures are having their intended effect.

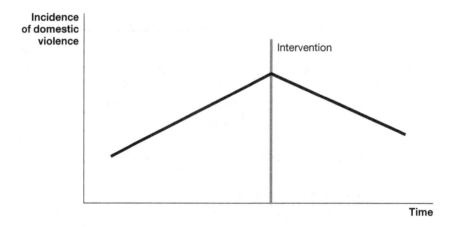

The drawback to this approach is that a simple before-and-after comparison can make it difficult or impossible to prove causality. The fact that a change in outcomes coincides with the introduction of the program does not necessarily prove that the program caused the change. If domestic violence has been a high-profile concern, it's likely that some other interventions might be going on as well, such as media campaigns or programs introduced by non-profit groups. Which of these factors caused the observed change in outcomes? A simple time-series analysis may also miss the positive effects of an intervention, if those effects take place with a lag. Suppose that domestic violence rates begin to fall several months, or even several years, after the program is introduced. It is plausible that programs such as domestic-violence education or legal reforms related to the treatment of abusive spouses might take some time to have a positive impact. If they prove successful in the long run, the time-series analysis may not detect this effect.

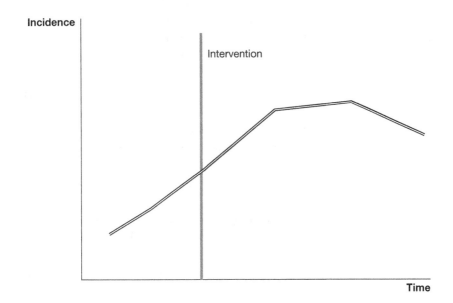

Political battles are often fought over different interpretations of time-series analysis. For example, Democrats routinely claim that the robust economic growth of the 1990s was caused by President Bill Clinton's fiscal reforms and balanced budgets. Republicans argue instead that the strong growth of the 1990s was caused by Ronald Reagan's tax reforms a decade earlier, which promoted investment and growth long after Reagan left the White House. Neither side can use simple longitudinal data to prove its case (not to mention that there may be some validity to both explanations).

····················| **POLICY IN THE REAL WORLD** |··················

Twin Studies: Are Psychopaths Born or Made?[16]

As our knowledge of human genetics becomes more complete, scientists are learning that genes, in conjunction with environmental factors, can shape everything from our health to our personality. One crucial methodological challenge is trying to separate genetic effects from environmental effects so that each can be understood more effectively.

Researchers have recently begun to study the extent to which psychopathy, which is defined as overt antisocial behavior and an extreme lack of empathy, may be influenced by genetic factors. Understanding psychopathy is particularly important from a public policy standpoint because it is highly correlated with adult criminal behavior. Individuals who demonstrate extreme antisocial behavior from childhood into adulthood—a pattern known as life-course persistent antisocial behavior—can be ten times more costly to society than the average person.

Yet probing the genetic and environmental roots of psychopathy is not methodologically easy; researchers cannot conduct experiments to determine the causes of psychopathic behavior. Researchers at the Institute of Psychiatry in London came up with a clever alternative: they studied twins. In particular, they exploited the difference between identical twins (who share an identical genetic makeup) and fraternal twins (who have the same genetic similarity as ordinary siblings). Because twins are raised in the same household, they presumably share the same environmental effects. That is what enabled the British researchers to probe the nature-nurture debate as it applies to psychopathy. If psychopathy is caused primarily by environmental effects, then pairs of fraternal twins should be just as likely to share the condition as pairs of identical twins. If there is an important genetic component, however, then identical twins will be more likely to share extreme behavioral tendencies than fraternal twins.

Once again, researchers have a longitudinal data set to thank for their insights. The data were drawn from the Twins Early Development Study

16. Adapted from "Psychopathy: Original Sinners?" *The Economist,* May 28, 2005, and Essi Viding, R. James R. Blair, Terrie E. Moffitt, and Robert Plomin, "Evidence for Substantial Genetic Risk for Psychopathy in Seven-Year-Olds," *Journal of Child Psychology and Psychiatry* 46, no. 6 (2005): 592–597.

(TEDS), which has been collecting data on a representative sample of thousands of twins born in the United Kingdom between 1994 and 1996. The data include a teacher assessment for 3,487 sets of twins at age seven that evaluates students on a scale for both antisocial behavior and callous, unemotional traits. For example, one indicator of antisocial behavior was "often fights with other children or bullies them"; meanwhile, callous, unemotional behavior is characterized by "lack of empathy, lack of guilt, shallow emotions." Students are considered to have psychopathic tendencies if they score high in both antisocial behavior *and* callous, unemotional traits.

How did the fraternal and identical twins compare? Antisocial behavior alone appears to have largely environmental causes, meaning that it is caused by life experiences (nurture) rather than genetics (nature). However, the researchers found that there is "remarkably high heritability" for callous, unemotional traits. The authors conclude, "Our results indicate that exhibiting high levels of callous unemotional traits at 7 years, as assessed by teachers at the end of the first year of school, is under strong genetic influence."

The authors found something else that was curious. Among those students who exhibit callous, unemotional traits, the likelihood of exhibiting antisocial behavior as well appears to have a strong genetic component. This is different than antisocial behavior among the population as a whole, which appears to be shaped mostly by environmental factors. Together, these findings suggest that the core components of psychopathy—a lack of empathy combined with extreme antisocial behavior—are present at birth, rather than shaped by life experience. The paper emphasizes that not all children with a combination of extreme antisocial behavior and callous, unemotional traits will become psychopathic criminals as adults. Still, the authors argue that their findings have "clear implications for research, treatment, and public policy." In particular:

1. Given "remarkably high heritability" for callous, unemotional traits and for antisocial behavior in children with these traits, molecular genetic research on antisocial behavior should focus on the callous, unemotional core of psychopathy.
2. A better understanding of how genetic influences translate into brain function will contribute to both pharmacological and environmental interventions so that psychopathy can be treated like other emotional disorders, such as depression.
3. Because psychopathy manifests itself early in life and has large social costs later on, intervention efforts need to begin in preschool.

13.3.5 Multiple Time Series (Difference in Difference)

Multiple time series, or **difference in difference,** compares longitudinal data for a treatment group with longitudinal data for a similar but nonrandom group that has not received the treatment. (This mechanism combines the two previous methodologies—a nonequivalent control group and time-series analysis.) The important assumption is that since the two groups used for the analysis are largely comparable but for the treatment, any significant difference in outcomes over time between the two can be attributed to the program or policy being evaluated. Consider the hypothetical case discussed above in which researchers are interested in the effectiveness of a program designed to reduce domestic violence. Simple time-series data are limited as an evaluation tool because of the many social forces that may have an impact on domestic violence over time. Even a reduction in domestic violence that coincides with the introduction of the program is not sufficient to prove causality. Conversely, even if domestic violence increases after the program is introduced, the program may still be effective in reducing domestic violence relative to what it would have been in the absence of the intervention.

Multiple time series can help us isolate the treatment effect. Suppose that the domestic-violence program is implemented at the county level and that we have time-series data both for the county in which the program is introduced and for a neighboring county that is demographically similar but has not implemented any kind of domestic-violence program. We can assume that the broad trends and social forces affecting the two counties are nearly identical. Thus, a researcher might reasonably conclude that a significant deviation in outcomes between the two counties that coincides with the introduction of the program was caused by the policy intervention. For the sake of example, assume that domestic violence has increased by 7 percent in the control county (where no program has been introduced) over a two-year period, while increasing by 2 percent in the county with the new program. We can evaluate the effect of the intervention by comparing the changes in the two counties over the period of study—the so-called difference in difference. If the control county is truly comparable, then researchers might reasonably infer that the program reduced incidents of domestic violence by 5 percent relative to what they would have been in the absence of the intervention. Because the incidence of domestic violence increased in the county with the new program by 2 percent over the course of the intervention, we might have overlooked its effectiveness without the comparison provided by a nonequivalent control group.

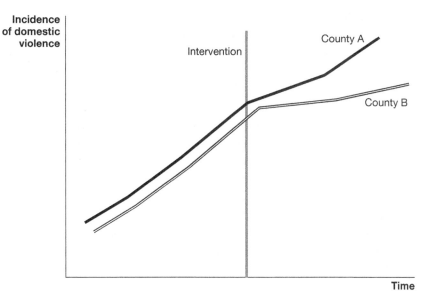

13.3.6   Discontinuity Studies

The primary challenge of most program evaluations is that the individuals who are recommended for some treatment are different in significant ways from those who are not recommended for the treatment. Thus, comparing outcomes for the two groups can't tell us much, if anything, about the effect of the treatment. People who seek psychological counseling are more likely to have serious mental-health issues than people who do not seek counseling— so we have no obvious way to determine the effectiveness of that counseling. **Discontinuity studies** exploit the fact that some treatments have a rigid cut-off, making it possible to compare outcomes for those who are just barely eligible for the treatment with the outcomes for those who just missed the cutoff and, therefore, did not receive the treatment. Since those who fall just above and just below some arbitrary cutoff, such as exam score or household income, will be nearly identical in many important respects, their outcomes can be compared in ways that provide meaningful results about the effectiveness of the relevant intervention.

Suppose that students who score below 70 on a midterm exam are required to attend a special study session with a teaching assistant, while those who score 70 or above are not eligible to attend. The professor would like to know if this study session has any value. Obviously, comparing the final exam scores for those students who did and did not attend the session would not be a valuable exercise. The students who attended the study session are those who are struggling most in the course; their final exam scores are likely to be lower than the rest of the class regardless of the value of the study session. Instead, the professor could exploit the eligibility cutoff: students who scored an even 70 on the midterm showed essentially the same proficiency as those who scored 69, except that the latter will attend the study session and the former will not. If there are enough students just above and below the cutoff, then the professor can compare the performance of the two groups on the final exam and reasonably attribute the difference to the mandatory study session. (As in any case, there is always the possibility that pure chance is responsible for some or all of the difference in outcomes. But the more data the professor has and the larger the difference between the two groups, the less likely it is that the difference can be explained by chance alone.)

Researchers used a more sophisticated version of this approach (regression-discontinuity analysis) to evaluate the effectiveness of a policy in the Chicago public schools requiring students who scored below a certain point on the Iowa Tests of Basic Skills in grades 3, 6, or 8 to attend a mandatory summer-school program.[17] At the completion of that program, students who still fell below a certain threshold on the standardized exam were required to repeat a grade. The authors explain:

> One can thus identify the impact of these programs by simply comparing students who scored just below and just above the promotional cutoff. For example, if students who missed the cutoff (and were thus required to attend summer school) learned much more than students who just made the cutoff (and thus avoided summer school), then one might conclude that summer school had a positive impact on student achievement.

The same basic methodology can be used to compare the outcomes for students who attended summer school and then narrowly passed the exam to advance to the next grade to the outcomes for those students who attended summer school but did not pass the exam and were required to repeat a grade. This is an important program evaluation, since the effects of forcing students

---

17. Brian A. Jacob and Lars Lefgren, "Remedial Education and Student Achievement: A Regression-Discontinuity Analysis," *Review of Economics and Statistics* 86, no. 1 (November 2004): 226–244.

to repeat a grade are not obvious. On the one hand, it may promote student achievement by holding students accountable for grade-level material; on the other hand, it has been shown to decrease self-esteem and raise dropout rates. The researchers who studied the Chicago program concluded that the net effect of the programs was "to substantially increase academic achievement among third-graders, but not sixth-graders."

13.3.7 Multivariate Analysis

Multivariate regression analysis is also a valuable tool for measuring a treatment effect. When regression analysis is done correctly, it enables researchers to isolate the association between a particular variable and some outcome of interest while controlling for other variables that might confound the analysis. For example, suppose that researchers are looking to see whether a particular sex-education program delays the onset of sexual activity. The dependent variable might be the age at which an individual first becomes sexually active. The independent variables would include data for a number of potential explanatory factors, or control variables, such as socioeconomic status, region of the country, religious background, and so on. In addition, the regression equation would also include a dummy variable that signals whether or not the individual participated in the sex-education program that is being evaluated. This variable is often called the **treatment dummy.** If the regression equation is specified correctly, then the coefficient on the treatment dummy should measure the relationship between participation in the sex-education program and the onset of sexual activity, controlling for other relevant factors.

Regression analysis is not a miracle worker, however. The quality of the analysis depends on ensuring that the observed relationship is actually causal—that the treatment variable causes the observed change in the outcome of interest. Regression analysis is prone to two common problems. First, the causality may run in the opposite direction (or even in both directions). Suppose, for example, that researchers are interested in the relationship between the crime rate in a particular location and the number of police on the street. A simple regression with the crime rate as the dependent variable and the number of police per capita would miss an important confounding factor: communities often put more police on the street in response to rising crime rates. The regression coefficient could easily (and wrongly) suggest that more police on the street is associated with more crime. Obviously, the police are not causing that crime; they are responding to it—though a mere statistical association cannot determine the difference between the two.

Second, regression analysis can present a misleading picture when an observed relationship between an outcome of interest and some intervention is in fact caused by some unobserved variable or variables associated with the intervention rather than by the intervention itself. To use the symbolism introduced earlier, the regression analysis might erroneously suggest that A is causing B, when in fact the missing variable C is causing both A and B. The highly competitive college question raised at the beginning of the chapter is a perfect example. Suppose that researchers are interested in whether or not attending an Ivy League college or university raises wages later in life. The dependent variable would be some measure of postgraduation income; the treatment dummy would measure whether or not the individual attended an Ivy League institution. But we know from the introductory example that highly competitive colleges select students who are extremely talented. The Ivy League dummy variable could be wrongly interpreted to mean that attending an Ivy League institution *causes* higher earnings later in life, when, in fact, a more likely explanation (or, at least, partial explanation) is that both attending an Ivy League school and making more money later in life are caused by other unobserved factors, such as intelligence, hard work, creativity, and so on.

In many cases, regression analysis can be used as a complement to the other tools discussed in this chapter. The program evaluation techniques discussed in this chapter can be used to solve what researchers often describe as the **identification problem,** which is the challenge of ensuring that the observed relationship between the treatment and the outcome of interest is indeed causal and not merely reflecting other extraneous factors. For example, one recent research paper used a natural experiment in combination with regression analysis to probe the relationship between television and test scores. Conventional wisdom, of course, is that young children who watch a lot of television will suffer academically. A simple comparison of test scores between students who watch television and those who don't would be misleading, since watching lots of television is likely to be correlated with other factors that dampen student achievement, such as inattentive parents. Even a regression analysis with a variable measuring television watching (such as number of hours a week) would likely be rendered inaccurate by missing information on the students being evaluated, such as the quality and attentiveness of their parents. Basically, this is the opposite of the Ivy League education challenge: Is it the television viewing that is causing lower test scores, or is it other factors associated with families whose children watch lots of TV? As one of the authors explained to the *Wall Street Journal,* "What are the reasons why some kids watch six hours of TV a day and some kids watch none?

Clearly it has to do with their parents and what kind of parenting they are doing; it has to do with how smart they are and how much they like doing other things like reading; it has to do with what socioeconomic resources they have. Do they have a nanny who's taking them to the museum every day versus sitting home alone?"[18]

Matthew Gentzkow and Jesse M. Shapiro, both economists at the University of Chicago Graduate School of Business, found a clever way to isolate the effect of television viewing.[19] Television was introduced in the United States in the late 1940s, but it came to different cities at different times, depending on when the Federal Communications Commission (FCC) granted the broadcasting licenses. The FCC granted no licenses between 1948 and 1952 because of problems in the way the broadcast spectrum was being allocated. As a result, there was a relatively long stretch when some cities had television and others did not, and it had nothing to do with the quality of parenting in those cities. The economists examined data on tests administered across the country to over 300,000 sixth-, ninth-, and twelfth-grade students more than a decade after this natural experiment (1965). But the authors did not merely compare the test scores of students in cities with television when they were young to students in cities without TV during the same childhood period; that difference could be explained by other sources of variation between the cities, such as income gaps or different levels of public spending on education. So the authors used multivariate regression analysis as well to control for other location-related characteristics.

What did they find? Controlling for factors such as population and income, exposure to television during the preschool years is associated with slightly *higher* test scores later in life. The effect is particularly strong for less educated households and for households in which English was not the primary language spoken. The authors caution that their results are limited to the effects of television viewing on young children as measured by achievement tests taken as adolescents. Similarly, they point out that the television content children are likely to watch today could be more or less educational than the content children watched during the 1950s. Nonetheless, the study is far more sophisticated—and, therefore, far more potentially valuable to policy makers—than an analysis that merely examines the correlation between television viewing and academic performance.

18. Justin Lahart, "A New View on TV," *Wall Street Journal*, September 6, 2008.
19. Matthew Gentzkow and Jesse M. Shapiro, "Preschool Television Viewing and Adolescent Test Scores: Historical Evidence from the Coleman Study," *Quarterly Journal of Economics* 123, no. 1 (February 2008): 279–323.

13.4 CONCLUSION

Program evaluation is a crucial component of policy analysis. Officials are often using public money to deal with important social problems. Citizens deserve an answer to the most basic question related to any program or policy: Does it work? That question is often more difficult to answer than it would first appear. The key to any accurate program evaluation is effectively isolating the treatment effect—the difference in outcomes that can be attributed to the relevant program or intervention. The "gold standard" of program evaluation is a randomized experiment in which the experimental group can be compared to a control group that is identical but for the treatment being evaluated. Since logistics and ethics often preclude such experiments in many situations related to public policy, researchers must instead adopt other strategies for measuring the impact of a policy intervention.

Rigorous program evaluation ensures that public resources are used as efficiently as possible. Program evaluation also makes it possible to replicate successful programs and abandon those that don't work. Indeed, the implementation of any new policy or program should include a mechanism for evaluation, including a process for collecting and analyzing relevant data.

FOR DISCUSSION

The Economics of Political Incorrectness: Does Abortion Lower Crime?

In 1999, two academics made a bold and controversial claim. John Donohue of Stanford University Law School and Steven Levitt of the University of Chicago (who would go on to write *Freakonomics*) presented evidence suggesting that much of the sharp drop in crime in the United States during the 1990s was caused by the legalization of abortion twenty years earlier as the result of the Supreme Court's *Roe v. Wade* decision in 1973. Donohue and Levitt argued that crime fell sharply in the 1990s because many would-be criminals were never born; they were aborted instead. Their original study on the subject argued that "legalized abortion appears to account for as much as 50 percent of the recent drop in crime."[20]

Donohue and Levitt based their argument on three strands of evidence:[21]

1. The precipitous drop in crime in the United States coincided with the period when the cohort born right after *Roe v. Wade* reached ages eighteen to twenty-four, which is the "criminal prime." Many prospective criminals who would have begun committing crimes roughly twenty years after *Roe v. Wade* were literally not born because abortion was a legal option instead. However, the crime rate for older cohorts, who would not have been affected by *Roe v. Wade,* did not drop during the same period.

2. Five states legalized abortion before *Roe v. Wade,* setting up a natural experiment. The states that legalized abortion in 1970 experienced drops in crime before the forty-five other states and the District of Columbia, none of which legalized abortion until required to do so by the Supreme Court in 1973.

3. A multivariate analysis found that states with higher rates of abortion in the 1970s and early 1980s had less crime during the period 1985–1997, even after controlling for other explanatory factors at the state level, such as income, poverty, unemployment, level of incarceration, and number of police.

Donohue and Levitt argued that abortion reduces crime through two avenues: "First, women who have abortions are those most at risk to give birth to children who would engage in criminal activity"—teenagers, unmarried women, and the economically disadvantaged. Second, abortion enables women "to optimize the timing of

20. John J. Donohue III and Steven D. Levitt, "The Impact of Legalized Abortion on Crime," *Quarterly Journal of Economics* 116, no. 2 (May 2001): 379–420.

21. "The Criminal Unborn," *The Economist,* August 12, 1999.

childbearing." When abortion is legal, a woman is more likely to have a child during a period in the life cycle when she can provide a nurturing environment; she is more likely to choose abortion when life circumstances are adverse to raising a child, such as when the father is not present or she has used drugs during the pregnancy. The result, the authors write, is that "children are born into better environments, and future criminality is likely to be reduced."

Donohue and Levitt emphatically point out that the findings are not meant as a justification for abortion. They write in the paper, "In attempting to identify a link between legalized abortion and crime, we do not mean to suggest that such a link is 'good' or 'just', but rather, merely to show that such a relationship exists. In short, ours is a purely positive, not a normative analysis, although of course we recognize that there is an active debate about the moral and ethical implications of abortion."

The "abortion reduces crime" argument set off an immediate backlash among social conservatives (despite the authors' admonition that the work was merely positive analysis). More relevant to this chapter, the paper also began a methodological debate that continues to the present. Does abortion really reduce crime, or do Donohue and Levitt merely confuse correlation with causation? Several strands of argument have been launched against the original finding, including the following.

Ted Joyce, a professor of economics at Baruch College, argues that the changes in criminal activity for cohorts born right after *Roe v. Wade* are not significantly different than changes in criminal activity for older cohorts, who were not affected by legalized abortion.[22] So, for example, if crime rates fell for twenty year olds roughly two decades after abortion was legalized, then we should also examine whether there is a similar pattern for thirty year olds—a cohort not affected by changes in the abortion laws. Joyce finds no significant difference among the cohorts. Instead, he attributes the Donohue and Levitt findings to the crack cocaine epidemic, which arose, peaked, and declined at different times in different places. Joyce also gives two reasons for why legalizing abortion may have little effect on unwanted childbearing: (1) many women were getting illegal abortions before the procedure became legal, and (2) although the number of abortions increased dramatically after *Roe v. Wade,* so did the number of pregnancies. The number of births per 1,000 women was essentially unchanged between 1973 and 1980.

The original paper was also indicted on technical grounds. Researchers at the Federal Reserve Bank of Boston found a computer coding error in the statistical analysis that compromises some of the conclusions.[23] (An article on Donohue and Levitt's statistical error in *The Economist* was entitled "Oops-onomics.")

---

22. Ted Joyce, "Did Legalized Abortion Lower Crime?," *Journal of Human Resources* 39, no. 1 (Winter 2004): 1–28.

23. Christopher L. Foote and Christopher F. Goetz, "The Impact of Legalized Abortion on Crime: Comment," *Federal Reserve Bank of Boston,* Working Paper No. 05-15, January 31, 2008.

Donohue and Levitt have responded in turn. They have acknowledged an inadvertent coding error in their original work but insist that their findings remain sound based on a "collage of evidence."[24] They have also "critiqued the critique" by Ted Joyce on the grounds that his study looks at crime rates for a narrow, anomalous period. In a follow-up paper, Donohue and Levitt present new evidence arguing "that Joyce's failure to uncover a negative relationship between abortion and crime is a direct consequence of his decision to focus exclusively on the six-year period 1985–90 without including adequate controls for the crack epidemic. We provide empirical evidence that crack hit the high-abortion early legalizing states harder and earlier. We then demonstrate that using precisely the same treatment and control groups as Joyce, but extending the data analysis to encompass the lifetime criminal experiences (as opposed to an arbitrary six-year window), the evidence strongly supports the hypothesis that legalized abortion reduces crime."[25]

Meanwhile, new evidence is coming from an unlikely source: Romania. In 1966, the leader of Romania, Nicolae Ceauşescu, banned abortion, which previously had been a common form of birth control. The birth rate rose from 1.9 to 3.7 births per woman in the course of a year—essentially setting up the *Roe v. Wade* experiment in reverse. Would more unwanted births lead to higher crime rates when those children reached young adulthood? The preliminary answer is yes, according to Cristian Pop-Eleches, a professor of economics at Columbia University. Romanian cohorts born after 1970 have higher crime rates during adulthood.[26] Of course, those children entered their criminal peak when other social phenomena were at work, namely the unraveling of Soviet dominance over Eastern Europe.

This correlation-versus-correlation debate is not over.

QUESTIONS

1. What are the policy implications of this dispute, if any?
2. Are you persuaded that there is a link between abortion and crime?
3. If you were convinced beyond a doubt that legalized abortion does reduce crime, would it change your views regarding abortion in any way? Why, or why not?
4. Can you think of any other natural experiments that might present research opportunities related to this question?
5. One argument in favor of this strand of research is that it can help to shed light on crime-fighting strategies that don't work. For example, in related work Levitt demonstrates that the sharp decline in crime between 1991 and 2001 can be

24. "Oops-onomics," *The Economist,* December 1, 2005.

25. John J. Donohue III and Steven Levitt, "Further Evidence That Legalized Abortion Lowered Crime: A Reply to Joyce," *Journal of Human Resources* 39, no. 1 (Winter 2004): 30–49.

26. Cristian Pop-Eleches, "The Impact of an Abortion Ban on Socioeconomic Outcomes of Children: Evidence from Romania," *Journal of Political Economy* 114, no. 4 (August 2006): 744–733.

attributed almost exclusively to four factors: increased imprisonment; the waning crack epidemic; increases in the number of police; and, of course, the legalization of abortion.[27] The implication is that factors most commonly mentioned in the media, such as more innovative policing and tougher gun-control laws, appear to have no significant effect. Does this line of reasoning change your view on the value of studying the abortion–crime link?

6. Would you object to the government funding research on this topic? Why, or why not?

KEY CONCEPTS

★ Program evaluation uses analysis and quantitative tools to determine the impact of a program, policy, or other intervention.

★ The treatment effect is the causal impact of a policy, program, or other intervention.

★ The counterfactual is what would have happened to the same set of actors under an alternative set of circumstances.

★ A selection effect, or selection bias, occurs when the participants in some treatment are significantly different in some important respect from the nonparticipants to whom they are being compared.

★ Two variables are correlated if a movement in one is associated with a movement in the other. Two variables have a causal relationship if a change in one brings about a change in the other. Good public policy depends on identifying and measuring causal relationships—when a certain intervention causes a certain outcome—but also recognizing when two outcomes do not have a causal relationship.

★ The dropout effect, or survivorship bias, can seriously skew the apparent outcomes of a program if a nonrandom group of participants quit or are removed from the program during the period of analysis.

★ Researchers sometimes have the luxury of designing experiments to test the effectiveness of a policy program. A large, eligible population is identified for some kind of policy intervention, and a random mechanism is used to separate those who will receive the treatment from those who will not. A difference in outcomes between the two groups can be attributed to the treatment.

★ Natural experiments occur when some unintentional intervention creates the opportunity to compare a group that participated in a program with another group that was similar in all important respects but was randomly excluded from receiving the relevant treatment.

---

27. Steven D. Levitt, "Understanding Why Crime Fell in the 1990s: Four Factors That Explain the Decline and Six That Do Not," *Journal of Economic Perspectives* 18, no. 1 (Winter 2004): 163–190.

★ In the case of a nonequivalent control, the subjects in the control group are thought to be largely similar to the subjects in the treatment group, but the assignment is not random.

★ Time-series analysis uses longitudinal data to compare some outcome of interest before and after a particular intervention or treatment.

★ Multiple time series, or difference in difference, compares longitudinal data for a treatment group with longitudinal data for a similar but nonrandom group that has not received the treatment. The important assumption is that the two groups are largely comparable but for the treatment and that any significant difference in outcomes over time between the two can be attributed to the program or policy being evaluated.

★ Discontinuity studies exploit the fact that some treatments have a rigid cutoff, making it possible to compare outcomes for those who are just barely eligible for the treatment with the outcomes for those who just missed the cutoff and, therefore, did not receive the treatment.

★ When regression analysis is done correctly, it enables researchers to isolate the association between a particular variable and some outcome of interest while controlling for other variables that might confound the analysis.

MAKING POLICY

CHAPTER 14

The Role of Institutions

A CONSTITUTION FOR IRAQ

The quick dispatch of Saddam Hussein's army in the 2003 invasion of Iraq almost immediately gave way to the larger and ongoing challenge of restoring order and building a civil Iraqi society. For a generation, Iraqi society had been ruled by dictatorship; the eradication of Saddam Hussein's autocracy left a governance vacuum. Drafting a constitution would be a crucial step toward building a democratic Iraq and a rejoinder to Saddam Hussein's boast that "a constitution is written by men so that another man can tear it up."[1] Nearly a decade after Hussein's autocratic regime was toppled, Iraq is still struggling to build and sustain democratic institutions.

The first step was drafting a constitution. In most democratic nations, a constitution is the blueprint for how society governs itself. In the case of Iraq, the constitution would have to address some of the most fundamental questions of political philosophy: the rights of individual citizens relative to the state; the role of religion in society; the rights of women; the balance of power between the central government and the provinces. In addition, the constitution would have to lay out the basic institutions for making democratic decisions, interpreting laws, and resolving disputes.

These are not mere technocratic issues that can be ironed out by legal experts. The challenge of building a civil society in Iraq was made difficult not only by years of dictatorship, but also by deep religious and ethnic schisms. Saddam Hussein's government was dominated by Sunni Muslims despite the fact that they made up less than 20 percent of the population. Iraq's Shia (or Shiite) Muslims had been denied power not only under Saddam Hussein, but for most of Iraq's history. The Iraq Study Group, the esteemed group of foreign-policy experts convened to advise the United States on the Iraq War, noted in their 2006 report, "The Shia, the majority of Iraq's population, have

---

1. Jonathan Morrow, "Iraq's Constitutional Process II: An Opportunity Lost," Special Report, United States Institute of Peace, Washington, D.C., December 2005.

gained power for the first time in more than 1,300 years. Above all, many Shia are interested in preserving that power."[2]

Meanwhile, Iraqi Kurds, concentrated in the north of the country, had also been oppressed under Saddam Hussein and were eager to gain autonomy or even independence. Thus, any constitution would have to balance democratic control by the Shia majority with institutional protections that reserved power for the Sunnis, Kurds, and other minority groups—in the face of centuries of distrust and bloodshed. In a report for the United States Institute of Peace, Jonathan Morrow explained that a successful constitution would be "a kind of intercommunal peace treaty." Iraq's large reserves of oil and natural gas compounded the constitutional challenge. The richest reserves of oil and gas are in the Kurdish north and the Shia-dominated southern provinces. Any agreement that left oil revenues substantially in the hands of the provinces would further disadvantage the Sunnis.

At best, a new constitution would provide an institutional framework for resolving long-standing disputes and building a peaceful nation going forward. Countries such as South Africa have used new democratic institutions to help heal deep societal wounds. At worst, the constitution would merely codify and deepen the existing schisms. Sadly, both the process for drafting and approving the Iraqi constitution and the agreement itself appear to have failed as tools for facilitating national reconciliation. The process for drafting a constitution was dictated by the Transitional Administrative Law (TAL), which was implemented after the coalition forces toppled the Hussein government. The TAL stipulated that Iraqis would elect a transitional National Assembly, which would be responsible for approving a draft constitution. The draft constitution would go into effect once ratified by a majority of Iraqi voters in a national referendum. However, TAL Article 61(C) also created a veto; the constitution would not be approved if two-thirds of the voters in three of Iraq's eighteen provinces voted it down.

Iraq's transitional National Assembly approved a draft constitution on September 18, 2005; it was approved by referendum on October 15, 2005. Yet at every turn, the constitutional process appears to have deepened wounds, more than healing them. The critique of the constitutional process stretches from the composition of the drafting committee to allegations of vote fraud in the national referendum:

- **The draft constitution was negotiated largely without Sunni input.** The National Assembly created a Constitution Drafting Committee with Sunni

---

2. James A. Baker III and Lee H. Hamilton, co-chairs, *The Iraq Study Group Report* (New York: Vintage, 2006), p. 13.

representatives. However, after only a month of work, this group was disband-ed and replaced by a Leadership Council with no women and no non-Kurdish minorities. According to Morrow's report for the United States Institute of Peace: "The expectation was quite clear: the Shia and Kurdish parties would agree to a constitutional text, which would then be presented as a fait accompli to the Sunni Arabs, who would be asked to take it or leave it."

- **The constitutional drafting process was not part of a larger national dia-logue on the future of the nation.** Security concerns limited access between representatives and their constituents. According to Morrow, "Every meeting on the Committee, the National Assembly, and the Leadership Council took place behind the blast walls, barbed wire, and gun turrets of Baghdad's International Zone. . . . The opportunity for Iraqis to communicate, either for-mally or informally, with their constituent representatives was practically nil."

- **Once the constitution was drafted, there was relatively little time allot-ted to explain and sell it to the nation.** The Iraqi "Outreach Unit" had eight weeks to explain and sell the proposed constitution. In other recent cases, East Timor had a six-month outreach process to introduce a new constitu-tion; Afghanistan took fifteen months.

- **The constitution was approved without any significant Sunni support, reinforcing rather than ameliorating a "fault line that profoundly divides Iraqi society."**[3] Shia and Kurdish regions approved the constitution with 95-percent supporting it.[4] Yet nearly every single voter (99.96 percent) in the Sunni-dominated Anbar province voted against the proposed constitu-tion. Over 80 percent of citizens voted no in the predominately Sunni Salah ad Din province. The constitution was also rejected by 55 percent of voters in Nineveh province, short of the two-thirds requirement that would have invoked the veto. (And that outcome was accompanied by credible allega-tions of electoral fraud.)[5]

The Iraqi constitution was an institutional success in the narrow sense that it created a parliamentary democracy supported by a majority of the nation's population. It was a failure in the broader and arguably more important mis-sion of building a society with institutions capable of making communal deci-sions viewed as legitimate by all participants, including those who disagree with them. In contrast, the U.S. Constitution and other constitutions around the world have endured because they are perceived as creating a fundamentally

3. Morrow, "Iraq's Constitutional Process II."
4. "New Constitution, Old Gripes," *The Economist,* October 29, 2005.
5. "New Constitution, Old Gripes."

fair process for making democratic decisions while simultaneously protecting certain individual rights. The Iraqi constitution cannot claim such legitimacy, which is one reason for the ongoing political violence. Many parties, including the Iraq Study Group, have recommended a process of constitutional review that would remediate some of the shortcomings described here. Of course, any review would be subject to the same political schisms as the first constitutional process; and any constitutional changes giving more power or autonomy to Sunnis would have to be approved by the Shia-dominated government set up under the existing constitution—essentially a voluntary divestiture of power. One thing is clear: to achieve peace and prosperity, Iraq will need effective institutions—laws, organizations, and commonly accepted practices—that make it possible for the nation to make communal decisions perceived as legitimate by all segments of society.

Institutions are the laws, organizations, and unwritten rules that make public policy possible. Groups ranging from a handful of homeowners to nations of hundreds of millions of people create institutions to facilitate their communal interactions. The federal government is obviously an institution; yet it is important to note that the Senate, House of Representatives, and Supreme Court are distinct institutions within that government, each with its own responsibilities, structure, and rules. School districts and neighborhood associations are institutions, as are the United Nations and the World Trade Organization. More broadly, institutions can also be a set of formal rules or even commonly accepted practices that govern human interaction. As the Iraqi-constitution example demonstrates, good institutions are a precondition for good public policy. This chapter will explore the attributes of effective institutions. It will also explain how an understanding of institutions and their limitations can help to explain policy outcomes that might not otherwise make sense.

CHAPTER OUTLINE

14.1 THE ROLE OF INSTITUTIONS

Groups—from neighborhood organizations to the sovereign nations of the world—create institutions to make and implement communal decisions. To that end, effective institutions must be capable of doing the following:

1. Aggregating the preferences of the members who make up the relevant group. How do the millions of citizens in the United States decide whether or not to invade a country? How do the member nations of the United Nations decide to impose sanctions on another country? How does a condominium association decide whether or not to plant flowers at the entrance to the building? Any group needs a process for translating the diverse views of its members into a communal decision. This can be anything from a show of hands at a public meeting to the elaborate procedures of the United Nations Security Council. One important insight is that different processes for aggregating preferences, such as using different voting rules, can lead to different outcomes, even when the preferences of the members of the group are unchanged. For example, it is arguable that Al Gore would have won the American presidential election in 2000 if the race were determined by popular vote rather than the electoral college, even without changing a single vote cast. The same voters with the same preferences would have selected a different president using a different (and perfectly reasonable) democratic process for aggregating their preferences.

2. Implementing and enforcing communal decisions. Effective institutions must have the capacity to carry out their policies in a way that achieves the intended effect. By definition, public policy involves changing behavior, often through coercion. Thus, public policy involves preventing some party or parties from doing something that they would otherwise choose to do (such as polluting or selling cocaine); or it involves compelling some party or parties to do something that they would otherwise choose *not* to do (such as planting flowers near the entrance to the condominium building or driving 25 miles per hour in a school zone rather than 45). **Public institutions** must have the capacity to design, operate, and enforce policies consistent with their members' preferences.

3. Protecting minorities and dissenting views. What mechanisms are in place to protect individuals or small groups from the "tyranny of the majority"? Most public institutions in the developed world are democratic, yet such institutions usually include nondemocratic mechanisms designed to safeguard certain minority rights or views. For example, the Bill of Rights explicitly protects the freedom of expression of all Americans, even if an overwhelming majority of citizens consider some of the views wrong or objectionable. Similarly, the United Nations was designed so that the five permanent members of the Security Council each have veto power over any United Nations resolution. No modern society would consider it acceptable for 51 percent of the electorate to vote to expropriate all the wealth and property of the other 49 percent of the citizens just because the majority would like to have it. Public institutions must strike a balance between carrying out the will of the majority and protecting smaller groups from that very same democratic process.

What Is a Public Company?

You've almost certainly heard mention of *public companies*. But that term should not be confused with our discussion of public institutions. A **public company** is a for-profit firm owned by its shareholders. Any member of the public can buy shares in a public company on a stock market, such as the New York Stock Exchange. Firms such as Microsoft, General Electric, and Starbucks are public companies. Despite the term *public company,* these firms are private for purposes of our discussion: (1) their goal is to maximize profits for the owners of the firm; (2) only those individuals who have opted to buy shares have an ownership stake in the firm; (3) members of the general public who are not shareholders have no more authority or ownership over these firms than they do over the local dry cleaner or any other private business.

14.2 WHY CAN'T GOVERNMENT OPERATE LIKE A BUSINESS?

One often hears the lament that public institutions are slow and inefficient, relative to the private sector. If basic economic analysis suggests that an employee at FedEx has more incentive to be helpful and courteous than a clerk at the Department of Motor Vehicles (DMV), then might one reasonably ask why we should have the DMV at all? Why can't we just turn over those responsibilities to a more efficient private firm? The answer to this question lies in the fact that public and private institutions are fundamentally dissimilar.

1. Public institutions are generally assigned tasks that the private sector will not or cannot do. To use an extreme example, if a public housing project were turned over to a profit-maximizing firm, the management would identify the key "problem" immediately: the public-housing project is full of poor people, who can't pay market-rate rent and often have social problems that make them bad tenants. The logical business decision would be to expel the low-income tenants and replace them with wealthier renters. But that's not the mission of public housing. As extreme as this example appears, the point is that public institutions are often created to provide goods and services that cannot or will not be provided cost-effectively by a private firm. Public housing is necessary in some places because the private housing market has not provided sufficient housing for individuals and families with little or no income.

2. Public institutions are often assigned a particular responsibility when a profit-maximizing firm doing the same task would have an incentive to behave in ways that might cause social harm. The profit incentive is usually a good thing; it motivates innovation, efficiency, better service, lower costs, and so on. In some circumstances, however, that same profit motive can have pernicious social consequences. Private firms maximize profits by pleasing customers; that should not necessarily be the goal of a building inspector, a health inspector, or the person who conducts driving tests at the Department of Motor Vehicles. Some applicants should *not* get their driver's license; it is in society's best interest that some customers leave the DMV disappointed or even angry. If private firms were allowed to grant driver's licenses, they would have an incentive to compete for customers by offering better service and lower prices—but perhaps also by making it easier to get a license. This last form of competition might please customers and earn extra profits for the firm, but it would be potentially dangerous for other motorists and pedestrians.

3. Private firms can measure success in dollars and cents, which makes it easier to define goals and measure success. What is the goal of Ford Motor Company or Microsoft? The answer: to earn profits for the owners of the company, who are its shareholders. Executives at both firms would say that they have many other objectives: producing good products, being a good corporate citizen, maintaining strong relations with suppliers and employees, and so on. But those are intermediate objectives, all of which are likely to maximize profits in the long run. The fundamental objective at these companies—and all other for-profit firms like them—is to maximize profits. Thus, if there is a decision to be made between a project that will produce a return of 9 percent on invested capital and a competing project that will produce a return of 6 percent, the answer is obvious: the firm will choose the project with the higher expected return. Similarly, a firm with a stock price that has climbed 50 percent over some long period is doing better than a firm with a stock price that has increased 21 percent over the same stretch, even if the latter firm has happier employees, higher market share, better relations with the community, or better marks on any other metric. Performance for a private firm is the proverbial "bottom line," which is easily measured (accounting chicanery notwithstanding) and compared across firms. This does not necessarily make managing private firms easy (as a Fortune 500 CEO would likely tell you), but it does help to define success and clarify the objectives of the firm.

Compare that to a public institution such as a school district. The objective of a school district is to maximize student achievement—but the seeming clarity of that "bottom line" dissipates quickly. Student achievement is not as easily measured and compared as dollars and cents. Test scores provide an objective measure of student achievement but only up to a point. Suppose a school district has improving math scores but weak writing? Or suppose that average scores are improving but that the gap between black and white students is widening? Public institutions rarely have an obvious "bottom line"; focusing exclusively on an indicator like test scores might give a misleading impression or create pernicious incentives for educators. Managing any institution is more difficult when there is no single criterion for defining and measuring success.

4. Private firms are not democracies; even public companies, which are owned by their shareholders, do not have elaborate protections for dissent. Private firms have no obligation to please anyone but their owners. The owners may find it strategically wise to build consensus within the firm, but they have no obligation to do so. Employees who subvert management decisions can be fired, or they can exercise their right to quit. This kind of hierarchical decision making is obviously faster and more efficient than any democratic process. Public companies, which are owned by their shareholders, do function in a nominally democratic manner. Shareholders elect a board of directors to govern the firm; shareholders vote directly on some items of business. However, such corporations do not have (nor do they need) safeguards that are explicitly designed to protect minority views from the will of the majority. That is a stark contrast to the U.S. Constitution, which grants any single person the power to repudiate a law or action that may be favored by hundreds of millions of citizens, if the majority have violated some constitutional boundary. These kinds of institutional protections make public institutions unwieldy; they can stall or derail actions favored by a majority of an institution's members, or even nearly all of them. But as the example of the Iraqi constitution should have made clear, these kinds of protections are also essential to building peaceful societies. They make institutions stronger in the long run but not faster or more efficient.

5. Public institutions are often given the responsibility of making individuals, firms, and even nations do things that they would otherwise choose not to do. If all fishermen would limit their catch and throw back fish under a certain size, then there would be no need for the U.S. Fish and Wildlife Service to impose such a requirement. And if all taxpayers voluntarily mailed checks to the federal government, then there would be no need for the Internal Revenue Service to conduct audits and prosecute tax cheats. The reality, of course, is that all fishermen do not abide by the conservation rules, and taxpayers do not make voluntary payments to the federal government. Instead, we have created institutions to enforce those rules, and we have granted those institutions sufficient power to coerce compliance.

This is a sharp contrast to market transactions, which are by definition voluntary exchanges. We need not require that customers line up to buy Starbucks coffee, nor do we need to compel Starbucks to sell certain drinks at certain prices. These kinds of decision are made voluntarily by firms seeking to maximize profits and by individuals trying to maximize their own utility. As long as those market activities produce socially efficient outcomes, there is no need to change behavior. Public institutions are usually only necessary when these kinds of voluntary exchanges do not produce a socially efficient outcome. For example, if some market activity produces a large negative externality, such as the CO_2 emissions and other airborne pollutants associated with driving, then society must somehow modify that behavior—through regulation, for example, or a tax that raises the cost of driving. Thus, a society may decide to reduce CO_2 emissions, but individual drivers would still prefer to drive more than the socially optimal amount. (If they didn't, there would be no need for the regulation or tax to change their behavior.)

Even in cases where some group unanimously supports a communal policy—such as a condominium association planting a communal garden or a nation fighting terrorism—each member of the group would still prefer to avoid *paying* for that shared good. You should recall from Chapter 4 that there is a strong incentive for individuals to be "free riders" when they cannot be excluded from sharing the benefits of a public good. In short, markets are in the business of giving people what they want. Public institutions are usually tasked with the opposite: preventing parties from doing something that they would like to do or making them do something that they would otherwise choose not to do.

14.3 INSTITUTIONS AND OUTCOMES

Institutions are frequently at the heart of good public policy—and bad. Institutional limitations are often one of the primary reasons that poor countries stay poor. For example, there is no doubt that many countries in sub-Saharan Africa would benefit from substantial investments in public health, education, and infrastructure. Economic analysis of such investments would almost certainly find that the social benefits exceed the social costs. But many poor countries do not have the institutions necessary to make these kinds of investments. They cannot collect taxes efficiently. They cannot prioritize investments so that the most socially worthwhile projects are done first (thus leaving spending decisions overly influenced by corruption or political favoritism instead). They may not have the capacity to ensure that a project—building a road or vaccinating children—is implemented as designed. They may not even have institutions capable of guaranteeing that funds donated from abroad are put to productive use.

All societies suffer from these problems to some degree, but impoverished nations tend to be plagued with singularly poor institutions. The quality of a nation's institutions is arguably one of the most important determinants of peace and prosperity. For that reason, students of public policy should recognize the important role that institutions play in shaping policy.

1. Institutional analysis can help us make sense of the outcomes that we observe. Many nations (and states and communities) fail to implement policies that would almost certainly make most citizens better off. Some government agencies fail in their public mission or deliver services in a way that leaves citizens frustrated or dissatisfied. These outcomes are often entirely understandable when viewed in an institutional context. Why has the United Nations proved ineffective in confronting many of the most serious global challenges, from genocide to global warming? Because the UN lacks both the authority and the resources to deal effectively with many international issues. In the case of global warming, for example, the UN has no authority to regulate CO_2 emissions or other kinds of polluting activities. In the case of genocide, the UN arguably has the authority to intervene, but it has no standing army and is, therefore, dependent on member nations to provide the troops for a peacekeeping intervention. (The United Nations will be explored in much greater depth in the For Discussion section at the end of this chapter.) A policy outcome often makes perfect sense when viewed in the context of the institution (or lack thereof) that produced it.

2. Institutional analysis can help us create institutions or reform existing institutions in order to get better outcomes. The goal of public policy is to improve lives. In many cases, that requires improving institutions in ways that produce better outcomes. One tragedy related to the September 11 attacks is that American intelligence agencies arguably had enough information to anticipate the terrorist attacks, but the disparate strands of information were not shared in a way that allowed analysts to piece together the plans of the attack. One response to the 9/11 attacks was a reorganization of America's many overlapping intelligence agencies. (In addition to the Central Intelligence Agency and the National Security Agency, each military branch has its own intelligence gathering agency.) The reorganization created a director of National Intelligence, or "Intelligence Czar," to sit atop all the intelligence agencies. The goal of the reform was to address the awesome challenge of gathering and distributing information around the world, combining it with other relevant data and expertise, and getting it all into the right hands as quickly as possible. These are all challenges related to institutional design; the intelligence bureaucracy needs to get the right decision makers enough information to enable them to connect disparate clues, but not so much information that they are overwhelmed by raw data.

Mike McConnell, the former U.S. director of National Intelligence, offers an example of the striking amount of cooperation necessary to act quickly on information gathered from different sources around the world:

> In the spring of 2005, the CIA and the military's Northern Command received information about two passengers aboard a plane flying from the Middle East to Mexico that would shortly cross U.S. airspace. Because the flight was not operated by a U.S. carrier and was not

scheduled to land in the United States, there was no requirement for the passenger list to be reviewed prior to takeoff. Although the airline's ticket agent thought the two passengers appeared suspicious, the flight departed before their names could be checked. The airline passed on the names and the flight information to U.S. authorities, however, and this information was funneled to the National Counterterrorism Center, the U.S. government's hub for all 30 separate government computer networks carrying more than 80 unique data sources. Within hours, the NCTC found information indicating that the two passengers had been placed on a "no-fly list" immediately after 9/11 because they had lived in the United States in the 1990s, had connections to two of the 9/11 hijackers, and possessed pilot's licenses. Based on this information, the plane was denied entry into U.S. airspace, and the pilot decided to return to Europe.[6]

That "real-time coordination and rapid-response" was the result of a specific institutional design. In the private sector, the market is the device that guides and motivates complex activities. Economists sometimes ask, "Who feeds Paris?" which is a rhetorical question designed to draw attention to the complex array of activities that happen every day just in the process of putting food on the table. As was explained in Chapter 7, these activities generally have no need for government coordination; the incentives created by the market ensure that information and resources are allocated as efficiently as possible. Public institutions are different. The market will *not* provide incentives for intelligence agencies and other relevant actors to share information that might avert a terrorist attack. Nor will the market stop a civil war in Africa or ensure that low-income children are vaccinated against polio. Accomplishing such objectives requires effective institutions—rules, procedures, budgets, and personnel that organize resources in order to achieve the task at hand. The quality and success of such institutions has a profound impact on everything from the cleanliness of a public park to the stability of the world order.

3. Institutional analysis can help us to act strategically to get the policy outcomes that we want. Successful policy actors will often exploit institutional rules and procedures in order to achieve a desired outcome—for better

6. Mike McConnell, "Overhauling Intelligence," *Foreign Affairs* 86, no. 4 (July/August 2007).

or for worse. A long-time politician will sometimes be represented as a "fierce bureaucratic infighter"; an agency veteran might be described as an expert at "cutting through red tape." These are individuals who are expert at navigating the formal and informal procedures of an institution or of multiple overlapping institutions. They succeed in getting what they want (or preventing what they don't want), where others—with the same goals and facing the same institutional structure—would not be successful.

In his role as majority leader of the U.S. Senate, Lyndon Johnson was legendary for his skills as a legislative tactician. One of his goals was to pass civil-rights legislation. Such bills had historically been blocked by powerful Southern Democrats who controlled the key Senate committees by virtue of their seniority. (Committee chairmanships were awarded to the longest-serving members of the party in power.) When Johnson became majority leader of the Senate in 1953, 61 civil-rights bills had been introduced into the Senate; not a single one had even made it to the floor for a vote of the full Senate.[7]

Johnson famously remarked, "I do understand power." What he understood was that the Senate as an institution would have to change before it would produce meaningful civil-rights legislation. Johnson used his formal power as majority leader to change the way that committee chairs were awarded. By eliminating the seniority system, Johnson stripped power from the hands of long-serving Southern Democrats and replaced them with committee chairs more favorably inclined toward his legislative agenda. Johnson passed civil-rights legislation not merely by changing minds, but also by literally changing the Senate as an institution.

In some cases, strategic considerations may dictate the choice *among* institutions. In the civil-rights era, for example, activists had many choices for changing American laws related to race and equality. Activists could pursue legal change at the federal level or at the state level. They could also seek judicial redress in federal or state courts. These strategies are obviously not mutually exclusive, but some institutional paths may prove more productive than others. In the case of civil rights, litigation in federal courts often proved more effective than seeking redress legislatively or in state courts. Modern policy advocates make the same kinds of strategic calculations. Advocates on all sides of issues like gun control, abortion, and climate change will pursue policy changes (or defend the status quo) using whatever institutional options are most likely to produce the outcome they want.

---

7. Jill Abramson, "A Soaring Johnson, Ruthless and Crude, but Compassionate," *New York Times,* April 24, 2002.

Institutions and Development:
The Institutional Legacy of Colonialism

Why are some nations peaceful and prosperous while others are ravaged by poverty and civil strife? This is perhaps the most fundamental question in public policy, since it lies at the heart of improving the lives of billions of people around the world.

Experts have long believed that the quality of a nation's institutions—its electoral system, judicial processes, regulatory regime, public infrastructure, and other mechanisms for governance—have a profound impact on its economic success. History provides illuminating examples. After World War II, Germany was divided into two nations, East Germany and West Germany. The two nations had shared a common language, history, and economy up to that point. But after the partition, the democratic and capitalist West Germany thrived while communist East Germany grew increasingly impoverished. The East German state ultimately imploded and was reunified with West Germany in 1990. The differences that evolved between East and West Germany can be attributed almost exclusively to their different governance structures.

The United States initially foundered under the Articles of Confederation, which proved to be an inadequate institution for governing the new nation. The Constitution changed the nation's governance structure to extraordinary effect. A different institution—the Constitution—organized the same people, the same geography, and the same economy into a more productive society.

To what extent can institutions explain the vast disparities in wealth across modern countries around the globe? This research question is trickier than it would first appear. Different parts of the globe have different physical attributes, some more conducive to prosperity than others. Poor countries may end up with bad institutions, rather than the other way around. Researchers have tried to sort out this causality by evaluating the quality of institutions imposed long ago by a colonial power and then examining the long-term economic impact of those institutions on the colonized nation. It turns out that the quality of institutions implemented by a colonizing power has a significant and long-lasting impact on economic growth even a century or more lately.

James Feyrer and Bruce Sacerdote of Dartmouth College examined the long-term economic development of 80 islands in the Atlantic, Pacific, and Indian Oceans, 79 of which were colonized by European powers at some point.[8] Specifically, they sought to examine the relationship between the nature and length of time spent as a European colony and current GDP per capita. Normally any empirical examination of this relationship would be confounded by the fact that the European powers were apt to colonize the most potentially prosperous islands first (e.g., those with the richest natural resources). Thus, any association between the length of colonization and subsequent economic performance would reflect the underlying attributes of the island, not the positive or negative impact of colonial institutions.

The authors cleverly avoided this problem by exploiting the fact that colonization patterns in the world's oceans prior to steamships were determined primarily by wind patterns and currents; the places settled first were simply the easiest to get to by ship. *The Economist* summarizes the subsequent findings: "Some islands were colonized early, some late, for reasons that had much to do with meteorology, and rather little to do with any other intrinsic attractions the islands might offer. The two authors show that the accessible islands, which lay on natural sailing routes, have prospered relative to the others. They put this down in part to the longer period these islands spent under colonial rule. A century as a colony is worth a 40% increase in today's GDP, they argue."[9]

The study does not endorse colonialism. Feyrer and Sacerdote explicitly note that colonization was often catastrophic for the islands' original populations. For example, the native population of Puerto Rico was essentially wiped out within 30 years of Spanish colonization, falling from 60,000 to 1,500. *The Economist* notes the important distinction, "The island may have since prospered, but the original islanders did not." Rather, the research reinforces the important role that institutions play in marshaling a society's resources—human and otherwise—for productive use. Strong and prosperous societies are built upon strong institutions.

14.4 THE ATTRIBUTES OF EFFECTIVE INSTITUTIONS

So what are effective institutions? Broadly speaking, they are laws, organizations, and accepted practices that enable a society to make the best possible use of its resources. An effective institution must have the capacity to carry out effectively the responsibilities that society has entrusted to it, whether that is making laws, collecting taxes, or killing mosquitoes. In general, effective public institutions share the following attributes:

8. James Feyrer and Bruce Sacerdote, "Colonialism and Modern Income—Islands as Natural Experiments," NBER Working Paper No. 12546, October 2006.
9. "Winds of Change," *The Economist,* November 2, 2006.

Authority. An institution must be vested with the requisite control or power to achieve the desired outcome. In most cases, the source and nature of an institution's authority is obvious. The Chicago Police Department is empowered by the citizens of Chicago, through their elected City Council, to enforce the city's laws. That elected government has given the police the authority to use force, even lethal force, if necessary. Chicago police officers have no authority whatsoever in Iowa or New York City. As with many institutions, the authority of the Chicago Police Department is confined to a specific political entity.

The U.S. Army has authority over the soldiers who have voluntarily enlisted. The nature of that enlistment is such that the army can exercise authority over its members at all times and in all places. The U.S. Army can also exercise authority over civilians in areas in which U.S. military forces are engaged, such as Iraq. But by law, the U.S. military has no authority over American civilians on American soil. The federal government, the source of the military's authority, has explicitly forbidden the military from performing any policing functions on domestic soil.

Authority can sometimes derive from the end of a gun. Fidel Castro exercised control over Cuba for nearly five decades. He, like many other autocrats around the world and throughout history, seized control of the apparatuses of the state and used that power to exert authority. Many leaders derive their authority from the loyalty of the armed forces or the effectiveness of the secret police, not from the will of the electorate. The distinction between *authority* (which such regimes have) and *legitimacy* (which they often do not) will be explored in the next section.

Many public policy challenges arise from situations in which there is no institution with adequate authority to deal with the full scope of the problem. Climate change, an issue that clearly transcends national boundaries, is one such challenge. The United Nations is the forum that the world's governments have created to deal with international issues, but the UN has no authority to deal with the behaviors that scientists now believe are associated with climate change. The UN has no authority to regulate carbon emissions. Instead, many nations signed the Kyoto Protocol, which is a treaty in which the signatory nations pledged to reduce their carbon emissions. The United States did not sign the treaty and, therefore, has no obligation to reduce its output of greenhouse gases. (The United States objected to the Kyoto Protocol in part because the treaty did not impose carbon restrictions on developing countries like India and China.) Climate change is a global issue without a corresponding global institution with the authority to impose changes in behavior that would likely lead to a better long-term outcome.

Legitimacy. Does an institution reasonably reflect the preferences of the people over whom authority is being exercised? In the developed world, democracy is the most common mechanism for bestowing such legitimacy. Democratic governments can exercise awesome powers. They can incarcerate citizens, impound their cars, remove children from abusive parents, and even impose the death penalty. These powers are generally seen as legitimate because they emanate from the citizens over whom they are exercised. Legitimate institutions "deserve" the authority they wield, however one may choose to define that. A brutal dictator may have far more authority than an elected politician, but that power is not likely to be seen as legitimate, either by the people over whom it is exercised or the rest of the world. Most authoritarian regimes have authority but not necessarily legitimacy.

Some institutions can acquire legitimacy through nondemocratic means, such as tradition or custom. The British monarchy is inherited, rather than being a democratic choice. No British citizen has ever cast a ballot for the queen, yet the monarchy remains a legitimate institution in the eyes of many (though by no means all) British subjects. Curiously, some figures acquire legitimacy without much formal authority, if any at all. Nelson Mandela represented black South Africans during the transition to a multiracial democracy, despite having been imprisoned for nearly three decades and having no formal authority in the South African government. It was obvious that his role as leader of the African National Congress bestowed on him a certain legitimacy to speak for black South Africans during that transition. Mandela obviously gained formal authority when he was later elected president.

Commissions such as the 9/11 Commission and the Iraq Study Group have legitimacy but no formal authority. Their recommendations carry far more weight than if they were made by ten people standing on the street or even by ten members of Congress (who are often seen as having less specific experience and more political motivation for their beliefs). Neither the 9/11 Commission nor the Iraq Study Group had any formal authority; it is up to Congress and the president to implement policies based on the commissions' recommendations.

Mission. A successful public institution must have a clearly defined purpose. It is difficult to do something well if there is serious disagreement about what that "something" is. Public institutions can be plagued by a lack of clarity in their mission or even by conflicting missions. Once again, this is an issue that is more easily sidestepped in the private sector, where the clear long-term goal is to earn the highest possible profits for the owners of the firm. True, firms may have mission statements that include "producing the highest quality product" or "improving the community," but these goals are almost always consistent with maximizing profits in the long run. (If a CEO produces a great product and contributes to the community but consistently loses money for the firm, his or her tenure is likely to be short.)

Public and nonprofit institutions do not have a "bottom line" to help define their mission and impose the discipline to stick with it. Consider the case of Amtrak, America's passenger rail service provider, which arguably has two conflicting missions. Amtrak is expected to provide extensive point-to-point rail service throughout the country *and* operate this rail service efficiently enough to cover its costs and avoid large public subsidies. Amtrak faces political pressure to serve small towns across the country that would otherwise be cut off from the transportation grid. Of course, the more remote a community, the more expensive it is to serve, both because of the distances involved and the relatively low number of riders getting on or off at that destination. Amtrak could operate profitably—if it jettisoned a high proportion of its routes and focused on service in high-density corridors such as New York–Boston–Washington and San Francisco–Los Angeles–San Diego. Or Amtrak could provide excellent service to and from every rail-accessible community in America, if Congress were willing to heavily subsidize the cost of providing that level of service. But it cannot do both.

Budget, personnel, and expertise. To be effective, an institution requires adequate resources (money, personnel, and expertise); the personnel within an institution must also have sufficient control over those resources to carry out any task for which they have responsibility. Once again, there are stark contrasts between private-sector institutions and public and nonprofit institutions. The virtue of markets is that they make capital and labor available to firms with the potential to use them productively. Even the smallest firm with a promising idea can tap credit markets for funding and attract high-quality employees by promising them a share of future returns. (The more risky the venture, the bigger the return they will have to promise.) This is the power of Adam Smith's so-called invisible hand. Good ideas (as measured by potential profits) will attract the talent and resources necessary to bring them to fruition.

Public and nonprofit institutions face different constraints. There is no mechanism through which worthwhile projects will automatically attract funding or personnel. Instead, resources must be allocated by the political process or through some other institutional mechanism. For example, fighting terrorism is clearly an endeavor for which the social benefits are likely to exceed the social costs. Yet capital and labor will not automatically flow to this task; there is no equivalent of the "invisible hand." The federal government must create counterterrorism organizations, allocate funding, hire personnel, set organizational objectives, monitor and evaluate performance against those objectives, and so on—all without the benefit of a "bottom line" to guide these institutional decisions.

The attacks of September 11 exposed failures in America's process for gathering and sharing intelligence. Congress responded by creating the new position of director of National Intelligence, who would sit atop the assorted intelligence agencies and be accountable for carrying out the core mission of protecting the United States and its citizens. But different is not necessarily better. In a 2005 op-ed in the *New York Times*, Richard A. Posner, a judge on the U.S. Court of Appeals for the Seventh Circuit and author of *Preventing Surprise Attacks: Intelligence Reform in the Wake of 9/11*, argued that any person occupying the position of director of National Intelligence would not have sufficient control over the intelligence-gathering apparatus to carry out the job he had been assigned.[10] Posner explained:

> So broad is [the director of National Intelligence's] mandate that should intelligence failures open the way to a new attack on the United States, he will be blamed.
>
> Yet he has not been given the wherewithal to prevent such failures. He can make a budget, true, but it is subject to the approval of the president and Congress. He can move some money and a few employees among agencies, and he can veto the appointment of some second-tier intelligence officials. But he cannot hire or fire the agency heads and he has no command authority—that is, he cannot tell an agency what to do. He has much less authority over the intelligence agencies than the secretary of the Homeland Security Department has over the agencies in his purview—yet after two years, no progress in molding those agencies into an organic unity is discernible.
>
> In short, the director of national intelligence can issue policies and guidelines to his heart's content. But if the agencies ignore (subvert, "interpret") them, he is helpless.

This kind of situation is not unique to the intelligence agencies. In public-school systems across the country, particularly large urban school districts, principals operate with the same constraints as the director of National Intelligence. Principals are routinely held "accountable" for the performance

10. Richard A. Posner, "Important Job, Impossible Position," *New York Times*, February 9, 2005.

of their schools, yet they often do not have control over things as basic as hiring, curriculum, and salaries (all of which are determined at the district level). Nor can they choose their students or determine when a particular student ought to be expelled. For many years, principals in Chicago public schools did not even have the keys to their own buildings. The building was opened and closed by an engineer, who was accountable to district officials, not to the principal of the building in which he worked.

················· **POLICY IN THE REAL WORLD** ················

Institutional Mismatch: Enron, OSHA, and Financial Whistle-Blowers[11]

Employees who report crimes within their own companies, or so-called "whistle-blowers," are an important tool for law enforcement, particularly when the alleged misdeed would otherwise be difficult to detect. Because whistle-blowers are exposing themselves to firing or retribution, lawmakers often create legal protections to encourage them to come forward and protect them after they do. In the wake of Enron and other major financial scandals, Congress passed the Sarbanes–Oxley Act to protect investors from fraudulent accounting; the act included a provision to protect the jobs of financial whistle-blowers.

But a seemingly unimportant institutional detail in the legislation has rendered the whistle-blower provision largely toothless. Sarbanes-Oxley vests authority for investigating and acting upon the claims of whistle-blowers with the Occupational Safety and Health Administration (OSHA) within the Department of Labor. At first glance, this makes perfect sense: OSHA has a long history of investigating employee complaints of corporate wrongdoing. The problem is that OSHA investigators have traditionally responded to whistle-blower complaints related to health and safety violations, such as illegal dumping of chemicals or unsafe working conditions on a factory floor. These transgressions have almost nothing in common with the sophisticated accounting schemes involved in securities fraud. OSHA investigators do not have expertise in accounting or securities law.

11. Deborah Solomon, "Risk Management: For Financial Whistle-Blowers, New Shield Is An Imperfect One; Claims of Employer Reprisal Go to OSHA Investigators Unschooled in Accounting; A Fired CEO Lingers in Limbo," *Wall Street Journal,* October 4, 2004.

"It's probably grossly unfair to ask OSHA to investigate Sarbanes–Oxley complaints because that's not their training or their background," says a lawyer representing a CFO who made a whistle-blower complaint to OSHA accusing his employer of improper accounting.

Several other institutional constraints have threatened the effectiveness of the Sarbanes–Oxley whistle-blower protection:

- OSHA inherited responsibility for investigating whistle-blower claims but was not granted additional funding to hire new personnel or to offer specialized training to existing staff.
- OSHA does not have the authority to issue subpoenas. Thus, the agency has limited power to compel firms to turn over documents that would support a whistle-blower's allegations. Similarly, OSHA cannot compel witnesses to testify under oath, which also limits its investigative capacity.

The Securities and Exchange Commission (SEC) or the Justice Department, both of which have greater financial expertise and more expansive legal powers, would have been more effective institutions for carrying out the whistle-blower provisions of the Sarbanes–Oxley statute.

· ·

Internal incentives. Institutions are managed and staffed by individuals whose incentives may or may not be aligned with the goals and objectives of the institution. Consider the following examples:

- A low-paid building inspector may have a stronger incentive to seek bribes from contractors than to ensure that a building conforms to code.
- A public-school administrator may be more concerned about preserving his or her job than cutting a program that is not working.
- An official in a regulatory agency may be hesitant to rule against a private firm because it will compromise a job opportunity when he or she leaves the public sector.
- Professors may shirk their teaching responsibilities because they are hired and promoted based on research output, not their performance in the classroom.

An institution will be most effective if the internal incentives for employees are structured to reinforce the organization's overall mission. A building inspector may be less tempted to take bribes if he is paid a higher salary (both because he will need the money less and because the cost of getting caught and fired is higher than it is when the job pays poorly). An administrator may be more willing to cut his own ineffective program if he is guaranteed a job somewhere else. University professors will pay more attention to teaching if course evaluations are considered in the tenure decision. It is crucial to get these kinds of internal incentives aligned with the broader mission of the institution.

Enforcement. An institution must have the will and capacity to enforce its decisions, often in the face of significant resistance. Consider two contrasting examples:

1. In 2004, the International Court of Justice ruled that the Israeli security barrier running through parts of the occupied West Bank violated international law. The court has both authority and legitimacy, since it is the judicial arm of the United Nations and was created by the UN charter in 1945. Israel is a member of the United Nations. Yet the court's decision had no impact on the security barrier—or "wall," as its global detractors call it. The International Court has no capacity to enforce its decisions, nor does any other institution take on that responsibility.

2. In 1954, the U.S. Supreme Court ruled in *Brown v. Board of Education* that public schools could no longer be legally segregated. Like the International Court of Justice, the Supreme Court has no independent enforcement power. However, the U.S. Constitution vests the executive branch of the federal government with the power and responsibility for carrying out judicial decisions. Dwight Eisenhower sent the National Guard to Little Rock, Arkansas, to enforce the Supreme Court's edict and integrate the schools, despite local opposition.

A law with no enforcement mechanism is not really much of a law. Clever legislators can exploit this fact by passing policies that give the illusion of action but will in fact have little impact because they contain no enforcement provisions. Violating the law may carry no serious penalty; or, if the penalty is steep, the law may not contain sufficient resources to catch and convict violators.

Rules. Every institution has rules that govern its operation. Often these rules are codified by a governing document, such as a charter or constitution. Some rules may also be dictated by tradition or custom. In any case, the rules have a profound effect on how power is allocated within an institution (such as vesting a great deal of authority with committee chairs or a legislative leader). They can also often affect institutional outcomes in ways that have nothing to do with underlying voter preferences. (In other words, different institutional rules can produce different outcomes, even when the attitudes of the individuals being represented have not changed at all.) For example, one powerful tool in the U.S. Senate is the filibuster, which allows a minority of legislators to kill a bill by discussing it endlessly (or until it is withdrawn).

The filibuster is made possible by Senate Rule 22, which requires 60 votes to pass a motion for "cloture," which is required to end debate on any bill. A group of 41 senators has the power to derail legislation that may be favored by a majority of the Senate. In fact, since Senate seats are allocated by state rather than population, it is entirely possible that a minority of senators representing a group of small states can override the preferences of the vast majority of Americans. If the Senate rules were different, then some bills killed by filibuster would be passed instead.

Is the filibuster a good thing? It depends on whether one is in the minority ("using the filibuster to force deliberation and prevent mob rule") or in the majority ("trying to overcome obstructionist tactics"). The minority party, Republican or Democrat, usually relies on the threat of filibuster to exert power when it could otherwise simply be outvoted. There is nothing in the U.S. Constitution protecting the filibuster; the Senate makes its own rules. But, of course, the process for changing the rules is dictated by the rules. Thus, it would be possible to filibuster any motion calling for an end to the filibuster!

Rules not only create order, they can vest extraordinary power in the hands of a small group or even a single individual. In many legislatures, for example, the Speaker has only one vote, making him or her appear to be one voice among many. In fact, the Speaker is often vested with the power to determine which bills are called to the floor for a vote. This amounts to veto power, since the Speaker can effectively kill any prospective legislation by refusing to call it for a vote. In 2007, Democratic legislators in Texas became so frustrated by their inability to maneuver around the powerful House Speaker Tom Craddick that they rushed to the front of the chamber and attempted to seize his microphone before being restrained by the House sergeants at arms.[12] What caused the revolt? Legislators had become disenchanted with House Speaker Craddick's autocratic style; a majority of House members wanted to get rid of him. The Speaker can be replaced at any time if a majority of members support a motion to "vacate the chair." However, according to the House rules, a motion to vacate is a "privileged motion," and all privileged motions must be recognized by the Speaker. Thus, Speaker Craddick was under no obligation to recognize the motion that would have led to his dismissal, regardless of how many members wanted him gone.

12. April Castro and Liz Austin Peterson, "Craddick Refuses to Surrender Post as House Unrest Boils Over," Associated Press via Yahoo! News, May 26, 2007.

14.5 INFORMAL INSTITUTIONS

Many of the most important institutions governing communal behavior are generally accepted procedures that evolve over time but are not formally codified. These are the "unwritten rules" that help to coordinate and organize human interaction: waiting in line, saving a chair by draping a jacket over it, or allocating picnic space in a park on a first-come, first-served basis. In societies with weak formal institutions, such as in the vast slums surrounding large cities in the developing world, these informal institutions take on a much more important role.

· · · · · · · · · · · · · · · ┌─── **POLICY IN THE REAL WORLD** ───┐ · · · · · · · · · · · · · ·

Informal Property Rights: Chicago Shovelers Protect Their Spots

Chicago is notorious for its cold winters and vicious snow storms. The city has learned to respond—both formally and informally. Formally, the city is responsible for plowing the public streets. Mayors are often evaluated (and sometimes voted out of office) based on how quickly they can get the streets plowed after a major storm. Residents also have informal customs for dealing with harsh winters. A visitor to the city after a major storm might be surprised to see furniture and other odd household items arrayed along public streets marking shoveled areas—everything from easy chairs to saw horses.

There is a method to this junk strewn about the streets. Unlike suburban areas, many Chicago neighborhoods don't have garages or driveways. Residents park their cars on the street near their homes. When the city plows the streets after a major storm, the cars parked on those streets are "plowed in" by dense drifts of snow that can be 3 or 4 feet high. People who have dug their cars out of this wall of snow don't want to do it more than once; so they leave an item of furniture behind to claim "their spot" for when they return.

There is no law allowing residents to protect a parking place on a public street, no matter how much shoveling is involved. In fact, it is technically illegal to place junk (or nice furniture) on a public street. Boston has cracked down on the practice; Chicago did for a brief stretch as well. In 2002, Chicago's mayor Richard Daley declared a halt to the tradition and instructed city workers to begin hauling away any items left on the street.[13] But several years later, he reconsidered; the city no longer hauls away personal items left to protect parking spots after major storms.

To the mayor and members of the City Council, having some junk strewn in the street is better than the alternative, which might be angry residents fighting over parking spaces. Mayor Daley explained at a press conference, "We don't want anyone to have any . . . fights or arguments in regards to those who clean in front of their houses." The mayor says that he gained respect for the "time-honored Chicago tradition" decades ago when his young son was hospitalized with a fatal illness. "I cleaned the whole front of my house because Kevin was very sick. I made sure that any car could get in and out. I didn't put anything there. But it had to be clean because we had to get to the hospital. I had to make sure we could get out of our driveway and out into the street."

City officials say they may reconsider the informal claim-staking if it gets out of hand—although, since there is no formal statute governing the practice, they would first have to define "out of hand."

14.6 CONCLUSION

Good institutions are a prerequisite for good public policy. The importance of institutions can be summarized in a handful of key points.

1. **The quality and nature of an institution will often dictate the quality and nature of the policy outcome.** Public policy requires a process for converting inputs—personnel, money, equipment, expertise—into outputs that improve lives. In cases where institutions are inadequate, poorly designed, or badly managed, the available resources will not be put to their best use.
2. **The same set of preferences filtered through different institutions will yield different outcomes.** One important purpose of institutions is to aggregate the preferences of the relevant group, whether it is a group of homeowners or the citizens of a state. But, as we learned in Chapter 6, there is no perfect mechanism for distilling the complex preferences of a group into a single course of action. As a result, different kinds of democratic processes will yield different results, even when the underlying beliefs of

---

13. Fran Spielman, "Chicago Letting Shovelers Stake Their Claim," *Chicago Sun-Times*, January 5, 2005.

the population represented are the same. The obvious example is the contrast between the U.S. Senate and the U.S. House of Representatives. Both are elected bodies representing all the citizens of the United States, yet they routinely come to different conclusions on the same issue.

3. **Different institutions give more or less power to different parties.** The U.S. Senate and the House of Representatives are not arbitrarily different; they were designed as a compromise between the populous states and the less populous states at the time the Constitution was drafted. The Senate, with two representatives from each state regardless of size, obviously grants more relative power to small states than the House of Representatives does with its proportional representation. The groups affected by any institution will be acutely aware of the power granted to them by the institutional rules and structure relative to other groups.

4. **The lack of an appropriate institution can often make it difficult or impossible to address a policy challenge effectively.** An effective institution must gather the input of its members, decide upon a course of action that is binding on the whole group, and then carry out that policy. If there is no institution with the authority and capacity to perform those three functions, then there is not likely to be an effective policy change. This institutional challenge often manifests itself in the international arena. Nations are loath to yield sovereignty to an international body such as the United Nations, but many policy problems that transcend international borders require a supranational solution.

5. **We explicitly create nondemocratic safeguards.** Nearly all democratic institutions contain features explicitly designed so that the majority will *not* get their way in some circumstances. The Bill of Rights protects the freedom of expression of a single person from hundreds of millions who might vote to silence him. Federal judges, including the Supreme Court, are appointed for life, putting them beyond the reach not only of the electorate, but of the politicians who appoint them. In the case of the Iraqi constitution, the key concern for Sunni Muslims was institutional protections from the Shia majority.

6. **Institutions are inherently difficult to change because the current power structure must approve the change.** When Senate reformers tried to suspend the filibuster rule in order to pass civil-rights legislation in the 1950s, their efforts were filibustered. Similarly, the UN Security Council—whose permanent members are not representative of the world's population by any reasonable standard—can only be reformed by a vote of the Security Council, whose permanent members each have a

veto. New rules must be approved using the existing rules; the beneficiaries of those existing rules are not likely to voluntarily relinquish their own power.

7. **Smart tacticians will manipulate all of this.** Public policy always has involved—and always will involve—pitched ideological battles. For any issue, there are competing visions of the "best" policy. As a result, rational actors will seek to design institutions that maximize their own influence; they will manipulate existing institutions to get favorable outcomes; and, when there is a choice of institutions through which they can pursue their goals (such as state or federal action), they will choose the route that is most likely to succeed.

FOR DISCUSSION

Global Governance:
Reform at the United Nations

The United Nations was created in 1945 to promote international cooperation and prevent the kind of global bloodshed that had twice convulsed the world in the first half of the twentieth century. Unfortunately, the United Nations has not necessarily lived up to its promise.[14] The UN is often described as unrepresentative, excessively bureaucratic, and poorly equipped to deal with the greatest global challenges of the twenty-first century. In 2003, UN secretary-general Kofi Annan appointed an outside panel of distinguished international experts to assess the UN's capacity to deal with global threats.[15] On the eve of the release of that report, *The Economist* pronounced that the UN and the rule of international law are "in crisis" and "increasingly seen as ineffective and anachronistic."[16]

The UN stands charged by many with failing to prevent the kinds of global crises that it was designed to prevent:

The war in Iraq. The UN proved ineffective in curtailing the transgressions of Saddam Hussein and, later on, irrelevant as the United States went to war without authorization of the UN Security Council.

Genocide in Rwanda and Darfur. The UN was created at a time when the world had been shocked by the horror of the Holocaust and was intended to prevent such crimes against humanity. Yet the UN failed to prevent genocide in Rwanda; some 800,000 people were killed in interethnic violence in 1994. Two independent commissions subsequently blamed the UN Security Council for its failure to act.[17]

Terrorism and weapons of mass destruction. The United Nations was chartered at a time when the primary threat to peace was conflict between nation-states. In the intervening sixty years, the nature of the threat to the world order has changed dramatically. September 11 highlighted the capacity of terrorist organizations and other so-called nonstate actors to carry out large-scale violence. The charter of the UN allows member states to employ violence only in two cases: when a country has

---

14. "Special Report: Fighting for Survival—United Nations," *The Economist*, November 20, 2004.

15. *A More Secure World: Our Shared Responsibility,* Report of the Secretary-General's High-Level Panel on Threats, Challenges and Change, December 2, 2004. The full report can be found at http://www.un.org/secureworld/report.pdf.

16. "Special Report: Fighting for Survival—United Nations."

17. Barbara Crossette, "Report Says U.S. and Others Allowed Rwanda Genocide," *New York Times,* July 8, 2000.

been attacked or when such an attack is "imminent."[18] The UN charter does not allow a "preventive" attack against a hostile power that is amassing forces that could be used to devastating effect in the future. The Security Council must explicitly authorize such a strike instead, which it refused to do in the case of Iraq. Iraq did not have weapons of mass destruction; other nations or groups with malevolent intentions may in the future. As *The Economist* has noted, "In a world of lethal weapons, where annihilation could come without warning at a press of a nuclear button, it is unreasonable to expect a country to wait until an attack is imminent." The UN was structured to mediate slow-developing disputes among sovereign nations, not dangers from groups like al-Qaeda that bear little similarity to traditional nation-states and may be armed with weapons that have the capacity to inflict catastrophic damage with little or no advance warning.

Insufficient Authority. The UN has four component parts: the Security Council; the General Assembly; the Economic and Social Council; and the Secretariat, headed by the secretary-general. Ann Florini and Carlos Pascual, foreign-policy experts at the Brookings Institution, have offered the following assessment of the UN's "fundamentally unsound institutional base":

> The fifteen-country Security Council, the only UN body with teeth, gives lopsided power to the victors in World War II, allowing China, France, Russia, the United Kingdom, and the United States each to single-handedly veto any decision. The General Assembly, wherein all 191 UN member countries theoretically have equal voice and power, has degenerated into a Byzantine chamber of largely pointless debates on an endless array of issues large and small. The fifty-three-member Economic and Social Council is, if anything, less effective than the General Assembly. The Secretariat—the staff arm of the UN—is hobbled by extreme micromanagement by member states and a long-standing tradition of weak general management and oversight within the Secretariat.[19]

While the Security Council may have "teeth," the five permanent members, each wielding a veto, say much more about the world in 1945 than they do about the world in the twenty-first century. (The other ten members of the Security Council are elected to two-year terms by the General Assembly and are not vested with a veto.) The simplest indictment of the Security Council is the list of countries that are *not* represented as permanent members:

18. "Special Report: Fighting for Survival—United Nations."
19. Colin I. Bradford, Jr., and Johannes F. Linn, eds., *Global Governance Reform: Breaking the Stalemate* (Washington, D.C.: Brookings Institution Press, 2007), p. 67.

- India, the world's largest democracy and home to more than a billion people, or roughly a sixth of the global population.
- Japan, which has the world's third largest economy.
- All of South America, Africa, and the Middle East.

So how can the UN be reformed to make it more effective and relevant? The Secretary-General's High-Level Panel on Threats, Challenges and Change was chaired by Anand Panyarachun, former prime minister of Thailand, and included fifteen other former heads of state, foreign ministers, and senior diplomats from around the world. Brent Scowcroft, national security adviser for President George H. W. Bush, was the sole representative of the United States. The panel released its report in December 2004 with 101 recommendations for how the United Nations could better address the global reality of the twenty-first century.

The panel exhorted the UN's member nations to tackle the underlying global challenges that lead to international conflict and instability. (Recommendation 1: "All States must recommit themselves to the goals of eradicating poverty, achieving sustained economic growth and promoting sustainable development.") The panel made seven different recommendations related to terrorism, including defining terrorism as "any action . . . that is intended to cause death or serious bodily harm to civilians or non-combatants, when the purpose of such an act, by its nature or context, is to intimidate a population, or to compel a Government or an international organization to do or to abstain from doing any act."

The panel proposed five basic criteria for the legitimate use of force by a member nation:

1. **Seriousness of threat.** Is the potential harm "sufficiently clear and serious"?
2. **Proper purpose.** "Is it clear that the primary purpose of the proposed military action is to halt or avert the threat in question, whatever other purposes or motives may be involved?"
3. **Last resort.** "Has every non-military option for meeting the threat in question been explored, with reasonable grounds for believing that other measures will not succeed?"
4. **Proportional means.** "Are the scale, duration and intensity of the proposed military action the minimum necessary to meet the threat in question?"
5. **Balance of consequences.** "Is there a reasonable chance of the military action being successful in meeting the threat in question, with the consequences of action not likely to be worse than the consequences of inaction?"

The panel proposed two options for enlarging the Security Council in order to "increase the democratic and accountable nature of the body." One approach would create six new permanent seats (without veto) and three new nonpermanent seats to be elected by region (e.g., Africa) for two-year terms. The alternative model for reform would not add any permanent seats, but would instead create eight new four-year-term seats (renewable) and one new two-year (nonrenewable) seat—all "divided among the major regional areas."

The world needs a more effective institution for coordinating global action; the High-Level Panel's recommendations are consistent with that goal. Yet major reform is unlikely in the near future. Any real reform would redistribute power. Pakistan would strenuously protest empowering India, its regional rival, with a permanent seat on the Security Council, just as China (empowered with a veto on the Security Council) would be wary of giving Japan a permanent seat. Indeed, all permanent members would likely look askance at any reform that dilutes their own power. The resulting inaction may be the kind of "collective irrationality" described in Chapter 4. Brookings Institution experts Florini and Pascual conclude:

> If multilateral institutions do not adapt to address today's threats more effectively, those institutions will not be used and they will become increasingly irrelevant. That, of course, would be the worst possible outcome, as it would suit the interests of no country. But it is the default position toward which the international community seems to be heading.

QUESTIONS

1. Did the United Nations fail the United States in the case of Iraq's supposed weapons of mass destruction? Or did the United States fail the United Nations? Or both?

2. Explain how the Iraq situation could have been handled better by the international community and how a more effective United Nations could have facilitated that process.

3. Do you see any similarities between the discussions over UN reform and America's Constitutional Convention? What are the parallels? What are the key differences? How might the compromises that made the Constitution possible inform the negotiations over a more representative United Nations.

4. Agree or disagree: The United States would be better off in the long run if it ceded some authority in international matters to the United Nations.

5. If you were to design a new United Nations from scratch, how would it look? How would decision-making authority be allocated among nations? How would UN decisions be enforced?

KEY CONCEPTS

★ Effective institutions must be capable of doing the following: aggregating the preferences of the members who make up the relevant group; implementing and enforcing communal decisions; protecting minorities and dissenting views.

★ Public institutions are often assigned tasks that the private sector will not or cannot do, such as providing services for the indigent.

★ Public institutions are often assigned a particular responsibility when a profit-maximizing firm doing the same task would have an incentive to behave in ways that would cause social harm.

★ Private firms can measure success in dollars and cents, which makes it easier to define goals and measure success; public institutions usually have broader and less easily measured objectives.

★ Private firms are not democracies; even public companies, which are owned by their shareholders, do not have the elaborate protections for dissent.

★ Public institutions are often given the responsibility of making individuals, firms, and even nations do things that they would otherwise choose not to do.

★ Institutional analysis can help us make sense of the outcomes that we observe, including serious public policy failures.

★ Institutional analysis can help us create institutions or reform existing institutions in order to get better outcomes.

★ Successful policy actors will often exploit institutional rules and procedures, or even change the institutions themselves, in order to achieve a desired outcome—for better or for worse.

★ Institutions are the laws, organizations, and accepted practices that enable a society to make the best possible use of its resources.

★ An institution must be vested with the requisite authority to achieve the desired outcome.

★ Institutions earn and maintain legitimacy by reasonably reflecting the preferences of the people over whom authority is being exercised.

★ A successful public institution must have a clearly defined mission.

★ To be effective, an institution requires adequate resources (money, personnel, and expertise); the personnel within an institution must also have sufficient control over those resources to carry out any task for which they have responsibility.

★ An institution will be most effective if the internal incentives for employees are structured to reinforce the organization's overall mission.

★ An effective institution must have the will and capacity to enforce its decisions.

★ Every institution has rules that govern its operation. The rules have a profound effect on how power is allocated within an institution; they can also often affect institutional outcomes in ways that are unrelated to underlying voter preferences.

★ Many of the most important institutions governing communal behavior are generally accepted procedures that evolve over time but are not formally codified. These are the "unwritten rules" that help to coordinate and organize human interaction.

CHAPTER 15

Policy Design

FIGHTING POVERTY IN BRAZIL

A large segment of the Brazilian population lives in poverty; many of the urban poor live in huge informal slums, or *favelas,* on the outskirts of cities like Rio de Janeiro and São Paulo. At the same time, Brazil has an extremely wealthy upper crust, creating one of the world's largest gulfs between rich and poor. At the beginning of the twenty-first century, the Brazilian government had several poverty-fighting programs in place, which policy makers were eager to reform and expand to make them more aggressive and more effective. But how? Transferring resources to the poor is simple in theory and complex in practice. Consider some of the following challenges:

- Who should be eligible for government assistance, and how much should they receive?
- How should the aid be distributed, given that many poor citizens have no formal address or documentation?
- Will the financial assistance cause behavioral changes that would diminish or perhaps even offset the benefits of the program, such as working less or dropping out of school?
- How can policy makers protect against fraud, both by government officials administering the program and by benefit seekers?
- What is "success," and how can it be measured?

In 2003, with the aid of the World Bank, the Brazilian government created the Bolsa Família ("family grant") program, which combined and expanded four existing antipoverty programs into a single, targeted effort. Bolsa Família had several key objectives: (1) to reduce current poverty and inequality by providing a minimum level of income for extremely poor families; (2) to break the intergenerational transmission of poverty by making the benefits conditional on behavior that will reduce poverty in the long run;[1] and (3) to

---

1. Kathy Lindert, Anja Linder, Jason Hobbs, and Bénédicte de la Brière, "The Nuts and Bolts of Brazil's Bolsa Família Program: Implementing Conditional Cash Transfers in a Decentralized Context," Special Protection Discussion Paper No. 0709 (Washington, D.C.: World Bank, May 2007).

link beneficiaries to other complementary social-service programs that may help them.

Bolsa Família provides cash benefits to over 46 million Brazilians—more than the population of many countries; it is the largest such program in the world. How does it work?

- The program is targeted toward the nation's poorest families. Families with children under age fifteen are eligible if their monthly income is below the government-determined poverty line (US$57 in 2007). The grants range from less than $10 a month up to $50, depending on the size and income of the family.
- Bolsa Família is conditional, meaning that beneficiaries must comply with assorted requirements in order to remain eligible for the cash transfer. All of a family's children must attend school (the quality of those schools is a different challenge); the children must be vaccinated and have regular health checkups; pregnant women must undergo prenatal care; and so on.
- The program is decentralized. Many parts of the program are administered by Brazil's 5,564 municipalities. Each municipality collects a list of eligible beneficiaries, which is submitted to the central government to be checked for duplication and against lists of workers who have jobs in the formal economy. Three national agencies provide formal oversight of the program.
- The Bolsa Família payment is most often made to the female head of household because research has shown that women are more likely than men to invest in the health and education of the family.
- Eligible beneficiaries are not given cash or checks. Instead, they have electronic bank cards (similar to ATM cards), which enable them to withdraw their benefits from a government bank as the funds become available. This lowers administrative costs (no checks to mail) and reduces theft (no checks stolen from the mail); it also introduces recipients to the formal banking sector, helping them to save and to become eligible for credit.

A 2004 survey of Brazilian households found that the Bolsa Família had an immediate and significant effect in reducing inequality and extreme poverty. A World Bank assessment concluded that the Bolsa Família was achieving its core objectives.

- The program raises consumption in a meaningful way. The Bolsa Família grants do not seem like much, but, as one farmer told *The Economist*, during the lean season, while the family awaits the harvest of cashew nuts, "it makes the difference between too little food and enough."[2]

---

2. "New Thinking about an Old Problem: Poverty in Latin America," *The Economist*, September 17, 2005.

- Those who were targeted, the poorest of the poor, are in fact receiving most of the benefits. The World Bank found that the poorest 25 percent of the population were receiving 80 percent of the Bolsa Família funds. Nearly all of the "leakage" (money that didn't go to the poorest Brazilians) went to the next quartile, or "near poor."
- The Bolsa Família does not discourage work among recipients. In fact, the World Bank found that the guaranteed minimum income provided the stability necessary for parents to find better work opportunities rather than scrounge for survival.
- The program promotes other virtuous behaviors. Healthier children and higher rates of school enrollment will strengthen Brazilian society in the long run.

The Bolsa Família is a classic example of the challenges inherent to program design. The question for Brazilian policy makers was not whether the government should help the extremely poor, but *how*. This chapter outlines a process for designing policies that are likely to achieve their objectives, while minimizing costs and unintended consequences. In a democratic system, this process does not happen in a political vacuum. An elegantly designed policy proposal that has no political support is no solution at all. On the other hand, the most politically expedient policies are rarely the most effective. Policy makers must balance substance and politics in order to create policies that are both effective and politically feasible.

CHAPTER OUTLINE

15.1 PROVIDING AFFORDABLE HOUSING: LET US COUNT THE WAYS

Let's suppose that the residents of some metropolitan region have decided that the local economy is being hampered by a shortage of affordable housing, meaning that many workers (or prospective workers) cannot afford to buy or rent homes reasonably near where they work. (Such a conclusion is likely to be debatable, but assume for the sake of example that a consensus has emerged around this need.) Policy makers are looking for a plan that would provide more affordable housing options for workers in the area. How can they accomplish that? In many different ways, it turns out. But each policy will have unique impacts—different costs, different degrees of effectiveness, different political supporters and opponents, and so on. In the case of housing, policy makers can also choose among different levels of government to implement a program. The federal government has an entire department devoted to housing policy: the Department of Housing and Urban Development (HUD).

Most state and local governments also consider housing policy within their purview.

Consider just a few of the possible policy options:

- **Public housing.** The local, state, or federal government could acquire land, build housing, and rent or sell it at subsidized prices to workers who cannot afford market-rate housing.
- **Rent control.** Local government could impose a regulation capping the rent that can be charged for some apartments or homes in the private rental market.
- **Subsidies for private developers.** Local, state, and/or the federal government could provide financial incentives, such as tax breaks, for private developers who build affordable housing units.
- **Changes in zoning laws.** Local government could relax zoning laws (the regulations that dictate what kinds of buildings can or cannot be built in a community) in order to make it easier to build certain kinds of affordable housing, such as apartment buildings.
- **Housing vouchers.** The local, state, or federal government could provide low-income residents with housing vouchers to supplement their incomes and make current market rents more affordable.
- **Do nothing.** Policy makers may conclude that market forces will eventually ameliorate the affordable-housing shortage or that workers or employers will adapt in some way. Or they may conclude that each of the above options has costs or other outcomes that are worse than the status quo. (There is an old policy aphorism: Don't just do something, stand there. It is a reminder that sometimes the wisest course of action is to avoid cures that may be worse than the disease.)

Each of the policies described above will impact the housing market differently. Subsidizing developers to build affordable housing will increase the supply of such units; so would constructing new public housing units or relaxing zoning laws. Giving out rental vouchers may or may not have any impact on the supply of affordable housing. In the short run, the vouchers will give low-income renters more purchasing power to rent existing units, bidding up the price of such units and making them less affordable for other renters. In the long run, developers may respond to this new purchasing power by adding new units (provided that the zoning laws allow such projects). Imposing rent control—requiring landlords to charge lower rents—would reduce the supply of available units in the long run. Developers would have less incentive to build new units (and investors would have less incentive to buy them), if the rent that they can charge is capped below the market rate.

Rent control makes some units more affordable (for those who are lucky enough to get a regulated unit), but it simultaneously constrains overall supply and makes other units less affordable.

Effectiveness aside, each of the above policies would have dramatically different political implications. Real-estate developers would strongly support changes in zoning laws because it would give them more flexibility to build different kinds of projects, such as denser developments or multiunit buildings. The same developers would bitterly oppose rent control because it curtails the profits that they can earn. Landlords—existing property owners who rent out their units—would also fight rent control, since the cap on rents would diminish their income. On the other hand, landlords would strenuously support rental vouchers; this subsidy would increase the purchasing power of renters and ultimately put more money in the pockets of landlords. Whether it is housing or any other issue, the organized interests that rally for or against a policy proposal do not necessarily care about the objective of the policy; they care about the specifics of the policy design. How are the costs and benefits allocated?

For policy makers, any issue has two considerations: (1) what the effects of different policy options will be, and (2) what the political ramifications of each of those options are.

15.2 STAKEHOLDER ANALYSIS

Policy makers must always ask two fundamental questions regarding any prospective policy change: (1) Who will be affected? (2) How will they respond? A policy change must be effective even after rational individuals and firms respond by seeking to protect their interests. Any new policy will require (or provide an incentive for) individuals or firms to do something that they would otherwise not do (e.g., pay taxes, dispose of waste in a certain way, put infants in car seats, etc.). Conversely, a policy may forbid individuals or firms from doing something that they would otherwise prefer to do (e.g., using certain drugs, hiring illegal immigrants, making products with lead paint, etc.). Thus, it is crucial to recognize that the policy must have an effective mechanism for changing behavior and that there will be natural resistance. After all, if individuals and firms were behaving in the desired manner without this mechanism for changing their behavior, then there would be no need for the policy change in the first place. The important exception to this, of course, is any policy change that removes or reduces some tax or regulation previously imposed by the government. If Congress votes to reduce the capital-gains tax, individuals will not need to be coerced to send less money to the government.

Policy makers must anticipate how any affected parties, the **stakeholders,** will seek to evade a policy change that imposes some cost on them. If the enforcement mechanism is weak, they may simply refuse to comply. For example, if motorists are asked to pay a higher toll, some may drive through the collection point without paying if the chances of getting caught are low or if the penalty is modest. More often, rational actors will find ways to evade the policy change legally; they will change their behavior in order to avoid incurring the costs imposed on them. This can be a good thing. If a higher toll is imposed on a congested highway during the peak travel times (e.g., 7:00 a.m. to 9:00 a.m.), some drivers will avoid the higher toll by postponing their travel until after 9:00 or by traveling earlier than 7:00. This response is one of the benefits of the policy; the higher tolls during peak travel hours will spread out some of the traffic and reduce congestion during "rush hour."

Not all responses will be healthy, however. Some motorists may choose to evade the toll by driving on local streets rather than on the highway where the toll is being collected. This is perfectly legal, but it is not how the transportation system was designed. Local streets are intended for short trips at low speeds; it can be dangerous and disruptive for residential neighborhoods to have large numbers of vehicles—especially large trucks—weaving through local roads in order to avoid paying a toll. These kinds of adverse consequences can usually be anticipated (and, therefore, dealt with) by analyzing the incentives created for the affected parties.

If policy analysts neglect to anticipate how stakeholders will react to a policy change, the resulting behavior of the stakeholders may detract from the effectiveness of a policy change or even impose unexpected costs that outweigh the anticipated benefits. This is often referred to as the **law of unintended consequences.** The same clever minds that make the market so effective through innovation and cost-cutting will seek to find ways to avoid doing things that they would prefer not to do. At a minimum, stakeholders who stand to lose from a policy change will seek out loopholes, exemptions, or other ways to continue doing what they were doing. Consider the amusing— but highly instructive—case of Boise, Idaho, where lawmakers sought to ban strip clubs. Because *strip club* is not a legal term, lawmakers instead banned complete nudity in public unless it serves some "serious artistic merit."[3] That was just the wiggle room that the owner of the Erotic City Strip Club was

3. BBC News, February 19, 2005.

looking for. He kept his club open, charging $15 for a sketch pad, pencil, and nude dance performance as part of "art club night."

In more serious cases, a policy change may introduce **perverse incentives,** which are incentives for stakeholders to respond in ways that cause harm. In one famous example, Mexico City introduced a policy to curtail air pollution by restricting driving; motorists were forbidden from driving on certain days of the week, depending on their license-plate number. (Even-numbered plates were allowed on some days, and odd-numbered plates on the others.) In theory, this policy would cut the number of vehicles on the road in half at any given time (and polluting emissions by half as well). In practice, motorists preferred to drive *all* of the days, or else the road-rationing plan wouldn't have been necessary in the first place. One way to evade the restrictions was to buy a second car, putting an even-numbered license plate on one and an odd-numbered plate on the other. This raised the demand for old cars that otherwise would have been junked or at least driven less. Because new cars are so much "cleaner" than old cars from an emissions standpoint, the net effect of the policy was to make air pollution worse, not better. Any new policy must be effective even when rational actors try to evade it, legally or otherwise. One of the most common policy-design errors is to assume that all behavior will remain the same except for the intended policy change. In reality, the process is dynamic, meaning that policy makers must also anticipate and plan for the changes in behavior that a policy is likely to cause.

Meanwhile, any policy change will invite some political resistance, no matter how large the expected benefits are relative to the expected costs. The reason is obvious, once you think about it: any policy change that makes society significantly better off without generating any political resistance would have been implemented a long time ago! Every elected official would like to make all voters happy. Such opportunities are rare, and politicians will seize them quickly; these rare political winners are the proverbial "low-hanging fruit" that is stripped quickly from most trees. Thus, it's far more likely that any policy change worth doing will generate social benefits but also significant costs. The parties who bear those costs will use the political system to fight the change. Successful policy makers must deal with this inevitable political resistance. Even deregulation invites political resistance, since it often exposes previously protected firms to new competition.

Finally, one must take account of the **distributional effects** of a policy change, which is the impact of a policy change on different groups—different income groups, racial groups, neighborhoods, or other relevant considerations. Policy makers must pay attention to the prospective winners and losers from any policy change, not just as a matter of politics, but also as a matter of fairness. Some policies that are highly attractive from an efficiency and cost-benefit standpoint may offend our sense of equity or fairness. For example, most economists would support an increase in the gas tax with some kind of offsetting cut in the income tax. The gas tax (or some other tax on carbon-based fuels) discourages behavior that harms the rest of society, such as pollution. The income tax, on the other hand, deters behavior that is good for society; high marginal income-tax rates will cause at least some individuals to work less. Thus, the gas tax, or something like it, is a far more efficient tax, meaning that it raises revenue without distorting behavior in bad ways (and may actually improve behavior from society's standpoint).

But a gas tax has serious distributional impacts. Low-income families spend a higher proportion of their income on energy than wealthy families do; conversely, an income-tax cut tends to benefit those with the highest incomes. (Many low-income individuals have no income tax burden.) Overall, a higher gas tax would increase the tax burden of low-income individuals relative to wealthier taxpayers, which may not make it an acceptable policy to some from an equity standpoint. Similarly, the gas tax has disparate geographic impacts. Residents of rural areas, particularly in western states, are likely to have lifestyles that involve driving longer distances; they also have fewer public transportation options or none at all. A gas tax would impose a disproportionate cost on certain parts of the country, certain industries, and so on.

There is no scientific formula for evaluating the distributional impacts of a policy change. Fairness is in the eye of the beholder. Nonetheless, the distribution of winners and losers can be be just as important as—if not more important than—a simple comparison of total social benefits to total social costs.

···············| **POLICY IN THE REAL WORLD** |···············

Balancing Substance and Politics: The "Wonks" and the "Hacks"

Americans have an expression for individuals with a studious appreciation for the elaborate substance of public policy, regardless of its political feasibility. They are called "policy wonks," or simply "wonks." The wonks usually have a deep understanding of the policy issues on which they work and a desire to create the most efficient, elegant, or comprehensive solution to a given challenge.

There is also an expression for those individuals who relish "winning" in the political process, without much regard for whether that victory makes the world a better place. They are called "political hacks," or simply "hacks." The hacks have a deep understanding of the political process and a keen appreciation for what is politically feasible at any given time.

Bruce Reed, a former staff member for President Bill Clinton, has written that the gap between the Republicans and the Democrats pales in comparison to the chasm between the wonks and the hacks. He says, "Wonks think the differences between the hacks and wonks are as irreconcilable as the Hutus and the Tutsis. Hacks think it's just like the wonks to bring up the Hutus and the Tutsis."[4]

Most academics are wonks. They toil in the world of "first best" solutions and often scorn lawmakers for embracing policy fixes that sacrifice substance for the sake of politics. Most lawmakers (by comparison at least) are hacks, if only because their job survival depends on it. Legislators and government officials are often frustrated when academic experts and other wonks cannot give them what they need most: practical answers to pressing policy questions in a reasonable amount of time.

Hacks recognize that if the first best solution does not have enough votes to pass, then a less elegant solution is often better than nothing. Wonks counter that a politic solution is often no better than doing nothing at all and may even be worse.

Public policy almost always involves a tension between wonks and hacks for the simple reason that it reflects the challenges of making public policy in a democracy. The most effective solutions are almost never the most popular; and the most politically expedient solutions are rarely the most effective. Of course, the two skills do not have to be mutually exclusive. Reed says of his former boss: "The secret of Bill Clinton's success was that he was the biggest wonk ever to hold the presidency, with political gifts that no hack could equal."

One purpose for studying public policy is to narrow the gap between the wonks and the hacks by appreciating the importance of both good policy and good politics.

....

4. Bruce Reed, "Bush's War against Wonks," *Washington Monthly*, March 2004.

15.3 MECHANISMS FOR CHANGING BEHAVIOR

The point of public policy is to change behavior in ways that produce better overall outcomes. Government has four broad tools for generating social outcomes that are different from the ones that the market would otherwise deliver on its own: regulation; taxes and subsidies (and other incentives); government provision of a good or service; or government financing of a good or service that is subsequently provided by the private sector.

15.3.1   Regulation (Deregulation)

Government has the authority to **regulate**—to require individuals and firms to act in a specified manner and to enforce that requirement with fines, confiscation of property, or even imprisonment. In other words, policy makers can change the behavior of individuals or firms by simply requiring them to behave differently. Obviously, different institutions of government are vested with authority over different kinds of activities.

> *Example:* **The federal government requires all new automobiles sold in the United States to be equipped with certain safety features.**

Many individuals or firms would presumably act differently in the absence of the regulation. As a result, one drawback of using regulatory power to achieve some outcome is that it requires extensive monitoring and enforcement. The regulated individuals and firms are being compelled to do something that they would prefer not to do, and some will avoid doing it—either legally through loopholes or illegally through forms of evasion that are hard to detect. A second drawback is that regulation can be a cumbersome, costly, and even ineffective mechanism for improving outcomes. In the private sector, the market naturally rewards efficiency and discourages inefficiency. There is no such mechanism to ensure the efficiency of government regulation. If a government regulation is not effective or if its costs exceed the benefits, firms and individuals must still abide by it because the law says they have to.

Deregulation occurs when policy makers decide that society would be better off without some regulation that currently exists because it is causing an outcome that is less desirable than what the market would deliver.

15.3.2   Taxes, Subsidies, and Other Incentives

Government has the capacity to raise and lower the prices of different goods and behaviors by using taxes and subsidies. A tax raises the cost of some activity; a subsidy lowers it. The change in price will, in turn, affect behavior—that is one of the core principles of economics.

> *Example:* **A gasoline tax raises the cost of driving; a subsidy for mass transit lowers the cost of taking a bus or train.**

All else being equal, we would expect a gas tax to encourage individuals to purchase more fuel-efficient vehicles and to drive fewer miles (perhaps by carpooling or using public transit). In the long run, a significant gas tax might encourage some families to buy homes in locations that require shorter commutes or have better access to public transit. A subsidy does the opposite by making some activity less costly or more profitable, thereby encouraging individuals or firms to do something that they would not otherwise do, if left to the market alone. Those who are willing to pay $2 to ride a subsidized municipal bus might not be willing to pay the $6 fare that would be necessary to operate the route, if it were not subsidized. Presumably, society is made better off when some people ride the bus (avoiding emissions and traffic congestion), rather than driving.

A **Pigovian tax,** named for English economist Arthur Pigou, is a tax designed explicitly to raise the private cost of some activity to equal the social cost. If the private cost of driving an automobile is $0.45 a mile (insurance, gas, car payments, etc.) but the costs imposed on the rest of society from driving are an additional $0.20 a mile (pollution, congestion, wear and tear on public roads, etc.), then the appropriate Pigovian gas tax would be $0.20 a mile. Obviously, the tax raises revenue, but its purpose is also to change behavior by raising the cost of an activity that policy makers would like to discourage.

Government can also alter incentives by changing the nonmonetary cost of an activity. A city that wants to promote environmentally friendly buildings can expedite the permitting process for new projects that meet certain "green" criteria. Or a government can promote carpooling by allowing vehicles with a minimum number of passengers to use dedicated high-occupancy-vehicle (HOV) lanes, where traffic moves faster. In both of these cases, the incentive involves saving time rather than money (though presumably that extra time can be put to productive use). Using incentives to change behavior is often easier than mandating the change through regulation. Consider the case of a state government that would prefer motorists to use electronic open-road tolling (such as E-ZPass) rather than paying tolls with cash. (Electronic tolls are less costly to collect, and they don't require stopping traffic.) The government could require that all vehicles be equipped with electronic transponders for electronic tolling; this would be difficult to enforce and would present logistical problems when cars from other states use the toll road. The more elegant solution is to charge a higher toll for cars and trucks that do not pay electronically—such as a $0.75 electronic toll but $1.50 for vehicles that pay the old-fashioned way. Most drivers will switch to the new system quickly, and the extra $0.75 from those who don't will pay for the infrastructure necessary to collect their coins and bills.

15.3.3 Public Provision of a Good or Service

Public goods, such as counterterrorism, mosquito abatement, or even a communal garden, can make the individuals who share them better off. However, as Chapters 4 and 8 discussed, individuals who do not pay for these kinds of public goods cannot be excluded from enjoying their benefits. This free-rider problem makes it hard for the private sector to deliver certain kinds of goods and services even when the total social benefits would vastly exceed the total social costs. Government (or some other communal entity such as a homeowners' association) can overcome the free-rider problem by providing a good or service and then compelling payment for it through taxation, membership dues, or some other mandatory fee. Whether it is policing the borders for drug traffickers or shoveling snow on a shared walkway, these situations have two common features: (1) the market is not providing some good or service that citizens believe would make them better off, and (2) government (or some other communal entity) pays for and provides that good or service.

Of course, not all activities undertaken by government necessarily make its citizens better off when the costs of taxation are taken into account. Policy makers can also undertake **privatization,** which involves devolving some function of government to the private sector. Citizens may decide that there is no economic rationale for government to be providing a good or service (e.g., operating banks or producing electricity) and that taxpayers and consumers would be better served by selling these businesses off to private investors. When the communist governments in the Soviet Union and Eastern Europe were overthrown, one key economic priority over the next decade was returning large segments of the economy to the private sector after years of government domination. When privatization is done right (in a transparent, noncorrupt way), it leaves society better off: governments shed money-losing businesses, private firms transform those businesses into profitable enterprises, and consumers get better-quality goods and services. Of course, even then there are likely to be losers and, therefore, political and social costs; employees who had comfortable government jobs are likely to find themselves out of work as private firms "transform" those businesses.

15.3.4 Public Financing and Private Provision of a Good or Service

If the market is not providing an important good or service, there is an alternative to having government provide it: a government (or other communal entity) can finance the provision of a good or service while leaving the private sector to produce it. Consider a classic public good such as a lighthouse. We know that the private sector will not likely invest in building a lighthouse, because the potential free-rider problem makes it hard to recoup the investment, even when the social gains far exceed the social costs. There is a strong economic case for public investment in a lighthouse (or national defense or any other public good). But the government does not have to build or operate the lighthouse; it merely needs to pay for it. The local government can overcome the free-rider problem by levying a tax on local residents; free riders have no choice but to contribute. (Historically, lighthouses have often been financed by levying a fee on boats moored in local harbors—which is essentially a local tax.) The money raised by government can then be used to pay a private firm to build and operate the lighthouse. The same is true with goods and services ranging from highways to military uniforms.

This distinction between public *financing* of a good or service and public *provision* is important. In some cases, a social objective can be achieved most efficiently by combining public funds with the market discipline of the private sector. If a government is building a highway, the department of transportation can put the project out to bid among many private construction firms. The highway would still be financed using public funds, but the bidding process would allow for the project to be built at the lowest possible cost (assuming some well-defined level of quality and an honest bidding process). Competition among private firms can lead to better quality, more innovation, and lower costs. Public employees rarely have the same incentive to innovate, cut costs, or finish the project on deadline.

15.4 DECIDING BETWEEN PUBLIC OR PRIVATE PROVISION

Given the benefits of competition, why shouldn't the government contract out all tasks to the private sector? It turns out that the incentive for private firms to cut costs and maximize profits can, in some cases, be counterproductive or even dangerous. In general, the benefits to having the government contract out the provision of a good or service to a private firm exist only when two criteria are met: (1) the task for which a private firm is being hired is clearly defined, and (2) the quality of the good or service to be delivered is easily observed and measured. If these conditions are met, then a government can give clear directions to private firms making bids to deliver the good or service (e.g., design a weapons system to certain specifications, operate a commuter train on a certain route, or collect the trash within a particular geographic boundary on a weekly basis). Policy makers refer to these criteria as **contractible quality,** meaning that the government can specify exactly what is to be done and then evaluate if a private firm is meeting that commitment. For example, if a government were soliciting bids to build a highway, the relevant agency would define the scope of the project: the kind of pavement, the requisite safety features, the timeline for completing the project, and so on. If the private contractor cut corners somehow, the government would be able to observe the problem and seek legal redress by comparing what was promised in the contract to what was actually delivered.

However, if the government's objectives cannot be specified clearly or if the quality of the good or service to be provided cannot be easily measured, then a private firm's incentive to maximize profits is a potential liability. Consider law enforcement. Suppose that a city would like to hire a private security force to protect its citizens. This assignment is vaguer than it would first appear. How many patrol cars should be on the street an any given time? How long should the force investigate a crime before giving up? How much effort should be devoted to teaching residents about crime prevention? Each of these activities is costly, so a private firm would be tempted to minimize them. A contract that spelled out all of the requirements for the firm to fulfill would be complicated and costly, if not impossible.[5] Even if the contract were created, some government entity would have to monitor all of the private firm's activities. Were there really three patrol cars on the street at midnight? How hard are the detectives working to solve crimes? A contract that specified outcomes, such as a 5-percent reduction in crime or an increase in arrests, would be impractical as well. Crime is determined by many factors; there would be no way to decide in advance how much effort and skill would be necessary to bring about such a reduction. In fact, it would difficult to allocate

---

5. Many stores, malls, and other public venues hire private security guards. You should recognize that the responsibilities assigned to such firms are more easily defined and measured than law enforcement in general. A security guard at a retail store need only stop shoplifters; he or she does not need to investigate crimes, make complicated patrol decisions, invest in crime reduction, or engage in other costly activities that are not easily contractible.

credit even after a crime reduction occurred (or to allocate blame after a crime increase). A very good private police firm might get blamed for a crime spree caused by forces far beyond its control—such as a national drug epidemic or a rise in terrorism—or credit where none is deserved. In a worse-case scenario, a private police firm may "hit its numbers" by arresting innocent people, being overly harsh on petty crimes (which makes for good arrest numbers), or tolerating crime over some period in order to facilitate later arrests. A profit-maximizing firm that had hit its arrest or crime-reduction target for the year would prefer to leave some criminals on the street so that they could be arrested next year.

The rule of thumb is straightforward: Can we tell if a private firm is doing a good job, or is it possible that the firm is making profits by cutting costs in unobservable but potentially harmful ways?

15.5 OVERVIEW OF THE POLICY PROCESS

Germany's nineteenth-century chancellor Otto von Bismarck is credited with saying, "There are two things you don't want to see being made—sausage and legislation." The policy process will vary, depending on the nature of the issue and the kinds of political institutions involved. Nonetheless, for any policy change that requires the approval of some political body, the process can be broadly summarized as follows.

Step 1   Identify the Potential Benefit

The first and most important step in the policy process is to identify the goal: What is the potential benefit from a policy change or the harm that might be ameliorated? As with any journey, the more you know about the destination, the more likely you are to get there. There are three common pitfalls that can derail the policy design process at the very beginning:

1. Vague or conflicting goals. Many policy objectives are far vaguer than they first appear: "better schools" or "fighting illegal drugs." Let's suppose that a commission meets to address the latter: the problems of illegal drug use. After a brief discussion, the group agrees unanimously that better policies are needed to deal with the social costs associated with drugs. This would appear to be an excellent start. In fact, the group has failed to answer the most important question: Which social costs of illegal drug use is the commission trying to ameliorate? There are several possible answers to that question, and each will suggest a different policy approach. Consider the following harms associated with illicit drug use:

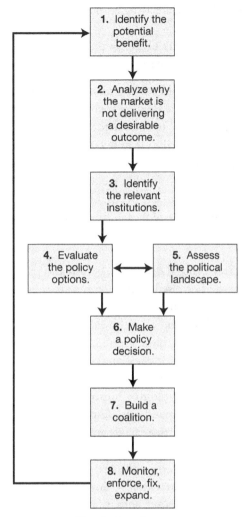

The Policy Process

- *Overdoses, loss of productivity, long-term health effects, and other physiological damage.* Drug users harm themselves; they impose a cost on society to the extent that some of these health costs are passed along to their employers or the public.
- *Transmission of HIV/AIDS.* The HIV/AIDS virus can be spread when intravenous drug users share needles—a major source of transmission of the disease.
- *Crime.* Illegal drugs are produced and distributed by violent criminal enterprises—from the drug cartels of Latin America to the street gangs in

America's cities. Meanwhile, drug addicts often turn to crime to support their habits.

- *Morality.* Some segments of the population believe that using mind-altering, addictive drugs is wrong and should not be tolerated by society.

A change in drug policy should address all of these harms. But that turns out to be nearly impossible, since dealing with some of them will make others worse. For example, one way to reduce the transmission of HIV/AIDS via intravenous drug use is to make clean needles more widely available. (The concept of "needle exchanges" was discussed in Chapter 2.) But such needle exchanges, or any other program that makes needles cheaper and easier to come by, also makes it easier to use drugs. Many needle exchanges take place in areas where the sale and use of illegal drugs is either implicitly or explicitly allowed in order to entice intravenous drug users to swap dirty needles for clean ones.

Or consider crime. Illegal drugs like heroin and cocaine are distributed by criminal enterprises because legitimate firms are prevented from doing so. There are no comparable criminal organizations distributing alcohol or cigarettes (though Prohibition did abet the rise of notorious criminals like Al Capone). Some economists have argued that the most efficient way to decrease the crime and violence associated with drug trafficking would be to make those drugs legal. They also point out that the resources spent on drug enforcement could be redirected to education and treatment programs that would help to reduce the demand for addictive drugs. Of course, legalizing drugs would deal a blow to drug cartels and street gangs, but it would also put the production and distribution of addictive drugs in the hands of profit-maximizing firms (or the government). We would expect drugs like cocaine and heroin to become cheaper, easier to buy, more potent, and more socially acceptable. Drug-related criminal activity would go down, but recreational drug use might go up, making the addiction and health effects worse (depending on the effectiveness of any education and addiction-treatment efforts). There is no single right policy in this case. The policy design process must begin by identifying exactly what policy makers hope to achieve.

2. Confusing intermediate measures with the real outcome of interest. Is society better off if test scores go up for fourth-grade students in the Chicago public schools? Perhaps. The answer depends entirely on the extent to which those higher test scores translate into outcomes that really affect students' lives: higher lifetime wages, improved college attendance, lower crime, greater life satisfaction, and so on. Higher test scores alone will not increase anyone's utility (except for perhaps the administrators in the school system). Test scores matter only to the extent that they are correlated with other outcomes that do make lives better. If higher test scores reflect the fact that students are learning more and that what they are learning will make them more successful in life, then higher test scores are a very important outcome. On the other hand, if higher test scores reflect rote memorization of skills that have little value, then they are not meaningful indicators. In fact, the time spent teaching for such tests will detract from time spent on more important educational tasks. As a society, we don't care about test scores per se; we care whether or not students are learning important and relevant skills—and, therefore, about test scores only to the extent that they accurately measure this. In this case and others, it is imperative that the policy affect an outcome that improves social welfare or is highly correlated with such an improvement.

3. Aiming for a "whole loaf" when the political timing is better for six slices. One must decide at the beginning of the policy design process how politically ambitious a proposal can be. Any democratic political process is binary, meaning that a proposal either passes or it does not. Aiming to do too much can often result in accomplishing nothing at all. It's true that there is room along the way for negotiation and compromise, but it must begin from a realistic starting point. (Politicians will often refer to an unrealistic proposal as a "nonstarter.") When President Bill Clinton sought to reform health care at the beginning of his first term, he sent Congress a 1,000-plus-page bill for a complete overhaul of the system. Months later, the entire plan was ditched, resulting in no change at all. In seeking to fix the whole health-care system at once, the Clinton administration missed an opportunity to make modest improvements with more political appeal.

Policy "wonks" appreciate what policy changes will be most effective; the political "hacks" appreciate what is politically feasible at any given time. Successful policy change in a democratic system requires both.

Step 2 Analyze Why the Market Is Not Delivering a Desirable Outcome

If markets are the primary mechanism through which rational people get what they want, why is it not working in this case? If there is some unmet social need, why hasn't an entrepreneurial firm filled the gap?

Understanding why the market is not delivering a socially desirable outcome can help the policy design process in two ways. First, markets are often **self-correcting,** meaning that disruptions or other problems usually set in motion their own solutions. The ideal strategy is often to do nothing, allowing firms and consumers to adapt. For example, rising gas prices will elicit a chorus of calls for government to "do something" even as those higher prices set in motion their own solution: conservation, new sources of supply, greater investment in alternative energy, and so on. Similarly, analysis may suggest that some existing government regulation is the cause of the undesirable outcome, in which case the appropriate remedy is to eliminate whatever regulatory barrier is precluding the market from delivering a better outcome.

Second, if the market, left to its own devices, will not correct a social problem, then the nature of the market failure will often suggest an appropriate remedy. For example, if an environmental problem is caused by some behavior that generates a negative externality, then one obvious remedy would be a Pigovian tax designed to raise the private cost of the offending behavior to its true social cost. The following are the basic rationales for government intervention, either to make markets work better or to make an efficient outcome more socially palatable:

1. **Promoting competition.** Effective markets depend on competition among firms. Government can intervene to promote competition and prevent collusion among firms.

   > *Example:* **Antitrust laws prevent firms in the same industry from fixing prices or even discussing prices in some cases.**

2. **Lowering transactions costs.** Markets depend on secure property rights, the rule of law, the free flow of information, a sound currency, and other institutions that make it cheaper and easier to conduct voluntary exchange.

   > *Example:* **All developed nations have national currencies so that commercial transactions can be conducted easily and predictably with a single unit of measure.**

3. **Ameliorating externalities.** Markets will not produce a socially efficient outcome when an activity imposes a cost on some party or parties that are not involved in the transaction. (The social marginal cost of the activity is higher than the private marginal cost, as was explained in Chapter

8.) Government may intervene to prevent or ameliorate such negative externalities or to promote activities that generate positive externalities.

> *Example:* **Environmental laws such as the Clean Air Act and the Clean Water Act place restrictions on the types and quantities of pollutants that can be emitted into the air or water.**

4. **Providing public goods (and overcoming other collective-action problems).** Government can help individuals overcome the free-rider problem by providing goods that make society better off but might not be provided in the absence of government intervention.

> *Example:* **The federal government is responsible for national defense and counterterrorism.**

5. **Equity and the social safety net.** Governments in all developed nations engage in some activities that redistribute income from rich to poor or otherwise protect against adverse outcomes.

> *Example:* **The Earned Income Tax Credit (EITC) uses the tax system to provide a subsidy to low-wage workers; workers whose income falls below a certain level are eligible for a tax credit that supplements their wages and raises their after-tax income.**

6. **Paternalism.** Government sometimes intervenes to prevent individuals from harming themselves. (Reasonable people disagree over the extent to which government should attempt to dictate individual behavior.) Nonetheless, all advanced societies have laws that restrict activities that would have little or no impact on the broader society.

> *Example:* **Many states require adult motorcyclists to wear helmets.**

Given the inherent power of markets, any policy maker ought to be able to explain explicitly why the market, left to its own devices, will not produce the desired outcome (or, conversely, why an existing regulation improves upon what the market would otherwise deliver). As the following example from India illustrates, government can do too much just as it can do too little.

··············· POLICY IN THE REAL WORLD ···············

Economic Growth in India:
Too Much Government—and Not Enough

India is one of the most populous nations on earth and also one of the poorest. Roughly 250 million Indians live on less than $1 dollar a day.[6] Policy makers in India are focused intently on economic growth, which creates jobs, raises incomes, and lifts households out of poverty. A recent report by the Organisation for Economic Co-operation and Development (OECD) concluded that policy reforms in India could improve the rate of growth and speed this process along.[7] The OECD report concluded that the Indian government needs to do more to help its citizens—and also less.

India has underinvested in infrastructure. Poor roads and unreliable power make the country a difficult place to do business. High-tech firms like Infosys (headquartered in Bangalore) must take on many of the responsibilities normally carried out by the government: generating power, purifying water, and even running buses to bring employees to work (all of which are expenses that firms in other countries do not have to take on). Road quality and congestion are so bad across India that it takes Hyundai seven days for trucks loaded with cars to deliver them from the plant in Sriperumbudur to New Delhi—roughly the same distance as Miami to Boston.[8] Ratan Tata, chairman of Tata, one of India's biggest industrial groups, told the *Financial Times,* "Unless India does something about its infrastructure failings, it will not be able to sustain even its current levels of growth."[9]

At the same time, the Indian government needs to do less in terms of regulating the economy, particularly the manufacturing sector. After gaining independence in 1947, India earned a reputation as the "license raj" because of the vast array of government permissions and licenses required to conduct business. Some of this red tape has been rolled back in recent decades; much of it has not. Each year, the World Bank ranks countries on their ease of doing business. In 2010, India ranked 133 out of 183—just behind Malawi and only a few spots ahead of the West Bank and Gaza (139).[10]

---

6. Mark Sappenfield, "India's Economy, Now with Muscle," *Christian Science Monitor,* November 1, 2006.

7. "A Himalayan Challenge," *The Economist,* October 11, 2007.

8. Sappenfield, "India's Economy, Now with Muscle."

9. Peter Marsh, "India 'Needs Big Infrastructure Drive,'" *Financial Times,* January 23, 2006.

10. The World Bank Group, "Doing Business 2010," www.doingbusiness.org/EconomyRankings/.

One particularly restrictive regulation is Chapter 5B of the 1947 Industrial Disputes Act, which requires manufacturing firms with more than 100 workers to seek government permission before laying off even a single employee. The government almost never grants such permission. As a result, firms are hesitant to grow beyond 100 workers for fear that they will not be able to downsize, if it becomes financially necessary. (The regulation also precludes the seasonal hiring of workers.) According to *The Economist,* "This partly explains why most firms are so small: 87 percent of employment in Indian manufacturing is in firms with fewer than 10 employees, compared with only five percent in China. Small firms cannot reap economies of scale or exploit the latest technology, and so suffer from lower productivity than big firms."[11] One example is textile manufacturing, where large-scale facilities are necessary to keep prices low. In 2005, India exported $17 billion in textiles, compared to China's $107 billion.

In India or anywhere else, good public policy is about using government to improve upon market outcomes in some cases and to leave markets alone in others. Good policy analysis is about telling the difference.

. . . .

Step 3 Identify the Institutions with the Authority and Capacity to Implement a Policy Change

The affordable housing example at the beginning of the chapter demonstrated that there is rarely a "right" policy solution. Instead, there are usually an array of options involving different institutions and different levels of government. Policy actors should ask three things when choosing the most appropriate institution for policy change: (1) What level of government is "closest to the people," while still having sufficient authority to encompass the full scope of the behavior to be changed? (2) What institution has the greatest capacity to act effectively? (3) What institution offers the greatest chances for political success? We will discuss each of these briefly in turn.

1. **Federalism.** A federalist system allocates power across different levels of government. In the United States, those governments are the federal government, the state governments, and the county and local governments. The Constitution explicitly reserves some powers for the federal government, such as the regulation of interstate commerce and the authority to enter into treaties with foreign nations. In many cases, however, all levels of government can claim some authority to act on a policy issue.

---

11. "A Himalayan Challenge."

Acting through local government—at the city or county level, for example—allows the greatest flexibility for accommodating local preferences. Local institutions are also most easily held accountable by voters. The federal government need not oversee trash collection, operate local libraries, or choose school textbooks. Local communities can choose how (and how much) to invest in such public goods.

On the other hand, any government implementing a policy change must have sufficient authority to deal with the full scope of the problem. A local community cannot affect behavior that originates beyond its boundaries, such as air pollution. A municipality—or even a state—does not have the authority to reduce emissions that are generated in a different political jurisdiction hundreds of miles away. In fact, this can be true even at the national level; Canadian officials have long complained that their acid-rain problems are caused by emissions from factories in the American Midwest. There may also be cost efficiency associated with offering a public service on a large scale at the state or federal level, as opposed to setting up hundreds or thousands of systems for service delivery at the local level. Of course, these cost savings can prove illusory if the challenges of operating a large bureaucracy overwhelm the theoretical economies of scale that come with size and centralization. The states play a middle ground in a federalist system, with broader authority than local communities but more room to accommodate diverse preferences than the federal government. Policy makers sometimes refer to the "laboratory of the states," an expression that reflects the idea that fifty different approaches are more likely to breed successful policy innovation than a single uniform approach. Federal programs like welfare reform have often been modeled on successful state programs.

2. **Institutional capacity.** One important consideration for policy design is the level of government, or the specific agency within some level of government, that has the capacity to act most effectively. Does a successful outcome require expertise, enforcement powers, or some other specific resources? The FBI has access to databases and expertise that state police departments do not; however, the FBI has no authority to investigate state and local crimes. Similarly, the U.S. Department of Housing and Urban Development (HUD) has a large budget that can be deployed to expand affordable housing; however, HUD cannot change local zoning laws, which are municipal regulations that often preclude certain kinds of housing, such as apartment buildings. What entity is most capable of changing behavior in a way that is consistent with the desired outcome?

3. **Strategic action.** Those who seek to change policy—either by introducing new laws and/or by getting rid of old ones—obviously hope to be successful. In a democratic system, political success is a prerequisite for policy change, and some institutional routes are more conducive to political change than others. Proponents of a policy change may find that the political party in control of the U.S. Congress is hostile to a particular idea, while many state legislatures are controlled by more friendly political forces. In that case, the proponents of change will seek state action, not necessarily because acting at the state level makes the most policy sense, but because that is where they have the greatest chance of "winning." Policy actors on both sides of the abortion issue are constantly acting strategically through many parallel institutional channels. They are battling over constitutional questions in the Supreme Court; they are battling in Congress over legislation that may limit or expand access to and funding for abortion in the United States and abroad; and they are battling in state legislatures over abortion policies that may deviate from what is happening at the federal level. These groups are not choosing strategies based on the finer points of federalism; they simply want their point of view to prevail and will pursue any and all institutional paths that make that most likely.

Step 4 Evaluate the Policy Options

Will it work? The most fundamental question is whether a policy remedy fixes the harm originally identified. If policy makers are concerned about student achievement, then there ought to be solid evidence that the remedy being proposed is likely to have a positive and significant impact on student performance. A shocking proportion of policy proposals fail this basic test. The primary difference between serious policy analysts and political "hacks" is the reliance on evidence-based solutions and the ability to anticipate perverse incentives and unintended consequences. Overall, a policy proposal must leave society better off, as measured by several possible criteria:

1. **Cost-benefit analysis.** Chapter 12 laid out the process for evaluating the total net social costs and benefits for a proposed policy change. If the total benefits exceed the total costs, then society will be better off overall—recognizing, however, that the process for attaching prices to certain costs and benefits is imperfect and that cost-benefit analysis does not take distributional effects into consideration.
2. **Cost-effectiveness analysis.** What policy achieves some defined objective at the lowest cost? Suppose the Environmental Protection Agency

directs a metropolitan area to reduce the emissions of a particular pollutant by 20 percent over a five-year time frame. Local policy makers have no choice but to comply with the directive; they should choose a policy that achieves the required objective as cheaply as possible.

3. **Some other improvement of the status quo.** If policy analysis were entirely scientific, then it could be turned over to computers, and society would be better off for it. In fact, "good" policy is often predicated on judgment, discretion, and ideology. A reasonable person could propose a policy that does not satisfy either of the criteria above. For example, a person or group may champion a policy with total social costs that exceed the total social benefits but for which the benefits accrue disproportionately to low-income groups. For those who believe that the marginal utility of income is much higher for the poor than for the wealthy—meaning that $1.00 in income generates more utility for a poor person than is given up when a wealthier person loses $1.50 or even $2.00 in consumption—then a policy that "shrinks the pie" can still leave society better off, depending on one's underlying worldview.

One crucial point is that steps 4 and 5 are usually done in tandem, rather than one after the other. The politics of policy change are never entirely separable from the substance; a strategic policy maker must be attuned to the political attractiveness of any proposal. A successful policy is not only one that works, but also one that has enough political support to get passed: a majority of votes in a state legislature; or 60 votes in the U.S. Senate (to survive a filibuster); or 4 votes in a seven-person town council; or the vote of a single committee chair who has the power to permanently table a bill not to his or her liking. Sometimes policy actors can "sell" what they consider to be an optimal policy by making it as politically attractive as possible and energizing the political interest groups that stand to benefit from it. At other times, that's not good enough, in which case the substance of a proposal must be modified to attract more supporters or to mollify opponents. Elegant ideas that don't get passed will never improve anything. Veteran policy makers must constantly navigate the interplay between substance and politics—between "first best solutions" and less-effective but more politically attractive compromises.

Step 5 Assess the Political Landscape

A policy proposal must have the requisite political support in order to get passed, whatever the relevant democratic institution. Strategic policy makers think about this consideration *during* the policy design process rather than *after* choosing some optimal policy. There is a reasonable analogy to designing consumer goods: it's better to ask consumers about their preferences during the product design stage than it is to build "the perfect product" in isolation and then try to convince consumers that they ought to love it.

Any political undertaking begins with three related questions: (1) How many votes does it require? (2) Where are they going to come from? and (3) Who needs to be persuaded of what? The answers to those questions will vary enormously. If a policy initiative is being undertaken through a referendum, such as a California ballot initiative, then the answer is that a majority of registered voters must be persuaded to support the proposal. The appropriate strategy in such a case would likely be a **grassroots campaign** in which a network of volunteers and paid staff target undecided voters using television advertising, direct mail, the Internet, door-to-door canvassing, and any other tools likely to win eligible voters over to their side. In other cases, a single person may determine whether a legislative initiative passes or fails. That person may be a veto-wielding executive, such as the governor, president, or mayor. Or it may be a legislator who is vested with procedural powers that make him or her uniquely powerful, such as a committee chair or the Speaker of the House. These legislators who wield disproportionate institutional power are often called **gatekeepers.** Effective policy makers will survey the political landscape to determine where the important political battles lie and how they can best be won.

One key to political success is effective communication. In particular, **framing** is the strategic use of language to broaden the appeal of a policy position (or lessen the appeal of an opposing position). Individuals and groups on different sides of a policy debate will choose language that is likely to make their position seem more attractive to undecided voters or politicians. Framing is effective because it shapes the way that individuals think about issues; different words can make the same content seem more or less attractive. Consider some examples that you will probably recognize:

- Americans who would like to curtail the number of workers who enter the United States illegally from places like Mexico are likely to speak about stopping **illegal aliens.** Groups who support such workers or who would like to expand immigration opportunities in general refer to the same individuals as **undocumented workers.** Notice how the two phrases have starkly different connotations. *Illegal aliens* emphasizes both the unlawful nature of the activity and the fact that those arriving are different and foreign. *Undocumented workers* emphasizes the fact that these immigrants have entered the country to work and merely lack the appropriate paperwork.

- Individuals and groups who believe that abortion should be illegal in the United States refer to themselves as **pro-life.** Those who believe that abortion should be legal refer to themselves as **pro-choice.** The choice of language reinforces the core arguments of the two sides. "Pro-life" emphasizes the belief that abortion ends a human life. "Pro-choice" focuses instead on the fact that a fetus is inextricably linked to its mother and that choices related to the pregnancy, including the decision to terminate it, should reside exclusively with a pregnant woman.

Effective policy makers frame their positions in ways that make them more appealing to those voters and legislators who do not have strong preexisting beliefs about the issue and are in a position to be persuaded one way or the other.

Step 6 Make a Policy Decision

The goal of policy analysis is to choose the most attractive policy from the available options. Sometimes the "best" policy is in the eye of the beholder. For example, most citizens would argue that the "best" location for a landfill or prison is in someone else's neighborhood. In other cases, there is a more objective measure of success. The best option is the one that makes most progress (relative to its costs) toward whatever goal was identified at the beginning of the policy process. However, that first best option may not be politically feasible. The optimal policy will be the one that offers the best hope for both substantive and political success. In many cases, that will be the proverbial half a loaf.

POLICY IN THE REAL WORLD

Cotton Subsidies: How Helping American Farmers Hurts West Africa

The federal government provides an array of direct subsidies and other indirect benefits to American farmers. The 2008 Farm Bill directs about $5 billion a year in direct payments to American farmers.[12] Most of these agricultural subsidy programs originated during the Great Depression, when

---

12. Carey Gillam, "Farmers Defend Direct Payment after Obama Remark," *Reuters*, February 25, 2009.

the government intervened to help struggling farmers. These programs are expensive for American taxpayers. They also have a less obvious cost: farm subsidies—particularly cotton—are potentially devastating for poor farmers in west Africa.

In 2003, Amadou Toumani Touré and Blaise Compaoré, presidents of Mali and Burkina Faso, respectively, wrote an op-ed in the *New York Times,* making the case that American farm policies are a serious threat to their economies: "Cotton is our ticket into the world market. Its production is crucial to economic development in West and Central Africa, as well as to the livelihoods of millions of people there. This vital economic sector in our countries is seriously threatened by agricultural subsidies granted by rich countries to their cotton producers."[13]

How can a policy designed to help American cotton farmers have such a significant adverse impact in Africa? U.S. farm subsidies encourage cotton farmers to expand production beyond what the market would otherwise dictate. This expanded supply drives down global cotton prices, which in turn lowers the incomes of West African cotton farmers. Since the United States is the world's largest cotton exporter, the impact on global prices is significant. A study conducted for Oxfam America, an international relief and development organization, concluded that eliminating subsidies for U.S. cotton producers would increase the global market price for cotton by 6 to 14 percent, which would translate into an increase in the household income for the typical west African cotton-producing household of $46 to $114.[14] That may not seem like a lot, but west African nations are among the poorest on Earth; some 40 percent of children under age five are malnourished. Small increases in household income are likely to be spent on health, education, or food—all of which can substantially improve lives.

. . . .

Step 7   Build a Coalition

In a legislative arena, the goal is to "get the votes." Effective policy makers build coalitions among the organized interests and other parties that support what they are trying to do; at the same time, they are working to mollify, subdue, or defeat the organized interests that are likely to oppose the action.

---

13. Amadou Toumani Touré and Blaise Compaoré, "Your Farm Subsidies Are Strangling Us," *New York Times,* July 11, 2003.

14. Julian M. Alston, Daniel A. Sumner, and Henrich Brunke, "Paying the Price: How US Farm Policies Hurt West African Cotton Farmers—and How Subsidy Reform Could Help," Oxfam (2007); based on key findings from the authors' study "Impacts of Reductions in US Cotton Subsidies on West African Cotton Producers," conducted for Oxfam (2007).

Savvy policy makers will recognize the broad potential coalition that can be built around some issue, even when many members of that coalition have little in common. Tom Grey, formerly the leader of an organization called the National Coalition against Legalized Gambling, ticks off his natural (but disparate) allies in that political battle: law enforcement, chambers of commerce, the restaurant association, the mental-health community, editorial boards of local papers. He explains:

> When I fight, I want a network. I want liberal, I want conservative, I want Republican, I want Democrat. I want all my bases covered. That's why we never talk about anything but gambling, because if you start to talk to one another about other issues, you'll all go out other doors. This issue unites people who fight each other on other things.[15]

The less obvious point is that the substance of the policy change must often be modified in order to build a sufficiently strong coalition. When the U.S. Senate was considering the abolition of the estate tax, the bill was broadened to include generous tax treatment for timber. The estate tax had no obvious connection to timber; rather, the Senate bill needed the votes of two Washington senators. The favorable tax treatment of timber was a sufficient sweetener to bring them on board. Conversely, provisions can be dropped from a bill if they engender overwhelming political opposition. Effective policy makers recognize their natural allies and opponents. They seek to build a coalition that strengthens the former relative to the latter.

Step 8   Monitor, Enforce, Fix, Expand

A policy change is just a first step. A sensible proposal should include a mechanism for gathering and analyzing data on the effects of the program relative to its objectives. It should also include a mechanism for monitoring compliance and sanctioning individuals or firms who are violating the new policy. Even with these mechanisms in place, the policy still may not produce the outcomes that were originally conceived. It may not work as designed; there may be unforeseen costs. Or a policy may work surprisingly well, in which case it can be expanded to include more people or additional jurisdictions. Policies are not perfect works of art. They are imperfect efforts, subject to constant improvement based on data, feedback, and changing circumstances and political climates.

15. Charles Wheelan, "No Dice," *Dartmouth Alumni Magazine* (July/August 2003).

15.6 CONCLUSION

The purpose of public policy is to change behavior in ways that lead to better social outcomes. In some cases, this is easy: policy makers can remove legal and regulatory barriers that preclude individuals and firms from doing things that will make them—and the rest of society—better off. In other cases, policy makers seek to change behavior in ways that individuals and firms would prefer to avoid; any policy change must be effective even after individuals and firms have reacted to protect their own interests. The most obvious goal of the policy design process is to identify a social harm and fix it to the greatest extent possible, using the fewest resources and causing the fewest disruptions or "side effects." In a democratic system, this process is always conjoined with politics. Policy analysts must constantly strike a balance between good substance and good politics.

FOR DISCUSSION

The Elusive Goal of Education Reform:
No Child Left Behind

Education is invariably one of our most important public policy concerns. Human capital is crucial to success in a modern economy, and public education is the most important mechanism for providing the next generation with the skills that they will need to succeed. However, America's public schools are not achieving their goals as effectively as they might.

- American students lag behind their peers around the world in a number of subjects.
- Poor and minority students are faring particularly badly.
- Real expenditures on education have risen steadily over the past several decades while student achievement has been essentially flat.
- A shockingly high proportion of students drop out of school, even though educational attainment is more important in the labor force than ever before. Meanwhile, the proportion of students who finish college—a primary source of U.S. innovation and prosperity for 150 years—has flattened (and even fallen for men).

Although support for education reform is nearly universal, there is very little agreement on how to make schools better. Does the existing system need more resources, or does the system itself need to be reformed—perhaps by giving students vouchers to attend the public or private school of their choice? Should the federal government set curriculum standards for the nation, or should the states be allowed flexibility to determine their own standards for what students need to know? Nearly everyone agrees that schools should be held "accountable" for student performance, but what exactly does that mean? Are standardized tests the best way to measure achievement? What subjects should be tested—and using what kinds of tests? What scores on those tests should indicate "proficiency"? Should students with special needs be held to the same standards? If not, who will define *special needs*? And so on.

President George W. Bush had no choice but to address all of these questions explicitly when his administration made education reform one of its first major initiatives. In 2002, President Bush signed the No Child Left Behind Act (NCLB), a bipartisan federal effort to improve student achievement across the country. The overall focus of the legislation was on assessment and accountability. States were instructed to define learning standards for students in different grades and then adopt tests to measure progress against those standards. Individual schools that failed to make progress would be sanctioned, as would states with a high proportion of students who were not meeting standards.

The final NCLB statute was 670 pages long. A key provision requires that all schools receiving federal funds administer a state-designed standardized test to determine whether student achievement is improving. Specifically, schools must demonstrate Adequate Yearly Progress (AYP), which means that students in a particular grade are doing better on the statewide exam than the students did in that grade the previous year. (In other words, the progress of any individual student is not evaluated; instead, the third graders in Wheelan Elementary School must do better in 2010 than the third graders in that same school did in 2009.) Schools that fail to make AYP are defined as "failing schools." Students in these schools must be offered special tutoring or the option to transfer to a different school.

Another provision of NCLB requires that schools collect data on the performance of different subgroups of students, such as racial and ethnic minorities, so that average test-score statistics do not cover up low performance by certain minority populations within a school or state. The overall philosophy of the law was straightforward: define what students need to know; evaluate progress for all students against those objectives; and take action when schools are not making sufficient progress.

Has it worked? NCLB has certainly not had the dramatic impact on student achievement that supporters would have hoped.

- Student test scores have gone up—dramatically in some cases. (For example, in 2005, America's nine year olds posted the best scores in reading and math in thirty years.) The achievement gap between black and white students has narrowed. However, the case that NCLB caused such progress is harder to make; these trends were underway before NCLB was introduced. A rigorous evaluation of one piece of NCLB, the Reading First program, found that schools that received Reading First grants did not have any greater gains in student achievement than schools that did not receive the grants.
- NCBL has a huge loophole: states are held accountable for ensuring that all students achieve proficiency by 2014—but the states get to write their own tests to determine proficiency. The easier the test, the better a state's students will look. (Imagine if a professor allowed you to write and grade your own exam; how rigorous would you make it?) According to a report released by the Department of Education in 2007, "Academic standards vary so drastically from state to state that a fourth grader judged proficient in reading in Mississippi or Tennessee would fall far short of that mark in Massachusetts and South Carolina."[16]
- Critics do not like the "teach to the test" mentality engendered by NCLB. Proficiency in the material tested may come at the expense of other subjects or activities like art and music. NCLB also rewards schools for getting students to a level of proficiency—but not for taking them beyond that. Gifted programs may

16. Tamar Lewin, "States Found to Vary Widely on Education," *New York Times,* June 8, 2007.

suffer as resources are devoted instead to getting the most number of students to some minimum level of proficiency.

No Child Left Behind was much more popular in theory than it has turned out to be in practice. George Miller, a congressman from California and one of the bill's architects, calls NCLB "the most negative brand in America."[17] As NCLB came up for reauthorization in 2007, the question was whether it ought to be fixed or scrapped entirely. The Aspen Institute, a policy think tank, created a bipartisan independent commission to evaluate NCLB and recommend improvements. The co-chairs of the commission were Republican Tommy Thompson, former secretary of health and human services and former governor of Wisconsin, and Democrat Roy Barnes, former governor of Georgia. The commission spent a year traveling the country, holding hearings and interviewing parents, teachers, researchers, and other policy makers at the local, state, and federal levels.[18] The commission produced scores of recommendations, including the following:

- Make AYP a less "blunt instrument." The commission noted, "Schools either make AYP or they don't. This method does not distinguish between schools that are moving in the right direction but have not yet reached the bar and those that are seriously struggling and show little or no progress. As a result, schools might be labeled in need of improvement despite substantial progress in student achievement, in some cases against considerable odds." The commission recommended better data collection on the progress of individual students, so that schools can be recognized for moving students toward proficiency, even if they have not yet hit the target.
- Improve teacher effectiveness. Education research has demonstrated three consistent findings: (1) high-quality teachers matter more than any other in-school factor in improving student achievement; (2) too many students, particularly low-income and minority students, have low-quality teachers; and (3) formal qualifications tell very little about a teacher's effectiveness. The commission recommended that NCLB focus on effectiveness rather than qualifications by collecting longitudinal data on student achievement with a "teacher identifier" that can be used to measure the long-term effectiveness of individual teachers. It is imperative to know not only which students are succeeding or failing, but which teachers are having the most impact on that success or failure.
- Make standards more rigorous and consistent. Watered-down state standards give only the illusion of student progress. Commissioner Andrea Messina told a congressional committee, "It would be a cruel hoax if students, teachers and principals did everything that NCLB asked of them and students still found

17. "Still at Risk," *The Economist,* October 2, 2008.

18. Andrea Messina, member of the Commission on No Child Left Behind, testimony before the House Committee on Education and Labor, hearing on the Miller–McKeon Discussion Draft of the Reauthorization of the Elementary and Secondary Education Act, September 10, 2007.

themselves ill prepared for success after high school." The commission recommended that NCLB create model national standards. States would be free to adopt these standards or use their own; however, the U.S. secretary of education would issue an annual report evaluating the relative rigor of the standards and assessments in states that do not adopt the national model.

No Child Left Behind highlights the challenges of policy design. Even when the objective is clear (improve student performance) and the political players agree on the need to act, the process of designing and implementing effective legislation can still be extremely difficult.

QUESTIONS

1. Based on your experience, what do you think are the most important elements of any policy effort to improve public education?
2. One result of America's decentralized public education system is that there are large disparities in the resources available to local governments to fund their public schools. In affluent communities, citizens are able to tax themselves sufficiently to provide a high level of per-pupil spending. Less affluent communities are likely to spend less on their public schools. Is this "fair"? Why, or why not?
3. Do you agree that schools should be held accountable for the performance of specific racial and ethnic subgroups? (In other words, a school can be considered as failing if average test scores are climbing but the scores of a subgroup, such as Latino students, are not.) Why, or why not?
4. Given what you know about the incentives of private firms, how do you think for-profit firms would operate schools differently than public entities? What would be the benefits of that competition? What might be the adverse consequences?
5. Agree or disagree: America's excellent system of higher education is driven primarily by choice and competition; this is evidence that K–12 should be based on competition as well.
6. Based on the NCLB experience, would you advocate a greater or lesser role for the federal government in public education reform? Why?

KEY CONCEPTS

★ For any issue, there will be a nearly unlimited array of potential policy options, each of which will have different impacts and different political implications.

★ Policy makers must always ask two fundamental questions regarding any prospective policy change: (1) Who will be affected? and (2) How will they respond? A policy change must be effective even after rational individuals and firms respond by seeking to protect their interests.

★ One of the most important rules of thumb in public policy is the law of unintended consequences: If policy analysts neglect to anticipate how stakeholders will react to a policy change, the resulting behavior of the stakeholders may detract from the effectiveness of a policy change or even impose unexpected costs that outweigh the anticipated benefits.

★ An ill-conceived policy change may introduce perverse incentives, which are incentives for stakeholders to respond in ways that cause harm.

★ One of the most common policy-design errors is to assume that all behavior will remain the same except for the intended policy change. In reality, the process is dynamic, meaning that policy makers must also anticipate and plan for the changes in behavior that a policy is likely to cause.

★ The distributional effects of a policy change measure the disparate impacts of a policy change on different groups—by income, race, geography, or any other relevant consideration.

★ Government has four broad tools for generating outcomes that are different from the ones that the market would otherwise deliver on its own: regulation; taxes and subsidies (and other incentives); government provision of a good or service; and government financing of a good or service with private provision.

★ Government has the authority to regulate—to require individuals and firms to act in a specified manner and to enforce that requirement with fines, confiscation of property, or even imprisonment.

★ Deregulation occurs when policy makers decide that society would be better off without some regulation that currently exists because it is causing an outcome that is less desirable than what the market would deliver.

★ Government has the capacity to raise and lower the prices of different goods and behaviors by using taxes and subsidies. A tax raises the cost of some activity; a subsidy lowers it.

★ A Pigovian tax, named for English economist Arthur Pigou, is a tax designed explicitly to raise the private cost of some activity to equal the social cost.

★ If the market is not providing some good or service that would make society better off, then one alternative is to have government provide it. Policy makers can also undertake privatization, which involves doing the opposite: devolving some function of government to the private sector.

★ If society would benefit from some good or service that the market is not providing, there is an alternative to having the government provide it: the government can finance the provision of a good or service while leaving the private sector to produce it. In general, the benefits to having the government contract out the provision of a good or service to a private firm exist only when two criteria are met: (1) the task for which a private firm is being hired is clearly defined, and (2) the quality of the good or service to be delivered is easily observed and measured.

★ The first and most important step in the policy process is to identify the potential benefit from the policy change or the harm that might be ameliorated.

★ The second step of the policy process is to analyze why the market is not delivering a desirable outcome. If the market, left to its own devices, will not correct a social problem, then the nature of the market failure will often suggest an appropriate remedy.

★ The third step of the policy process is to identify all the institutions with the authority and capacity to implement a policy change.

★ The next step is to simultaneously evaluate the policy options and the political landscape. A successful policy is not only one that works to the greatest extent possible, but also one that has enough political support to get passed.

★ Effective policy makers make a policy decision and then build a coalition among the organized interests and other parties that support what they are trying to do; at the same time, they are working to mollify, subdue, or defeat the organized interests that are likely to oppose the action.

Glossary

Boldfaced terms that appear within definitions are themselves defined in the Glossary.

absolute advantage. The ability of a person, firm, or nation to produce something more efficiently than another person, firm, or nation.

absolute figures. Statistics or data that are presented in a defined unit of measure, such as dollars or degrees.

absolute poverty. A measure of poverty that reflects the degree to which a person's basic needs are being met—food, housing, health care, and so on.

actuarial fairness. When the premium charged by an insurance company (or the price of any other contract involving uncertainty) is set equal to the expected loss.

adverse selection. When individuals or firms use private information to sort themselves into or out of a **market** transaction. Markets do not necessarily function smoothly in the face of this kind of **asymmetry of information.**

aggregating preferences. The process in which the beliefs and opinions of many actors—i.e., their individual preferences—are organized into the preferences of the group as a whole, often as a prerequisite for making a communal decision.

alternative hypothesis (H_a). The hypothesis that must be accepted if the **null hypothesis** is rejected. If the null hypothesis is that substance-abuse counseling has no impact on the recidivism rate for federal prisoners, then the alternative hypothesis would be that substance-abuse counseling does affect the recidivism rate.

arms race. A variation on the **prisoner's dilemma model** in which rational actors behave in a way that makes them all worse off. An arms race describes any situation in which the outcome is strictly a function of relative performance, rather than absolute performance. In the case of a literal arms race, the strategic outcome is determined by which party has more or better weapons. Of course, all nations have the same incentive to seek this strategic advantage. The likely outcome is that countries spend increasing amounts on armaments (to the exclusion of other goods and services) without changing the party that ends up with the strategic advantage. All parties would be better off if they could spend less in order to achieve the same relative outcome (e.g., country A has one nuclear weapon and country B has none, rather than country A has 1,000 nuclear weapons and country B has 500).

Arrow's theorem. The proof by Nobel Prize–winner Kenneth Arrow that there is no optimal mechanism for **aggregating preferences** of a group when there are three or more alternatives from which to choose. Specifically, any voting system will violate one of the following criteria: unrestricted domain, completeness, transitivity, Pareto optimality, nondictatorship, and independence of irrelevant alternatives.

asymmetry of information. When one party to a transaction has more information than the other. If the information gap is significant enough, it can hinder the way **markets** operate or even cause them to fail entirely.

at-large legislative districts. Districts in which all of the representatives are elected by all of the eligible voters in the relevant geographic area.

averting behavior. Behavioral responses that minimize or eliminate the harm associated with some adverse outcome.

barter. A **market** transaction in which one good or service is exchanged directly for another.

behavioral economics. A subfield of economics that examines the imperfect processes by which humans make decisions. Behavioral economics suggests that individuals are not always as rational as economic **models** assume them to be, which has significant implications for **public policy.**

biased sample. A data sample that is not representative of the population of interest and will, therefore, produce inaccurate or misleading results.

binary variable. A variable that can take only two possible values, such as 0 or 1.

bivariate regression analysis. An analysis of the linear relationship between two variables, such as height and weight.

branding. Investments by a firm in building an identity around a product or products that convey important information about quality, durability, style, safety, or other attributes that might not otherwise be easily observable.

Byrd rule. A Senate rule created by Senator Robert Byrd of West Virginia stipulating that only legislation germane to the budget should be included in the budget reconciliation bill. The purpose of the Byrd rule was to prevent the budget reconciliation process (which is immune from **filibuster**) from being used for legislative purposes other than expeditious budget completion.

cap-and-trade system. A process for reducing pollutants in which a **government** or some other regulatory body sets a cap for the total emissions of a certain pollutant. The regulatory body then distributes emissions permits, or allowances, up to that cumulative level. No individual or firm without a permit is allowed to emit the pollutant; the total allowable amount of a particular pollutant is fixed and can be reduced (by withdrawing permits) over time. The government can auction off emissions permits or allocate them in some other way. Once the permits are issued, they can be bought and sold, ensuring (like any other market) that the permits are put to their most efficient use.

cartel. A group of firms that agree to collude, usually by holding prices above the competitive **market** price.

causality. See **causal relationship.**

causal relationship (causality, causation). A relationship between two variables in which a change in one variable brings about a change in the other.

causation. See **causal relationship.**

central limit theorem. A theorem that states that the **sample means** for any population will be distributed roughly as a normal distribution around the true **mean** for the population. The larger the number of samples, the more closely the distribution will approximate a normal distribution.

central planning. An alternative to a **market** economy in which **government** officials decide how the productive resources within an economy ought to be put to use.

certification. A **market** mechanism for overcoming information problems in which an independent third party attests to the quality of a good or service.

ceteris paribus. A Latin term meaning "all other things being equal." The *ceteris paribus* assumption is important when researchers and policy analysts are focusing on the importance of a single factor.

club goods. A category of goods in which the costs and benefits of maintaining a resource can be spread over some group, and those who do not pay for the resource (such as a health club) can be excluded. Thus, these goods are nonrival and exclusive.

cluster sample. A sample created by dividing the population of interest into many similar or identical clusters, such as rural counties or high-income zip codes, and then drawing **observations** from one or several randomly chosen clusters.

coalition government. The **government** formed in a parliamentary system when no single party controls a majority of parliamentary seats. Two or more parties must join together to support a prime minister.

Coase Theorem. The insight, posited by economist Ronald Coase, that externalities will be corrected by the **market** without **government** intervention if (1) **property rights** are clearly defined, and (2) **transactions costs** are nonexistent or very low.

coefficient. A constant produced in a regression equation that quantifies the effect of a one-unit change of an **independent variable** on the **dependent variable** *ceteris paribus.* In the equation $y = a + bx,$ b is the coefficient that expresses the effect on y of a one-unit change in x.

coincidence. When two variables move together over time by chance. There is no underlying association between the variables, causal or otherwise.

collective-action problems. Cases in which the members of a group are unable or unwilling to organize themselves to conduct some activity, even though that activity would make all members of the group better off.

collusion. The process by which a group of firms in the same business or industry agree not to compete based on price. The effect is to hold prices above what they would be in a competitive market, enabling the colluding firms to earn higher profits. Collusion is generally prohibited by antitrust laws.

committee markup (marking up). The process in which congressional committees do much of the work related to writing and revising legislation before a bill is voted out of committee for consideration by all of Congress.

common-pool resource. A resource for which it is difficult or impossible to exclude any party from using. However, the resource is not infinite and can be used up or overexploited. Thus, a common-pool resource is rival and nonexclusive. An international fishery is a common example.

comparative advantage. The ability of a person, firm, or country to produce a good or service at the lowest **opportunity cost** relative to other individuals, firms, or countries.

comparative politics. The study of how different political systems operate around the world.

compensating differential. The risk premium that must be paid to induce workers to take jobs that involve risk or unpleasantness. The compensating differential can also be negative—workers may accept lower wages for jobs that are comfortable, prestigious, or otherwise attractive in nonpecuniary ways.

confidence interval. A probability-based inference that expresses the likelihood that the population **mean** lies within a certain distance of the observed **sample mean.**

contingent valuation. A method for placing a **value** on some cost or benefit in which individuals are asked in a survey or questionnaire how much they would be willing to pay to receive an intangible benefit or, alternatively, how much they would be willing to pay to avoid some harm.

contractible quality. An attribute of a good or service that can be observed and measured objectively, making it possible to write a contract specifying a certain level of quality (e.g., the cement on a highway must be 5 inches thick).

control for. When researchers use statistical tools to hold constant other factors that may influence the outcome of interest, thereby making it possible to isolate the influence of a single variable. For example, researchers looking at the link between obesity and heart disease would control for other lifestyle factors, such as smoking, education level, access to health care, etc.

control variable. An **independent variable** that is likely to have an effect on the outcome of interest but is not the primary focus of inquiry. Researchers must include it in the **regression analysis** to improve the validity of the results.

correlation. A measure of the degree to which two variables are associated with one another. Variation in one is associated with variation in the other, positively or negatively.

cost-benefit analysis (CBA). The process by which the total benefits of a project are tallied up and compared to the total costs.

cost-effectiveness analysis. A process that evaluates or ranks policies based on their costs for achieving some defined objective.

counterfactual. The outcome that would have been observed under an alternate set of circumstances—that is, had a different decision had been made.

creative destruction. The constant process in a **market** economy in which innovation makes older skills, technologies, or processes less valuable or even useless.

cross-sectional data. Data comprising **observations** for a set of individuals, countries, or some other unit of observation at a particular time.

culture of dependency. The idea that extensive **government** aid can cause recipients to rely on charity, rather than working to improve their own circumstances.

data mining. The process of loading a **regression analysis** with many **explanatory variables** for which there is little or no theoretical support. Simple probability suggests that some of these junk "explanatory" variables will appear to be correlated with the **dependent variable,** even though the relationship is spurious.

data observations (data points). Individual **observations** that collectively make up a data set.

data points. See **data observations.**

deadweight loss. A measure of the inefficiency caused by a policy change when the loss of welfare imposed on one party exceeds the gain in welfare afforded to another party.

decile. An interval that contains one-tenth of the **observations** in a distribution, after the distribution has been ranked in order and divided into ten equal parts. For example, the bottom decile of households by income in the United States would comprise the 10 percent of American households with the lowest incomes.

decision tree. A tool that maps all possible contingencies, the probability of each contingency, and the payoff for each contingency. As a result, the decision tree provides a graphic description of all possible outcomes and their relative likelihoods.

degrees of freedom. A measure of the quantity of data on which the results of a **regression analysis** are based relative to the number of parameters to be estimated in the equation. Specifically, the degrees of freedom in a regression analysis would equal the number of **observations** in the sample (n) minus the number of **independent variables** in the equation plus the constant (k), or $n - (k + 1) = n - k - 1$.

dependent variable. The outcome of interest in a **regression analysis** that is explained by one or more **independent variables.**

deregulation. A policy change in which regulations previously imposed by a **government** are removed or reduced.

difference in difference. See **multiple time series.**

diminishing marginal returns. A relationship in which each additional unit of input (e.g., hour of studying or pound of fertilizer) produces less incremental increase in total output.

direct democracy. A system that enables all actors with a voice in the decision-making process to vote directly on whatever matter is being considered.

discontinuity studies. Studies that take advantage of the **fact** that some treatments have a rigid cutoff for inclusion. Thus, a comparison can be made between the outcomes for those who were just eligible for some treatment and the outcomes for those who just missed the eligibility cutoff and, therefore, did not receive the treatment. The two groups are likely to be broadly similar, despite being on opposite sides of the eligibility cutoff.

discount rate. The interest rate that is used to place a present dollar **value** on some future sum. The higher the discount rate, the lower the present value of any future cost or benefit.

distributional effects. A measure of how the costs and benefits for a given policy or program are spread across society.

dominant strategy. A strategy that is the best option for one player, regardless of what any other player chooses.

double-blind. A study in which neither the participants nor the evaluators are aware of which participants are in the control group and which are in the treatment group.

dropout effect (survivor bias; survivorship bias). A skewing of outcomes caused when a nonrandom group of participants quits or is removed from a program during the period of analysis.

dummy variable. A variable that can take on only two possible **values,** 0 or 1.

dynamic behavior. Behavior that adapts to circumstances, such as when a firm reacts to a policy change or when an individual's behavior is shaped by the behavior of those around him or her.

earmarks. Specific projects that are attached to pieces of legislation by individual lawmakers, usually to appease their local constituencies. Projects funded by earmarks can skirt the traditional process for approving and funding public ventures.

economic benefit or cost. A measurable pecuniary gain or loss (e.g., loss of income) as opposed to a noneconomic gain or loss (e.g., the destruction of a scenic mountain view).

economic rent. An extraordinary profit that is not bid away by normal competitive forces.

efficiency. The degree to which resources are used to generate the most productive outcome.

efficiency–equity trade-off. The idea that more **equity** often comes at the expense of **efficiency** and vice versa. Or as economist Arthur Okun notes, "We can't have our cake of market efficiency and share it equally."

elasticity. A measure of the degree to which supply or demand change in response to a change in price.

elasticity of supply. See **price elasticity of supply.**

empirical question. An issue for which a hypothesis can be accepted or rejected based on **observation,** experiment, or some other objective analysis.

endogenous variable. A variable affected by the outcome that it is being used to explain.

endowment effect. The tendency for individuals to demand more compensation to give up something than, if the circumstances were different, they would be willing to pay to acquire it.

equilibrium. A situation in which there is a relatively stable outcome even in the face of changing behavior or circumstances.

equity. A measure of fairness, however one may define it. See **horizontal equity; intergenerational equity; vertical equity.**

error term. The portion of the variation of the **dependent variable** not explained by the (unobservable) true regression equation for the full population of interest.

evaluator bias. A skewing of outcomes caused by an evaluator's potential tendency to treat the control group differently than the treatment group.

exogenous variable. A variable affected by factors outside the system.

expected loss. The **mean** loss from a series of events for which we know the probability of all possible outcomes and the "payoff" for each of those outcomes.

expected value. The **mean** outcome, positive or negative, from a series of events for which we know the probability of all possible outcomes and the "payoff" for each of those outcomes.

explained sum of squares (ESS). The amount of variation in the **dependent variable** explained by a regression equation.

explanatory variable. See **independent variable.**

fact. An objective reality or truth, generally informed by **observation,** measurement, or calculation.

fertility rate. The average number of children that would be born to a woman over her lifetime.

filibuster. The procedure in the United States Senate by which a senator can speak for as long as he or she wishes about any topic, usually in an effort to stall legislation. A filibuster can only be ended by the invocation of cloture, which requires the vote of 60 senators (rather than the majority of 51).

fitting a line. A method by which a line is drawn through a cluster of **observation** points, so that the **residual sum of squares** is minimized. This line will best express the relationship between the **independent variable** and the **dependent variable.**

for-profit firms. Firms that operate to earn a profit for their owners.

framing. The strategic use of language to broaden the appeal of a policy position or to lessen the appeal of an opposing position.

free riders. Individuals who enjoy the benefits of group action without contributing to the effort.

***F*-test.** A test of **significance** for a regression equation overall. It examines the likelihood that all of the coefficients in the regression equation collectively have no **value** in explaining the outcome of interest (the **dependent variable**).

future value (*FV*). The **value** to which a given quantity will grow at a certain time in the future, given a specific rate of growth.

FV. See **future value.**

game theory. The study of strategic interactions between individuals, or "agents," which facilitates the understanding of group behavior.

gatekeepers. Individuals whose institutional powers give them disproportionate influence over legislative outcomes.

gerrymandering. The process of drawing electoral boundaries in ways that give a political advantage to a political group or individual.

goodness of fit. The extent to which a regression as a whole explains the outcome of interest.

government. A body that exercises authority over some political jurisdiction—a town, a county, a state, a nation, or a union of countries. Government is the only entity legally empowered to compel individuals to do things that they might otherwise choose not to do.

grassroots campaign. A "bottom-up" campaign strategy in which a network of dedicated activists use a wide array of tools, often inexpensive and low-tech, to win support for their cause.

gross domestic product (GDP). The **value** of all goods and services produced in a country.

gross domestic product (GDP) per capita. The **value** of all goods and services produced in a country, divided by the country's population.

hedonic market analysis. A method of isolating the **value** of a specific cost or benefit using **regression analysis.**

horizontal equity. A measure of the degree to which similar persons and situations are treated equally.

human capital. The sum of all skills and positive attributes embodied within an individual, such as education, perseverance, experience, and so on.

hypothesis testing. The process of proposing a hypothesis and then testing its validity through experimentation or data analysis.

identification problem. The methodological challenge of observing and quantifying a **causal relationship** between a treatment and an outcome when that relationship is obscured by many other extraneous factors.

illegal aliens (undocumented workers). A characterization of persons who enter the United States illegally that is commonly used by political groups seeking to put a negative spin on this kind of immigration. This is an example of **framing.**

independent. Events or **observations** with no statistical **correlation;** uncorrelated.

independent variable (explanatory variable). A factor that researchers believe has some **causal relationship** with an outcome of interest (the **dependent variable**).

index. A single measure created by combining multiple **indicators** in some way, such as the windchill factor (which combines temperature and wind speed) or the United Nations human development index (which is created by combining measures of educational attainment, income, and life expectancy).

indicators. Quantitative measures of performance, such as test scores or **per capita** income.

inelastic. A situation in which the supply or demand for a product is relatively invariant to price.

informal institutions. Generally accepted organizational procedures that evolve over time but are not formally codified; "unwritten rules" that help to coordinate and organize human interaction.

initial endowment. The beginning allocation of resources, before any **redistribution** or **market** transactions have occurred.

initial endowment of resources. The beginning distribution of land, wealth, **human capital,** and other assets—the "hand that is dealt" to a person, nation, or other entity.

institutions. The laws, organizations, and unwritten rules that govern human interaction and, therefore, make **public policy** possible.

intellectual property. Intangible assets that are creations of the mind—such as art, music, or ideas—and can be offered many of the same kinds of legal protection that physical property is, such as restrictions on use by nonowners.

intensity of preference. A measure of how strongly a person or group feels about a certain issue or situation. If two individuals share a belief (such as support of free trade), one party may have a much greater intensity of preference than the other, meaning that he cares more deeply about his position.

intergenerational equity. A measure of the degree to which policies treat different generations fairly.

intertemporal. Situations or decisions involving trade-offs at different times.

iterated game. A game that is played over and over, allowing the players to build up some kind of trust and predictability.

law of supply and demand. A **model** which states that, holding all else constant, (1) producers will supply more of a good or service at higher prices and (2) consumers will demand more at lower prices.

law of unintended consequences. The tendency for policy makers to attempt to fix one problem and, in the process, inadvertently create another one or make the original problem worse.

logrolling. The process in which politicians trade and withhold favors in order to advance their own political goals.

longitudinal data (time-series data). A series of data consisting of **observations** for some unit of analysis at multiple times.

marginal product of labor. The incremental output produced by one additional unit of labor, holding all other inputs constant. In a competitive labor market, the marginal product of labor is closely related to the wage rate.

margin of error. A **confidence interval** for a **poll.**

market. An **institution** that facilitates voluntary exchange.

market equilibrium. The price and quantity for which supply is equal to demand. Firms have no incentive to raise prices or add capacity, and consumers are willing to buy the quantity supplied at the **market** price—no more, no less.

market failure. A situation in which **market** transactions do not lead to a socially efficient allocation of resources.

market power (pricing power). The power of a monopolist or **cartel** to determine the **market** price and output of a good. This power to raise prices above what they would otherwise be in a competitive market comes from dominance in a particular market and allows the monopolist or cartel to earn higher profits than it would in a competitive market.

marking up. See **committee markup.**

maximizing profits. The assumption that the owners of a firm seek to make as much money as possible over the long run.

maximizing utility. The assumption that individuals seek to make themselves as well off as possible, however they may define that.

mean. The sum of a given set of numbers divided by the number of **observations;** the average.

measure of dispersion. A measure of how widely a set of **observations** are dispersed around their **mean** or **median.**

median. The midpoint in a distribution of numbers that have been arranged in increasing or decreasing order. The median does not give weight to how far observations are from the midpoint and is, therefore, not sensitive to **outliers.**

median voter theory. A **theory** suggesting that under certain circumstances politicians can maximize the number of votes they receive by adopting the positions favored by the **median** voter.

model. A simplified illustration of how systems operate that can be used to gain greater insight into some more complex process or situation.

monopoly. A situation in which one firm controls the entire **market** for a specific good or service.

moral hazard. A situation that occurs when an individual or firm is protected against some kind of loss and, therefore, acts with less caution than it otherwise would, thereby making a bad outcome more likely.

multicollinearity. The problem that occurs when two **independent variables** in the same regression are so highly correlated with one another that it is difficult or impossible to ascertain their independent effects on the **dependent variable.**

multiple regression analysis. A statistical method that quantifies the linear relationship between a **dependent variable** and more than one **independent variable.**

multiple time series (difference in difference). A method of statistical analysis that compares longitudinal data for a treatment group with **longitudinal data** for a similar but nonrandom group that has not received the treatment.

multivariate regression analysis. See **multiple regression analysis.**

n. The number of **observations** in a data set.

natural experiment. A natural occurrence that closely approximates a controlled experiment. Circumstances create two groups that are nearly identical but for some policy intervention that affects only one of the groups, thereby creating a natural treatment and control group.

negative externality. The difference between the social cost of an activity and its private cost. If this gap is large, an individual or firm (weighing only private benefits relative to private costs) will engage in "too much" of an activity from the standpoint of overall social welfare.

negative feedback loop. A situation in which some negative development induces behavior that makes the situation even worse; a vicious cycle.

negative-sum game. A situation, or "game," in which participants compete for shares of a shrinking pie.

net present value. See **present value.**

nominal figures. Data or statistics that have not been adjusted for inflation, making them potentially inaccurate when compared with **real figures** from other time periods.

noneconomic benefit or cost. An intangible gain or loss (e.g., the destruction of a scenic mountain view).

nonequivalent control group. A study in which the subjects in the control group are thought to be largely similar to the subjects in the treatment group but the assignment is not random.

nonprofit firms. Firms that are not operated for the purpose of earning a profit and can, therefore, undertake activities for which the revenues do not necessarily exceed the costs.

nonuse value. An intangible **value** that is attached to a resource for reasons that do not stem from its direct use, such as the value placed on potential future use or even utility derived simply from the knowledge that the resource exists.

normative analysis. Analysis that introduces one's **values** or ideological beliefs and makes explicit conclusions about what should be done.

null hypothesis (H_0). The **theory** or proposition that is being tested. Statistical inference is used to accept or reject the proposition with some level of statistical confidence.

observation. (1) A single unit of data. For example, in a data set of test scores for 1,000 students on a single exam, the test score for each one of the students would be a single observation. (2) An act of recognizing and noting an occurrence.

omitted variable. A variable left out of a statistical analysis that has a significant relationship with the variables being examined and can, therefore, render the results inaccurate because of its omission.

omitted variable bias. An inaccuracy that is introduced when an important **independent variable** is left out of the regression equation and the independent variables included in the analysis are merely proxies for the omitted variable. If a relevant **explanatory variable** is not included and that variable is correlated with other independent variables that are included in the analysis, then **causality** might be erroneously attributed to the proxies included in the regression equation. For example, a **regression analysis** may find that a particular vehicle is particularly dangerous (e.g., a high rate of driver fatalities per mile driven). But if the analysis does not include data on the kind of person most likely to drive such a car (e.g., young males), then the analysis may wrongly blame the design of the vehicle for poor safety outcomes when the kind of person likely to buy and drive the vehicle may play a significant role.

opportunity cost. The cost associated with forgoing one's next best alternative. For example, one significant opportunity cost often associated with attending graduate school is forgone wages as the result of time spent out of the labor market.

ordinary least squares (OLS). A statistical method of determining the best fit for a regression line by minimizing the sum of the squares of the **residuals.**

outlier. An **observation** that lies particularly far from most of the observations in a distribution. For example, in a data set of student heights, a student who is 7 feet tall would likely be an outlier.

outside the range of the data. The idea that regression results should not be used to make inferences about populations not included in the data set and, therefore, likely to be different in key respects from the population for which the data were collected.

oversampling. A data-gathering strategy in which members of a subgroup of a population are included in the sample in excess of their share of the larger population in order to ensure that the sample has sufficient data to draw meaningful conclusions on the subgroup of interest.

panel data. Data comprising **observations** for a set of individuals, countries, or some other unit of observation at multiple times; a combination of **cross-sectional** and **longitudinal data.**

Pareto-efficient. A situation in which it is not possible to make any individual better off without making another individual worse off.

participant bias. A skewing of outcomes caused by participants' tendency to behave differently if they know that they are part of an experimental group.

paternalistic policies. Policies that seek to improve overall social welfare by preventing individuals from doing potentially harmful things that they might otherwise choose to do. Paternalism essentially protects individuals from themselves.

"pay as you go" program. A program, such as Social Security, in which benefits are paid to current recipients from revenues paid by current contributors.

per capita. A statistic that has been divided by the relevant population. For example, **gross domestic product per capita** is a nation's **gross domestic product** divided by the nation's total population.

percentage change. A mathematical representation of the extent to which some number or quantity has changed relative to its initial **value.**

percentile. A subset of a distribution containing one one-hundredth of the **observations,** after the distribution has been ranked in order.

perverse incentive. An inadvertent effect of a policy that causes rational individuals and firms to behave in ways that are not consistent with the policy and may even cause serious harm.

Pigovian tax. A tax levied on an activity that generates a **negative externality.** In **theory,** the tax should equal the difference between the **private marginal cost** of the activity and the **social marginal cost,** producing a socially optimal level of output. (A *Pigovian subsidy* could be employed when dealing with a **positive externality.**)

plurality. A system in which the candidate with the most votes wins, regardless of whether that candidate achieves a majority or not.

points of entry (for policy change). The places in the policy process that a party can seek to influence or change in order to achieve some overarching objective.

poll. A form of statistical inference that uses a sample of the population to calculate a **confidence interval** for the proportion of the population that shares some attribute or opinion.

positive analysis. A statement of **fact,** finding, or **theory** that is devoid of judgment. A conclusion is made about what did or will happen without introducing an opinion as to whether this is a good or bad thing.

positive externality. A situation in which the public benefit of some activity exceeds the private benefit, creating a positive "spillover" that is not taken into account by the individual when he or she weighs the private marginal costs and benefits of the activity. Thus, the **market** will provide "too little" of the activity from the standpoint of society overall.

positive feedback loop. A process in which some behavior or incident causes a positive outcome that induces additional positive behavior.

positive-finding bias (positive-publication bias). The tendency for studies with positive findings to be published and read more often than studies looking at the same question but finding no significant results. The net effect is to overemphasize positive findings, possibly suggesting a statistically significant relationship when in fact none exists.

positive-publication bias. See **positive-finding bias.**

positive-sum games. Games in which the participants can increase the total payoff, or "size of the pie," if they behave in certain ways.

poverty rate. The fraction of the population living at or below established **poverty thresholds.**

poverty threshold. A level of income, based on household size, at or below which one is said to be living in poverty. This is sometimes referred to as the *poverty line.*

present discounted value. See **present value.**

present value (net present value; present discounted value; *PV***).** The **value** of a particular future quantity converted into what is it worth today. This allows for the comparison of costs and benefits that occur at different times. Converting a future sum to its present value requires an assumption about the appropriate **discount rate.**

price discrimination. The practice of charging different prices to different consumers, based on their willingness to pay.

price elasticity of demand. The percentage change in demand associated with a 1-percent increase in price.

price elasticity of supply (elasticity of supply). The percentage change in supply associated with a 1-percent increase in price.

pricing power. See **market power.**

principal–agent problems. Potential conflicts that arise when one party, the *principal,* expects another party with different motivations, *the agent,* to act in a way that is consistent with the principal's goals and objectives. However, the principal does not have sufficient expertise or resources to monitor the agent's behavior.

prisoner's dilemma. A **model** depicting how two rational agents, each trying to maximize his own utility, can end up behaving in a way that makes both of them worse off.

private marginal cost. The cost borne by a firm to produce one additional unit of a good or service. Alternatively, the cost to an individual of consuming one additional unit of a good or service.

privatization. The process of devolving some traditional functions of **government** to the private sector.

pro-choice. A common characterization, or **framing,** of the belief that abortion should be legal.

productivity. A measure of the **efficiency** with which inputs are converted to outputs; the single most important determinant of our standard of living.

program evaluation. The use of analysis and quantitative tools to determine the impact of a program, policy, or other intervention.

pro-life. A common characterization, or **framing,** of the belief that abortion should be illegal.

property right. The legal right to exercise control over some resource or asset.

public company. A **for-profit firm** owned by its shareholders.

public good. A category of goods that (1) is not "used up," meaning that additional users can enjoy the good at zero marginal cost, and (2) for which it is difficult or impossible to exclude those who do not pay to use the resource. Thus, public goods are nonrival and nonexclusive.

public institutions. See **institutions.**

public policy. The process by which groups act collectively, such as making communal decisions that are binding on all members of the relevant group.

PV. See **present value.**

p-**value.** The probability of observing a particular **value** for a test statistic if the **null hypothesis** is in **fact** true.

quartile. A subset of a distribution containing one-quarter of the **observations** after the distribution has been ranked in order.

randomized experiment. An experiment in which a large eligible population is identified for some kind of policy intervention and a random mechanism is used to separate those who will receive the treatment from those who will not.

real figures. Numbers that have been adjusted for inflation, making it easier to compare statistics meaningfully across time periods.

redistribution. Transferring resources from one portion of the population to another portion of the population, often for reasons of **equity.**

referendum. A direct vote among the entire eligible voting population that accepts or rejects a proposition or measure.

regression analysis. A statistical analysis of data that seeks to explain some outcome, the **dependent variable,** as a function of one or more **independent variables.**

regulation. Government exercise of authority in which individuals and firms are required to act in a specified manner and in which that requirement is enforced with fines, confiscation of property, or even imprisonment.

relative figures. Statistics that are compared to some other quantity or statistic.

relative poverty. A measure of an individual's consumption or well-being relative to other members of society.

rent seeking. The process by which political interests use the powers of **government,** such as **regulation** or taxation, to secure some kind of economic advantage.

reporting legislation. The process by which a bill goes from committee to the full legislature for consideration, along with a committee report that includes background information on the legislation.

representative democracy. A form of **government** in which voters choose representatives who make decisions on their behalf.

representative sample. A data sample that accurately represents the population of interest.

residual. The unexplained variation in the **dependent variable** in a regression equation; the difference between the observed **value** and the predicted value for an **observation** in a regression equation.

residual sum of squares (RSS). The sum of each **residual** squared for all the **observations** in the sample. This reflects the amount of variation in the **dependent variable** not explained by the regression equation.

revealed preference. A method for placing a **value** on intangible attributes or outcomes by observing the actions of individuals and calculating the implicit price they are willing to pay to obtain some outcomes or to avoid others.

revenge. Deriving satisfaction from imposing a cost on another party, regardless of whether or not it makes the party seeking revenge materially better off.

reverse causality. When the direction of **causality** is the opposite of what was expected or believed. A was thought to cause B when, in fact, B causes A.

risk aversion. The tendency of many people to choose to pay a regular, fixed amount to avoid the possibility, however small, of some catastrophic event. More generally, a risk-averse party will prefer to receive a fixed amount with certainty rather than an uncertain amount with the same expected **value.**

roll-call vote. A vote that requires every member of a legislative body to go on record "for" or "against" a measure (as opposed to a **voice vote**).

R^2. A measure of how much variation in the **dependent variable** is explained by the regression equation as a proportion of the total variation in the **dependent variable.**

sample mean. The **mean,** or average, for any sample set of **observations.**

sample size (n). The number of **observations** in a sample.

sampling. The process of selecting a set of individual **observations** from some larger population, often with the intent of using the sample to make inferences about the full population.

sampling bias. Flawed results caused by the selection of a sample that does not accurately represent the population of interest.

sampling error. The natural variation that is the result of making inferences based on a sample instead of the whole population.

scarcity. Finite supply. Scarce resources must be rationed, using some mechanism.

screening. A **market** mechanism for overcoming information problems in which one party to a transaction designs a mechanism that elicits private information from another party to the transaction.

selection bias. A methodological flaw that can occur when the process used to collect data generates a non-representative sample.

selection effect. A methodological flaw that can occur when the participants in some treatment are significantly different in some important respect from the nonparticipants to whom they are being compared. The composition of the treatment and control groups, rather than the treatment itself, may account for some or all of the difference in outcomes between the two groups.

self-correcting market. The idea that disruptions and other problems usually set in motion their own solutions in a **market** system, often by changing prices in ways that elicit a "healing" response.

self-selection bias. A methodological distortion that occurs when individuals sort themselves in or out of the group being studied in a way that will affect the composition of the treatment group relative to the control group.

sensitivity analysis. The process of evaluating how the analysis is affected by changes in some of the key assumptions.

separation of powers. The distribution of power across different governmental **institutions** to provide a system of "checks and balances."

shadow price. A monetary value that is assigned to an input or output that does not have an observable **market** price.

sign (of the coefficient). The direction of the effect of an **independent variable** on a **dependent variable.** If positive, the variables have a positive **correlation;** if negative, the variables have a negative correlation.

signaling. A **market** mechanism for overcoming information problems in which individuals or firms undertake activities with no direct **value.** Instead, their activities "signal" intangible information to other parties about the quality of a good or service.

significance (of the coefficient). A measure of the likelihood that an observed relationship between two variables is merely a product of chance, rather than of some true association.

significance level. A measure of **statistical significance** that reflects the likelihood that some observed occurrence or relationship is a product of chance, rather than the result of a true association. For example, a researcher may find that there is a positive association between sun exposure and skin cancer, and that "the results are significant at the .01 level." This statement means that there is less than a 1-percent chance that the observed relationship in the data between sun exposure and skin cancer is a **coincidence.**

simple random sample. A sample drawn from a population in such a way that any individual **observation** in the population has an equal probability of being included in the sample.

single-member legislative districts. A method of electing a legislature in which the relevant geography is divided into individual districts, with one representative elected by the members of each district.

sin tax. A tax designed to discourage the consumption of a good that has broader social costs.

size (of the coefficient). A measure of the degree to which a change in an **independent variable** affects the outcome of the **dependent variable.** If large in absolute value, a unit change in the independent variable causes a large movement in the dependent variable (in the relevant units). If small in absolute value, a unit change in the independent variable causes relatively little change in the dependent variable.

social discount rate. The interest rate used to discount costs and benefits to the present when doing **cost-benefit analysis** from a public perspective. The **discount rate** selected can have a profound impact on cost-benefit analysis, particularly when costs of benefits occur in the distant future.

social marginal cost. The cost borne by all of society, including the private costs borne by producers and consumers, when one more unit of a good or service is produced and consumed. Social welfare is maximized when the social marginal cost of any activity is equal to its social marginal benefit.

socioeconomic status. A comprehensive measure of affluence and social standing, including such things as income and education.

stakeholders. The affected parties in any policy decision.

standard deviation. A **measure of dispersion** around the **mean.** A large standard deviation indicates that the **observations** are spread relatively far from the mean, while a small standard deviation indicates that the observations are more tightly clustered around the mean.

standard error. A **measure of the dispersion** of **sample means.** For some population with **mean** μ and **standard deviation** σ, the standard error of the sample means is $\sigma/\sqrt{n}$, where n is the size of each sample.

standing. An assessment of which parties should be included in the **cost-benefit analysis** of a potential policy decision.

statistical sampling. The process of gathering an unbiased sample from a larger population in order to make statistical inferences.

statistical significance. A statistical association between two variables of interest that cannot be easily explained by chance. Statistical significance alone does not imply **causality.**

status-quo bias. The tendency toward inaction in policy making due to the inherent uncertainty surrounding change.

stratified sample. A method of **sampling** in which **observations** are randomly chosen from within a set of defined subpopulations, or strata, to ensure that observations from each stratum are represented in the sample in proportion to their share of the overall population.

survivorship bias (survivor bias). See **dropout effect.**

theory. A general principle supported by data or analysis. A theory can be supported or disproved by subsequent inquiry.

time-series analysis. A statistical method that uses **longitudinal data** to compare some outcome of interest before and after a particular intervention or treatment.

time-series data. See **longitudinal data.**

time value of money. The idea that payment today is preferred over payment in the future because of things such as the ability to invest money in the present for greater gains in the future, fears of inflation, and general uncertainty about what the future may bring.

total sum of squares (TSS). The sum of the squared difference between each **observation** for the **dependent variable** and the **mean** for the **dependent variable.**

tragedy of the commons. A common **collective-action problem** in which a shared resource is overutilized or despoiled (contrary to the interests of all parties using the resource) because, in the absence of effective monitoring and enforcement, individuals have an incentive to cheat on a voluntary agreement that protects the resource in ways that maximize its long-term communal **value.**

transactions costs. All of the costs associated with conducting an exchange of goods or services, such as the costs of gathering information, bargaining, drawing up contracts, monitoring an agreement, and so on.

treatment dummy. A **dummy variable** in a regression equation signaling which **observations** have received the "treatment," which can be any outcome, attribute, or intervention that separates them from the control group, such as graduating from high school or participating in a drug treatment program. If the regression equation is specified correctly, the **coefficient** on the treatment dummy quantifies the association between the treatment and the **dependent variable,** *ceteris paribus.*

treatment effect. The causal impact of a policy, program, or intervention.

t-statistic. A measure of the size of a **coefficient** relative to its **standard error** that can be used to determine whether or not a coefficient has **statistical significance.**

type I error. A situation in which the **null hypothesis** is rejected even though it is true and the alternative hypothesis is falsely accepted; a false positive.

type II error. A situation in which the **null hypothesis** is accepted when it is in fact false and the alternative hypothesis should have been accepted; a false negative.

uncertainty. Imperfect information regarding current circumstances or future contingencies.

undocumented workers. See **illegal aliens.**

unit of observation. The nature of the unit on which one is collecting data. For example, if a researcher is interested in educational outcomes, the unit of observation (or unit of analysis) could be individual students, in which case data would be collected on each student in the data set: test scores, demographic information, etc. But the unit of observation could also be individual schools, in which case data would be collected on each school in the data set: average test scores, demographic profile of the student body, etc.

use value. The **value** derived from the ways in which a resource can be used directly, either for recreational or commercial purposes.

utility. A theoretical concept that measures overall well-being. Utility is not directly observable or measurable.

value. (1) A strongly held belief rooted in faith, life experience, or ideology that is generally not "right" or "wrong," or at least cannot be proved empirically as such. (2) Worth.

value of a statistical life (VSL). The monetary **value** assigned to a human life as part of a **cost-benefit analysis** when loss of life is a possible cost or preventing the loss of life is a potential benefit.

variance. A **measure of dispersion,** calculated by taking the sum of all of the squares of the difference between each **observation** in the data set and the **mean,** and then dividing this sum by the number of observations.

veil of ignorance. A philosophical construct, first put forth by John Rawls, arguing that decisions regarding social welfare should be made by individuals who have no idea what role they will be assigned in the society they are designing.

vertical equity. A measure of fairness that reflects how the privileged are treated relative to the less privileged.

voice vote. A vote that merely records whether or not a measure has passed, rather than recording the specific vote cast by each legislator.

vote of no confidence. An action taken by the governing party or parties in a parliamentary system to remove a prime minister and replace him or her with a new leader.

weighting. A statistical process in which a subgroup or subgroups are oversampled in a data set to ensure that there are sufficient data on the group. Each **observation** from the relevant subgroups are subsequently given less weight in the statistical analysis to avoid distorting the analysis as a result of the **oversampling.**

willingness to accept (WTA). A tool used in **cost-benefit analysis** that places a monetary **value** on a benefit based on how much an individual would have to be paid in order to give up that benefit. Conversely, a monetary value can be placed on some harm based on how much an individual would have to be paid to be voluntarily subjected to that harm.

willingness to pay (WTP). A tool used in **cost-benefit analysis** that places a monetary **value** on a benefit based on how much an individual would be willing to pay to acquire such a benefit. Conversely, a monetary value can be placed on some harm based on how much an individual would be willing to pay in order to avoid it.

"winner take all" labor markets. The idea, first observed by Sherwin Rosen, that in certain markets one need be only slightly better than the competition in order to win most or all relevant gains (such as television viewers). In such markets, individuals with even a tiny advantage over their peers in the labor market can demand a very large wage premium.

zero-sum games. Games in which potential gains ("the size of the pie") are fixed. Any gain by one party must come entirely at the expense of someone else.

z value. A measure of distance from the **mean** in terms of **standard deviations**.

Index